Praise for *Radicals for Capitalism*

"Deftly sort[s] out the various competing strains of thought, the rise and fall of organizations and movements, and the complicated relationships between libertarians and their ideological rivals."

—*Chicago Sun-Times*

"[Doherty] presents a sympathetic picture of a movement that emerged as a significant force over the past half-century. . . . Doherty writes entertainingly about the movement's infighting and schisms. . . . Doherty's book provides valuable background on the origins and development of ideas that have helped shape the world of today and tomorrow." —*New York Post*

"An astute, entertaining history of thinkers as diverse as Ayn Rand and Milton Friedman, who both believed that the best government was the one that involved itself least in the life of its citizens."

—Bloomberg.com

"A serious look at the movement as well as an entertaining tell-all about the LP's movers and shakers, the book sheds light on an eccentric and misunderstood political party. . . . [I]f you want to grasp the intellectual root system of libertarianism I can't think of anything written remotely recently that comes close."

—JONAH GOLDBERG, *National Review*

"Those with a keen interest in the modern history of minimal government philosophy couldn't ask for a more comprehensive account than Doherty's . . . the encyclopedic volume would make a worthy addition to the collection of anyone who possesses some background in libertarian thought. . . . This is a really good book, a really important book, a fascinating book." —The Politico

"Libertarian ideas have a long and rich tradition, which Doherty unearths, to great effect, weaving a narrative that carries the reader along . . . with its many sub-plots peopled with idiosyncratic dramatis personae of rebels with a cause. . . . It will surely succeed in its apparent task of becoming the definitive history of the modern libertarian movement. . . . [Doherty] has performed a great service to libertarians, and political scientists, as well as the interested public, in detailing the storied history of the freedom movement." —AntiWar.com

"A massive, lively history. . . . An appreciation of even the most gnarled branches of the ideological family tree." —*Commentary*

"Modern libertarians see themselves as the loyal opposition to the totalitarian tendencies of centralized power, in an American tradition reaching back to the anti-Federalists. Doherty's astute history shows where that consensus comes from and where it fractures along personal, political and practical lines. . . . [C]onveys an insider's understanding in clear, confident prose. . . . Doherty's well-researched history avoids polemics in outlining a vital political orientation that cuts across the political spectrum." —*Publishers Weekly*

"Fascinating characters fill *Radicals for Capitalism*. . . . Mr. Doherty, an able researcher and writer, has produced a book that is not just readable but enjoyable. Mr. Doherty's evident passion for his subject makes the book sparkle." —*Washington Times*

"*Radicals for Capitalism* is going to be the standard history of the libertarian movement for years to come. And it tells a story libertarians can be proud of." —DAVID BOAZ, Cato Institute

"Doherty recounts the history of this tension between ideological purity and necessary compromise in absorbing detail. . . . *Radicals for Capitalism* maintains its momentum, illuminating a quintessentially American story that has not yet found the audience it deserves. Doherty's fascinating and, indeed, freewheeling history reminds us that curmudgeonly people can shape the world, too." —*The American*

"Doherty . . . has written what should be the standard intellectual history of libertarianism for many years to come. Most laymen can probably offer a reasonably accurate definition of libertarianism's core premises . . . [b]ut Doherty's history makes clear that libertarianism is a political philosophy anchored in a robust intellectual tradition. His examination of that tradition is both comprehensive and insightful." —*City Journal*

RADICALS *for* CAPITALISM

A FREEWHEELING HISTORY OF THE MODERN
AMERICAN LIBERTARIAN MOVEMENT

BRIAN DOHERTY

PUBLICAFFAIRS
New York

For Angela Keaton

Freedom Fighter, Wife

Published in the United States by PublicAffairs™, a member of the Perseus Books Group.

Public Affairs books are available at special discounts for bulk purchases in the United States. by corporations, institutions, and other organizations.For more information, please contact the Special Markets Department at the Perseus Books Group, 2300 Chestnut Street, Suite 200, Philadelphia, PA 19103, or call (800) 810-4145, ext. 5000, or e-mail special.markets@perseusbooks.com.

Designed by Timm Bryson

Library of Congress Cataloging-in-Publication Data
Doherty, Brian.
  Radicals for capitalism : a freewheeling history of the modern American libertarian movement / Brian Doherty.
     p. cm.
  Includes bibliographical references and index.
  ISBN-13: 978-1-58648-350-0 (hardcover : alk. paper)
  ISBN-10: 1-58648-350-1 (hardcover : alk. paper) 1. Libertarianism—United States—History—20th century. 2. Capitalism—United States—History—20th century. I. Title.
  JC599.U5D64 2007
  320.51'2—dc22
2006036915

10 9 8 7 6 5 4 3 2 1

PBK: ISBN 978-1-58648-572-6

"We must make the building of a free society once more an intellectual adventure, a deed of courage. What we lack is a liberal Utopia, a program which seems neither a mere defense of things as they are nor a diluted kind of socialism, but truly liberal radicalism which does not spare the susceptibilities of the mighty . . . which is not too severely practical and which does not confine itself to what appears today as politically possible."

—*F. A. Hayek*

"Western civilization is based upon the libertarian principle, and all its achievements are the results of the action of free men."

—*Ludwig Von Mises*

"Neither the origins nor the essential principles of free-market ideas have anything to do with a defense of any of the established regimes of the world. Quite the contrary, the ideas themselves speak for a fundamental transformation of the world."

—*Don Lavoie*

"*Laissez-Faire* was and is revolutionary, and we have come to fulfill the work begun by the martyrs who have gone before; we have come to complete and resuscitate the Revolution."

—*Murray Rothbard*

"The revolution in public opinion which this cause requires is not to be expected in a day, or perhaps in an age."

—*Albert Jay Nock*

"To work for libertarianism—to oppose the growth of government and aid the liberation of the individual—used to be an idealistic choice taken for purely idealistic reasons. Now it is an act of intelligent and almost desperate self-defense."

—*Robert Anton Wilson*

"For radicals to deny their own past is to insure their future defeat."

—*David DeLeon*

CONTENTS

REVIVING AN AMERICAN RADICAL TRADITION

As the twenty-first century dawned, the most characteristic American government program of the twentieth century—Social Security—was on the ropes.

Social Security was wreathed in the highest-sounding motives and had become such a foundation stone of post–New Deal America that to speak ill of it had become the definition of political suicide. The program was designed to create unity, to ease suffering, to bind us all into one people. The policymakers behind Social Security took it upon themselves to manage the future and savings of all Americans intelligently and rationally. But what they set in place was a system that would eventually bind the coming generations to promises they could not reasonably afford. It was, in other words, the foundational political program of the twentieth century—well meaning, choice eliminating, and ignoring obvious secondary effects. And it was headed for failure.

A group of intellectuals and activists had long seen the need for an escape route from the Social Security system and had offered a solution two decades before most American politicians or citizens realized that a crisis was coming. The Cato Institute was a think tank for libertarian intellectuals and publicists, named after a pair of American revolutionary-era pamphleteers who wrote of inalienable rights and human liberty under the pseudonym Cato (an act of anonymous political speech—

also largely restricted by modern government under the guise of campaign finance laws).

One way to rescue America from the potential fiscal wreckage of Social Security, said the libertarians at Cato, was to give citizens personal control over their own savings and their own retirement. Let them keep at least a portion of their own money to invest however they thought best (in a nod toward political reality, the modern Cato plan would allow government to limit the choices of what private investments citizens could make with Social Security money), rather than force them into a complicated and doomed pyramid scheme by which the next generation was mortgaged to make good on government promises to the previous one.

Another program central to Western government had essentially died in the waning years of the previous century. The notion of welfare as a permanent entitlement, the idea and practice that it was the state's obligation to take care of (and manage) the lives of the poor, had been replaced by short-term assistance with work requirements. The new regime in welfare, shepherded by Democratic President Bill Clinton, seemed tailor-made to answer critiques by scholar Charles Murray in his influential 1984 book *Losing Ground*. In 1997, Murray wrote a book that laid out the intellectual roots of his successful critique of the welfare state: *What It Means to Be a Libertarian*.

The conspirators behind this libertarian movement suspected that it would take a perceived crisis to make their ideas seem sensible. Leading libertarian intellectuals from Murray Rothbard to Milton Friedman (two men who disagreed on many things) knew that a prime mission for libertarian intellectuals and activists would be to prepare solutions for problems that would arise from government programs before those problems became obvious to most politicians or laymen. As Friedman put it, "We [libertarians] do not influence the course of events by persuading people that we are right when we make what they regard as radical proposals. Rather, we exert influence by keeping options available when something has to be done at a time of crisis."[1]

Libertarians have ambitious goals for America. The movement's efforts include well-funded public policy research institutes, political opinion magazines, syndicated talk radio shows, training and funding centers for college professors, and America's most successful, long-lasting third political party.

Its eventual goals include the abolition of all drug laws (not just those against currently illegal narcotics and hallucinogens, but an end to prescription laws and the Food and Drug Administration as well), the abolition of the income tax, the abolition of all regulation of private sexual relations (from marriage to prostitution and everything in between), an end to public ownership and regulation of the airwaves, an end to overseas military bases and all warmaking not in direct defense of the homeland, an end to the welfare state, and an end to any legal restrictions whatsoever on speech and expression.

Libertarians' policy prescriptions are based on a simple idea with very complicated repercussions: Government, if it has any purpose at all (and many libertarians doubt it does), should be restricted to the protection of its citizens' persons and property against direct violence and theft. In their eyes, most modern government functions, if done by private individuals, would be seen as violence and theft. Libertarians' economic reasoning leads them to the conclusion that, left to their own devices, a free people would spontaneously develop the institutions necessary for a healthy and wealthy culture. They think that state interference in the economy, whether through taxing or regulation, makes us all poorer rather than richer.

Their ideas and policy prescriptions seem unbelievably radical in the current political context. But in many ways, libertarians argue, the United States was founded on libertarian principles. The Constitution defined a role for the federal government much smaller than what it practices today, and it restricted government to a limited set of mandated powers. This vision of America has been lost, libertarians argue, through a series of expansions of centralized federal power dating back at least to the Civil War (if not to when the Constitution replaced the Articles of Confederation), and including as cusp points Progressive Era reforms, the New Deal, and the Great Society.

Although it hearkens back in spirit to the American Founding, the libertarian vision is not backward looking or reactionary. By extending individual liberty into radical areas of sex, drugs, and science (no restrictions on stem cell research, cloning, or nanotech), libertarianism is the most future looking of American ideologies. It sells the promise of a world mankind hasn't yet fully known, one with personal liberty limited only by preventing damage to other people or their property. It's a world that would be freer, richer, and even cleaner.

Because libertarian proposals tend to seem, as noted above, unbearably radical to most Americans, who are relatively satisfied with their government, libertarianism has been a shadowy movement through twentieth-century intellectual history. Only since the mid-1970s has it begun attracting money, numbers, and attention to the degree that it is clearly an intellectual and ideological force to be understood and reckoned with. In a postcommunist world where the tyranny and poverty that accompany supposedly benevolent attempts to create a paradise of economic and political equality have been made abundantly clear, after a century where governments have killed more millions than a sane mind can comprehend, in a new century where international power politics and medieval religious throwbacks threaten a world of unremitting chaos, where the inevitable fiscal doom of the twentieth-century's entitlement state looms ever closer, libertarian ideas have more appeal than ever. Advances in technology have made possible new wired worlds where governments might be unnecessary, new biological abilities have expanded our potential power over ourselves and our environment to almost godlike status. We may even be on the cusp of creating new societies off the surface of the planet itself. All that makes the history, ideas, and ideologues of this movement of unrestricted human liberty, both mental and physical, and unleashed human abilities, both scientific and social, more relevant than they've ever been.

This book tells the libertarians' story and functions as a shadow ideological history of the twentieth century. While the world has undoubtedly turned in some ways in a more libertarian direction—and in some ways directly because of the thinkers and activists whose story this book tells—in many ways the libertarian movement remains a radical underground whose true influence is yet to come.

Libertarians believe either or both that people have a *right* to be mostly left alone to conduct their own affairs inasmuch as they don't harm others, or that things will on balance work out *best* for everyone if they are. They define "work out best" to mean creating the most varied and richest culture and economy. In a sense, that very freedom is part of what constitutes "best"—people will flourish and be happiest to the extent that they are free to choose their own life plans and pursue them as best they are able. In that pursuit, the libertarian believes, people will discover new ways of living, new ways of meeting human needs and desires, even new ways of understanding what it means to be human, that will enrich us all.

Libertarianism combines appeals to practicality and the way the world really works, through its reliance on economic logic to dissect the efficacy of state economic intervention, and a burning call to a higher justice, with its sense that there are certain things one human should not be able to force another human being to do, even if it is allegedly for her own good. Libertarianism thus provides an ideological package that is intended to resonate with both mind and heart. Some libertarian thinkers claim to rely more on freedom's good consequences in judging it right; some rely on a more purely moral argument about rights and justice. In fact, most of them rely on a combination, sometimes smooth, and sometimes rough, of both ideas, since their vision of rights tends to be rooted in what is best for human flourishing. Rights and consequences get linked, then, in a happy congruence.

This book will explain what libertarians believe and why through the stories of the people who invented, advocated, and spread libertarian ideas. Without libertarian activists, libertarian ideas would likely disappear, and certainly find no traction in the real world. Many libertarian intellectuals included in this book are scholar-activists. What's the point, as libertarian economist and philosopher Murray Rothbard wrote, of setting forth economic and philosophical truth with no context for achieving victory for that truth? To the truly impassioned libertarian, educating the public in libertarian theory is vital. Yet "just as the theory needs to be carried to the attention of the public, so does the theory need *people* to hold the banner, discuss, agitate, and carry the message forward and outward to the public. . . . both theory and movement become futile and sterile without each other; the theory will die on the vine without a self-conscious movement which dedicates itself to advancing the theory and the goal. The movement will become mere pointless motion if it loses sight of the ideology and the goal in view."[2]

"A COMPLEX ORDER RESTS ON A SIMPLE BUT SECURE FOUNDATION."

Libertarians can believe, with some justification, that we are in some sense already living in their world. Although tens of millions were killed in the name of his dream in the twentieth century, we are not living in Karl Marx's world or the world of his followers, either the intellectuals or the thugs. We live in a world energized and shaped by the beliefs of Marx's political–economic rivals and enemies—the classical liberals, the thinkers who believed a harmony of interests is manifest in unrestricted markets, that free trade can prevent war and make us all richer, that decentralized private property ownership helps create a spontaneous order of rich variety.

Liberalism in the nineteenth century meant simply the movement toward greater liberty. In the twentieth century liberalism has come to mean the expansion of state power in the pursuit of perceived social welfare, not necessarily liberation of the individual from outside control. The ideas and those who advocate them, which in the nineteenth century would have been known as liberal, are now "classical liberal."

Modern libertarians include both those carrying on that classical liberal tradition and radical heirs of that set of ideas who try to take those ideas as far as they might go: If private property is good, why have public property at all? If individual liberty is conducive to flourishing, then why should government regulate our use of weapons or drugs, or force us to pay for the indoctrination of our children in public schools, or steal from some in order to benefit others? The people and institutions whose story this book tells asked these questions, questions that barely seemed worth asking to most people, and helped cement them in our culture in the form of such vital movements— most only halfway measures by libertarian standards—as the medical marijuana movement, the press for homeschooling and vouchers, welfare reform, and the fight against eminent domain and campaign finance regulations that stifle speech.

Classical liberal values have shaped and defined modernity in many ways. Our role in life is no longer dictated by the status we were born into; to a large degree (though not entirely), legally protected guilds no longer define what we are able to do for a living; skin color and gender no longer restrict where we can live or work by the enforced order of men with guns. (For those who don't see the power of men with guns behind every law, libertarians say, just wait and see what ultimately happens if you refuse to obey one, even the most picayune one.) Churches no longer have power over secular life; the dream of total economic planning is over, the Berlin Wall has fallen, and the liberating wealth of capitalism is sought by millions to whom government policy had previously denied it in Asia and the Third World.

These are the ideas and animating principles from which libertarianism arose; the ideas of libertarian heroes such as Henry Maine, who celebrated the historical shift in human society from status to contract; the nineteenth-century free traders who wanted everyone to be able to buy and sell on mutually agreed terms with anyone, anywhere; the Scottish enlightenment figures who saw that a complex and valuable order could arise in human affairs without planners bossing everyone around.

Rather than creating a world of atomistic individuals, as its enemies have predicted accusingly, these classical liberal ideas have created a world in which networks of trust and interdependence are omnipresent and worldwide. Libertarian author David Boaz, an executive at the Cato Institute, explained what that means in practical terms: "My father's good reputation didn't extend much beyond the small town where we lived, and he would have had trouble borrowing money in a hurry even a few towns over, much less across the country or across the world. But . . . I have instant access to cash and credit virtually anywhere in the world—not because I have a better reputation than my father, but because the free market has developed credit institutions that extend around the world. As long as I pay my bills, the complex financial networks of American Express and Visa . . . allow me to get goods, services, or cash wherever I go. These systems work so well that we take them for granted, but they are truly a marvel. . . . The network of trust and credit relies on all the institutions of a free society: individual rights and responsibility, secure property rights, freedom of contract, free markets, and the rule of law. A complex order rests on a simple but secure foundation."[3]

The interconnected networks of the free market—which is the living apotheosis, in many ways, of the full libertarian vision—disciplined by free competition, motivated at its best by a desire for personal gain that generally translates into building long-term relationships based on trust rather than taking the money and running, while never even close to perfect in a world of imperfect humans, becomes, the libertarians argue, the closest to paradise that man can ever know.

Libertarianism qua libertarianism has mostly failed to garner extended attention in American political and ideological history. One reason for this is the complicated overlaps, both intellectual and institutional, between it and better-known and more successful right-wing conservatism. Modern American conservatism was constituted from three often warring tendencies in its formative years in the 1950s— traditionalism (often religious, with strong European and Catholic strains), sometimes rabid anticommunism and cold warriorism (usually cheer-led by ex-communists), and antistate libertarianism. However, libertarianism remained only a tendency within the modern conservative right, and never the dominant one. Traditionalism, anticommunism, and then fealty to a Republican Party that was seen as the right's standard-bearer in real-world politics, almost always overwhelmed the libertarianism.

Clear connections still exist, both personal and institutional, between libertarians and the right. But libertarian institutions have a separate identity from their occasional comrades, friends, and sparring partners among conservatives. This book tells the story of that distinctly libertarian set of thinkers and institutions. There is not a one of them who wouldn't tell you you were wrong, and very sharply, if you called them conservative.

Five thinkers form the spine of the story this book tells, five people without whom there would have been no uniquely libertarian ideas or libertarian institutions of any popularity or impact in America in the second half of the twentieth century. Those five are—in the order in which they are discussed in this book—Ludwig von Mises, Friedrich A. Hayek, Ayn Rand, Murray Rothbard, and Milton Friedman. Four men and one woman; four Jews and one Catholic; four economists and one novelist; four minarchists (the libertarian movement term for those who believe in a government mostly limited to defense, adjudication, and perhaps a limited range of public goods) and one anarchist (who believes we need no government at all); two native-born Americans and three immigrants; two Nobel Prize winners and three who remained not only aloof from most professional and intellectual accolades but generated a heated hostility from cultural gatekeepers; three best-selling authors and two secret influences.

The Austrian émigré economist Ludwig von Mises could fairly be considered the fountainhead of modern libertarianism, not only because of the strength of his own ideas, his unreconstructed nineteenth-century liberalism, and his mostly unyielding free market economics, but also because of his important role in the education and shaping of other important libertarian thought-leaders. F. A. Hayek was an early disciple of Mises's (though never technically his student) in Austria in the 1920s, and received his first professional job through him. Rothbard was an eager student (though a non-degree-seeking one) at Mises's New York University seminars in the 1950s and strayed little from the Misesian catechism in economics. Even the imperious and independent novelist Ayn Rand chose him as her most-recommended free market economist (though she did not embrace him in every respect).[4]

In addition to his influence on the new generation of American libertarians that arose in the 1960s—one couldn't escape Mises no matter your angle of approach to libertarianism; the movement's flagship think tank the Foundation for Economic Education honored him and relied on his ideas; the Nathaniel Branden Institute, pushing Ayn Rand's philosophy, recommended his books, and Murray Rothbard, who tried to keep in touch with every libertarian he could, evangelized on his behalf everywhere, in person and in print. He was also considered a formidable figure in the contemporary conservative movement, earning himself a place of honor toward the front of George Nash's history, *The Conservative Intellectual Movement in America Since 1945*. But, as with Hayek, who felt compelled to write an essay explicitly spelling out "Why I Am Not a Conservative," Mises didn't really fit into the burgeoning and more conventionally successful traditionalist/anticommunist American right wing.[5]

Murray Rothbard spelled out some of the reasons conservative mandarins ought to mistrust Mises in an article aptly called "The Laissez-Faire Radical," which limns many of the factors that distinguish libertarian free market economists such as Mises from the standard right-winger. Rothbard laments the attempts to claim Mises, during his centennial year 1981, as "a quintessential *National Review* conservative." Rothbard points out that Mises was rather "a proclaimed pacifist, who trenchantly attacked war and national chauvinism, a bitter critic of Western imperialism and colonialism; a believer in nonintervention with regard to Soviet Russia; a strong proponent of national self-determination, not only for national groups, but for subgroups down to the village level—and in theory, at least, down to the right of individual secession, which approaches anarchism; someone so hostile to immigration restrictions that he almost endorsed war against such countries as the United States and Australia to force them to open up their borders; a believer in the importance of class conflict in relation to the State; a caustic rationalist critic of Christianity and of all religion; and an admirer of the French Revolution."[6]

Mises had influence beyond economists and movement libertarians. Three of his associates, highly influenced by him, played major roles in the economic reconstruction of postwar Europe: Ludwig Erhard in Germany, Charles De Gaulle's economic adviser Jacques Rueff in France, and Luigi Einaudi, one of Italy's presidents. President Ronald Reagan often cited Mises as an inspiration (not that you could tell from his accomplishments). Mises's wife Margit relates that, upon meeting Reagan, he told her he was honored: "You don't know how often I consult the books of your husband before I make a speech." Lest that be interpreted as mere gallantry to the bereaved widow, Reagan had already spoken of loving Mises before his presidency.[7]

F. A. Hayek belonged to a wave of younger Austrian economists and social scientists whose lives were changed from a youthful attraction to socialism by Mises's 1922 attempt to demolish the theory in all its manifestations, *Socialism*.

Hayek's most famous book, *The Road to Serfdom,* appeared in 1944, during the period when a unique set of arguments and heroes began to coalesce, marking the dawn of modern libertarianism—a dawn then difficult to make out against the suffocating darkness of fascism, communism, and world war. Hayek combined a wide range of intellectual approaches to the question of liberty (his work covered economics, intellectual history, cognitive science, and evolutionary biology), and in the rarified fields of academia he is the most respected of libertarian thinkers.

He has also been more successful than most in influencing politics. Former British Prime Minister Margaret Thatcher once visited her Conservative Party's research division and, aggravated by their half measures toward freer markets, pulled out Hayek's 1960 epic *Constitution of Liberty* and slammed it down, announcing "This is what we believe."[8] Hayek's varied body of work has spawned an academic cottage industry, getting more active by the year, and his insights on the evolution of spontaneous orders have made him a favorite intellectual for a new generation of artificial intelligence theorists, computer mavens, and business management gurus.

The Russian-born novelist and philosopher Ayn Rand was the most popular libertarian of all and simultaneously the most hated. As a libertarian, if you don't love her, you are apt to feel embarrassed by her, burdened by her omnipresence and the occasional fanaticism of her followers. When Jerome Tuccille wrote his semifictional odyssey of a libertarian activist through the 1950s, 1960s, and early 1970s, he picked a title that seemed inevitable: *It Usually Begins with Ayn Rand*. It was true in 1971, when Tuccille's book appeared, and retains a hint of truth today, though less of one as more varied paths to libertarianism open.[9]

Ayn Rand is the most influential libertarian of the twentieth century to the public at large. She is a cultural force of impressive heft; a 1991 joint Library of Congress/Book of the Month Club poll found her magnum opus *Atlas Shrugged* to be the second most influential book on Americans' lives, after the Bible.[10] Yet her status within and relationship to the movement she was essential to spawning is a paradox. A is A, Aristotle taught us and Rand reminded us relentlessly; but the culturally immense libertarian novelist and philosopher would remind anyone who asked that she was *not* a libertarian. In fact, she disdained them more fiercely than most of her other (and many) ideological foes, calling them her "avowed enemies."[11] Her devoted official followers have continued this tradition. More libertarian movement activists and devotees consider her more integral to their intellectual and ideological development than any other thinker; yet Rand stood intentionally and proudly aloof from the movement that would not exist in anywhere near its current size and strength without her.

To understand Rand's disdain toward her most abundant and active intellectual children, you must understand the airtight world of her philosophy—Objectivism. She invented the name when she discovered, to her horror, that some would-be followers were referring to themselves as Randists. She is "much too conceited," she related, "to allow such a use of my name."[12] While she lived, she didn't even allow people outside her immediate circle to call themselves Objectivists, for fear that she would be thought responsible for any intellectual or moral errors they committed (and in Rand's eyes, those categories overlapped). "Students of Objectivism" was the proper phrase.[13]

Rand, more than any other libertarian thinker but Murray Rothbard, was a system builder. Not content, as were Hayek and Mises, to situate themselves as contributing fresh thoughts to an ongoing Western tradition of political and economic liberalism, she thought she was recreating philosophy from the ground up. Her political libertarianism was not based merely on the idea that laissez-faire capitalism was the most efficient social system or created the most wealth. Politics was at the end of her system (though some critics argue that her philosophical base was more rationalization for previous political convictions than purely rational).[14] She insisted that a philosophical system must be one airtight unified structure, and generally had contempt for those who reached the same conclusions as she without the same base. The self-assured iconoclasm that led Rand to angrily reject her largest and most active band of followers was central to almost every decision she made in her dramatic and tempestuous life.

New York–born economist, philosopher, and journalist Murray Rothbard is both loved and rejected with great passion by various fellow libertarians. He was equally at home in the scrum of institution building and movement politics and in rarified realms of economics and political philosophy, and equally capable of making enemies in either area. He possessed the pugnacious New York Jewish intellectual style, passionate, funny, certain, and scabrous. He'd have made a great, characteristic communist and then neocon intellectual if only he hadn't been an anarchist libertarian.

Rothbard intersected Rand's orbit and became sold on the natural rights tradition from her after his initial background in Mises's utilitarian economics. Yet while Rand is the libertarian figure with the highest profile outside the movement, Rothbard is the major libertarian whom a typical American, layperson or academic, is least likely to know about.

He is, though, the most uniquely and characteristically *libertarian* of libertarians; the one whose influence explains most about what makes the ideas, behavior, and general flavor of American libertarianism unique; the most illustrative and paradigmatic of the foundational figures of modern libertarianism. He lacks Milton Friedman's almost universal respect as an economist and commentator. He lacks Rand's huge cult following. He lacks Hayek's academic influence. He came to intellectual maturity in the late 1940s and 1950s with work by the other four major libertarian influences affecting his own thinking, whether as positive influence or foe to grapple with. He had the least affinity for Friedman, because of disagreements on economic method and the proper role of the state; and the most for Mises, whose New York University seminars Rothbard attended for many years and whose distinct "Austrian" style of economics Rothbard advocated and furthered.

Rothbard strove to create, in his own words, a "thorough and systematic theory of liberty."[15] He built his system from varied materials: the Austrian economics of Mises, a natural-rights ethic that came to him first from Rand;[16] a yen for seeking libertarian lessons in history, particularly regarding the alliance between big business and the state, and the state's bloody history of warfare; a rehabilitation of the mostly forgotten nineteenth-century American individualist anarchist tradition as exemplified by Lysander Spooner and Benjamin Tucker; and a delight and fascination with the mechanics of movement building and down-and-dirty politics that the other four major libertarian influences abjured.

Rothbard was the most radical exponent of an anarchism that was latent in many of the important figures of 1940s and 1950s libertarianism, even though none of them dared speak its name—not even Rothbard, at first. While to many, both libertarian and nonlibertarian, "libertarian" means a dedication to a small government, a night watchman state in the popular formulation, one restricted to the protection of citizens' life, liberty, and property, limited for the most part to the police and court functions, Rothbard advocated a fully anarchist libertarianism. He argued that even the functions of defense and courts could, and should, be provided through voluntary transactions in a free and competitive market.

Rothbard affected the libertarian movement not only through his writings but also through personal influence on those he met, befriended, tutored, formed organizations with, and in many cases feuded and broke with. For all his undoubted influence, Rothbard's edge-seeking radicalism and many strategic turns and bridge burning earned him many detractors in the movement.

Milton Friedman is a figure of world-historical importance, the American libertarian who will (further victories for libertarianism or no) clearly be recognized as one of the most important intellectuals of the twentieth century. For that reason, right-wing conservatives have tried to claim him as their own. Friedman is having none of it; he knows he is a libertarian, though if he had his way he'd be able to call himself, and be understood, as a liberal—in the classical nineteenth-century tradition, that is, someone who believed in individual autonomy above the perquisites of states, unions, guilds, or church.

He arose from a traditional, almost archetypal, American background, the son of an immigrant peddler and restaurateur, befitting a scientist and polemicist advocating what he considers a traditionally American philosophy of governance. But from those beginnings the depth and breadth of Friedman's impact on both economics and public policy is undeniable by friend or foe. As economist and polemicist, he has been the most widely respected libertarian of the twentieth century. Rand sold many more books, but she is not recognized by the opinion makers of her fields, literature and philosophy, as a great; precisely the opposite. Mises's economic contributions were more architectonic; but it is Friedman of whom the *New Palgrave* writes: "In effectiveness, breadth and scope, his only rival among the economists of the 20th century is Keynes."[17] Rothbard was a more colorful and hardcore libertarian polemicist; but Friedman had a triweekly *Newsweek* column to expound his policy views in his dry, but authoritative and convincing, prose before millions of readers from 1966 to 1984.

Friedman was a highly sought-after adviser of presidents and potentates around the globe for decades; he is proximately responsible for some major constitutive aspects of the modern world, from America's volunteer army to its income tax withholding system; from floating exchange rates to a Federal Reserve that tries to keep a tight lid on money supply growth. Ronald Reagan considered Friedman's 1980 book *Free to Choose* a must read, as does that younger actor-turned-politician, California Governor Arnold Schwarzenegger. Friedman is a remarkable example of radicalism in action, a hard-core libertarian who has never been shy about end goals that are still far in the future, while ideologically entrepreneuring politically achievable steps that will—*probably*—lead further in the direction he seeks.

"Radicals for Capitalism."

Libertarianism is based in economic theory, as economic science teaches how workable order can arise from the seeming chaos of free actions uncoordinated by a single outside intelligence, and how government intervention is apt to upset that balance. It is based in moral theory, positing what is or is not right when it comes to a human being, or group of human beings, using force or coercion on another. It is based in political theory, exploring the likely effects of granting human beings power over others. It is ultimately a delicate ecological balance of all these, with history in the mix as well, to further understand how the constant struggle of liberty versus power tends to play out in the real world.

But as much as it is economic, moral, and political, the most significant thing about libertarianism, the element that distinguishes its unique place in modern American thought, is that it is *radical*. It takes insights about justice and order and the fight between liberty and power farther and deeper than most standard American liberals, patriots, or Jeffersonians. It is a uniquely American radicalism whose goals can be described in many ways. Libertarians are radicals for liberty; they are radicals for choice; but a phrase, first used by Ayn Rand, characterizes the movement's prickliness, its willingness to take on terms from their enemies and turn them to their own advantage: Libertarians are "radicals for capitalism." They are radicals who believe in the system of private property and free exchange that has been demonized by its enemies as "capitalism"—the tool of capital. But the libertarian radicals for capitalism argue that that system is good not just for capital, but for everyone.

A general aura of unlovely suspicion surrounds the libertarian movement—that in its railings against state power it produces nothing but rank apologetics for market power; that those who finance or participate in libertarian agitation of whatever variety do so merely out of a gross desire for specific pecuniary advantage in this world; that, in the crudest Marxist sense, anyone who advocates these ideas is doing so under the influence of, and merely to protect, privilege.

But libertarianism, this book will show, is a radical doctrine; one that would upset any existing concentrations of state *or* market power to such a degree, sever so many tangled and long-spun links between business and government, that anyone supporting it out of pecuniary interests is a fool. Certainly, many, even most, financiers of libertarian causes have been big businessmen—they do tend to possess the concentrations of money that make large-scale philanthropy of any sort possible. But in doing so, they are following a personal interest in these ideas, not seeking quick advantage. Take, for example, textile king Roger Milliken, who has spent a great deal of money agitating for tariffs to protect his industry—as unlibertarian a cause as one could imagine, and one that does redound to his direct pecuniary interest.

But for decades, Milliken also spent a great deal of money supporting, and insisting his own employees sit through, the pacifist-anarchist lectures of libertarian educator Robert LeFevre, a cause that very likely could hurt his bottom line.

The biggest financiers of libertarian causes in the past few decades, the billionaire Koch brothers Charles and David, indulge in more standard political philanthropy as well, such as funding Republican candidates; their funding of libertarian causes is a labor of ideological love. Those who do believe simultaneously that a world of laissez-faire would be only to the benefit of existing plutocratic structures, and that plutocrats are generally effective conspirators in their own interest, must explain the comparative paucity of funding of specifically libertarian advocacy—not much more than $125 million a year, and while growing, not growing by leaps and bounds. (The Cato Institute, by far the largest and most influential libertarian organization, is currently a $22 million a year operation.) Another libertarian foundation, Liberty

Fund, is worth over $350 million, but spends only 5 percent or so of that a year, mostly on scholarly activities not designed to directly influence public policy. While no longer completely subterranean, and with very real effects on the world, libertarianism is still a radical, outsider movement.

This is a story of thinkers and activists who felt the need to pursue their beliefs through alternative institutions, living out something of a shadow history against the "great" actions of politicians and major parties and the idea books and publications that constitute mainstream American intellectual history in the twentieth century. Not entirely of course—it is hard to accuse Ayn Rand or Milton Friedman of living in the shadows, as much as their opponents might wish to keep them there. Friedman in particular has always tried, while remaining radical in his goals, to work within and among the institutions whose gears mesh with the wheels of the "real world"—focusing his energy mostly on the GOP, not LP (Libertarian Party); on *Newsweek* and not the movement magazine *Liberty*.

Chapter 1 will explain aspects of the intellectual roots of modern American libertarianism in prerevolutionary Whig radicalism in England; in the patriotic American revolutionary tradition itself; in nineteenth-century French economic and philosophical radicalism and the classical liberal tradition of peace and free trade between nations; in the native anarchism of various curious nineteenth-century American abolitionists, free lovers, and alternative community builders. While many thinkers central to modern Western civilization, from John Locke to Adam Smith, had ideas of great importance to the modern libertarian tradition, this chapter will focus not on them—widely and thoroughly discussed in hundreds of other places beyond my powers to add or detract—but on more obscure characters who tend to be remembered and honored only by libertarians nowadays. Chapter 2 will discuss the early careers and radical free market economics of the Austrian School, a dominant intellectual influence on modern American libertarianism. (But not the only one. The Chicago School, with Milton Friedman its most famous exponent, has also added tremendously to the movement's arsenal of economic thought on the benefits of free markets. The differences between the two, which will be discussed at greater length, are in method—the

Chicagoites tend to be more empirical, the Austrians more theoretical; the Austrians focused only on microeconomics, the choices of individuals; the Chicagoites more willing to think in terms of macroeconomics, the shifts and changes in inflation rates, gross national products, and the like; the Chicagoites embrace the standard tools of the economic profession such as equilibrium analysis and assumptions of perfect information; the Austrians think of markets as an eternally shifting process in which equilibrium is at best a useful mental exercise and at worst a lie, and also as a realm in which the search for information is one of the key problems; the Austrians tend to be more aggressively and consistently libertarian in their economic policy positions.)

Chapter 3 will introduce the three founding mothers of modern libertarianism—Rose Wilder Lane, Isabel Paterson, and Ayn Rand—independent and fierce women creating a fresh ideological tradition with some tools from a dying classical liberalism. With Chapter 4, the institutional history of modern libertarianism proper begins, with the founding of the first modern libertarian education institution, the Foundation for Economic Education. Chapter 5 discusses the anarchist strain in the modern movement and the rise of Ayn Rand's Objectivist movement. Chapter 6 tells of the triumphs and travails of the movement during the 1960s, when squads of radical youngsters embraced libertarianism, only to be condemned by their heroine Ayn Rand as "hippies of the right." Chapter 7 discusses the rise of the Libertarian Party and the entry into the movement of billionaire financier Charles Koch, and the aftereffects of that sudden injection of cash. Chapter 8 relates the story of libertarianism in the Reagan and Gingrich eras and beyond, and limns its influence on philosophy, culture, economics, and even psychiatry. Chapter 9 discusses the final days of the major libertarian heroes, and the epilogue assesses the controversies and prospects for this set of ideas now and in the future.

This is an insider's history. I have worked for, or with, or appeared at conferences sponsored by, or written for publications issued by, many of the major libertarian institutions discussed herein. I am currently a senior editor of *Reason* magazine, a full-time staff position. I have been an employee of the Cato Institute (from 1991 to 1994) and managing editor of one of its magazines, *Regulation* (from 1993 to 1994). I received a fellowship from the Competitive Enterprise Institute in 1999 and spoke at conferences under the sponsorship of, and received small writing prizes from, the Institute for Humane Studies. I've attended Liberty Fund–sponsored seminars and I've written for publications of the Foundation for Economic Education and the Ludwig von Mises Institute.

In other words, I'm hip deep in this world. My understanding of the ideas, institutions, and thinkers whose story this book tells is informed by seventeen years of study and labor from the inside, and is shaped by libertarians' own sense of the thinkers and institutions that they see as part of their team. Not everyone who has ever advocated a libertarian idea counts as part of the "libertarian movement" per se, not as understood within it. And there are people and institutions whose stories will be told here—including such luminaries as Nobel Prize–winning economists Hayek and Friedman—to whom radical libertarians might deny the label. But this book is rooted in a detailed and internal understanding of how libertarians have understood themselves over the past half century.

Like obscenity, libertarianism is something I know when I see, and other libertarians feel the same way. Many a movement libertarian's favorite pastime is reading others out of the movement for various perceived ideological crimes. As Fred Smith, head of the libertarian think tank Competitive Enterprise Institute, says, "When two libertarians find themselves agreeing on something, each knows the other has sold out." Libertarians are a contentious lot, in many cases delighting in staking ground and refusing to move on the farthest frontiers of applying the principles of noncoercion and nonaggression; resolutely finding the most outrageous and obnoxious position you could take that is theoretically compatible with libertarianism and challenging anyone to disagree. If they are not of the movement, then you can enjoy having shocked them with your purism and dedication to principle; if they are of the movement, you can gleefully read them out of it. Libertarians (not all libertarians, certainly, and not even many) have advocated on libertarian principle private ownership of nuclear weapons; the right of parents to starve their children; and that, if you fell off a building and grabbed onto a flagpole and didn't have the explicit permission of the person who owned the balcony, you ought to let yourself fall rather than violate their property rights by crawling to safety.

For all its occasionally zany radicalism, libertarianism is not a utopian ideology. More than any other set of political ideas, it recognizes and is based in the limits that economic reality and human nature place on attempts to use the state to accomplish grand goals. It instead "places its restricted faith in the unpredictable and unplanned consequences of the individual decisions of free men and women."[18]

Libertarianism is deeply rooted in the impulses of America's founding, and could easily be seen as its apotheosis and fulfillment. We live in a world with citizens riven over issues that almost always come down to angry debate over government action, issues in which much of the conflict would disappear if government action were removed from the table—from immigration policy to public schools to entitlements to value wars in the public square to abortion to war. In that world, the ideas promulgated by the people and institutions whose story this book tells may seem a reasonable and achievable basis for a conceivable next American revolution.

1

PATRIOTS, UNTERRIFIED JEFFERSONIANS, AND SUPERFLUOUS MEN

The libertarian vision is all in Jefferson. Read your Declaration of Independence: We are all created equal; no one ought to have any special rights and privileges in social relations with other men. We have, inherently, certain rights—to our life, to our freedom, to do what we please in order to find happiness. Government has one purpose: to help us protect those rights. And if it doesn't do that, then it has to go, by any means necessary.[1]

Hard to imagine a more libertarian document; and there it is, one of the nearly sacred founding documents of the United States of America. Of course, not everything about the American founding meets complete libertarian approval; lingering affection for the antifederalist cause is one of libertarianism's many interpretive peculiarities in the modern American context. The antifederalists saw in the U.S. Constitution a dangerous return to the sort of tyrannical powers on the part of the national government that we had fought the British to free ourselves from. Antifederalists were particularly alarmed by Congress's power under the Constitution to tax almost without limit, to alter the time and manner of elections, and to raise and support armies.[2] And they understood, as does the modern libertarian, that state power is always trying to overwhelm political liberty, and that defending it requires the unwavering diligence of free citizens. But overall, the modern American libertarian, if so inclined, can feel unambiguous stirrings of patriotic fervor when contemplating the covenantal purpose of this nation.

Lessons about the benefits of free markets are embedded in American history, not merely American ideology; the famines and travails of the Plymouth and Jamestown colonies in their beginnings were the result of unfortunate experiments in agricultural communism, providing grim lessons in the necessity of private property and free trade.[3]

Murray Rothbard, who wrote the only explicitly libertarian history of colonial America, leads the reader into a wonderland of libertarian example making. He paints a portrait of people who gleefully tarred and feathered customs inspectors, juries that refused to convict on unjust laws, and a citizenry that refused to buy government-confiscated property; Rothbard identifies swaths of essential and mostly blissful anarchism at certain places and times (Pennsylvania in the 1680s, for example). Some colonial Americans were so uninterested in politics that they didn't bother sending representatives to assemblies; they were so devoted to personal rights and justice over state power that they enjoyed justice that was dedicated to compensating the victim, not merely giving governments the power to punish. In prerevolutionary history Rothbard finds Americans fighting against any encroachment on their liberties, with a strong streak of religious liberty (rare at that time), inspired by radical Whig notions of inalienable and natural rights to life and liberty, as well as the elimination of tyrants. While Rothbard's narrative history has a distinct agenda, it provides a fair amount of convincing evidence for a powerful libertarian streak in the character and behavior of early Americans.

All ideologies try to create a usable past; libertarians have often relied on the philosophical spirit of the American Revolution to support the modern libertarian vision of the proper role of government. To counter this, conservatives rightly point at elements of early American civic life that would strike a modern as the worst sort of tyranny, things most colonials seemed to accept sanguinely enough, from sumptuary laws to state-established religions to vagrancy statutes that made moving into certain towns nearly impossible. The American past is complicated, and libertarianism's apotheosis remained a task for the future—and remains so today.

"THE PEOPLE ARE THE MOST IMPORTANT, THE STATE IS NEXT, AND THE RULER IS THE LEAST IMPORTANT."

The idea of human political liberty, of restrictions in the power and reach of government, goes back forever. One can play the game, as libertarians sometimes do, of finding libertarian-sounding rhetoric from such hoary and venerated figures as Confucius's disciple Mencius, who wrote that "in a nation, the people are the most important, the state is next, and the ruler is the least important."[4] That idea about the state's circumscribed role, however, never led to the development of an effective mechanism to create regime change, much less real system change, in Confucian China—nor was there any widespread urge to do so.

In the Western tradition, Judaism contained the idea that the king rules beneath God, is subject to God's rules, and is in no sense divine. The existence of a separate priestly caste meant that the king wasn't necessarily responsible for interpreting what was his business or his mandate. The heart of Judaism was the contract between Jehovah and the Jews. Even God, the highest source of government, owed obligations to man, or at least to the Jews, as long as they kept up their end of the bargain.[5] Christian intellectual history has a natural law and natural rights tradition that recognizes discoverable, rational standards for behavior and human control of behavior that are above and beyond the decisions of earthly governments. This tradition can have strong libertarian implications.[6]

The notion of a higher law that binds government or even God was not a purely Judeo-Christian innovation. Some Greeks believed that, as historian Mario Attilio Levi put it, "the king, even if he were a God, was fallible. They continued to believe that the law was the product of reason, not revelation."[7] *Prometheus Bound* by Aeschylus (featuring Prometheus steadfastly and heroically defying Zeus in the name of a justice higher than the gods), *Antigone* by Sophocles, and plays by Euripides attacking slavery and the barbarity of war, indicate a people who understood the distinction between what earthly or even divine authority commanded and what was right and just.[8]

The idea of limits on state power antedate the Western heritage. Levi writes of the concept of *ma'at* in ancient Egypt: "Ma'at was a limitation imposed on God by himself. Just as, in theological terms, God begat himself in the form of the king, so 'ma'at' became the Law that even the King-god had to respect, and which was therefore separate from him as the son was separate from the father."[9]

The *idea* that state power is not the last word in justice is ancient; the yearning for liberty against power and attempts to figure out what it means and how it can be actuated are not restricted to a particular religious tradition, though in practice the set of ideas and institutions that arose from certain cultures seemed more amenable to liberty than others did, despite what Mencius said. The notion of a king imposing restrictions on himself would remind a modern libertarian of a constitution whose limits are judged by the same government empowered by that constitution. Modern American history, libertarians argue, shows that government is not apt to work for liberty, considering the enormous expansion of government power since the Progressive Era and New Deal, supported by excuses such as the Constitution's Commerce Clause, which is alleged to mean that even wheat grown on your own farm for your own consumption falls under federal power because you *could* have sold it in an interstate market.

Libertarian ideas about human politics go back to the creation of the state itself. While a strictly modern libertarian historical anthropology has not been fully developed and a theory of the origins of the state is merely implicit in most libertarians, it is fair to characterize the vision of German anthropologist Franz Oppenheimer in *The State* (1922) as a dominant libertarian story of how we ended up with the state and what it's all about in origin and essence.[10] Oppenheimer says that the state was born in blood and conquest, as conquerors lived off of the efforts of the conquered through taxation and in return provided "protection." In Oppenheimer's classic distinction, the state reified the practice of the "political" means of survival—predation—as opposed to the "economic" means—production.

The history of Western civilization, however bloody and tyrannical in practice, provides succor for libertarian belief in the power and rightness of liberty and free markets. That relatively free markets and capitalism have produced the wealth and liberty we enjoy today is central to the libertarian story of Western culture. However, no state, guild, church, or bastion of aristocratic privilege has ever allowed those forces to operate totally unrestricted. A common interpretation has it that the urbanization and mechanization created by the relatively free flow of labor and capital known as the Industrial Revolution made millions miserable. The libertarian counterargument is that those millions would not have been alive at all had not free markets, mechanization, and urbanization created surplus wealth above mere agricultural sufficiency.[11]

"IF SOCIETY COULD BE BUILT AND KEPT ENTIRE WITHOUT GOVERNMENT, THE SCAFFOLDING MIGHT BE THROWN DOWN, WITHOUT THE LEAST . . . CAUSE OF REGRET."

The twentieth-century movement for limited government—very limited government, extremely limited government, at times totally limited government—began in America, and American libertarians won't let you forget it. Lots of America's sacred iconography is co-opted by libertarians—Liberty Bell, Statue of Liberty—hey, it's right there in the name. Liberty is this country's shibboleth.

Americans were Englishmen first, and, as historian Gordon Wood wrote, "no people in the history of the world had ever made so much of [liberty]. Unlike the poor enslaved French, the English [in colonial American days] had no standing army, no letters de cachet; they had their habeas corpus, their trials by jury, their freedom of speech and conscience, and their right to trade and travel; they were free from arbitrary arrests and punishments; their homes were their castles."[12]

The progress of markets and wealth in the past centuries has eliminated many aspects of day-to-day early American life that strike us today as tyrannical, from the sharp distinctions of rank, the religion-based social control in the towns, and of course the most prominent stain on America's libertarian heritage, the status of blacks and women. (In the form of social pressure as opposed to strict state action, such problems have not entirely disappeared.) As nineteenth-century libertarian hero Henry Maine noted, the history of Western civilization and Western liberty has been the shift from status to contract—from being locked into positions based on who you were at birth, to being able to live, work, do what you wish, deal with others as you please, based on mutually binding contracts—commercial, residential, or marital—chosen by both parties.

More than just Englishmen, Americans were Englishmen who zealously protected their liberties, enflamed by pamphleteers like John Trenchard and Thomas Gordon, of the famous *Cato's Letters* (after which the modern libertarian think tank the Cato Institute is named). Trenchard and Gordon, identified by historian of American revolutionary thought Bernard Bailyn as probably the best-read and most widely regarded pamphleteers of prerevolutionary times, believed in inherent natural human rights that no government may violate. These rights, they maintained, come from God and cannot be alienated; the function of government is solely to defend citizens' persons or property. The capper was, as their hero Whig martyr Algernon Sidney said, free men always have the right to resist tyrannical government.[13]

Thomas Paine, a leading radical of the founding generation, knew that this antimonarchical revolution in the colonies was also something new; that the band playing as British General Cornwallis surrendered was correct: The world had turned upside down. As Paine put it, "we see with other eyes; we hear with other ears; and think with other thoughts than those we formerly used."[14] As embodied in the Declaration of Independence, American revolutionaries were fighting for the natural rights of all mankind, not just their own particular rights as a people.[15] To the early American revolutionary, "English rights were the legal application of natural rights."[16]

Magna Carta or no, the rights of Americans were not not theirs *only* because of any ancient "contract." As James Wilson put it, using ancient legal terms, "The fee simple of freedom and government is declared to be in the people."[17] Thus the people always had the right of revolution against a repressive government. This too was part of a grand Whig British heritage that the colonists were upholding even if king and Parliament (the latter of whom many colonists thought they owed no fealty to regardless) were ignoring it.[18] The Declaration of Independence was Americans' way of reminding them, and the world, of the rights of a free people.[19]

Using ideas echoed by later French liberals, Americans had a fresh vision of civic virtue; no longer based only in participation in public (i.e., governmental) matters, the new virtue, as historian of the revolutionary era Gordon Wood put it, "flowed from the citizen's participation in society, not in government, which the liberal-minded increasingly saw as the principle source of the evils of the world. . . . People were wrong to consider society as merely the scaffolding of government; [as James Wilson said,] 'in the just order of things, government is the scaffolding of society: and if society could be built and kept entire without government, the scaffolding might be thrown down, without the least inconvenience or cause of regret.'" An early statement of classic American anarchism, that.[20]

In early America, commerce—that great libertarian emollient of all social ills, that creator of wealth and happiness—was breaking free of the old-fashioned strictures and attitudes that denied it respect. We were to be a great commercial republic and, to the best of our ability, a free republic. In other words, a libertarian republic.

If it had actually worked out that way, the modern American libertarian movement would not exist. There is no room here for a detailed discussion of the long history of the diminution of American liberties, though some libertarian or libertarian fellow-traveler historians of American thought and politics have tried to supply it.[21] Still, even as the contrary impulse toward federalism and nationalism overshadowed these radical founding notions, libertarian ideals surfaced now and again as a counterweight to the impulses toward centralization and statism.

Libertarian historians have detected libertarian strains in the Jacksonian fight against centralizing institutions of federal control such as the national bank, even in aspects of the Confederacy, though that's tricky and controversial ground for libertarians because of human slavery. Many libertarians tend to be sensitive to the quasi-tyrannical means Lincoln used; while not necessarily sympathetic to Confederate values, they sense that the issues involved are more complicated than Lincoln's triumphalism and regret some of the powers of the centralized federal state that arose in the aftermath of, and to a large degree as a result of, the Civil War.[22]

Libertarians find political heroes from the second half of the nineteenth century, though it was hardly the golden age of laissez-faire. Dug up for praise on occasion in libertarian publications is Supreme

Court Justice Stephen Field. A former chief justice of the California Supreme Court, Field was named a justice in 1863 and served for thirty-five years in, ironically, what could be seen as a court-packing scheme by Lincoln (ironic because both court packing and Lincoln were things that libertarians in the 1930s and 1940s were not enthusiastic about), a rare tenth justice (the court was reduced back to nine in 1869, but Field stayed).[23]

Field was one of the pioneers of the concept (beloved by many libertarian legal thinkers) of substantive due process—the notion that the due process protected by the Fourteenth Amendment applied not merely to procedures but to the substance of laws as well. Thus the courts could overturn state laws that regulated private property. As slavery was abolished, the Fourteenth Amendment tried to guarantee that no state government could violate the "privileges and immunities" of an American citizen. Field argued, as one libertarian journalist put it, "the phrase 'privileges or immunities,'. . . describes those 'natural and inalienable rights' that 'belong to the citizens of all free governments.' Furthermore, 'among these must be placed the right to pursue lawful employment in a lawful manner, without other restraints than such as equally affects all persons.'"[24] This idea that the Fourteenth Amendment gave the federal government the power to overturn state laws that violated rights is a cornerstone of twentieth-century liberal constitutional jurisprudence. However, hardly any judges use it as Field and other late nineteenth-century judges did, to overthrow economic regulation.

For example, through substantive due process doctrine a court could declare and protect the right to practice a trade, noting that without this doctrine "there be no protection, either in the principles upon which our republican government is founded, or in the prohibitions of the constitution, against such invasion of private rights, all property and all business in the State are held at the mercy of a majority of its legislators."[25]

Field believed in economic rights unspecified in the Constitution (which he linked with the Fourteenth Amendment, but which could be placed in the libertarians' favorite amendment, the Ninth, which specifically roots the Constitution in a natural rights tradition that says we are born with more rights than any constitution could ever list or specify). His intellectual enemies linked this belief with popular late-nineteenth-century Yale political scientist and sociologist, William Graham Sumner. Sumner opposed imperialism, advocated strict business laissez-faire, and celebrated the right of entrepreneurs to accumulate as much as they can in an honest way. Sumner was a social Darwinist who thought the best should be left to succeed and others left to fail in a free economy. He celebrated the notion that the market order was so brain-bustingly complex that government attempts to manipulate it are apt to lead to unpredictable and likely negative results.

Sumner celebrated "the forgotten man," the independent middle-class man who falls between the cracks of the plutocrats on the one hand and the paupers who receive benefits from government reformers and planners on the other. Yet he has to pay for the schemes that help them. Sumner also rightly predicted that the twentieth century, given the burgeoning combination of socialism and warmongering, would be "a frightful effusion of blood in revolution and war."[26] He eloquently celebrated liberty's intimate connection with peace: "The great reason why all these enterprises which begin by saying to someone else, We know what is good for you better than you know yourself and we are going to make you do it, are false and wrong is that they violate liberty; or, to turn the same statement into other words, the reason why liberty, of which we Americans talk so much, is a good thing is that it means leaving people to live out their lives in their own way, while we do the same. If we believe in liberty, as an American principle, why do we not stand by it"[27] when it comes to foreign affairs? Sumner mordantly noted in his anti-imperialist essay "The Conquest of the United States by Spain" that the United States, despite its apparent victory in the Spanish-American War, allowed Spain's imperial system to conquer it. "We have beaten Spain in a military conflict, but we are submitting to be conquered by her on the field of ideas and policies."[28]

A crude version of American history paints the nineteenth century as an era of the unbridled laissez-faire that libertarians call for—an era that the American people found intolerable and rebelled against with a series of sensible Progressive Era laws that rescued the American dream of opportunity and equality from the villainous plans of the robber barons.[29] Just because the occasional ideologue like Field or Sumner worked on the American mind during the nineteenth century does not mean that era actuated the eternal libertarian dream. Before the

Civil War enormous state subsidies went into internal improvements, most of them regrettable[30] as the state interfered with people's business and personal lives.[31] Historian Sidney Fine, who celebrates America's departure from laissez-faire in the twentieth century, writes that "the doctrine of laissez faire . . . appears to be of relatively slight import in the formulation of state policy before the Civil War . . . but . . . those who argued for or against laissez faire between 1865 and 1901 generally spoke little of the earlier, varied activities of government in the United States, and tended to assume that laissez faire had been the determining factor in the formulation of government policy."[32] By the second half of the nineteenth century, as Fine points out, big business wanted and got "a national banking system, a high protective tariff, generous land grants to railway corporation" among other government giveaways and interventions on behalf of the wealthy and powerful.[33] As Arthur Ekirch, a historian of American liberal decline beloved by libertarians, noted, "Instead of the limited state desired by Jeffersonian believers in an agrarian society, the post-Civil War era was characterized by the passage of a stream of tariffs, taxes, and subsidies all unprecedented in their volume and scope."[34]

A libertarian movement functionary debating with Murray Rothbard in the late 1950s opined that libertarians should not allow the left to spread the myth of nineteenth-century laissez-faire. Libertarians must stake their ground as true revolutionaries, a stance that is "rightly and accurately ours!"[35] The nineteenth century was a world of interventionism and mercantilism, with government a useful tool for big business, if not for the less well off. Libertarianism is the ultimate future revolution, the truly liberal, truly free world of tomorrow, for a mankind liberated from all yokes of status and privilege. Rothbard thought, strategically, that libertarians should "praise the American tradition of free enterprise" while maintaining that "we are revolutionaries and not reactionaries because we want to go all the way . . . . *Laissez-Faire* was and is revolutionary, and we have come to fulfill the work begun by the martyrs who have gone before; we have come to complete and resuscitate the Revolution."[36]

The general sweep of the American experience is to a large degree disheartening to the modern libertarian because of the horrors of war and statism unleashed by the Civil War,[37] the invention of the Federal

Reserve, the income tax, Progressive Era business regulations (arising, as historians and theorists both libertarian and leftist have stressed, more from business desires for rational control over their own industry than from an impulse to empower or help the citizenry), World War I and World War II, the New Deal, and the Great Society. American government has steadily shifted toward less reliance on the free play of commercial republican virtue as it moves toward a traditional pattern of a god-king government, unrestricted by constitutions, dedicated to caring for and managing people in all their activities. This is why a gang of economists, novelists, theorists, pamphleteers, and politicians founded the libertarian movement in the first place.

"THE STATE IS THE GREAT FICTION BY WHICH EVERYBODY TRIES TO LIVE AT THE EXPENSE OF EVERYONE ELSE."

Libertarianism arose in America from distinctly American roots. Yet in its soul it is a cosmopolitan philosophy, celebrating a world united in spirit, ideas, and trade, while reveling in the wide panorama of freely chosen local peculiarity that only relatively free polities can provide. Modern libertarians sought solace, inspiration, and insight from radical liberals of Europe in the eighteenth and nineteenth centuries and even earlier. Montaigne's good friend Etienne de la Boétie, in his *Discourse on Voluntary Servitude* (1577), tackled the question of *how* governments keep command over people who command more force than the government ever could. He realized that government's control over us is ultimately ideological—that people believe they ought to obey the state before the state can command obedience. His insight helped drive modern libertarianism's mission to educate the public as to the true nature and effects of the state.

The first major postrevolutionary liberal in France was Benjamin Constant (whose novel *Adolphe* is better remembered than his political writings), who celebrated what he called "the liberty of the moderns" (actual liberty in day-to-day private affairs) in contrast to the classical "liberty of the ancients" that the French revolutionaries relied on overmuch, which merely meant "equal powerlessness before the state and equal participation in public affairs."[38]

Unlike the free market French economists of the Turgot School (the Physiocrats), Constant was one of the first liberal figures to see the state as always and everywhere the enemy, rather than as a useful instrument for liberal reform against Church, guild, and other power centers. "With Constant, the chief articulator of his generation's liberal ideas, we see the beginnings of classical liberalism's 'state-hatred,' which, after the 18th century's ambiguous attitude, marks its theory to the present day," noted modern libertarian and historian of classical liberalism Ralph Raico.[39] A consistent antistatist, Constant rejected both Jacobinism and conservatism, since "both involved violent interference with the individual's private judgment and action, the seedbed from which emerge the things that make social life worthwhile."[40]

Early-nineteenth-century French liberal economists created a libertarian class analysis that was later warped by Marx. In the view of this school of French *economistes,* the relevant class distinction, as Franz Oppenheimer hinted, lay between the productive and the predatory—with the productive being anyone working in the market in any capacity, and the predatory being the state and its agents and dependents who steal from the productive. Here we see the vital libertarian distinction between *society* and *state;* between the forces of productive human cooperation and those who prey on it; between, as Comte put it, "farmers, manufacturers, merchants, and scientists, and . . . courtiers, office holders, monks, permanent armies, pirates, and beggars."

That distinction was the key libertarian insight of these nineteenth-century French radical liberals. As economist Destutt de Tracy, one of the inspirational figures centered around the publication *Le censeur européen,* put it, "Society is purely and solely a continual series of exchanges . . . an exchange is a transaction in which the two contracting parties both gain . . . . It is this unnumberable crowd of small particular advantages, unceasingly arising, which composes the general good, and which produces at length the wonders of perfected society."[41]

Following in this tradition of French liberal economics was the greatest libertarian publicist of the nineteenth century, Frederic Bastiat, a free trader who wrote witty pamphlets against protectionism and tariffs. Bastiat came from a banking family; he followed closely the actions of Richard Cobden and John Bright, the English liberal politicians and publicists who succeeded in overturning Britain's Corn Laws (tariffs and restrictions on imported grain) in the 1840s. Their influence helped shape his writings and agitation on behalf of free trade in France (though he was less successful than Cobden and Bright).[42] Bastiat's writings have been reprinted by libertarian publicists and educational institutions in the twentieth century. In fact the most popular book of libertarian economics in the twentieth century, Henry Hazlitt's *Economics in One Lesson,* is a contemporary updating of Bastiat's style and approach to looking at the secondary and tertiary effects of government economic intervention beyond the apparent good they might do.

Bastiat was a great epigrammist for freedom; for example, "The State is the great fiction by which everybody tries to live at the expense of everyone else." He mocked anti–free trade arguments, proving that under protectionist logic, France as a nation is better off if its exports sink at sea before they can be sold, and the profits turned into imports that make the balance of trade worse. He composed the perfectly logical (on protectionist grounds) candle makers' petition against the sun, arguing that for the benefit of French industry and craft the nation must bar this dastardly source of free, imported light. Bastiat's general tone, an important contribution to the spirit of modern libertarianism, was to celebrate the abundance markets create and mock the blinkered small-mindedness of producer-centered economics, which ultimately makes human life less abundant, human beings less rich. Operating in an environment of nineteenth-century socialists, he tried to show how free markets achieved what the socialists hoped to achieve through the state: more abundance and a better life for all.[43]

The most radical of the nineteenth-century European liberal economists (and thus a particular favorite of Murray Rothbard's) was Gustave de Molinari. Molinari was the first, apparently, to explain how the principles and practices of the free competitive market could apply to military defense, thus kicking the props out from under any need for government. He was a young follower of French liberal economists Bastiat and Charles Dunoyer, and gave a speech and published a paper in the *Journal des economistes* in 1849 that shocked them by reasoning

that if free competition works in other fields, we ought not assume beforehand that it could not work with defense.

As Molinari wrote in his 1849 book *Les Soirees de la Rue St. Lazare*,
"Aren't there men whose natural aptitudes render them specially fitted
to be judges, policemen and soldiers? On the other side, haven't the
property owners a need to protection and justice? . . . If there are on
the one side men fitted to attend to the need of society, and on the
other side, men disposed to attend sacrifices upon themselves to obtain
the satisfaction of that need, doesn't. . . . Political economy . . . say if
such a need exists it will be satisfied, and it will be better under a
regime of full liberty than under any other?" Molinari hit on the most
significant point anyone questioning the "anarchy" of the free market
must understand, in the libertarian view: "How will this industry organize itself? What will be the operating techniques? Here is where political economy cannot know the answer. Also I am able to affirm that
if the need to feed itself is manifest at the heart of society, this need
will be satisfied. . . . Things will arrange themselves in absolutely the
same manner if it is a matter of security rather than food."[44]

The German Wilhelm von Humboldt, much relied on by John Stuart Mill in his more famous writing on liberty, is another European
liberal admired by modern libertarians. He argued in *The Spheres and
Duties of Government* (1792) that providing security was government's
only proper function, and that social progress required that people be
free to conduct cornucopian experiments in living from which we can
learn the manifold possibilities and pleasures of human living.[45]

According to modern libertarian and historian of European liberalism Ralph Raico, Humboldt was possibly the first to summon certain
arguments for liberty (e.g., the almost metaphysical one, going beyond
politics to the nature of what it means to be human). As Raico put it,
Humboldt explained it is "only when men are placed in a great variety
of circumstances that those experiments can take place which expand
the range of values with which the human race is familiar, and it is
through expanding this range that increasingly better answers can be
found to the question, 'In exactly what ways are men to arrange their
lives?'"[46] Only under liberty, Humboldt argued, and Mill would later
repeat, can the true manifold glories of human possibility be discovered and expressed.

Herbert Spencer was the most influential of nineteenth-century European philosophical radicals. He based his first major work of political philosophy, *Social Statics* (1851), on what he saw as innate social laws that make liberty as essential to human life as understanding scientific laws is for mastering nature. This social law of liberty is so unyielding that it led Spencer to anarchism, announcing the "right of people to ignore the state." (He backslid from this radical anarchism, however, and in later editions of the book he excised that chapter.)

Spencer rose from a humble Quaker background and an early career as a railroad draftsman to become one of those energetic Victorian intellectuals who wrote massive books summing up all his thoughts on various sciences, physical and moral. He was an early evolutionary theorist who invented the phrase "survival of the fittest," coined the term "law of equal freedom" to sum up the libertarian message that we have a right to all the freedom we can enjoy that does not infringe on another's freedom, and was largely responsible for whatever laissez-faire feelings dominated elite intellectual thinking in the late nineteenth century. Historian Sidney Fine writes, "It would be difficult to overestimate Spencer's popularity in the United States during the quarter-century after the Civil War" (over 350,000 copies of his works were sold in America between 1860 and 1903).[47] In 1864, the *Atlantic* declared that "Spencer . . . represents the scientific spirit of the age" and that his ideas "will become the recognized basis of an improved society." Andrew Carnegie was so impressed and heartened by Spencer's explanation of the advantages of free markets and business that he gifted him with a grand piano.[48] Spencer is perhaps best known in American legal-intellectual circles for Oliver Wendell Holmes's summoning of him darkly, in his dissent in the 1905 *Lochner* case (which overturned a maximum-working-hours law on principles of economic liberty that Holmes felt the Constitution did not protect), that "the 14th Amendment is not an enactment of Mr. Herbert Spencer's *Social Statics*." Spencer was the most prominent name to drop when it came to a libertarian vision of unrestricted economic rights. Holmes had elsewhere written that no writer but Darwin had done more to shape the thinking of his age.[49]

Auberon Herbert, a disciple of Spencer's, stayed truer to Spencer's original anarchist vision and was a direct inspiration to a squad of

1950s American libertarian anarchists who adopted his term "voluntaryism." Herbert was that rare anarchist philosopher who was a practicing politician before his ideological maturation. He served as Liberal representative in the House of Commons for Nottingham between 1870 and 1874; in Parliament he fell under Spencer's spell to the point that he began to doubt the propriety of staying in government.

By 1879, deciding that his political values did require representation in Parliament, he tried again, but the Liberal party found his new radical views uncongenial. He had become a leading anti-imperialist by then. Convinced that he was taking a purified Spencerianism further than the increasingly cynical Spencer himself dared in the last decade of the nineteenth century, he started a Party of Individual Liberty and a journal, *Free Life*, "the organ of voluntary taxation and the voluntary state." Herbert argued passionately against state education and against the notion that the majority had any more right to run a man's life than "either the bayonet-surrounded emperor or the infallible church."[50] He foresaw the explosion of wealth that truly free trade would bring for all in a realm of inviolable private property, recognized that pollution was a rights violation, and, apparently detecting the likes of Murray Rothbard on the horizon, theorized that someday a philosopher of liberty would explain why libel law is an unjust diminution of freedom.[51]

He saw his anarchistic libertarianism as the final apotheosis of everything good in the human moral sense, a world in which force and violence can legitimately be used for nothing other than protecting "self-ownership"—the root of all human rights.[52] An unjustly obscure figure, in his style and in the far places he took his libertarianism, Auberon Herbert sounds the most twentieth-century of all the nineteenth-century individualists.

"A COMMUNIST SAILING UNDER THE FLAG OF ANARCHISM IS AS FALSE A FIGURE AS COULD BE INVENTED."

Modern libertarianism has an American tradition to lean on that continued past the era of Paine and Jefferson. This is fortunate for libertarians, as some radicals among them consider the Constitution itself and the Federalist movement from which it arose a betrayal of America's tradition of decentralized liberty.[53]

The prehistory of modern American libertarianism will of necessity be surveyed lightly here, alighting on certain figures of unique influence on the modern movement, particularly those less widely noted in other surveys of American intellectual history. Not every American intellectual or political figure whose beliefs are echoed by modern libertarianism will be discussed here. Given the libertarian roots of American political theory, that would require nothing less than a shadow history of American thought itself. Henry David Thoreau, for just one prominent example, professed impeccably libertarian beliefs when he wrote "that government is best which governs least" and asserted the less famous but explicitly free market "this government never of itself furthered any enterprise, but by the alacrity with which it got out of the way." But more obscure heroes that only modern libertarians are apt to remember, and whose intellectual resources and spirits only the libertarians call on, will be discussed here.

The American individualist anarchists represented a small and by the late 1940s almost forgotten sidestream in nineteenth-century American radicalism. The linchpin of this movement (or tendency) was Benjamin Tucker, a Bostonian (born in South Dartmouth in 1854) from a well-to-do Unitarian family. He blended the beliefs of his various American anarchist forebears and dedicated his life to a plumb-line, no-retreat, and no-sellout defense of them. Tucker's role for his radical intellectual movement presaged Murray Rothbard's in his. After reading Tucker in light of Rothbard, one seems to hear eerie echoes sounding backward in time. They shared a similar tone, a passionate belief in the moral illegitimacy of the state, and a brave (some might think foolhardy) tendency to remorselessly follow the logic of their chosen premises to any end, however bitter it might seem even to those who agreed most of the way.

The modern libertarian movement is the only political tendency that honors these individualist anarchists, keeping their ideas alive and in some cases (like Lysander Spooner) openly embracing them.[54] Despite this, not much contemporary scholarship analyzes the individualist anarchists in the light of how their ideas have been revived and maintained by libertarians.[55]

Tucker saw himself as continuing and expanding a tradition launched by Josiah Warren in America and Jean-Pierre Proudhon in France.[56] Their antistate radicalism arose in a different intellectual environment than did the mid-twentieth-century libertarian movement. Although Warren and Proudhon said many things that would generate enthusiastic nods of assent from a modern libertarian, much in their thinking is alien to its main thrust. Both Warren and Proudhon saw themselves as figures in a worldwide socialist revolution, though Warren's catchphrase, which Tucker said summed up *his* mission as well, was "individual sovereignty." The main goal of their movement was to eliminate the causes of exploitation and oppression that keep the laborer from what is properly his. Tucker and the other individualist anarchists thought, contrary to the other socialists of their day, that eliminating the state was the clearest, most just path toward that goal.

Although intellectual history provides few clear-cut examples of innovators with no discernible precursors (making any declaration that anyone was *the first* when it comes to ideas a mug's game), Josiah Warren is a suitable starting point for the history of a uniquely American anarchism. Historians such as Eunice Minette Schuster and William Reichert trace back American anarchism's roots to Anne Hutchinson's resistance to Puritan authority in Massachusetts in the 1630s, and her brother-in-law Reverend John Wheelwright's belief that spirit always trumps law.[57] Active around the same time as Warren were such American rebels against authority as Thoreau, John Humphrey Noyes and his perfectionism,[58] William Lloyd Garrison, the Non-Resistance League end of the antislavery movement,[59] and Adin Ballou of the utopian colony in Hopedale, Massachusetts, who believed that the Bible advocated anarchism.[60] All of these ideas arose in a subterranean American environment of social ferment over free love, temperance, slavery, women's suffrage, and the liberty to speak and worship freely. Eventually everyone but the anarchists ended up winning their battles.

Garrison's natural rights–based radical assault on slavery—which insisted on immediate abolition, with no "compensation to the slaveholders" (what about compensation to the *slaves?*)—led to victory for his ideas within a generation, as inspirational an example as we have of a radical libertarian activist whose cause prevailed, even though through the troublesome means of Civil War. (It is hard to be precisely certain to what degree intellectual agitators inspired or caused real-world events that follow their prescriptions.) His journal *The Liberator* helped turn escaped slave Frederick Douglass into an ideological anti-slavery crusader. Garrison also won that ultimate compliment to the antistate agitator: a bounty on his head in various states. His life shows modern libertarians that uncompromising radicalism in defense of justice, even if most of your culture sees your cause initially as more madness than justice, can enflame souls and effect real change.[61]

Born in 1798, Josiah Warren was a New England man who traveled west to Cincinnati. His first brush with radicalism was joining Robert Owen's experimental community of New Harmony, Indiana, in 1825. Warren moved his family into that community, which collapsed after two years. Owen's approach failed, Warren thought, because individuality and difference were stifled among the residents.[62]

After the collapse of New Harmony, Warren, who loved empiricism in social theorizing, tested his contribution to anarchist economics: the idea that cost should always be the limit of price. One should not sell something for what its value is to the buyer, but rather for the cost of making it (or obtaining it) to the seller. He first tried this out at his Time Store in Cincinnati in 1827. He ostentatiously activated a clock at the beginning of every transaction to measure how much time he dedicated to selling you what you wanted.[63]

In 1833, Warren published the first American journal of anarchism, *The Peaceful Revolutionist*, wherein he made such pronouncements as, governments "commit more crimes upon persons and property and contribute more to their insecurity than all criminals put together."[64] Warren was an inventor as well as a social theorist. He came up with an innovative lard-burning lamp and a new kind of continuous-printing press (which was destroyed by an angry labor union in Evansville, Ohio, in a fit of Luddite rage in 1840).[65] His influence spread to Europe as well; John Stuart Mill credits Warren with influencing his own conception of individualism.[66]

Warren didn't want to overthrow existing society; he merely wanted to create alternative communities where men could ignore the state. He eventually decided to enter the experimental community business and do it right. Warren's family and five other families settled on four hundred acres in Tuscarawas County, Ohio. Poor drainage drove them out within a year.[67] His next colony, started in 1847 in Ohio, was called, appropriately enough, Utopia, also sometimes known as Trialville. Most of the residents were ex-Fourierites, whose own colony, the Clermont Phalanx, had failed. The community tried to run on Warren's "equitable commerce" principles, using labor notes, and by most accounts succeeded remarkably for a while.[68] Eventually Warren decided that taking someone's labor in exchange was awkward; what if you had no particular use for it? Deciding that corn was better than metal "with respect to ease of determining its cost of production in man hours," labor notes became payable in a certain amount of corn as well as in labor.[69]

Warren's biggest experiment in a new kind of human community commenced in 1851 on a 750-acre patch in the township of Islip in Suffolk County on Long Island, about forty miles outside New York City. The community was called, portentously enough, Modern Times. By now Warren had picked up one of his most prominent disciples: Stephen Pearl Andrews, a man with an already illustrious and notorious libertarian past.

Andrews, born in 1812 in Templeton, Massachusetts, to a roving Baptist minister, became a firebrand lawyer and abolitionist. By 1839, Andrews and his wife were living in Houston, helping translate the Republic of Texas's constitution and laws into Spanish.[70] Andrews had become an ardent abolitionist while living in New Orleans and witnessing the institution's baneful effect on both slave and master. He developed a scheme to keep Texas, then an independent republic, from entering the United States as a slave state: convince Britain to buy it. He set sail in 1843 on his mission, but the Texas government had already warned the British that Andrews represented no one but himself. He failed to seal the deal.[71]

His opportunity to strike a historic blow against slavery a failure, Andrews realized (after being driven from both Texas and New Orleans by angry mobs who didn't cotton to abolitionist agitators) that it was the North for him. He settled in Boston and indulged in another of his lifelong interests: a more compact and convenient language. He invented a new phonographic shorthand and began teaching it. Around this time he discovered Josiah Warren's *Equitable Commerce* (1846) and became an enthusiastic convert to the cause of individual sovereignty and cost-the-limit-of-price. He wrote a huge work explicating Warren and adding some of his own wrinkles, called *The Science of Society* (1852). Benjamin Tucker thought this book "the most important political and economical work ever printed in the English language."[72] Andrews's socialism was by no means antimarket or anticompetition; he had a fairly sophisticated, Austrian-sounding theory of how truly free competition will automatically lead every worker to find the place where he can be most productive and earn the most he is capable of.[73]

Modern Times attracted more than those into cost-the-limit-of-price and living in communal but individualistic liberty; it was catnip as well to the full range of mid-nineteenth-century experimenters in living.[74] Although Warren and Andrews allowed people in by invitation only at first, with future residents needing the approval of at least one of the first ten settlers, Modern Times became famous not as a land of the free but as a land of the peculiar. Warren, more bourgeois in outlook when it came to *that* kind of experimental living, wrote despairingly of the dietary crank in Modern Times who would eat nothing but beans. "She tottered about a living skeleton for about a year," Warren recalled, "and then sank down and died (if we can say that there was enough left to die)."[75] Nudists and polyamorists flocked to the Pine Barrens of Long Island. The Spiritual Affinity movement found a home there. The town's reputation as a hotbed of radical kookery spread. Henry Edgar, a disciple of Comte's socialist positivism, tried to make Modern Times a Comtean redoubt.[76] After the Civil War Modern Times was no longer a functioning experimental community; it had ceased using Warrenite labor notes for currency and existed as the town of Brentwood, New York.[77]

After Modern Times, Andrews went on to a colorful career as a full-service nineteenth-century American kook. He invented his own language, Alwato, which he taught to his acolytes; he became a fervent advocate of free love and invented his own gaseous all-encompassing "science" called Universology and declared himself "pantarch." Despite embracing the idea of individual sovereignty and spreading it to later generations, in his waning days Andrews became convinced that he should be ruler of the world and that he was in all likelihood the reincarnation of Christ.[78] Famed suffragette, presidential candidate, and free love advocate Victoria Woodhull became an acolyte of Universology and invited Andrews to contribute regularly to her early-1870s journal the *Woodhull and Claflin's Weekly*. (When Andrews and Woodhull joined the socialist First International, they were promptly booted for "bourgeois" tendencies.)[79]

Both Andrews and Warren became personally acquainted with the man most responsible for their ideas surviving their century: Benjamin Tucker, an enthusiast from the first after attending an 1872 meeting of the New England Labor Reform League (NELRL), a group largely dedicated to Warrenite principles.[80] Reading Warren's *True Civilization* was a conversion experience for Tucker. He was led from there to Proudhon. Tucker had freshly translated and published some of the French socialist-anarchist's work. Anarchist theory was then mostly dedicated to the problems of the working man. Whether individualist or communist, anarchists of the nineteenth century thought their beliefs were a social tool they could use to rob the plutocrats of their dominion over the mind—and surplus labor—of men.

Tucker was certain who the primary enemy was: "The State is said by some to be a 'necessary evil;' it must be made unnecessary," he declared. "This century's battle, then, is with the State: the State, that debases man; the State, that prostitutes women; the State, that corrupts children; the State, that trammels love; the State, that stifles thought; the State, that monopolizes land; the State, that limits credit; the State, that restricts exchange; the State, that gives idle capital the power of increase and, through interest, rent, profits, and taxes, robs industrious labor of its products."[81]

Tucker the individualist anarchist, no less than Johann Most the communist anarchist, embraced the Marxian concept of the surplus value of the laborer stolen by the bosses. But Tucker identified four monopolies, all of which he thought would die when the state died: currency monopoly, tariff monopoly, land monopoly, and the patent and copyright monopoly. In the pages of his short-lived publication *Radical Review* (1877–1878) and later in *Liberty* (1881–1908), Tucker and his coterie of fellow individualist anarchists quarreled, fussed, speculated, and explored the policies and implications of a world with no states and the four-legged monopoly beast slain. (Despite his opposition to monopoly, the anarchist Tucker didn't believe in antitrust law.)

Ezra Heywood, one of Tucker's first mentors and an energetic NELRL member, sometimes reached 100,000 people through his pamphlets.[82] Tucker became an associate editor of Heywood's publication *The Word* in 1875, but quit in frustration at the end of 1876 when he concluded that Heywood was more concerned with freedom of speech and sexual relations than with more important labor and economic reform matters.

Still, when Heywood was arrested in 1877 by famous bluenose Anthony Comstock for printing his essay "Cupid's Yoke" (which questioned the necessity of marriage and suggested that women should be free to have sex under any circumstances they wished), the estranged Tucker stepped forward to keep the magazine coming while Heywood languished in durance vile. (President Rutherford B. Hayes later pardoned Heywood.)[83]

Free love advocates and unionists swirled through Tucker's world, though he was not necessarily one with them. (He lost his virginity to an aggressive Victoria Woodhull.)[84] Tucker put his money where his mouth was regarding opposition to censorship, publishing an edition of the banned *Leaves of Grass* by Walt Whitman. (He was never prosecuted.)[85] The world of American radicalism was small; the utopian socialists and the free lovers and the new languagers and the labor syndicalists and the Marxist rabble-rousers all minded each other and argued with each other as the outside world persecuted and laughed. As the various revolutions—Soviet, sexual, and other—of the twentieth century would show, the kooks were indeed visionaries, even if not always right. A feminist individualist anarchist in his wide circles, Voltairine de Cleyre, is heralded and anthologized these days by modern libertarian feminist thinker Sharon Presley (who ran the Association of Libertarian Feminists) for her bold combination of politico-economic anarchism and radical feminism and sexual liberation for women. A sign of the different ways history has treated the individualist anarchists versus the communist anarchists is how little known de Cleyre is compared to her occasional sparring partner Emma Goldman.[86]

Tucker played the role of movement leader and enforcer, dictating what he called the "plumb line" of individualist anarchism.[87] In the Tucker line, Proudhon and Warren were heroes and wise forefathers;

Marx tried to be a friend of labor but was ultimately an authoritarian rather than a lover of liberty, though Tucker did accept much in Marx's economics.[88]

Tucker tried to clear a more consistent path to liberation than did either state socialists or bourgeois liberals. As *Liberty* anthologist Frank H. Brooks put it, "In *Liberty* . . . liberals and anarchists could argue together as fellow libertarians, while state socialists and anarchists could argue together as fellow socialists."[89] The pages of *Liberty* were frequently filled with Tucker and others distinguishing their libertarian anarchism from the communist variety. "A Communist sailing under the flag of Anarchism is as false a figure as could be invented," Tucker insisted.[90]

"THERE IS NO REAL LIBERTY SAVE THAT ONE TAKES FOR ONESELF."

Like socialists, Tucker and *Liberty* fulminated against concentrations of wealth and the rise of monopolies; like libertarians, they admired private property and competition. But Tucker held no truck with the violence of the stereotypical bomb-throwing anarchists, though all anarchists were stained by that association after the Haymarket incident of 1886, in which an anarchist labor gathering in Chicago was disrupted by explosions that killed seven and wounded dozens more. (It quickly turned into a riot of police violence after that.) Whether set off by anarchists or police provocateurs is still uncertain, though almost all now agree that the men who were hanged for the crime—anarchist activists Albert Parsons, August Spies, George Engel, and Adolph Fischer—were in no way responsible.[91] Tucker was no pacifist, but he considered bomb throwing to be a less productive strategy than education.[92]

In his strategic focus on how an anarchist could achieve social change, Tucker presaged Rothbard and through him modern populist libertarianism; much of his rhetoric reads exactly like Rothbard's (or vice versa). From Tucker, Rothbard (and through him the libertarian movement) got arguments about how most of the ills of society, rather than requiring a state solution, are caused by the state itself. Consequently there is no practical reason to tolerate government. But the individualist anarchists disagreed with the modern anarcho-capitalists in economics. While a Rothbardian thinks a landlord can be as productive as anyone else in a free society, Tuckerites thought that only occupancy grants a right to land ownership. All absentee landlords should—and would, with the death of the state that acted as their praetorian guard—lose any right to extract rent.[93]

Similarly, Tuckerites embraced notions about banking and currency—largely from the influence of William B. Greene—that seem sheer crankery to the Mises-marinated anarcho-capitalists of today. They agreed on eliminating state monopoly control over currency. Unlike most anarcho-capitalists, who believe that nothing less than a hard metal can serve as an appropriate currency in a free market, Tuckerites under Greene's influence believed in bringing monetized debt to the people, creating mutual banks where all personal property could back currency. This would ensure, they argued, that no one would ever lack for purchasing power.[94]

Though Tucker moved in the radical socialist circles of his day and thought of himself as a socialist, he was aware that the quest for enforced equality leads to tyranny.[95] Summing up his movement's self-image within the American tradition, he declared himself and his associates "unterrified Jeffersonians"—people unfrightened by the radical implications of the American idea of freedom.[96] As individualist anarchist historian Eunice Minette Schuster wrote, "The Individualist Anarchist . . . crystallized the traditional individualism and lawlessness of America into a universally applicable, systematic philosophy. And they were conscious of their heritage. Almost without exception they were the descendents of old New England families, particularly of Massachusetts, and in some cases of Revolutionary War heroes . . . American tradition was their inheritance and European philosophies reinforced their convictions, particularly those of John Locke, Adam Smith, William Godwin, Jeremy Bentham, Proudhon, John Stuart Mill, Max Stirner and Herbert Spencer."[97]

The *Liberty* crowd prefigured the concerns of modern libertarians. Victor Yarros was already defending anarcho-libertarians from the accusation that in opposing government, they opposed society and civilization. Yarros posited the anarcho-capitalist idea of competing defense agencies in a market replacing a government monopoly on defense. "Society would cease to exist if life and liberty were not protected against invasion, external or internal," Yarros admitted. "But it would not cease to exist if the governmental method were abandoned."[98]

Tucker's *Liberty* was not strictly dedicated to American anarchism; it also discussed the work of such British fellow travelers as Auberon Herbert and Herbert Spencer. In the early days of *Liberty* Spencer and his law of equal freedom were highly praised. But Tucker ended up criticizing both Spencer and Auberon Herbert for what he saw as an obsession on their part with only the liberties that benefited the bourgeoisie, and not matters of equity to labor.[99]

By the early 1890s, Tucker had discovered a new foundation for his anarchism. He abandoned his initial belief in natural rights and embraced the egoism of German writer Max Stirner (real name Johann Kasper Schmidt), as explained in *The Ego and Its Own*, translated into English by *Liberty* contributor Stephen Byington. "There is no real liberty save that one takes for oneself," Stirner declared.[100] Stirner rejected morality entirely; arguments based on "rights" struck him as superstitious hoodoo. To be truly free, the individual must be free of any mental "spooks," as Stirner called them, that would become more important to him than *him*, full stop.[101] Tucker came to insist, after Stirner, that contract alone creates obligations; morality or rights has nothing to do with it. *Liberty* contributor John Kelly countered that contracts themselves posit a moral system, else whence came the obligation to obey them?[102]

Tucker believed in education, not political action or mass demonstrations; in the quiet conversion of minds, one at a time, to anarchistic thought. Eliminating the state through revolution without first convincing people that they don't need one merely guarantees that another state will quickly arise in its place. Tucker wanted anarchy in a wholly modern, urban context; not for him the Warren idea of experimental anarchist communities separated from the rest of the world.[103]

In reading through old *Liberty* articles, a modern libertarian will find many familiar arguments and issues. Like libertarian periodicals from the 1960s to 1990s, they contain discussions of whether libertarians are, or ought to be, harder on slightly deviationist fellow libertarians than they are on statists; arguments over whether a certain libertarian conclusion rubs so violently against most people's beliefs that it is better not to emphasize it; debates about whether libertarians must first start living libertarian principles, proving that voluntary individual effort can meet needs most people think only the state can handle; controversy over whether Christianity is inimical to or essential to libertarianism; a hue and cry over whether a libertarian ought to vote; all these internal movement dialogues essentially began in *Liberty* and went underground for over fifty years, resurfacing in the libertarian periodicals of the postwar era.

After a while, his circle's failure to significantly turn America in an anarchist direction began to wear on Tucker. His brand of individualist anarchism suffered from having no clear constituency that directly benefited from it, unlike labor agitators' attraction to socialism or big business's attraction to progressive centralization.

Schuster summed up the difficulties of the Tuckerite program within its historical context well: "[Individualist anarchism's] demands to secure the just distribution of wealth did not please the capitalists. Its pacific, un-class conscious program left the proletariat cold. The capitalists wanted nothing of absolutely *unrestricted* unprotected competition and individualism. What it wanted was class solidarity, cooperation and the distribution of the goods of this world irrespective of the accident of birth and inherited capacity. Its complete anti-governmentalism made them all tremble. But the lack of a definite means of destroying the present forms of inequalities made it impractical."[104]

Tucker never promised a utopia, something the social agitators of his time seemed to crave. "There are some troubles from which mankind can never escape," he admitted. "[The anarchists] have never claimed that liberty will bring perfection; they simply say that its results are vastly preferable to those that follow from authority. . . . As a choice of blessings, liberty is the greater; as a choice of evils, liberty is the smaller. Then liberty always says the Anarchist. No use of force except against the invader."[105]

Tucker gave up on *Liberty* after a 1908 fire claimed his print shop and most of his papers. Taking his wife and young daughter, he moved to France, a country he grew to adore. This love for France led him to support the allied forces in World War I, a move many of his old fans and friends saw as a sellout of his principles. He despaired of his anarchistic values ever finding a congenial place to take root and grow in the modern world. The communist anarchists surrounding Emma Goldman and Alexander Berkman were victims of a powerful state backlash in the late 1910s and early 1920s. Being an anarchist and an immigrant became a crime, and hundreds were arrested and dozens deported—the final act in the post-Haymarket drama of fear and distrust of anarchists.[106]

In 1925, Tucker wrote to a friend who asked him what he, Tucker, had achieved of lasting value: "To that question 'Nothing' is the only truthful answer," Tucker glumly replied. "I aimed to contribute a stone to a social edifice, a cathedral if one may call it so, which I expected to be carried to completion, slowly but surely, through the ages. I have contributed that stone. . . . But I see now that the cathedral will never be finished, and that the portion already built is destined soon to tumble into ruins."[107]

> "A GOVERNMENT, PROFESSEDLY RESTING ON
> CONSENT, WILL EXPEND MORE LIFE AND TREASURE
> IN CRUSHING DISSENT, THAN ANY GOVERNMENT,
> OPENLY FOUNDED ON FORCE, HAS EVER DONE."

Tucker's greatest contribution to the individualist anarchist tradition was publishing in *Liberty* and befriending the nineteenth-century individualist anarchist most revered by modern libertarians: Lysander Spooner.

Spooner was born in 1808 on a farm outside Athol, Massachusetts. He became an enemy of the state early on and succeeded in repealing a state statute that prevented him from practicing law without college training.[108] Before beginning his copious writings on the criminal nature of the state, he practiced some competitive anarchism: running a private post office. Spooner's American Letter Mail Company, launched in 1844, was cheaper and more efficient than its government competition, and was driven out of business by Congress.[109] For those who want to explain Spooner's relentless assaults on every ethical excuse for the government as arising from personal pique, one could look to that, and to the fact that the state of Ohio drained a river and damaged land that Spooner owned on the shore.[110]

Spooner developed a vision of the inherently criminal nature of government that strikes many with a powerful and liberating force (as it struck me when I came across Spooner's 1870 pamphlet *No Treason: The Constitution of No Authority* in high school). His arguments are firmly based in the standard Western moral order, and yet his relentlessly logical conclusion proves that the state by its very nature always and everywhere destroys justice, even though nearly everyone in the West believes in the state as much as they believe in justice. This sense of the utter criminality of all government action can be traced through Rothbard's polemical writings on government: a furious indignation that government, nothing more than a band of brigands and killers, should command so much obedience and carry so much moral weight. While Spooner was not a violent revolutionary, he believed in the natural right to use force, up to and including deadly force, against those who would deny you your rights.[111]

Spooner grew into his mature opinion that there was no legitimate authority behind the U.S. government, or any government not based on complete consent. He was especially caustic on the pretended consent in which the U.S. government cloaked itself, especially after the Civil War. "The North exults beyond measure," he wrote, "in the proof she has given, that a government, professedly resting on consent, will expend more life and treasure in crushing dissent, than any government, openly founded on force, has ever done."[112]

He began his polemical career as a standard abolitionist who argued *for* America against the fervent opinion of abolitionist leader William Lloyd Garrison: Since the U.S. Constitution countenanced slavery, it was a compact with Satan and not to be respected. Garrison inflamed crowds by setting fire to copies of the Constitution.[113] Spooner used his lawyerly constitutional analysis to prove Garrison wrong—to show that the U.S. Constitution properly interpreted could not permit slavery. History was more on Garrison's side, as it took the destruction of aspects of the U.S. Constitution—particularly the idea that it was a voluntary joining together of independent and sovereign states—and its official amendment to finally end slavery. Despite his abolitionism, Spooner thought the Civil War was a worse crime than slavery, since it cemented the principle "that men may rightfully be compelled to submit to, and support, a government that they do not want; and that resistance, on their part, makes them traitors and criminals."[114]

Spooner agitated for the basic individualist anarchist line on mutual banking and free currency.[115] In one of his unique contributions, he was the patron saint of the lively movement for jury nullification. His longest work of legal/historical scholarship was *Trial by Jury*. In it, he demonstrated that historically in Anglo-Saxon society juries were not merely meant to decide who was or wasn't telling the truth on the witness stand, but to be the people's final council and bulwark against the possible tyranny of king and parliament. Spooner insisted that juries always had (and must always have, to protect citizens' liberties) the power to judge both the law and the facts. Even if a defendant did in fact perform the alleged act, the jury must have the power to decide to refuse to convict anyway—in modern language, to "nullify" the conviction.[116]

Spooner later went a step further, in effect saying, screw the jury; none of the laws enforced by U.S. courts have any validity whatsoever. In a series of essays called *No Treason*, he argued that only consent can give moral validity to the government's use of force. The alleged consent of our forefathers when they ratified the Constitution can by no acceptable legal logic bind anyone living in the present to allegiance unless they personally vow such allegiance. Thus "no treason," since treason is betraying that to which one rightfully owes allegiance—and no one owes the U.S. government such allegiance.

At best, Spooner says, the Constitution could only bind those men who ratified it, which was never even all the people living then. For Spooner, elections were merely the illegitimate deputizing of politicians to act as thieves and marauders.[117]

In a quote beloved by libertarians, Spooner tried to prove that the state is in fact of *lower* moral standing than a common brigand.

The fact is that the government, like a highwayman, says to a man: *Your money, or your life.* . . . [But] the highwayman . . . does not pretend that he has any rightful claim to your money, or that he intends to use it for your benefit. . . . He has not acquired impudence enough to profess to be merely a "protector.". . . Furthermore, having taken your money, he leaves you. . . . He does not persist in following you on the road, against your will; assuming to be your rightful "sovereign" on account of the "protection" he affords you. He does not keep "protecting" you, by commanding you to bow down and serve him; by requiring you to do this, and forbidding you to do that; by robbing you of more money as often as he finds it for his interest and pleasure to do so; and by branding you as a rebel, a traitor, and . . . shooting you down without mercy, if you dispute his authority, or resist his demands. He is too much of a gentleman to be guilty of such impostures, and insults, and villainies as these. In short, he does not, in addition to robbing you, attempt to make you either his dupe or his slave.[118]

Spooner demolishes the arguments that paying taxes or voting—or not leaving the country—imply agreement to the "social contract" that legitimizes the U.S. government. He provides the most furious yet lawyerly argument yet seen for a bourgeois anarchism, one that takes bourgeois reasoning and propriety to their ultimate limit and shows that, properly interpreted, they allow no room for a state. More than any of his nineteenth-century individualist anarchist brethren, Spooner is still an active influence on the libertarian movement— reprinted, quoted, honored, and relied on.[119]

Whether there is any direct ideological lineage from Josiah Warren through Stephen Pearl Andrews and then to Benjamin Tucker and on to modern libertarianism is a controversial question.[120] To the extent that such an influence exists, Rothbard is its major conduit.[121]

The Tuckerites' opposition to absentee land owning and their belief in monetizing everything are absent from modern libertarianism.[122] Stirnerism is far less popular than arguments that are either moralistic, such as Rand's and Rothbard's, or don't make a point of antagonizing moralists, such as Friedman, Mises, and the "government doesn't work" pragmatic mentality that frequently undergirds the arguments of libertarian organizations such as the Cato Institute and the Libertarian Party.

Still, one can detect the spirit—certainly the thoroughgoing opposition to any and all government action—of Tucker and especially Spooner in the libertarian movement today. As William Gary Kline said in his book about the individualist anarchists, "They took the ideals of the liberal tradition more seriously than most Americans."[123] That is also true of modern libertarians.

"THE MAIN TRADITION OF AMERICAN INDIVIDUALISM . . . INDIVIDUALIST RADICALISM."

Even before a recognizable movement of institutions, funders, and writers dedicated to libertarianism in its modern sense coalesced in the 1940s, scattered public intellectuals in America in the first half of the twentieth century were already advocating ideas similar in many respects to the radically antistate individualism that defined the postwar American libertarian movement. Journalist, biographer, and belle lettrist Albert Jay Nock is frequently cited in attempts to establish a prewar pedigree for modern libertarian thought, and he is a hero to many of the modern movement's founders. His book-length essay on political philosophy and American political history, *Our Enemy, The State* (1935), was brought back into print by libertarian-themed presses in both the 1970s (Free Life Editions) and 1990s (Fox & Wilkes).

Nock's final book, *Memoirs of a Superfluous Man*, was a best-seller in 1943, and he contributed regularly to such popular–intellectual American magazines as the *Atlantic* and Mencken's *American Mercury*. He was widely praised for his fine style. Post-Mencken *American Mercury* editor Paul Palmer called him "the greatest stylist among American writers . . . no American ever wrote a purer prose."[124] But Nock is mostly forgotten outside libertarian circles today, although conservative kingpin William F. Buckley also considers him a personal hero.[125] Michael Wreszin (who specializes in hard-to-pigeonhole American public intellectuals with biographies of Oswald Garrison Villard and Dwight MacDonald) wrote in his 1971 Nock biography that Nock's memory was kept alive by "a small body of eccentric libertarians who championed his cause in obscure subterranean journals."[126] Nock's public profile hasn't risen since.

Nock was an anarchist, though he carefully distinguished the state, to which he was bloodily opposed, from government—the necessary functions for an orderly civilization historically usurped by the state.[127] His anarchism was, as Wreszin put it, an "extrapolitical poetic vision" more than a considered political program or theory.[128] Nock considered the stuff of humane culture—art, literature, good living—more important than political ideology.

Nock was honest enough to admit the curious fact that "I have to recognize, with searchings of heart, that the sense of whatever in human society is enviable, graceful and becoming has been bred by a regime so monstrously unjust and flagitious that it had no right ever to exist on earth." This, he wrote, made him "a little circumspect about the imposition of one's theories. . . . I am an individualist, anarchist, single-taxer and free-trader. . . . I think also that the general course of things is in those directions. But whenever I feel inclined to hurry up the course of things, I ask myself how much at home I should feel in a society of my own creating."[129]

Nock was born in 1870 in Scranton, Pennsylvania, the son of Joseph Albert Nock, a clergyman. Nock himself was an ordained Episcopal minister, active from 1897 until 1909.[130] He kept his religious career secret in later life and didn't even mention it in his memoirs. Nock was notorious for extreme reticence about his personal life. Libertarian journalist and Nock protégé Frank Chodorov wrote, "It was only after I was appointed administrator of his estate that I learned of the existence of two full-grown and well-educated sons."[131] After leaving the priesthood, Nock drifted into journalism. He became a staff writer at the *American* magazine, edited by John S. Phillips and staffed largely by refugees from the original home of American muckraking journalism, *McClure's*. The *American*, as Nock biographer Robert Crunden put it, attempted to "improve and educate, not to shock or irritate."[132]

Nock was already devoted to Henry George, a political and economic philosopher, author of *Progress and Poverty* (1879), who came into vogue in the late nineteenth century. George combined a basic libertarianism with a belief that government should be funded by a "single tax" on the unimproved value of land. Nock wrote a long series of articles for the *American* on the inequities of America's existing, non-Georgist system of property taxation.[133] He left the *American* in 1914 after claiming he wrote a deliberately bad article about Edison that was accepted and published.

In 1915, on a supposed mission (mysterious to all his biographers) in Europe on behalf of Secretary of State William Jennings Bryan, Nock met and befriended Francis Neilson, a British member of Parliament who had written an early work of World War I revisionism called *How Diplomats Make War*. The book was a pioneer in arguing against the Allies' notion that the full load of war guilt rested properly on Germany. Nock wrote an introduction to the first American edition and helped find a publisher for it. Nock's association with Neilson was his entrée into the world of twentieth-century war revisionism, discussed below. Nock wrote his own book on German war guilt, *The Myth of a Guilty Nation* (1922).

Neilson and his wife, Helen Swift, an heiress to the Swift meatpacking fortune, were major funders of *The Nation* during Oswald Garrison Villard's editorship. The Neilsons bought a staff position for Nock on the magazine.[134] Nock wrote a story criticizing labor leader Samuel Gompers that got the September 13, 1918, issue temporarily banned from the U.S. mail.[135] (Gompers was a favorite of the Wilson administration for helping keep the labor movement supportive of World War I.)[136]

The Neilsons also financed the *Freeman*, a publication Nock edited for its entire run (1920–1924). Its circulation never exceeded 7,000.[137] *The Freeman,* in Nock's vision, opposed the mealy-mouthed equivocations of the standard liberal press as represented by Villard's *Nation* and Herbert Croly's *New Republic*. When Villard wrote a piece welcoming Nock's *Freeman* to the community of liberal magazines, Nock responded that "we loathes liberalism and loathes it hard," insisting that his magazine was *radical*.[138] The magazine maintained and retained a high reputation as a home for serious writing on culture and politics, with Nock's Georgist–reformist slant showing through. *Freeman* contributors included Charles A. Beard, Conrad Aiken, Carl Sandburg, Bertrand Russell, Lincoln Steffens, and John Dos Passos.[139]

Nock's overall political/intellectual slant was unique, although parts of it were strongly influenced by earlier writers. Nock biographer

Robert Crunden astutely characterized the Nock intellectual mix as "spirit and object from Matthew Arnold, philosophy and politics from Herbert Spencer, economics from Henry George, and history and sociology from Franz Oppenheimer."[140] Libertarian historian Charles Hamilton noticed that Nock's uniqueness left observers of the *Freeman* "struggl[ing] to fit the journal into a political procrustean bed. They couldn't decide if it was liberal, conservative, Bolshevik, revolutionary, anarchist, or Georgist. Lillian Symes and Travers Clement were probably closest when they placed *The Freeman* within 'the main tradition of American individualism . . . individualist radicalism.'"[141]

In 1924, with Nock's relationship with the Neilsons strained, *The Freeman* went under.[142] One of his assistants, Suzanne LaFollette, revived the publication under her control as the *New Freeman* in 1930. Nock wrote a regular column for it, but it folded within a year.

Nock biographer Wreszin makes much of the two Nocks—the early muckraking radical journalist with his innocent belief in the perfectibility of man and society, and the later Nock who, under the influence of largely forgotten architect (and pop anthropologist) Ralph Adams Cram, came to believe that the majority of people aren't human in any meaningful sense, and are beyond reform.[143]

This Cram thesis colored Nock's writings from the mid-1930s on. Nock wrote extensively during that period about education, contending that most of what passed for education in the United States was training. This was perfectly appropriate, because, as per Cram, most people weren't capable of being educated in the true sense, which involves the inculcation of a refined wisdom pursued for its own sake, not mere utility. Nock thought universal literacy a useless goal, as most people can't do anything valuable with it anyway.[144]

Nock's belief in the uneducability of most men led to one of his strongest influences on the modern libertarian movement. He introduced to movement thinking the concept of the Remnant—an idea of vital influence to the sense of mission of the Foundation for Economic Education, the first libertarian think tank and a great conduit for Nockian ideas and attitudes into the modern movement. The Remnant belief is that the ideas of human liberty might not become dominant at any given historical moment, but that the movement's task is to keep the ideas alive, a flame of truth flickering in dark ages. It is, as Nock styled it in a famous essay, akin to "Isaiah's job," preaching to those few with ears to hear. And the Remnant *will* find the true-hearted prophet. "They will find him without his doing anything about it; in fact, if he tries to do anything about it, he is pretty sure to put them off."[145]

Nock's most extended political thoughts are found in *Our Enemy, The State*, derived from a series of lectures he gave in the early 1930s at Columbia University. This is one of the few libertarian classics shot through with the thinking of Henry George. This is sometimes sold as a great introductory work to the libertarian tendency; it was introduced to me as such when I was a college student. But the book's focus, which attacks landlords and the evils of rent (as per George) almost as much as the state, would strike most modern libertarians as somewhat strange.

Georgists and libertarians have been uneasy fellow travelers and sometime allies for over a century; significant libertarian figures such as Nock and later Frank Chodorov arose from the Georgist movement, and many Georgists to this day insist that libertarians should just make peace with the idea that has come to define Georgism, the so-called single tax—that all government functions can and should be funded through a tax on the basic value of land (*not* on improvements on it). Theoretically such a tax would have the virtue (among others) of having no negative incentives on wealth creation, since humans can't make new land (though they can, of course, make new *usable* land). Georgism would lead, then, to a very libertarian society indeed, with government taxing little and doing little. (Georgism remains an obscure strain in libertarianism today, though in its day it was a significant Progressive Era reform movement.)[146]

Our Enemy is also rooted in Oppenheimer's theories of the state as a parasitic excrescence on social power, and his important distinction between the economic means of satisfying human desires (production) and the political one (theft and depredation).[147] Nock analyzes American history through Charles Beard's lens, excoriating the merchant state that held no truck for natural rights or popular sovereignty. His analysis provided little hope for short-term change in American circumstances. As Nock noted, he was "oppressed with a great sense of futility in publishing it. Any good critic would say that the main object of the book is to show that there was no use in writing it."[148]

Though Nock was patrician in manner and attitude, he was not a rich man. He survived for his last couple of decades off the patronage of wealthy fans of the *Freeman*.[149] Nock's goal, his attorney Abraham Ellis said, was to die with no money, "and he succeeded in his goal." He would only work when he needed the cash.[150]

While Nock is usually slotted as a member of the pre–Cold War right, many of his stances and attitudes would make modern conservatives condemn him as the worst sort of pink—continual naïveté about the good intentions and prospects of Soviet Russia; a belief that youngsters during his dotage were not rebellious enough, complaining that they "seem to cherish none of the resentment wherewith their Creator endowed them as an inalienable right;"[151] and a fussy bachelorhood that extended to believing that standard domestic family relationships were the enemy of the human race.[152]

Nock was firmly opposed to social pressure that might limit the freedom of alternative lifestyles. It wasn't enough, he insisted, for a judge to refuse to convict girls for walking naked down the street; true freedom would mean no one even noticed. He argued not merely for legal freedom but for the necessity of an overarching spirit of liberal tolerance.[153] He hit on the idea, later also touched on by Hayek, that a busybody state doing things both *for* and *to* its citizens damages a people's character. "The best argument for free speech," Nock wrote, "is what the suppression of it does to the character of a people."[154]

But Nock did possess one of the most important constitutive elements of the old right/protolibertarian temperament: a contempt for Franklin Roosevelt bordering on bloody hatred.[155] Like many cranky individualist writers of the time, he recognized no substantive difference between the various governments clashing during World War II. "Rooseveltism, Hitlerism, Stalinism, are all only local variants of the common doctrine that man has no natural rights but only such as are created for him by the state . . . [this is] State absolutism, formulated by the German idealist philosophers."[156]

In his last years, his *Memoirs of a Superfluous Man* became a surprise best-seller. In one of his more Menckenian moments (H. L. Mencken was a longtime friend and fan of Nock's), Nock wrote that he best approached the mentality of the average American when horribly ill—then he achieved the "enervated mind, debilitated nerves, no power of concentration and an intense desire to be rid of the burden of my circumstances" that characterizes his countrymen.[157]

The *Memoirs* were useless for the facts of Nock's life, but a great introduction to his detached, cultured, patrician persona, his stoic self-reliant strength that rose above the problems of merely political life. Meeting this mind—coolly adjusted to the reality that his attitudes and beliefs rendered him superfluous in FDR's welfare/warfare state—was a delightful and often formative experience for many readers.

After Pearl Harbor, Nock's anarchism and opposition to war could find no home in standard American journalism. The outbreak of World War II killed or neutered a generation of individualist writers who could not gin up the enthusiasm for FDR and the New Deal that the war suddenly made a social necessity—some of them will be discussed further on. Nock's friendship with anti–New Dealer and anti–World War II journalist Lawrence Dennis earned him a visit from the FBI.[158]

Nock had never stopped thinking of himself as a radical. He found it bitterly ironic that in the post–New Deal era, conservative businessmen became his primary audience. He had never imagined them his natural constituency. He was disconcerted by the notion that he was now being feted by "Wall Streeters, oil magnates, and . . . steel baron[s]."[159]

"The simple truth," he wrote, "is that our businessmen do not want a government that will let business alone. They want a government that they can use. Offer them one based on [Herbert] Spencer's model and they would see the country blow up before they would accept it."[160] He lamented, as Roosevelt's New Deal solidified, that it was doubtful "how many people in this country would read a treatise on liberty, written by a disinterested hand; I would put it at perhaps a thousand . . . anyone who mentions liberty for the next two years will be supposed to be somehow beholden to the Republican Party, just as anyone who mentioned it since 1917 was supposed to be a mouthpiece of the distillers and brewers."[161]

Nock died on August 19, 1945. He represented a strain of old right thinking that wins sentimental praise from modern libertarians—for the ragged glory of his fully imagined fight against the modern megastate—

but which is no longer clearly recognizable in the active movement or intellectual tendency.

For example, a celebratory love for modernity, for the material benefits of a cornucopian market society, permeates the modern libertarian movement. The patrician Nock had no use for such an attitude. He had powerfully expressed prejudices that few libertarians in the early twenty-first century would share. Nock saw commerce as vulgar and uncivilized; he was adamantly opposed to the automobile and even the electric light; his Remnant philosophy, though of vital importance to the Foundation for Economic Education's sense of mission, is no longer widely embraced in the libertarian movement, which strives to be more ecumenical and reach out to a wider mass audience.

Nock represented an apolitical, cultural, and intellectual approach to anarchism. He eschewed attempts to change policy or strenuously push his views. One of the "most offensive things" about FDR's America, Nock wrote, "was its monstrous itch for changing people."[162] Nock's attitude toward affecting political change could be seen in something he once told Leonard Read, the founder of the Foundation for Economic Education, regarding his Georgism. He was not an *advocate* of the single tax, Nock said—merely a *believer* in it.[163]

Nock was in no sense an activist—political or intellectual. As libertarian historian Walter Grinder summed it up in an introduction to the 1973 reprint of *Our Enemy, The State*, Nock's "plan of action" was "a plan of no action at all. To Nock there was clearly only one path to follow, and that was to learn, to think, to write, to informally teach, and then, simply wait."[164]

"ALL GOVERNMENT IS EVIL . . . AND . . . THE DEMOCRATIC FORM IS AT LEAST AS BAD AS ANY OF THE OTHER FORMS."

The decades from the 1920s to the 1940s saw a gang of individual thinkers who have been adopted by a certain segment of modern libertarians as ancestors; from H. L. Mencken at the most famous to Garet Garrett at the most obscure. The term of art for them has become "the

Old Right" though they didn't think of themselves as or call themselves that. One could argue there was no "they" at all—they were a squad of journalists, novelists, politicians, and publicists who can be seen in retrospect as standing for many of the same values, pushing in the same direction. Aspects of their stance and style fed into the words of Ayn Rand, Isabel Paterson, and Rose Wilder Lane (see Chapter 3), though none of these old right figures were across-the-board libertarian in the modern sense.

Their institutional homes included the *Saturday Evening Post* under George Horace Lorimer and the *Chicago Tribune* under Colonel Robert McCormick. Their political heroes—mostly for their opposition to Roosevelt on various matters, from the National Recovery Administration to court packing to entry into World War II—included Senators Robert Taft, William Borah, and Burton Wheeler—not all conservatives in a modern sense, certainly not all libertarians, but the only opposition to important aspects of the major shifts toward statism in the 1930s and 1940s. The one quality that united them was opposition to some, most, or all of Roosevelt's New Deal, disdain for its quasi-fascist centralization, and disgust for his maneuverings of America into yet another European war.

Some modern libertarians love to laud them, but major differences exist between them and the radical, principled, philosophically and economically rooted antistatism that constitutes modern libertarians. Yet in books such as Justin Raimondo's *Reclaiming the American Right* and monographs such as Sheldon Richman's "New Deal Nemesis: The 'Old Right' Jeffersonians," modern libertarians make a convincing case that the old right was a real movement, not made up entirely of libertarians in the modern sense but containing strong strains of similarity. It was an important (though ultimately failed) force in American politics during the New Deal era.

What links the old right to modern libertarian ideas was a call for "a return to first principles: the U.S. Constitution, separation of powers, checks and balances, decentralization, limited popular rule, individual autonomy; in a word, republicanism."[165] They were in some ways a new antifederalist movement, as are modern libertarians. These movements are as American as whatever pie Americans gave up in order to choose the apple pie. Old right and modern libertarians continue a tradition of endless opposition, the perpetual "other party," the anima haunting America since the founding. In a sense, they have been the American establishment's most loyal enemy, waging war over American hearts and minds in distinctly American language; all the while knowing that they are fighting an uphill battle.

An important institutional arm of the old right was the controversial Liberty League. It was formed by businessmen, including J. Howard Pew of Sun Oil and Alfred Sloan of General Motors, who would be prominent supporters of libertarian causes in the 1940s and 1950s. The league agitated strenuously to defeat FDR in 1936, through pamphleteering and sponsoring a professional lawyers association which argued that certain aspects of the New Deal were so clearly unconstitutional that no one need obey those laws. The organization fizzled out after its 1936 failure to unseat Roosevelt. Its reputation was on the ropes already, first because of its powerfully plutocratic makeup during times of mass privation and second because General Smedley Butler fingered it as a group of conspirators secretly plotting a fascist military coup against the president.[166]

World War II was another reason some old right characters have been subsumed into a protolibertarian coalition by later libertarian thinkers. Since antimilitarism is a constitutive element distinguishing modern libertarians from supposedly "free market" conservatives (though even antimilitarism has become controversial within the libertarian big tent post 9/11), any antiwar force exudes some libertarian flavor. Most of the antiwar forces ended up opposing Roosevelt fully, not limiting themselves to his foreign policy.

Thus the America First Committee movement, though a single-issue group not dedicated to larger libertarian principles, is considered proof of a popular antiwar tradition in American culture surviving into the twentieth century, an actual mass movement standing up for a principled noninterventionism and preservation of classic American republican virtues. We are a nation out to preserve our own political virtue, not expend citizens' lives and treasure trying to remold the world. Despite the fact that we have waged war after war in our history mostly with popular approval, and in this century all of them away from the homeland, the America First movement indicated that our national character retains some link to classic Washingtonian virtues of peaceful

isolation from the rest of the world's wars. Peace is a constitutive libertarian principle; the vision of the state's role in libertarianism remains,
for the most part, the nineteenth-century classical liberal one, of a
world linked by cosmopolitan principles of free trade, not international warfare *or* welfare. That vision leaves no room for acting as a
world superhero, regardless of motive. Although peace may be a libertarian principle, not all peace forces are thorough libertarian forces.
Still, some of the arguments America Firsters proffered for their opposition—such as the centralization and aggrandizement of government
power inherent in waging huge wars—recognize the libertarian roots
of peace.

John Flynn, chair of the New York branch of the America First
Committee and one of its most tenacious defenders against the encroachment of pro-Nazi forces into its antiwar ranks, though often
feted and praised by modern libertarians, never really grew out of his
roots as a *New Republic* columnist on finance matters into a detailed
and sophisticated understanding of the importance of free markets.
Flynn won a permanent place in the hearts of anti–New Dealers with
his detailed shredding of FDR's political career, *The Roosevelt Myth*
(1948), and his account of the similarities between New Dealism and
European fascism, *As We Go Marching* (1944), though Flynn later
turned into a severe Cold Warrior.[167]

Other old right hands had direct connections with modern libertarians. Garet Garrett, one of the *Saturday Evening Post's* leading anti–New
Deal writers in the 1930s, was an early mentor to Richard Cornuelle,
later of the Volker Fund, the major funder of libertarian causes during
the 1950s. Garrett contributed a (not very useful) sense of Jacobite
tragedy to libertarianism with his stirring paean to the fact that American liberties are beyond protection and were lost after the New
Deal.[168] Garrett came from a classic Americanism, not a purist libertarianism. He had a soft spot for national autarchy (the idea that America
ought to be as independent as possible of international trade) and an
anti-immigrant streak. He thought that importing foreign ideas—even
from Europe—damaged the American character and polity.[169]

Libertarians have had to fight for their past. H. L. Mencken, a spiritual forefather to these old right figures in his love of traditional American liberty and hatred for Roosevelt, was as popular an intellectual as
America knew in the 1920s, forger of a distinctive sense of good-

humored, whooping liberality and keen eye for the comedy of cant, political, literary, or social. Yet he is rarely thought of as libertarian. His outrageous sense of humor, his contempt for religious obscurantism, censorship, and any variety of Puritanism made many identify him as a protoprogressive lefty. As libertarian journalist John Chamberlain noted, Mencken's guffaw, as even many of his devoted young fans failed to notice, "had Voltairean undertones. It stemmed in good part from an outraged appreciation of true libertarian political principles, not from mere love of watching the clowns behave idiotically in the anterooms of Capitol Hill. Mencken had read his Jefferson, his John Stuart Mill, and we had not."[170] Murray Rothbard was correct in noting that Mencken was first of all a radical individualist libertarian, who believed, in Mencken's own credo, that "all government is evil, in that all government must necessarily make war upon liberty; and that the democratic form is at least at bad as any of the other forms."[171]

Albert Jay Nock represented the beginning of libertarian linkage with a cause that some early libertarians adopted as part and parcel of their antimilitarism: twentieth-century war revisionism. That connection was honored and extended by such libertarian institutions as the Institute for Humane Studies and the Cato Institute; movement magazines like *Reason* would devote respectful issues to it in the mid-1970s. These days, war revisionism is ignored by most mainstream libertarian institutions. Arguing against the Leviathan state seems far enough beyond the pale to trouble yourself further by linking yourself with such lost causes as arguing that America should not have entered World War II or even the milder version, that Roosevelt's means for getting us into it were underhanded, antidemocratic, and antirepublican in the real, not partisan, sense.

Nowadays, only some writers associated with the Ludwig von Mises Institute and the libertarian-run website Antiwar.com are apt to link libertarianism and revisionism. But especially in the old right days, and in a line continuing through Rothbard and those he directly influenced, libertarians cheered and embraced war revisionism, even if the war revisionists were not libertarians. (In many cases they were disillusioned left progressives, such as Charles Beard.) The term "revisionist" refers to attempts to "revise" the standard, triumphalist understanding of our century's wars and their causes spread by the victors. Leading revisionist writer and cheerleader Harry Elmer Barnes says the term arose from the fact that their initial second looks at World War I and its aftermath had the polemical purpose of seeking revisions in the terms of the treaty of Versailles and its overly punitive measures that (as even John Maynard Keynes agreed) helped create the resentments and conditions that led to World War II.[172]

World War I revisionism was successful, and its viewpoints—in broadest terms, that war guilt did not belong to Germany and its allies alone in World War I, and that the war's aftermath was unnecessarily punitive—became standard liberal-progressive opinion by the end of the 1930s.

But when a squad of historians and polemicists—including some of the same men, like Barnes, who had been a well-known and widely relied on sociologist and historian prior to his war revisionist work—tried to do the same with World War II, they made no headway with acceptable opinion. While many Americans opposed American entry into World War II, that opposition mostly sank to the bottom of the sea along with American ships at Pearl Harbor. (Raising questions about how much FDR knew in advance about, or even welcomed, the Pearl Harbor attack became a popular pastime for war revisionists.) In Barnes's mind, men such as him, Charles Tansill (author of *Back Door to War: The Roosevelt Foreign Policy, 1933–1941,* 1952) and Charles Beard (author of *President Roosevelt and the Coming of the War,* 1948) were victims of what he called a "historical blackout"—ignored, mocked, reviled, in some cases, Barnes accused, blocked from access to government historical papers. Barnes became the revisionists' main spokesman and propagandist. Historian of American anarchism James Martin also became an enthusiastic Barnesian, writing self-published books on war revisionist themes in the 1970s.[173] Their major polemical point could be summed up as follows: World War I, theoretically fought to make the world safe for democracy, resulted in fascism and communism overtaking much of Europe; World War II, fought to stop aggressive totalitarianism, extended the scope and control of one of the worst totalitarianisms known to man, communism, in both Europe and Asia.

World War II revisionism fit snugly with the anti–New Deal, anti-regimentation attitudes that defined the old right and shaded over into postwar libertarianism. Roosevelt's sneaking us into war was all of a piece with his creation of unconstitutional agencies to institute his plan for overall regimentation of the U.S. economy and his court-packing scheme to make sure no other branch of government would stop it. To classic American republicans, wishing to preserve the power of Congress—the institution closest to the people—over foreign affairs and holding tight to the power of the people over their own economic affairs, Roosevelt seemed to be setting up the equivalent of the most ancient forms of tyranny, the god-king—combining magic and religion, as anthropologist Gordon Childe put it, with magic being "a way of making people believe they are going to get what they want" and religion "a system for persuading them that they ought to want what they get." The combination of alphabet agencies, Social Security, and relentless barrages of war whooping and propaganda, plus a reign that seemed to be growing as long as any pharonic family with term after unprecedented term—what did this all add up to? All hail God-King Roosevelt![174]

The old right's end was inherently, sadly, crepuscular. They saw themselves lose and lose and lose and lacked the optimism of some of the next generation who looked up to them. The waning of their personal fortunes as their ideological fortunes dissipated must have added to their crankiness; John Flynn, who started his career as a favorite in high standing of standard American liberalism as a financial columnist for the *New Republic*, ended it accused of fascist sympathies and driven from most standard sources of American opinion, his work lauded and distributed only by disreputable right-wing groups.[175] Garet Garrett no longer wrote for one of America's most widely read publications, the *Saturday Evening Post,* but edited *American Affairs*, the journal of the National Industrial Conference Board, a businessmen's pressure and education group. Mencken lost his voice in the contemporary American conversation over politics and more long before he lost it in reality through a stroke in 1948. Roosevelt and his forces won the war, and they won World War II. Those who opposed it were losers, and inevitably seen as sore ones at that.[176]

Roosevelt's successful revolution formed the constitutive elements of American politics and government, creating a veritable one-party state. Even such supposed Republican reactionaries as Ronald Reagan and Newt Gingrich admired FDR and paid him fealty. The forces arrayed against Rooseveltism, including the protolibertarian elements of the old right, lost; but their ideas—in most cases, purified and intensified versions of their ideas—formed the soil from which modern libertarianism grew.

As modern libertarians recognize, America never really had an era of true laissez-faire—at least not since the antifederalists lost their fight over ratifying the Constitution. Modern libertarianism is a vision of a radical and just future—but one whose contours are inherent in the meaning of the American Revolution, arising from European traditions of natural law, natural rights, a relationship between man and the state that ought to be contractual and reciprocal; and a vision of man that is rooted in the best of the Western Christian tradition. That vision sees the individual soul as so worth saving that God-made-man would sacrifice himself to do so. And that individual soul is responsible for the choices that can guarantee its own salvation.

America in the twentieth century developed an alternate version of individualism. This new version argued that the full flowering of the individual came in material security and a technocratically managed culture that gave man, through the government, control over what had heretofore been seen as beyond human control. Politicians would do for us what we would do for ourselves, if only we were able. What could be more liberating to the individual than that? This new vision sold itself as modern and scientific, the apotheosis of reason. It held out the promise of managing our way to a benevolent and equal wealth.

The twentieth century had no room for an apparently outmoded political philosophy. This was now a world of crises, big machines, war, and economics. Carping about the propriety of the methods used to muddle through these crises seemed antiquated, in the midst of interlocking national wars of communism, fascism, New Dealism. The state's ability, the state's need, to manage the big machinery of the modern economy went largely unquestioned.

Thus it was appropriate—and probably necessary—that the first pair of major intellectual leaders for a recognizably modern libertarianism made their reputation as economists, with a scientific vision rooted in the nineteenth century. Their mission was to show that technocratic management and manipulation of the economy is not a path toward a just equality and unprecedented wealth but to instability, chaos, and serfdom.

Austrian Roadblocks on the Road to Serfdom

A true American wants to have liberty, to be free of arbitrary controls, to have no one demanding his papers, to be rid of officious busybodies poking in his business for whatever reason, to buy what he wants to buy and sell what he wants to sell, to whomever and on whatever terms he chooses. This seems easy enough to grasp, and the libertarian wing of the old right could only wonder what was wrong with any American who'd deny it. But the ideas that could explain, in ruthless but glorious scientific logic, why state intervention in people's economic affairs was counterproductive if wealth, efficiency, and freedom were your values, were imported to America by a pair of old-world Austrians, Ludwig von Mises and Friedrich A. Hayek.

"Whosoever foresees so clearly before the age of forty the disaster and the destruction of everything he deems of value . . ."

Ludwig von Mises was an accomplished economist and political philosopher. He was one of the few prominent thinkers in the first half of the twentieth century doggedly defending the values of nineteenth-century liberalism: tolerance, peace, and unrestricted free markets and free international trade.

As an economist, he was the chief of the third generation of the Austrian economics tradition. After Mises and Hayek, and because of their influence in America, most economic "Austrians" were Americans. The Austrian economics tradition began with the 1871 publication of a book known in English as *Principles of Economics*. Its author, Carl Menger, was born February 28, 1840, in Galicia, now part of Poland but then part of the Austro-Hungarian Empire. Menger "came from an old family of Austrian craftsmen, musicians, civil servants and army officers" and became a journalist covering economic issues after receiving his doctorate in law from the University of Cracow in 1867.[1]

Soon he was working in the press department for a division of the Austrian Civil Service. Menger, in writing about markets for an official newspaper, "was struck by the glaring contrast between the traditional theories of price and the facts which experienced practical men considered as decisive for the determination of prices."[2]

Menger's book was one of a trio of major works that, appearing independently within a few years of each other, shook the foundations of classical economics and formed modern economics. (The other two were William Stanley Jevons's *Theory of Political Economy* and Leon Walras's *Elements of Pure Economics*.) These three books all shattered the classical conception of value, solved problems the old theory couldn't solve, and set the stage for all subsequent developments in modern economics.[3]

The three books take subtly different approaches. While they all contributed to the invention of what is known as marginal utility analysis, the Mengerian tradition had a distinct focus, which Austrian scholar Erich Streissler identifies as resolutely subjectivist, based on the inescapable fact of limited human knowledge. People do not know everything they need or want to know, and they face an inherently unknowable future. This led Menger to stress uncertainty rather than certainty; the processes that lead to price formation rather than specific prices. While there is scholarly debate as to how central such ideas were in Menger, the further unfolding and exploration of subjectivism and uncertainty defined the Austrian tradition Menger fathered. It still exists today, opposed to the mainstream mathematical, equilibrium-obsessed neoclassical consensus that evolved from the Jevonian/Walrasian tradition.[4] (The notion of a mathematically calculated equilibrium in an economy, used by most modern economists, ignores the Mengerian reality that markets are a continuous process with causes and effects created by human choices and valuations. Thus equations from which human action has been removed are not the best means to model an economy.) Menger's tradition has been connected intimately with modern libertarianism. However, many still heatedly debate, in scholarly journals and on e-mail Listservs, whether this link between Austrian economics and libertarianism is inherent in Menger's theory or merely a sociological aberration produced when Mises linked his passionately held nineteenth-century liberal political values with Menger's value-free economics.[5]

Before Menger, Jevons, and Walras, an object's value was generally thought to arise from the labor that went into making it. Economists tended to consider the value of objects as a class, which led to the apparent diamond/water paradox. If water is indispensable for human life and diamonds are a frippery, how is it that diamonds cost more than water under most circumstances?

The innovation of *marginal utility* cut to the solution: We don't make valuational decisions regarding diamonds and water in general or in total, but on a specific given amount of either up for our immediate consideration. And we value any given unit of a good for the least valuable possible use to which we could put that unit. Thus the more units of something available to us, the less valuable any given unit of it is.

For (a Mengerian) example, if a farmer has five bags of corn, he may use the first two to feed his family—its most valued use. He may store the third for possible future food needs, the fourth to feed his horse, and the last to feed chickens. To that farmer, feeding chickens is the least valuable use for a bag of corn. But if he lost one bag, he would give up the least valued use to him. Thus the farmer values a bag of corn only equal to its use as chicken feed.

Similarly with water; there is so much of it at our disposal that the least valued use tends to be letting it run down a drain. That's how abundant but essential water ends up being less expensive than rare but frivolous diamonds. Still, we are often willing to pay dearly for bottled water from a faraway spring, while letting tap water spill away. This illustrates another subjectivist insight: Goods that are the same physically or conceptually are not necessarily the same economically. Value arises from human interpretation, not objective reality.

Menger's theory of value and price formation places the consumer at the center. Value and price are dictated by what the consumer wants, on his "valuations at the margin" in economics lingo. This was a momentous shift. Before the 1870s, economics could rightly be called plutology, the science of wealth. After Menger and his fellow marginalist revolutionaries wrote, it became a science of human wants and desires, studying the ever-changing prices and markets that arose as the spontaneously organized result of millions of individual choices.

Followers of the Mengerian/Austrian tradition remained truest to this original source of the 1870s marginalist revolution: Economics is about the desires and valuations of the individual consumer. Consumers, not producers, are at the heart of the market system, in the sense that producers cater to consumer tastes. The best results for everyone tend to emerge from allowing this free play of consumer desires. Because it takes that idea very seriously, Austrian economics has been one of the strongest intellectual props for the benefits of free markets, and a powerful, occasionally dominant strain in the modern libertarian movement.

After the publication of *Principles*, Menger began lecturing at the University of Vienna, where he achieved the rank of professor in 1873. He became prominent in Austrian court affairs, and was appointed tutor in economics to the Austro-Hungarian Empire's Crown Prince Rudolf in 1876. Menger's lectures to Rudolf, strangely, glossed over Menger's theoretical innovations, but do show a protolibertarian attitude embedded in the Austrian tradition from the beginning, even if Menger's published works didn't exhibit it.[6]

Menger wrote almost nothing on economics after *Principles*. Most of his intellectual energy was taken up by the *Methodenstreit*, an ongoing intellectual duel with the dominant German historical school of economics. Although immensely complicated, the debate was rooted in arguments over whether there were predictable theoretical regularities in economics, as Menger believed, or if there were nothing but a disconnected set of historical facts to study that said nothing definite about the future.[7] That school was far more successful in filling high academic positions in Germany and Austria with its type of economist than Menger was. Mises, writing out of his own World War II–era melancholy, speculates that Menger, the great liberal, lost his zest for life and productivity because he foresaw the decades of world war caused by the abandonment of liberal policies. Mises's conclusion: "Whosoever foresees so clearly before the age of forty the disaster and the destruction of everything he deems of value, cannot escape pessimism and psychic depression."[8]

"THE MOST POWERFUL OPPONENT OF MARXISM IS THE AUSTRIAN SCHOOL."

The second generation of the Austrian economic tradition was dominated by a pair of brothers-in-law: Eugen von Böhm-Bawerk (1851–1914) and Friedrich Wieser (1851–1926). Neither studied directly under Menger, but both embraced and extended his methods. Both did more to spread and popularize Menger's ideas than Menger did himself.

Wieser was born into a family of Austrian civil servants. Like most of the important figures of the Austrian tradition, he was first attracted to economics by a chance reading of Menger's *Principles,* after graduating from the University of Vienna with a law degree. He became friends with Menger, and at Menger's recommendation got his first teaching position in political economy at the University of Prague in 1884. Wieser went on to assume Menger's chair at the University of Vienna in 1903 and became Austria's minister of commerce in August 1917 in the waning days of the war. After the Austro-Hungarian monarchy collapsed, Wieser taught for a few more years at Vienna, retiring in 1922.

Wieser is credited with coining the term "marginal utility" for the concept already implicit in Menger and others.[9] He added "opportunity cost" to the modern economist's arsenal: the notion that the cost of something is best conceived as the next best option forgone in choosing it. Wieser also extended Menger's work in factor imputation—calculating the value of a production good (a good used to make another good that is ultimately used by a consumer—for example, a slicer in a bread factory) based on the consumer good (for example, the bread we eat) that it helps produce. Since all value boils down to consumer choice, production goods only have value because of the value of the consumer goods they help make. If no one wanted to eat the bread, no one would value the bread slicer.[10]

Politically, Wieser was the least liberal and least subjectivist of the early Austrians. His student Hayek, who thought the world of him, admitted that Wieser's liberalism "already included a good deal of argument for [government] control [of the economy], certainly so far as problems of the labour market and social policy are concerned."[11] Wieser believed that his marginal utility theory provided an airtight justification, for example, for a progressive income tax, and he gave credence to the notion that prices in a capitalist society could deviate from "natural value" in a manner that government planners might be able to fix.

Böhm-Bawerk was married to Wieser's sister and had also studied law at the University of Vienna. He served three times as Austria's minister of finance, in 1895, 1897, and 1900. He began teaching his famous seminar at the University of Vienna in 1904 and continued until his death in 1914. Böhm-Bawerk is most famous for early Austrian work in capital theory, introducing both the importance of time and the higher productivity of roundabout forms of production. The reason we have a capital-heavy economy is because machinery, for example, while a roundabout way to the goal of making whatever the machine makes, makes so much *more* of whatever it is than we could make without it that the wait is more than worth it. He used Mengerian methods to discover why interest exists, and came up with an answer that combined time preference with productivity. That is, humans are thought to inherently value something now more than something later, other things being equal, so they demand payment for waiting, which is what interest is in one sense. But Böhm-Bawerk thought this was not enough to explain interest, which also existed because in waiting, because of roundabout means of production's extra productivity, we can have more later by investing, rather than spending, a given amount of resources now.[12]

Menger was disappointed with the theory and Mises rejected it in favor of a pure time-preference theory, with productivity playing no role. That version of interest theory has come to be the more distinctly Austrian position, though in fact it is only Misesian.[13] By keeping the cause of interest limited strictly to time preference, a personal and subjective phenomenon, and excluding productivity, a more objective one, the pure time-preference theory of interest is truer to the Austrian tradition of subjectivism.[14] As Hayek, Austrian economics' only Nobel laureate, said, "It is probably no exaggeration to say that every important advance in economic theory during the last hundred years was a further step in the consistent application of subjectivism."[15]

Böhm-Bawerk also began the Austrian tradition's war with Marxism, writing *Karl Marx and the Close of His System* (1898), which attacked—in a manner that convinced even many previously Marxian socialists in Austria and Germany to turn against his economics—Marx's attempt to prove that consumer prices were in fact based in labor, rather than, as Böhm-Bawerk insisted (and almost all economists now agree), in subjective marginal valuations. And if the labor theory of value was wrong, as Böhm-Bawerk proved, then pretty much everything else in Marx was wrong, since his intellectual edifice was built on that labor theory of value. As Böhm-Bawerk wrote, Marx produced "a most ingeniously conceived structure, built up by a fabulous combination, of innumerable stories of thought, held together by a marvelous mental grasp, but—a house of cards."[16] This led Bolshevik theoretician Bukharin to assert in 1919, "It is well known that the most powerful opponent of Marxism is the Austrian school."[17]

Hayek and Mises would be the most widely read and highly regarded twentieth-century exponents of the Austrian tradition. Hayek was a student and devotee of Wieser; Mises, of Böhm-Bawerk. But the early Austrians did not succeed, despite their power base within the Austrian government and high bureaucracy, in crafting a solid academic berth for their tradition. Mises lamented that Menger and Böhm-Bawerk failed to develop a "school" in a traditional sense; they lacked the requisite killer instinct for successful academic infighting. "They never attempted to propagandize their theories. Truth will prevail by its own force if man has the ability to perceive it. . . . Carl Menger never tried to extend favors to his colleagues, who would then return such favors through recommendations for appointments." Böhm-Bawerk actively promoted professors who disagreed with his approach.[18]

"IT TURNS OUT, OF COURSE, THAT MISES WAS RIGHT."

Ludwig von Mises was born on September 29, 1881, in the Austro-Hungarian city of Lemberg, which, like Menger's birthplace, was in Galicia. (The city is now known as Lvov, Ukraine.) He was the son of Arthur von Mises, a construction engineer in the Austrian Ministry of Railroads, and Adele Landau von Mises.[19] His family was well-connected politically; his great-grandfather Mayer Mises was a leader in the fight for Jewish legal equality in Galicia during the revolutionary year of 1848. And in the 1873 elections to the Austrian parliament, all three of the Jewish members elected from Galicia were close relatives of Mises's.[20] The family moved to Vienna when Mises was young, and he attended the University of Vienna from 1900 to 1902, studying law and political science. He then took a year off to serve as an artillery officer trainee in the Austrian army.

Mises returned to the University of Vienna and received a doctorate in law in 1906. His interest in economics had already been piqued by reading Menger's *Principles,* sometime around Christmas 1903. Even before getting his doctorate, Mises had economic research essays published and even a book, though he had not yet developed his distinctive style and radical free market approach.[21] Reading and contemplating Menger's vision of the inherent beneficial order of free markets turned him away from the standard interventionism of the intellectuals surrounding him at the University of Vienna and toward old-fashioned liberalism. His shift to hardcore liberalism was gradual, helped along by Mises's attendance at Böhm-Bawerk's seminar, a legendary center of Austrian intellectual firepower. (Böhm-Bawerk so fascinated Mises that he, like other students, continued to attend Böhm-Bawerk's seminars even after he graduated.)

Upon graduation, this apostle of governmental noninterference in the economy spent eight months working for the empire's internal revenue service. He then put his degree to use clerking in various courts and joining a Viennese law firm. Mises began his long career as a teacher inauspiciously in 1908 at the Viennese Commercial College for Women, teaching constitutional law, public finance, and economics. He kept that post until 1912. In 1909, he also attained a position at the Austrian chamber of commerce, which was not an organization representing private business interests to the government but a quasi-official economic advisor to the government.[22]

Mises maintained his position at the chamber, rising in influence as a public economist, until 1938. He also began teaching at his alma mater, the University of Vienna, in 1913. He was not an official faculty member paid by the university—he was a *privatdozent*, paid from student fees. (This was not an unusual fate for innovators in the Viennese university system; Sigmund Freud languished similarly.)

During his first university seminar, Mises, the complete free trader, set his students to studying the effects of the protectionist trade policies of the divisions of the Austro-Hungarian customs union. World War I began, and prewar plans became so much cannon fodder. All four students Mises set to work on this problem were killed, went missing, or were taken prisoner during the war. He never saw any of them again.[23]

Mises himself served as an artillery captain at the front for three years. He contracted malaria and ended up in a desk job in the economics division of the War Department by 1917.[24]

After World War I, Mises worked on a book that contained almost every argument made by advocates of free markets and enemies of socialism throughout the twentieth century, though sometimes in truncated or merely suggestive form. The book, *Socialism*, came out in 1922. Hayek was then working for Mises as an assistant in a special chamber of commerce office, the Bureau of Claims Settlements, dedicated to supervising the terms of a World War I treaty.

Hayek remembers Mises as a "tremendously efficient executive, the kind of man who . . . does a normal days work in two hours."[25] Despite working with him day to day, though, Hayek had no idea that "Mises was also writing the book which would make the most profound impression on my generation. . . . Much as we had come to admire Mises's achievements in economic theory, this was something of a much broader scope and significance. It was a work on political economy in the tradition of the great moral philosophers . . . . there can be no doubt whatever about the effect on us who have been in their most impressionable age. To none of us young men who read the book when it appeared the world was ever the same again."[26]

Socialism contrasts socialism with liberalism, in the nineteenth-century sense. Mises parses out every extant variety of socialism, and flays them all. He examines socialism's devastating effect on the constitutional order, the family, foreign trade and foreign relations, and the economy. More than a mere work of comparative economic systems, *Socialism* presented the case for a liberal social order. It explained Mises's vision of how human societies develop (a vision that, at different times, can seem both similar to and different from the more famous evolutionary one presented by his friend and colleague Hayek) and debunked every aspect of Marxist theory.[27] To Mises, the attitude behind all varieties of socialism is "destructionism"—a spirit of resentment and envy that tears down the productive social relations of free market liberalism.

Socialism's most famous contribution was Mises's hotly debated demonstration that socialism in a dynamic industrial economy would lack the ability to rationally calculate—or, as it is generally known, his proof that socialism is "impossible." Mises first raised this idea in a 1920 essay, but it was presented in its most detailed form here. As with most scientific ideas, it can be traced back in some form to many earlier thinkers, including Wieser.[28] It launched what came to be known as the "socialist calculation debate."

Socialist economist Oskar Lange once mocked Mises, claiming that "a statue of Professor Mises ought to occupy an honorable place in the great hall of the . . . Central Planning Board of the socialist state" because of Mises's service in showing them the problems they had to (and would) solve on the way to performing efficient economic calculation without private property and money prices.[29] A more apt object of honor, perhaps, would have been one of those heavy chandeliers Khrushchev once complained about, in an economy where meeting a physical quota imposed by the party by making things heavy, or light (if more of a specific object was what was demanded), was more important than meeting consumer demand.[30]

Some of Mises's modern-day devotees have attempted to back-pedal from the sheer boldness of this assertion. Don Lavoie, a student of the debate, insists that Mises meant something more limited than it sounds by "impossible"—just that socialism couldn't meet its stated goals of keeping an industrial economy running with a high level of productivity.[31]

In the 1920s, a significant portion of the Western intelligentsia saw huge possibilities (if not inevitability) in socialism following Russia's Bolshevik revolution. Even economists were taking socialism seriously, which struck Mises as bizarre. As modern Austrian economist and student of the Soviet economy Peter Boettke noted, "Mises would say that a noneconomist might advocate socialism, but once you were an economist you wouldn't. Then Oskar Lange came along and started trying to use an economic argument to defend socialism. It hit Mises and Hayek like a 2 x 4 to the head."[32]

Choosing among different production methods was more than just a technological problem, Mises insisted, despite claims by some socialists. It was an economic problem of figuring out in what proportions and to what extent certain things are valued in order to use them most, well, economically. And without private property and prices to reduce comparisons between different and incommensurable objects to a common denominator—a money price—that economic calculation problem was insoluble. For example, you may have steel at your disposal, but you need food. In a market economy, the money price becomes the great equalizer that tells you what everything is worth in terms of everything else. If steel is, say, selling for $40 a pound, and apples for $1 a pound, you know that steel is worth forty times what an apple is. And you can trust that prices approximate, as closely as anything could, a correct estimate of the entire society's valuation of things, because if apples were "really" worth $2 a pound (if people were willing to pay that much), you can be sure that in a market economy where people own property and can keep what they get from selling it intelligently, someone will realize this and begin raising the price, which, if he keeps selling them at the higher price, signals other private property owners seeking profit to raise their prices, and so on, until it actually reaches the price at which the most apples can be sold profitably. This process is continuous and never-ending, never reaching the modern economists' perfect model of an equilibrium where no more trades need be made, since people's relative valuations of things shift constantly.

Without a world of people able to bid and compete for the use of resources, bringing their own subjective valuations to bear and able to profit from their choices, there is no way to make an intelligent choice about what to do with any given resource, since there would be no way to actually know what people want most out of that resource. Thus, with one set of planners owning everything and making all allocation decisions without market prices, economic inefficiency will ensue that will come nowhere near actually reflecting people's desires. Without the money prices and the incentives of private property, an advanced industrial economy would never know what things were actually valued at, and the waste of resource to meet political needs, not consumer needs, would be inevitable.

Mises defined socialism, as did most socialists of the time, as full public ownership of the means of production. Partially, no doubt, in response to some of the strength of Mises's arguments, the definition of socialism as public ownership of the factors of production has almost disappeared today. The word is now often applied merely to welfare states with a good deal of state ownership and management. In Mises's day though, his definition was uncontroversial, and even his opponents accepted it.[33]

The fight to refute Mises on the question of whether a socialist economy could solve this calculation problem was heated and intense, with Oskar Lange, Henry Dickinson, and Abba Lerner the biggest names on the socialist side; Mises, Hayek, and Lionel Robbins of the London School of Economics were on the other. In the short run, Mises's side was seen to have lost. Says David Ramsey Steele in his book on the controversy:

> When I began reading about economic calculation in 1970 the dominant view was that Mises was a nonentity whose simple-minded criticism of socialism had been deservedly buried. In theory, Mises had been refuted by Lange, and in practice by the Sputnik. Among mainstream economists it was the rule, when making an occasional passing reference to the debate over the Mises ar-

gument, to state that Mises was wrong, perhaps obviously wrong, and possibly so obviously wrong as to approach silliness.[34]

Lange and other socialists believed that if economic planners could simply find out what everyone had and could get continuous reports on what everyone wanted, they could use mathematical equations to figure ways to successfully emulate the calculations and decisions that are made in an uncoordinated and scattered way by every economic decisionmaker, and effectively emulate what free market prices do in terms of squaring supply and demand without actually having free market prices. What free market prices do, in the Austrian theory, is spread information about every person's subjective valuations of needs and desires for goods; and they do so by depending, as Hayek has emphasized, on local, individual knowledge of specific circumstances that no central planner could ever gather through any means other than the very system of free market prices that planners think they can replace.[35]

Contemporary scholars have covered the history of the socialist calculation debate from many different angles, and even among Austrians strong differences of opinion still exist. As Mises's most widely discussed idea, it deserves some extended attention. Ironically, the staunchest of modern Misesians, represented by Murray Rothbard and Joseph Salerno, end up agreeing with the perspective of Mises's opponents in the 1930s, who claimed that Hayek and Robbins retreated from Mises's strong claim of impossibility for socialism later in the debate. They merely concluded, it was said, that because of the knowledge problem (the inability of any one planning board to know everything about the resources available and people's expressed desires for things) and the complications of the simultaneous equations a "market-imitating" socialist computing state would have to solve, socialism would be horribly impractical.[36]

Don Lavoie attempted to unravel this complicated question in his book *Rivalry and Central Planning* (1985). He concluded that Mises and his colleagues did not retreat; that in fact Hayek's later arguments, while merely an elaboration of what Mises originally said, shifted emphasis slightly in order to counter new arguments brought forward by the socialists after Mises's first attack.

Mises was necessarily directing his critique at the dominant form of socialism of the day, Marxism, and thus devoted much of his argument to the point that the price system is necessary for rational calculation and cannot, for example, be supplanted by calculation in units of labor hours. Nevertheless, his critique contains the essential elements of the subsequent critiques of market socialism by Hayek and Robbins. Mises anticipated both the view that the problems could be handled "mathematically" and the attempt to reconcile a "competitive" exchange economy with common ownership of the means of production. The former misunderstands the dynamic nature of the problem, and the latter neglects the fact that it is only through the rivalrous bidding of independent owners of the means of production that prices tend to have the coordinative "meaning" necessary for their function in economic calculation. . . . All of [the market socialists'] arguments are essentially "static" in the sense that they completely abstract from any complications entailed in the existence of continuous, unexpected change. In all three arguments it was assumed that the knowledge necessary for the Walrasian equations is available and that the only problem remaining is that of finding, whether by algebra or guesswork, the equilibrium set of prices.[37]

Debate continues over the precise meaning and conclusions of the socialist calculation debate. A certain popular understanding of the argument won Mises renewed cachet after the collapse of the Soviet Union and other communist economies. This led popular economics journalist Robert Heilbroner, no fan of Mises, to declare in the *New Yorker*, "It turns out, of course, that Mises was right."[38]

A strict Misesian would have to note that the a priorist Mises would bristle at the suggestion that events in the world "proved him right." To Mises, economic theory is proved by logical deduction from true premises, not empirically. If Mises was right, it was the logic and rigor of his argument that proved him so, not history.

To Mises, the so-called socialist economies never achieved a true functioning socialism, which was not possible to begin with. The Soviet Union and other communist countries suffered from a particularly virulent form of interventionist state capitalism larded with hampered markets. To the extent that the Soviets attempted to centrally plan, they approached the disaster that Mises promised for anyone making the attempt. But they never achieved full socialism, so their collapse arguably has little to do with proving Mises's position in the socialist calculation debate.[39]

"ONE CANNOT PERMIT THE PEACE TO BE DISTURBED BY PRIESTS AND FANATICS."

Mises recounts his adventures as an Austrian chamber of commerce economist during the turbulent interwar years somewhat grandiosely in his slim memoir, *Notes and Recollections* (1940). In his capacity as economic adviser to the government, Mises thought that he alone persuaded Otto Bauer, head of the Marxist Social Democratic Party that was in charge of Austria during the grim postwar winter of 1918–1919, not to allow a complete Bolshevik takeover of the recently demonarchized Austria.[40]

Mises spent much of the late 1910s and 1920s and early 1930s at the chamber of commerce fighting frantic attempts by the Austrian government to buy its way out of various economic crises by printing more and more banknotes, threatening hyperinflation and banking crises. Despite long and difficult labor in chaotic postwar Austria, Mises mostly failed in his long-term attempt to stop inflation and halt what he saw as ruinous foreign exchange controls in his beloved homeland.[41]

Mises had established his reputation in Austria as a prominent monetary economist with *The Theory of Money and Credit* (1912).[42] Menger had already delivered a brilliant bit of speculative sociology in his *Principles*, explaining how money could have arisen in an unplanned, spontaneous way from a barter system. Barter runs into the problem of the mutual coincidence of wants: Before you can make a trade, you must find someone who not only has what you want but wants what you have. This would likely be rare. After a while, people would get the idea that certain items seem more desirable to more people for trade, and would trade for those items even if they didn't need them, in the hope that they could later trade such widely valued items for something they *do* need.

That's how, in the Mengerian theory, certain items would eventually end up accepted universally in payment, becoming money. In the modern world of central government banks and fiat legal tender paper currency, money might seem an inevitable tool of government. But Menger explained that free humans spontaneously trading to meet their needs could have developed a monetary system without central planning or state involvement.

Mises went further, with a logical argument that Menger's speculation is *necessarily* true—that money could *not* have developed any other way. Mises used a regression theorem to bring money into the general system of subjective marginal value. He had to do so to unravel a paradox: People valued money based on its purchasing power, and its purchasing power depended on how people valued it. So how did people decide how much money to hold? That decision, Mises declared, was based on an estimation of money's purchasing power *yesterday*.

This might seem to replace a paradox with an infinite regress. But at a certain point in the history of, say, gold, there was a day *before* it became used entirely as money, and had inherent value from consumption and industrial uses—people's desire to own it to make things, or for the sheer pleasure of contemplating its beauty as an ornament. Thus the infinite regress of monetary value had to end with something that was valued as *something else* before it was valued as money per se. If Mises was correct, this meant government could not create a pure fiat money from nothing. This sort of argument is key to why many libertarians believe that gold or some other metal that government can't create from essentially thin air is the best, safest, truest money. (Scratch a goldbug, expose a libertarian, in most cases.)

Mises eventually lost his fight for integrity and security in the Austrian banking system. By 1931, Austria's major bank had collapsed. Mises realized that much, if not all, was lost for Austria. Within a few years he was eager to take a teaching job that would rescue him from a country that he suspected—rightly—was ripe for a Nazi German takeover. In the spring of 1934, Mises moved to Geneva as a lecturer at the Graduate Institute of International Studies.[43]

After publishing *Socialism* but before leaving Vienna, Mises wrote *Liberalism,* the best short explanation of Mises the social philosopher, as opposed to economist. However, Mises, despite his fierce insistence on economics as a science independent of its practitioners' values, sometimes blurred this distinction himself. "Liberalism," Mises wrote:

> is derived from the pure sciences of economics and sociology, which make no value judgements within their own spheres and say nothing about what ought to be or about what is good and what is bad, but, on the contrary, only ascertain what is and how it comes to be. When these sciences show us that of all the conceivable alternative ways of organizing society only one, viz., the system based on private ownership of the means of production, is capable of being realized, because all other conceivable systems of social organization are unworkable.[44]

While there may be no political values in Mises's economics, there are most certainly economics in his political values.

Mises presented in that short book a vision that remains the modern libertarian movement's (nonutopian) ideal to strive for. Mises's liberalism is materialistic; "it has nothing else in view than the advancement of [man's] outward, material welfare."[45] It is capitalistic but recognizes that a true liberal capitalist system is driven not by capitalists per se but by the desires of consumers—every man. It is democratic for pragmatic reasons: Violent upheavals in government are bad for man's welfare, and democracy is the best means of ensuring peaceful turnovers of state power. It is utilitarian; Mises does not support economic and personal liberty out of any spiritual or metaphysical doctrine of rights, but because he believes it can be demonstrated, both in theory and by observation, that liberalism ensures the greatest wealth and physical abundance for all. His liberalism is a doctrine of peace, for the same reason. Mises argues here, as he does elsewhere, that universal liberalism is the only sure means for international peace. Only in a world where all men are allowed to benefit from each other's productivity through universal free trade can the resentments, grievances, and cries for colonialism and lebensraum that triggered this century's bloody wars be avoided.[46] It is a doctrine of tolerance.

> Liberalism . . . must be intolerant of every kind of intolerance. If one considers the peaceful cooperation of all men as the goal of social evolution, one cannot permit the peace to be disturbed by priests and fanatics. Liberalism proclaims tolerance for every religious faith and every metaphysical belief, not out of indifference for these "higher" things, but from the conviction that the assurance of peace within society must take precedence over everything.[47]

Private property is the cornerstone of Mises's liberalism—"All the other demands of liberalism result from this fundamental demand."[48] If property is respected and protected by law, the other attributes of Mises's liberalism will naturally flow. Mises saw his liberalism as a revival of the dominant social philosophy of the nineteenth century, eclipsed in the twentieth by false, bloody doctrines like statism and nationalism.

"PRAXEOLOGY SHOWS ONLY WHAT CANNOT BE DONE AND WHY IT CANNOT BE DONE."

Mises was deeply worried that science as well as politics and society were corrupted by false doctrines in the twentieth century. Thus in 1933, he issued his first methodological work, *Epistemological Problems of Economics*, a coherent whole formed from earlier journal articles. This book explains how Mises set himself apart from the trends that dominated economic method during the rest of the twentieth century.

Mises held firm to his peculiar methodology throughout his career, despite the tectonic shifts in the economic profession that went on around him throughout the mid-twentieth century. The rest of his profession ultimately concluded that his views were antediluvian, unscientific, almost absurd. He stuck to them, continuing to believe them of the utmost importance, and repeated them in detail in his late 1940s magnum opus *Human Action*. Then he returned to the issue, which became all the more vital to him as his ideas about it became more unpopular, in his last book, *The Ultimate Foundation of Economic Science* (1962).

Mises was an enemy of logical positivists, who also arose out of his interwar Vienna milieu. Logical positivists believe that all human knowledge has to be reduced to empirical sense impressions, rejecting theory entirely. Mises rejected their standard of proof and defended a purely logical method in the social sciences that doesn't rely on empirical evidence at all. He called this purely logical science of human action *praxeology*, a term neglected by most, beyond Mises's own students and devotees. Economics was the most developed branch of praxeology, and Mises often referred to it as *catallactics*, a term Hayek also used, to indicate the entire system of individual economizing plans that make up what others call "the economy."

Proper praxeological economics to Mises was concerned not with the macrovariables and curves and equations of the contemporary economist; what does any of that have to do with acting, choosing man, which is what economics is properly the study of? The purely logical method of economics was appropriate, Mises insisted, to acting man, making choices to increase his perceived well-being in the face of an uncertain future and scarce means.

Mises's method, heavily derided by his critics, was purely a priori, requiring nothing in the way of empirical observation or verification. From the indisputable notion that human beings act, using scarce means to achieve goals (indisputable because disputing it is itself such an action—it requires using one's time, one's energy, one's breath, the calories from the food you eat, all scarce resources, to achieve your chosen goal of disputing the fact that human act to achieve goals), Mises deduces all economic concepts. As Mises explains it:

> As thinking and acting men, we grasp the concept of action. In grasping this concept we simultaneously grasp the closely correlated concepts of value, wealth, exchange, price, and cost. They are all necessarily implied in the concept of action, and together with them the concepts of valuing, scale of value and importance, scarcity and abundance, advantage and disadvantage, success, profit, and loss. The logical unfolding of all these concepts and categories in systematic derivation from the fundamental category of action

and the demonstration of the necessary relations among them constitutes the first task of our science. . . . There can be no doubt
whatever concerning the aprioristic character of these disciplines.[49]

That's the Misesian method in a nutshell. Since economics is a deductive science, working logically from the indisputable ("apodicti-
cally certain" was Mises's favorite catchphrase for the idea) fact of
action, gathering statistics or appealing to history or empirical testing,
the methods that comprise so much twentieth-century economics, is
not economics to Mises. It is either history, which admittedly has its
own use, or it is nonsense. This would surprise anyone who has
thumbed (incomprehensibly, certainly, if not an initiate into the discipline) through an economics journal in the past sixty years, where
equations and graphs challenge the eye at every turn. But Mises insisted economics was a verbal deductive system, and he wrote his economics in graphless, equationless English (or German). When it comes
to equations, Mises believed, the arid, abstract mathematical equiva-
lences they promise are meaningless in a science that is about constantly changing human choices, a world where there are no constants
and nothing remains equal for long.

It can be difficult for those not steeped in his thinking to grasp exactly how theoretical and nonempirical Mises was, how stubbornly
opposed to the intellectual trends of his time he remained. He defi-
antly insisted that "examining the facts" cannot settle questions in economics. He returns to this issue again and again throughout his work,
but one of his earliest takes on the topic is in *Epistemological Problems*.
His comments on it doubtless seem counterintuitive to someone
raised in a culture where the Joe Friday "just the facts, ma'am" attitude
seems the apotheosis of good Yankee common sense.

Still, anyone who has plowed through op-ed page debates, listened
to dueling economic analysts on TV, or just argued with a recalcitrant
friend, might recognize the wisdom in Mises thinking:

> [A] proposition of an aprioristic theory can never be refuted by ex-
> perience. Human action always confronts experience as a complex
> phenomenon that must first be analyzed and interpreted by a
> theory before it can even be set in the context of an hypothesis that
> could be proved or disproved; hence the vexatious impasse created

when supporters of conflicting doctrines point to the same historical data as evidence of their correctness. The statement that statistics can prove anything is a popular recognition of this truth. No political or economic program, no matter how absurd, can, in the eyes of its supporters, be contradicted by experience. Whoever is convinced a priori of the correctness of his doctrine can always point out that some condition essential for success according to his theory has not been met.[50]

This logical, experienceless method, and its apodictic certainty, frustrates Mises's opponents and some supporters as well. Intellectual gambits like titling a section of *Liberalism* "Capitalism: The Only Possible Form of Social Organization" bring sighs from those who would joust with him and have led former Misesians, such as David Prichytko, to question the base of his whole edifice:

> The claim of "apodictic certainty" tends to break down into a kicking, stomping, unreasonable and apoplectic certainty in the face of criticism. In fact, it is but a small step (or logical deduction, as it were) to conclude that those who do not fully embrace the praxeological system are either morally suspect (that is, they really do recognize the truth within praxeological thought, but refuse to endorse it) or nihilist (that is, they reject logic and the primordial fact of human action), or just plain stupid. . . . This approach to the community of social scientists leaves praxeology with little evolutionary potential and may merely attract those who are predisposed to dogmatic thought or its ideology.[51]

Economic methodology was no dry, academic issue to Mises. It was vitally connected to public policy, and thus to human flourishing. Mises felt justified in calling his methodological opponents, the European historical economists and the American institutionalists, "the harbingers of the ruinous economic policy that has brought the world to its present condition and will undoubtedly destroy modern culture if it continues to prevail."[52]

Mises also explained in *Epistemological Problems* the logical connection between economic science (as understood by Mises) and political libertarianism:

> The development of economics . . . did more to transform human thinking than any other scientific theory before or since. Up to that time it had been believed that no bounds other than those drawn by the laws of nature circumscribed the path of acting man. It was not known that there is still something more that sets a limit to political power beyond which it cannot go . . . in the social realm too there is something operative which power and force are unable to alter and to which they must adjust themselves if they hope to achieve success.[53]

Unfortunately, neither the government nor most citizens are inclined to accept these limits to the possibilities of social engineering that economics dictates. Mises glumly grants that economics is indeed, in a sense, the dismal science: "[People] see in the teachings of the sciences of human action only the depressing message that much of what they desire cannot be attained. The natural sciences . . . show what could be done and how it could be done, whereas praxeology shows only what cannot be done and why it cannot be done."[54] What government cannot do is one of libertarianism's most important messages.

"MY THEORIES EXPLAIN THE DEGENERATION OF A GREAT CIVILIZATION; THEY DO NOT PREVENT IT."

While Mises taught classes as a *privatdozent* at the University of Vienna, his most significant pedagogical contributions came through a private seminar he ran out of his chamber of commerce office, with no official connection to the university. Every other Friday between 1920 and 1934, from October to June, Mises and the cream of interwar Vienna's economists and social scientists gathered, more or less as equals, to discuss the methodology and epistemology of the social sciences, logic, and (less frequently than might be assumed) economics.

Often someone, not necessarily Mises, would present a paper and discussion would follow, or Mises would just throw out a topic inspired by a newspaper story or current event. Mises was not lecturing at his fellow seminar members, who included at various times Hayek,

Fritz Machlup, Oskar Morgenstern, Gottfried Haberler, sociologist Alfred Schutz, political scientist Erich Voegelin, philosopher Felix Kaufmann, and, as occasional foreign visitors, economist Lionel Robbins and British politician Hugh Gaitskell. Machlup, later a prominent economist and teacher at Harvard, who received his doctorate under Mises, "wonder[s] whether there has ever existed anywhere a group from which so large a percentage of members became internationally recognized scholars," though none held full professorships in Vienna at the time.[55] Hayek recalls the meetings over which Mises presided as "at least as much the center of economic discussion in Vienna as the university."[56] Many who attended remember these days fondly in printed reminiscences. It was the sort of exuberant youthful intellectual gang of which one member, Kaufmann, wrote bits of celebratory comic song.[57]

Mises thought the world of his colleagues and students. "I consider the real success of my work as a professor of economics in Vienna was that I made it possible for a number of very gifted and able men to find a way to devote their lives to scientific research," Mises said in 1962.[58] (This was especially kind, as by that point almost all of them had positions of greater prestige in America than Mises did.) Mises's longtime secretary says that the reason Mises pulled together Rockefeller money to float the Austrian Institute for Business Cycle Research, which Hayek ran from 1927 until he left Austria for England, was "because he had to help Hayek find the right start in life."[59]

Mises resented his inability to get an official salaried professorship at the university. After Wieser retired from Menger's old chair, the remaining official economics professors at Vienna were Ferdinand Degenfeld-Schonburg, Hans Mayer, and Othmar Spann—three men whom Mises disliked intensely. Mises claimed Mayer did all he could to bedevil Mises and his students, which led many of the students attending his class to not officially register, so as not to flag to Mayer their connection with Mises. Mises's students were forbidden to use the Economics Department library, though Mises made up for this by letting them use his, "incomparably better than that of the University economics department."[60] Mises thought most students at the university to be of low quality anyway, and "many professors could not even be called educated men."[61]

Mises had a lot to trouble him—the Austrian economic disasters during which his advice was not taken, his situation at the university. His emotional life was complicated as well. Mises's father had died in 1903, while Mises was still in college. Thereafter he lived with his imperious mother. His friends and associates—who tended to think of Mises, in his forties, as "the old man"—assumed he would remain the proper, fussy, homebound bachelor for life.

But at a dinner party in 1925 at the home of his student Fritz Kaufmann, Mises met a widowed ex-actress named Margit Sereny and began a curious courtship—long stretches of no contact, Mises calling Margit on the phone then saying not a word. He never permitted her to meet his mother, with whom he lived. Only after she died did Mises insist Sereny marry him. They were wed on July 6, 1938, in Geneva. Margit, in her curious and sometimes ill-spirited memoir of their relationship, mentions that after their marriage Mises refused to bear any discussion whatever of their thirteen courtship years.[62]

By then, Mises had left Vienna for Geneva. Margit was still stuck in Vienna when the Nazis took over but managed to get out shortly thereafter with her two children from her previous marriage. Mises's teaching load in Geneva was light, just two hours of lecturing a week on Saturday morning. This gave him plenty of time to work on *Nationalokonomie* (1940), the first German-language version of the book that was to become, when revised and written in English, his magnum opus setting forth his economics from the foundations up—*Human Action*.

As German military victories mounted and France fell, the Miseses thought it wise to escape Switzerland. In the summer of 1940, they began difficult machinations to emigrate to the United States. Mises implored a friend with the Chase Manhattan Bank to get his family nonquota visas for the United States. But escape required them to pass through France, Spain, and Portugal, and obtaining visas for all three countries was difficult. (Famous modernist composer Darius Milhaud, whose wife had been tutoring Margit's daughter from her previous marriage, pulled strings for them in France.) After a harrowing trek across Europe, finally, on July 25, 1940, a boat left Lisbon for the United States with the Miseses onboard. They landed in New Jersey, greeted by Mises's old private seminar friend, the phenomenologist

Alfred Schutz.[63] From previous arrangements, he had hoped to get a teaching position at the University of California–Berkeley, but it fell through at the last minute, as did an attempt by friends working with the Rockefeller Foundation to set him up at UCLA. His failure to find meaningful work—even at the New School for Social Research, a place where his own efforts had helped set up programs for émigré scholars fleeing the Nazis—added to his general depression during his early days in America.

To begin with, he was dispirited at having to abandon Europe as it seemed to sink beneath the weight of the antiliberal forces Mises had dedicated his professional life to fighting. He wrote his pessimistic memoirs *Notes and Recollections* just after arriving in America. Mises was at a low ebb of hope for liberalism's future then; when he wrote the book *Liberalism* in the 1920s, he was confident enough to declare that "it is . . . superfluous to trouble oneself especially about the spread of liberalism. Its victory is, in any case, certain."[64]

By the time he wrote these memoirs, he glumly declares, "I have come to realize that my theories explain the degeneration of a great civilization; they do not prevent it. I set out to be a reformer, but only became the historian of decline."[65] Later, after years in America and witnessing the growth of a nascent libertarian movement, his attitude improved, and he expressed hope that the mentality of intellectual leaders can be changed, and the masses will follow suit—a central strategic vision for much of the libertarian movement throughout its history, usually associated with Hayek.[66]

But in the early 1940s, he was certain it was all over for him and his work. He mordantly noted in a letter to Hayek: "I have been very busy these last months in writing my posthumous works."[67]

Despite his low emotional state, Mises developed a new circle of friends in New York. The most helpful and fateful of them was the American economics journalist and *New York Times* editorialist Henry Hazlitt. While Mises's writings were often slow to be translated into English, which affected their reception and impact in America, a select few had already noticed Mises here, Hazlitt prime among them. Even before Mises arrived in the United States, Hazlitt was one of his leading promoters. In his 1938 *Times* review of *Socialism*, Hazlitt called it "an economic classic in our time." When he first spoke to Mises on the phone, he was as shaken up, he said, as if he had picked up the phone to hear, "This is John Stuart Mill speaking."[68]

Hazlitt became the most successful popularizer of Mises's ideas, with his book *Economics in One Lesson*. Hazlitt had the most respectable intellectual pedigree of any American Misesian. He had been a reporter for the *Wall Street Journal*, a critic and editor at *The Nation,* a book critic for the *New York Sun*, and was Mencken's handpicked successor in editing the *American Mercury* in 1933 (but lasted mere months, probably because of personality conflicts with the magazine's publisher, Alfred Knopf). He was a trusted editorial writer on economics for the *New York Times,* that bastion of respectable middle-of-the-road opinion (though occasionally his libertarian views on topics such as Bretton Woods were overridden by higher-ups). Hazlitt was the best connected of libertarian writers; hanging out at the Bohemian Grove retreat, pulling strings in the State Department to help Margit von Mises's daughter escape Nazi-occupied France and get to the United States, corresponding with nearly every president of the century. Ronald Reagan was "proud to count myself as one of your students."[69] He reached enormous audiences for two decades with his free market opinion column in *Newsweek* (1946–1966), as well as writing classics in utilitarian ethical theory (*The Foundations of Morality,* 1964) and an almost page-by-page refutation of Keynes (*The Failure of the "New Economics,"* 1959).

Mises began a series of lectures by invitation in the New York area at such institutions as Columbia, the New School for Social Research, and Princeton. He spoke at Harvard at the invitation of his brother Richard, a statistician teaching there. His entire Viennese seminar gang had ended up in New York, and Mises continued to enjoy their company. Mises's doctoral student Fritz Machlup, who taught at Princeton for many years, says Mises's foresight regarding the eventual fate of Austria helped many of his students escape in time. Machlup related an absurdist fantasy Mises developed (which seems to belie the image some presented later of Mises as grim and impersonal) about the fate of their group in the new world. "We pictured ourselves founding a nightclub. . . . In this envisioned cabaret, Kaufmann would be a crooner; I received the doubtful role of a gigolo, doing my very best to give a good time to young ladies (and those who would have loved to still be young) . . . and Mises himself would wear the distinctive attire of a doorman."[70]

Through another of his old Austrian seminar friends, John Van Sickle, who worked with the Rockefeller Foundation, Mises got funding from Rockefeller for a position with the National Bureau of Economic Research. This grant was continued through 1944. During this time, Mises wrote *Omnipotent Government*, his history of Germany in the past century. Germany's problems, in Mises's telling, arose from its abandoning liberalism for statism and nationalism.[71] Hard as it is to believe, considering the paper's attitude toward unreconstructed classical liberalism today, he also wrote the occasional unsigned editorial during the wartime years for the *New York Times*, thanks to his friendship with Hazlitt.[72]

However, Mises was unable to find a paid academic berth commensurate with his stature in Europe. While many of his supporters blame prejudice against his firm libertarianism, Mises's age may have been as much of a problem—he was approaching the standard retirement age of sixty-five when he arrived in America.[73] He was also reluctant to relocate to any city less grand than New York.

Mises began working with political activist groups in America as the war years waned, notably the group of industrialist free enterprise boosters, the National Association of Manufacturers, whose Economics Principles Committee Mises joined in 1943. Mises worked there with the likes of J. Howard Pew of Sun Oil, B. F. Hutchinson, vice chairman of Chrysler, and Robert Welch, later founder of the John Birch Society.[74] He began lecturing to business groups on free enterprise, and in Los Angeles met a strongly libertarian chamber of commerce general manager named Leonard Read, eventual founder of the first libertarian advocacy institution, the Foundation for Economic Education.

Austrian economist and historian of Austrian economics Karen Vaughn blames these links with political and business activist groups for Mises's problematic reputation in America:

> Mises's refusal to join in the contemporary economic conversation was partly cause and partly effect of another aspect of his American life. Largely because he was known as a staunch advocate of free markets at a time when the enthusiasm for them had reached a

nadir in American intellectual life, Mises quickly attracted a following among the "old right." He became a spokesman for an economic point of view that was largely absent in professional
economic circles . . . and was a rallying point for free market
groups who were looking for intellectual leadership.[75]

Vaughn points out that in a 1956 Mises Festschrift, all the participants were either old colleagues, disciples, or libertarian activists—not
a single representative of mainstream American economists, among
whom Mises was thought a relic from bygone days.

"ECONOMICS AS SUCH IS A CHALLENGE TO THE CONCEIT OF THOSE IN POWER."

Mises's major work during his first decade in America, in most estimations the major work of his life, was a nearly 900-page thoroughgoing
treatise on every aspect of economic science, called *Human Action,*
published by Yale University Press. Almost every idea Mises ever ex-
pounded is in this book, though not always in its most detailed form.
Praise from individualist circles was as monumental as the book. One
individualist critic, Rose Wilder Lane, opined that "this book begins
and will stand for a new epoch in human thought, therefore in human
action and world history."[76] Hazlitt in his *Newsweek* column called it "a
landmark in the progress of economics . . . . If a single book can turn
the ideological tide that has been running in recent years so heavily
toward statism, socialism, and totalitarianism, *Human Action* is that
book. It should become the leading text of everyone who believes
in . . . a free market economy."[77]

Outside the circle of libertarian sympathizers, though, the reaction
was equal and opposite in its intense aversion. The *New Republic*
thought it "not acceptable . . . frivolous . . . even those who agree
may be embarrassed . . . a holocaust of straw men."[78] The *Economist*
found it "irrelevant to the point of craziness . . . the arrogance with
which Professor von Mises dismisses all contemporary economics
without ever condescending to meet his adversaries on their own

ground is nevertheless remarkable."[79] One German-language newspaper in the United States, *Aufbau*, declared it "the most stupid book so far this year. . . . The book presents an inner inhumanity, mixed with a dash of intellectuality, such as one finds only among Jewish European reactionaries, who translate their own Ghetto inferiority complexes into economic theory."[80]

Human Action demands a strong reaction, if one can digest it. It is dense, filled with unusual ideas and interpretations on almost every page, and stars Mises's often remarked on "apodictic" tone. Its scope encompasses far more than merely economics; the reader has gotten through nearly one hundred pages of methodology and philosophy (and even some analysis of probability theory and its applications) before he gets to issues most would normally consider "economic."

Mises begins where he insists economics must begin: with acting man, facing an uncertain future and necessarily scarce means, with a shifting set of values and choices, striving, though not necessarily succeeding, to further his own perceived well-being. Mises explains the importance of his economics for libertarianism: "It is impossible to understand the history of economic thought if one does not pay attention to the fact that economics as such is a challenge to the conceit of those in power. An economist can never be a favorite of autocrats and demagogues."[81] Mises explains marginal utility, how the economic division of labor created human society and culture, and the meaning of subjective value. He discusses what prices mean and how they develop, and what they can and can't do. He explains the use and misuse of imaginary constructions in economics. He explains the importance of the entrepreneur as "the driving force of the market" (though always in thrall, in a sense, to consumer desires).[82] He explains capital (always heterogeneous and subjective, its value dependent on human estimations of the value of the things it can be used to make) and interest (which exists because of subjective time preference for things now instead of in the future). He explains how and why profit and loss exist, how they function in the economy, and how they always tend to disappear but never actually do so, as the market changes constantly. He discusses monopoly and where and when it exists, concluding it only becomes a problem when the monopolist can extract a monopoly *price*, which is rare. (That is the situation where the monopolist can make *more* money by selling *less* of something, which depends on a certain lack of elasticity in people's demand curves, a structure that doesn't always apply.)[83]

Money and banking are explained, as are the dangers of inflation; his theory of the trade cycle as caused by unnatural expansion of credit by banks (or the government) is spelled out. (This theory was expanded famously by Hayek, and is discussed in more detail in the section dealing with him below.) Mises grapples with foreign exchange rates and the setting of wages, and he revisits the impossibility of economic calculation under socialism. Toward the end, he analyzes the (ill) effects of government intervention in the workings of the economy, including taxation, restriction of production, price controls, legal tender legislation, credit expansion, and foreign exchange controls. He presages later economic and policy insights like the Laffer curve (which says that at certain levels of taxation, raising taxes will decrease the revenue governments get from taxation) and elements of rational expectations theory (which says that government manipulations in the economy often fail when people begin to figure out what government is trying to accomplish and react in a way that frustrates the planners' intentions). Through all this he sprinkles brilliant aperçus about government and society, not obviously related to the general economic issue under discussion.

His analysis in *Human Action* is, as always, utilitarian and value-free; he always insists that government interventions fail *on the terms of those who desire them* to achieve what they want. Price controls remain his favorite example. Those who set them desire the controlled item to be cheap and plentiful, but drive it out of the market altogether by making production of the item uneconomical. Lower prices both raise demand and lower supply as some suppliers on the margin can no longer profit at the artificially lowered price, leading to shortages. He also analyzes how government interventions tend to lead, if the desired result is still chased after an initial failure, to more and greater government interventions, on an inevitable path to complete government control. Thus he denies the possibility of a viable "third way" between free markets and socialism.

Throughout, Mises's economic analysis is in the classic Austrian style: subjective, individualistic, free of math. All economic phenomena are explained in terms of individual choices and valuations, which are necessarily subjective. Aggregates such as "national income" and the "unemployment rate" do not react or cause anything, and are thus meaningless for the economist. And mathematical equations, since they often blur the key economic issue of causation and can never give any more information than can also be provided verbally, are unnecessary for the economist (as opposed to the statistician or economic historian).

While Mises had trouble finding a prestigious academic post, he had no trouble finding publishers for his books. Through Hazlitt, Mises began a relationship with Yale University Press in 1944, when they published both his history of German statism and nationalism, *Omnipotent Government*, and his monograph *Bureaucracy,* about how the bureaucratic method—by Mises's definition, a system in which workers must act not on their own judgment but on rules and regulations laid down by their superiors—was inevitable in any operation, such as government, in which there is no market price for the service being provided, and thus no price signals to tell people when they are or are not meeting their goals. (The same bureaucratic logic would apply, Mises thought, to any nonprofit organization.) Mises then brought to his editor at Yale, Eugene Davidson, the idea of publishing a heavily revised English language version of his *Nationalokonomie.* After being convinced by various other prominent figures, including Hayek, of such a project's value, Yale agreed. *Human Action* was published in May 1949. Despite its size, difficulty, and controversial stances, it was in a third printing by October. It was an alternate selection of the Book-of-the-Month Club. Yale then published new English editions of *Socialism* and *The Theory of Money and Credit.*

Mises's relationship with Yale went swimmingly, until his old editor and the director of the press both left. The second edition of *Human Action* was botched, to a degree that became a cause célèbre among right-wingers. In *National Review* Hazlitt excoriated Yale for the shoddy printing and editing job. Mises was not even permitted to see galley proofs. Margit remembers what a blow this botched second edition was to Mises.

> Outsiders may have considered the misprinting of *Human Action* an
> episode in the life of a great man, accepted and forgotten. But it was

not so. It was the only time in his life that he had sleeping problems, though he steadfastly refused to take any pills. He was angry. It was an ice-cold, quiet anger directed against what he felt was an unknown enemy at Yale University Press, menacing his great book, his creative strength, his very existence.[84]

Mises threatened to sue and eventually won the rights to the book back from Yale. He felt the bad job was "a purposeful design to prejudice both the circulation of the book and the reputation and the material interests of the author."[85] The book is kept in print by the Ludwig von Mises Institute in Auburn, Alabama.[86]

While *Human Action* was as successful as a nearly thousand-page treatise on economics could be, the mentor was exceeded in his popular influence on American politics and philosophy by his student Hayek, who came to America after him, not as a homeless émigré but as a best-selling controversialist and the most prominent public voice for economic liberalism in the 1940s.

"POINT OUT BARRIERS TO FURTHER ADVANCE ON THE PATH CHOSEN BY OTHERS."

Though Friedrich August von Hayek was Mises's most important disciple, he was by no means a slavish one. Hayek became the most complicated, nuanced, and wide-ranging of the great libertarian thinkers of the twentieth century. In his influence, inspiration, and achievement, he is widely regarded as the most significant libertarian intellectual of modern times (though never the best known).[87] He is also, in some ways, the least *libertarian* of the major libertarian influences of the twentieth century, by many other libertarians' lights.

During the surprising American popular success of his 1944 book *Road to Serfdom,* Hayek was swept against his expectations and almost against his will on a whirlwind publicity and polemical tour the likes of which the quiet, abstract Austrian-by-way-of-England had never before experienced. His book had been condensed and reprinted in America's bible of periodicals, *Reader's Digest.* (The condensation was made by famous Marxist turncoat Max Eastman.) Hayek became temporarily famous in America.

During this tour, he squared off against a couple of typical American intellectuals of the era, Professors Charles E. Merriam and Maynard C. Krueger, both from the institution that would soon become Hayek's home, the University of Chicago. During that debate, Krueger told Hayek, after failing to make Hayek endorse various antigovernment stances that Krueger clearly hoped the audience would find absurd, "It seems to me that you do allow far more of public planning than most of the readers of your book in this country have assumed."[88]

Indeed. While almost all of his consistent admirers call themselves libertarian (those who might prefer to call themselves conservatives are kept at arm's length by one of Hayek's most famous essays, "Why I Am Not a Conservative," which concluded his thorough exploration of his vision of the free and prosperous commonwealth, *The Constitution of Liberty* [1960]), Hayek's thought does not necessarily provide ammunition for a philosophy of consistent and uncompromised freedom. Still, he unquestionably contributed both original concepts and revivals of old truths that have been central to the contemporary libertarian project, such that the editor of the highest-circulation libertarian magazine of today, *Reason*, saw fit to dub him "capo di tutti capi" of modern libertarianism.[89]

Hayek's vision of individualism and liberty is not based on a belief in human grandeur, ability, or strength. It's based on our limits and weakness, particularly the limits and weakness of our reason. Hayek didn't base his belief in strict and severe limitations on the power of the state on a judgment of the state's evil, as with the more philosophically passionate Rand or Rothbard and many contemporary libertarian activists. Instead, Hayek stressed the state's inefficacy: the essential and in Hayek's mind insurmountable limits of what a state can hope to do, owing to the insurmountable limits of what man's reason and knowledge can do.[90]

Well into the 1930s Hayek was not yet a full-blooded champion of freedom. Before writing *The Road to Serfdom,* his first strong public declaration against the powers of the contemporary socialist state in all its manifestations, Hayek wrote, "If our conclusions on the merits of [planning] . . . are essentially negative, this is certainly no cause for satisfaction. . . . Nothing . . . could do more to relieve the unmitigated gloom with which the economist today must look at the future of the world than if it could be shown that there is a possible and practicable way to overcome [planning's] difficulties."[91]

No mention here of the positive virtues of freedom. Perhaps in camouflage, Hayek takes on the persona of the unhappy bearer of bad tidings who *wishes* socialism could work but is driven by the exigencies of pure science to admit that it seemingly can't.

Hayek's economics was also rooted in man's ignorance, what man can't do or know. Hayek summarized his own contribution to economic science thus: "What I had done had often seemed to me more to point out barriers to further advance on the path chosen by others than to supply new ideas which opened the path to further development."[92]

"A TIME WHEN THE NEW THEORIES OF HAYEK WERE THE PRINCIPAL RIVAL OF THE NEW THEORIES OF KEYNES."

Hayek came of age in a time when utopian visions of what man could accomplish were shattered or tarnished during the madness of World War I. The glories of Western civilization seemed burned to ashes and smothered in trenches, never to rise again. Hayek fought in the war that was to end all war, and came out of it with an abiding interest in the creation and preservation of social orders[93] and, after learning later of all the things his government did *not* tell him about the war, a burgeoning mistrust of the intentions of the governing class.[94]

Hayek was born in Vienna, capital of the Austro-Hungarian Empire, on May 8, 1899, shortly before the century many call the American century but which could also, with some justice, be called the Austrian century.[95] He was the son of August Edler von Hayek and Felicitas von Juraschek. The Jurascheks were a wealthy bourgeois family, and the Hayeks had gained and lost a fortune and generated a number of scholars. Hayek's father was a plant geography professor at the University of Vienna and a doctor.[96] Philosopher Ludwig Wittgenstein was a cousin and a friendly acquaintance.[97]

The young Hayek was an unenthusiastic student, though he showed signs of a scientific bent early by emulating his father's interest in plant classification.[98] World War I interrupted his life, as it did the life of his civilization. He joined a field artillery unit in Vienna in March 1917 and seven months later was sent to the Piave River front in Italy. He saw little fighting but managed to contract malaria.[99] Someone then gave Hayek his first economics texts, which were so bad that "I still marvel that the particular books did not give me a permanent distaste for the subject."[100]

After returning from the war, he entered the University of Vienna during a period when it was a hotbed of many of the ideas that would shape twentieth-century Western civilization as it dragged itself up from the Great War: psychotherapy, Marxism, logical positivism, and, less influential but most relevant to Hayek, radically subjectivist Austrian economics. He earned two doctorates from the University of Vienna, one in law in 1921, the other in political science in 1923. All along, though, his passions and interests were in economics and psychology.[101]

At Vienna he studied under Friedrich von Wieser, leader of the second generation of Mengerian economics. Hayek's first professional job, obtained the month before he received his first doctorate, was at the Austrian Office of Claims Accounts, working under Mises, star of its third generation. Mises taught Hayek his first lessons in why socialism doesn't work—lessons that Hayek spread as the major focus of his life's work. Hayek had a letter of introduction from Wieser to show Mises, plugging Hayek as a most promising young economist. A skeptical Mises replied, "I've never seen you at my lectures" but took him on anyway.[102]

In spring 1922, Hayek met a traveling American economics professor, Jeremiah W. Jenks of New York University, who promised Hayek work as a research assistant in the United States. In March 1923, Hayek dragged himself to New York City, discovered Jenks was on vacation, and was about to begin work washing dishes in a Sixth Avenue restaurant when Jenks returned. While working for Jenks and seeking another doctorate at NYU (never completed), Hayek "gate-crashed a good deal into lectures at Columbia University, especially the lectures of W. C. Mitchell on the history of economics."[103]

Here Hayek was first exposed to the atheoretical, data-collecting method of American economics as represented by Wesley Mitchell. (Mitchell's method, and the organization he founded, the National Bureau of Economic Research, also seduced the young Milton Friedman, later Hayek's fellow Nobel laureate libertarian giant. Friedman's approach to economics as a science, though it comes to largely similar policy conclusions, is thus radically different from Hayek's and Mises's.) Hayek then became fascinated with the problem of business cycles and their cause, which would loom large in his work for a decade.

Even after he returned to Austria (he had run out of money, and the Rockefeller fellowship he won arrived too late to prevent him from hopping on a boat back to Europe), Hayek still was embroiled in the dilemmas of trade cycles. In 1927, with Mises's fund-raising help, Hayek started the Austrian Institute for Business Cycle Research. Hayek directed the organization, later with the help of game theory pioneer Oskar Morgenstern and money from the Rockefeller Foundation. During this time, applying his theory of business cycles, he predicted a forthcoming end to the 1920s economic boom in a February 1929 report for the institute.[104] And indeed, the predicted end was not long in coming.

He began lecturing in economics at the University of Vienna in 1929, while running the institute.[105] He also began work on what was to be a complete history of money and monetary policy, and some of that work fed into his first book, *Monetary Theory and the Trade Cycle* (1929 in German, 1933 in English). His background in monetary policy history served him in good stead when he ended up teaching in England in the 1930s. "When I came to England it turned out that I knew much more about the history of English monetary theory than any of the English professors themselves, which caused a great impression."[106]

Hayek was invited to lecture at the London School of Economics in 1931 by his friend Lionel Robbins, which led to a long-term appointment there. Hayek's theorizing on the cause and cure of business cycles spurred on his career. It also spurred him into a long and heated clash with his personal friend and intellectual adversary, John Maynard Keynes, the most influential economist of the twentieth century. The clash occurred among the LSE faculty and in the pages of learned economics journals throughout the 1930s. Keynes was a man who, according to Hayek, "was neither a full master of the body of economic theory then available, nor really cared to acquaint himself with any development which lay outside the Marshallian tradition. . . . His main aim was always to influence current policy, and economic theory was for him simply a tool for this purpose."[107]

The storied clash between Keynes and Hayek was at its root over Hayek's and Keynes's alternate theories of the cause and cure of business cycles. It was bogged down in sometimes maddening technicalities that a noneconomist will doubtless find confusing. The educated layman ought to despair of even beginning to understand the debates in contemporary professional economic journals. The obfuscation and mathematization of the discipline is to some degree a result of the victory of Keynes's method over Hayek's. The Keynes/Hayek debates are mercifully free of mathematics and can be followed, with difficulty to be sure, by a noneconomist willing to slog through it.

The battle lines were drawn over such issues as whether the unemployment caused by business cycles could be cured through manipulating aggregate demand—trying to give consumers more (or less) purchasing power as government managers thought it was needed—and whether saving and investment can fall out of balance through any means other than an expansion of bank credit. Keynes thought yes, Hayek no, representative of a general disagreement over Hayek's belief, in line with the classic discoveries of traditional economics such as Adam Smith's fabled "invisible hand," that an unfettered economy tended to create stable orders, and Keynes's belief that a free market would be rife with errors and crises that government could and must step in to solve.

Hayek's Austrian business cycle theory said that if banks or government pumped more credit into the economy without people deciding that they wanted to save from their current consumption in order to have more capital goods and consumption goods later, then more long-term production processes would end up in motion than people really wanted—in a process Hayek called "forced savings," that is, savings that don't reflect real changes in people's desire to save versus their desire to consume. That would lead to those long-term capital goods eventually proving uneconomical—bad decisions that would not have been made if people's true desires for future goods had not been disrupted by the inflation, leading to unemployment and capital consumption.

As Hayek scholar Caldwell explained it, "In the Austrian theory of the cycle the lengthening of the structure of production, begun under a regime of forced savings, never gets completed. It is always the case that rising consumer prices signal firms that their earlier decision to employ more roundabout methods was in error. Firms abandon their incomplete capital projects and thereby precipitate the crisis."[108] This was the "bust" following the "boom" of the initial inflationary burst of more money and credit in the economy.

Keynes thought unemployment was caused, rather, by insufficient aggregate demand from consumers—that if people had enough money to buy all the goods produced, then people would always find work producing those goods. If the free market economy on its own wasn't generating enough aggregate demand to keep everyone gainfully employed, then it was up to banks or the government to supply cash or credit to increase demand.[109]

Hayek gave a relatively concise explanation of the process through which that sort of inflationary credit manipulation leads to economic imbalance and eventual bust in his 1928 essay "Intertemporal Price Equilibrium and Movements in the Value of Money." Some version of this argument is key to the libertarian case against government attempts to prime the economic pump or otherwise use its fiscal powers to ameliorate economic difficulties. Milton Friedman made similar arguments from his own macroeconomic monetarist perspective.

When Hayek says "gold," read "any money or credit."

> Persons whose products and services are first demanded because of new gold inflows will initially enjoy a rise in their money incomes, which for them signifies a rise in their real income as well. But this nominal rise in income will not in any sense imply an enduring change in their market position, since similar rises in nominal income will take place successively with all other persons, and hence in the final analysis the share of social output falling to each individual will not have undergone any essential change. Nevertheless, the temporary rise in the profitability of the sectors of production

first effected by the gold inflow will have led to their expansion, an expansion which must show itself to have been unjustified as soon as the gold inflow slackens off, a part of the extra output stimulated by it will no longer be able to be sold at prices which cover costs but only at a loss. Hence the branches of production concerned will ultimately have to be contracted back to their level at the beginning of the gold inflow.[110]

To express the same point in Keynesian terms, any attempt to heighten aggregate demand through credit expansion or inflation merely creates booms inevitably followed by busts—the central assertion of Hayek's business cycle theory. Its libertarian implication is that government should not mess around with fiscal and monetary policy.

Hayek thought Keynes's definitions of saving and investment were confusing and skewed, that his theory depended on the most *uneco-nomic* assumption that society always had unused resources.[111] Keynes's ultimate goal, Hayek asserted, was to fool workers into accepting a real wage cut through inflation that they would not accept if it were obvious in monetary terms.[112] Hayek later decided that what really separated him from his friend Keynes was that the latter always believed that certain advanced thinkers (Keynes among them, of course) could skillfully and accurately manipulate the social order to their own ends, without ill effects. Hayek was always too skeptical about the limits of human knowledge and ability to believe that.[113]

Hayek lost the battle with Keynes but in some ways won the war, though to the average undergraduate of the past forty years, the name Keynes is emblazoned on every introductory economics student's notepad, and Hayek is most likely mentioned not at all.[114] In 1967, contemporary economics great John Hicks was able to write, truthfully, "When the definitive history of economic analysis during the 1930s comes to be written, a leading character in the drama (it was quite a drama) will be Professor Hayek. Hayek's economic writings . . . are almost unknown to the modern student; it is hardly remembered that there was a time when the new theories of Hayek were the principal rival of the new theories of Keynes."[115] Keynes's underconsumptionist theories of how to alleviate business cycles (he believed that individuals' lack of sufficient purchasing power, which could be alleviated by government spending, helped cause the cycles) have not proven as universally applicable as many believed at the end of the 1930s. The idea that government manipulation of aggregate demand is not enough to solve economic problems is respectable again.

"IN THE EARLY 1930s, EVERYBODY WAS A HAYEKIAN; AT THE END OF THE DECADE THERE WERE ONLY TWO OF US."

In a sense Hayek won the first battle. Keynes backed away from some of the specifics in his analysis in *A Treatise on Money* (1930), and retreated to work on the book for which he is most famous, *The General Theory of Employment, Interest, and Money* (1936).

Hayek neglected to mount a public criticism of that work, and in essence it took over the world. Hayek offered many different reasons for failing to launch another full frontal assault on Keynes, ranging from his frustration with Keynes's tendency to simply say he had changed his mind after a powerful critique, to the realization that the bigger problem behind his disagreement with Keynes involved a disagreement with macroeconomic method (and that the larger problem was more important), to realizing that fully explaining what was wrong with Keynes would require patching up existing holes in capital theory.[117]

The Keynes–Hayek duel ended, as the 1930s ended, with Hayek in tatters, ready to leave the discipline entirely, and Keynes ascendant, triumphant, his sweet nostrums filling the ears of the leaders of the Western world. As Hayek's fellow Austrian economist Ludwig Lachmann once noted, "When I came up to the LSE in the early 1930s, everybody was a Hayekian; at the end of the decade there were only two of us: Hayek and myself."[116]

Hayek exited the Keynes controversy bruised but not defeated. He concluded that the entire macroeconomic approach that Keynes embodied, not merely the particulars of his theory, had to be fought. So Hayek returned to revising Austrian capital theory after the pioneering, but incomplete, work of Böhm-Bawerk. To this end he produced

The Pure Theory of Capital (1941), which unfortunately came out when war matters monopolized everyone's attention and the international economics community was shattered and scattered. In that book, Hayek seemed to abandon his confidence in the standard equilibrium model of neoclassical economics, the model that he had used in different versions in his previous economic work, and found he had nowhere to go from there in economics.[118] As he summed up the problems he had come to see in the mathematic general equilibrium model, "Any approach, such as that of much of mathematical economics with its simultaneous equations, which in effect starts from the assumption that people's *knowledge* corresponds with the objective *facts* of the situation, systematically leaves out what is our main task to explain."[119] While this shift away from equilibrium theory in favor of a more market–process approach made him more of an Austrian purist in a certain sense, he had simultaneously shifted further away from a belief in Misesian praxeology as the path to economic knowledge. He had come to think that while the logic of individual choice may be a priori, once you start dealing with the interactions of many choosing agents in real economies, empirical observation was needed.

He did not become a pure positivist who felt that observation and prediction were the only hallmarks of true science. Hayek continued to believe (because of the complexity of the orders that resulted from human interactions, most of them spontaneous) that prediction in the social sciences such as economics could only be of general patterns, not specific events—making the number of events that can "falsify" social science theory in the Karl Popper sense small. (Popper's famous definition of science has it that the only truly scientific statement is one that can be conceivably falsified by empirical observation.) The vaguer the prediction—a necessity, not a flaw, when it came to social sciences, Hayek insisted—the harder it is to falsify. These questions of method in the social sciences engaged Hayek in many interesting (but beyond our scope) oppositions to both his old mentor Mises and his later good friend Popper.[120]

Pure Theory turned out to be Hayek's last attempt at sustained serious work in economics, though he was to return to the question of inflation with some brief, more polemical, and radically libertarian pamphlets and essays in the 1970s. He advocated ending the government's monopoly of money production—a position that the younger Hayek had condemned as essentially crazy.[121]

Hayek's first move after departing the economics wars after *Pure Theory* affected the world more than had any of his professional economic work. During World War II, when the world was exploding and burning from the results of totalitarian ideologies, he crafted the twentieth-century nonfiction libertarian work most likely to live on as a social science classic, *The Road to Serfdom* (1944), a polemical argument for old-fashioned liberalism against the then-current mania for planning and socialism in the West. The book turned him into a temporary cause célèbre and an American lecture circuit star, even as it scarred his reputation as a scientist.

The Road to Serfdom, despite what could be seen as half measures and idiosyncrasies in purist libertarian terms, and despite the temptation of dismissing its dire predictions as falsified by history, was an epochal work in forging the modern libertarian mind. Milton Friedman, Hayek's fellow libertarian Nobel economics laureate, wrote in an introduction to a later edition of the book, "Over the years, I have made it a practice to inquire of believers in individualism how they came to depart from the collectivist orthodoxy of our times. For years, the most frequent answer was a reference to [*The Road to Serfdom*]."[122] Hannes Gissurarson, the Icelandic translator of *Serfdom*, wrote, "Little did [Hayek] know what his book was destined to become: the source and inspiration of a new political philosophy."[123]

My own experience tends to confirm this, though the more radical the libertarian, the more likely that libertarian would consider Rand or Rothbard a truer inspiration. *Serfdom* has sold over a quarter million copies in its English language edition and been translated into more than twenty foreign languages—and that's just authorized versions. Underground translations in Russian, Czech, and Polish circulated behind the Iron Curtain before it fell. Though the Russian occupying authorities in postwar Berlin tried to ban its import into Germany, tenacious admirers of Western liberty smuggled copies in that were reproduced and spread.[124]

The socialism at which Hayek aimed *Serfdom* (with its famous dedication, Hayek's declaration of independence from all contemporary factions, to "the socialists of all parties") has become moribund since he wrote it. Back then, "socialism meant unambiguously the national-ization of the means of production and the central economic planning which this made possible and necessary." Nowadays, "socialism has come to mean chiefly the extensive redistribution of incomes through taxation and . . . the welfare state."[125]

The book's central warning still applied, Hayek asserted in his preface to a 1976 edition of *Serfdom*: that central economic planning, no matter how well-meaning, would inevitably lead to a loss of most liberties and a general trend toward sinister tyranny in government. The roots of the hated Nazis were in the same sort of economic planning embraced by the very Westerners fighting those Nazis. He acknowledged that the road of Western economic interventionism is a slower trudge than the Nazis', but he thinks the final destination is the same.

To those who reduced his book's message to an easily disproved ab-surdity—that any socialism leads inevitably to complete tyranny—Hayek said in the same introduction, "It has frequently been alleged that I have contended that any movement in the direction of social-ism is bound to lead to totalitarianism. Even though this danger ex-ists, this is not what the book says. What it contains is a warning that unless we mend the principles of our policy, some very unpleasant consequences will follow which most of those who advocate these policies do not want."[126]

While attacking central planning, Hayek also condemns collectivism in general, defends the information-transmitting powers of the free price system (a way for everyone everywhere to understand the col-lective subjective desires of everyone else as those desires relate to the material goods and services available, desires and knowledge that scat-tered individuals might not even be able to articulate themselves), de-limits the power of democracy, defends the classic idea of the Rule of Law as better than the arbitrary rule of Men, explains how economic control must lead to total political control, details how unequal market rewards inform people how they can best serve the larger social good, insists on the inevitability of gross nationalism and dubious moral virtue in the leaders of a fully planned society, worries over how plan-ning inspires a tendency toward government thought control, and pro-vides some intellectual history of how Nazism grew from socialism, rather than, as many assert, being a capitalist reaction *to* socialism. Most of the ideas Hayek would work out in greater detail in his later political philosophy works are present in nascent form—laid out in a stark outline that makes them easier to quickly perceive and grasp.

Despite its importance to libertarianism, *Serfdom* is no full-bore assault on government; it merely condemns government attempts to take complete control of the national economy. Hayek is generous with the powers he grants government and is contemptuous of "laissez-faire" as a philosophy of government and economy. In the final chapter he makes an impassioned plea for world government, even calling it the apotheosis of nineteenth-century liberalism.[127]

Hayek is willing to grant government the power to restrict production methods, as long as such restrictions are enforced fairly and equally; he supports sanitary laws, working-hour laws, disaster relief, provision of certain social services, and a welfare state to supply a minimum standard of living for all. His standard of the proper working economy is "competition," not laissez-faire, and he thinks there is a lot government can do to ensure that competition works properly.

Serfdom has a kind, even tone, an obvious hatred of tyranny tempered with willingness to grant a large role to government. Yet Hayek's implication that well-meaning socialists might destroy the very social order we all rely on enraged them, and they turned on him bitterly— despite the fact that the even-tempered and gentlemanly Hayek never even suggested that his intellectual opponents were any less than well meaning, until very late in his life. He stressed over and over again that he and the socialists shared the same values.[128] They merely had a scientific disagreement over what social order was best for achieving those values.

Still, Hayek garnered praise from some fellow intellectuals who were more modern liberal than libertarian—mostly those who still had classical liberal leanings, such as George Orwell and even Hayek's old friend and adversary Keynes, who claimed to find himself "in agreement with virtually the whole of it; and not only in agreement with it, but in a deeply moved agreement."[129]

Of course, Keynes didn't really mean it. In the same letter he went on to talk about how the real key was to make sure the right people were doing the planning and everything would be fine. And Keynes's spirit continued for decades to animate an elite of planners, regulators, and restrictors of social orders and markets. A war still raged over the nature of government and of economic management. Keynes was still winning and Hayek was still losing—and America was on Keynes's side.

Other fronts had to be manned in the war against Keynes-style economic management and the vision of government inherent in it. As Hayek's *Road to Serfdom* prepared to hit the world, three women, each a combination of novelist and political philosopher, brought to bear their own moral, literary, and historical weapons in that war.

3

THE THREE FURIES OF LIBERTARIANISM

The modern American libertarian movement can convincingly be traced back to the work of three women—all friends, at least for a time. Their first major works on political and ideological matters all appeared in 1943, predating Hayek's *Serfdom,* while America was enmeshed in wartime centralization. As journalist John Chamberlain put it, "It was three women—Mrs. [Isabel] Paterson, Rose Wilder Lane, and Ayn Rand—who, with scornful side glances at the male business community, had decided to rekindle a faith in an older American philosophy. There wasn't an economist among them. And none of them was a Ph.D."[1] They continued to be hailed for their foundational contributions within the libertarian movement. More recently, David Boaz of the Cato Institute wrote, "In 1943, at one of the lowest points for liberty and humanity in history, three remarkable women published books that could be said to have given birth to the modern libertarian movement."[2] Rand's classic was her third novel and first success, *The Fountainhead*; Lane's was *The Discovery of Freedom*; and Paterson's *The God of the Machine.*

Chamberlain was not the only one to note this curious concatenation of female individualist writers, even at the time. Old right mainstay Albert Jay Nock declared of the two nonfiction works by Paterson and Lane that they were "the only intelligible books on the philosophy of

individualism that have been written in America this century." Nock
noted that these two women had "shown the male world of this
period how to think *fundamentally*. They make all of us male writers
look like Confederate money. They don't fumble and fiddle around—
every shot goes straight to the centre."[3]

"IF PEOPLE CAN STAND HER AT ALL, THEY EVENTUALLY BECOME VERY FOND OF HER."

While she is little read or remembered today, Paterson helped set the
tone, timbre, content, and style of modern libertarian assertions and
arguments.

In *The God of the Machine*, her one work of political philosophy, she
tried to explain American exceptionalism—the historical mystery of
why this country was uniquely prosperous. Paterson was herself,
though, a native Canadian, born Isabel Bowler (or possibly Mary Isabel Bowler—even her biographer was unable to ascertain her birth
name) on an island in the middle of Lake Huron on January 22, 1886,
one of nine children. Her family moved to America shortly thereafter,
spending time in Michigan's Upper Peninsula and the Utah territory.
Her girlhood was spent farming, ranching, and communing with Indians in the American West. She had only two and a half years of formal
education but was a voracious reader. She had no respect for her father, an irresponsible bounder, but internalized many useful, if eccentric, lessons from her frontier childhood.

"She would never regard the frontier as the breeding ground of puritan virtues," Paterson's biographer, Stephen Cox, wrote. "She was
aware that other people did. Those people, she could only suppose, had
'never lived on the frontier,' where freedom to loaf was more highly
prized than hard work and stern ambition."[4] She did not think of her
fellow frontiersmen and women as necessarily at the apex of virtue
and acumen. But she recognized that "frontier society offered 'the
most civilized type of association'. . . because it had 'the absolute minimum of external regulation' and therefore 'the maximum of voluntary civility and morality.'"[5] While she was aware of the popular theory
that "America's chief inheritance from its frontier past is 'aggressive-

ness,'" she considered that theory "nonsense . . . on the frontier you have to be polite to your fellow men, and it won't get you anywhere to be aggressive to a blizzard.' What worked out west wasn't aggressiveness but 'a peculiarly individual, mind-your-own-business confidence.'"[6] She cultivated that quality in herself.

As a young woman she returned to Canada and worked as a secretary for R. B. Bennett in Calgary, a lawyer who was premier of Canada between 1930 and 1935. In 1910, she married a Canadian real estate agent, Kenneth Birrell Paterson. By 1918, she apparently had no idea what had become of him. Through the 1910s, Paterson worked on various newspapers in the Pacific Northwest and in New York, writing editorials and drama criticism. She published her first novel, *The Shadow Riders*, in 1916. (It was faintly praised by H. L. Mencken, who credited it with "a certain readableness" and "an occasional mark of respect for the reader's intelligence.")[7] In 1921, she was introduced by a mutual friend to Burton Rascoe, literary editor of the New York *Tribune* (later the *Herald Tribune*). He didn't like her at first, but she went on to become his assistant and worked there as a columnist and critic from 1924 to 1949.[8] After Rascoe departed, she worked under Stuart Pratt Sherman and Irita Van Doren.

Paterson became an influential literary critic, staking out a position somewhere between an open embrace of "naturalism, 'realism,' and literature as sociology" and a hewing to America's old genteel tradition.[9] She became famous in literary circles from her berth at the *Herald Tribune,* with a unique voice and a cheeky, biting reputation. As her biographer Cox summed up her critical stance, "her insistence on the variety of ends and means kept her from critical dogmatism; her insistence on the sufficiency of means to ends kept her from going soft on either the avant-garde or the conservatives" in American literature.[10] She wrote a weekly column in the paper's book supplement, called "Turns with a Bookworm."

The *Herald Tribune*'s supplement was a powerful national force; in the mid-1930s it had 30,000 copies distributed to bookstores nationwide and an overall circulation of half a million; critic Frances Newman judged that it "reach[ed] more important people than any other review."[11] Novelist John O'Hara, at the time *Appointment in Samarra* was published, admitted to being "very much afraid of Isabel Paterson."[12] Her job required her to be well read and well informed, and she was;

and she was not afraid to let everyone around her know it. But, as one friend told a newspaper writer profiling Paterson in 1953, "If people can stand her at all, they eventually become very fond of her."[13] She once condemned a friend as a "low grade imbecile" for the crime of voting for Herbert Hoover in 1928; his economic interventionism and embrace of Prohibition maddened her.[14]

She lived alone, rode tugboats for fun, and would gather a crew of friends and acolytes to turn her Monday night exertions putting the latest issue of the book supplement to bed into an impromptu literary salon. Believing you got the best of creative people in their work, she never took to the whirl of Manhattan literary social life, though she had intimate friendships with a small circle of writers that included humorist Will Cuppy, who dedicated two books to her.

She continued to write novels through her career as a critic, most of them set in the past. One contemporary romance of sorts, *Never Ask the End*, was a best-seller in 1933. Throughout the 1930s, politics concerned her more and more, though she didn't fall into the didactic trap of letting politics dictate her literary and critical judgments. In common with most individualists and protolibertarians of her day, Roosevelt and his New Deal drove her to distraction. (She voted for him in 1932 because he was against Prohibition. In 1920, she voted for socialist Eugene Debs, who was in prison at the time. She admired his brave dedication to his principles.)[15] Drawing on analysis from old right stalwart Garet Garrett as well as her own thinking, she concluded that government action, particularly efforts to buoy commodity prices in the 1920s, led to the Depression, and that the Depression persisted mostly because of government attempts to end it. She was appalled at the love for state planning that seduced most of the literary intellectuals of the 1930s. The political themes that were fully expressed in *God of the Machine* began showing up in her columns (which were never strictly about reviewing books) through the 1930s and early 1940s. Her occasional political comments led Edmund Wilson to tell her that she was "the last surviving person to believe in those quaint old notions on which the republic was founded."[16] Her growing sense of alienation led her to spend most of her time at a rural home near Stamford, Connecticut, and less time in the thick of the scene in New York.

Paterson had become friends with two other feisty individualist women, novelists Rose Wilder Lane and Ayn Rand, with whom she could speak sympathetically on her political beliefs. Paterson's biographer Cox thought that common experiences might have led the three women down similar ideological roads. "She started as an outsider, and she remained one; she had to struggle for life, then for identity and recognition. Much the same could be said of Lane [and] Rand . . . . People who were used to doing for themselves might have a larger conception than other people of the things that individuals can and ought to do for themselves."[17]

Paterson and Lane commiserated and visited with each other as war engulfed Europe in 1940. "The second war, like the first one, disturbed her so profoundly that she could hardly bear to think about it," Cox wrote.[18] Still, she refused to join either isolationist organizations or a government-sponsored organization called the Free Company, intended, as Cox wrote, "to propagandize for 'the basic civil rights of a democracy' . . . she was startled to find that the 'spontaneous' movement has been hatched in meetings at the Department of Justice and approved by the solicitor general and attorney general of the United States."[19]

Alarmed at the parlous state of Western civilization, Paterson turned to writing a book that would explain why she thought it was special and what was worth preserving in it. She published *The God of the Machine* with G. P. Putnam in 1943. Although it was not a success, it has been reprinted over the years because of ideological interest by publishers like Caxton, Robert Hessen's Palo Alto Book Service, the Arno Press series on American individualism edited by Murray Rothbard and Jerome Tuccille, and most recently by Transaction due to the efforts of Paterson's biographer, the libertarian English professor Stephen Cox.[20] The book's title, as Cox wrote, could be interpreted to mean either human intelligence, which rules the machine economy; or God himself, "the original 'Source of energy' for the human dynamo and the guarantor of the principles from which human liberty proceeds."[21]

God was a radically individualist attempt to answer the question, Why was America so rich and powerful? The book was built around a unique and eccentric metaphor of society as a machine. The most healthy and wealthy of cultures, said Paterson, were those that built the most elaborate and stable "long circuit energy systems," which had to run on "absolute security of private property, full personal liberty, and firm autonomous regional bases for a federal structure."[22]

"Personal liberty," Paterson explained, "is the pre-condition of the release of energy. Private property is the inductor that initiates the flow. Real money is the transmission line; and the payment of debts comprises half the circuit. An empire is merely a long circuit energy-system. The possibility of a short circuit, the ensuing leakage and breakdown or explosion, occurs in the hook-up of political organization to the productive processes."[23]

While her metaphors were mechanical (to an almost absurd degree), her philosophy was by no means materialist. She begins her long-view march through human history with the Romans. She writes that

> neither their location nor their material progress, no economic clue, accounts for their function. . . . What the past shows, by overwhelming evidence, is that the imponderables outweigh every material article in the scales of human endeavor. Nations are not powerful because they possess wide lands, safe ports, large navies, huge armies, fortifications, stores, money, and credit. They acquire those advantages because they are powerful, having devised on correct principles the political structure which allows the flow of energy to take its proper course.[24]

Paterson tried to demonstrate throughout *God* what those correct principles are, and to show how various cultures rose or fell based on their adherence to them, and how America became unprecedentedly—almost impossibly—powerful and wealthy by approximating the purest application of those proper ideas for structuring human society.

She is in awe of the political genius of the Founding Fathers, calling the Constitution "the greatest political document ever struck off at one time by the mind of men."[25] In her survey of American history and political life, she defends classical republican principles against pure democracy (a consistent libertarian bête noire, because it gives citizens the power to violate anyone's rights or property merely by majority rule); pinpoints slavery as the "fault in the structure" the

Founders built; and radically assaults the growth in government since the Progressive Era and the New Deal. In doing so she stakes out a set of positions on economics and politics that have defined the libertarian movement ever since.

Paterson attacks antitrust law, asserts that without the right to produce and exchange freely you have no real right to even exist, and stresses that the logical end of public ownership of property is "long trains of prisoners transported in cattle cars to a place where they do not wish to go."[26]

Her position on money and credit, presented in two chapters of *God,* fits in neatly with the Austrian economic tradition that shaped modern libertarianism, though there is no evidence she ever read Mises or Hayek. Paterson came to most of her political and economic ideas independent of contemporary influences; Lord Acton was her favorite political philosopher.[27]

She advocated a straight gold standard, as it best facilitates money's role as a long-term "repository of values [that] carries exchanges through time on the long circuit of energy."[28] Proper money was as important to a healthy, wealthy culture as liberty and private property were. "Private property, money, freedom, engineering and industry are all one system . . . when one element is taken out, the rest must collapse, cease to function."[29]

Libertarian theorists usually tout the clearly manifest ethical and practical advantages of liberty, which raises a question: Why do so many people fail to see these obvious advantages of unfettered liberty? Paterson provided an answer in the chapter most remembered among libertarians, brutally titled "The Humanitarian with the Guillotine."[30] She concluded that

> if the primary objective of the philanthropist, his justification for living, is to help others, his ultimate goal *requires that others shall be in want.* His happiness is the obverse of their misery. If he wishes to help 'humanity,' the whole of humanity must be in need. The humanitarian wishes to be a prime mover in the lives of others. He cannot admit either the divine or the natural order, by which men have the power to help themselves. The humanitarian puts himself in the place of God.[31]

Because the psychological desire to help requires others to *need* help, "the humanitarian in theory is the terrorist in action."[32] Paterson maintains that nonstandardized, noncentralized private charity, though admittedly "random and sporadic" and unable to "prevent suffering completely," at least does not "perpetuate the dependence of its beneficiaries" and manages to keep deprivation from becoming too widely spread—at least in a culture enough in command of the long-circuit energy system to be wealthy. The United States, she notes, is such a country—"the only country on record that has never had a famine since it became a nation."[33]

But charity, whether centralized and managed by the state or decentralized and private, pales in comparison to the greatest thing one man can do to help another: Launch an enterprise that can employ him. "If the full roll of *sincere* philanthropists were called, from the beginning of time," Paterson notes, "it would be found that all of them together by their strictly philanthropic activities have never conferred upon humanity one-tenth of the benefit derived from the normally self-interested efforts of Thomas Alva Edison, to say nothing of the greater minds who worked out the scientific principles which Edison applied."[34]

God is a sprawling book. Paterson seemingly tried to cram in all the political ideas she had and apply them to human history as well as current controversies that interested her. She wrote of the history of Rome and of the medieval Church (which she thought was "the only long-circuit heavy-road system for the transmission of energy" during medieval times. "Energy flowed into and through the church because the church afforded the only means of emancipation from status, and therefore a release of individual talent")[35]; of public schooling ("there can be no greater stretch of arbitrary power than is required to seize children from their parents, teach them whatever the authorities decree they shall be taught, and expropriate from the parents the funds to pay for the procedure. . . . A tax-supported, compulsory educational system is the complete model of the totalitarian state"); and application of her ideas to the ongoing world war.[36]

She argued that it was foolish and counterproductive for the nation that had mastered the long circuit of energy—the United States—to force men to fight, since that deflected them from the economic production machine that made the United States rich, powerful, and capable of winning the war in the first place. "A free economy invariably wins against a closed or status economy or 'totalitarian state,'" she noted. "*But it must fight as a free economy.*"[37]

God ends as a valentine to America. In the book's conclusion, Paterson writes that

> with the establishment of the Republic of the United States of America, a great landmark in secular history was erected. The most profound scholar of the past century, Lord Acton, who devoted his life to the study of the history of human liberty, said it "was that which *was not*, until the last quarter of the eighteenth century in Pennsylvania." The event he denoted was unique in that it was the first time a nation was ever founded on reasoned political principles, proceeding from the axiom that man's birthright is freedom. And as long as those principles were maintained, it succeeded beyond all precedent. . . . Whoever is fortunate enough to be an American citizen came into the greatest inheritance man has ever enjoyed. He has had the benefit of every heroic and intellectual effort men have made for many thousands of years, realized at last. If Americans should now turn back, submit again to slavery, it would be a betrayal so base the human race might better perish.[38]

That statement exemplifies a consistent tension in modern American libertarian thought. Libertarianism is a philosophy that is quintessentially—perhaps uniquely—American (though its principles could and would, libertarians mostly insist, apply to the entire human race, if adopted by them). Yet it is also uniquely critical of the many ways in which the modern American state has betrayed its libertarian birthright.

Paterson has few direct disciples on the libertarian scene today. At the time her book thrilled scattered devotees of the freedom philosophy. John Chamberlain wrote in the *New York Times* that *Machine* showed "individualist liberals are beginning to recover their poise" and that it was a "brilliant, searching, and closely reasoned" book.[39] Rose Wilder Lane wrote to her pen pal Herbert Hoover that "it seems to me a book ranking with the best of Paine and Madison."[40] When Lane reviewed it, she declared that "anyone who has read it comfortably has not read it adequately, and should read it again and again until he experiences an earthquake."[41] Ayn Rand raved that it "does for capitalism what *Das Kapital* did for the Reds" and "what the Bible did for Christianity."[42] R. C. Hoiles, publisher of the Freedom Newspaper chain, bought one hundred copies of the book, musing that women might "have to lead us out of the wilderness."[43] Nebraska Republican congressman Howard Buffett was also a big fan.

Paterson's most significant libertarian disciple was Ayn Rand, who acknowledged intellectual debts to no one but Aristotle. Nonetheless, Rand told Paterson in a letter that "you were the very first person to see how Capitalism *works* in specific application. That is your achievement, which I consider a historical achievement of the first importance. . . . I learned *from you* the historical and economic aspects of Capitalism, which I knew before only in a general way, in the way of general principles."[44] In a rhetorical gesture that readers of *The Fountainhead* will understand as having deep emotional significance, Rand inscribed a copy of the novel to Paterson, "You have been the one encounter in my life that can never be repeated."[45]

But their relationship deteriorated and their correspondence ended in a series of arguments. Rand thought that Paterson misunderstood her philosophy and refused to give Rand proper credit for her unique contributions besides.[46] Rand complains, "You say in your letter: 'It almost seems as if nobody, dead or alive, ever did know or does know how Capitalism really works, except Me.' Does it really seem to you that I have not been born yet? It seems to me that I was born as long as 43 years ago, and it almost seems that you had noticed the fact."[47] (While Paterson respected Rand's politics and philosophy, Rand the novelist did not impress Paterson the literary critic.) A few months later, Rand ended their friendship over what she considered intolerable rudeness to one of Rand's friends while Paterson was visiting Rand in her California home—and for discovering that Paterson had refused to review *The Fountainhead* in the *Herald Tribune*.[48] Paterson, in what her biographer Cox insists must have been the sort of mordant joke that would be lost on Rand, said of Rand's Hollywood friends, "I don't like Jewish intellectuals."[49]

Even had those conflicts not arisen, the once close Paterson–Rand relationship (Rand used to join Paterson on Monday evenings to help her proof her column in the early 1940s) would have likely come a cropper over religion, an issue about which Rand brooked no disagreement. Rand was a committed and principled atheist; Paterson had written that "the axiom of liberty cannot be postulated except on the basis affirmed by Christian philosophy."[50]

Paterson adhered to no specific Christian sect. Her religious views are best characterized as deist.[51] In one of their epistolary arguments, Rand wrote that Paterson believed "that unless I [Rand] accept God, I will have betrayed the cause of individualism, that the case for individualism rests on faith in God—and on nothing else. To the best of my rational understanding, the opposite is true."[52]

The God of the Machine was not a financial success. Like most libertarians of the time, Paterson became more and more alienated from the mainstream beliefs of her culture—and most importantly, from her employers at the *Herald Tribune*. While her editor there, Irita Van Doren (a lover of Wendell Willkie's), according to Paterson's biographer Stephen Cox, "intimated to inquiring readers that Paterson had 'been retired,' Paterson stated, more straightforwardly, that she had been fired for her political views."[53] Her last "Turn of the Bookworm" column appeared in late January 1949.

She retreated to a farm in New Jersey, close to Princeton. She found few places to publish after that. John Chamberlain, a former *New York Times* book review columnist who crossed swords with Paterson about politics but ended up being converted to her philosophy, wanted Paterson to write for *The Freeman*, the libertarian monthly he edited with Henry Hazlitt and Suzanne LaFollette in the early 1950s. Paterson felt insulted by the meager two cents a word he could afford to offer her, and refused.[54] She was weary and annoyed by the rest of the world by then, certainly the rest of the ideological world, even the parts closest to her. When Henry Hazlitt wrote her to praise *The God of the Machine* but intimated that "I do not pretend to agree with you in every point and in every statement; I do not imagine that you expect that kind of agreement," the libertarian newsman was merely advertising his lack of imagination. Paterson responded that "it isn't a

question of *agreement*" with *God*. "I tried to set forth axioms, principles, facts and deductions of a logical nature. They are either true or
not true, but they don't depend on agreement; they are so *per se*. Do
you 'agree' with Euclid's statement that 'a straight line is the shortest
distance between two points?'"[55]

Having established that disagreeing with her was on the same intellectual level as disagreeing with Euclid, it is not surprising that Paterson wearied of the attentions and questions of the free market
businessmen who adopted her as a heroine. She had already decided
that the modern world was a vast ruin that held little interest for her
anymore. Anyway, so long as America has direct election of senators
and no property qualifications for voting, it was all hopeless anyway. As
for these businessmen who wrote to her, well, "They send clinkers to
Newcastle. Their opinions are of no use to me—or to anyone else.
They own all the newspapers, periodicals, publishing houses. They use
those facilities to spread Communism. They give me a pain, and I hope
they get their God-damn necks broke, as they will."[56]

When *National Review* started in 1955, William F. Buckley, who
greatly admired Paterson's writing, brought her into his fold. But they
bickered over pay and editorial changes. Buckley wrote to her in
frustration over an editorial squabble, "I did not agree (as you imply)
that my function as editor would, where you are concerned, reduce
to the act of redirecting your manuscripts to the printer."[57] Paterson
was also appalled by Whittaker Chambers's notorious attack on
Rand's *Atlas Shrugged* in *National Review*, telling Buckley, "Mister
[Chambers] has supplied ample grounds for a libel suit. And though I
haven't communicated with Ayn Rand for many years, nor do I expect to, I shouldn't be surprised if she took it that way. . . . It's not a
good review anyhow. [Rand's] novel is open to some stringent criticism, but I can't think of anyone less capable of doing the job than
[Chambers]; and I will add that I don't think it was decent in any case
to commission him to do it."[58]

Her final break with Buckley came over a commissioned article on
the DuPont corporation. Buckley thought it "brilliant, amusing, readable and uncharitable and that we should publish," but then dared "suggest a few minor changes aimed at dissapating [sic] the impression that
you are pursuing a vendetta."[59] (Paterson aimed some sharp criticism at

her former friend, DuPont executive and libertarian financier Jasper Crane, in the manuscript.) Paterson refused to allow any changes, and she never wrote for Buckley again.

Whittaker Chambers certainly didn't miss her; he once told Buckley he was aggravated by the respect she commanded among some on the right. "Almost anything she says is likely to be wrong," he insisted, and if the Republican Party ever dies, people would avoid its grave "because of the banshee screams, heard there even at noonday—Isabel Paterson, of course."[60]

Paterson died, largely forgotten, on January 10, 1960, at the home of friends in Montclair, New Jersey. In retirement she tried (and failed) to sell another novel. Like her friend Rose Wilder Lane, she refused to take money from Social Security.[61]

Because of its enduring interest to libertarians and students of American individualist philosophy, *The God of the Machine* is still in print. Recognizing and celebrating America's unique system of strictly limited republican government and the necessity of untrammeled private property rights for a healthy, wealthy society (in an age when such ideas were considered radical and absurd), it helped cast the template for modern American libertarian thinking and polemics.

"I AM NOW A FUNDAMENTALIST AMERICAN."

Rose Wilder Lane, although little remembered compared to her friend and libertarian colleague Rand, has a (contested) claim to popular literary fame even greater than Rand's, with her tens of millions of novels sold. Lane was the daughter of (and possibly ghostwriter for) Laura Ingalls Wilder, author of the immensely popular series of children's books known as the *Little House* series, after *Little House on the Prairie*.

While Lane's authorial responsibility is still debated, she undoubtedly lived the American adventure her mother wrote about, at least in part. (One of her mother's novels, *The First Four Years*, explicitly includes Rose as a character.) Rose, author of the 1943 libertarian classic *The Discovery of Freedom*, was born on December 5, 1886, in DeSmet, in the territory of South Dakota. Her early years were a hardscrabble settler's

life not unlike her mother's childhood, which was the subject of the
Little House books. Rose was the only surviving child of Almanzo and
Laura Ingalls Wilder. Almanzo grew up on a farm near Malone, New
York, and moved with his family to Minnesota when he was a teen-
ager. Eventually he met and married Laura Ingalls in DeSmet.

Rose's early years included many a dusty, drought-plagued summer,
the death of a young brother, and covered wagon peregrinations from
South Dakota to Minnesota to Florida to Mansfield, Missouri, in the
Ozarks. There she and her parents settled more or less permanently.[62]
They made a home on Rocky Ridge and started a farm. In the hard
early years they lived in town for a while, Almanzo minding horses
and Laura providing boarding for men building a nearby road.

Farm girl Rose didn't fit in with the more refined townie girls of
Mansfield, and she found grade school stultifying. She graduated from
high school in 1903 while living briefly with an aunt in Louisiana, under whose influence she developed a youthful infatuation with Eugene Debs and socialism.[63]

Rose worked for a few years as a Western Union telegraph operator
in Kansas City and Indiana and then drifted out to San Francisco,
where she had a short marriage to traveling salesman Gillette Lane. In
1909, she miscarried a pregnancy; by 1915, Gillette was out of her life
for good, though she was never officially divorced and retained Lane's
name.[64] (This situation mirrored Paterson's—a youthful marriage to a
man who quickly disappeared from the picture but whose name she
kept.)

Rose's career as a journalist and novelist began in earnest after she
got rid of Gillette. She lived a bohemian life as a free young woman in
San Francisco, writing for the *San Francisco Bulletin* and penning often
fictionalized popular biographies of figures such as Jack London,
Charlie Chaplin, Herbert Hoover, and Henry Ford. She socialized
with young reds and considered herself one of them.

As World War I wound down, Rose sought a piece of the action by
joining the Red Cross. She intended to write articles for American
magazines on the food troubles in England. But the armistice inter-
vened, and Rose spent the waning days of the 1910s living with a female roommate in Greenwich Village, writing articles and fiction for
the women's magazines of her day.

In 1920, she finally made her way to Europe under Red Cross auspices. She spent much of the decade adventuring across Europe and
parts of the Middle East, usually with close female friends such as Red
Cross nurse Helen Boylston and Dorothy Thompson, a young journalist who later married Sinclair Lewis and become a well-known and
influential newspaper columnist.[65]

During her travels Lane fell in love with Albania and quasi-adopted
a young Albanian man (beginning a pattern of supportive relationships
with youngsters that the childless Lane would continue with various
people throughout her life, sometimes with success, sometimes with
heartache). Also in Albania, she developed a deep love and respect for
Muslim ways, which informed *The Discovery of Freedom*, providing it
with one of the many interpretive eccentricities that make it such a
rich and fascinating book.

She had a couple of long-term relationships with men during her
traveling years but never remarried. Lane developed a modern feminist
view of marriage after her experience with Gillette; one of her early
novels, the quasi-autobiographical *Diverging Roads*, is to some degree
about the stultifying effect of marriage on a young woman.[66]

By the end of the 1920s, her adventures in Europe and the Middle
East mostly over, Rose ended up back at Rocky Ridge in the Ozarks,
somewhat resentfully caring for her parents. Helen Boylston moved in
to keep her company. Rose often fantasized about returning to her
beloved Albania but never did. Her parents lived in a newly built cottage on Rocky Ridge, Rose and Boylston in the old farmhouse. Rose
had earned a pile of cash writing popular fiction in the 1920s, but she
lost most of it in the 1929 stock market crash.

During the 1930s, she stayed at Rocky Ridge and began what could
charitably be called collaboration, or possibly ghostwriting, on her
mother's series of children's books.[67] Certainly the *Little House* books
show signs of Lane's particular adoration of liberty. Lane's biographer,
William Holtz, points to a Fourth of July sequence in *Little House* in
which young Laura realizes that "Americans won't obey any king on
earth" and when she is grown "there isn't anyone else who has a right
to give me orders."[68] Lane also published in 1933 (serialized in the *Saturday Evening Post* in 1932) her own most popular novel, a story based
on her family's life as Dakota pioneers, called *Let the Hurricane Roar*. In

the midst of the New Deal, of which the former socialist sympathizer was beginning to grow suspicious, she considered this evocation of old American pioneer virtues subtly antiauthority.

Rose was among the most popular fiction writers for the 1930s *Saturday Evening Post*, a leading bastion of anti-Roosevelt, anti–New Deal sentiment under the editorship of George Horace Lorimer. Lane occasionally worked with old right journalist Garet Garrett, touring farming country with him for a *Saturday Evening Post* article. Rose was appalled at the level of constriction and control New Deal policies imposed on the American farmer. By 1935, the former socialist had solidified the American revolutionary fervor that informed *The Discovery of Freedom*. She wrote in the *Post* that "I am now a fundamentalist American, give me time and I will tell you why individualism, laissez-faire, and the slightly restrained anarchy of capitalism offers the best possibilities for the development of the human spirit."[69]

While traveling with Garrett through farm country, Rose was impressed with American farmers' disdain for New Deal agricultural policy. In one southern Illinois county that the government had tried to take over for a demonstration project on rural redevelopment, none of the locals "would speak to Garet or to me until we *proved* that we did not come from the Government. . . . And these are the people said to be demanding subsidies!"[70]

She explained her new Americanism in a very popular *Post* article called "Credo," published in March 1936. This article so impressed Los Angeles chamber of commerce manager Leonard Read that he and some friends began a publishing imprint called Pamphleteers, Inc., in order to reprint it under the title *Give Me Liberty*.

Lane's hatred for Roosevelt and the New Deal intensified through the 1930s. She once admitted hoping that he'd be killed.[71] She feared that the sort of old-fashioned Americanism she and Garrett (with whom her biographer speculates she had a brief, unsuccessful romance) stood for was on the ropes, ready to fall.[72] She wrote one last hugely successful novel, *Free Land* (1938), harkening back to the homesteading days that she thought cemented the American character with self-reliance and love of liberty. Some thought the novel worthy of a Pulitzer, but it proved to be her last major public splash. Disillusioned by the state of the country, and with her mother financially independent because of the success of the *Little House* books, Rose bought a farmhouse in Danbury, Connecticut, to which she retreated for her remaining days.

After Lane moved to Danbury in 1938, libertarian advocacy and activism became her whole life. Her only nonpolitical writings for her last few decades were articles on needlepoint for *Women's Day*. Even there she slipped in individualist messages.[73] Her only book-length work from then on was *The Discovery of Freedom*.

Both Lane and Paterson were popular novelists making first forays into the nonfiction treatise; both took a world historical view on the development of human potential, and both tried to explain the link between liberty and the unprecedented prosperity of mid-twentieth century America. Both built their books around an overarching metaphor; for Paterson, it was society as a machine; for Lane, it was human energy as only fully usable when men are individual and free: "This is the nature of human energy; individuals generate it, and control it. Each person is self-controlling, and therefore responsible for his acts. Every human being, *by his nature*, is free."[74]

The Discovery of Freedom is a paean to human growth and change. Lane's vision is ideological—nothing about the laws of nature, or human nature, changed in America to make it unique; the necessary change, she insisted, was ideological. People began realizing the power of free human energy. (Lane uses the term "religious faith" somewhat eccentrically, to mean what most people mean nowadays by "ideology." She used her peculiar definition to deny that atheism was even possible, since believing in *anything*, supernatural or not, was religious to her—any "standard of value" is tantamount to God. One sees hints in *The Discovery of Freedom* of why her friendship with the militantly atheist Rand couldn't last.)

Lane's ideology seems largely self-created; there are few references to other writers or thinkers in *Discovery*, and many areas of disagreement with other libertarian thinkers. (Paterson biographer Cox accuses Lane's of being a slightly dumbed down version of Paterson's more sophisticated work, and thinks she was mostly presenting a watered-down version of ideas she picked up from her friend Paterson.)[75] Though she knew of Mises's work, she never accepted his notion that a communist economy must necessarily collapse. Lane thought they could survive indefinitely and would merely stagnate without the flow of free human energy.[76]

Tightening economic controls caused the fall of all great nations, Lane argued.[77] She wrote at length of three attempts in human history to establish and build a culture on the notion, as she interpreted it, that man is and must be free: the biblical Israelites, the Saracen (Muslim) empire created in the centuries after Muhammad, and the United States. She credits the biblical Israelites with being the first to realize that man is free; the Saracens with creating the first technologically sophisticated, scientific civilization. (She credits the European Renaissance to Italy's exposure to the Saracen world.)

The Saracen vision of human freedom, though, "was not quite as pure . . . as it was among the Israelis," and Lane thought their lack of civil law doomed their civilization to eventually fade.[78] She thinks the collapse of post–exploration era Spain can be explained by the expulsion of the Moriscos, the remnants of the great Saracen civilization who were the only ones in the country to understand the nature of free men.

Although she was often lumped in with the old right and was resolutely anti-European, Lane was not a typical patriotic devotee of the old American republic. She was a revolutionary, and while she believed that America's experiment in liberty arose organically from its experience as a frontier nation, she thought that revolution could and should be worldwide. America, she wrote, "is a totally new world . . . that has nothing to do with races, creeds, classes, or nations. It abolishes all barriers between human beings. . . . This new world is an intricate interplaying of dynamic energies, a living network enclosing the whole earth and linking all human beings in one common effort, one common fate."[79]

She was utopian in a manner almost redolent of modern-day neoconservative crusaders for American internationalism, except for her contempt for democracy. ("The superstition that all men have a right to vote is a triumph of Old World reasoning . . . extensions of the franchise are dangerous to individual liberty and human rights."[80])

Discovery is an eccentric and spirited statement of a certain strain of the modern libertarian character: historically visionary, rooted in

American experience yet foreseeing a whole world transformed by a political/ideological spirit that could and should be universal in character. She never lets the reader forget the essentially murderous nature of government controls; to Lane, both American and world history provide abundant lessons to indicate that only laissez-faire is fit to keep men alive and thriving. She tosses out handfuls of interesting historical incidents and observations to support her sweeping points, in the end, not enough to fully buttress such a huge and weighty thesis.

Rose didn't do much writing after *The Discovery of Freedom* but kept up a voluminous correspondence with fellow libertarians young and old, people who had discovered her unique views through *Give Me Liberty* or *The Discovery of Freedom.* The last of her young charges and her eventual heir, Roger MacBride, was the son of a *Reader's Digest* editor who was working on condensing a Lane book for that magazine. Lane met him when he was fourteen, and they became fast friends for life. MacBride brought his new best friend Lane to lecture at his New England prep school, and his American government teacher was enthralled; he "sat up half the night talking with Mrs. Lane, because, as he told me later, he had no idea that people *actually existed* who thought the way she did!"[81] Lane taught her young friend well: MacBride led student libertarian groups at Princeton and Harvard, and became a state representative in Vermont who bedeviled his fellow legislators with piles of libertarian bills to save his constituents money.[82] (He played an important role in the Libertarian Party in the 1970s.)

Another of her faithful correspondences was with financer of free market causes Jasper Crane of the DuPont Corporation. A huge selection of their letters—and a better view of the mature libertarian Lane than is present in *The Discovery of Freedom*—can be found in the MacBride-edited book *The Lady and the Tycoon.*

Most of Lane's later writings consisted of book reviews for the National Economic Council's *Review of Books,* a position she inherited from Albert Jay Nock in 1945. Lane, like Paterson, refused to accept a Social Security card. When the NEC insisted on taking out Social Security taxes from her pay, the largely self-sufficient farm lady stopped writing for them in 1950. She kept her official income as low as possible to avoid taxes.

In her later life, Lane once wrote a postcard to a radio host fingering Social Security as the sort of socialist Bismarckianism we supposedly fought against in World War II. A sedition-sniffing postmaster alerted the FBI, who sent a state police officer to investigate, a young man. Lane asked him if expressing such an opinion was subversive. He said yes, ma'am, it was.

Lane thundered back, "Then I'm subversive as all hell! . . . I say this, and I write this, and I broadcast it on the radio, and I'm going to keep right on doing it 'til you put me in jail. Write that down and report it to your superiors!" Canned vegetables and slaughtered pigs were *true* social security, she insisted. The NEC distributed an account Lane wrote of this little contretemps as a pamphlet, helping make her a folk hero among antitax forces.[83]

Her libertarianism turned anarchistic, and except for Laura Ingalls Wilder fans (many of whom still love her, though some resent latter-day attempts to horn Rose in on her mother's glory), only libertarians remember or honor Lane.[84] So it is strange—or a sign of the lack of respect that the intelligentsia accords libertarian ideas—that Lane's only serious biographer, William Holtz, writes off this portion of Lane's life as little more than pathology. He wrote that her later political beliefs resulted from "a failure of maturity"[85] and that "the social scientist, reviewing the list of symptoms, would find a clear case of American right-wing pathology" and refers to the "pathos of her journey to that position" as if libertarianism were an inherently sad fate.[86]

Rose was a movement-conscious libertarian early, always interested in the activities of student groups like those led by her protégé MacBride, and commiserating with Jasper Crane on his moribund attempts to start a free market economics journal to be run by Hans Sennholz (a student and devotee of Ludwig von Mises's) or an academy to teach nothing but proper free market economics. In a 1947 letter to Crane, she uses the phrase "libertarian movement" to identify herself and those who thought like her—the first example I've found of the phrase in its modern sense.[87] She encouraged the young because she knew the philosophy of individualism "hasn't had its Plato yet. I'm betting that the oncoming youngsters will produce one."[88]

Lane was already optimistic about the movement's growth by the late 1950s. She wrote to Crane in 1958 that there are many, many more efforts of all kinds being made now. Twenty years ago, do you remember? It was almost impossible to find *one*. I used to spend all my time, every day, at my typewriter following up every least little "lead" that I could find. Example: I heard a high-school "debate" among all pro–New Dealers on the radio, and wrote to each of them. One replied, with all the Welfare State collectivist notions that had been put into his head, but he didn't seem wholly unintelligent, so I kept on writing to him for some months, apparently with no effect, finally getting no answer. Now he turns up as publisher of *National Review*, telling people that I—i.e., my letters—changed his whole life. . . . The whole "climate of opinion" is changing. And every least little thing that you have done has helped to change it; never think that a bit of it failed, even when it seemed to.[89]

She was, however, a keen-eyed heresy spotter; her special metaphor for the bad ideas that sometimes infected even libertarians was the dead rat found in the middle of a delicious cherry pie. As Richard Cornuelle, who worked with Lane during his days at the libertarian funding foundation the Volker Fund in the 1950s, remembered, because of Lane's metaphor, "for years we called heresies of whatever dimension 'dead rats' and were forever on the lookout for them. Rose summarily revoked Robert Taft's provisional libertarian credentials when he endorsed federal aid to education—his dead rat. When someone suggested that her failure to forgive the Senator this fashionable transgression showed a lack of Christian charity, she said, "I know perfectly well Jesus said, 'Go and sin no more.' But the operative word was 'go.'"[90]

Lane clearly understood the difference between her individualist antistatist position and the stances of famous right-wingers of her day. In a 1953 letter to Crane, she wrote that the "'Conservative' (so-called) movement in the universities seems to me little more than a scramble; it is a back-to-medievalism movement, and I cannot see these millions of young veterans and their wives renouncing television, motor cars, radios, deep freezes, and airplanes for the placidity of, as Professor [Russell] Kirk [the ultratraditionalist author of the 1953 book *The Conservative Mind,* the ur-text of the contemporary intellectual right wing] imagines and says, 'a society of status.'"[91] Nor did her opinion improve; in 1958, she told Crane that the "so-called 'conservative' movement, of the Russell Kirk ilk, impresses me as not only trying to scuttle backward, crabwise, to medievalism, but as being singularly asinine on the way."[92]

As with many libertarians, cold war matters separated her from the more mainstream *National Review* conservatives. She scoffed at the notion that the socialist Soviet Union could seriously threaten the free United States, deciding that they wouldn't dare allow their armies to leave their shores for fear of mass defection.[93]

Her last major influence in the libertarian movement was on Robert LeFevre, founder and operator of the Freedom School (later Rampart College), a major institution of 1960s libertarianism. LeFevre was converted by *The Discovery of Freedom*,[94] and Lane became an enthusiastic booster and financial supporter of his school, keeping it from going out of business at a particularly bad time in the late 1950s with a cash donation of almost her entire bank account.[95]

Rose died in 1968. In her last years, she became, without apparently trying to jibe her new opinions with her old anti–cold war belief, an enthusiast for the Vietnam War with a rather typical domino argument of the sort she once disdained. She was even sent, under State Department auspices, to cover the war for *Women's Day* in 1966.[96]

Her influence is mostly secondhand these days, though *The Discovery of Freedom* is kept in print by libertarian mail-order house Laissez-Faire Books. She was the initial conversion experience, however, for the likes of MacBride, who learned directly at her feet, LeFevre, and libertarian editor and publicist Roy Childs, who became active and central to the movement in the 1970s. And the *Little House* books were, according to many letters she received, integral to "bringing up . . . children to be real Americans, in spite of other influences."[97]

Lane knew that the intellectual work she and her fellow 1940s and 1950s libertarians did was akin to "one of those little ripples that begin the turning of an ebb tide and forecast the coming Wave of the Future."[98] But her faith in the American character and the power of the unleashed energy of free people made her "as certain as anyone can be of anything in the future that the twentieth century will end as the eighteenth did, with a great revival and resurgence of individualism."[99]

"TELL THEM THAT RUSSIA IS A HUGE CEMETERY AND THAT WE ARE ALL DYING SLOWLY."

Ayn Rand was self-made down to her name. She was born Alyssa Rosenbaum on February 2, 1905, in St. Petersburg, Russia. She was the daughter of shop-owning chemist Fronz Rosenbaum and his wife, Anna. While the family was reasonably well off in Alyssa's youth, being shop owners did not serve the Rosenbaum family in good stead after the Bolshevik revolution tore Russia apart. The shop was taken from them, and during the height of the wars between the Red and White armies in 1918, the family relocated to the Crimea. There Rand taught soldiers to read and write, and witnessed firsthand the nature of forced collectivization as dresses were taken from all the girls and redistributed according to official whim, forcibly "socialized" among the grade school girls.[100]

The family returned to St. Petersburg in time for Alyssa to receive the benefits of a free proletarian education at the University of St. Petersburg. She graduated in spring 1924 with a degree in history and worked as a tour guide for the Soviet state for extra money. As the daughter of a class enemy, she barely evaded being booted from college during a student purge at the university in 1923; only those entering their senior year among the children of nonproletarians were allowed to finish their education.[101]

Her student years, as well as her family's (and nation's) privations and struggles, informed her first novel, *We the Living* (1936). Its indomitable and vaguely Nietzschean heroine Kira Argounova reflects Alyssa Rosenbaum, another young girl, Soviet by cruel fate but not spirit, with little to motivate her but the desire to escape. Kira's desire ended in tragedy; Rand's in triumph.

After years of trying and with the help of relatives in Chicago, Rand got a coveted passport out of Russia in 1926. She was supposed to visit her American relations and then return to the motherland. Rand pretended to have a Soviet sweetheart to help convince an official at the American consulate in Latvia that she was sure to return. But Rand boarded the train for Berlin with no intention of ever returning to the trap she'd escaped.[102] For years she'd tell a story that limned the mission she saw for herself as a fortunate escapee.

Someone approached her at her farewell party, she says, and told her, "If they ask you, in America—tell them that Russia is a huge cemetery and that we are all dying slowly." "I'll tell them," Rand remembers promising.[103]

And she did, most concretely in *We The Living* and more abstractly throughout her entire body of work. The young Alyssa, who was using her self-chosen identity of Ayn Rand by the time she got to America, never intended to found a philosophic or political movement. She was a dazed and devoted fan of American movies, finding them a rare and precious drop of emotional fuel when she managed to see one in Russia. They were a concrete embodiment of her fantasies about the wonderland she escaped to: wealthy, shining, romantic, alive, free. She wanted to be part of that tradition. Though she first stayed with an aunt on her mother's side in Chicago, she was Hollywood bound. With a loan from her relatives, she made it there in the summer of 1926.[104]

Though she was still struggling with English, she was intent on becoming a movie scenario writer. This was the tail end of the silent era. Visual imagination could still carry a writer even if a grasp of complicated dialogue was out of reach. Rand holed up at a boarding house for young ladies trying to make it in the movies, called the Hollywood Studio Club.[105]

Rand was trying to sell stories of brave architects unjustly accused of endangering the public, of an army of Chinese bandits laying siege to a hotel in order to capture an American lady who caught their leader's eye.[106] Rand recalls being rebuffed often with the complaint that her stories were outrageous and unrealistic. Her love of the grand fictional gesture stayed with her through her novels, gifting the world with such scenes as Howard Roark's dynamiting of his botched public housing project in *The Fountainhead* and the evil Project X of *Atlas Shrugged* reducing hundreds of miles to rubble with force rays. Rand was contemptuous of those who scoffed at her fiction for lacking realism and answered them in a later exposition of her theory of romantic fiction, *The Romantic Manifesto* (1970).

From the beginning, Rand practiced the theory she later consciously formulated. To her, fiction should not be about re-creating life as it is; it should present life as it could be, and ought to be. Wild romanticism in fiction was her love. While that won her no friends in

Hollywood production houses in the 1920s, it earned her enormous wealth and fame decades later.

Her earliest writings also had flashes of an almost antinomian love for the rebel, the man everyone else hated. The hero who saved the Americans from the ravening Chinese gang was a common cat burglar. The star of her first planned novel, a hatefully Nietzschean work called *The Little Street* that never progressed beyond a set of notes, was a killer who, in Rand's own words, was "perfectly cynical. Stone-hard. Monstrously cruel. Brazenly daring. No respect for anything or anyone." He was the *hero*.[107]

Cecil B. DeMille was one of the kings of Hollywood in 1926, and one of Rand's favorites. In a suitably romantic twist, Rand found herself running into the Great Man himself by accident on the studio lot. The awestruck young Russian girl charmed DeMille. He nicknamed her "Caviar" and by his leave she began working as an extra on his sets. Rand can be seen, if you look very closely, in crowd scenes in DeMille's epic *The King of Kings*.

On the set Rand met another extra, a midwestern boy named Frank O'Connor also trying to make his way in the film business. Rand saw him on a bus and liked his looks. She found to her delight that he was going to DeMille's studio too. It was love at first sight for Rand. She lost track of O'Connor for nine months because she never got the nerve to ask him for a phone number or address when his work on the film was over. But she met him again by accident in a library and married him on April 15, 1929. Now, as the wife of an American, Rand no longer needed to fear a visa-related forced return to the Soviet Union.[108]

Her dogged apprenticeship on DeMille's sets eventually paid off. Rand was given a writing job in his operation. She reviewed literary properties for which he had purchased film rights, and made outlines for screenwriters to use in developing scripts. The work was unfulfilling; Rand disliked most of the stories she dealt with. DeMille closed his studio, and Rand worked odd waitressing jobs until after her 1929 marriage to Frank, when she found work in the wardrobe department at RKO Pictures.

She continued her own screenwriting and began her first novel, eventually published as *We the Living*. The dominant theme in her

work was Soviet misery and tyranny. She maintained, with her cus-
tomary insistence, that principles and conceptual thinking were more
important than concretes, that the theme of *We the Living* was not just
that the Soviet Union was a hellish nightmare, but that collectivism as
a principle is the enemy of the human mind and spirit. While Rand
the philosopher of Objectivism was still decades away, Rand the enemy of political tyranny lived in her first public works.

She was already self-conscious about the kind of philosophy she
stood for. As early as 1934 she had sent H. L. Mencken a prepublica-
tion copy of her *We the Living* manuscript (then titled *Airtight*), and
praised him as

> the greatest representative of a philosophy to which I want to dedi-
> cate my whole life. . . . I have always regarded you as the foremost
> champion of individualism in this country. . . . Perhaps it may seem
> a lost cause at present, and there are those who will say that I am
> too late, that I can only hope to be the last fighter for a mode of
> thinking which has no place in the future. But I do not think so. I
> intend to be the first one in a new battle which the world needs as
> it has never needed before, the first to answer the many—too
> many—advocates of collectivism, and answer them in a manner
> which will not be forgotten.[109]

It took years, but Rand did all she hoped to do, and more.

As the 1930s wore on, Rand began selling screenplays. They didn't
always end up being filmed—a very common fate for screenwriters.
Red Pawn was her first sale, to Universal Studios. It was another take
on Soviet inhumanity with a plot, as in *We the Living*, of a woman pretending to love a Soviet official in order to save the man she really
loved—and the emotional complications that arise as the faked love
turns subtly real.[110] In 1934, Rand, in the grip of a more contemptuous
and Nietzschean[111] individualism than she evinced in her official
philosophical writings later, wrote and sold a play that was not set in
the Soviet Union and did not, on the surface, deal with politics.

Rand called the play *Penthouse Legend*, though it would end up on
Broadway in 1935 (altered by the director into a form that Rand despised) under the title *The Night of January 16th*.[112] The play nonethe-

less contains hints of Rand's antinomian Nietzscheism. Her offstage hero is said, admiringly, to have "never thought of things as right or wrong. To him it was only: you can or you can't. He always could."[113] The later Rand, the preeminent moralist, would never praise *not thinking* of right and wrong.

Rand relocated to New York City to work on the Broadway production of *Night*. New York was the metropolis whose filmed images had married her heart to the American ideal, the city she loved most. Despite trouble selling *We the Living* (which Rand attributed to its anti-Soviet theme in an American literary culture that she found surprisingly, and appallingly red), Macmillan bought and published it in March 1936. The book was a flop, earning Rand $100 in sales on the initial hardback. The novel quickly went out of print, reappearing twenty-three years later in a paperback edition in the wake of Rand's best-selling fame with *The Fountainhead* and *Atlas Shrugged*. That edition has since sold more than 2 million copies.

Primed by her childhood love of adventure heroes, Rand's ultimate goal with her romantic literature was to create her image of an ideal man. Finally feeling comfortable with the English language and with a first accepted novel behind her, she began creating a man who would be realized on the screen a decade later by Gary Cooper, one of her movie idols. This first great Rand creation was Howard Roark, hero to millions of young men and women over the years. She placed him in the world of architecture and consequently thought she must learn as much as she could about the topic. Despite her antinaturalism, Rand did research her novels' milieus. She went to work for a New York architectural firm for a while in 1937 to get a feel for that world.[114]

She worked on *The Fountainhead* on and off for nearly six years. She also tossed off a brief novella called *Anthem* (1938), another adumbration of her theme of the individual versus the collective—this version highly stylized and set in a future dystopia. The *Anthem* world is so collectivized that people can't make their own decisions about what to study, what job to perform, or who to love; they can't even conceptualize the first person pronoun.

The novel's hero falls in love, rebels, escapes, reinvents the electric light, and in his final and greatest achievement, understands the meaning and glory of the forbidden and forgotten word "I." The book is

unlike anything else Rand wrote, and is the most charming and unvar-
nished representation of her philosophic sense of life.

It was originally published only in Britain. Finally in 1945 libertarian booster Leonard Read, later founder of the first modern libertarian
think tank, the Foundation for Economic Education, published an
American edition under his Pamphleteers imprint.[115] Unlike her other
tomes, *Anthem* can be read in an afternoon; but like all her works it has
mental and emotional repercussions that can extend across a lifetime.
While Rand has many virulent critics, none gainsay her writing's ability to change minds and lives. Some may lament it and some may
cheer it; no one can deny it.[116]

Rand also wrote two more plays during these years, *Think Twice* and
Ideal; neither was produced.[117] She did get a play version of *We the Living*, retitled *The Unconquered*, produced in February 1940, but it closed
in five days.

As she continued to struggle with *The Fountainhead*, Rand had her
first and last experience with political activism during the 1940 Wendell Willkie versus Franklin Roosevelt presidential election. Rand, like
other right-wing and individualist intellectuals of the time, hated
Roosevelt. Though she ended up disillusioned with the unphilosophi-
cal Willkie as well (eventually concluding that he "did more to destroy
the Republican Party than did Roosevelt"), she thought the Roosevelt threat severe enough that she spent days doing old-fashioned
street corner haranguing on the Republicans' behalf, even though she
and Frank were almost out of money.[118]

Rand found that "I was at my best among hecklers, on street corners
and on 14th Street," lamenting that "I'm no good at all as a polite
speaker to an audience that agrees with me."[119] She also ran the research department for the national headquarters of Associated Willkie
clubs. There she discovered that literature in support of individualistic
capitalism was sorely lacking.

During her Willkie experience, Rand began socializing and com-
municating with a loose band of right-wing and individualist intellectuals, including Isabel Paterson, the biggest influence on Rand's
mature political philosophy.[120] Rand also met and socialized with
Rose Wilder Lane, and with remnants of the old right, such as Albert
Jay Nock.[121]

Rand began agitating for a specific movement consciousness on the part of her intellectual compatriots. Together with drama critic Channing Pollock, she began planning a new national organization of individualists. In 1941, she wrote a manifesto for this nascent group. Many of the right-leaning businessmen whom she and Pollock tried to recruit doubted that any new group espousing what they referred to among themselves as Americanism was needed. After all, didn't the National Association of Manufacturers (NAM) stand up for the interests of business and free markets? Rand was aggravated by the concrete-bound mentality behind such dismissals. "What organization of our side has defined a concrete ideology of Americanism?" Rand wrote to Pollock:

> None. The first aim of our organization will be intellectual and philosophical—not merely political and economic. We will give people a faith—a positive, clear and consistent system of belief. Who had done that? Certainly not the N.A.M. They—and all other organizations—are merely fighting for the system of private enterprise and their entire method consists of teaching and clarifying the nature of that system. It is good work, but it is not enough. We want to go deeper than that. We want to teach people, not what the system of private enterprise is, but why we should believe in it and fight for it. We want to provide a spiritual, ethical, philosophical groundwork for the belief in the system of private enterprise.[122]

While the later Rand would doubtless bridle at the use of the word "faith," she already recognized her political and ideological task—establishing a defense of individualism and capitalism that went deeper, more to the roots—more radical in the true sense—than any in existence. As a struggling novelist, she was beginning to see the outlines of her task as a radical for capitalism. Rand recruited DeWitt Emery, head of the National Small Businessmen's Association, to pull together this unique organization of advocates of individualism, but it never happened. It would be Rand's last attempt to get involved in a group activity that did not fully sing her tune.

Selling *The Fountainhead* proved as difficult as finding easy commissions for architect Howard Roark. Her agent quit in despair after twelve rejections from major publishers. Desperate for money, Rand was working as a script reader for Paramount. Richard Mealand, a story editor there, was enchanted by the unfinished manuscript of *The Fountainhead* and sent it to an editor he knew at Bobbs-Merrill, Archibald Ogden.

In another of those Randian touches that mysteriously dotted her real life, Ogden put his new job on the line by telling his boss, who was dubious about the novel that Ogden loved, that "If this is not the book for you, then I am not the editor for you." The editor caved in to Ogden's enthusiasm, and Bobbs-Merrill bought the book in December 1941, giving Rand a year to complete it.[123] During her rush to finish this difficult work, she began to take Dexamyl, a combined barbiturate and amphetamine, which some have speculated might be to blame for some of her peculiar behavior later in life.[124] Her friend Paterson warned her in no uncertain terms that she must "stop taking that Benzedrine, you idiot. I don't care what excuse you have—stop it."[125]

The Fountainhead is a strange and wonderful book, and it has been in print since it was published in 1943. While it rarely gets respect as a literary classic, it is a modern "underground" classic—if that term can be applied to a book that has sold more than 4 million copies.

The Fountainhead dramatized the theme of secondhand lives—Rand's working title for the book. The inspiration for the concept of the secondhander came from a conversation with a fellow employee at RKO. Rand admired the woman's ambition, but when she asked her what she wanted to achieve in life, the woman's answer perplexed Rand: "I'll tell you what I want. If nobody had an automobile, then I would want to have one automobile. If some people have one, then I want to have two."[126] Rand wondered what sickness of soul could lead someone to link her own ambitions to what everyone else had or wanted; and that wondering led her to the central conflict in *The Fountainhead*.

The plot revolved around the lives and careers of two architects, the individualist and heroic Howard Roark and the glad-handing, uncreative, craven Peter Keating. They are college acquaintances and housemates, as we learn in the novel's opening scene when Roark is booted from college for his intransigence and unwillingness to parrot the stale bromides of architectural classicism.

Losing the status ticket of a university degree doesn't bother Roark a bit; he has full confidence in his ability to succeed on his own terms. Roark and Keating's lives continue to intertwine as Roark begins an erratic career, sometimes toiling in quarries to support himself; working for small, dying firms; getting few commissions but producing spectacular work when he does.

Keating gets the big-money positions at highly reputable firms but secretly relies on Roark to ghost for him when talent or originality is required. Roark goes along with Keating's deceptions, since he believes that getting the building built is more important than who gets the credit. A resolute individualist, he does not need or desire the world's acclaim; he is the only judge that matters.

Roark's and Keating's lives are complicated by Dominique Francon, a strange woman disgusted with the poor chances for greatness in a corrupt and mediocre world. She goes out of her way to destroy greatness where she does find it, both in herself, when she condemns herself to a pointless marriage with Keating, and in Roark, whom she dedicates herself to ruining even as she secretly becomes his lover.

Dominique is one of the most curious and compelling characters in Rand's oeuvre; her passion for the good and the depth of her twisted confusion at finding it thwarted is fascinating; few actual humans could feel as strongly as she does, strongly enough to understand the motivation for her seemingly bizarre behavior. Rand once confessed that Dominique represents herself on a bad day—when her hatred of the small and the evil overwhelms her belief in the inherent benevolence of the universe and the constant possibilities for human greatness.[127]

Critics often slam Rand for her unrealistic characters. In the literal sense this is true; they are romantic, living evocations of ideas. Her heroes and villains personify the principles of heroism and villainy as Rand sees them. She romanticizes the modern collectivist intellectual in the person of Ellsworth Toohey, a witty and intelligent architectural and social critic of great influence who realized that disarming man's soul through unrelenting attacks on the great and elevating of the mediocre left them open for manipulation by the likes of him.[128]

Keating becomes part of a crowd of confused young acolytes who take Toohey's word on everything from ethics to politics to art. Rand delights in mocking the pretensions of modern writers such as Gertrude Stein, whom she thought a fraud, in the person of a Toohey acolyte who writes a nonsensical novel called *The Gallant Gallstone*, about an overly individualistic gallstone who comes to a bad end after being hit with a dose of castor oil. Toohey, in his newspaper column, praises the book to high heavens.

That the collectivist villain is a critic rather than a politician gives telling insight into Rand's concerns. The enemies of the individual and of liberty, she knew, are not just those who openly advocate political tyranny, but anyone who chips away at the foundation of individual greatness. She always contended that evil is inherently powerless, and only wins by the acquiescence or cravenness of the potentially good. Toohey, the great villain of *The Fountainhead*, and Roark, its hero, meet only once, and anticlimactically. Toohey, eager with curiosity, asks Roark what he, Roark, thinks of him. Roark replies, "But I don't think of you" and then ignores him.[129]

Rand expiates her earlier flirtation with Nietzscheism in the character of Gail Wynand, a Hearst-like newspaper magnate who employs Toohey and also becomes Dominique's lover. Wynand, a man of stunted greatness, shares Dominique's contempt for the average man, which he manifests by manipulating them, becoming an opinion leader by catering to lowest-common-denominator mass taste. When Wynand meets Roark and realizes that greatness *can* exist and *does* have a chance, he dedicates his newspapers to defending Roark during his climactic trial. Wynand discovers too late that by reducing his ambitions to dominating the public, he became their slave more than their master. The stupid beast of the public he catered to was now beyond his control.

Roark found himself in the dock for a marvelously Randian gesture. He was doing one more secret job under Keating's name—designing a public housing project called Cortlandt Homes. The design realized Roark's innovative notions for more attractive, inexpensive, and resource-efficient housing. Various bureaucrats had mucked up his design and created a monstrosity. Roark, seeing no other legal option for the vindication of his rights as creator, dynamited the (unoccupied) buildings. Roark convinced the jury that his rights as a creator had been violated by the alterations—that his actions were just.

"It is said that I have destroyed the home of the destitute," Roark said at his trial. "It is forgotten that but for me the destitute could not have had this particular home. . . . It is believed that the poverty of the future tenants gave them a right to my work. That their need constituted a claim on my life. That it was my duty to contribute anything demanded of me. This is the second-hander's credo now swallowing the world.

"I came here to say that I do not recognize anyone's right to one minute of my life. Nor to any part of my energy. Nor to any achievement of mine. No matter who makes the claim, how large their number or how great their need.

"I wished to come here and say that I am a man who does not exist for others.

"It had to be said. The world is perishing from an orgy of self-sacrificing.

"I wished to come here and say that the integrity of a man's creative work is of greater importance than any charitable endeavor. Those of you who do not understand this are the men who're destroying the world. . . . I recognize no obligations toward men except one: to respect their freedom and to take no part in a slave society."[130]

The jury acquits. Toohey loses his job when Wynand, crushed by the realization that his life has been futile and that true greatness could have been within his grasp, closes down his papers. Roark goes on to build one more great building as a commission for Wynand, in honor of what he might have been. The conclusion, in Rand's mind and those of most of the book's fans, is an unalloyed triumph for the individual.

Rand's novels have a curious way of subtly—and unintentionally—undercutting their own messages; hints of the Dominique in Rand's soul shine through. Roark doesn't go to jail, but the world remains the same world Toohey dominates. It's easy to believe that Roark will be lucky if he manages to get another commission, while Toohey will undoubtedly keep his destructive mission rolling at some other publication, his reputation and power intact, if not growing.

Rand believed in the glory of the individual; she seemed to believe equally that most of the world was made up of the evil and mediocre and those who through their incomprehension and inaction allow the evil to flourish. In her mind, her novels are meant to honor and emphasize the heroic. But in his own sinister way Toohey is as grand a character as Roark, and the novel by no means shows him ultimately beaten. Under the surface, Rand seems to argue in *The Fountainhead* that what happens to the world at large is insignificant compared to the wonders that creative individuals like Roark—the fountainheads of all human progress—can achieve.

The Fountainhead became a slow but inexorable success, despite what Rand saw as mostly uncomprehending reviews and ad campaigns that soft-pedaled the novel's controversial themes. Rand believed in art as a self-standing absolute, but she also realized that *The Fountainhead* was a powerful salvo in a philosophical and political war, one in which her side had long been thought routed from the field. As early as 1935, she realized that "Capitalist democracy has no ideology. That is what this book has to give it."[131] She later complained to DeWitt Emery of the National Small Businessmen's Association that no businessman or group of conservative/individualist inclinations was willing to stand up publicly for her book.

"I performed a miracle in getting a book like this published in these times," Rand wrote, "when the whole publishing world is trembling before Washington. Now let the reactionaries help me spread the book. If the book goes over big, it will break the way for other writers of our side. If it's allowed to be killed by the Reds—our good industrialists had better not expect anyone else to stick his neck out in order to try to save them from getting their throat cut."[132]

Her book was not "killed by the Reds." Nor were Paterson's or Lane's, although they did not succeed commercially as Rand did. And Rand herself would go forward to fight political and intellectual battles in defense of libertarian principles even more fervently than she did in *The Fountainhead*. But as grim as it might have seemed in 1943 to Rand, Paterson, and Lane, others in the wings were prepared to stick their necks out in the name of individualism and economic liberty.

The revolution launched in its modern form by the two Austrian economists and the three women writers had more fronts on which to fight. Leonard Read, the man who created the institutional framework for that revolution with the first educational think tank dedicated to pushing what he called the "freedom philosophy," had been directly inspired by the works of all of them. He loved Lane and Rand so much that he started a small publishing house to print their work. Thanks to their influence, the first modern institution dedicated to libertarian education, the Foundation for Economic Education, was born in 1946. The splash they made with their books in 1943 would ripple in ways they could never have predicted.

FIGHTING FOR THE FREEDOM PHILOSOPHY

Ayn Rand's American fantasy came full circle. *The Fountainhead* made her a hot commodity in the movie industry, which had attracted her young soul to the United States in the first place. She returned to Southern California to write the screenplay for a film adaptation of *The Fountainhead*. The $50,000 she earned ended her financial struggle for good. She moved into a house outside Los Angeles designed by modernist architect Richard Neutra. (Frank Lloyd Wright, assumed to have inspired *The Fountainhead*, once designed a home for her, but it was never built.)[1] She nabbed a rare half-year renewable contract (giving her the other half to work on her own projects) to write screenplays for producer Hal Wallis.[2] She began socializing occasionally with a crowd of Southern California individualist businessmen, among them Leonard Read, then general manager of the Los Angeles chamber of commerce.

"THE PROBLEM WARRANTS IT AND I AM JUST RECKLESS ENOUGH AND CONFIDENT ENOUGH TO TRY."

Leonard Read was born to farmer Orville Read and his bride Ada in 1898 in the Michigan township of Lebanon. He was handsome

enough but affected no airs. "The Reads I came from were probably
more horsetraders than gentlemen having a coat of arms."[3] His father
died when he was eleven. Leonard worked hard to keep the household going as a teen, then served in World War I as a mechanic in the
aviation section of the Signal Corps. He was aboard the SS *Tuscania*
when a torpedo sank it near Ireland, and the lifeboat assigned to him
was shredded in the torpedo explosion. In Read's recollection, he was
the last living man to leave the ship, escaping in a collapsible boat
with others who had resisted the temptation—as many had not—to
leap into the dark, churning ocean in hope of rescue. Those men
found nothing but a swift, icy death.[4]

After the war Read returned to Michigan, where he launched and
ran a successful produce sales company. He'd drive to Detroit in the
middle of the night to fill his truck with vegetables coming in by train.
Eventually he was driven out of business by pressure from chain stores
that turned violent; one of Leonard's friends was murdered gangland
style in the wholesaler wars. He figured it was time to go someplace
more congenial.[5]

Read rode a cresting wave that brought hundreds of thousands of
Midwesterners to California, the perfumed fruit orchards and rolling
hills promising a fragrant future that went on forever. He sold business
and home and shot off to this utopia of good weather and endless options, on the locomotives built and run on a tangled mix of state privilege and private grit. He went into real estate, selling off bits of
paradise to other American pilgrims. He was well liked in his community and joined the chamber of commerce in Burlingame, a small
town between Palo Alto and San Francisco. He rose through the ranks
in the chamber and embarked on a normal, petit bourgeois life of
shilling for American business interests. In 1939, he became general
manager of its Los Angeles branch.

Read had started off believing in Roosevelt and the New Deal, sort
of, because that was the sort of thing decent Americans did in those
days. Even the chamber of commerce, that hidebound bastion of
middle-class business values, tried to go along to get along with National Recovery Act codes and the demands and restrictions of the
new form of American economic governance. By 1943, its new president announced that "only the willfully blind can fail to see that the

old-style capitalism of a primitive, free-shooting period is gone forever. The capitalism which . . . fought against justified public regulation of the competitive system is a thing of the past."[6]

But Read was no longer willing to go along unreservedly with this version of chamber doctrine. In the mid-1930s, William C. Mullendore, a former lawyer, former assistant to Herbert Hoover during his secretary of commerce days, and then vice president of Southern California Edison, turned Leonard Read's life around by explaining in great detail how Roosevelt's alphabet agencies violated the principles of good sense and the U.S. Constitution and would lead our nation to economic and moral ruin. Under Mullendore's influence, Read wrote a popular anti–New Deal book in 1937, *The Romance of Reality*, shot through with anti–central control ideas from Spencer, Sumner, and Nock.[7] Mullendore changed Read's life and laid the groundwork for the creation of the first modern libertarian think tank.

Mullendore had worked with Herbert Hoover (in the American Relief Administration) and Robert Taft (in the U.S. Food Administration). He couldn't bear to hear anyone, anywhere spout socialism without speaking up in firm opposition. He was also obsessed with the worlds of spirit and psychic energy, and he thought modern America's rot was as much spiritual as economic. As president of SoCal Edison, he achieved fame for his union busting during an early 1950s strike.[8] Mentor Mullendore was in some respects ahead of student Read, and in some respects behind, when it came to libertarian attitudes. Mullendore was, for example, far more glum about the immediate prospects of Western civilization, looking at the future through Misesian lenses and espying an economic apocalypse always looming ahead because of government mismanagement of the economy and credit manipulations, a doom forever drawing closer, closer. For decades he had been warning correspondents that the piper must soon be paid—and that any industrialist or businessman who dared express optimism was betraying the cause of true liberalism.

Mullendore was slower than Read to give up on standard partisan politics, although he glumly assented to Garet Garrett's insistence that free marketers in the late 1940s were not fighting, as some foolishly thought, to *prevent* some government power grab or some fatal blow to the American constitutional order, but to roll back one that was already a fait accompli. "The Revolution Was," as Garrett's influential essay put it. When Robert A. Taft—beloved by many of these individualists far beyond his true laissez-faire bona fides[9]—lost the GOP presidential nomination in 1952, it was Mullendore's final moment of despair with politics as usual. "The final elimination," he moaned, "of any real opposition to the revolution which I have been doing my best to try and fight for twenty years."[10]

What marked Mullendore's vision of Western decay as distinctly libertarian was his certainty that U.S. military might and its careless extension was a bloated symbol of what he was fighting against. As president of SoCal Edison, he was invited on a Defense Department propaganda junket intended to acquaint—and awe—captains of industry with the scope and majesty of America's imperial forces.

Mullendore sourly but proudly noted that none of it worked on *him*. "I am not sympathetic with our foreign policies, or with the idea that American youth is a mere pawn of the State to be used and ordered about throughout the world in support of policies devised by such men as Roosevelt, Acheson and Truman."[11] When Henry Ford II pleaded with his fellow plutocrat to kick back a little something to World Brotherhood Week (one of those bits of 1950s postwar IGY gee-whiz euphoria that made Mullendore cringe), Mullendore refused. Such charity missed the point utterly: U.S. militarization itself was the greatest danger to world brotherhood.[12]

This was the man who transformed Read into a free market, anti–New Deal crusader who, within the limits of national chamber policy, fought against statist control. A former Harvard economics professor with free market leanings, Thomas Nixon Carver, advanced Read's libertarian education by introducing him to the works of Frederic Bastiat. Read began to suspect, though, that merely refuting specific bits of government intervention is akin to refuting the fallacy that the earth is square—good enough for what it's worth. But until you explain how the earth actually *is* shaped, an infinite number of false notions may arise to freshly refute—no, it isn't a cylinder either, flat, or a cone, or . . . Refuting false principles wasn't good enough for Read; he had to inculcate true ones.

When Read left the L.A. chamber in 1945, a left-leaning labor newspaper, the *Hollywood Press Times*, cheered the departure of this fiend who had transformed the bourgeois chamber into a den of "Nazi-like propaganda" and reaction. With that sensitive signal intelligence possessed by creatures living in a tight, constrained underground, Read was corresponding with Rose Wilder Lane and was now pals with Rand. With Mullendore at the center, a gang of Leonard's friends from the chamber world joined with him to form a publishing concern to distribute individualist writings, called Pamphleteers Inc. That imprint became the first American publisher of Rand's pre-*Fountainhead* science fiction fable of the rediscovery of individualism in a collectivist dystopia, *Anthem*.[13]

Read's work with the chamber, his growing passion for defending the free market cause in any venue, his round and loud condemnations of the "plunderbund" bearing down on America with the force of a "plunderstorm" (two Read neologisms that never got much traction) earned him admiration and friendship from businessmen small and big across the country. They were still doubtful, confused, and concerned by the New Deal and war socialism, and the possible aftermath.

Journalist Rick Perlstein, writing on the origins and development of the Barry Goldwater movement in his book *Before the Storm* (2001), summed up the mentality that fed into a fascination with Goldwater and the likelihood of agreeing with Leonard Read and his work: You were likely to live in the Midwest, in a smallish town with factories on the outskirts of town; to work in a business your father or grandfather started, with old friends and associates in the local bank that loaned you money when you needed it; to admire Coolidge and think people ought to work for a living. But you were watching times change, watching unions shatter the old bonds of comity that your father had built with his workers; you had to go to New York for loans; you watched Franklin Roosevelt bankrupting the country and imposing all sorts of rules that seemed a lot harder on you than they were on your bigger competitors.

And you wondered why the heck it was the United States that had to fight England's quarrels in a war that FDR was elected to an unprecedented third term swearing he'd keep us out of, and why swarms of bureaucrats were now dogging your every move, eating out your substance. And then after the war you watched what you probably thought of as Your Party, the Republicans, buying into the same controlling, bureaucratic one-worldism you hated in FDR. You would likely appreciate the sort of no-nonsense defenses of America's freedoms—especially America's economic freedoms—that Read offered.[14]

The more distinctly libertarian types might read *Road to Serfdom* and find someone speaking to their secret heart, encouraging and compelling them to walk on an ideological path that among businessmen in the postwar era marked one as a bit of a queer duck, old-fashioned and possibly outmoded. But they were also imbued, many of them, with a sense that they *couldn't, mustn't* be quiet about these vital truths. The civilization they loved and fought to preserve and wanted to pass on to their children was at stake. It was hard to explain to your neighbor or someone seated next to you at a dinner party why legalizing narcotics or prostitution, say, or ending public education was vital to the future of a free America; but it had to be said. You could get many friends and associates to nod along with you about domestic communism and about the excesses of the New Deal, but not some of these more outré ideas. But you had to express the whole truth: If your movement merely positioned itself as being against *socialism* (conceived as complete state ownership of the means of production), you were playing into the hands of the gradualist left in America. Although leftists were for heavy taxation and regulation and interference in employer-employee relations, they could truthfully say that they were against socialism too.

Read's relationships with men who thought this way, including bigger industrialists who kept up the old-time faith, won him his next gig—executive vice president at the National Industrial Conference Board (NICB), a group founded in 1916 to promulgate pro-business and usually pro–free market (not always the same thing) ideas, with a special emphasis on reaching schoolteachers. Virgil Jordan was the NICB chief who brought Read onboard; Jordan had hard-core leanings, having also brought in Garet Garrett to edit the journal *American Affairs*. Because Read wanted to be a skilled apostle to the worlds of the chamber and the NICB, any untoward softness on matters of economic freedom among the business community would wound him. "Most people in our country today," he figured, "regard as soundly free enterprise anything which emanates from businessmen or business-supported organizations. For them to have any part whatsoever in these coercive, collectivist ideas, is to give more harm than all of the radical and communist front organizations put together."[15]

The NICB had a policy Read couldn't abide by. To maintain an aura of impeccable integrity and fairness, it insisted that the public educational events it sponsored present both sides of any given political or economic issue. Read's biographer (his longtime employee Mary Homan Sennholz) describes his feelings on this weak-sister policy:

> The "other side" was everywhere—in government, education, and communications. Even businessmen had come to rely on government for restrictions of competition, for government contracts and orders, easy money and credit, and other favors. Everyone was looking to government for the ultimate solution to his problems. How do you represent "both sides" when "one side" is all around you, preempting the public discussion, and the "other side" is barely audible in the deafening noise? . . . How do you state your case for individual freedom and the private property order when the other side is monopolizing the stage?[16]

Read, burning with libertarian evangelical fervor, wanted no part of it. In March 1946, after only eight months, he quit NICB, disappointed at not being given free rein to blast collectivism on a national scale. *He* needed to be in charge if he was to agitate effectively for what he called the "freedom philosophy." War socialism and its horrible aftermath left him sick at heart; after the atom bomb was unveiled, he lamented to a friend that "Savagery returns in a more frightful manner than . . . has ever been known. At a time when bandits are rising to power and when the banditry even in the good of us is manifesting itself we would have to discover the most destructive device ever known to man. Had I been the president of this country and obligated to announce what we had done I would have released to the press only a copy of my prayer asking forgiveness."[17] Read was, as John Chamberlain called him, "a curious mixture of American go-getter, Tolstoyan Christian, Herbert Spencer libertarian, and dedicated medieval monk."

In early 1946, he began calling in chits collected during his chamber years and NICB stint to gather money and a board of trustees for a curious new institution he wanted to create, which he called the Foundation for Economic Education. He found support and encouragement, tinged with some friendly (though ultimately supportive) doubt, from manufacturers small and large, insurance magnates, steel barons, car makers, insurance and banking firms, and privately owned electric utilities. When retired oil man H. B. Earhart initially failed to get his foundation board to give to Read's new passion, he kicked in a $10,000 personal check. (The Earhart Foundation later became a major FEE supporter.) Read's plan seemed promising. Truly individualist businessmen had realized by then that neither the chamber nor the National Association of Manufacturers was a reliably tenacious and radical defender of the meaning of free enterprise.[18]

Read hoped FEE would educate for liberty on every level, perhaps become a publishing house to reprint individualist classics of the Bastiat variety and give them wide—free if necessary—distribution; reach out to Americans from students to industrialists, from storekeepers to politicians; to repeat, in every different form and format, the eternal verities of encouraging "Anything That's Peaceful"—the title of one of Read's most enduring homiletic essays.

Read's vision of what FEE could do was influenced by a consultation he and Henry Hazlitt, already the favorite economics journalist of market reactionaries everywhere, had been granted with General Motors bigwig Alfred Sloan. Sloan wanted the pair to help him think through what might be the best way he could further freedom with the $10 million he had given to the Sloan Foundation.[19] B. F. Goodrich (of the tire company), who had donated to Read at NICB, encouraged him to do whatever he thought best to spread the ideas of freedom and promised that the money would be forthcoming.[20]

Mullendore warned Read that his plans were too ambitious, but Read had spent too many years proselytizing from the chamber bully pulpit and had seen too much continual growth in government economic intervention to think small. Free enterprise needed an uncompromising fighting force, and Leonard Read was going to supply the analytical and polemical ammo. To Mullendore's nay-saying, Read cried out, "I only want to give this damned field in which I have been working just one final grand uninhibited fling. The problem warrants it and I am just reckless enough and confident enough to try."[21]

Read called his organization the Foundation for Economic Education because he was certain, in the beginning, that America's crisis of governance arose from people not properly understanding free market economics, not grasping why government intervention in peaceful transactions is both counterproductive and wrong. The first meeting of FEE's founding incorporators was convened in Manhattan on March 7, 1946, in Room 3012 of 230 Park Avenue, the offices of the B. F. Goodrich Company. On the same day in Washington, a House special committee decided price controls needed to remain in place for at least the next fifteen months, the city of Detroit was begging for federal aid with an ongoing General Motors strike, and an assistant secretary of state was haranguing the Senate for further credits for Great Britain, though their war debts were still huge. These men knew they had a long, arduous fight ahead.[22]

By July FEE was settled in a sprawling mansion on seven acres in Irvington-on-Hudson, New York, that had fallen into desuetude, about forty minutes north of Manhattan on the Hudson Line. A horse stable on the grounds was turned into a storeroom for a growing collection of books, pamphlets, magazines, and clippings, and a house was built, owned by FEE, for Read and his wife Gladys to live in out back. (FEE presidents still live in it.)

FEE had healthy financing from the start, thanks to what the name Leonard Read meant to free market–loving businessmen. By May 1947, FEE had received $254,000 in donations (around $2.4 million in current dollars). Read was earning $25,000. He had carefully selected the board and it was—and remained—loyal to him. It was Read's show, from beginning to end. He wanted the board to be a mix of business and educational leaders, preferably scattered as widely as possible around the country to increase the number of potential donor communities he might tap. Of course he wanted all his trustees to be hard-core libertarians. His board loved and trusted him. One day, J. Howard Pew of Sun Oil called Read to tell him that he had $136,000 that he had to get rid of, for some arcane tax reason, in the next twenty-four hours—and would Read, along with Howard Kershner of Christian Economics (a more right-wing religious education group Pew also supported) figure out among themselves what they could best do with it? Thanks. And they did.[23]

Read developed a curious but successful soft sell approach to filling the coffers. He would never explicitly scrape for funds; none of these modern direct mail letters warning people of the imminent passage of this or that horrible legislation if they didn't give generously to FEE, and by return post! He never directly asked anyone to give anything, he proudly insisted, and while FEE would sell literature to all comers, it was also free to anyone who asked.

His attitude toward money was Zen, sometimes hilariously so. When asked how FEE was doing financially, his favorite reply was, "Just perfectly." So far as he knew, every person who wanted to give FEE money was doing so. When people would tell Leonard that they were not going to (or not going to continue to) support FEE, he'd write them. "I am pleased that there still exist areas where one is free to choose how one expends his own money. That these areas are being rapidly narrowed is self-evident. In view of the fact that FEE is attempting to widen the areas where one is free to choose, we cannot consistently complain when someone chooses not to support our work."[24]

Read wanted no endowments and frowned on any donation meant to be held in reserve for some future need. Human energy (a rhetorical and philosophical obsession with Read, as it was with Lane and Paterson) needed to be fed *now*, while it was alive, vital, on the move. What was FEE worth, after all, beyond the brains, tenacity, and effort of its staff—and who knew what might become of them in the future? FEE as an institution is but a disembodied idea. But the men who constituted it needed to act, and needed the resources to be able to act *now*. It was never money the freedom movement lacked, Read insisted, but good ideas and good people to do good things with whatever money there was. He always believed the money would follow the good work, not precede it. Institutions qua institutions didn't mean much. "Even if the libertarian cause prospers after the days of Clise, Pew, Hutchinson, [three FEE board members] Opitz, Mises, Harper, Poirot, Curtiss [FEE staffers] and others of us, it is almost certain to do so under roofs other than FEE," he wrote a FEE board member.[25]

"THERE ISN'T A GOD-DAMN BOOK IN THERE THAT IS NOT LEFT."

The crew surrounding FEE had no sophisticated model of social change. Many of them seemed bewildered by how the world had gotten the way it is, except that—somehow—the wrong ideas, and in some cases the wrong people, had taken over the culture, the government, even the world of business in which most of them moved. A couple of wealthier ones got it in their heads that what America needed was one blockbuster book that would *really explain* what was wrong with collectivism, and what was right about freedom and free enterprise. Their general attitude was a winning (though naive) belief that what led to big government was not competing interests or a desire to gain advantage at the expense of other citizens; they thought if their fellow citizens and politicians just *understood* free markets, all would eventually be well.

They gathered a conclave of all the individualist businessmen and intellectual warriors they could muster on February 8, 1946, a month prior to FEE's official launch, to figure out who might write this book and what it might say. Read, Mises, Hazlitt, Garrett, and an economist from Cornell who would later work at FEE named F. A. Harper were in attendance. The circulated transcript of the meeting has most of the speakers' names blocked out, but one cranky fellow who sounds very Garet Garrettish complained about the smallness of this "great book" plan.

He (everyone present was a he) noted that when valuable books such as John Flynn's, Herbert Hoover's, or ones by the speaker are issued, the left-dominated reviewing and bookselling trade keeps them from reaching reader's eyes. He notes that it isn't people *reading* Marx or Keynes that really pollutes the climate of opinion; it's thousands of people writing *about* Marx and Keynes, and talking about them, and having newspaper and radio accounts that uncritically accept their premises.

> You tell these people who have the money to finance one book, that they have to get a press, they have to get . . . a radio network, they have to get publishing houses. God-damnit, they have to create an

atmosphere in which what we call sound economic thought will function, and in functioning it will produce a book, and now a book, and those books will go up in the window. Whereas now, if you will just walk down the street and look in bookshop windows, there isn't a god-damn book in there that is not left.[26]

When the success of Hayek's *Road to Serfdom* was brought up as a counterexample, one pointed out that that book got as far as it did only because Hazlitt, their mole in the mainstream media, got his positive review of it on the front of the *New York Times* book review section, which calls the tune for all the intelligentsia.

Mullendore, among others, knew this "great book" plan was naive. The problem clearly went beyond a lack of good books explaining the truth about America's situation, what was wrong with it, and how to get back to the right path. The likes of Spencer, Bastiat, even (mostly) John Stuart Mill had said most of the important things about the proper scope of government. The problem was, who was reading them? And who had ears to hear?

Read himself couldn't be certain of the answer to *that* one; but he had a Nock-inspired faith that some Remnant—of what size, it would be foolhardy to guess—out there had ears to hear, and would seek and find and learn from and appreciate what FEE was doing.[27] (Read was a Nock fan and friend. Nock inscribed a copy of *Memoirs of a Superfluous Man* to Read with the comment, "If this book is good enough for Leonard E. Read, it is good enough for me.") Distinct from other groups on what was still then thought of mostly as the far right, FEE indulged in "no disparagement of persons or organizations; discussion is limited to ideas and principles. No telling people what to do; simply present the facts and let others draw conclusions, if any, for action."[28] They did not aid politicians or fight commies. They were for, in Read's inspirational phrase, Anything That's Peaceful— and against things like price controls of any sort (including of rents and wages), public housing, loyalty oaths, forced unionism and union intimidation, and conscription.

Read would try to find his Remnant, whoever they might be, through extensive travel and speaking, usually set up for him by local friends and FEE supporters, who would write the attendees afterward and mention that FEE did, after all, depend for survival on the voluntary support of those who believed in its mission. In a two-month period in 1951, Read traveled 18,000 miles explaining how the miracle of the free market waters your lawn while you sleep and makes your car while you practice music; of how the only meaningful action when it comes to restoring liberty is the intellectual action of increasing your own understanding of liberty.

Read was enough of a Nockian to dislike appearing on mass media like radio; and though speeches were a necessary evil in reaching people, he thought talks to large groups were inferior to one-on-one or tiny group discussion in selling the merits of liberty. The most effective proselytizing for the freedom philosophy, he insisted, was person to person, from someone whom the proposed student had reason to believe in, whose judgment and probity he had reason to trust. Speaking to big groups was at best a way to get people to begin to know him, as a preface to the face-to-face encounter. Woe betide someone sitting next to Leonard Read on an airplane, who wasn't in the mood to hear about how coercion could never generate creative activity or how various government officials ought more properly be called, say, secretary of external violence, secretary of interior violence, secretary of fraud, or secretary of predation.

Read's vision of the Remnant was not elitist; anyone could be a vital thought leader on some level. Reaching that person, whoever it might be, with the right ideas could have incalculable effects for the cause down the line. He raged at one of his early senior staffers who blew off a particular speech engagement, certain that the crowd would be too small to bother with. To Read, any and every person might end up being the most important person the freedom movement could ever reach.

Yet he did not have a Pollyannaish belief that just because some vital and important convert might be found *anywhere*, that this meant they were *everywhere*. He was still a Remnant man. "If we could not save our situation except as the millions come to master the complexities of economic, social, political and moral philosophy, I would not spend a moment of my life in this work—it would be like expecting a majority of adult Americans to become symphony composers or conductors."[29] He thought FEE needed to reach opinion leaders most of all. He was just more ecumenical than Hayek about who those opinion leaders might be, where they might be found, not just professors but bartenders; not just high government officials but bright high school kids. (Sometimes Read described FEE as a sort of grammar school of liberty; at other times as working on deep levels of inquiry that had to be dug and foundationed before mass education could begin.)

It did happen, over and over again, that a businessman would be dragged by a buddy to a luncheon speech at a local Kiwanis and find that the unheard-of words issuing from this curious evangel resonated with him, that some strange metaphor about how the dimmest light of truth could be seen even in what had been utter darkness, was telling him what he hadn't realized he already believed. And then later at the office he'd dictate a letter to that man in Irvington and get one back. It would contain some startling yet homey metaphor that made his thoughts about freedom seem sensible. And then he'd order one hundred copies of Henry Hazlitt's *Economics in One Lesson* to mail to all *his* business associates, lodgemates, relatives, and fraternity brothers. And then next time Leonard Read was coming through town, *he'd* be dragging along some unsuspecting soul and just maybe it would all happen again. Some FEE board members came to the foundation that way.

Then maybe the new recruit would set up a weekend seminar where Read and his crew would come out and talk all day and on into the evening, preferably in a retreat situation, far from the distractions of family and day-to-day business. It was best to invite only people already inclined in their direction. Read knew this kind of ideological immersion is more apt to make the cold prospect run screaming than snuggle closer to Irvington. And hopefully by the end that inclination would turn to a conviction that one must be an active part of the FEE team. Read was skilled at finding and making true believers. And it takes one to make one. One old FEE board member said of Read, "Another man speaking the same words might sound like a phony making a political speech, but not Leonard—it came straight out of his heart."

Read possessed that strange human power on which so much history, both exalted and regrettable, hinges—to tell you an idea or suggest a path and make you think that it is, however strange or troublesome, a very good idea that is worth acting on. The resort to charisma as explanation, however scientifically exasperating, is the only way to understand what might otherwise seem somewhat mysterious: how, from the mid-1940s aftermath of World War II until the early 1980s dawn of Reaganism, Read managed to gather over $1 million a year in donations from some of America's biggest businessmen in the name of "economic education" to talk of the mysteries of the creative spirit, to explain how the purpose of man on earth is to expand consciousness into harmony with infinite consciousness, to write and distribute curious passion plays. In his pamphlet *Conscience on the Battlefield,* Read imagines himself dying in a bloody mire in Korea and being visited by his conscience, who tells him murdering amid an army in the name of the state does not absolve him of his sins. No overseas communist military could really harm the United States, so he should abandon this "self-defense" excuse and delusion.

This darling of a very old-fashioned brand of American businessman was a nearly pacifist mystic, meditating on our ignorance of all but one trillionth of the universe's vibrations—a secular Zen libertarian saint who believed that the only way to change the world was through relentless self-education and self-understanding, not politics as commonly understood. In a speech commemorating FEE's twenty-fifth anniversary, the man whom Read hoped would succeed him (but who died before Read did), Wabash College economics professor Benjamin Rogge, was candid about how unsatisfying Read's message could seem on the surface. "I suspect (I know) that this aspect of FEE's thinking has been occasionally irritating to many of you and particularly to the more activist-minded of you. . . . Not only does Read not promise us a win in the *near* future; not only does he not guarantee us a win in the *distant* future; he has the unmitigated gall to tell us that we still don't even fully understand the game or how to recognize a win when we see one."[30]

Read had some interests besides liberty, including curling, golfing, roasting his own coffee beans, glazing his own porcelain plates, and testing out recipe after recipe on his wife Gladys and friends. He loved mailing recipes and the occasional kitchen tool to his far-flung correspondents. He tended to carve deep and lasting marks in the minds and souls of those he spoke to. Part of it came from the fact that he would neither argue nor pretend to agree when he didn't, but stick to his own principles with unshakable equanimity. But his power is not, alas, fully potent in most of the written words he left behind in his dozens of books, almost all collections of short essays he wrote for FEE, and published by FEE.

Read was no great intellectual. Some colleagues whispered scoffingly that you couldn't get Leonard to read anything longer than a handful of pages. Longtime FEE employee Bettina Bien Greaves says he was never comfortable with long talks on economics with the likes of Mises. He preferred the parable, the striking metaphor, the colorful and folksy example, to detailed economic argumentation. Read just wanted to offer his own way of understanding the freedom philosophy, in a manner more preacher than teacher. This very quality made him so valuable to his businessman supporters, who often used his simplified approach to proselytize to their employees. FEE supporter C. H. Shaver of U.S. Gypsum made his salaried supervisors and staff listen to record albums of Read explaining "the essence of Americanism" and "the clichés of socialism," while noting that hourly wage workers would probably be perplexed by words like *monetize, concomitant*, and *affluence*.

Read was a spiritual man without any particular allegiance to any Western form of honoring or propitiating that spirit. His sexual exploits, allegedly on a par with Wilt Chamberlain's, are the stuff of whispered legend among libertarians (and in the nature of such things, it's hard to be certain how much of it is indeed merely legend). But his unpatrician and impassioned sincerity won him enduring affection and admiration, bordering on awe, that has lasted beyond his own lifetime. In the *Reader's Digest* terms that Leonard might appreciate, he was the "Most Unforgettable Character" for many friends and associates. Fading beauties still get misty eyed remembering the wonders of Leonard. And many an activist libertarian adult, whether college professor or think tank executive, remembers the intense seriousness with which Mr. Read, or one of his staffers, weighed the questions and concerns of gawky teenagers trying to understand life, liberty, and the universe, and how that dedication to finding principled, consistent answers animated their own careers.

Leonard Read wrote a piece in the *Freeman* arguing against the right of striking airline workers to forcibly prevent anyone else from doing the jobs they chose to stop doing. It was a standard FEE piece. Objections to union violence and coercion were a common thread in the minds and writings of early libertarians. Read received an angry three-page diatribe from a labor union organizer, a fellow known as Whitey. Read replied carefully and with scrupulous politeness. The labor organizer wrote back to apologize for his rudeness. Read sent him a couple of FEE pamphlets, including F. A. Harper's *Why Wages Rise*. (The answer, you can bet, was not "union agitation.") Whitey was fascinated and wanted to know more. After a couple more rounds of correspondence, he told Read that he'd love to read anything the sage from Irvington might deign to send him, and include whatever invoice Read thought appropriate.

Soon they were fellow libertarians and good friends, and Whitey was no longer a labor organizer. Read revealed to him the simple wizardry he'd performed to nip their feuding in the bud. He'd *removed the tension*, given the angry man nothing to push against. When the former union man was hospitalized after an auto wreck, he wrote his friend Leonard to tell him that "you should see the interest my three doctors are showing in *our* philosophy."[31]

And that, many of his old friends would say, is the kind of man Leonard Read was.

"THE FIRST BOOK EVERYONE ON EARTH SHOULD READ."

FEE published works of many different types, from small pamphlets for racks in break rooms to hefty but understandable books such as Hazlitt's *Economics in One Lesson*; long studies on real-world topics like the Tennessee Valley Authority to abstract meditations on principle and simple homilies about right and wrong, and how government often did not know the difference. All rights were happily unreserved. FEE wanted anyone and everyone to reprint or spread their words for any reason they wished. *Reader's Digest* took them up on the offer so often they began to ask for advanced notice of what FEE was up to so they could be the first to reprint. In its first four years, FEE mailed out over 4 million bits of literature, saw its work appear in four hundred newspapers, and compiled a mailing list over thirty thousand strong.

FEE's thought spread through this unjealous casting bread upon the water attitude. Some idea might occur to Read from a comment made to him at a dinner party. It would feed into his essay in the next *Notes from FEE* newsletter, sent out to all who asked; a small-town newspaper editor, perhaps part of the Pulliam family or Hoiles family chains (two small publishers amenable to libertarian ideas), might reprint it on their editorial page, where it would be clipped and sent by a reader to an acquaintance in editorial at the *Saturday Evening Post*—who would reprint it. Finally, at a dinner party, Read would have someone sitting next to him hit the very interested Mr. Read with the same idea he had launched into the world a year earlier.

The writers FEE promoted most tenaciously in its early days were Bastiat and his modern acolyte, Henry Hazlitt. Over the years FEE gave away and sold half a million copies of Bastiat's *The Law* and Hazlitt's *Economics in One Lesson*—his 1946 updating of Bastiat's central insight of "things not seen" when it comes to government economic intervention. After reading it, you will understand why it is *not* a good thing that some hoodlum breaks a window. Of course it isn't. But some smarty-pants Keynesian might come along and convince you you're a sucker, because while you see only a broken window, *he* sees all the work created and money changing hands as the shop owner has to hire a glazier, who pays his workers, who use that money at their corner store, and so on.

But Hazlitt took it further. Sure, it makes work for the glazier, who then might use the money to buy some new piece of machinery, and so on. Anyone who sees those benefits might think themselves clever indeed for seeing behind surfaces to the secret economic boon of destruction. (Reading news reports in the aftermath of any natural disaster, you'll inevitably find this idea, this "broken window fallacy," as Hazlitt made it famous, presented quite seriously.) What they *don't* see are all the things—more inventory, perhaps, a newer lighting system, a more attractive awning—that the shopkeeper *would* have bought with the money he now has to spend on a window—and all the things that the people he patronized would have then done with that money, and down the line—while still having the window, doing its service, unshattered, yet contributing nothing obvious to the national economy.

The book was a simple but vivid lesson in looking at the extended effects of economic choices and human actions. Its libertarian implications lay in how it showed how the surface good that government intervention might seem to create has behind it, and down the line, other effects that cancel out or unbalance that seeming good. Taxing and spending is analogous to that broken window; you might see what government does with the money, but you don't see what the money's original holder *would* have done with it if the government hadn't taken it. Hazlitt's book, which is still in print, has for generations now served as a first eye-opening to the thoughts behind free market economics (as it did for this author), to seeing through the veil of good intentions and grandiose plans of state economic intervention. Robert Hessen, later a member of the inner circles of both Murray Rothbard and Ayn Rand, enthusiastically says "I regard it as the first book everyone on Earth should read. It was an incredible revelation."[32]

Although Rose Wilder Lane was a favorite of Read's, her book *The Discovery of Freedom* was out of print by her own desire. She planned to revise a book she saw as terribly flawed, but never did. A dedicated fan, Henry Grady Weaver, a General Motors employee, wrote a popularization of it, fixing some of what he saw as exaggerations or mistakes in her history, and published it as *The Mainspring of Human Progress* (1947). For decades, it was one of FEE's most widely distributed works, though it remained controversial because of its historical interpretations, particularly Lane's insistence on the libertarian qualities of high Muslim civilization in the Middle Ages. General Motors bought the book in bulk and gave it to all supervisory employees.

Anyone who cared enough about liberty to write FEE with a question got a detailed and intelligent answer, neither hostile nor condescending. Read was proud that hours of research and staff consultation often went into a single answer. Convinced that a lack of mutual understanding between town and gown threatened American education and the American economy, FEE sponsored college professors on six-week summer field trips to investigate the inner workings of participating businesses, to give sometimes uncomprehending eggheads a firsthand look at the factory floor, at the complications of the accountant's ledger.

Bettina Bien (who married Percy Greaves, another Mises follower in the FEE orbit) was Mises's most loyal American seminar participant and ran FEE's high school debate program, making sure libertarian analyses got to young forensicists across the nation. For one young libertarian, Williamson "Bill" Evers, writing to FEE for help in a debate regarding apartheid opened his eyes to fine gradations in the ideological spectrum he hadn't suspected. He had assumed FEE and *National Review* were mostly on the same side. He was surprised when the material from FEE was for unrestricted free markets with no truck for Boer sensitivities or fear of what mischief the unregulated Negro in South Africa might commit. In the late 1970s, Evers became editor of the left-outreach libertarian magazine *Inquiry.*[33]

For its first decade FEE's staff was dominated by a quartet of free market mavericks who had known each other at Cornell University. There was Paul Poirot, a former Office of Price Administration economist who got his doctorate from Cornell in 1940; Ivan Bierly, who taught agricultural economics there from 1938 to 1948; W. M. Curtiss, a marketing professor from 1936 to 1946; and Floyd Arthur Harper, known as "Baldy."[34] Harper was a young economist who had his eyes opened by Hayek and then dedicated his life to propagating the morality and propriety of unrestricted free markets, helping train and educate others in the catechism at various institutions. Harper, a man about whom his associates and colleagues had almost no complaints, was the most energetic and productive of FEE's early staffers. He was also the one who most quickly bridled at Read's management style. Before FEE published an essay, it would make the rounds of the entire senior staff for comments, often resulting in a morass of talk and debate and memos from which lots of written work never arose to see public print. Read would listen to other views before making an arbitrary decision.

This grated on his colleagues, who expected to see the writings they labored over published. People churned in and out of FEE freely in its first decade and a half, even though there were few professional options for libertarian agitators in that era. Harper and Ivan Bierly both went from FEE to the Volker Fund (a financer of libertarian causes, more on which below) in the mid-1950s; Dean Russell left to become a political adviser for the Ingersoll Milling Machine Company of Rockford, Illinois, run by a libertarian, and then to teach college, before returning later to FEE. By 1960 or so, the staff stabilized and remained mostly stable (some said stagnant) until Read's death.

Read is remembered as a secular saint of principle, friend to potentate and pauper, spreading the light in the darkness and in sweet intellectual comity with all liberty lovers. At the same time, Read annoyed close associates, lost many of them, and in some cases failed to lose them merely for lack of other comparable options. This type of thing is inevitable in a radical political movement made up of eccentrics with extraordinary self-confidence in their own intellectual judgments. Certainly the rest of the world wasn't reassuring them they were right, or even sane.

"THE COMMUNIST CONQUEST OF EASTERN EUROPE MUST NOW BE RECOGNIZED BY AMERICANS AS A *FAIT ACCOMPLI* "

Surveying the roots of the libertarian movement after Lane and Paterson but before Buckley's *National Review* is tricky. For the most part, the anti–New Deal coalition had not yet figured out who was who. From the beginnings of the self-conscious "conservative" movement in the postwar era, unmitigated love for free markets was not necessarily welcome. See, for example, Pulitzer Prize–winning poet (and son of a convicted Nazi conspirator) Peter Viereck's turn to political lucubration of a Burkean variety in his influential 1949 book *Conservatism Revisited*.[35] Viereck, contemptuous of Manchesterite laissez-faire, wanted to unite middling leftist and rightists for an international war against totalitarianism under the name "conservative." (Viereck is widely credited with the first use of that term in its contemporary postwar sense.) He, joined by many others calling themselves conservative (especially Russell Kirk, who in 1953 took over Viereck's role as leading self-consciously conservative intellectual), had only small, instrumental use for what they might call the soulless, traditionless machinations of the unrestricted market.

The beginnings and quick shifts of the story of *Human Events,* now unreservedly a journal of the right, limn the shape of the conservative-libertarian struggle as the cold war moved into gear. *Human Events* founder Felix Morley arose from the Brookings Institution and the *Washington Post* (where he was editor from 1933 to 1940), and Haverford College (a Quaker institution). He was not someone whom most movement conservatives would find congenial today, and not just because of those associations. As one of his last acts before he left the presidency of Haverford in 1945, he invited socialist presidential candidate Norman Thomas to be commencement speaker. He admired Thomas's "unflinching moral courage and independence which the college sought to inculcate."[36]

As the war wound down, Morley, a respected Washington insider, was offered a military government commission to help oversee postwar Europe and a Senate gig as chief of staff for postwar planning. He declined both offers in favor of an opportunity, suggested to him by freelance military journalist Frank Hanighen, to start a small newsletter in which he could express himself freely about how to guarantee the end of the war and secure a congenial aftermath, and bring American military might back to its own shores. With initial funding from Sun Oil's Joe Pew and a title taken from the Declaration of Independence, *Human Events* was launched in 1944.[37]

Morley shared with mainstream conservatives a belief that the glory of America's republican institutions demanded not just freedom but a rigorous civic virtue. He explored this idea in his most popular book, a libertarian favorite for decades though little read now (and out of print), *The Power in the People* (1949). That book resulted from one of the mid-1940s attempts by financiers of individualist causes to find *the book* that would make America come back around to its traditional devotion to liberty.

Though he had already begun working on it without his help, Morley received financing from Jasper Crane of DuPont, Rose Lane's faithful correspondent, to help complete *Power in the People.* The book was vetted by a squad of small-government superstars including

Leonard Read, J. Howard Pew, and Lane, whose "individualist enthusi-asms" Morley found useful, but whose "loquaciousness . . . perhaps ex-plained why a reputed love affair between her and King Zog of Albania had lapsed."[38]

Unlike Lane's world-historical and universalist vision in *Discovery of Freedom*, Morley in *Power* was a particularist for America. He did not necessarily believe that American republican institutions could work well in any culture; and he certainly did not believe it was any duty of America to ensure that they did. He tried to show the ideological and historical roots of small, divided government, painting the anti–New Deal coalition as the true patriots, keeping alive traditional American virtue. He insisted that American republicanism must be based in Christian religious virtues, but he remained an old-fashioned liberal, with no role imagined for the state in enforcing such virtue, either at home or abroad. Morley did, though, lack the firm background in Austrian-style free market economics that many of his friends had, and seemed to think that state action against monopoly and concentrated economic power is often warranted if not always prudent. He even thought nationalization of industry might sometimes make economic sense, though perhaps not political sense.[39]

While working on *Power*, Morley realized he was increasingly at log-gerheads with his partners in *Human Events*, Hanighen and budding right-wing publishing magnate Henry Regnery. When the journal was launched in 1944, with Morley as the main essayist and Hanighen as on-the-ground reporter in Washington and business manager, it fo-cused on laying the intellectual groundwork for a sensible peace and a stable postwar Europe. Other contributors included William Henry Chamberlin, Herbert Hoover (far more of an individualist, and far more popular among the libertarian minded, as a disgraced ex-president then as a president), and Norman Thomas. Albert Jay Nock, in his last year of life, became excited about the magazine, seeing it potentially as a new *Freeman*. It found 5,000 subscribers in its first four years. But by 1947, especially after an eye-opening experience at the first Mont Pelerin meeting (an international organization of free market thinkers, more on which below), Morley could no longer abide by Hanighen's increasing cold warriorism. Hanighen, Morley notes, "was particularly critical of my belief that the Communist conquest of

Eastern Europe must now be recognized by Americans as a *fait ac-compli*. This, in the unanimous opinion of the Germans at Mont Pelerin, was the only alternative to the unthinkable prospect of another major war."[40]

Richard Nixon tried to recruit Morley as a journalistic witness to the takedown of accused Russian spy Alger Hiss; again frustrating Hanighen, Morley decided *Human Events* should steer clear of that story. By 1950, Hanighen and Morley realized that Hanighen's desire to focus on the overseas communist threat and Morley's on defending American liberty at home made them unfit partners. Morley gave in and allowed Hanighen and Regnery to buy him out, and *Human Events* became a leading journal of Who Lost China?, communist hunting, and Soviet baiting. As Morley noted in his memoirs nearly three decades later, "In retrospect I see [his split from *Human Events*] as symptomatic of that which has come to divide the conservative movement in the United States. Frank and Henry . . . moved on to associate with the far Right in the Republican Party. My position remained essentially 'Libertarian,' though it is with great reluctance that I yield the old terminology of 'liberal' to the socialists."[41]

Morley notes that after jettisoning the baggage of his isolationist libertarianism, *Human Events*'s circulation soared.

"THE FACT THAT HOILES IS NOT IN JAIL IS A HIGHLY ENCOURAGING TESTIMONY TO THE CURRENT AMERICAN SCENE."

Early financial backers of FEE included the Earhart Foundation, the Volker Fund, the Mott Foundation, and an obscure newspaper from south of Read's old chamber stomping grounds, the Santa Ana *Register*, from the heart of Orange County. The *Register* was owned and operated by an eccentric anarchist newspaper magnate named Raymond Cyrus Hoiles, a compact man with a face often puckered quizzically (Why? was one of his mantras). Known for legendary physical and mental toughness, a multimillionaire in tattered off-the-rack suits from Penney's who carried a worn briefcase, Hoiles was the kind of dedicated, unheeding, and unreconstructed eccentric whose destiny is to be called "crusty."

In his first bout of newspaper ownership in his home state of Ohio, Hoiles exposed crooked bidding by local government and contractors. Soon bombs started going off in his house and were found attached to his car. Although the perpetrators were never apprehended, Hoiles always suspected the crooked contractor, who also went into the newspaper business in Hoiles's towns to spite him and ended up owning one of Hoiles's papers. Hoiles moved his family to Southern California, and in 1935 bought an interest in the *Register* of Santa Ana.[42] Orange County became known, to a large degree thanks to Hoiles himself, as "nut country," the hotbed of the rightest of the right wing, the source of Barry Goldwater's primary victory in California in 1964. Orange County is an idyllic land of fruit groves, gorgeous beaches, and tract houses in planned suburbs carved out of rolling hills—and a hotbed of radical dissatisfaction with the size and direction of the state fueled by, as cheap irony would have it, an aerospace and military economy dependent on Big Government to thrive.[43]

Hoiles's *Register* became the newspaper of record for Orange County and flagship of a minichain, mostly small dailies scattered around the Midwest and Southwest. No Hearst or Gannett or Scripps, Hoiles named his company after what he valued most in the world: Freedom Newspapers (now Freedom Communications). His devotion to his principles exceeded his devotion to his own reputation. When he was once arrested for speeding, his own papers reported it on the front page.[44]

Hoiles was a hard-core modern libertarian before anyone knew what one was, before Read and FEE had begun codifying their beliefs and linking their far-flung adherents. He characterized his belief as the "single standard of conduct," meaning that government shouldn't have the power or right to do anything an individual doesn't have the power or right to do. This means no taxation, not even for supposedly "necessary" services. Hoiles once wrote, "Any time a man has to pay for something he does not want because of the initiating of force by the government, he is, to that degree, a slave."[45]

In 1944, Hoiles paid to freshly translate and publish some Bastiat classics. During World War II he was one of the rare newspaper publishers to editorialize against the internment of Americans of Japanese descent. "Few, if any," he wrote,

> ever believed that evacuation of the Japanese was constitutional. It
> was a result of emotion and fright rather than being in harmony
> with the Constitution and the inherent rights that belong to all cit-
> izens. . . . we should make every effort possible to correct the error
> as rapidly as possible . . . convicting people of disloyalty to our
> country without having specific evidence against them is too for-
> eign to our way of life and too close akin to the kind of govern-
> ment we are fighting. . . . we are on the road to losing our
> democracy.[46]

He also believed in ending all immigration restrictions or quotas.

Beyond being a dedicated and premature civil libertarian and loving French classical liberalism, Hoiles was an earthy and simple man and a notorious union-busting anarchist cuss, who'd thrust himself into picket lines surrounding his property to tell the union boys why they were all wet. If people do *not* cross a picket line, he thundered, "it is only a question of time until they are taken over by a Hitler, Stalin, or Mussolini."[47] Unions hated Hoiles and tried to bring down this crazy old man who refused to deal with them and thundered against them from his paper pulpit. (He was mad at Hazlitt's *Freeman* for being printed by a union printer.) He'd notoriously engage anyone and everyone in his company, from editors to janitors, in nerve-wracking sessions of "close reasoning," his favorite kind of talk—the rigorous discussion of the nature of man and liberty, with a dogged insistence that his interlocutors define their terms precisely and continuously. If he stumbled across a bright young libertarian mind (more frequently, attracted by the light of the *Register*, they'd find him), he'd try to find a place for him in his company. When a failed former protégé of Ayn Rand's, Thaddeus Ashby, read about Hoiles in *Time* and sent him some articles echoing the Hoilesian line on education, Hoiles hired him. Then he sent Ashby, who was recuperating from tuberculosis, to the congenial climes of Colorado Springs to write editorials for the Freedom Newspaper there, the *Colorado Springs Gazette-Telegraph*.[48]

If Hoiles hated anything worse than unions, it was public schools (though his own children attended them). He preferred whorehouses, which, he'd point out, were voluntary, while public schools were not. Schools were the root of every other evil in our statist culture. As long as the government grabs us when our minds are fresh and unformed and forces us through a twelve-year indoctrination of its own design, he felt, forcing our parents and everyone else to pay for it, how can American kids grow up to understand the true meaning of our Declaration of Independence or Constitution, whose spirits are grossly violated by public schools? Hoiles floated an open challenge to school officials in any city with a Freedom paper: publicly debate the propriety of public schools in a format where they must answer every question asked. Hoiles was certain no self-respecting person could stand up in public and defend the tyranny of the public schools, and despite his $500 offer no one ever did.

It maddened Hoiles that Read and FEE shied away from open assaults on the public schools. Hoiles saw it as a sign of cowardice and fear of stepping outside the boundaries of acceptable opinion. He harangued Mises for years over the old Austrian economist's rejection of voluntarily funded competing defense agencies as a substitute for coercive government police powers, sad that the great libertarian would "continue to advocate any form of socialism, or any form of tyranny. And when you are advocating that the free market is not the better way of protecting men's lives and property, I think you are seriously in error."[49]

Hoiles had personal grudges against government as well. He blamed FDR and the end of the gold standard for lowering the value of a contract he made for the sale of a newspaper in 1931 that stretched out payments through to 1935, across the New Deal's great gold divide. The feds fined him for violating wartime wage control laws by giving an illegal *raise*. Hoiles once refused to stand in the courtroom of a judge who refused to define and defend his values, and was willing to take a contempt charge too. The judge wearily let it ride.

Old R.C. was too eccentric to escape the occasional, sneering notice from the mainstream press. The *New York Times* in 1964, while granting that *maybe* other people walked the earth with his curious views, such as abolishing licensing laws and compulsorily supported police and fire departments, "none has the combination of status, wealth and possible public influence of Mr. Hoiles."[50] By the mid-1960s, he was reaching 300,000 readers with his Freedom Newspapers and had a net worth of around $50 million. (By the early twenty-first century, with R.C. dead, his company, still family owned, was worth nearly $2 billion.)

For fellow old-school newspaper magnates, some still holding firm to anti–New Deal verities, Hoiles was the "worseniam," defined by columnist and Freedom Chain employee D. R. Segal as the guy you can point to and say, you think we're outrageous? Hoiles is "worseniam." Segal notes that many old-school publishers, those who owed allegiance to themselves and their families rather than stockholders or corporate paymasters, told him privately that they agree with crazy old R.C. but *couldn't* say what he says—unions would strike, advertisers would cancel, subscribers would dump them, economic apocalypse would be inevitable. Yet Hoiles's chain, and his income, kept growing, despite his eccentricities.

Hoiles corresponded with his fellow libertarians and sparred with most of them. Each stance he took appeared to arise full-grown in his own head, though he admired predecessors from Bastiat to Lane to Mises, and would often make his column—which he wrote daily for decades—consist of long quotes from authors he admired. That was a blessing to anyone who tried to read them. An ex-employee who dearly loved the old man and his philosophy couldn't help but note that "his writings are about the most cumbersome, unwieldy and unreadable in print. . . . it was a good thing that R.C. owned some newspapers because no independent publisher would ever accept anything he wrote. Nor, so far as I know, has anyone ever done so."[51]

The Hoilesian tenet that most amazed his audience (and even fellow libertarian Leonard Read) was that compulsory taxation for any reason is not to be countenanced. When asked how government can be supported without compulsory taxation, Hoiles would (quite accurately) reply that we can't seem to support it *with* compulsory taxation. In his early days, he would say his morality and politics were based on the Golden Rule and the Ten Commandments. His obligation to hector his readers and the world on matters like the crime of "gun-run education" and any interference with freely competing currency was biblical. His reading of Ezekiel told him that he would bear the burden of his fellow citizens' statist sins if he didn't call them on it, as continuously and sharply as possible. He stressed root principles and their ruthless application and once nudged Leonard Read, "the man who sanctions public education has no basis for opposing compulsory health insurance."[52]

Murray Rothbard summed up the spirit of almost awed admiration Hoiles engendered in many libertarians, contemplating this wild radical's wild success as a businessman, and in the media business at that, where his opinions were reaching hundreds of thousands daily: "The fact that Hoiles is not in jail is a highly encouraging testimony to the current American scene."[53]

"I HAVE NO FEAR AT ALL OF THE MOSCOW APPARATUS BUT, RATHER . . . MY OWN INADEQUACY."

Leonard Read was generally friendly to everyone else in what was known by many, even sometimes among themselves at the time, as the extreme right. But he always knew that his objectives differed from the standard right wingers', the people who were beginning to think of themselves in the early 1950s, after the success of books by Peter Viereck and Russell Kirk, as "the conservative movement." By 1956, Read had noticed Kirk condemning the likes of him and FEE as "ossified Benthamites" because of their dedication to untrammeled liberty above rooted tradition-based order.[54] The terminology was loose, and the battle lines had not yet been drawn. Those within the anti–New Deal coalition often referred to themselves as "conservative" in those days, though the term "libertarian" was already in use as well. The anarchist-leaning ones were toying with the term "voluntaryist," derived from Auberon Herbert—or "100 percent Voluntaryist." Read never seemed completely satisfied with the term "libertarian" in the 1950s either. He called what he was pushing the "freedom philosophy" more often than not, and at times floated such potential substitutes as the "willing exchange economy" for the idea FEE stood for.

His rightist friends pursued certain activities that seemed pointless
to Read, such as exposing, protesting, and boycotting supposedly anti-
American or anti-market college textbooks. When asked candidly, he
would privately warn associates off of such groups as Fred Clark's
American Economic Foundation, which had a similar strategy as
FEE—publishing and distributing pamphlets and articles on the benefits of free markets—but on what Read saw as a lower intellectual
level; Merwin Hart, of the National Economic Council (a market
propaganda outfit which had Nock, and later Lane, writing its book
review newsletter), who infected his free market thought with anti-
Semitism; and, later, the John Birch Society (JBS), the legendary es-
piers of communist conspiracy everywhere, up to, and including the
Eisenhower White House.[55]

Now Bircher economics were in the mainstream of the FEE vision—the JBS American Opinion bookstores across the country sold
Mises's books in large numbers.[56] Still, Birch leader Robert Welch's
obsession with communist conspiracies and the tight control he exercised over his organization and its members vitiated any benefits that
might arise from the group's understanding of free market economics,
in Read's mind. He explained his attitude toward the JBS to a friend
and supporter in the guise of Leonard the humble Zen monk. Welch,
Read wrote, "sees a communist under every bed and blames our
whole socialistic mess on the Moscow apparatus. . . . No doubt your
friend, Read, is just as obsessed as is Bob Welch, but my obsession takes
a different turn from his. I have no fear at all of the Moscow apparatus
but, rather, my own mind, my own inadequacy."[57]

Read saw *Human Events* post-Morley as too militaristic and protectionist for his taste and understood the Crusade for Freedom, an attempt at a popular grassroots market advocacy group, as too
vituperative. Any linkage of the freedom philosophy with a mindless
patriotism, a simple Americanism, was not for Read. *Reader's Digest*
once asked him to contribute to a regular feature entitled "The Day I
Was Proudest to Be an American." Read declined. His sense of pride
had nothing to do with national boundaries, and he noted wryly that
there were plenty of devotees of Earl Warren and Joe Stalin among his
fellow Americans, so how proud could that make him feel? Neither
was he a Republican partisan, even before the 1952 Taft disappointment that turned many old right types away from the GOP in disgust.

For a while he was a confirmed nonvoter, though he confessed in his journal that it was slow going convincing most of his friends on that point. (He later admitted that in 1956 he wrote in a vote for right-wing third party candidate T. Coleman Andrews, a former IRS commissioner who turned radically antitax and had sought advice from FEE seven years earlier on how to be a successful crusader for restoring lost liberties.)

In the early 1950s, Read began to realize that he was surrounded by anarchists. And it worried him. Anarchism, he was certain, wasn't correct. Government was not merely a necessary evil, much less, as Baldy Harper had come to think by the early 1950s, a completely unnecessary one.[58] It was vital to human society, when kept to its proper limits, and Read thought it important to explain that, mostly to his fellow libertarians.

He worked on a manuscript that he circulated in draft form to most of his fellow libertarians, originally called "In Defense of Government." He intended to put his thoughts on paper regarding the subject of anarchism versus government and to stimulate education and debate within the movement. In 1954, he issued it as an official FEE publication under the title *Government: An Ideal Concept*. He explained upfront that it had become necessary to defend government.

> The reason has to do with the ineffectiveness of one's anti-statist allies. For it is an observed fact that numerous students of liberty, particularly those who became extremely devoted to their cause, falsely reason past properly limited government to the abolition of all formal government—as though limited government were nothing more than a convenient compromise for ideological weak-hearts who have no stomach for the whole truth. In short, some students of liberty arrive at philosophical anarchy and, in so doing, may well lose their effectiveness as libertarians.[59]

The short book contains examples of Read's bizarre energy metaphors and thoughts,[60] and explains that since we need to protect our lives, and lack the ability to do so by ourselves, we must of necessity ally with our fellows for mutual defense, with everyone treated equally.[61] Read explains that it can be proper, even on libertarian grounds, to pay forced taxes, as long as they are used *only* for an equally applied protective service.

We are all obligated to pay taxes for mutual defensive services because

> others have a moral right to protect themselves against anyone
> who would burden their energy . . . against anyone who would
> siphon off their livelihood. A person who by failure to attend to
> his own obligation, thereby loading it onto all others, engages in
> an inhibitive action against the society of which he is a member.
> He is not returning an equivalent for benefits and services ren-
> dered—this equivalent being an equitable tax. Thus the agency of
> society must, in justice, collect from him. This collection does not,
> therefore, classify as aggressive force, but rather as repellent or de-
> fensive force.[62]

Because of man's inherently social nature, Read maintained, man-as-
society can morally do things that man-as-individual cannot—as long
as it is to protect "society" from freeloaders on its "energy." Baldy
Harper likened what Read did in this book to building a grand ship
named *Liberty* and then setting sail—after boring holes in the bottom
and giving the majority an augur and carte blanche to bore however
many more holes they have a mind to. One old friend from his chamber of commerce days wryly noted that Read now knew what it felt
like to be on the receiving end of very Read-like jabs for the crime of
weakening the case for freedom.

Read's apostasy on forced taxation disturbed many of his friends,
board members, and colleagues. They were especially annoyed that he
chose to publish the finished product under FEE's imprimatur (after
apparently telling some of them that he had no such intention).
Read's radical associates were disappointed and outraged over a book
that, among other things, stood firmly against any government role
whatsoever in issuing money or providing education. But that just
wasn't hard-core enough for many libertarians of the time.

His anarchist staffers were disappointed that Read did not permit
their opposing views to similarly appear under FEE's aegis, and that he
hid attacks on *Government: An Ideal Concept* mailed to FEE and addressed to all of them. Harper hinted that the pamphlet and its aftermath made him hate Read briefly. Read's attitude toward taxation
made any protestations on his part that he was a true libertarian but

bitter gall. "You can define and redefine 'justice' any way you wish. . . . but so long as you give another party the right to tax you under a monopoly power to govern you, they are empty words indeed." But his emotional reaction turned into "a sadness akin to losing a friend. A person with rare potential . . . is frantically riding a horse in a direction . . . that he does not perceive. . . . What can be done with [Read's theory of government] to enslave me makes my bald hair curl! If I am going to be enslaved, I don't want it to be done by my friends."[63]

Eventually Read stopped reading critiques of *Government: An Ideal Concept*; his heart had hardened to anarchistic arguments. Read violated what some purist libertarians saw as a cardinal rule: Although you were not obligated to take libertarianism to its farthest reaches in all your public pronouncements, you at least must ensure that nothing you write directly violates the principle of noninitiation of force. Thaddeus Ashby (then writing editorials for Hoiles's Freedom Newspapers in Colorado Springs) wrote a scabrous fifty-page attack on Read's book that Hoiles circulated among the boys. Hoiles himself accused Read of evasion. "I know of no person who will answer questions without evasion who so believes [in forcing a man to pay for protection]."[64] This gang of businessmen Read had gathered around him thought nothing of taking the time to dictate to bewildered secretaries five-page letters back and forth, chewing over recondite issues of social philosophy, because they were certain that a proper understanding of such issues, for them, their children, their loved ones, their community, was vital to the nation's survival. Precious few of them were left who understood or cared.

"THE VOLKER PEOPLE LEARNED THAT I ORDERED SOME RUSSIAN DRESSING ON MY SALAD . . . AND WILL HAVE NO MORE TO DO WITH ME."

During the early FEE era and throughout the 1950s and early 1960s, the largest and most dedicated financier of libertarian causes was an obscure charitable organization called the Volker Fund. And the Volker Fund did what it did because of a man who can be thought of as the

Ur-source for the funding of American libertarianism, Loren "Red" Miller. Miller was a toiler in the field of privately funded "good government" research foundations, at (among other such organizations) the Bureau of Governmental Research in Detroit under the tutelage of Lent D. Upson. Miller, a hard-drinking, unpretentious man with a disarming sense of humor and an almost magical ability to win the deepest trust from the wealthiest of men, inherited the helm of the bureau from Upson on his 1944 retirement, and turned most of his energy to spreading an inchoate modern libertarian doctrine among friends and colleagues. Miller made some key converts, although his own libertarianism may have been an Athena-like accretion straight from his own brow.

Old associates speculate that Miller's years of examining, from a citizen's perspective, the problems of government management may have led him to decide that an efficient, well-run government was impossible. All his hires at the Bureau of Government Research had to read a ten-plus page, single-spaced memo that set forth the libertarian gospel according to Miller, and agree to use that document as the rudder for their work. Among the young libertarian firebrands Miller brought on and tutored in Detroit were Herbert Cornuelle, who became Leonard Read's first right-hand man at FEE, and William Johnson, who later edited the religious-libertarian journal *Faith and Freedom*.

Miller got around in the early libertarian movement; he advised everyone, met everyone, and made sure everyone met everyone else who might be able to educate or support them. He became a trusted adviser to major foundations funding libertarian and right-wing causes, including the Earhart and Relm Foundations (both started by H. B. Earhart) and the Volker Fund. It was Miller who helped Read come up with the money to buy the Irvington-on-Hudson mansion as FEE's headquarters. And it was Miller who introduced Hayek, whom he glommed onto as a treasure for the small-government cause during his first American visit post-*Serfdom*, to Harold Luhnow, who helmed the Volker Fund.

Luhnow was a businesslike Baptist running the charitable foundation set up by his uncle, William Volker. Volker had been proprietor of a successful Kansas City company that wholesaled material for home interiors. (Luhnow and Volker had been part of the eventually successful campaign to overthrow that city's notorious Pendergast machine.)[65] The Volker Fund from the 1940s to early 1960s was the prime paymaster for libertarian causes, spending about $1 million a year to search out and support carriers of the individualist flame, the only self-conscious forger of a libertarian intellectual movement with cash to burn. Volker Fund employee Herb Cornuelle, who first worked for Miller and then for Read at FEE before ending up at the fund, wrote a Boy Scout–dull biography of the famously reticent philanthropist Volker, called *Mr. Anonymous,* that shows little evidence of Volker's passionate interest in a strictly limited state.[66] The political turn in the Volker Fund's interests seemed to come from Luhnow, who ran the fund after Volker's death, via Loren Miller.

Because of Miller's influence on Luhnow, the Volker Fund became the driving force and money behind sending a squad of American economists and popularizers of libertarianism to the first meeting of Hayek's Mont Pelerin Society (more on which below). Most importantly for the future of libertarian ideas in America, Miller convinced Luhnow to use Volker Fund money to pay for American university berths for the two great Austrian libertarian economists, Mises and Hayek.

Miller's influence went beyond just Volker. In the early days of another big money organization, the Earhart Foundation, when the family was torn over what causes it ought to support, Miller arranged for Leonard Read and Felix Morley—whose establishment credentials were impeccable—to meet with one of Earhart's skeptical daughters to convince her that libertarian economic education was worthy of Earhart money, even though the daughter was on record as opposing the "radical right."[67]

Miller's friendships with Earhart and Luhnow were the most significant ones in the first phase of the American libertarian movement because of the wealth the two men controlled through their charitable foundations. Those foundations became vital supporters of antigovernment and individualist causes, though only Volker stayed on a mostly recognizable libertarian line. Earhart became a more standard right-wing funding source as the years went by.

The Volker Fund sponsored conferences, had books published and distributed to libraries, and built connections and networks among the scattered devotees of a hated philosophy. In this way it gave the nascent movement self-consciousness and intellectual depth, and helped find the few far-flung libertarians, bring them together, and make sure they got to work where they'd be most useful.

The mission and tactics of the Volker Fund were informed by Hayek's famous essay "The Intellectuals and Socialism." In it Hayek pointed out that socialism began as an intellectual movement before it became a mass one. Despite socialist rhetoric to the contrary, it did not arise from an angry, aggrieved working class defending its interests. Hayek explained how a class of people he identifies as "secondhand dealers in ideas" dictates ideology to the masses by a process "almost automatic and irresistible." And that class of people in the 1940s, not through "evil intentions" but through "honest convictions," was socialistic.[68]

To the extent that capitalism's defenders fail to recognize and understand the reasons why socialists are socialists, they will fail to convince them. Hayek analyzes how intellectuals tend to apply interesting, even truthful ideas from the cutting edge of science to areas where they don't belong, a phenomenon Hayek condemns as "scientism," helping form a general "climate of opinion" to which intellectuals try to fit and against which they judge every other idea that comes their way. And that climate in the 1940s was a socialist one, certain that the intelligently planned is always superior to the seeming accidents of the spontaneous order of free markets whose glories Hayek analyzes and praises. Libertarian intellectuals also had working against them the fact that they sought improvements and furtherance in an already largely successful nineteenth-century liberal program—thus their ideas "can have none of the glamour of a new invention."[69]

Richard Cornuelle, Herbert Cornuelle's younger brother, who worked for the Volker Fund in various capacities for most of the 1950s, recalls that Hayek essay was "like the Holy Bible." But like the Bible, it was sometimes difficult to authoritatively parse. "I used to think it said take a hard, unyielding line, then later I realized it said that's what we *shouldn't* do."[70] Cornuelle's confusion is understandable. It arises from a tension in Hayek between stressing the importance of remaining intellectually open, of never judging by "conformity to a fixed set of opinion" (an idea he presented on the next to last page of the essay), and the importance of sticking to principle no matter how remote its chances of implementation in the real world, of bravely arguing for full freedom rather than the weak-tea ameliorism of "reasonable freedom of trade" and "relaxation of controls" (an idea Hayek presented on the last page of the essay). Hayek seems to say, be radical in pushing the limits of what you think is right, but always be open to the idea that you may be wrong. That indeed made for a paradoxical action program for the likes of foundation funders.

The idea implicit in Hayek's essay—which has been a dominant strategy for libertarian organizations and funders ever since Volker days—is that intellectual change occurs via ideas percolating down from a top layer of intellectual elites—mostly in academia—to what Hayek calls "secondhand dealers in ideas"—journalists, ministers, secondary and elementary teachers, even artists—and then down to the masses at the base.

In the 1950s intellectual milieu it could be seen as unwise and unsafe to openly declare allegiance to this curious set of libertarian ideas they were promoting, and consequently the Volker Fund and its program officers—at different times Herb and Richard Cornuelle and then later Kenneth Templeton and Ivan Bierly—worked craftily, in the shadows, searching for people to support. Unlike most charitable foundations, Volker didn't have people coming to it and looking for support—the ideas it was pushing were so alien then that the fund had to go out and find people worthy of its support. (In line with founder William Volker's wishes, the fund kept its support activities out of the public eye.) The Volker Fund helped people in different ways, at different levels; for masters like Mises and Hayek, fully funded academic berths; for lower-level promising professors, seminars where they could meet, hear each other's ideas, hone them off of each other; maybe get enough money for a year off to write a book, for which Volker would help subsidize publication and distribution; for students, fellowship aid to study at the feet of libertarian masters.[71] Volker helped keep libertarians such as Murray Rothbard and Rose Wilder Lane (and fusionist conservative Frank Meyer, part of William Buckley's *National Review* team) afloat with paying gigs reading books and journals, and letting the fund know about any promising articles and thinkers.

Some academics Volker approached rebuffed it haughtily—I'm not *that* kind of a thinker, sir! But more commonly, Richard Cornuelle remembers, Volker encountered a "tearful recognition that there *was* someone else out there [who believed in libertarianism]—everyone thought they were the last one." These efforts to spin webs of communication among this scattered band of ideological outliers, helping them find each other, thrilled Volker's employees, and they all remember it with great affection decades later. It got ingrown, admits Cornuelle, but was still "very gratifying. We were a delightful bunch, all serious, dedicated, interesting misfits."[72]

As obscure as it was in its time, the Volker Fund had its monied hands on the future's pulse, at least in economics, the area where libertarian ideas have always had their greatest spread and success. Its directory of active contacts, intellectuals Volker supported and could rely on to appear at sponsored conferences, included six future Nobel laureates in economics—Hayek, Milton Friedman, Ronald Coase, James Buchanan, Gary Becker, and George Stigler. The field of law and economics, an intellectually rich though controversial field of economics in the past few decades (the field in which Ronald Coase worked to receive his 1991 Nobel in economics), was launched under Volker auspices, with its support of Friedman's brother-in-law Aaron Director, as he started the first academic journal devoted to the portmanteau field in 1958. The Volker Fund also paid for student fellowships to study in the new program at the University of Chicago.

Volker Fund people were trying to craft a libertarian identity distinct from the larger right-wing conservative movement, and they worried that people didn't understand the difference between its brand of free market radical libertarianism and the free market views of the NAM/right-wing/business elite crowd. For one thing, the libertarians *really meant it* about free markets, completely and totally with no exceptions, but that wasn't enough somehow. Cornuelle thought Volker had to boldly stake out ground distinct from that of a standard postwar big business apologist. They contemplated foregrounding aspects of their libertarian intellectual project such as attacks on the medical monopoly and occupational licensing, and on business subsidies and tariffs, to distinguish themselves.[73]

The stern demand for libertarian bona fides on the part of the people and causes they supported did make the Volker Fund seem less than intellectually open and honest to some. Revisionist historian

Harry Elmer Barnes, in advising a colleague who sought some Volker support, warned him he "should make it clear that he does not believe in public schools, highways, police departments and other evil statist enterprises! . . . the Volker people learned that I ordered some Russian dressing on my salad on a trip to the West Coast in 1919 and will have no more to do with me."[74]

"THE ROOT OF THE WHOLE MODERN DISASTER IS PHILOSOPHICAL AND MORAL."

Ayn Rand spent much of the second half of the 1940s working in Hollywood, fighting quixotic battles for individualist principles while gestating what was to become her magnum opus, the final concretization of her philosophy and aesthetic, *Atlas Shrugged*.

One of her projects was an aborted propaganda film about the invention of the atomic bomb. She agreed to work on it only after convincing her boss, producer Hal Wallis, that the film's message had to be that only free men in a free society could have invented the atom bomb. Its technological ingenuity made it a victory over brute force by men of the mind. If state power was ultimately the cause of victory, she asked, why then didn't the more stringently state-managed Nazi Germany invent the bomb?[75]

Rand also plunged into the bubbling cold war ferment over communist influence in Hollywood. While she firmly opposed government censorship and even official industry codes, she wrote *Screen Guide for Americans* for the Motion Picture Alliance for American Ideals, a Hollywood anticommunist group, with advice for those who wanted to make sure their films didn't, intentionally or not, support communism. Its thirteen points of advice were:

> 1. Don't take politics lightly. 2. Don't smear the free enterprise system. 3. Don't smear industrialists. 4. Don't smear wealth. 5. Don't smear the profit motive. 6. Don't smear success. 7. Don't glorify failure. 8. Don't glorify depravity. 9. Don't deify "the common man." 10. Don't glorify the collective. 11. Don't smear the independent

man. 12. Don't use current events carelessly. 13. Don't smear American political institutions.[76]

Rand didn't limit her denunciations to films containing direct pro-Soviet propaganda. Her keen sense of the dark implications behind seemingly innocuous attitudes led her to excoriate the multiple-Oscar-winning *The Best Years of Our Lives* (1946), a tale of the abuse heaped on a returning World War II hero. The movie is antibusinessman and anticapitalist, she snarled, because it denounced a banker for refusing a loan to a vet because the vet lacked collateral. It was also, she argued, unforgivably anti-anticommunist because it portrays an obnoxious character as simultaneously anti-Soviet, antiblack, and anti-Jewish, thus linking anti-Sovietism with racism and pro-Nazism. She notoriously testified before the House Un-American Activities Committee (HUAC) in October 1947. Rand wanted to stick to what she saw as deeper and more important issues, including her attack on *Best Years of Our Lives*. That "was the big hit of the period and the movie I particularly wanted to denounce. . . . It was much more important to show the serious propaganda about America—not some musical about Soviet Russia [1944's *Song of Russia*] that would not fool anybody, and that had failed at the box office. . . . But the Congressmen told me that they would not dare come out against a movie about an armless veteran—there would be a public furor against them."[77]

Rand agonized over her HUAC experience and ultimately concluded that "it was a very dubious undertaking. I think that legally and constitutionally they had the right only to ask factual questions, such as party membership and Communist penetration of organizations. If their focus was to expose communism, it had to be done ideologically—but it's improper for a government agency to do it."[78] She thought that giving communists an opportunity to publicly answer or evade the question of being communists did not per se violate their freedom of speech, since they had no right to be communists and avoid the consequences of people disapproving of that fact.[79]

Her first attempt at a huge project after *Fountainhead* was a nonfiction treatise on morality, to be called *The Moral Basis of Individualism*.[80] She was bored by the task and realized quickly that to her style of thinking, a theory of morality unmoored by a fully fleshed out metaphysics and epistemology wouldn't work. Her conclusions on those subjects became the backbone of her next and last great work of fiction.

A Rand essay that touched on these same topics, "Textbook of Americanism" (appearing in *Vigil,* a magazine for screenwriters, in 1946), thrilled the scattered gang of early libertarians in FEE's orbit. Leonard Read noted admiringly that her simple and unobjectionable principle that no one ought to initiate physical force against another would, if applied "to present-day practices . . . be shocking to many persons. What a repeal of laws and decrees this would mean!"[81] The individualist business community mostly loved this fearless, impassioned Russian novelist, who gave a soaring and exalted voice to their labor, which others did not love them for and which even they sometimes darkly suspected was not the highest ideal to which they might aspire.

The love some businessmen felt for her wasn't entirely reciprocated. Rand was becoming more certain that her approach to politics had little in common with most of the so-called conservatives she met. They weren't consistent enough; they relied too much on religion and tradition, while Rand had already concluded that only a thoroughgoing devotion to reason could firmly ground a belief in individual liberty. She admired Read's mentor, Mullendore of SoCal Edison, and paid him what was for her the ultimate intellectual compliment: He was "the only businessman that I know of—then or in fact now—who was completely uncompromising. He was for free enterprise, laissez-faire, with no middle of the road, none of that conservative compromising."[82]

But Mullendore was a rare and shining jewel in Rand's gimlet eye. Hayek, for example, was to Rand "real poison"[83] who does "more good to the communist cause than to ours."[84] Mises and Hazlitt, though friends, were in many ways fools in her eyes, with their utilitarian ethic, their deeply mistaken belief that morality was essentially social, only mattering in interactions with other people.[85] To Rand, every choice, even if you were living alone on a desert island, has moral implications. The desert island is where man needs a moral code the most—that code being "*rational control* of himself and his actions . . . the rational choice of his purpose and how to achieve it."[86]

The business interests then dominating the conservative movement earned Rand's vituperation through what she saw as personal slights. She complained to Isabel Paterson about how, early in *The Fountainhead*'s publishing history, "it looked as if the book had been most efficiently murdered—and none of our goddamn 'conservatives' would lift a finger about it. . . . I've done more for free enterprise than the NAM [National Association of Manufacturers] with their million-dollars-a-year budget—and those so-and-so's will now pat me on the back—yet where were they when the book needed them? But to hell with them."[87] Most right-wingers were pushing an unmoored, tradition- and religion-based defense of the capitalist order that was not only weak, Rand thought, but actively detrimental. "God save capitalism from capitalism's defenders! Nobody can defeat us now—except the Republicans!"[88]

Rand was contemptuous of a substantial strain of modern conservative thought, from William Buckley to Ronald Reagan—what she derisively called the "God-family-tradition swamp."[89] To Rand, all associations should be rational and intellectual, not arising from the sheer chance of family and nationality. Hecklers during her street corner days pumping for Wendell Willkie would ask why she, an obvious foreigner, was lecturing them. She valued her American citizenship more, she'd announce ferociously, because she *chose* to be an American.

God, of course, was beyond the pale. Before Rand was anything, she was an atheist. "The concept of God is degrading to man," she decided, before coming up with more rational explanations for why a supreme being didn't exist.[90] In that early formulation, Rand is the archetype of the Luciferian atheist, rejecting God out of overweening pride.[91]

Leonard Read, to Rand, was no mere right-winger. Here, she thought, was an extraordinarily talented man, potentially Roark like.[92] She allowed herself, upon contemplating this accomplished real-world man with a seemingly peerless understanding of politics and economics, one last fling with hope for reformers other than herself.

But she wouldn't have been Ayn Rand if she didn't have some criticisms, starting with the name of Read's organization, Foundation for Economic Education, and the beliefs implied by it. FEE's name made it sound, she lectured Read, "that the cause of the world's troubles lies solely in people's ignorance of economics and that the way to cure the world is to teach it the proper economic knowledge. This is not true—therefore your program will not work. . . . The root of the whole modern disaster is philosophical and moral. People are not embracing collectivism because they have accepted bad economics. They are accepting bad economics because they have embraced collectivism."[93]

Still, she was willing to work hard advising Read "because I consider an organization created by you as potentially of tremendous importance. I consider you the only man in my acquaintance who has the capacity to translate abstract ideas into practical action and to become a great executor of great principles."[94] Her vetting and advising him on early FEE publications lead her to jokingly refer to herself as his "ghost."[95]

But Rand's support of, and hope for, FEE was short-lived. The Hazlitt-inspired FEE, approaching economics mostly in the Misesian/Austrian style, had an initial controversy presaging the quiet underground duel between Austrian and Chicagoite approaches that has continued through the libertarian movement's history. FEE's second published booklet, *Roofs or Ceilings?* was written by University of Chicago economists Milton Friedman and George Stigler. (Rand referred to them as "two reds" in her condemnation of the essay.)[96] Friedman, whose role as a public libertarian would later grow to gargantuan proportions, was as yet a small player on the scene, not that any prominence on his part would have caused Rand to spare him a syllable of her invective. The pamphlet about rent control was, to Rand's eyes, "the most dreadful thing ever put out by a conservative organization. . . . I never expected that from Leonard Read. He was really my one last hope of a conservative who would act on the proper principles, and take some positive practical action for our cause; and it is awfully hard to see a last hope go."[97]

Rand felt especially betrayed that her standing offer to ideologically vet all FEE publications—as a gratuitous donation to the cause—was ignored. The Friedman/Stigler pamphlet was positively evil, she thought, since it implied that rationing by government command was the moral equivalent of "rationing" by a free price system, with the only important difference being efficiency.[98] That is, they tried to explain why rent control was bad not by arguing that it was always and everywhere wrong to order other people about what they could or could not charge for their property or services, but merely that doing so led to certain inefficiencies in terms of lowering the amount of available rental property that even advocates of rent control would realize are not what they wanted. As with any price control, the effect of rent control is to make the object whose price is being controlled, in this case apartments, less available. This conflict over emphasizing efficiency versus emphasizing morality when making libertarian arguments remains a fault line to this day, with Chicago school types more likely to emphasize efficiency over morality, the Randians and Rothbardians morality over efficiency. However, they also recognize that market interventions, in addition to being wrong, tend to be inefficient; they do not achieve the goals they ostensibly aim for.

While Rand was a particularly keen heresy spotter, she was not the only one in the FEE orbit who found Friedman and Stigler's soft-core approach to government intervention nettlesome. Read and others at FEE were disturbed by a paragraph suggesting that the authors agreed with the goal of equalizing income, and thought policy measures aiming at that goal were preferable to manipulating how people are allowed to spend the unequal incomes they have, which is what housing price controls do.[99] That is, they suggested that rather than trying to make certain things like rent cheaper by law in order to help those with lower incomes, it was wiser to come up with long-term economic policies that would tend to make everyone's incomes more equal and then let them spend that income in a market where prices were allowed to freely carry out their function of allocating people's efforts toward the goals that society as a whole most valued.

Friedman's and Stigler's hackles rose at the idea of cutting that part out, and they steadfastly refused to do so. The FEE staff settled on a solution that ensured everyone involved was at least a little bit peeved. They let Friedman and Stigler's statement stand but appended a footnote spelling out FEE's official objections. "The authors fail to state whether the 'long-term measures' which they would adopt go beyond elimination of special privilege, such as monopoly now protected by government. In any case, however, the significance of their argument deserves special notice. It means that, even from the standpoint of those who may put equality above justice and liberty, rent controls are the height of folly." Leonard Read wanted it on the record. Who can say where these gentlemen from Chicago stand, but let it be known, the Foundation for Economic Education does *not* consist of those types, who would make justice and liberty a secondary consideration to equality.[100]

Read was always consulting and hectoring his circle of friends, board members, and supporters about FEE's activities. They were a concerned and involved group, bound tight by the constant exchange of long, philosophically and politically dense letters. Industrialists and intellectuals across the land found themselves judging the potential heresies of the Chicagoites, and the Russian firebrand's intolerance of same. Mullendore first thought Rand was going too far, being too picayunely purist, in her attacks on Friedman and Stigler, but then found himself agreeing with her. Others, like Orval Watts, who had worked as an economist for Read in his chamber days and later did work for FEE as well, thought Rand was dancing perilously close to the anarchism that bothered him more and more as he noticed it among his fellow libertarians. Rose Wilder Lane and R. C. Hoiles, along with Rand, were going too far in the antistate direction as far as he was concerned.

Beyond her seeing evil where none was intended, Watts found Rand's moralistic rights-based arguments ultimately unconvincing. Libertarians needed to show thieves *why* they shouldn't steal in practical terms, not just scream that they are violating some sort of so-called inalienable right. Why should they care about *that?* Then too Rand's tone and quick conclusions were illiberal in the social sense, Watts argued. Libertarians can't win hearts and minds by reading people out of polite company and tossing them into the outer darkness to wail and gnash their teeth with all the other evil collectivists for one deviation from Randian purism.

In the early days FEE was seen as a source of intellectual weaponry for its business sponsors. Although this never became a typical modus operandi for FEE, the idea for the rent control booklet had been suggested to Read by the National Association of Real Estate Boards, who bought a half million copies to distribute.[101] FEE never sent its work to anyone who hadn't asked for it. If Read wanted a particular book or pamphlet to be seen by more eyes, he would suggest that a board member or supporter send them to friends and associates personally, so it had a direct connection with someone they had reason to respect, not merely appearing as unsolicited propaganda from some operation in New York.

FEE would never, for example, deluge politicians with pamphlets. But politicians would sometimes order thousands to educate their constituents on some matter or to explain a position they had taken.[102] Read's own congressman was one of the last solidly old right, mostly antiwar and antistate Republicans, Ralph Gwinn, a man with libertarian instincts if not always libertarian actions. (He would, though, send copies of Nock's *Our Enemy, the State* to constituents to explain what he believed, which couldn't help but endear him to Read.) Gwinn advised other constituents to hear Read speak and would mail out (at no taxpayer expense, he'd stress) copies of Read's letters to him to illuminate issues. Read explained his, and FEE's, attitude toward the burgeoning cold war, the new obsession of what had once been a reliably antistatist anti–New Deal coalition, in a letter to Gwinn—a sterling example of Read's folksy, simple but compelling style, and his growing isolation from the waves swaying the postwar Right: "If I had stood up to a demented bully and had 'told him off' and had invited him into the alley and, then, had discovered that the fracas would destroy both of us and, plus this, had been informed that he would suffer destruction at his own hands anyway, I am one who would turn to other pursuits and let the matter pass," Read wrote. "Communism or socialism—or the same thing, state interventionism here at home—is a philosophy to be despised and *explained* away. It is not a military threat to be feared and *shot* away."[103]

Their warm relationship, and Gwinn's congruence with a fair amount of FEE principle, never led Read to go easy on him. Read, who pushed Hazlitt's writings on the topic, was anti–Marshall Plan and anti–aid packages to postwar Europe.[104] Gwinn had what he thought was a somewhat more market-oriented European recovery plan, but Read wanted to be served no alphabet soup from his congressman and friend.

He mockingly wrote a version of what Gwinn's call for European aid really meant: "I, Congressman Ralph Gwinn, advocate that my constituent, Leonard Read, and others, be made to pay a disproportionate part of $500,000,000 to the socialist governments of Europe because, in my judgement, my Plan is not as bad as other plans. Further, that the payment from Read and others be assured by bringing to bear the police force of the United States government, even to the extent of confiscating their homes."[105]

"WHO FINANCES THESE GANGS OF LITERATE GOONS?"

FEE's relentless pursuit of principle made it a detriment at times to the business interests whose support it hoped for. Even on FEE's own board, J. Howard Pew of the Sun Oil family thought FEE went too far in condemning all tariffs. Although it didn't make Pew cut off support (though he thought about it), that policy did lead some FEE funders, including one who had given Read $5,000 to help launch the foundation, to abandon it. FEE could be pointed to, some less radical business interest groups feared, as an example of the unmasked true radicalism of all this blather about the free enterprise system. While some group might be calling to eliminate or ease a certain price support, FEE was out there proving that the *real* goal was the elimination of all price supports. That was indeed FEE's stance, but not necessarily that of the more equivocating business rights groups of the NAM variety.

FEE, although obscure to those outside the movement, did not escape the baleful eye of outside forces. Eleanor Roosevelt slammed FEE in her syndicated column in 1951 for calling the welfare state "communism–socialism." A FEE board member felt obliged to quit when FEE published an early pamphlet attacking the Tennessee Valley Authority. He (like many early FEE supporters) ran a private electric utility and had a delicate understanding with TVA to not engage in any public attack in exchange for being left alone in return.[106]

FBI agents came snooping around FEE in June 1948, took some files, and then returned them; and in 1950, a congressional committee investigating lobbying by propaganda, helmed by Rep. Frank Buchanan (D-Pa.), a man unsympathetic to the individualist cause, called Leonard Read and FEE to the dock to reveal to the interested congressmen exactly who was supporting these strange, seemingly unAmerican, ideas. Read allowed agents of Buchanan's Committee on the Investigation of Lobbying to dig around without serving their sub-poena, then decided he had failed in his duty to his board of trustees by so doing. After meeting with Buchanan and other committee members, Read reluctantly went along with the investigation, confident that nothing in FEE's files could condemn the organization as a conscious lobbying group. Read noted with alarm, however, that the subpoena's definition of "lobbying" seemed to embrace any communication of thought whatsoever.

When Read was preparing to testify on July 18, 1950, a WOR radio newsman, rebroadcast on a national network, gleefully anticipated how Buchanan's committee would "rip the cover off one of the biggest and best financed pressure outfits in America. . . . Who finances these gangs of literate goons?" and named Montgomery Ward, B. F. Goodrich Tire, U.S. Steel, Sun Oil, Sears Roebuck, and Westinghouse as complicit in Leonard Read's efforts to, among other things, "save the slums for the wealthy real estate operators who thrive on human misery." The newsman also hinted that FEE's propaganda techniques were similar to those "that enabled Hitler and big business to seize Germany."

Everyone remembers McCarthyism and the outcry it caused a few years later, when leftists were called to the dock and required to name names. But the Buchanan Commission is a little-remembered spectacle, when the avatars of right-wing reaction were similarly, and earlier, forced by subpoena to name names to congressmen hungry for flesh, and contemptuous of Americans who thought they had the right to refuse to offer any. Demands for lists of who they were, or had been, giving cash to in regard to "any attempt to influence, directly or indirectly, the passage or defeat of any Federal legislation," to be replied to forthwith, were dispatched to 166 captains of industry, including Read's mentor Mullendore.

The FEE crowd was appalled but not necessarily surprised. In an age when sob sisters were always on hand to weep about and offer tissues to the victims of red scares, they were morally certain, as Ayn Rand would articulate for them a decade later, that one of the most persecuted minorities in American life—all the more persecuted because no one even stood up to defend *their* rights—was the undaunted and uncompromising defenders of laissez-faire. FEE employee Reverend Edmund Opitz called libertarians in the 1950s the "unorthodox dissenters," those whose dissent was so far beyond the pale of convention that respectable folk hardly knew it existed.

Mullendore did not take Representative Buchanan's request lightly. He snapped back via telegram with his "deepest resentment and indignation at this brazen attempt at thought-control." He sharply reminded the congressman that he was a servant, not master, of any American citizen. It was proper, Mullendore explained, for private companies to invest what was, after all, often stockholders' money in causes such as FEE. The protection of corporate property, part of their fiduciary duty, required fighting the damaging depredations of government. Since Buchanan's government had its grubby paws in almost every aspect of life and business, it would be difficult indeed to ascertain what comments or actions by the company or its officials, or those it supported financially, did *not* have some connection to some federal legislation, either existing or proposed.

And finally, Buchanan's request was rancid with the stench of unwarranted power: "the power, if it exists, to require reports and an itemized accounting of the costs of a private citizen's proper exercise of the right to attempt to influence legislation is the power to that extent to inhibit, to burden, and to regulate such right . . . If the citizen's constitutional rights to petition Congress for the redress of grievances, to freely speak and freely publish arguments and facts for the purpose of influencing opinion upon public issues is to be subjected to harassing and burdensome inquiry, and detailed, itemized accounting as to costs and expenditures, then these rights will be in the process of extinguishment." Mullendore promised to send his reply to all of SoCal Edison's stockholders, in order to make them as angry at Buchanan as he was. With a cavalier flourish, he signed off by telling the congressman and his cronies to "review their early American history and learn therefrom what caused the revolt in which this Nation was born."[107]

Such conflicts only cemented the resolve of 1950s libertarians. The libertarian movement, in the immediate postwar years as FEE ramped up, is perhaps better conceptualized as a gang than as a movement. Its activists, journalists, propagandists, and significant financiers amounted to a group of substantially fewer than one hundred people. (Though if you count those reading regularly, whether enthusiastically or disgustedly, the work they produced, the numbers are far larger, in the tens of thousands at least.) They were all aware of each other, most corresponded with each other, and discovering more of them was an intellectual adventure and, for the Volker Fund, an expensive project.

These men (despite the huge influence of Rand, Paterson, and Lane, they were still mostly men) were in regular contact, forming committees of correspondence to lament Rooseveltism and its stepchild Eisenhowerism and muse over strategies about how to combat it, all of them sure the answer was not grabbing the muskets for armed revolution, but searching for a new Tom Paine—but one whose vision of what government could properly do was even more limited than that of the Founding Fathers.

"Ultimately it will separate us."

FEE did not begin what eventually became its most prominent activity until the end of its first decade in business. The roots of this project began in 1950, when Henry Hazlitt, in collaboration with John Chamberlain and Suzanne La Follette (who had worked with Nock on the original), revived the title *Freeman* for a mostly individualist fortnightly that strove to be an all-purpose ecumenical magazine for the entire inchoate libertarian–conservative gang of the time.[108] It didn't necessarily succeed, since the attempt at ecumenicism gave everyone in their potential audience something to be annoyed with. This *Freeman* could celebrate war in Asia in a way that discomfited the likes of Read and Mullendore; an article in the first issue cheered war in Korea as "the first, epochal stand of the United Nations armed forces against the insidious, continuous encroachment of Communism upon free peoples" and noted humbly that "no campaign was every more brilliantly conceived and executed."[109]

At the same time the *Freeman* was celebrating war in Korea, Read expressed his point of view regarding the *previous* war in this letter to his congressman, Ralph Gwinn (which Gwinn reprinted and mailed to his constituents):

Did you ever try to squash out, with the slap of the hand, a puddle of mercury? And find that nothing was squashed at all, but that you had splattered the metal all over the place? Well, that is about what happened in World War II. We tried to promote freedom by force. In so doing we got rid of several totalitarian items—Hitler and his gang—but splashed totalitarianism all over the globe, a lot of it in the United States of America itself. We succeeded only in changing the label and our concept of totalitarianism from nazism to communism, the stuff itself being more prevalent than ever.[110]

The *Freeman* swallowed up *Plain Talk,* a mostly anticommunist but not necessarily warmongering little journal that published Rand and Mises among exposés of Soviet gulags and teeth grinding over Western giveaways to Stalin in the aftermath of the war. *Plain Talk* was financed by China Lobby industrialist Alfred Kohlberg, a man obsessed with the idea that the United States was selling out China to the communists, and edited by Isaac Don Levine, a Russian-born journalist who had been sent to cover the aftermath of the Russian revolution for the *Chicago Daily News* and picked up a lifelong animus toward the Soviet regime because of what he learned about it.[111]

While Hazlitt wanted his *Freeman* to stay above the fray and be devoted to economic issues, his colleagues enjoyed the scrum of day-to-day politics. A split over that issue, as well as petty personal matters, destroyed his partnership with Chamberlain and La Follette. Hazlitt, who wanted the magazine to stay clear of McCarthy and obsession with anticommunism rather than general libertarianism, ended up the only member of the original troika running the magazine in 1953. Meant as a for-profit operation, the *Freeman* had hemorrhaged $400,000 (in early 1950s dollars) in just three years.[112]

Something had to be done. Read, who was on the magazine's board of directors, stepped forward and launched a small for-profit company called Irvington Press to take over the *Freeman*, which Hazlitt had now walked away from. Read named Frank Chodorov the editor and the new *Freeman* was launched with the July 1954 issue.

In the mid-1940s, Chodorov had been a one-of-a-kind tenacious representative of the general spirit of the Three Women of 1943, writing boldly antistate articles arguing, for example, that "universal suffrage and representative government obscure but do not mutate the character of politics," which is "loot[ing] without ritual."[113] He pointed out that the fine businessmen associated with such groups as the chamber of commerce, ostensibly fretful and fearful of communist infiltration, were in fact the vanguard in seeking the communist goal of ultimate centralization of decisionmaking power in the state, for the purpose of guaranteeing their own rate of return and protecting them from competition and losses.[114] He wrote all this, and more, in the pages of a mostly one-man, self-owned, four-page broadsheet named (lowercase and all) *analysis.*

It had few readers, never more than a couple thousand. But to those few it was the most important journal in their lives, because it told them that they were not alone, not mad, that some stranger in New York with a courageous twinkle was willing and able to say things they thought but no one else was saying. Some of them were things that alienated individualists could hardly imagine anyone was even *thinking*, like "Don't buy bonds!" and "Taxation is robbery," and that the best way to get communists out of government jobs was to get rid of the jobs.

Chodorov was born on New York's Lower East Side, the eleventh child of Russian immigrants, son to an immigrant peddler and small restaurant operator.[115] In 1936, Chodorov met and befriended Albert Jay Nock while playing pool at a gentlemen's club. He ended up executor of Nock's estate when Nock died in 1945. Shortly before he died, Nock delightedly shared with Chodorov strangely individualistic pamphlets issued from the Los Angeles chamber of commerce—the work of the yet unknown Leonard Read. "To understand his enthusiasm and my astonishment," Chodorov wrote, "you must understand that there was at that time no current literature of freedom, and that if you wanted to read on the subject you had to dig up and dust off books of ancient vintage."[116]

Chodorov was an independent thinker in the Nockian mode, with a profound disgust toward our enemy, the state. He advocated the social ostracism of government workers. Government buildings, he said, should be thought of, and treated as, charnel houses. His first taste of notoriety and acclaim came through a public act of union busting, beating a strike by the Amalgamated Clothing Workers of America at a clothing factory he was running in 1923. This got him speaking engagements at Harvard's Graduate School of Business, where he was distressed over how all the students were Marxists.[117]

During the Depression, Chodorov (like Nock) was attracted to Henry George's free market philosophy. After some years as a traveling salesman, Chodorov edited a magazine published by the Henry George School of Social Science in New York, also known as the *Freeman*, but was fired for his isolationist views during World War II.[118] Like Leonard Read, he had to create his own institution to address issues of man and state as he pleased, so he launched *analysis* in 1944. He couldn't have imagined much of an audience for a newsletter that, as the cold war ramped up, would paint anticommunist agitation as pure empire-building propaganda for the benefit of an America that has decided to create a world situation where "a lot of people are under compulsion to hand over a good part of what they produce to a handful of people who employ the soldiery that does the compelling."[119] But Chodorov had what his mentor Nock called the essential ingredient of the successful pamphleteer: a fundamental philosophy to apply rigorously to events and, more importantly, a streak of cussed certainty of the importance of his message, and great pleasure in explaining it, that sustained him through a career when it was never obvious that many cared or understood. He was accused by some readers as being obviously in the pay of Hitler; by others of obviously being in the pay of the National Association of Manufacturers.[120] His fellow Georgist (and Nock's lawyer), Abraham Ellis, recalls lending Chodorov $500 for the project, asking him to please pay it back out of any profit the little journal made. "I never got that $500 back."[121]

Chodorov's strategy for social change was a populist variant of the Hayekian model, aimed at changing the minds of the next generation of thought leaders, college students. (Chodorov thought it was already too late for the faculty.) The intellectual and political victories of the planning mentality in the United States were caused, Chodorov maintained, by student groups advocating socialism in the early twentieth century, capturing students' attention by adopting an aura of idealism, radicalism, and pacifism. The individualist counterrevolution would have to do the same, assiduously planting individualist thought in the minds of the young, slowly turning the wheel that would change the world's direction away from collectivism, toward individualism. A return to thoroughgoing individualism culturally could take another fifty years or more, he realized.

The individualist's task, said Chodorov, was to "polish up our ancient arguments, apply them to the current scene and offer them as brand-new merchandise. We must do a selling job."[122] In 1951, he had given up on *analysis* as a separate magazine, folding it into *Human Events*. In 1953, with an unsolicited $1,000 check from J. Howard Pew, who had read an article Chodorov wrote in *Human Events* about his "fifty-year plan" to turn the socialist tide, and with FEE promising to supply good literature in bulk to any individualist students Chodorov could recruit, he launched the Intercollegiate Society of Individualists (ISI) to actuate his educate-the-young strategy.[123] The idealistic young would not be attracted by a backward-looking mentality. His libertarian individualism was, and had to be sold as, "first-class radicalism."[124] Within a year or so, FEE was mailing 24,000 pieces of literature to 2,500 ISI members at 210 colleges.[125]

FEE's relationship with ISI became strained as Read tried to assume authority over literature going out under ISI's aegis, and more or less tried to swallow the whole operation and turn it into a wholly-owned FEE subsidiary. Chodorov's executive vice president, Vic Milione, especially bridled at this. He was more of a Kirkian traditionalist conservative with little love for unbridled free markets than he was a Chodorov–Read libertarian individualist anyway. Milione got the ISI board to agree that it deserved an existence independent of Read, and the relationship was severed.[126] ISI moved in an increasingly Kirkian direction from there; it even changed its name to the contentless Intercollegiate Studies Institute to retain its initials but eliminate the stink of Chodorovian individualism. Its relevance to the libertarian movement, as opposed to the conservative one, was minimal from then on. Chodorov's more consistently libertarian friends would forever after look on ISI and sigh about what might have been. With its new conservative dispensation, ISI has grown to a nearly $8-million-a-year op-

eration, teaching the verities of Western civilization and Christian order to 50,000 college kids across the nation.[127]

Chodorov made the *Freeman* a more explicitly libertarian magazine
than was the Hazlitt version, proudly using the term. While not banning cold warriors from the coalition, he did write an editorial pointing out why they didn't dominate it, and what libertarianism should
be all about in the early 1950s.

He could fill every issue with submissions about the foreign commie threat, he noted, but he chose not to. This was not merely to avoid
"the deadly fault of dullness."

> We are . . . opposed to communism . . . no more so than we are
> opposed to fascism or socialism or any other form of authoritarian-
> ism. . . . To stress the threat of communism is to divert attention
> from the threats of equal potency and nearer home. We cannot help
> seeing in the concentration of power in our own Executive an at-
> tack on freedom; in the drive for government schooling we see the
> menace of collectivist indoctrination; in taxation and inflation we
> recognize the gradual abolition of private property. . . . If under
> cover of our preoccupation with communism these threats to free-
> dom are permitted to go unchallenged, what is accomplished?

Chodorov finally voiced the libertarian suspicion of the right-wing
cold warrior starkly and directly: "Sometimes as I read these anticommunist manuscripts, the unkind suspicion comes upon me: are
these writers *for freedom* or only *against communism*?"[128]

Not that Chodorov ignored cold war issues. When he did address
them, he tended to spell out that what we do when we go into places
like Korea to "fight communism" is more properly described as
"slaughtering natives." He similarly pointed out that communism is
"to vest all property rights in those who wield political power, the
State. This, then, is the idea that we who believe in the American tradition should try to kill, and let all natives live."[129] He allowed room in
the same issue for his young friend Bill Buckley, already beginning to
design in his mind what would debut a year or so later as *National Review*, to present his prescient essay "A Dilemma of Conservatives."

In that article the soon-to-be father of modern conservatism predicted that fights over how to handle the Soviet threat would divide
the anti–New Deal, antistate right. He called, with the subtlety that
men must adopt when publicly advocating mass murder, for a strike
against communist Russia *now*, no matter what the cost, on the somewhat libertarian-sounding grounds that what the United States would
be obliged to do in order to be properly prepared for fighting them
later would involve so much bureaucracy, so much conscription, so
much taxation, that it "would mean that readjustment to private property and limited government would be nothing short of revolutionary." All this small-government pacifism might be well meant, but a
true conservative must be made of sterner stuff. "The issue is there,
and ultimately it will separate us," Buckley declared. And with him
helping the separation along, it ultimately did.[130]

Buckley loved Chodorov, and the radical Georgist libertarian is often embraced as a historical father of Buckley's conservative movement. But Chodorov's libertarianism was too extreme for that, and he
knew it. "I will punch anyone who calls me a conservative in the
nose," he wrote to *National Review* in its first year. "I am a radical."[131]
Read couldn't make the Chodorov *Freeman* turn a profit, since there
was no mass audience for Chodorov's radicalism. Read despaired that
Irvington Press would bring down FEE and questioned the legality of
the nonprofit subsidizing the theoretical for-profit.

The Chodorov *Freeman* was in peril, and Buckley, who even then
was working on funding and strategy for what became *National Review*
(and was then imagined as *National Weekly*) offered to the Irvington
Press board to assume the *Freeman*'s assets and debits for a nominal
dollar and essentially fold it into his operation. Jasper Crane and J.
Howard Pew, dedicated Presbyterians, scotched this attempt to give
the store away to the famously Catholic Buckley.[132] The *Freeman* was
turned from a magazine dealing with contemporary politics and issues
into a controlled-circulation organ for FEE, publishing the same sort
of things FEE had been publishing as stand-alone pamphlets, dedicated
to quiet, nonconfrontational expositions of the core principles of liberty as applied to any given issue.

Having a regular, branded outlet for its assorted efforts was a magic
bullet of sorts for anything that might have been ailing FEE. While its

donor base had stabilized at around 4,100 since 1952, within two years of relaunching the *Freeman* under its nonprofit aegis with its January 1956 issue, they had around 9,000 donors, and nearly 42,000 people receiving the magazine.[133] From that day to this, the *Freeman* has been a presence in any youngster's pilgrim's progress to libertarianism. Scratch anyone who came of age from the late 1950s through the 1980s, who works professionally in either a libertarian or even in many cases conservative think tank or other organization for political activism, and you will find someone who sent away at some point to Irvington—or had some relative or mentor send away for them—either $10 or $5, or even just a sincere request, and started receiving monthly doses of measured, simple, direct, unironic and uncomic, homey (and often strikingly peculiar), timeless explanations of why things worked better if you let the eternal order of the Creator, in whatever of his manifestations, act itself out through unbridled human creative energy. The authors and articles would be respectful, but not slavishly so, of American tradition, carefully debunking the "clichés of socialism" that FEE knew its readers encountered every day, helping them see another world, a sane, moral, successful, sensible world that freedom could lead to. The sight of that imagined world was often enough to make that young man—it was usually a man—dedicate his intellectual or political life to those ideas.

"IT WAS MORE THAN CONTEMPT THEY FELT FOR MISES. THEY THOUGHT HE WAS DANGEROUS."

As FEE got off the ground, its favorite economist, Ludwig von Mises, after a few years of languishing in his new, strange land, finally landed a teaching position at New York University's Graduate School of Business Administration in 1945. In 1948, he began his second series of lauded seminars.[134] This seminar (and not so much the regular course work) was the wellspring that ensured the survival of the Austrian economics tradition in America. Nearly everything that contributed to its continued vitality can be traced to students Mises inspired during his twenty-one years of NYU seminars. As of 1949, his salary was paid not by the university, but mostly by the Volker Fund, a sign of American academia's low opinion of Mises, an insult that his admirers point to with the almost perverse antipride of the dedicated outsider radical. Later other sources were gathered through the efforts of such friends as Hazlitt, Read, and NYU board member Lawrence Fertig. (Mises *was* past the normal retirement age by then.)

Mises attracted students from all over the world, not just NYU. Many of them came just for Mises. One such student was Richard Cornuelle, whose brother Herb was mentored by Loren Miller and then became Leonard Read's first righthand man at FEE. Cornuelle had been working as Garet Garrett's assistant in Garrett's last days, helping him edit the National Industrial Conference Board magazine *American Affairs.* "I didn't take a degree, I just took Mises's seminar," Cornuelle remembers. "The first year I tried taking other courses, but then realized I was only interested in Mises. I stayed three years."

NYU wasn't highly regarded as an economics school. Still, "we felt lucky to find some place that would take him," Cornuelle recalls. "It's hard at this distance to realize, but it was more than contempt they felt for Mises. They thought he was dangerous. They thought he was pushing a vicious, inhuman position that appealed to capitalists but didn't deserve any encouragement. It was an outcast position."[135] Israel Kirzner, Mises's graduate assistant during the 1950s and 1960s, recalls that "during those years I became aware that he was not treated as part of the mainstream faculty. He was just a visiting member, paid from the outside. There may have been cases where students were advised against taking his classes. The real tragedy was not so much that Mises was marginalized by the rest of the faculty at NYU, but that he was never able to obtain an academic position suitable to his international prestige."[136] The mistreatment extended to his students. Robert J. Smith tells horror stories about how the NYU administration jerked him around as a Volker-funded grad student studying under Mises, a tale that progresses in grimness from being forced to take accounting courses he didn't care about—he only wanted to study with Mises— to being turned in to the draft board for not taking a full course load. "It was a total nightmare. In two years it went from bad to worse— from having to take accounting to about to be sent off to Vietnam, all because I wanted to study under Mises."[137]

Few professors inspire such fascination and devotion that a non-degree-seeking adult would attend their lectures constantly for eighteen years. While Bettina Bien Greaves, already an employee at FEE, was by far the most devoted of Mises's seminar acolytes (she never stopped attending until the end and kept copious lecture notes to boot), she was not unique.

As Robert Nozick, Harvard philosopher and author of the libertarian political philosophy bombshell *Anarchy, State, and Utopia,* said, "In 18 years of teaching at Princeton and Harvard, I never encountered any professor teaching a seminar where non-degree-seeking adults would continue to attend year after year . . . [Mises was] unique in attracting mature minds without demanding discipleship." What attracted them, says Nozick, was "the content of his ideas and their power and lucidity."[138] Many of Mises's nondegree students were set on, as Greaves remembers, "carrying on the Mises teachings in some way in their professions." A restaurateur, for example, would sponsor dinner meetings for Mises and his friends.[139] Mises's friend George Koether, an editor at *Look* magazine, commissioned a bronze bust of the great scholar.

"The seminar wasn't really a seminar," Cornuelle recalls. "Mises would lecture, we'd sit around a table. He'd make a long, long statement but there was no give and take like in a real seminar, where everyone puts their cards on the table. Mises didn't think that way, didn't work that way. If you asked a question, he'd just repeat that portion of the lecture he thought you didn't quite grasp."[140]

Greaves, whose experience with the seminar extended longer than Cornuelle's, remembers more give-and-take on occasion. She recalls Mises marching in to his classroom shortly before 7:25 P.M. every Thursday of the school year,

> straight and erect and . . . with a firm step. He always dressed very properly in suit, vest, and tie. His grey hair and moustache were always neatly brushed. He was serious, no nonsense or frivolity toward his subject, but his eyes sparkled.
>
> A half-dozen words, no more, neatly and precisely written in Mises's old-fashioned European script, on a small piece of paper,

usually about 2" x 3", were sufficient to remind him of the important points he wanted to cover in an evening's discussion.

Mises encouraged participants in his seminar to ask questions. They should not accept his every statement as absolute truth, or, he said, he might as well be a dictator.[141]

Greaves also recalls that

sometimes people would ask questions and he'd say it's not pertinent to what we are talking about. But sometimes lively discussion came from traditional students with backgrounds in Keynes and aggregate economics. He'd also talk about anarchy sometimes—[George] Reisman and [Murray] Rothbard and a few anarchists came. He'd tell them to write a book, he didn't want to argue.

But he would say, "Don't be afraid to ask questions. Even very intelligent people ask stupid questions." One guy would always challenge him with something he had read in the paper that day, asking Mises what he thought of *that*. You could always ask a fact question, an information question. But to Mises economic theory was so precise that if you question it, you are just wrong. So if a question would seem stupid, he'd say, "You are just wrong."[142]

Mises's audience at NYU was not wholly made up of fascinated devotees. Many degree-seeking NYU students were eager to study under Mises because he offered a notorious "gut" course. At first, Mises gave everyone As. When told this wasn't the way things were done in the United States, where grades serve a different purpose than in Vienna, he would give all As and Bs. Merely showing up guaranteed a B—and no papers, tests, or specific readings were required—which guaranteed a good number of uninterested dullards signed up. As Cornuelle recalls, even those types "began to suspect that they were in the presence of quite a different breed than the usual asshole who might be teaching accounting. This was a formidable character."[143]

Many blame Mises's inability to get far in American academia on his manner—intolerant and arrogant. Milton Friedman delights in telling a story of Mises cutting off relationships for years with his old friend

Fritz Machlup over a disagreement about the gold standard, and angrily condemning a gaggle of his fellow Mont Pelerin free market mandarins as "a bunch of socialists."[144]

Different students have different memories of Mises's comportment. One of Mises's five Ph.D. students at NYU was Hans Sennholz, who holds a unique distinction among libertarian thought leaders: He once served as a soldier for a totalitarian power. He was a Luftwaffe pilot during World War II, shot down over Africa. He insists, as a point of pride, that no other air gunner managed to nail him; a lucky fellow on the ground with an antiaircraft missile shot his tail off.

The resourceful Sennholz ended up in a POW camp in Texas. With the help of some aunts already living in America, he took correspondence courses from the University of Texas, studying economics. Sennholz ended up with a year's worth of college credits that he used later in Germany. After the war, he was shipped as a prisoner to England, where he starved himself into illness to win an early dismissal from the POW camp. By fall 1946, he was in college in Germany, studying under Wilhelm Röpke, an old cohort of Mises's and founding member of the Mont Pelerin Society. Sennholz credits the greatest part of his early economics education not to class work, but to popular articles by Röpke from newspapers clipped to bulletin boards.

In 1948, Sennholz first came across Mises's *Theory of Money and Credit.* "At that time, among students, it was said that if you wanted to understand rational economics, you've got to read Mises. And so I read *The Theory of Money and Credit.* I didn't at that time see the ideological implications, the scope of Mises. I just saw him as a monetary theorist, as the one rational theoretical economist a young student could follow."[145]

Sennholz came to the United States, and chose NYU as a graduate school for the chance to study under Mises. "Sometimes at the beginning of a class, the other professor was still using the classroom. When the other one, usually younger, would try to say hello, Mises would look the other way or stare at the ceiling. He didn't care to talk to the other professor. And when I first went to him and said I'd like to do a thesis under you, he was short and discouraging. He said, 'Oh, everybody wants to do that, but very few can do it.' He cut me off. It was not a friendly interlude.

"But I already had a Ph.D. I wasn't shattered. The second one would be of lesser value as far as Ph.D.s go. So four weeks later I was able to go back to him, and lo and behold he was very friendly. We developed family relations. I married a classmate [Mary Homan, a secretary at FEE], introduced to me by Mrs. Mises. She claimed credit when we had a boy, and became godmother. Mrs. Mises and Dr. Mises went to baptism classes, and from then on he was always considerate and nice and fatherly. We had such an excellent relationship that whenever he went on a speaking tour to Central America, if they invited someone else to accompany him it would be me. There's the original shell, but once you succeed in getting through the shell he would be kind to you. He wouldn't bother with the ones who weren't interested.

"When Mises was ninety or ninety-one, I was giving a speech at FEE. This was 1972. Mises came out with his wife. I was honored that the old man would come when I would speak. And he would go to sleep. That was our relationship on some level."[146]

Greaves contrasted Mises with Hayek. "Hayek was a gentleman and a diplomat. Mises was a gentleman, but I'm not so sure he was a diplomat. If he didn't like somebody, he would walk out, or argue with them, or ignore them."[147]

Margit Mises reinforces Greaves's view in her memoir. "When friends talk about my husband, they spoke of him as being polite, distinguished, and gentle. . . . He was gentle with me because he loved me. But actually he was not gentle. He had a will of iron and a mind like a steel blade. He could be unbelievably stubborn, but people would not detect that in daily life, for he had excellent manners."[148]

The oft-repeated tales of Mises as a suffering-no-fools grump during his American days don't jibe with the vision of the gentle and respectful group leader of his Vienna seminar. The Viennese Mises Circle, however, truly were his equals, or at least playing in the same arena, in age and intellect. They were not composed almost equally of uncaring business students and semi-worshipful younger men. One of Mises's five Ph.D. students (and the only one to land a tenured job at NYU), Israel Kirzner, speculates on the difference: "In his Vienna seminar he had been by all accounts open to all possible points of view. But by the time I was at his seminar, he was of advanced age and had heard all of the arguments in favor of other points of view. There's no doubt he felt convinced that he knew what was valid and invalid. That awareness on his part was fairly obvious to anyone, from body language if you like, and it could be that some members of the seminar might have felt put off. But I don't believe he was arrogant. That's an unfair characterization. He was self-confident, and brooked no nonsense, but I always found him extremely encouraging to myself. I would ask questions and never felt put down. There was, though, always a difficulty in approaching him across the seminar table, because of his slight hearing problem.

"Another aspect of those years that has to be kept in mind is that for various sociological reasons Mises became surrounded by people who were very eager to protect him. Some of those well-meaning individuals may have projected an image that Mises is not to be criticized, not to be disagreed with. That was unfortunate, and in my own work I've tried to treat Mises's ideas as scientific ideas that must be treated with the respect they deserve—which means being questioned and criticized."[149]

Margit remembers: "One of his former students . . . told me: 'Four or five students had formed a group in order to protect the professor against dissident students who opposed his views. They occupied a table ahead of the class next to the professor in order to be ready to protect him against any possible violence.'"[150]

Kirzner and Murray Rothbard shared a sense of sadness over the pass that one of the shining lights of European intellect had come to in the United States. "However wonderful the seminar experience for knowledgeable students," Rothbard wrote in his brief Mises biography, "I found it heartbreaking that Mises should be reduced to these frowsy circumstances. Poor Mises. There was scarcely a Hayek or a Machlup or a Schutz among these accounting and finance majors, and Childs' Restaurant [where the interested would repair after the class was over at 9:30] was no Viennese Cafe."[151]

Despite some grim trappings, the seminars were central to the future of Misesianism. "It's true that if you count noses or the number of Ph.D.s who arose from Mises at NYU, it doesn't seem so impressive," Kirzner says. "But remember that Rothbard, who has made enormous contributions to economics, was there, though not as an official student. It is true that the majority of participants at any one evening would be people coming in because everyone knew Mises gave everyone a B. People at brokerage houses on Wall Street would come sit in the corner and fall asleep and get a B.

"But that's not the spirit of the Mises seminar. You must look beyond the registered students. The seminars maintained the vitality of Austrian economic thought at a time when it would have died."[152]

Hayek said—with strange prescience—at a 1956 tribute to Mises, referring to the likes of Machlup and Haberler, "You have seen your pupils reap some of the rewards which were due to you but which envy and prejudice have long withheld."[153] After Mises died, Hayek reaped the greatest reward his profession had to offer, which many thought Mises deserved: the Nobel Prize in economics.

"I AM NOT SO SURE THAT IT WOULD BE A MERITORIOUS THING TO BRING A LOT OF LEFT-WING ECONOMISTS TO OUR COUNTRY AT OUR EXPENSE."

As World War II wound down in 1944, Hayek worried about its possible aftermath. Germany had to be reintegrated into the larger Western world, Hayek thought, for a peaceful and prosperous postwar world to function. Accomplishing this, as well as restoring his beloved lost liberalism of the nineteenth century to the center of Western culture, required the creation of an interdisciplinary and international society of scholars who shared a belief in individualism and liberty. He wanted to name the group the Acton-Tocqueville Society, after his channel-crossing pair of nineteenth-century liberal heroes.[154]

Hayek's star was high in the scattered community of intellectuals and organizers dedicated to classical liberal ideas in the wake of *The Road to Serfdom*. Although Hayek had connections and respect, organizing an international conference took money, and Hayek found it amid the rubble of an aborted journal of classical liberal ideas that Wilhelm Röpke, a German economist of traditionalist but largely free market leanings, was attempting to launch. Albert Hunold was a Swiss businessman who had raised funds for the Röpke project and then abandoned it when he was unable to raise the full amount needed.

Hunold got the donors' permission to redirect the money into Hayek's conference idea.[155]

Hayek, on a promotional trip for *The Road to Serfdom* in America, had been introduced by Loren "Red" Miller to Harold Luhnow of the Volker Fund, who was a fierce admirer of *The Road to Serfdom*. (Luhnow offered to pay Hayek to prepare an American version of *Serfdom*, which, though popular in America, had been written to apply to Britain. Hayek declined.) Luhnow financed the participation of leading American libertarians and classical liberals such as Milton Friedman, Aaron Director, Henry Hazlitt, F. A. Harper, Chicago school of economics founder Frank Knight, Felix Morley, and Leonard Read.

The first meeting of Hayek's new society was held over ten days in April 1947. It came to be known as the Mont Pelerin Society, after the Swiss resort where the first meeting was held. (Leonard Read credited himself with that argument-sparing name, which did not require the society to seem publicly attached to any particular idea or intellectual. However, the official minutes say Karl Brandt was responsible.)[156] Hayek was elected president of this elite gathering of classical liberal/libertarian minds. The statement of principles decried how "the position of the individual and the voluntary group are progressively undermined by extensions of arbitrary power."[157] It pledged allegiance to no "meticulous and hampering orthodoxy . . . with no particular party."[158] This first meeting had panels discussing liberalism and Christianity, wage policy and unions, agricultural policy, the future of Germany and a possible European federation, and government efforts in poverty alleviation and countercyclical economic manipulations.

The presence of Read and some of his FEE associates limned an important distinction between the American radical libertarians and the merely classical liberal Europeans. (Hayek in some respects could be said to belong in the latter category, but was—mostly—warmly embraced by the former.) Europeans, such as Röpke, Maurice Allais, and William Rappard, accepted some government actions, short of central planning, to deal with unemployment, poverty, and other social problems. To Read, the commonsense American businessman who saw the truths of libertarianism starkly and simply, these European professors were simply squishes, not worthy of being considered part of any international freedom movement.

After the first Mont Pelerin meeting, Read was appalled. "So far as I am concerned, I can see no hopes whatever for [MPS] to become a useful force in the fight for freedom . . . the philosophies range all the way from middle-of-the-roaders to one who is an out-and-out social-ist."[159] (To anyone familiar with MPS's reputation in the world outside the libertarian movement, the radical severity of Read's judgment will be apparent. Suffice it to say, Pelerines are *not* seen as middle-of-the-roaders—hidebound reactionary right-wing free market fanatics is more like it.) After the 1949 meeting, Read was even more exasper-ated, lamenting that had the meeting gone on longer, "I would lose whatever sanity I possess. Not once have I heard an expression of an idea of aid to the liberal philosophy." The European members thought themselves good liberals, in Read's mind, only because they were a smidgen more freedom-minded than the socialists and collectivists surrounding them in Europe.[160]

A pair of Pelerines, Ludwig Erhard and Walter Eucken, even if not properly hard-core in the eyes of Irvington, achieved real victories for economic liberalism in Germany. Erhard, as chief economic adminis-trator for the Allied occupation zones in Germany after the war, man-aged to push through—sometimes over the weekend while others weren't around—free market policies, including freeing up prices, that created a postwar German "economic miracle." Many of his associates in German economic management were also Pelerin members.[161]

Read and his associates wanted a purist, hard-core Pelerin, but they had no support across the pond for such an organization. Over its first decade Read would often decide Pelerin was beyond saving, but he saw renewed glints of light through the 1950s. In preparation for the first American meeting of the society in 1958, Read wrote to an im-portant funder, Pierre Goodrich,

> Hayek's approach is considerably different than yours and mine, as relating to the conduct of the Mont Pelerin Society, even though his personal views are apparently quite similar to yours and mine. I gave up a long time ago arguing my point of view with Hayek. I held that the Society should be only for the purpose of developing a bet-ter understanding of the libertarian philosophy; that the other side of the argument shouldn't be introduced into the program at all; that

the other philosophy had plenty of platform [sic] all over the world. On several occasions I was tempted to resign from the Society, but I noted an increased trend toward libertarian thinking year after year and decided that the Society was probably worthwhile.[162]

Read recalled once arguing about conscription with Hayek. He noted that thanks to the military draft, the two men might well have ended up killing each other during World War I.

Hayek eventually became annoyed that so many FEE-type journalists and propagandists were in Pelerin at all, and he questioned Luhnow about concentrating too much on such FEE characters in Luhnow's funding of Pelerin travel for Americans. To Hayek, the perfect Pelerine not only believed in old-style liberalism but also had a liberalism fully honed and tempered with a detailed understanding of the strongest objections of the antiliberals.

Though Mises was himself a European liberal, he fell on the Read side of the divisions in Pelerin—only fitting, as FEE had adopted Mises as its patron saint of economics and was paying him a salary, if mostly honorary. He often gave lectures and speeches at Irvington, and sometimes on the road, for FEE. Mont Pelerin helped widen the divide that the rent control pamphlet controversy had opened between the Chicagoites and the Read crew. The former thought the latter unsophisticated ideologues; the latter thought the former equivocating squishes. If pushed to the limits of applying libertarian thought, Read was convinced, not even a dozen Pelerines would pass muster in the eyes of FEE.[163]

In 1958, MPS met in America for the first time, at a Princeton conference largely funded by hard-core Americans. The funders ensured Mises had an honored slot to speak on the nature of freedom. From the perspective of Sun Oil magnate J. Howard Pew, Mont Pelerin was all about exposing the straying Europeans to the pure quill of American libertarianism. However, when contemplating paying the expenses of the American meeting, he told Read that "I am not so sure that it would be a meritorious thing to bring a lot of left-wing economists to our country at our expense."[164]

As Read wrote to FEE board member Jasper Crane, he had the temerity to tell Aaron Director, Milton Friedman's brother-in-law, that the writings of Chicago school founding father Henry Simons, which the Chicagoites thought were a thorough defense of market freedom, were "from the standpoint of the philosophy to which you and I subscribe . . . perfectly awful and made more so by Simons being represented as a devotee of laissez-faire."[165]

The treatment Mises received at Pelerin meetings, as well as Mises's personal attitude toward the society, helped shape American businessmen's attitude toward it. Even before the first meeting, Mises was writing concerned letters to Hayek about the society and complaining that he had no desire to visit Europe in 1947: "I have seen enough decline already." The main problem with MPS would be the same one Read saw: "It relies upon the cooperation of many men who are known for their endorsement of interventionism." He named Röpke, Karl Brandt, Henry Gideonese, and Max Eastman as bad eggs.[166] A friend of Read's recalls Mises referring to most Pelerines as "entrepreneurial Marxists," and Milton Friedman famously repeats a story of Mises storming out of a room of his fellow Pelerines condemning them as "all a bunch of socialists." Some of the Americans had begun to suspect Mises was not well regarded or properly minded by his European colleagues, whose libertarianism was less unrelenting than Mises's.

Hayek, not so obsessed with ensuring that no ground be given to statism on any front for any reason, was far more pleased with his child. "Americans have done me the honour of considering the publication of *The Road to Serfdom* (1944) as the decisive date," he wrote, "but it is my conviction that the really serious endeavor among intellectuals to bring about the rehabilitation of the idea of personal freedom especially in the economic realm dates from the founding of the Mont Pelerin Society in 1947."[167]

Mont Pelerin survives today. Many who joined it when it was smaller and more distinctive wonder if it still serves a valuable purpose. After all, people believing in old-style liberalism, at least in economics, are no longer a scattered and lonely band, and there are many other specialized groups for market-oriented (or at least anti–modern liberal) intellectuals in America, including the Philadelphia Society (created as a sort of junior American Pelerin) and, for lawyers and legal scholars, the Federalist Society. MPS meets yearly in international and local meetings to allow its members to exchange thoughts, deliver papers, socialize, share ideas, cement alliances. Being tapped for membership remains the highest honor that the libertarian/conservative intellectual world has to offer.

Read's complaint about MPS not being hard-core libertarian holds true today, though it is at least consistently free market. It has become as much a right-wing or conservative institution as a libertarian one, and is perhaps more influential in the Spanish-speaking world these days than the English-speaking one. From time to time founders such as Hayek and Friedman were prepared to lay MPS to rest in the wake of absurdly drawn-out personality conflicts. They thought the society had grown too large for personal scholarly interactions to be optimally close and fruitful. Since it succeeded in its initial goal—perpetuating a set of ideas in academia and politics that no longer needs such support—why not lay it to rest?[168] One measure of the society's success in reviving and spreading liberal ideology and scholarship is that the first meeting was attended by four future Nobel laureates—all in economics. In that field, at least, libertarian ideas are free to speak their name without fear.

"LIBERTY IS NOT MERELY ONE PARTICULAR VALUE BUT . . . THE SOURCE AND CONDITION OF MOST MORAL VALUES."

After acclaim for *The Road to Serfdom* faded and his retreat from economics was nearly complete, Hayek returned to psychology and produced a curious and difficult tome reviving ideas about human mental structures that he first played with in the 1920s at the University of Vienna while trying to grapple with the ideas of Ernst Mach.[169]

The book that resulted, *The Sensory Order* (1952), is an anomaly in Hayek's career, yet to Hayek it provided the necessary base for all of his future sociological and political speculations. The human mind, Hayek posits, is an essentially interpretive and classifying organism; pure perception not filtered through mental categories doesn't exist. Classification is thus inherent in the physiological act of perception. This idea underlies some of the key tenets of the evolutionary social philosophy

Hayek adumbrated at great length and with slight variations in emphasis in all his major works afterward: *The Constitution of Liberty* (1960), *Law, Legislation, and Liberty* (3 vols., 1973–1979), and *The Fatal Conceit* (1988): the notion that modern man in the market order is burdened with moral categories formed over millennia of tribal life, and that much of the modern ennui over markets and desire for socialist order is an atavistic longing for (and entrapment in) mental categories that are no longer appropriate but are (somehow—Hayek in his characteristic abstraction is vague on the precise mechanism) embedded in the structure of the mind. "There can thus be nothing in our mind which is not the result of past linkages (even though, perhaps, acquired not by the individual but by the species)," Hayek wrote in *The Sensory Order*.[170]

Hayek revisited some of the themes of his early 1940s essays in intellectual history, and collected the results in 1952 as *The Counter-Revolution of Science*. In it he attacks what he calls "scientism," or the illegitimate application of the methods of the physical sciences to the social sciences. Scientism as a method can lead, in Hayek's thought, to the unfortunate application of what he called "constructivist rationalism"—the false belief that human social orders can be planned and controlled through human reason, without relying on tradition or the spontaneous orders that arise in free markets. Alas for Hayek, many so-called liberals in the twentieth century adopted that method and those tools, in a pattern arising from the positivism that dominated Viennese intellectual culture in his youth, which dictated that only empirical sense impressions could be the source of useful or proper knowledge, leaving clumsy locutions like "classical liberal" for Hayek and his brethren. "Libertarian" has come to dominate as the term for Hayek and Hayekians.

Hayek in *The Counter-Revolution* traces the roots of modern socialism back to Henri de Saint-Simon, the early-nineteenth-century French pseudomystic, cult leader, and prophet of the scientific recrafting of human society according to rational principles. The key concepts of modern socialism, Hayek shows, come from Saint-Simon's work or that of his disciple Auguste Comte, one of the founders of sociology.

Saint-Simon preached that man had both the power and the need to rationally reshape his environment. His followers were predicting in 1829, pre-Marx, that in a wonderful world to come "individuals will be classed according to their capacities and remunerated according to their work." Consequently "the right of property, as it exists, must be abolished." They wrote of laws of history, as implacable and unavoidable as those of physics, and of the class struggle between bourgeoisie and proletariat.[171] Sounds familiar?

By the time *The Sensory Order* was out, Hayek was ensconced in his new home on the Committee on Social Thought at the University of Chicago. (He had also divorced his first wife and married his second.) He officially left the London School of Economics at the end of 1949, taught a semester at the University of Arkansas, and then started at Chicago in October 1950.[172] His reputation in economics was at such a low ebb, his methods and theories completely eclipsed by Keynes, that a seat in Chicago's Economics Department was scotched.[173] Hayek, by then eager to branch out into larger philosophical issues, was satisfied with where he ended up at Chicago.

> The post at the Committee on Social Thought at the University of Chicago offered me almost ideal opportunities for the pursuit of the new interests I was gradually developing. As professor of social and moral science, I was allowed there to devote myself to almost any subject I cared and to do as much or as little teaching as I wanted. I had . . . become stale as an economist and felt much out of sympathy with the direction in which economics was developing.[174]

He lectured on the history of economic thought and gave small seminars on specific books.[175] During his decade at Chicago, he wrote the book that most thoroughly explains his political philosophy, *The Constitution of Liberty* (1960).

Hayek wrote *Constitution* with a certain sense of mission, perhaps even fear, inspired by the cold war. The world needed a total vision of a classically liberal society that stretches beyond economics, he was certain. His goal is telegraphed in the title. He wants to explain liberty—why we want it, what it's good for, the institutions the West has developed to preserve it, and how they are threatened.

His defense of liberty is instrumental; like most from the original Austrian economics tradition, Hayek didn't lean his defense of liberty on a notion of natural rights. "Some readers will perhaps be disturbed," he admits in the introduction, "by the impression that I do not take the value of individual liberty as an indisputable ethical presupposition and that, in trying to demonstrate its values, I am possibly making the argument in its support a matter of expediency . . . if we want to convince those who do not already share our moral suppositions, we must not simply take them for granted. We must show that liberty is not merely one particular value but that it is the source and condition of most moral values."[176] This necessary entanglement of moral and practical, or deontological and consequentialist, is threaded throughout most libertarian scholars and polemicists, even if they think they are arguing only in one way and not the other. There are almost none who don't simultaneously seem to believe that liberty works best and is also morally proper. Far from illegitimate deck stacking, as some opponents of libertarianism charge, this is generally because libertarian visions of moral propriety are rooted in a notion of human rights, and their notions of human rights in a vision of what is necessary for human flourishing, thus closing the circle between what is right and what works. Indeed, what works is a necessary constituent of what's right.

Hayek defines *freedom* as the absence of coercion, and he defines *coercion* as "such control of the environment or circumstances of a person by another that, in order to avoid greater evil, he is forced to act not according to a coherent plan of his own but to serve the ends of another. . . . Coercion is evil precisely because it thus eliminates an individual as a thinking and valuing person and makes him a bare tool in the achievement of the ends of another."[177]

Hayek's definition of liberty is purely negative; it guarantees you nothing but your own sphere in which your choices are your own. His definition, when left that loose, almost implies anarchism. But Hayek is far from an anarchist. When government indulges in actions that would clearly be coercion under Hayek's more general definition, its actions can be justified by ensuring that they are rule based and affect everybody equally. Thus not even forced taxation and conscription sink to the level of coercion by his definition in *Constitution*. (He changed his mind on this later.)

Rules, defined by Hayek as "simply a propensity or disposition to act or not to act in a certain manner, which will manifest itself in what we call a *practice* or custom," are the sine qua non of both civilization and government; we could not possibly achieve what we have achieved without following them.[178] It is only when rules are followed that what Hayek calls the "spontaneous order" can develop.

Here Hayek brings in his other overarching idea: man's ignorance. We can never know for sure what the end results of our actions will be. Consequently our extended social order depends on following certain end-independent rules instead of taking the act-utilitarian path of trying to figure out in every circumstance what action might have the best results. Because we can never know all the results of any action, following rules is the best bet—even when we have to follow them in a way that those Hayek calls "constructivist rationalists," who think we can restructure society at our whim using the power of our reason, would consider blind.

The root of socialist folly, the folly of any who believe man's intelligence gives him the power to craft any sort of social order he desires, lies in not realizing the limitations imposed by man's ignorance. Following rules is also the very blood and marrow, to Hayek, of that most difficult of social theoretical concepts, justice. Hayek defines *justice* in the same way many laymen might define *fairness*: as the application of equal abstract rules to everyone, irrespective of the particular content of those rules. The only way to judge the justice of individual rules is in how well they fit in with the overall order of other rules; we can't otherwise objectively determine whether a rule is just.[179]

Both individuals and governments must obey rules, and any culture's ability to survive depends on the details of the rules it chooses to follow, or more accurately, the rules it inherits from its cultural tradition. Where these rules originate is obscure in Hayek. He either implies or directly states that they mostly result from accidents that somehow, without us knowing why or even really *that* they are advantageous, help the groups that adopt them to survive and thrive where other groups don't. Hayek is an intellectual whose vision of human progress leaves little room for the intellect. To Hayek, the rules we follow, knowingly or not, shape us and our minds far more than we consciously shape our rules.[180]

In *Constitution,* Hayek presents evidence for most of his big ideas: the value of liberty, how market prices in a free economy bring all the dispersed individual knowledge in a society together in the only way it *can* be brought together; the glory of a civilization that maximizes the ability for accidents to happen, since it is only through such accidents that man progresses. He first essayed this idea—considered by many the most important in the Hayekian intellectual arsenal—in his 1945 essay "The Use of Knowledge in Society." Despite the pretensions of modern neoclassical economists, there is no such thing as perfect or given knowledge from which the economic problem is merely one of logic or simple calculation. The relevant knowledge of specific circumstances is spread around everyone in an economy; no central planner has that knowledge or conceivably can have it. Thus any attempt at planning will fail from lack of knowledge on the planners' part. And it is prices, in a system of economic liberty, that transmit the relevant information about relative scarcities and wants that make an economy work.[181]

Hayek lauds progress, even uneven progress, and makes an ingenious defense of the utility of what some call the obscenely wealthy as advance shock troops pioneering new methods, new products, even new arts and philosophies. Only the wealthy, Hayek argues with some historical evidence, can afford to subsidize the new and radical in any field.

Hayek also presents in *Constitution* a more detailed exposition of his views on the intellectual history of liberalism, oft repeated over the course of his writings: the distinction between the Scottish/British liberal tradition, as exemplified by Hayek's heroes David Hume, Adam Smith, and Adam Ferguson, and the French/Continental tradition, as exemplified by Descartes and his apostles Rousseau and Voltaire. The distinction is philosophical, not merely regional; Hayek tosses Brits like Hobbes and Jeremy Bentham into the French constructivist tradition.[182]

The Scottish tradition was evolutionary, and, unlike the French constructivists, it recognized the limits and weaknesses of reason. Scottish tradition liberals understand the value of tradition and don't try to remake the world from first principles through the unaided power of intellect. Hayek saw himself as carrying on this tradition, and he is its most prominent and successful twentieth-century advocate. Most of the major ideas associated with Hayek—spontaneous order, social evolution, the necessity of the rule of law, property as the key to justice,

justice as applying only to deliberate individual human action—are derived from these Scottish forebears.[183]

A couple of quotes from Hayek's honored predecessors contain, in précis form, much of what is most valuable in Hayek's contribution to twentieth-century intellectual debates. Bernard Mandeville, a seventeenth-century Dutch precursor to the later Scottish moral philosophers whom Hayek credits with being the first to realize the evolutionary character of social institutions, wrote, "We often ascribe to the excellency of man's genius, and the depth of his penetration, what is in reality owing to the length of time, and the experience of many generations, all of them very little differing from one another in natural parts and sagacity."[184]

And from the Scot David Hume: "The government, which, in common appellation, receives the appellation of free [is] that which admits of a partition of power among several members whose united authority is no less, or is commonly greater, than that of a monarch, but who, in the usual course of administration, must act by general and equal laws, that are previously known to all members, and to all their subjects. In this sense, it must be owned that liberty is the perfection of civil society."[185]

Constitution, a dense and rich work, also has expositions on free will and responsibility (where Hayek makes an instrumental defense of responsibility, concluding that whether or not we are in any metaphysical sense "responsible for our actions," it is valuable to treat everyone as such); the necessity of legal equality, and why it's incompatible with material equality; the distinctions between liberalism (which deals with what law ought to be) and democracy (which deals with how decisions are made about the law, and which can sometimes be the enemy of liberalism if left unchecked); the dangers posed to liberalism and market freedom by the mentality of the employed (like Jefferson, he saw a society of freeholders far more congenial to successful liberty than a society of employees). Hayek also provides disquisitions on what law has meant historically, from ancient Rome to America, and the proper nature of law as distinguished from command; detailed thoughts on what a government under law ought to be able to do (and what it ought to be prohibited from doing) in the market. The book's final section applies his vision of the rule of law and ordered liberty to a range of specific modern political questions, including the welfare state, state provision of certain public goods, social security, taxation, monetary policy, housing policy, agriculture policy, labor unions, and public education.

Constitution clarifies Hayek's many differences with other strains of twentieth-century libertarianism.[186] Hayek makes this distinction between him and other libertarians quite clear toward *Constitution*'s end. He pledges no fealty to liberty for its own sake or for the sake of rights or justice. If anything is an unquestioned and unquestionable good to Hayek, it is diversity, growth, change, and progress, in both knowledge and material goods. The free market and the unhampered price system are good, then, because they allow dispersed knowledge to be transmitted and brought to bear on the real world.

But a different strain of libertarianism fed into the movement and shaped its flow, a strain that could acknowledge the truth of Hayek's thoughts on free market advantages in terms of solving knowledge problems but valued free markets for deeper reasons. Free markets are, in recognition of man's nature and of the standards of justice, the only proper economic system. And a free market meant a *free* market—one unhampered by any act of government whatsoever. Hoiles, Harper, and others in the movement already thought this way, but none were systematizers. The man who would do the systematizing was already among them in the 1950s, though not yet widely published: Murray Rothbard, conceptualizer and promoter of anarcho-capitalism.

5

Objectivism, Anarcho-Capitalism, and the Effects of Psychedelics on Faith and Freedom

The nascent libertarian movement argued over compulsory taxation, the morality of the cold war, and such recondite free market economics debates as the gold standard versus managed central banking, passing around (and ruthlessly editing) suggested reading lists for the proper understanding of individualist ideas and history. But Ayn Rand was no longer contributing her barbed ex cathedras into the fray. She had removed herself from the organizations and controversies of her fellow individualists after Leonard Read and FEE disappointed her over the Friedman/Stigler rent control pamphlet. She had not, though, removed herself from the fight for liberty as she waged it—through art and through a rigorously developed philosophy consistent with the facts of reality.

"What if all the creative minds of the world went on strike?"

Rand spent the last years of the 1940s and most of the 1950s working on what was to become *Atlas Shrugged*, the ultimate melding of her art and philosophy. Her working title was *The Strike*. The germ for the novel came from a conversation she had with Isabel Paterson before their final break.[1] Paterson commented that the world needed Rand to write a nonfiction treatise detailing her philosophy. Rand, appalled at any appeal to the needs of others as a claim on her efforts (and how could the mother of Howard Roark feel otherwise?) roared back, "What if I went on strike? What if all the creative minds of the world went on strike?" Her husband Frank O'Connor, overhearing this, is said to have told her that that would make a fine idea for a novel. Rand ran with it—and ran far.[2]

Atlas ended up a stunning dramatization of the real-world effects of airy and abstract philosophic principles, a tour de force that inspires both life-changing awe and deep and powerful repugnance. One hears—often—that the book changed a reader's life; yet you can also hear of people, upon discovering a copy in a loved one's room, throwing it out a window "for their own good"—and someone in the yard, seeing what the offending book was, running over it again and again with a lawnmower, shredding it, ensuring that *this* copy at least could wreak no more harm, pollute no more minds.[3]

The plot is labyrinthine and horrifying. It's the story of a genius named John Galt, who is brought to harm by a foolish experiment in collective worker ownership of a factory. He decides that a world philosophically corrupt enough to believe in the worthiness and efficacy of communism does not deserve his gifts. He withdraws from society and leads a clandestine crusade to encourage all other geniuses and men of ability—the industrialists and philosophers and financiers and artists and thinkers who do the important work of mankind—to join him in unyielding refusal to contribute to a corrupt culture. Galt leads men of the mind in their first strike. As Rand would have it, civilization collapses into ruin and misery without their genius and ability. Then the Great Men return from their hidden valley individualist paradise to remake the world anew, built only on the strictest principles of Aristotelian logic, reason-based epistemology, individualist ethics, and laissez-faire capitalism.

Atlas is a mystery, unveiled slowly and deliciously; the full contours of what's really going on don't become clear until the 1,100-page story is two-thirds over. The plot's tension pivots on two creators whom the strikers cannot convince to join them—Dagny Taggart, the beautiful young brain behind Taggart Transcontinental railroads, and

Hank Rearden, steel magnate and inventor of Rearden metal, an amal-gam that's lighter, cheaper, and stronger than steel. The novel relates in hideous detail the ruin to which a world run by mediocre, bureau-cratic secondhanders will come. Dagny is stymied by her spineless brother Jim, titular head of Taggart Transcontinental; Hank is bedeviled by his shrewish wife, ne'er-do-well brother, and useless mother.

Atlas was meant to be the final knitting of Rand's philosophy, and its concretization. She shows us the real-world effects of embracing her philosophy—and her enemies'. We see her philosophy leading to well-being, grand achievements, wealth, brotherhood, and peace; her oppo-nents' leading to corruption, rot, failure, self-hate, and eventually destruction and death. Rand believed all this ferociously, and that helps explain the equally fierce revulsion her work inspires in those who can't cotton to her philosophy.[4]

Rand and her fans think *Atlas* presents an inspirational vision. Rand's aesthetic philosophy says that art is meant to provide emotional fuel for man by showing him values made real, by providing him with the joy of living temporarily in a world where everything is as it should be. However, the novel is for most of its length literally night-marish. It focuses more intensely on the terror of destruction and de-cay than it does on the glory of achievement and growth. While Rand clearly spoke in the name of peace, liberty, and achievement (though her ideological enemies have rarely granted her the respect of noticing that's what she explicitly stood for), the novel supplies plenty of am-munition to those who accuse it of being written in a spirit of hate.[5]

Atlas is to some extent as much a wallowing in a sewer as the worst modern naturalistic literature Rand hated—possibly even *worse*, since she portrays the most pathetic evil causing more destruction than it ever managed to do in real life. She romanticizes the evil as much as she romanticizes the good. Yet *Atlas* contains passages of glorious po-etry as well, pure hymns to human greatness. But she can't keep her mind on her fabled Atlantis (the heroes' hidden home), can't keep from giving the weak and pathetic more attention than her intellect would grant they deserve. This subconscious struggle makes the book more harrowing than necessary to anyone who can't instantly click with Rand's philosophy and sense of life.

Characters who have no moral or philosophic failings, who merely lack any spark of creative greatness, are punished. Take Eddie Willers, a

Taggart employee and Dagny's lifelong pal and assistant. Instead of making it to the strikers' Atlantis, where his lack of unique genius would make him unuseful, Eddie ends the novel, in one last horrific punch in the gut after civilization has collapsed (when the government strangles and mismanages the economy, natch), weeping helplessly beneath a vast uncaring night sky, beside the last stalled and useless Taggart Transcontinental train. Rand's utopia was not for those who understand that *A* is A, you can't fake reality, and you must not initiate force; it's only for the Great. In her choices as a novelist, if not explicitly in her nonfiction, Rand retained a streak of Nietzsche.

Rand thought *Atlas* important for those it praised, not those it blamed. The good inherently deserve more attention than the evil, she maintained. As Barbara Branden put it in her Rand biography: "This was to be Ayn's gift to America. A moral sanction. The philosophical demonstration that to live for one's own rational self-interest, to pursue one's own selfish, personal goals, to use one's mind in the service of one's own life and happiness, is the noblest, the highest, *the most moral* of human activities. . . . Speaking to the unnamed, unchampioned, beating heart of her new land, Ayn was to say: 'Yours is the glory.'"[6]

In *Atlas* Rand detailed the philosophy that would come to be known as Objectivism. She has strike leader John Galt give a fifty-seven-page speech over government radio waves to explain to a world heading to ruin exactly where things went wrong. The only significant part of Objectivism barely touched on by Galt is her theory of concept formation, the only aspect of her philosophy she considered important enough to write an entire book about *(Introduction to Objectivist Epistemology)*.[7] Galt famously went on at length, but Rand, when challenged, was able to deliver a précis of her philosophy while standing on one foot: "Metaphysics: Objective reality. Epistemology: Reason. Ethics: self-interest. Politics: capitalism."[8] Galt's exposition gave substance, context, and drama to this bare presentation. It showed how the nightmare world of *Atlas* arose from people's rejection of Rand's principles.

Rand spent the rest of her life spreading and elaborating Objectivist philosophy and its implications. Though she lived another twenty-five years, she never wrote another novel, only making desultory notes toward one in the late 1960s.[9] Eventually Rand returned the advance she received from Random House for the novel she never wrote.[10]

"SHE HOPED I HAD LEARNED THAT SHE BELIEVED IN LAISSEZ-FAIRE CAPITALISM."

Rand's second career as philosopher-activist would have been unlikely had she not met and befriended a young fan named Nathan Blumenthal and the woman who later became his wife, Barbara Weidman. The couple became known as Nathaniel and Barbara Branden. Their energy, belief, and encouragement turned Rand and Objectivism from a subject of merely literary interest to linchpins of a philosophical-political movement.

Blumenthal was a Canadian who discovered *The Fountainhead* at age fourteen. He was an archetypal young Rand reader: smart, alienated, too serious and cerebral to get along well with his peers, filled with a sense that there was something more important to life than the inanities of high schoolers and the petty dreams of those who surrounded him in Toronto. "I wanted to like and admire people," Branden wrote in his 1989 memoir, *Judgment Day*, "but I was indifferent to the values and concerns of my contemporaries: winning love from mother or father, being popular, or cloning oneself in the image of whatever was currently fashionable. I suspect that others my age probably thought my indifference was an affectation. I knew no one to whom I could talk about what mattered to me, no one who felt as strongly about the importance of ideas or the great questions of life."[11]

The young *Fountainhead* fan daringly wrote his hero a letter speculating about her political convictions. (Despite Rand's intentions, many of her readers were capable of reading and even loving *The Fountainhead* without piecing together the political implications of the thoroughgoing individualism Roark represented.) Nathan had the temerity to insist that whatever she believed in, it was "certainly not capitalism."[12] Earlier he had begun and ended a love affair with another Canadian *Fountainhead* fan, Barbara Weidman of Winnipeg. Both of them enrolled in UCLA, Nathan to study psychology, Barbara philosophy. Still lonely and alienated at UCLA, distressed over the failure of his love affair with Barbara, he wrote Rand again, this time an innocuous letter asking if she had any books in print he might not know about.

"A couple of months later," he wrote in his memoir, "I received a brief note from her with the information that those were the only books she had published. She added that she could not say when she would complete her next novel. Then she asked me if I was the gentleman who had written her from Canada asking about her political convictions. If I was, she hoped I had learned that she believed in laissez-faire capitalism."[13] Emboldened by this direct communication, Nathan wrote Rand a longer letter, "asking her a number of questions about *We the Living,* the nature of free will, and capitalism."[14]

Frank encouraged Rand, who was busy with *Atlas,* to write back to this young man; he seemed bright, worth encouraging. Rand wrote a long letter back, and Nathan responded and included his phone number. In February 1950, Rand called him and invited him to stop by her Neutra home in the San Fernando Valley. Their meeting was fateful for them and for the libertarian movement. Though neither could know it, Rand was meeting her St. Paul. (Nathan might have suspected he was meeting his Jesus.)

Rand was impressed with this young acolyte—his seriousness about ideas combined with a willingness to boldly test her consistency. He also had "completely the face of my kind of man."[15] Nathan, using their mutual love of Rand as a bond between them, brought Barbara to the next meeting. Soon the two became regular visitors, among the few Rand still entertained. She became philosophical and personal mentor to both through their regular Saturday night visits. Barbara's young cousin Leonard Peikoff, another *Fountainhead* admirer, was also introduced to Rand.[16] After the friendship had matured, Rand extended the most honored intimacy she could imagine—letting her new young friends read *Atlas* in manuscript as she wrote it. By 1951, Nathan and Barbara, dating again, moved to New York City after Barbara got into the philosophy graduate program at NYU. Rand felt so close to them that she and Frank moved to New York a few months later, despite her previous insistence that she needed to stay settled until *Atlas* was finished.

With Rand mentoring them through their relationship problems, Barbara and Nathan decided to marry in January 1953.[17] Nathan changed his name to Nathaniel Branden. Nora Ephron later wrote that this name was deliberately chosen because it's an anagram of "ben Rand"—son of Rand in Hebrew. Both Brandens deny this, although it has been repeated often.

Rand's opinion of Nathaniel mounted higher. He began applying Objectivist thinking to his work in psychology and developed the concept of social metaphysics, which became a key weapon in Objectivism's arsenal of condemnation. The social metaphysician is the secondhander par excellence, depending on other people's thoughts and reactions to define reality for him, rather than his own senses and reason.[18] Rand was delighted with this new concept; "You've gone far deeper than my idea of the second-hander in *The Fountainhead*," Branden says Rand told him. "You've really gone into the root of human rottenness."[19] Though she was socializing a bit with other New York–based libertarian intellectuals, particularly Mises and Hazlitt, Rand thought that no one else saw things with her clarity, her depth. She had given up on conservatives and the conservative movement, and she saw herself as a "radical for capitalism." She was unalterably opposed to Mises's and Hazlitt's utilitarian ethics, though she tended to be soft on Mises as a person. (She didn't feel it necessary to harangue a man in his eighties who had achieved as much as Mises had.) Mises once warmed Rand's masculinist heart by referring to her as "the most courageous man in America." "Did he say *man*?" Rand wanted to know, and was delighted the answer was yes.[20]

In September 1954, the implicit became explicit. Rand and Nathaniel announced to Frank and Barbara that by the logic of who they were and the Randian theory of romantic love (love arises from the search to possess the human who most exemplifies your highest values), they were in love and would require some time alone together each week. The arrangement was initially nonsexual, but that changed by the beginning of 1955 (also explained beforehand to their spouses). Their affair continued as Rand wrote the final parts of *Atlas*, mostly Galt's speech laying the foundations of Objectivism. That speech took the painstaking Rand almost two years to write.[21]

Rand's circle had expanded thanks to Nathaniel and Barbara. A small gang of mostly worshipful youngsters would gather in Rand's home in the evening to listen to her speak on philosophy and to read segments of *Atlas* as they were written. Most of them were related to the Brandens or were friends of relatives. Members of the inner circle included Barbara's cousin Leonard Peikoff; Nathaniel's cousin Allan Blumenthal, a psychiatrist and would-be concert pianist; Nathaniel's sister Elayne Kalberman and her husband Harry; and an earlier husband of Joan Mitchell, who eventually married Allan Blumenthal—a young economist and financial adviser named Alan Greenspan, one of only two of the original group Rand never kicked out of her life, and later the chairman of the Federal Reserve Board.[22] The group was known as the Class of '43, after the year *The Fountainhead* was published; or, with a humorous irony that turned out to have a ring of bitter truth, the Collective.[23]

"SHE GOT HOPEFUL ABOUT WHAT MIGHT BE POSSIBLE."

Rand sold *Atlas* to Random House, and it was published in late 1957. Despite the novel's studied and deliberate opposition to the culture of its time, it became an enormous best-seller that has been in print ever since. It has changed tens of thousands of lives and become a cornerstone of the modern libertarian movement. *Atlas* achieved everything Rand wanted aesthetically—presented her vision of the perfect man in John Galt; gave vivid, colorful concretizations of her philosophy; and was written and published exactly as she wanted it. At her insistence, the editors at Random House did not change a word.[24]

Yet *Atlas* seemed to ruin her as much as fulfill her. Her closest confidantes, the Brandens, look back on the publication of *Atlas* and its reception as marking the end of Rand's joyous spirit. While she lived for another twenty-five years and produced a body of nonfiction essays that also remains in print, she never revived her zest for life, for work. Writing *Atlas* was Rand's mission, and it was over. She came to resemble the character in the only short story she published during her lifetime, a writer's self-indulgence that only appeared at the back of her collection of essays on aesthetics, *The Romantic Manifesto*. The story's hero had written a masterpiece, but the world didn't notice. He was perplexed and confused. The book got some attention, but people noticed all the wrong things. "He knew that it was there, that it was clear and beautiful and very important, that he could not have done it any better—and that he'll never understand [why his book was ignored or misunderstood]. That he had better not try to understand it, if he wished to remain alive."[25]

Atlas was a cry to the culture: May I find real-life embodiments of the men I write about! Its immense mass popularity was all well and good. But Rand wanted approbation from men of influence and accomplishment, from men of achievement whose judgment of her work and love for it merited her respect. She was too much the elitist to be satisfied by mere best-sellerdom.

That respect was not quick in coming. *Atlas* declared that the dominant cultural, philosophic, political, and artistic trends were the prelude to mass death and the complete collapse of civilization. Rand insisted that the enemies of her philosophy were in fact death worshipers, and sniveling and weak ones at that. This did not, strangely, endear her to the culture barons. They struck back the only way they could: with cynical contempt and total incomprehension.[26]

Rand beat an emotional retreat, but Nathaniel Branden had other plans for her. Rand called her philosophic system Objectivism (a word that does not appear in *Atlas*). The term, Branden writes, "was applicable to her theory of existence, of knowledge, and of values. In metaphysics, she held that reality is Objective and absolute, existing independently of anyone's consciousness, perceptions, beliefs, wishes, hopes or fears—that that which is, is what it is; that 'existence is identity'; that A is A. In epistemology, she held that man's mind is competent to achieve objectively valid knowledge of that which exists. And in ethics, she held that values appropriate to human beings are objectively demonstrable—in other words, that a rational code of morality is possible."[27]

Branden thought that the world needed to understand Objectivism, and that Objectivism needed something more than Rand's novels to spread and extend it. He proposed giving a lecture series that explained the basics of her philosophy. Rand agreed, but not enthusiastically. The Nathaniel Branden Lectures (in 1961 incorporated as the Nathaniel Branden Institute, NBI) debuted at the Sheraton-Russell Hotel on Park Avenue in New York City in January 1958.[28] Branden became a freelance market intellectual operating outside the confines of academe and the standard publishing industry.

"She couldn't quite see it when I began NBI," Branden says. "She was worried I'd be hurt. She couldn't visualize that it would be a success. As it began to build and grow, she got hopeful about what might be possible. Then we had the newsletter [*The Objectivist Newsletter*] and magazine [*The Objectivist*] which grew out of NBI after she saw there was this market, so she got progressively more hopeful. But she wasn't the person really to lead such a movement because—and I think she would agree with this—because she didn't really know how to lead people. She was very morally severe, very moralistic, very much concerned with matters of personal loyalty. So she watched the growth of NBI with good-natured fascination, but she was always concerned that somebody would call themselves an Objectivist and say or do something that she wouldn't agree with, and that attitude, which I was obligated to transmit on her behalf, became a terrific inhibitor because you can't have that much control over an intellectual movement: Independent people will get turned off by it, they'll drift out and all you'll have left are true believers with nothing original to contribute."

"For further details," says Branden, "visit the Ayn Rand Institute [Leonard Peikoff's organization representing the "official," Rand-heir-approved Objectivist movement]."[29]

With the founding of NBI, Randism/Objectivism became a movement. In order to maintain the purity of the philosophical product, far-flung groups outside New York (where the Objectivist inner circle lived) gathered in lecture halls or hotel meeting rooms and listened to tape recordings of lectures made by the Brandens or Rand or Peikoff.[30] Rand tried to get an old Hollywood friend, novelist Ruth Beebe Hill, to supervise the playing of NBI tapes in Los Angeles. When Hill suggested she'd like to hear the tapes before committing, Rand angrily ended the friendship over this unforgivable questioning of her judgment.

By the end of 1964, taped versions of the lectures were being played formally in 54 cities in the United States and Canada, with 3,500 students per year paying for the full course and thousands more auditing individual lectures. The *Objectivist Newsletter* had a circulation of 15,000.[31] One year later, courses were being given in 80 cities in North America, and many outside it, and 5,000 students a year were taking the courses.[32] The *Objectivist Newsletter* morphed into a digest-sized magazine called *The Objectivist,* with a circulation of 21,000 by 1967.[33]

Rand became a genuine public phenomenon, particularly on college campuses, where in the 1960s she was as much a part of the cultural landscape as Tolkien, Salinger, or Vonnegut, though because of her outré political orientation she is rarely mentioned in the same breath with them. She could attract over a thousand people to see her on rare trips to Los Angeles, and her annual Ford Hall Forum talks in Boston usually filled the hall and overflowed into other rooms where people huddled to listen over loudspeakers.

"AYN RAND IS THE GREATEST HUMAN BEING WHO HAS EVER LIVED."

While Rand worked on the Objectivist newsletters and magazines through the 1960s, NBI and her circle of influence were growing. The lore of the implacable and impossible Ayn Rand cult grew, helped along by non-Randian libertarians. An amusing fictionalized autobiography of a young libertarian's Pilgrim's Progress, Jerome Tuccille's It Usually Begins with Ayn Rand (1971), was rife with risible representations of cigarette-smoking, cape-wearing young women spouting Randian catch phrases thoughtlessly; endless worries about whether this or that novelist or composer was properly "rational" or had the right "sense of life"; banishment for trivial disagreements with any element of Randian dogma, which extended beyond the official Objectivist philosophy to any opinion or judgment Rand ever expressed, however personal or off-the-cuff.[34]

Some survivors of the Rand/NBI experience think the cult accusations are overblown and shouldn't be blamed on Rand herself. Ronald Merrill, author of The Ideas of Ayn Rand and an NBI follower living outside New York, thinks the crazy stories have been exaggerated for comic effect, and were only true, to the extent that they were, of the New York circle that had direct contact with Rand—and Nathaniel Branden.[35] Some think (and Branden's memoir gives some credence to this) that he was more of a moralistic terror than was Rand herself. Robert Hessen, an employee of NBI and later a historian at the Hoover Institution, recalls that "Nathan had a wonderful way of calling people and saying, 'I want to have lunch with you,' and you knew you were being called on the carpet for some failing and it struck terror into people's hearts. Nathan was quite sadistic in his handling of people. There was a lot of backbiting, people would report lapses and it would get to Nathan and you'd be called to explain why you had done something."[36]

NBI's lectures and advice on all aspects of life, as befits the totalistic nature of Objectivism, added to the cultlike atmosphere. Proper Objectivist stances were laid out on the arts as well as on political and ethical issues. Branden attempted to provide fuel for his students' intellectual and emotional needs, sponsoring NBI dances and film screenings, socials, and softball teams, as well as philosophic lectures, in an attempt to provide a fully rational context for living.

NBI founded its own press to reprint books of Randian interest, including Rand's favorite old romantic novels. It began a book-selling service—one of the major sources through which masses of people were exposed to and encouraged to buy books on libertarian economic theory by Ludwig von Mises. Soon NBI was selling reproductions of properly Objectivist art (clean, clear lines and realism are best) and began an NBI Theater Group. Tuccille writes of Rand's fascination with a "rational dancer."[37]

Joan Kennedy Taylor was part of a 1960s crew of Randian insiders, along with journalist Edith Efron and economist Martin Anderson, later a leading domestic policy adviser to Richard Nixon and Ronald Reagan. Taylor remembers "lots of insularity, absolutely" among New York Objectivist circles. "I remember a story about a patient of Allan Blumenthal's. She was a very shy girl and he was trying to get her out of her shell. At one point she went a little far and picked up a man off the street. She was telling Allan about this and it was fairly risky behavior, but his first question was: 'Was he an Objectivist?' There was a great deal of insularity; NBI socials were their entertainment, there was an Objectivist-appropriate person in every profession [who you were supposed to patronize]. Many of the people attracted to Objectivism were not intellectuals, but technicians, engineers—bright, accomplished people, but rather than go on to Columbia and read books, many hadn't really read at all in philosophy or fiction or the humanities. People thought Ayn invented laissez-faire capitalism."[38]

Rand demanded nearly complete (not to say thoughtless) obedience from her inner circle. Branden reports Rand telling him, "If, by your own statement, I am the highest, most consistent embodiment of your values, then I expect your first consideration always to be given to me. I expect not just you but the whole collective to make me their highest loyalty, so far as any other people are concerned, if it ever comes to a conflict. Otherwise, what do you imagine the principle of loyalty to one's values mean?"[39]

In his 1989 memoir Branden admitted, with regret, the cultish nature of Objectivism in the 1960s, and wrote of the "implicit premises" of Rand's inner circle, "which we transmitted to our students at NBI.

- Ayn Rand is the greatest human being who has ever lived.
- *Atlas Shrugged* is the greatest human achievement in the history of the world.
- Ayn Rand, by virtue of her philosophical genius, is the supreme arbiter in any issue pertaining to what is rational, moral, or appropriate to man's life on earth.
- Once one is acquainted with Ayn Rand and/or her work, the measure of one's virtue is intrinsically tied to the position one takes regarding her and/or it.
- No one can be a good Objectivist who does not admire what Ayn Rand admires and condemn what Ayn Rand condemns.
- Since Ayn Rand has designated Nathaniel Branden as her "intellectual heir" and has repeatedly proclaimed him to be an ideal exponent of her philosophy, he is to be accorded only marginally less reverence than Ayn Rand herself.
- But it is best not to say most of these things explicitly (excepting perhaps, the first two items). One must always maintain that one arrives at one's beliefs solely by reason.[40]

Joan Kennedy Taylor remembers that Rand reserved her stern attitudes for her students.

She was much harder and much less respectful to anyone who wanted to be her student. People like Mickey Spillane, my father [composer Deems Taylor, whose work Rand respected; she once encouraged him to turn *Anthem* into an opera], Henry Hazlitt, who didn't necessarily agree with her about anything, she would just admire what she saw in them that was good. People who wanted to be her students, she had a totally opposite orientation: She looked for mistakes and constantly threatened not to speak to them anymore.

I remember once I said I could understand why Bill Buckley would be attractive as a candidate for mayor of New York City. He was articulate; he brought up interesting points no one else talked about. Ayn said, "If you never want to speak to me again, go ahead and consider voting for him."[41]

Robert Hessen remembers that lesser members of the inner circle—including eventual heir Peikoff—were regular victims of minipurges. Rand would stop speaking to them over such sins as expressing respect for intellectual enemies of Rand or approving of a movie Rand thought evil (without even seeing it).[42]

The stringent set of Objectivist rules and the accusatory, moralistic manner in which Rand and Branden enforced them could be dehumanizing, not least to the Brandens themselves. They once wondered, after enjoying a night out dancing, why Rand disapproved of their innocuous, unintellectual fun and what Rand meant when she said such a disagreement indicated "a gulf in values" between them.[43] Objectivism built a shelter that insulated young acolytes from the corrupt world, complete with art on the wall, books on the bookshelf, and agreeable companions for dinner parties. But that home could seem small and constrained, with no free space. Through the building's complicated architecture the movement essentially dictated what members could or couldn't (or should or shouldn't) do.

Life in the Objectivist movement offered opportunities to approach rational glory—as well as experience terrible embarrassment. Hessen remembers an evening in the mid-1960s as the most awkward of his life. Rand and the Brandens gathered the rest of the collective to condemn members for not doing enough for the Objectivist cause, leaving too much for the troika to accomplish. "We were scolded, all of us, for leaving to Ayn and Nathan the burden of saving the world. All of us were in effect parasites, going about our own lives and concerns, children, careers and the like, while they were doing all the hard work. But there was one exception among us: Bob Hessen. He's the only one carrying his weight."

It wasn't because of his NBI work.

> I wasn't really a great typist or organizer. But I had a creative mind for practical suggestions. They listed 10 things I'd done to put Objectivism on the map, the most important and obvious being I noticed in paperback mysteries there were bind-in advertising cards for cigarettes. I told Ayn, I bet you are such a big author they'd let you put in cards advertising Nathan's lecture series in your books. It was mainly from those bind-in cards that NBI got on the map.
>
> That evening I was like a Stakhanovite, one who produces far above the rate and made everybody else look like a slacker. It was the most embarrassing experience of my life. . . . So then Edith Efron came up with the brilliant suggestion that she will compile a list of 100 books each of us have to read to carry our weight— 10 in political philosophy, 10 in economics, 10 in European fiction, 10 in American fiction. One person's heart sank, because he's struggling to have a life and career and he's not an academic and the thought of having to master 100 books and be responsible for applying their insights to the real world—it was like telling a horse it has to carry another load of bricks.
>
> That was all a big part of the atmosphere—lots of scolding.[44]

But most of the rank-and-file NBIers, not directly exposed to Rand's and Branden's demands, didn't mind. During question-and-answer periods at lectures, where Rand would frequently show up after Branden's talk as a special treat, her answers could be sharp and harsh. Once an eager young acolyte asked Rand's opinion of the art of Maxfield Parrish, clearly seeking some validation of her favorite artist from her favorite writer. Rand's one word reply: "Junk!" The girl was crushed.

But Rand was usually forgiven, no matter her rudeness, no matter her sharpness. "If she occasionally lost her temper, most of them seemed to feel, what of it?" wrote Branden in his memoirs. "As one former NBI student put it . . . 'Look how much she had to offer! Look how much I was learning! If she got a little berserk now and then, *so what?*'"[45]

"GENTLEMEN, LEAVE YOUR GUNS OUTSIDE!"

As Objectivism grew through the 1960s, Rand focused on nonfiction essays for her newsletter.[46] Rand's first post-*Atlas* book, *For the New Intellectual* (1961), was a collection of philosophical passages from her novels with a new introductory essay spelling out Rand's colorful view of the philosophical history of Western civilization. She called for an alliance of the businessman and the intellectual—to finally realize and explicitly defend the values of the Founding Fathers: every man's right to "his own life, his own liberty, to the pursuit of his own happiness—which means: man's right to exist for his own sake, neither sacrificing himself to others nor sacrificing others to himself."[47] The practical corollary of this is capitalism, which the new intellectual must defend not on pragmatic grounds, but because it is the right and moral way for men to interact. The two main ideas that these new intellectuals—the army of scrappy intelligentsia that rallied to Rand's books, that was trained by NBI—were supposed to inculcate into the culture at large were (1) that emotions are not a means of cognition and (2) that one must never initiate physical force against another man. Her exhortatory closing links the necessity for peaceful relations among men to the threat of atomic annihilation with powerful moral force. The great principle of civilization, she writes, is "Gentlemen, leave your guns outside!"[48]

While her long-term reputation will undoubtedly rest on her novels, Rand's essays provided a rich and often invoked set of libertarian arguments against collective morality and state action. From her nonfiction, along with Galt's speech (which, in one of those Randian touches that can seem charming or ridiculous depending on one's charity, is regularly quoted and cited as if it were academic support—or holy scripture—in Rand's nonfiction writing), a larger picture of Rand's philosophy and sense of life comes into focus.

To Rand, everything depends on three unquestionable axiomatic primaries, which you cannot deny without affirming: existence, identity, and consciousness. Like Mises, she deduces her philosophy from necessary truths. But unlike Mises, her bedrock, unquestionable truth was ontological, rooted in the very nature of reality, not just a function of how the human mind and human action work. To Rand, politics can't come first. It is impossible, she thought, to effectively fight collectivism without attacking altruism, its moral base—and equally impossible to defeat altruism without first striking against irrationalism, its epistemological base. And the ultimate irrationalism is denying that existence exists—that a thing is what it is—that A is A.[49] If you understood what reality *is*, what men *are*, and you applied noncontradictory reason to it, then you would come, she insisted, to the proper libertarian economic and political considerations. Man's nature requires him, in essence, to be free.

Her essay collection *The Virtue of Selfishness*—the title chosen because she knew it would offend people—begins with an explication of Objectivist ethics that try to solve, in a bold stroke, the ancient moral philosophical problem of how to derive an "ought" statement from an "is" statement—how to make the facts of reality lead to an undeniable moral conclusion. "The fact that a living entity *is*, determines what it *ought* to do."[50] A human being must choose to think and reason, and a human being *must* think and reason to survive. Otherwise we are not well equipped to outcompete our mammalian competitors for food. We are not faster than the gazelle or stronger than the lion, yet by using our reason and intelligence, we can surpass them in the struggle for survival. Ethics involves the choice of the proper values to pursue—and values, Rand says, only have meaning in the context of choice—only to living beings. Nothing can make any difference to an inanimate object, or a dead one.

Thus, Rand reasoned, the proper value for a living being is *its own life*. If your life is the ultimate value, certain other values are integral means to that end: reason, purpose, and self-esteem. You cannot survive without using reason to grasp the nature of the world around you. "Nature, to be commanded, must be obeyed" is a popular Objectivist epigram. You cannot act consistently or to any effect unless you have chosen a purpose. And since man is "a being of self-made soul," as John

Galt put it, self-esteem is necessary for man to feel qualified to continue living, as the problems of neuroses and suicidal depression show.

And because a human being must be free to use his mind and to homestead property, as per Locke, a reality-rooted political ethic says that no man ought to interfere with another's ability to think, act, and appropriate property—and freely trade that property once justly obtained. That is the basics of how Rand derives her libertarian conception of human rights. Some rights scoffers have pointed out that Rand, in the context of attacking welfare statism and forced income redistribution, said that "a need is not a claim" and then based her whole view of human rights on the fact that man *needs* other men to respect them in order to survive and thrive.[51]

Rand's view of man's nature was based in a nonreligious natural rights/natural law tradition; she respected Thomas Aquinas as an Aristotelian despite his Catholicism.[52] Man's standard of life isn't mere animal survival but survival as "man qua man." This makes assessing man's proper behavior less "objective," less reducible to unquestionable observed sensory reality. Rand realized early in her philosophical speculations that her version of the proper nature of man is not something man "naturally" is. "Man must remain man through his own choice. Nature guarantees him nothing, not even his own nature."[53]

In her essays Rand dealt with more than the technicalities of her philosophy and ethics; she also applied her thinking to current events and the theory and practice of fiction writing and other arts.[54] On current events she could be prescient, such as her early evaluation of the student uprisings in Berkeley that largely predicted what right-wing critics have said ever since about the leftist/nihilist takeover of college campuses.[55] She condemned nationalism/tribalism, which she despised as the most primitive forms of collectivist thinking. In her 1970s writings she predicted the necessity (if not the specifics) of war in areas like the Balkans, where differing ethnically conscious groups are crammed together in one powerful state. Like Mises, she realized that state power exacerbates cultural tensions in polyglot nations by making the question of who controls the state vitally important. Without powerful central states, ethnic groups would lack a key issue to quarrel over.[56]

Rand was at her polemical best when she had a culturally powerful foe to joust against. She didn't try to deal with her opponents' positions on their own explicit terms but used what Peikoff once characterized as her "intellectual Hercule Poirot" qualities.[57] She saw the necessary though often unspoken philosophic implications of the likes of B. F. Skinner and Pope Paul's *Popularum Progressio*, which she read as hating man's intelligence and desiring to enslave man to the most basic requirements of the body: reproduction and other people's bare physical needs.[58] She also notes—as she noted of the growing thickets of government regulatory policy in a different context—that the pope's proscriptions were not meant to actually be obeyed, but to inculcate constant moral guilt (or in the case of regulations, potential legal guilt) in everyone all the time in order to morally (or legally) disarm them.[59]

Man, Rand notes, is an essentially moral animal. If he thinks something is *right,* he is willing to put up with enormous practical hardships to pursue it. This, she thought, is where Mises and other economist defenders of liberty went wrong. They thought people only need to understand that collectivism and statism don't *work,* don't deliver the goods. Rand knew that people don't *care* if something doesn't work, as long as the dominant morality of altruism tells them that it is *right.*

"FOR ME THERE WAS ONLY ONE CHOICE . . . TO GO ON TO ANARCHISM."

Though she stood aloof from most other libertarians, Rand generated a mighty gravitational pull in the 1950s that propelled other libertarians out of what might have seemed their natural orbit. Murray Rothbard, the man known by many in the 1970s and 1980s as "Mr. Libertarian," for example, saw his path intersect hers three times, before he finally spun away forever—but not unchanged.

Murray Newton Rothbard was born in the Bronx on March 2, 1926, the son of David Rothbard and Rachael Babushkin Rothbard, Jewish immigrants from Poland. He was a short, stout, bookish child, and a contrarian one. One of his favorite memories from his childhood was of a family gathering in which his overwhelmingly socialist extended family discussed the Spanish Civil War in the manner typical of a group of socialist-leaning progressive Jews in the 1930s. Young Murray piped in with, "What's so bad about Franco, anyway?"[60]

"I had two sets of Communist Party uncles and aunts, on both sides of my family," Rothbard recalled. "But more important, the one great moral question in the lives of all these people was: Should I actually join the Communist Party and devote the whole of my life to the cause, or should I remain a fellow-traveler and 'selfishly' devote only a fraction of my energy to communism? That was it; any species of liberalism, let alone conservatism, was nonexistent."[61]

Still, Rothbard's early rightist tendencies were not antinomian rebellion from family—he agreed with his father's pro-market, anti-left politics even as a boy. Father and son commiserated, for example, over the depredations of labor unions when David, who managed a Tide Water oil refinery in Bayonne, New Jersey, was trapped there during a long strike in 1952. His father's troubles, Rothbard wrote a friend, were "a direct result of gangster-unionism (and believe me, these two words deserve a perpetual connection)."[62] The police refusal to do anything about what he saw as union crimes during that strike supported Rothbard's skepticism about government law enforcement: "Here, in the failure of the police force, is another living example of the necessity of Right-Wing An— . . . (oops, I mean) . . . Voluntaryism."[63]

Rothbard entered Columbia University in September 1942 and earned his master's degree in economics and math in 1946. He was twenty years old, and the foundations for his lifelong ideological commitments were already in place. His beliefs arose not from immersion in any libertarian movement per se, which had barely formed at this point, coming to birth even as Rothbard's intellectual awakening occurred. Rothbard was temperamentally and ideologically formed by the loose quasi-movement (more like a tendency) now known as the old right, which he championed in different contexts throughout his career. (See Chapter 1.)

Rothbard was educated by the great old right newspapers, the *New York Sun* and the *Chicago Tribune* under Colonel Robert McCormick. Rothbard referred to his philosophy as "true liberalism" in the mid-1940s and still believed certain parts of the Republican Party exemplified it. He was an active member of New York's Young Republican Club in the immediate postwar years. Even then, his "true liberalism" had lost any serious influence within the party. Until 1946, Rothbard remembered, he did not meet a single other "rightist."[64]

In a curious irony, a leading light of the Chicago school of free market economics, which Rothbard would eventually fight against for dominance of libertarian thinking, first linked Rothbard with the intellectual movement that would sustain him for the rest of his life, even as he worked to purify, strengthen, and expand it according to his own lights. Professor George Stigler, long associated with the University of Chicago, was teaching at Columbia in fall 1946. His lectures touched on his opposition to rent control and the minimum wage.

This delighted Rothbard, especially when he saw how it maddened his fellow left-leaning students to hear such heresy in the halls of Columbia. The young Rothbard was alternately aggravated and amused by Columbia's leftist atmosphere. He enjoyed the shock he caused by being a young New York Jew for Strom Thurmond in 1948. He admired Thurmond's state's rights position and could only giggle when a stern young Stalinist assured him that Rothbard could not be a true jazz lover, since jazz is the people's art and Rothbard was a reactionary.

Stigler had just written his controversial pamphlet against rent control, in collaboration with his friend Milton Friedman, for FEE (see Chapter 4). Stigler told Rothbard about the pamphlet and about FEE. Rothbard was delighted to learn of an organization promoting his political and economic values. The peculiarity of his strongly held views was already alienating him from the political–cultural scene surrounding him. In a letter he noted that "anyone who dares support the principles of the Rule of Law, of political and economic freedom, is immediately accused of being a 'Fascist,' a 'black reactionary,' a 'paid agent of the NAM [National Association of Manufacturers],' and is forthwith ostracized from 'intellectual' society."[65]

Murray Rothbard was not born a cold war revisionist, though he would later become one; he was writing letters in 1946 to New York newspapers cheering calls for an end to Soviet aggression. But by 1947, after exposure to Irvington thinking, the mature Rothbard isolationism had solidified. Close friends were already warning him that his dogged purism would doom the free world to communist slavery—the sort of imprecation he'd hear from erstwhile pals and supporters on the right for the rest of his checkered, strange career. By

1948, Leonard Read had already noted young Rothbard's deep knowledge of market economics and libertarian principles (and their history) and began to lean on him to vet articles for FEE.

Rothbard was in the doctoral program at Columbia, researching a thesis on the bank panic of 1819. Reading FEE literature and making personal visits to its Irvington headquarters opened up a larger world of intellectuals and activists who shared his beliefs. How could the pugnacious young Rothbard, surrounded by ideological enemies, not feel his heart sing upon discovering the likes of Frank Chodorov and his pamphlets such as *Taxation Is Robbery*?

Rothbard met Chodorov at a FEE party. He made a great early mentor for Rothbard, versed as he was in the old right libertarian tradition of his friend Nock. Chodorov helped introduce Rothbard to the works of Nock, Herbert Spencer, Garet Garrett, and Isabel Paterson, among others. Rothbard become immersed in the libertarian tradition that predated him, which he relied on through the rest of his intellectual life: Mises, Nock, Mencken, Tucker, Spooner, and Spencer (whose *Social Statics* Rothbard called "the greatest single work of libertarian political philosophy ever written").[66]

Rothbard produced his first professional writings for Chodorov's *analysis* newsletter. They included reviews of Mencken, old-right mainstay John Flynn, and Mises's *Human Action*. Before the 1940s ended, Rothbard would take a step beyond most of his old right and classical liberal mentors in what was then called the "freedom philosophy" by FEE types. Though Rothbard was an economist, he didn't oppose the state just because he knew that government intervention rarely achieved its desired end. His economics certainly dovetailed with his politics—a state of affairs common among libertarians, and one that often makes its intellectual opponents suspicious. A dovetailing of practical and ethical stances is exceedingly common, almost universal, among all varieties of political thinking, but it was ultimately considerations of ethics and justice that led Rothbard to reject the state entirely.

Rothbard was embroiled in one of his usual debates over his free market radicalism, he recalled, when his interlocutors asked him a question: If a social contract can justify a legitimate minimal state, then "why can't society also agree to have a government build steel mills and have price controls and whatever? At that point I realized that the laissez-faire position is terribly inconsistent, and I either had to go on to anarchism or become a statist. Of course for me there was only one choice: that's to go on to anarchism."[67] He spent the winter of 1949 going back to his anarcho forebears such as Spooner, Tucker, and Auberon Herbert; he was discovering Mises's *Human Action* around the same time. His fate was sealed: "In the fall of 1949 I was a free-market minarchist of no particular school of thought; by the spring of 1950 I was a hard-core Misesian and anarcho-capitalist, as well as an 'isolationist.'"[68]

"WHEN IT COMES TO *POLITICS*, SOME OF US CONSIDER MISES A MEMBER OF THE NONCOMMUNIST LEFT."

Libertarian movement handlers seized on Rothbard as a treasure. The Volker Fund's Richard Cornuelle thought him "unquestionably the most gifted young economist I know anything about."[69] Mises agreed with Cornuelle's recommendation to have Rothbard write a textbook-style simplification of *Human Action*. The Volker Fund relied on Rothbard to vet manuscripts and scour academic journals for congenial ideas and writers, glomming onto him as the brightest and best educated of a (nearly nonexistent) rising generation of libertarians. While working for Volker and occasionally for FEE (where he produced essays on money and the Great Depression that Read, as was his wont, chose to sit on), Rothbard chugged slowly along on his doctoral thesis, published in 1962 as *The Panic of 1819*. It applied Austrian business cycle thinking, which blamed banks for creating excess money and credit and thus creating cycles, to this early American economic crisis. Despite dueling faculty advisers, Arthur Burns (later chairman of the Federal Reserve) and Joseph Dorfman, he finally won his doctorate in 1956.

But Rothbard was set on goals loftier than a doctorate earned through study of a single historical episode, even if that task did require bringing praxeological, economic, historical, and political science skills to bear. Rothbard wanted to use his multidisciplinary fascination with libertarian ideas to forge a unified "science of liberty."

By the start of 1954, he was telling Cornuelle at Volker Fund of the glories of "a comprehensive science which rests on many foundations: praxeology, economic history, philosophy (especially ethics and epistemology)," even "psychology, biology."[70] His correspondence of the time reveals a young man burning to make sense of the world and history, reduce all the conundrums of the social and ethical sciences to liberty and property, the banners he waved.

Always conscious of movement strategy, Rothbard looked to successful ideological revolutionaries of the past, such as Lenin, for strategic insights into how to effect ideological change on a national level. One of Rothbard's pet Leninist tropes was the idea of the cadre—the dedicated inner circle of revolutionaries, 100 percent reliable in ideology and action, around which a movement could crystallize.

The masses would not be turned quickly, although Rothbard didn't see them as a major threat to liberty, as conservatives influenced by Ortega y Gasset might. "I do not see the masses as evil at all," he was telling his friend Frank Meyer, an ex-communist who became a leading light at *National Review* and tried from there to effect a "fusion" between conservatives and libertarians. "Rather I kind of like them. I look at the masses this way: competent to run their daily lives, but unable to think for themselves on abstract issues, such as political ideologies. They therefore take their ideologies from the intellectuals."[71]

In the early and mid-1950s, Eisenhower took over the GOP. Unreconstructed classical liberal peaceniks, anarchists, and near-anarchists, such as Rothbard and his New York City friends, united by their then-peculiar ideological dedication to liberty, realized that they had no comfortable place on the American political scene. In that atmosphere, Rothbard formed his first real cadre, turning most of them (though not all) into fellow "right-wing anarchists" or "voluntaryists."[72]

Leonard Read's bold, heretical declaration in his book *Government: An Ideal Concept* that citizens can be forced to pay taxes for their own protection engendered a cross-national flood of anger, revealing the tensions that existed between the anarchists and "minarchists" (those who believed in a "minimal" government restricted to protecting citizens' life and property against force and fraud. The term "minarchist" to describe such libertarians entered the movement vocabulary a decade or more later, courtesy of movement gadfly Samuel Konkin.) In terms of significant power centers, the anarchists had the minarchists outnumbered and included most of the Volker Fund's program offi-cers, the Freedom School (the only purely libertarian educational in-stitution, run by a man named Robert LeFevre), and the Hoiles Freedom Newspaper chain. Leonard Read and his small-government men were holding on to their Irvington redoubt, still the most influ-ential part of the libertarian world. FEE's Baldy Harper had become frustrated with the ideological stagnation that he thought Read's dis-dain for anarchism imposed. He was frustrated as well with Read's management style, which left lots of writing languishing in file draw-ers. He left FEE for the Volker Fund in 1958, working with Richard Cornuelle on one of its side projects, the Foundation for Voluntary Welfare. That organization tried to make an end run around the state by exploring how social needs could be met through freely chosen voluntary activities, not state violence. (As anarcho-libertarians, they saw the gun behind every state welfare program. After all, what hap-pens to people who refuse to play along with state demands?)

The libertarian movement in the 1950s was not a purely constitu-tionalist limited-government gang of respectable patriots; anarchism was woven intricately and thickly throughout it. (Ayn Rand and Isabel Paterson remained dedicated to their limited state, and Rose Wilder Lane vacillated between anarchism and statism, though she identified herself as an anarchist on occasion.) FEE's Edmund Opitz found it un-sporting of anarchist libertarians (such as Hoiles) to speak the language of the Founding Fathers and claim a Yankee Doodle heritage for their heresies; none of the Founding Fathers believed in this voluntary competing defense agency stuff. Opitz feared (as happened with Ben-jamin Tucker and his nineteenth-century individualist anarchist move-ment after he embraced Max Stirner) that anarchism among his comrades would lead ineluctably to amoralism, which Opitz was cer-tain would be fatal to the libertarian cause.

None of the libertarian anarchists back then fully embraced the term. Even Rothbard held on to Auberon Herbert's "voluntaryist" for a while, though he joked about "right-wing anarchism" among his friends. Some of them, like FEE donor Mercer Parks and Robert LeFevre, thought that anarchists advocated the violent overthrow of all constituted authority, and that certainly didn't describe *them*.

But Rothbard's new cadre didn't worry about such niceties. On April 23, 1953, at a Mises NYU seminar meeting, Murray Rothbard met two high school students, George Reisman and Ralph Raico, who amazed him with their advanced understanding of libertarianism, which jibed with his. Reisman was already asking why the government needs to have anything to do with money. The boys met Rothbard's economist mentor Mises one day when they knocked on the Great Man's door, hoping to capture his attention by claiming to be selling *Freeman* subscriptions door-to-door. Professor Mises politely announced he already received the journal, apparently thinking nothing amiss about the notion of door-to-door libertarian journal saleskids.

Raico and Reisman got to meet Mises under more normal circumstances, at his seminar, because of a letter Raico had written to "a little pocket-sized magazine called *USA*" in which he praised Mises.[73] Leonard Read, always alert for signs of libertarian life in the political–cultural desert, called Raico and invited him to Irvington. Raico brought his friend Reisman along, and they were taken in limos from the Waldorf in Manhattan after a FEE board meeting to Irvington, meeting Read and Baldy Harper, and the rest of the FEE crew of supporters and staff—Jasper Crane, Paul Poirot (who edited the *Freeman* for decades), Edmund Opitz, Percy Greaves, and his future wife Bettina Bien. They were introduced to Mises himself, who invited the boys to attend his NYU seminar, so long, in recognition of their youth, as they did not make any undue noise.[74]

Raico's memory of that first meeting with Rothbard shows a gang delighting in their own head-spinning radicalism—not uncommon among free-spirited youngsters feeling their libertarian oats. After their first Mises seminar meeting, Rothbard invited Raico and Reisman out for coffee. "My friend and I were dazzled by the great Mises, and Murray naturally was pleased to see our enthusiasm," Raico recalled. "He assured us that Mises was at least the greatest economist of the century, if not the whole history of economic thought. As far as politics went, though, Murray said, lowering his voice conspiratorially: 'Well, when it comes to *politics*, some of us consider Mises a member of the non-Communist left.' Yes, it was easy to see we'd met someone special."[75]

Rothbard was already tiring of FEE's lack of radicalism. But given its role in introducing him to these budding young anarchists, he thought it did have its uses—as long as youngsters didn't get trapped at a FEE-level understanding of libertarianism. It is telling of the nature and extent of the libertarian movement at the time that this discovery of two high school kids in New York with anarchist leanings was the event of the year and buoyed Rothbard's spirits for months. He rushed to describe his new finds to friends like Cornuelle at Volker. News of two high school kids bedeviling their commie social studies teacher with bon mots and arguments from *Human Action* was as exhilarating as news of a barricade smashed, a province taken, would be for more militant radical movements. Theirs was a battle for minds, and every keen one they captured was worth a regiment.

From that trio of Rothbard, Raico, and Reisman a larger gang of feisty, absurdist, anarchist kids with a mock-revolutionary fervor formed, mostly from people already linked to Reisman or Raico. Most of them avidly attended Mises's seminars, though only one, Reisman, became a registered student at NYU. "Our frequent informal gatherings," Rothbard remembered decades later, "combined learned discourse, high wit (most of it contributed by [Ralph] Raico and [Ronald] Hamowy), song composing, joint moviegoing, and fiercely competitive board games. It all added up to a helluva lot of fun."[76] It also supplied the libertarian movement with its first influx of twenty somethings. "Before Murray started reproducing himself through his first generation of disciples, the movement had no youthful tinge," Cornuelle recalls. "I was just a ringer myself, coming in on my [older] brother [Herb]'s coattails."[77]

Rothbard and his friends formed a self-conscious intellectual and activist salon, a beleaguered band of brothers cetain of ultimate triumph. They named themselves the Circle Bastiat, to cement the continuity of their radical ideas with the nineteenth-century classical liberal tradition. The circle composed tongue-in-cheek polemical battle tunes, including this one, to the tune of "America the Beautiful": "It's ours to right the great wrong done, ten thousand years ago./The state, conceived in blood and hate, remains our only foe./O Circle Brothers, Circle Brothers, victory is nigh./Come meet your fate, destroy the state, and raise the banner high."[78]

Most circle members remained friends for life (except for one schism to be detailed later), and all of them went on to play important roles in the libertarian movement. Raico, Reisman, and Robert Hessen were pals from the Bronx High School of Science. A fourth, Ronald

Hamowy, had gone to grade school with Reisman. Raico went on to study under Hayek at the University of Chicago's Committee on Social Thought in the early 1960s, and later became a historian at SUNY–Buffalo.[79] Reisman got his economics doctorate at NYU under Mises and currently teaches economics at Pepperdine University in California. He remained a part of Ayn Rand's inner circle for years and wrote a massive, *Human Action*–style summation of economic science from the ground up, in a mostly Austrian style, called *Capitalism* (1996). Robert Hessen also worked with Ayn Rand through the 1960s and later became a fellow at the Hoover Institution at Stanford University.[80] Ronald Hamowy also studied under Hayek at Chicago, and with Raico founded and edited the *New Individualist Review*, the first and still most accomplished student journal of classical liberal and libertarian scholarship and commentary. It was published from 1961 to 1968.[81]

Another circle member was Leonard Liggio, a freelance intellectual and sometime college professor who became Rothbard's partner in the mid-1960s in publishing *Left and Right,* trying to forge a radical anti-state coalition across standard left–right barriers. Liggio wrote extensively on such topics as the history of classical liberalism and the anti-interventionist tradition in America.[82] The Circle Bastiat became their social center, with Rothbard and his wife Joey as the hub and host. Rothbard had met JoAnn Schumacher, a young woman from Virginia, through mutual friends at Columbia, and they married in 1953. Circle members were mostly night owls; Rothbard liked to talk, play, and work until dawn.[83] Cornuelle recalls delightful nights when he, Rothbard, and others composed scathing letters to industrialists thought to be selling free enterprise down the river by their support for government actions.

Social circles rooted in personal affection are key to the strengthening and spreading of ideological movements. Following an intellectual path that the rest of the world finds peculiar or frightening is lightened by the knowledge that one is fighting not only for truth but also for an affectionate circle of comrades. The Circle Bastiat engaged in grandiose, *mostly* mock assertions of their own world-historical importance, thinking of themselves as an analog and antidote to Marx and his gang of revolutionary communists in 1848.

As Hamowy recalls, the circle "was around 90 percent of my social life. We were regarded by most of the world as being fascists or Nazis or

crackpots for having our political beliefs. It became clear very quickly
in discussing politics with anyone that we were taking a position people
had a very strong visceral reaction against. So we all palled around a
great deal. We all liked to stay up late and play games and go to movies
and badmouth the left—all the usual fun things."[84] The favorite circle
game was Risk, a strategy game in which armies fought for control of
countries. Rothbard suggested that only anarchists could freely enjoy it
without too much anxiety about the outcome, since they were the
only ones who didn't want to conquer the world. Hamowy recalls an
excursion to a horror movie whose villain was a man-eating tree.
Rothbard relentlessly cheered the tree. "The people he ate were aggres-
sors," Rothbard insisted. "They kept trying to set the tree on fire or
chop it down, when the tree hadn't done a damn thing to them!"[85]

"You are *for* public schools? Where did you get such strange ideas?"

Some circle members were more natural-born individualists than others. Hessen recalls being turned by Raico and Reisman during bull sessions at the high school lunch table. "I remember saying that if the
government didn't deliver the mail, we wouldn't get any letters. Ralph
said that if the government didn't build cows, we would never get
milk." Hessen recalls that Raico and Reisman discovered they shared
beliefs during a United Nations Celebration Day at Bronx High
School of Science. "Everyone was supposed to jump up and sing about
'the U.N. on the march with flags unfurled, we're going to make a
brave new world.' Ralph and George were the only ones in the class
that remained seated, and they immediately glommed onto each
other."[86]

Many of the circle participated in the dying days of the old right,
anti–New Deal, anti–foreign intervention tendency in the Republican
Party, as part of a Youth for Taft group. Leonard Liggio was a New York
kid weaned on the early *Human Events* with its essays by Morley,
Mises, Hayek, Hazlitt, and Chodorov, with a strong interest in the
World War II historical revisionism of the likes of Charles Tansill and
Harry Elmer Barnes. Those scholars questioned the official story of

how and why the United States became involved in World War II, in
ways that made the United States look less noble than did the official
version. Liggio went to Georgetown University to study under Tansill.
"Jesuit institutions were more into private property at that time" than
the Ivy League was, Liggio recalls.[87]

While active in Youth for Taft in 1952, Leonard would frequently
spend weekends in New York City where he met Raico and Reisman,
fellow youths for Taft. Raico recalls that as a Republican, "I identified
very much with the Midwestern wing of the party. I used to go to
Times Square to pick up the *Chicago Tribune* [published by old right
hero Robert McCormick]. They used to have front-page color editorial cartoons in those days. A typical one would show the blue UN flag
and underneath it simply say, 'The Traitor's Flag.' Not much in the way
of subtlety, but I identified with that."[88]

After Taft lost the nomination to Eisenhower, Raico convinced Liggio that they must forge on to the next political–ideological adventure: overturning Social Security. "I thought that was too extreme,"
Liggio remembers. "The Republicans hadn't raised it as an idea. 'What
are you saying?' I thought. Ralph told me we had to convince the
public that it was neither just nor workable in the long term. Then he
told me, 'You have to read *Human Action*—no one can breathe another
day without reading *Human Action*.'"[89] Thus another libertarian entered the fold.

With both Taft and their next favorite, General Douglas MacArthur,
out of the Republican running, they worked with a new student
group called Students for America, in which Liggio, Raico, and Reisman were eastern regional organizers. At the time, Liggio recalls, being
openly right-wing on college campuses was as dangerous as being
communist. "Students who were considered right wing got kicked out
of school all over," Liggio says. "This was not uncommon."[90]

Among the right-wing enthusiasms of the time that the circle embraced, somewhat surprisingly given their general opposition to cold
war madness, was McCarthyism. Rothbard approved of investigating
the possible communist ties of government employees (he'd approve of
anything that bedeviled *them*). Besides, he liked to tweak the "respecta-
bles" in the Democratic mainstream who wanted to walk the line between being properly anticommunist and pro-McCarthy, those who

talked of approving his ends—the elimination of communist subversion—but being repulsed by his means. "The glory of McCarthy, as far
as I'm concerned, was his *means,* not his ends: his populist reaching
over the heads of the Establishment and its intellectuals to mount a
crusade against the Establishment itself."[91]

The Circle Bastiat boys were also pranksters who liked to disrupt
other people's realities for their own amusement and occasionally for
moments of libertarian Zen wisdom. When talking to young socialists, they enjoyed turning some of the socialists' predictable rhetoric
back on them, for example, soberly explaining that socialism might
have been all right in the primitive conditions of the eighteenth or
nineteenth centuries. But in today's complex, modern machine era,
surely they could see that we must have laissez-faire—it's just the irresistible motion of history, the inevitable wave of the future, no point
in fighting it.

One of their favorite stunts involved filling the audience at a talk by
the governor of New Jersey aired on a TV program called *Youth Wants
to Know,* and hitting him with their brand of questions from all sides,
which included adopting the attitude that *their* ideological universe
was the norm and *his* some sort of aberration. "What, governor? You
are *for* public schools? Where did you get such strange ideas? Can you
recommend any books on this subject?"[92] A favorite technique of
theirs was to dominate the social reality in any gathering of right-
wingers or leftists. By appearing en masse (but not obviously as pals)
and talking their libertarian talk, they thought they could make their
opponents see them as a legitimate and real "other side" of some issue
and force the majority to grapple with their viewpoint. They'd go to
any right-wing meeting they could and loudly air an antidraft or anti-
Eisenhower viewpoint. Rothbard loved the technique of pushing
people who might be on the correct path further toward libertarianism. He suggested that the Volker Fund should run more conferences
in which the hard-core anarcho-capitalists made up more than half of
the attendees. Creating an atmosphere in which the less hard-core
were an embattled minority, he thought, might help turn some
thinkers who were inclined in the proper direction all the way around.

One of their pranks injected the Circle Bastiat into McCarthyist history. They managed to infiltrate a testimonial dinner for Roy Cohn

under the aegis of Students for America, and offered the idea that small grassroots groups (like themselves) should laud Cohn and give him awards of their own design. Rothbard composed a speech for Reisman to deliver, with the purpose of turning the meeting from a merely anti-communist one "to an anti–Socialist, anti–New Deal meeting. . . . The speech followed the old Communist principle of turning every meeting, every forum for discussion. . . . into a weapon for agitation. . . . all the other awards had been completely insipid, and speeches had been confined to denouncing 'atheistic Communism.' At the last minute, George and I, discussing how we could make the speech even more extreme, slipped in a direct denunciation of Eisenhower—the only one of the evening, and which got the biggest applause."

> Why the intensity of the hatred against Cohn and McCarthy by the self-styled 'intellectuals' of the Left? It is because any threat to expose Communists in high places is also a threat against the Communists' blood brothers—the Socialists and New Dealers who have been running our political life for the last twenty-one years—*and are still running it!* Communism, after all, is simply a brand of Socialism; the Communists and the New Dealer may have their family quarrels at times, but essentially they have been united.[93]

Rothbard was thrilled by the wild applause the speech got from the crowd, and the coverage it got from *Time* magazine. He sourly noted that the masses were far more radical and correct than their leaders. The organizer of the Cohn testimonial told Rothbard that had he known the content of the speech beforehand, he wouldn't have allowed Reisman to deliver it.

"THE WAR-PEACE QUESTION IS *THE KEY* TO THE WHOLE LIBERTARIAN BUSINESS."

The distinctions between individualist libertarians and their conservative counterparts sharpened and multiplied as the 1950s wore on. The right wing as represented by William F. Buckley's rising conservative movement held no appeal for the Circle Bastiat. Rothbard was an early contributor to Buckley's *National Review*, mostly of book reviews, but was always leery of the fanatical anticommunism that he saw as overpowering the antistatism in the new conservative mix. Still, he remained a member in good standing of the larger *National Review* circle, at least as far as Buckley was concerned, even after Rothbard sent him numerous long letters upbraiding Buckley for his betrayals of liberty or trying to explain to him that a revolutionary *seeking* power has a different set of incentives and desires than an apparatchik *in* power; consequently the men running the Soviet Union weren't necessarily loyal to old Leninist saws about pursuing world revolution at any cost. Rothbard and Buckley were old buddies, though. Rothbard had helped with the parts of Buckley's *Up from Liberalism* concerning economics and was being cheerily invited to *National Review* editorial meetings as late as April 1960.[94] Others in the FEE circle felt the same aversion to *National Review*. A onetime chairman of FEE's board of trustees wrote Buckley, upon reading the first issue, that "I have a little bit the fear that too much attention may be paid to being anti-Communist and not enough being against communism."[95]

By the end of 1956, Rothbard was complaining of the "clerical–fascist" tinge of the magazine and mocking its obeisance to an organic connection to England and France, its interpretation of the Hungarian revolt as a call for Habsburg restoration, and its pro-colonial attacks on Egypt's Abdel Nasser during the Suez crisis. When the journal ran an article by Portuguese dictator Antonio Salazar, Rothbard darkly suggested that merely being an anticommunist Catholic was enough to earn you *National Review*'s laurels, whether or not you were a dictatorial mass murderer.[96] Even his old loves, *Human Events* and *Chicago Tribune*, had palled on him, with their incessant nuclear sabre rattling.

Rothbard enthusiastically watched the bubbles and flare-ups and crackups, too numerous to be worth mentioning, as right-wingers disgusted with Eisenhower tried to make third-party end runs around the Republican Party. Rothbard kept up with it obsessively, writing long memos on what he found to his friends at Volker. He was especially enamored of maverick Utah governor J. Bracken Lee, finding him "the only candidate whom I would risk compulsory jury slavery to vote for for President."[97] As mayor of Price, Utah, Lee managed to run the city for three years of his twelve-year reign without imposing any city taxes.[98] Lee was also an outspoken foe of the Sixteenth Amendment (which allowed the creation of an unapportioned federal income tax), and in 1955 while governor of Utah decided to withhold some taxes to protest the use of his money in foreign aid, placing the bucks in a trust account pending a court decision on whether he really owed the money. Lee insisted he got thousands of letters of support, though some opponents painted their own negative reactions on the front steps of the governor's mansion, such as "Grow up, Gov." Bracken coolly noted that they did "a very good paint job."[99] The Pulliam papers and David Lawrence at *U.S. News & World Report*, then the more right-wing of the national newsweeklies, supported Lee. Chodorov compared him to Thoreau in the *Freeman*.[100] Lee was clearly too good for the 1950s GOP.

In 1956, Rothbard supported the third-party candidacy of T. Coleman Andrews for president. As he described it, "The last political manifestation of the Old Right was the third-party, Andrews-Werdal ticket of 1956, which called for the repeal of the income tax and the rollback of the New Deal. Its foreign policy was the last breath of the pre–Cold War Old Right: advocating no foreign war, the Bricker Amendment, and the abolition of foreign aid."[101] (The Bricker Amendment would have restricted the president's ability to unilaterally commit the United States to foreign treaties that might violate provisions of the Constitution. It was a favorite right-wing cause in the 1950s, with fear of the United Nations and one world government riding high.) The T. Coleman Andrews campaign brought together a whole gang of rightist groups disgusted with Eisenhower, including Clarence Manion's For America, Kent Courtney's New Orleans group, something called the Constitution Party, and some dodgy outfits whose main concern was keeping segregation going in the South.

Andrews's antitax program didn't ring bells for the Buckley right, as Liggio recalls. "In 1956 I wrote an article on the French election in which an anti-tax movement got a lot of seats. I wrote about that because I knew a lot about French politics, and *National Review* rejected it because they were not in favor of tax protest movements," he says. "I submitted it to *Human Events* and they rejected it. This was in 1956 when there was a presidential campaign by T. Coleman Andrews against the income tax, and the two major so-called conservative publications were not supporting the idea of tax protest."[102]

Rothbard had begun to tire of the standard right as a vehicle for his energy even before he became angry with Buckley. He had been complaining of the right's lack of support for free immigration (also lacking among standard liberals of the time, as well).[103] He was maddened by the right's support for censorship and laws regulating marriage or sex.[104] By the middle of 1955, months before *National Review* would, in Rothbard's mind, slam the door forever between him and the standard conservative movement, he had decided that he liked the left better than the right on a range of issues, from Formosa (should we go to war over it?) to the Smith and McCarran Acts to immigration, free trade, censorship, and divorce law.[105] He still had comrades among the presumptive right, even in high echelons of Republican politics. Former Republican congressman from Nebraska (and father to superinvestor Warren Buffett) Howard Buffett was a big Rothbard fan and admired his writing on the cold war.[106] But most right-wing intellectuals struck Rothbard as having a shallow understanding of true human liberty and defending it timidly. And the right-wing masses were in some ways worse than the intellectuals. "The Right-wing masses care little and know nothing about liberty or economics; they are 'for' Christ and the Constitution, and they are against foreigners, Communists, atheists, and Jews."[107]

The shadow of nuclear annihilation, the most evil aspect of an evil institution, weighed heavily on Rothbard, and he was willing to embrace strange allies and forbidden causes to try to dispel it. He joined the mostly left–liberal Committee for a Sane Nuclear Policy[108] and actually did office work for the Adlai Stevenson organization. He enthusiastically supported the idea of having Khrushchev visit the United States, thinking it might help end the nuclear brinkmanship between the two nuclear powers.[109]

"I am getting more and more convinced," he wrote Kenneth Templeton of the Volker Fund in 1959, "that the war-peace question is *the key* to the whole libertarian business, and that we will never get anywhere in this great intellectual counter-revolution (or revolution) unless we can end this Verdamte cold war—a war for which I believe our 'tough' policy is largely responsible."[110]

The Buckleyite right positioned itself as the snide older brother to the more radical and irresponsible libertarian individualists, even though when it came to antistatism, most of his crew of former communists were Johnny-come-latelies compared to the FEE circle. Buckley mocked what he saw as the libertarians' effete and useless disengagement from the cold war, scoffing at them for shuffling off from serious geopolitics to their little intellectual seminars on demunicipalizing garbage removal.

In 1963, FEE board chairman E. W. Dykes, an Ohio architect, responded to this line of attack by taking Buckley's critique for a given and defending libertarians on those seemingly outrageous terms.

> War is the culmination of the breaking of libertarian principles, not once, but thousands of times. We are challenged to jump in at this point and apply our principles to get out of the unholy mess, built up over years and years of error on errors. I suggest it would be a very little different challenge had he posed this proposition: "You are a second lieutenant. Your platoon is surrounded. Your ammunition is gone. Two of your squad leaders are dead, the third is severely wounded. Now, Mr. Libertarian, let's see you get out of this one with your little seminars."
>
> My answer—"demunicipalize the garbage service."
>
> Now wait, don't give me up as a nut yet. I have a point. That second lieutenant is a goner. And so is the prospect of a lasting peace until man learns *WHY* it is wrong to municipalize the garbage service. You can't apply libertarian principles to wrong things at their culmination and expect to make much sense. It is too fundamental. You have to start back at the very beginning and that is precisely what our little seminars are for. There are people who build for tomorrow; there are people who build for a year; there are people who look forward a generation—the libertarian, a part of "the remnant," takes the long view—he is looking forward to the time when war will be looked on as we now look on cannibalism, a thing of the past. . . . What do we do in our little seminars? We make the case for freedom which cannot coexist with interventionism. . . . Again I say: We will never end wars until we at least understand why the garbage service

should be removed from the jurisdiction of the police force—that is, government."[111]

"THE ANTI-LIFE HABIT OF FALLING ASLEEP ON HER COUCH."

In addition to butting heads with the Buckley right, Rothbard and at least half of the Circle Bastiat had the distinction of being among the first to get purged from Ayn Rand's Objectivist circle.

Rothbard had known about Rand before the publication of *Atlas Shrugged*. Herbert Cornuelle had introduced them, and Rothbard hung around her in the early 1950s, then again in 1954, before Rand started associating only with the Branden-centered collective. Rothbard had not been terribly impressed then. He saw in her thinking a belief in one rational purpose that all men ought to share, which to him implied that human individuality was to be shunned—that everyone should basically be the same perfectly rational Objective man.[112]

In 1954, Rothbard noted that under Randian premises "there is no reason whatever why Ayn, for example, shouldn't sleep with Nathan, or Barbara with Frank. Since they all have the same premises, they are all the same people, or rather interchangeable parts in a machine." If reason can dictate proper behavior, and Randians possess the firmest grasp on reason, then "the case really becomes very good for a complete Statist tyranny that will plan everybody's lives, educate them from the cradle in rationalist tenets, enforce mating, etc." He credits Reisman, after Rothbard brought his new circle friends by for a 1954 meeting with the Randian collective, with deciding that "Ayn's system is a perfect engine for complete totalitarianism, but . . . Ayn herself is a libertarian out of an irrational prejudice, and that fifty years from now some smart Randian disciple will see the implications and convert the thing into a horrible new Statist sect."[113]

But when *Atlas* came out, Rothbard, despite his bad experiences with Rand, adored it. He decided he had been wrong to write her off so quickly. He wrote one of the first *Atlas* fan letters Rand received, and it could hardly have been more adulatory. He told her that the whole Circle Bastiat was convinced that *Atlas* was the greatest novel ever written. (Bastiat member Hessen worked in an airport bookstore and was able to supply his friends with copies before the official release date.)

Rothbard admitted that he had never liked novels much until *Atlas*, finding them "at best, a useful sugar-coated pill to carry on agit-prop work amongst the masses who can't take ideas straight."[114] Rothbard shows an open-hearted vulnerability in the letter to Rand that he rarely showed in any public context, confessing that he had avoided her for the past few years because talking with her depressed him. But now he felt this was because he found the strength of her mind and intellect so overpowering that he feared losing his own personality, his own independence. He thanked her for leading him in the direction of natural rights thinking, since he had always felt that was one thing the strictly utilitarian Misesian edifice lacked. Reading *Atlas* had made him a better person, and he no longer laughed at the Randians as cultists for declaring her one of the greatest minds of all time.

He'd be laughing again soon enough. Rand loved the letter and invited Rothbard back to the fold for long nights talking philosophy and the wonders of *Atlas* in her living room on East Thirty-Sixth. Rothbard brought along the expanded Circle Bastiat and even took on Branden as his therapist, in the hope that a strong dose of psychological Objectivism could cure some of his crippling phobias about traveling, bridges, and planes.

As Rothbard recalls it, after a couple of months he and most of the circle found Branden's officiousness and humorlessness aggravating and laughable. He began noticing political deviations in Rand that he found hard to take, particularly her refusal to realize that the logical and moral corollary of voluntary taxation (which she did believe in) was private anarchist justice (in which the need for adjudication and protection were provided by private businesses in a competitive free market), which she rejected violently. One night, back at the Rothbards' apartment, the circle's usual jackanapes turned toward an impromptu skit imitating Rand and Branden attempting to convince a young woman (a therapy client of Branden's) that following the Branden–Rand line would guarantee her happiness. Word of this mockery, daring to make light of the designated right-hand mind to the most brilliant woman of all time, got back to Branden. War was on the horizon between the Brandenites and the Rothbardians.

During one evening at Rand's, as Rothbard recalled, everyone was indulging in "an orgy of Holy-Roller type testimonials in which each person, in turn, was expected to tell the assembled acolytes the answer to one crucial question: 'Who has been the most intellectually important person in my life?' The answer, of course, was foreordained."[115] Bastiat member and philosophy student Bruce Goldberg had the temerity to say that his friend Ralph Raico, who had converted him to libertarianism, had been most important. Branden reacted angrily and had both Goldberg and Raico banished from the Randian presence.[116] Leonard Liggio, meanwhile, began exhibiting the "anti-life habit of falling asleep on [Rand's] couch whenever she was speaking at any length" (as Jerome Tuccille put it).[117]

Things were unraveling fast. Branden began wondering why Rothbard and his pals didn't come by more often. "The reason I didn't see this crew more often," Rothbard recalled, "is that I couldn't stand these people. Any of them. Posturing, pretentious, humorless, robotic, nasty, simple-minded jackasses. I couldn't very well say: 'I don't want to see more of you because I can't stand you.' Not only would such a statement have been socially unacceptable, it would have been considered philosophically erroneous and evil. According to Randian doctrine, these were the most 'rational' people in the country, if not the universe. *If* you wish to be rational yourself . . . it follows ineluctably that you'd want to spend as much time as possible with these Most Rational People. I should be dying to spend *eight* days a week, if that were possible with these super-men and super-women."[118]

The Randians, Rothbard says, held up his wife Joey's belief in God as a sign of a deep problem, one that reflected poorly on Rothbard for remaining married to such an irrational woman. When exposure to Branden and Rand's airtight argument against the possibility of God's existence failed to elicit sudden apostasy on Joey's part, the rift widened even further between the Rand circle and the Circle Bastiat.

Rothbard was glum; he had been stunned by *Atlas*, but he regretted getting enmeshed in the Branden circle again. It was sullying the insular joie de vivre and pleasing comic darkness of the Circle Bastiat. They were acutely aware of the absurdity of their position in the world and held nothing as sacred from their acidic humor, parodic songsmithery, and general self-aware absurdist wit. "This is a time of testing," he wrote to circle member Bruce Goldberg, then in the army, as pacific relations with Branden degenerated to war. "But my love for the Circle, my faith in the Circle, and—I hope—my rational under-standing of the Circle, leads me to affirm that the Circle will, as always, emerge triumphant, a little wiser and I hope not sadder." (He was too hopeful.) He ended the letter with fresh Circle song lyrics, including, "Remember Mises' sacred trust. . . . Thou wilt not yield the Branden toll, Circle my Circle/Thou wilt not bow to his control."[119]

In their account of relations with Rothbard, the Brandens stressed a separate incident as the cause of Rothbard's banishment from their Manhattan Galt's Gulch and denied that Joey's theism was an issue. Rather, they claim that in his essay "The Mantle of Science" Rothbard plagiarized from both *Atlas* and Barbara Branden's master's thesis.[120] Branden ordered Rothbard to appear at a Randian trial at a time spec-ified, but Rothbard failed to deliver his body and mind up to Objec-tivist justice. That was it; Rothbard and all who stood by him were banished from the Presence.

But Branden did not stop there. He had Rand's lawyer write to Hel-mut Schoeck, head of the Volker Fund conference at which Rothbard was to deliver the paper, telling him the whole story. Branden expected that exposing Rothbard's perfidy would cost him his place in the con-ference and even his job with the Volker Fund. Schoeck was shocked by the letter. "Their primary aim," he decided, "seems to be the destruc-tion of Dr. Rothbard as a human being." Because it was from a lawyer, he suggested that "Dr. Rothbard . . . with our help, get quotes for each of the disputed paragraphs of course preceding in time the publications of the plaintiffs. They can be found easily."[121]

"The ideas which you charge me with taking from *Atlas Shrugged* and Barbara Branden's essay," Rothbard replied to Branden, "are neither theirs nor mine; on the contrary, they are a part of Western civilization, and can be found in innumerable rationalist writers. Of the many people at all versed in philosophy who have read my paper, not one thought these ideas were original, and not one failed to state that these were ideas that he had encountered many times before."[122] As Rothbard recalls, "Every once in a while, someone would ask me, 'it's a good arti-cle, but why do you have all those footnotes to points that are a basic part of Western philosophy?' And then I tell the story."[123]

The plagiarism accusations broke up not only Rothbard's relationship with Rand, which he was quite ready for, but the Circle Bastiat as well. Reisman and Hessen thought Rothbard's refusal to defend himself at the hearing was an implicit admission of guilt. Rothbard mailed them back tattered dollars in his keeping, their official circle dues. "It was like having your buttons torn off and sword broken," Hessen recalls.[124]

Rothbard remained scabrous on the subject of Rand (and Branden) forevermore, producing in letters and occasional articles a thick and often hilarious body of commentary on the peccadilloes of her and her circle, some public, some private. On Kant, that philosophical supervillain who Rand maintained "deliberately set out to destroy the human mind," Rothbard shared with correspondent Kerry Thornley that "I seriously question whether *anyone,* outside of Dr. Fu Manchu and other such sources for Randian aesthetics, ever 'set out deliberately to destroy the human mind.'"[125] He also noted dryly that with NBI's list of recommended books, Randians were doing the Catholic Church one better. While the Church had an index of prohibited books, the Objectivists in essence had an index of *permitted* books.

To this day, the Brandens attribute Rand's apparently irrational aversion to the libertarian movement to her assumption that modern libertarians were all like Murray Rothbard. He wrote an absurd one-act play parodying how Rand and the Brandens behaved and treated visitors, called *Mozart Was a Red.* Unpublished officially, it has circulated for years as a libertarian movement samizdat classic, and has even been performed on occasion for libertarian audiences.[126]

"TO DEMONSTRATE HOW A TOTALLY FREE, STATELESS MARKET MIGHT OPERATE SUCCESSFULLY."

Rothbard's main source of income through the 1950s came from reading and reviewing manuscripts and journals for the Volker Fund, searching for undiscovered individualists. He was also their go-to man for bibliographical information on any subject, from the Sixteenth Amendment to rent control to monopolies to compulsory education.

The rest of the movement seems to have decided that Rothbard knew (or could learn) much of what any of them needed to know. His unwillingness to leave New York City (due to a crippling travel phobia, which he did not fully overcome until the 1970s) frustrated his attempts to find an academic teaching berth. He declined an invitation to apply for a postgraduate fellowship at the University of Chicago.[127]

He did a part-time stint with FEE in 1956 and worked briefly in fall 1957 with a quickly scuttled organization called the Princeton Panel, funded by Claude Robinson, the head of the Opinion Research Corporation. Princeton Panel was meant to educate businessmen about liberty. Shortly after Rothbard took the position, however, Robinson took ill and the program fell apart. Rothbard researched public housing and federal aid to education for Leonard Read's congressman, Ralph Gwinn, briefly in 1957 and 1958.

In the meantime he finished the book Volker had commissioned in 1951, the textbook-style popular summation of the Misesian economic edifice.[128] What Rothbard finally produced was more ambitious than that. Most of it was published in two volumes in 1962, after many years of failing to find a publisher, as *Man, Economy, and State*.

Like *Human Action*, it presented economic science as a totality, building through verbal–logical deduction from the unquestionable premise that men act to improve their circumstances, using scarce resources and swimming in uncertainty. Rothbard's book was more of a straight-line economics treatise than Mises's sprawling work. Rothbard's reasoning, of course, largely agreed with Mises's. He took a nonmathematical deductive approach to the discipline and followed the Misesian line on the regression theory of money, a pure time-preference theory of interest, and a subjective marginal utility theory of prices. *MES* could be understood as a mere gloss on Mises.

But Rothbard provided more understandable organization and a step-by-step logical approach to the Mises project of reducing all economic phenomena to the subjective valuations of individuals. He took Misesian reasoning further than Mises did in certain directions. For example, Rothbard shows that following Mises's reasoning in the socialist calculation debate, we can say not only that socialism cannot function but that firms in the free market could never grow larger than a certain size (or else they'd run into the same calculation difficulties that face socialist governments).[129] He also differed from Mises on some of his conclusions (in a radically libertarian direction, of course), for example, regarding monopoly price.

Mises granted in *Human Action* that a monopoly price *could* exist. He defined it as a price charged by a monopoly "at which it is more advantageous for the monopolist to restrict the total amount to be sold than to expand his sales to the limit which a competitive market would allow."[130] Rothbard, an anarchist where his mentor Mises was a classical liberal, delighted in using economic reasoning to kick the props out from under any possible excuse for state intervention. A "monopoly price" cannot be ascertained in a free market, Rothbard insisted; the most we can say is that a given price is, or isn't, the price that arose in an unrestricted market.[131]

Rothbard's banking theories took the Austrian school in a more extreme direction, condemning fractional reserve banking, the current practice whereby banks keep on hand only a small portion of the money deposited in them, loaning the rest out, thus essentially creating money where there was none before and risking, Rothbard argued, dangerous credit bubbles as per Austrian business cycle theory. Rothbard considered the practice inherently fraudulent and maintained that it should be illegal in any libertarian society, since it involves promises to repay money deposited that can never be all honored.[132]

While always insisting, as per Mises, that economics is purely scientific and value-free, Rothbard explained why his economic reasoning tends to buttress libertarian conclusions about the errors of state intervention.

> One reason why economics has tended to concentrate on the free market is that here is presented the problem of order arising out of a seemingly "anarchic" and "planless" set of actions. We have seen that instead of the "anarchy of production" that a person untrained in economics might see in the free market, there emerges an orderly pattern, structured to meet the desire of all individuals, and yet eminently suited to adapt to changing conditions. In this way we have seen how the free, voluntary actions of individuals combine in an orderly determination of such seemingly mysterious processes as the formation of prices, income, money, economic calculation, profits and losses, and production.[133]

To Rothbard, the greatest revelation of praxeological economics is the hidden order of free markets and the foreseeable chaos of intervention.

MES questioned the wisdom or efficacy of government intervention in the economy and threw in bits of libertarian legal theory on matters such as contract, property, and even libel law. (Rothbard did not think libel should be punishable, since no one can be said to have ownership over his or her reputation, as it consists of thoughts in other people's heads.) The last segment of the original *MES* manuscript was dedicated to spelling out the deleterious effects of government intervention. That part of the book was originally longer and more explicitly anarchist. It was reconfigured and published in 1970 by Baldy Harper's Institute for Humane Studies as a separate volume called *Power and Market*.

Power and Market is Rothbard's first thorough defense and explanation of how market anarchism would work.[134] As the first detailed exposition of the anarcho-capitalist idea that would dominate the libertarian movement in the late 1960s and 1970s, *Power and Market* deserves extended attention. It starts off by observing that any study of economics in the real world inevitably involves the study of the exchange of property, and thus it requires an underlying ethic that says what property *is*. "An economist cannot fully analyze the exchange structure of the free market without setting forth the theory of property rights, of justice in property."[135]

He then launches into the most difficult part of anarchist theory: an explanation of how a truly libertarian society would extend free markets even to personal defense. Many argue that defense of property and person is a necessary precondition of a free market, and thus it cannot be handled *by* a free market. After all, everyone needs defense, right? Similarly, everyone needs food, but that doesn't mean the government must supply it as a necessary precondition for a free market to function. That argument about defense, Rothbard argues, requires denying the notion of marginality in economics, the insight from Austrian school of economics founder Carl Menger and others that explained why unnecessary diamonds are more valuable than vital water: We must not treat defense as one unitary good that we either have or don't have, but as something whose marginal services can be bought. We can't buy a whole justice system, but we can hire the services of an arbitrator to adjudicate our personal disputes; we can't buy "the police" but can hire someone to defend our property or track down some miscreant who has wronged us.

Having established the idea that a free market can supply anything human beings need, Rothbard goes on to analyze and critique the various types of state intervention.[136] He defends a libertarian class analysis derived from an early-nineteenth-century American vice president, senator, congressman, and political philosopher—John Calhoun: the idea that the real classes in contemporary society are not boss and worker, but taxpayer (those who are mulcted by the state) and tax consumer (those who gain through the state's organized theft).[137]

The bulk of *Power and Market* explains how and why, from Rothbard's perspective, government intervention never increases human utility and always fails to meet its stated goals. Rothbard insists that by any valid standard of utility—where we must presume that in any freely entered exchange both parties benefit, or at least anticipate benefiting—no government intervention could ever be authoritatively said to increase utility for society at large. (Certainly one person can benefit in a transaction where one is robbing the other, but Rothbard assumes most good-hearted devotees of the state assume that its existence somehow improves things for society as a whole.) Thus, since the state is always stepping in to create or manage an interaction people did *not* freely choose to enter into, from creating public schools to a welfare state, Rothbard insists that a free market maximizes social utility, while "no act of the state can ever increase social utility."[138] (Since Rothbard insists all utilities must be manifest in action—we can't rely on people's mere reports about what they want and don't want—he says that, for example, envy over someone else's success in the market cannot be said to lessen social utility, since all preferences are unknowable unless manifested in action.) Rothbard also grants that, given the unknowability of "social utility" we cannot authoritatively and scientifically say that any state action decreases social utility either. We simply can't say anything meaningful about the concept.[139] But since we can know that every state action decreases at least one person's utility, since it forces them into a transaction they did not freely choose to enter into, any argument that the state provides an overall improvement for society as a whole fails.[140]

The last section of *Power and Market* is a potpourri of defenses of a completely free market from a grab bag of critiques—from the accusation that it will lack security, charity, or morality to the notion that a free market is merely a hotbed of other types of coercion from nature and unequal economic power. Rothbard disposes of the "free rider" problem—the notion that suppliers of some goods such as defense cannot ensure that they collect payment from all those who benefit without a taxing power—essentially by asking, Who cares?[141]

This anarchist work won praise from Senator Mark Hatfield, who wrote that "not only does he argue persuasively against the economic functions of government, but also suggests alternative means of dealing with problems normally assumed by government. In other words, one cannot off-handedly reject the thesis of this book as a flight of fancy."[142]

Rothbard's next book after *MES*, like his doctoral thesis, was an attempt to apply Austrian business cycle analysis to a specific historical event. It arose from work he did for FEE in the 1950s that languished on Read's desk for years and never saw print. The Great Depression, Rothbard set out to prove, far from being a failure of the free market, resulted from inflationary policies followed by the Federal Reserve throughout the 1920s. Other analysts, including Milton Friedman, deny that inflation was any sort of problem during the 1920s, because consumer prices did not rise appreciably.

Rothbard relied on the Misesian insight that the distorting effects of inflation need not manifest themselves first or only in consumer prices. The Federal Reserve's looseness with the money supply, as Rothbard insisted his data showed, created the conditions (as predicted by Mises and Hayek's business cycle theory) for an imbalance in production goods: with people's actual demand for the consumption goods produced too small and resources invested in production processes making goods that people ultimately did not want. That, he argued, is what caused the economic collapse of the late 1920s and early 1930s.

Contrary to the standard story that blamed the severity and pain of the resulting Depression on a misguided and religious adherence to outmoded laissez-faire on the part of President Herbert Hoover, Rothbard argued that Hoover's reaction to the burgeoning depression was in fact a wave of government intervention in farm policy, tariffs, public works, and other areas that stymied the necessary and proper economic adjustments that would have ended the crisis soon enough.[143]

"NO ONE FROM AGRICULTURE? HOW DO YOU FARM? NO ONE FROM JUSTICE? WHO KEEPS YOU FROM HARM?"

When talking about libertarian institutions in the movement's early days, who can forget Spiritual Mobilization?[144] Everyone, it seems. But in the early 1950s, Leonard Read and his FEE crew and their general universe of funders and supporters saw this pamphleteering group of libertarian outreachers to Protestant clergy (and to those who listened to Protestant clergy) as one of their most significant peers. But few, among even the highest echelons of active movement libertarianism, remember Spiritual Mobilization today.

Part of the reason may be a residual aftereffect of Ayn Rand's fiercely atheistic legacy to the movement. She laid brick after brick on a mighty wall of separation between libertarianism and religion. But Spiritual Mobilization, which reached more people with more radical libertarian ideas than any other group in the late 1940s and early 1950s, was an explicitly religious educational group. Its official name was Mobilization for Spiritual Ideals, but it was better known in shorthand as Spiritual Mobilization. Members had their hands in the pulpit as well as all available media, including a syndicated newspaper column and a nationally broadcast radio program, *The Freedom Story,* which featured short radio plays dramatizing lessons in libertarianism. One lesson has kids in a classroom socialize the grading process. They make the mistake of telling a wise free market teacher that socialism sounds quite fair and kind. Then the teacher knowingly forces them to suffer the chaos that results as everyone stops working hard as the incentive provided by personal gain melts away. Spiritual Mobilization also maintained a journal called *Faith and Freedom,* which was sent to tens of thousands of pastors and laymen worried about America's future in the face of a rising socialist tide (or those Spiritual Mobilization hoped it could make worry).

Spiritual Mobilization advised its flock to judge every political candidate or government action against a checklist of criteria, including

- ○ Does it (the program, platform, or act) encourage the Christian principle of love or the collectivist principle of compulsion?

- ○ If it proposes to take the property or income of some for the special benefit or use of others, does it violate the Commandment: "Thou shalt not steal"?
- ○ Is it necessary to use the compulsion of political means in this instance, or could the ends be accomplished by Christian cooperation and non-political voluntary associations?[145]

Spiritual Mobilization was founded in Chicago in 1935 by Reverend James Fifield and two friends. Fifield soon headed west and became pastor of the large First Congregationalist Church in Los Angeles (Leonard Read's parish during his days running the L.A. chamber of commerce). Read's Pamphleteer pals lawyer James Ingebretsen and SoCal Edison executive W. C. Mullendore were also part of Fifield's flock. Spiritual Mobilization's mission was inspired by a resolution that came out of a meeting of the General Council of the Congregational and Christian Churches in 1934, which called for the abolition of America's "destructive" free enterprise system. That was the beginning of what Fifield saw as the evil "social gospel/social action" philosophy that came to dominate the Protestant National Council of Churches in the 1940s and 1950s. He didn't want those antimarket heresies to spread unopposed.

A trio of financiers from the Spiritual Mobilization/FEE world—J. Howard Pew, Jasper Crane, and B. E. Hutchinson of Chrysler—were high-level players on the National Lay Committee, a group of businessmen in the 1950s who fought a rear guard (and ultimately failed) action against the socialist trends they saw taking over American clergymen and churches. For a while, they tried to ensure that any pronouncement on political or social issues coming from the National Council of Churches would be vetted by the free market businessmen on their committee. (They failed.)[146]

After World War II, Fifield hoped that the climate would turn propitious for libertarian thought. He confided to his friend Norman Vincent Peale that his philosophy suffered a "serious setback . . . when we entered the war and it seemed un-American to do anything but applaud everything that was done or said in Washington."[147] With the war over, Fifield prepared for a fresh burst of activity. He started the magazine *Faith and Freedom* in late 1949, edited by anarcho-libertarian William Johnson, another veteran of Loren "Red" Miller's operation in the Midwest. *Faith and Freedom* was similar to the later *Freeman* in its FEE days, with its quiet, homiletic approach and radical devotion to peaceful social intercourse. It published many of the same authors as the FEE *Freeman*.[148]

Unlike many of their compatriots on the "Christian right," *Faith and Freedom* did not focus on foreign enemies or conscious conspirators, but rather, in the classic FEE style, on the mistaken ideas that underlay the communist menace. They knew the fight for true liberalism had more fronts and would stretch longer than any single presidential election; that socialism had crept into American life before FDR; and that in the nature of things the libertarian ought not let the political events of the day either plunge him into gloom or propel him to jubilance.

Some action items were in order. Spiritual Mobilization tried to organize tens of thousands of its subscribing ministers to preach on the topic of freedom on Columbus Day. But they were mostly preachers, not fighters; *Faith and Freedom* ran an article by Leonard Read on the Korean war that said this: "I have yet to find a single person who is in favor of the present war, which is to say, I have yet to find an individual who is anxious himself to give up home, family, fortune, and even life, shoulder a gun, and go forth to kill Chinese."[149]

Faith and Freedom was the first national journal to run a regular column by Murray Rothbard. Since Rothbard, under the concerned eyes of his Volker Fund handlers, was mindful of his future academic reputation as an economist, he wrote this column of fierce political opining under the pseudonym "Aubrey Herbert" after the great British voluntaryist Auberon Herbert. Also, since he was titularly *Faith and Freedom*'s Washington editor (Frank Chodorov held the title before Rothbard), he didn't want anyone to notice that Murray Rothbard of Manhattan was posing as an editor from a city he never even visited, much less lived in. (Aubrey Herbert's radical libertarianism, with its attacks on war and Eisenhower, struck many *Faith and Freedom* readers as disturbingly leftist, or at least not right, and he was canned because of reader complaints at the end of 1956. The editors and writers of *Faith and Freedom* were far more radically libertarian than their audience.)[150]

Spiritual Mobilization had its enemies. A 1953 book called *Apostles of Discord* slammed it as promoting a "kind of economic royalism dedicated to the extreme view that no positive governmental action of any kind is justified."[151] The author pulled out all the usual gripes about radical free marketers—they are reactionaries who want a return

to discredited nineteenth-century verities; they are unaware that economic liberty is "outdated by the increasing complexities of modern
society."[152] The CIO called Fifield "a neo-fascist enemy of organized
labor and the New Deal."[153]

More important than enemies, though, Spiritual Mobilization had
pamphlets—folksy ones making antistate points with a Midwestern
sort of charm, distributed in bulk to churches across the country. A long
look at one reveals a lot, and entertainingly to boot, about its beliefs and
approach. The pamphlet celebrates, in song, the glories of Armstrong
County, South Dakota. At the time it was a 518 square mile county
with fifty-three residents—and the only county in the United States, as
of 1950, containing not a single civilian federal employee. Sing along!

> All Hail to Armstrong, South Dakota,/Land of the Free/You have
> yet to fill your quota/With a Federal Employee!/No one from
> Agriculture?/How do you farm?/No one from Justice?/Who
> keeps you from harm?/No one from Veterans?/By whom are you
> paid?/No one from Commerce?/How do you trade?/No one from
> Housing?/Who buildeth your shacks?/No one from Treasury?/
> Who takes your tax?/No one from Post Office?/Who sells your
> stamp supply?/No one from Military?/Who keeps your powder
> dry?/And no one from Security?/How, then, can you be Social?/If
> you have no single bureaucrat/To decide things equivocal?/Even
> the Department of the Interior/Is from Armstrong's roster
> missed./Tell me, Armstrong County,/How do you exist?/All Hail
> to Armstrong County,/Where there's no 'share the pelf,'/And de-
> spite the Welfare Staters,/Each does things for himself!

Copies available for a dime per, and a quantity discount of 100 for $4.[154]

"LSD STEPS UP OUR VOLTAGE AND FREQUENCY. TO USE THE NEW VISION THUS MADE AVAILABLE ONE MUST BE ABLE TO 'PLUG IN,' 'GET IN TUNE.'"

The FEE/SM scene was made up of men who had climbed to the
highest reaches of American business and society. They were aware,

acutely and sometimes painfully, that they were an embattled minority. Some were certain that civilization as they valued it was descending into a Dark Age that might be frightfully long, even endless. For that reason, perhaps, many of these men were riven with deep spiritual dissatisfactions, possessing a yen for mystical enlightenment that went far beyond the standard Protestant Sunday school verities of their era. Perhaps there is no singular explanation, and perhaps in this they were not much different from more standard organization men of the supposedly conformist 1950s.

Spiritual Mobilization head Fifield didn't seem to have these tendencies. He retired from active leadership of SM in 1954 and handed the reins to high-powered L.A. lawyer (and one of Read's partners in Pamphleteers) James Ingebretsen, "Inx" to his dear ones, of the firm Musick, Burrell & Ingebretsen. Occasionally Ingebretsen mixed his libertarianism and his lawyering, representing the parents in the 1953 *Turner* case in California, which challenged (but failed to defeat) laws requiring parents to send their children to school.[155]

Despite being president of an explicitly religious libertarian organization, Ingebretsen believed "that religion was balderdash."[156] He wasn't particularly disturbed by apparent hypocrisy. "I didn't come to Spiritual Mobilization as a minister: I came as a lawyer and a libertarian. Fighting the forces that wanted to abolish the free enterprise system was my mission, not promoting Christ!"[157]

Correspondence with his libertarian friends indicates that this cosmopolitan atheist politico had occasional yearnings for a mystic's life, something that would take him away from cities and civilization to a lonely natural setting, a place for contemplation and self-knowledge instead of constant war against the ways of the world. But as he confided decades later in his memoir, he was not ready to feel repentance and grace overtake him in the battered Salvation Army church he dropped into on a mysterious whim during a business trip to New York. Later that night, he was similarly surprised to see Jesus appear out of a mosaic at St. Patrick's cathedral—a rather angry Jesus.

Things were whirling in his soul, unexpectedly, high on nothing stronger than his usual steak and dry martini. Ingebretsen decided he was possessed by the spirit of a dead daughter, Kristi. He adopted a glyph as his new identity, which in English would be pronounced "Kristifer." Waves of rapture replaced his fear and uneasiness, and he began giving his cash to bums in the street. (This all happened over the course of a day or so.) Shortly thereafter during a meeting at the home of a Spiritual Mobilization funder, he scrawled "Kristifer" in large letters on his host's table, where he usually collected the small signatures of famous guests. The host was not amused.[158]

Spiraling into what felt like insanity, Ingebretsen called on an old colleague from Spiritual Mobilization, Edmund Opitz, a Unitarian minister who was working with Leonard Read at FEE. Opitz was at a loss when he heard this story of possession and rebirth and told Ingebretsen that what he needed to do, in the midst of this apparent super-accelerated spiritual evolution, was talk to their friend Gerald Heard.

Of course! Leonard Read was the first of the libertarian circle to know of Gerald Heard. Read was a general devotee of semipopular metaphysical literature, and Heard purveyed such literature in the 1950s. The gaunt, red Vandyke-sporting Briton wrote weird mystery tales and was erudite to the point of pain. He was the son of a high church Anglican and good friend and guru to fellow exile Aldous Huxley out in Southern California. He impressed everyone with his habit of answering questions with seemingly unrelated observations or questions and with the hours he spent in silent contemplation. Heard had played the role of spirit guru to British intellectuals, including Christopher Isherwood and W. H. Auden in addition to Huxley. Heard became Ingebretsen's guide through his strange new mystic dispensation—and led him far beyond the set free market frontiers of what Spiritual Mobilization and the libertarian movement had been.

Read had questioned his membership on the Spiritual Mobilization advisory board, noting he was never really asked for advice (quite common, as these things go, with such masthead-filling names). But Read was in many ways a spiritual leader in the psychological-mystical trends that overtook Ingebretsen, his mentor Mullendore, and *Faith and Freedom* editorial staffer Thaddeus Ashby (veteran of stints with Rand and the Hoiles newspaper chain—the libertarian movement was a small world in those days).

Read was an early surfer of an interesting cultural wave, one that has not traditionally been associated with ex-chamber of commerce men running a "far right" propaganda outfit. A vaguely eastern spiritualism became linked in the 1960s with callow youths and hippies, lost, alienated, desperate for guidance. But gaseous spirituality, since the days of Madame Blavatsky and Anne Besant in late Victorian times, if not before, was often a preoccupation of the well-to-do leisure class (which, come to think of it, the hippies and 1960s kids also were), and Read and his pals followed in this tradition.

Leonard Read had long been an eager spiritual seeker, and it was he who discovered and loved the writings of Gerald Heard. But he did not hoard these spiritual treasures, always turning his old mentor Mullendore on to his latest metaphysical conjectures and guides. Even before his weird conversion experience Ingebretsen was often involved in spiritualist discussions through Reverend Edmund Opitz as an intermediary. The exact lines of influence are difficult to untangle, but all these men shared many interests in libertarianism and other subjects, and corresponded tirelessly. So now James Ingebretsen, a respectable lawyer and linchpin of a religious libertarian advocacy group, was a new man with a new identity. At Opitz's recommendation, he turned to Gerald Heard to shepherd him through his unexpected spiritual rebirth. As he tells it in his memoirs (and anyone actually trying to read Heard's writing would agree), it might seem mad to follow this curious but brilliant man, with his bizarre interests and ways of expressing them.

But Heard had a gift. "An astonishing number of people considered Heard to be the most brilliant man they had ever met," wrote one journalist, who added that "the brilliant Heard, the voluble Heard, was missing from the written Heard. His writing tended to be pedantic, 'practically unreadable' according to Huxley," and Aldous had a point.[159] Among the "astonishing number of people" who adored Heard were libertarian activists Mullendore, Read, and Ingebretsen.

The man dazzled them. Heard was given a regular column in *Faith and Freedom*, and an entire issue was dedicated to Heardianism. Read, after going to a Detroit area meeting where Heard did his thing (Heard was hosted by FEE trustee and Chrysler executive B. E. Hutchinson, through a local Episcopal parish), told Mullendore that "I agree with everything you say about Heard. I wonder if there exists another with such a synthesis of knowledge."[160]

These libertarians were primed for Heard's eclectic, hypereducated world-historical spiritualism. A yearning for larger meaning, a wider understanding, an expanded consciousness consumed these men—

lawyer Ingebretsen, private utility chairman and union buster Mullendore, world-changer-through-self Read. What they had mistakenly pegged as a political crisis might in fact be a spiritual one. Mullendore had suffered a serious heart attack in 1952, perhaps making him more inclined to contemplate larger vistas than those of the material world. A general desire to understand not just politics, not just their own business, but the very nature of reality consumed them; and being political radicals who were unhappy with the standard verities of their time, they tended toward spiritual radicalism as well. In where this interest, with the guidance of Heard, took them next, they were a decade ahead of their time, and a lifetime ahead of their class.

Read's sense of the divine was vague and gaseous. Although Read and FEE have kept a reputation as a beachhead of traditional religiosity and morality in a sometimes antinomian and libertine libertarian movement, Read's sense of religion was more mystical than Christian. He once wrote to R. C. Hoiles, "I assume you consider the Bible as much and as little an authority as I do. What then is authority? Where does it reside? In my case it is my own judgement, the results of my own free will."[161] He was no atheist or materialist but far more a seeker of spiritual truth than someone confident he had found them in a Western tradition.

Read was not unique in this among his libertarian friends. Hoiles was fascinated with Krishnamurtri, and other FEE board members along with Read found theosophists and metaphysicians from Rudolf Steiner to Alfred DeNouy to Stewart Edward White and Franz Winkler endlessly worth delving into and contemplating. Mullendore was Read's special spiritualist buddy. They shared their opinions and enthusiasms in the field in their correspondence for years. But the libertarian businessman/intellectual circle found their personal guru in Gerald Heard.

Read introduced Heard's writings to Mullendore. Read had met Heard personally in New York in 1951. But Mullendore, Ingebretsen, and others took off running with him, since they lived in Southern California where the wizard also resided. They began hosting Heardian meetings at Idylwild, a wooded retreat in the mountains east of Los Angeles. The cream of the libertarian movement went for weekends to listen to Heard talk on evolution of the spirit, to encourage quiet meditation. It's culturally disorienting, reading these high-powered, though doubtlessly eccentric, businessmen, ex-managers of big city chambers of commerce, chairman of big city utilities, in the supposedly staid, constrained, and conformist 1950s—and these men by all accounts representatives of the most Neanderthal right—waxing like nothing so much as stoned college kids might have been imagined to lucubrate more than a decade later. Read wrote to Mullendore in March 1955, "I will have to amend my use of the term 'Self-realization' unless I define it to mean a realization of my potential to perceive. Harmony with the Divine Purpose can improve only as perception opens, widens, deepens. It is the process 'of becoming,' the road to oneness. Or, so it seems to me now."[162] After an Idylwild retreat in August 1956, Mullendore wrote to Read, "The meeting was helpful in my growth, and your attendance was a contribution of importance to the whole effort. I feel we are all making progress, in that we are extending the 'focal length of our consciousness' and growing in humility, i.e., breaking the stranglehold of the ego."[163]

In the mid-1950s, they all would gather at the Bohemian Grove, a secretive nature retreat for the wealthy and powerful in Northern California. They'd kibitz with Herbert Hoover and Henry Hazlitt, swooning beneath the ancient trees and even more ancient stars, wondering how far consciousness and spirit and energy can evolve and grow—along with how to get the damn Eisenhower government to shrink itself. It was a heady time for them, and it got even headier. Gerald Heard, along with his friend Aldous Huxley and another friend, UCLA medical researcher Dr. Sidney Cohen, was not just a leading metaphysician, but also one of the leading Los Angeles evangels for mescaline and later LSD.

Heard seems to have played a similar role in the lives of his new libertarian friends, especially Mullendore, Ingebretsen, and Thaddeus Ashby, the former Hoiles employee then working for *Faith and Freedom*. (Ingebretsen in his memoir admits to only one Heard-hosted LSD session, but Ashby was by the end of the 1960s writing guides to lovemaking on mushrooms filled with hippie language derived from *Stranger in a Strange Land,* the successful novel of another libertarian hero, science fiction writer Robert Heinlein.) It is widely whispered in the libertarian community that Read joined his friends in acid explorations; it is worth noting that Read goes out of his way to deny this in his journals.[164] In 1962, Read had his own mystical experience, undrugged, from which he concluded that "there was nothing whatsoever I could do about the mending of the mess we are in. Further, doubt came as to anyone else's ability to 'do' . . . I have not been given the world to manage nor should it be among my ambitions." It was an end of sorts to his burning sense of mission and made him feel a little uneasy about FEE—until he remembered that FEE never did promise to change the world.[165]

Mullendore found LSD a fascinating tool, talking of its wonders like a true electric utility man: "LSD steps up our voltage and frequency. To use the new vision thus made available one must be able to 'plug in,' 'get in tune'—to 'harmonize' with this new environment which LSD opens for us to 'correspond with.'"[166] Mullendore's son-in-law, Louis Dehmlow, was a huge LSD enthusiast by the early 1960s, and his reaction to it sums up the interesting way this squad of spiritually seeking high-bourgeois industrialists and professionals lived out a first wave of psychedelic adventurism, before the more populist one of the mid- to late 1960s. Dehmlow wrote a friend about how LSD, rather than making him "drop out" in Timothy Leary's sense, made him even more intensely, but pleasurably and lovingly and awarely, focused on his business, his children and their schooling, and his everyday life. It affected his business philosophy toward the solvent company he worked at; he decided they must help each employee to be free as an individual and "respect . . . his right to choose his own way toward perfection."[167]

Those outside the range of Heard's mystic gaze watched from afar with a perplexed squint as their libertarian comrades sank into Heardianism. Dehmlow failed to get Ayn Rand to say any good words about Heard. Rothbard found that "I . . . have never been able to read a Heard article through. On the rare occasions when I have, I've never been able to find a point, or any sort of concrete addition to knowledge. I get the impression of a kind of vague and wooly mysticism, and I have yet to see the connection with libertarianism."[168] Rothbard was alarmed by late 1956 that Heard was making his fellow libertarian leaders think that politics is not the Way, that cultivating an inward spiritual orientation is more important than trying to change the world.

Ingebretsen and Opitz started a Heardian spiritual self-awareness group called the Wayfarers, which they convinced Spiritual Mobilization's board to finance. More and more of Ingebretsen's energy went into promoting Heard, trying to buy a college for Heard, pushing an orientation inward to the spirit rather than outward to this fallen world's political structure. To the decidedly unmetaphysical Rothbard, Heard's influence "spread . . . like a miasmic blight, sapping both the will and the rationality of libertarians."[169] The anarchist William Johnson was squeezed out of his editorship of *Faith and Freedom* in the heyday of Heardianism, as one prominent libertarian maintained, for "refusing to genuflect to the east whenever Gerald Heard waggled his beard."[170]

As Ingebretsen's interests shifted toward the Heardian realm, he gave *Faith and Freedom* an antiunion focus—not necessarily any more spiritual, but he decided this was one libertarian issue where his team might have enough traction to win. He named Edward Greenfield as new editor, a Presbyterian preacher from Princeton, Indiana, famous for union-busting exploits.[171] Greenfield summed up the spirit behind Spiritual Mobilization as "the Liberating Spirit"—an ecumenical, almost deist-sounding principle of liberty.[172]

Any sort of active presence in the libertarian movement was over for the people and organizations from California who became enmeshed in Heard, psychedelics, and the quest for spiritual enlightenment. Mullendore was still writing letters warning of economic apocalypse to friends, but Ashby and Ingebretsen were lost to the movement. Spiritual Mobilization petered out in 1961. Its corporate supporters from the Midwest withdrew as the 1950s wore on, uneasy with Ingebretsen's new turn and seeing little energy or activity, with *Faith and Freedom* appearing only sporadically and the radio show and newspaper column dead. Ingebretsen shifted his attention toward being a full-time New Ager, convinced he was a hermetic avatar of sorts after his "Kristifer" experience, and sponsored retreats at his new 270-acre Mount San Jacinto hideaway for Sufis, depth psychologists, and t'ai chi masters.

Rothbard just shook his head sadly. This inner spiritual liberty thing was nonsense; there was a state to smash, right here in the material world. The spiritualism and the psychedelics had drawn away some comrades, and his cause was weakened.[173]

"I, PENCIL, SEEMINGLY SIMPLE THOUGH I AM, OFFER THE MIRACLE OF MY CREATION."

While Rothbard may have seen no merit in the spiritualism his comrades indulged in, Read's interest in cosmic awareness energized and enriched his libertarian work; see, for example, Read's singularly curious book *Elements of Libertarian Leadership* (1962). He writes of the wonders of the theologically unspecified "Creative Force" that Rudolf Steiner said we could all master to some degree, with the proper spiritual and mental disciplines. Read in his inimitable manner set forth some of his own rituals for our potential improvement—rituals that lead to one of his most famous essays.

Read's success over decades in winning the affection and cash of representatives of the upper reaches of America's plutocracy becomes even more fascinating in light of the sort of thinker the mysterious Mr. Read was, as evidenced in that book; or, rather, some thoughtless presuppositions as to what sort of materialist, hidebound philistines these men were, who had succeeded in business and industry and fretted about the New Deal and its aftermath, may be banished.

Read stressed that the methods he offered in *Elements of Libertarian Leadership* for summoning and controlling the Creative Force *must become habits*. Any laxity in discipline will cancel the potential benefit. Examining one of these in detail illuminates the curious way Read's mind worked. This particular discipline inspired Read's most successful single piece of writing—one that sums up in a colorful and unforgettable way the most important and foundational lesson of the libertarian intellectual project. It was an essay called "I, Pencil," which first appeared in the *Freeman* in 1958. Milton Friedman spread its message to millions of viewers decades later in his *Free to Choose* TV series. Some academics insist it is as classic an example of metaphorical economics as any from Adam Smith.

Read advises the seeker to "concentrate for not less than five minutes each day on some object of your own choosing . . . think of everything you possibly can about this object. . . . It should be *your* exploratory thinking, no one else's. One purpose of this exercise is to fix or identify you with reality. . . . It helps to free one from exterior influences like traditions, social positions, professions, nationalities."[174] The reader must engage in this exercise every day for one full month without fail.

In the second month, the seeker is instructed to pick every day some action "which has no utility whatever" and *do it*. Read suggests, "Do something as useless as walking around a room once the first day, twice the second, and so on. The thirtieth day you will make thirty loops! Better do this one in the privacy of your own boudoir!"[175]

For the third month, the seeker reflects daily in quiet solitary contemplation on something that happened to him and tries to glean what instructional message the event is trying to impart. For the fourth month, he contemplates what good can be found in some event that may seem bad at first. Read offers a legend that uses Jesus as an example: "Christ was warned not to cross a road because on the other side was something bad: the rotting carcass of a dog. Christ crossed the road and observed the good: 'The dog has beautiful teeth.'" (Devotees of Zen fables will be excused for wondering about the Christian provenance of this lesson.) In the fifth month, Read advises, resolutely "refuse to draw a conclusion from gossip or hearsay."[176] Month six has the seeker repeating the first five exercises for six days each.

Read then warns: "No one should even consider these exercises who is not temperamentally and spiritually ready and determined to become an improved person, *at whatever cost*. . . . To 'toy' with these untapped and potentially powerful forces within one's own person is actually dangerous."[177] Yes, this is the work of a man whose organization was more commonly concerned with wage and price supports, tariffs, taxation, union perfidy, the provision of public services, and other mundane manners.

But underlying Read's entire project was always the belief, as any old sensei might tell you, that there *is no* changing the world—there is *only* changing ourselves. As Read adds, after presenting the spiritual exercises, "a precondition to any realization of one's creative powers is the recognition of one's impotency. We must know how utterly powerless we are to cast others in our own images before there can be any emergence of our latent powers. For, be it remembered, we have not been given mankind to improve and reform, but only man—*one's manhood, if that can be found!*"[178]

Read's powers of metaphor in defense of markets were brought to their zenith when he performed the first exercise listed above, about contemplating an everyday object, on a pencil. The essay "I, Pencil" emerged. In a stunning combination of what read as an acid head's awed appreciation of the latent wonders in the everyday and an economist's grasp of the unutterably complex workings of the spontaneous order of the market, Read assumes the voice of a pencil (a Mongol 482, assembled and finished by Eberhard Faber in Wilkes-Barre Pennsylvania) to explain an amazing paradox: though Mongol 482 and his brothers exist in such profusion that we can break or lose them without a second thought, *nobody can make one.*

That is, no single body, no single mind, can. Read traces the arts and sciences that must be invented, commanded, and brought to bear on your way to the pencil—the saws and trucks and rope and other gear that goes into harvesting the trees, and everything that goes into making all of *those* things, then all the techniques and knowledge and raw materials, and the food that goes into fueling all the people who make and do all those things. The mind boggles. Read tells of how graphite from Ceylon gets mixed with clay from Mississippi and waxes from Mexico through machinery that required years of thrift and saving with parts from dozens of other places, and the same story can be told about each one of those parts.

And that's before one has even begun to contemplate the ferrule— the bit of brass that holds in the eraser—and all the metallurgy and mining that went into *that.* Every step of this complex chain, from the person who makes the coffee for the logger to the scientist who figured out how to apply black nickel to a ferrule, is essential; and there are so many of them that, not only can no one make a pencil, no one could even set forth in full how one would go about doing so if they wanted to.

Read wants us all to look into any object, any window, any pencil, any day, and see manifest not only the unimaginable wonders of God's creation but also the ineffable glories of the free market's spontaneous productive order. The essay is absurd, profound, an all-around bravura performance. It ends: "I, pencil, seemingly simple though I am, offer the miracle of my creation as testimony that this [faith in unfettered markets] is a practical faith, as practical as the sun, the rain, a cedar tree, the good earth."[179]

"EDUCATION FOR THE CAUSE OF HUMAN LIBERTY IN THIS COUNTRY HAS GOTTEN NOWHERE."

Though he adored his cadre, the Circle Bastiat, Rothbard was overall depressed at the state of the movement as the 1950s ended.[180] He thought the new FEE *Freeman* dull and weak, lamented the departure of Lane, Paterson, Chodorov, Garrett, and Morley from the scene; he considered Rand's nascent Objectivist world an objectionable cult; add the drug-drenched slow death of *Faith and Freedom* on top of all that, and contemplate Eisenhower still in firm control of the GOP and Russell Kirk and William Buckley of the conservative intellectual movement—well, he wasn't brimming with optimism. But it did create an entrepreneurial opportunity.

The old right was dead. Rothbard knew exactly who he and his budding cadre were, and detailed it in March 1956.

> What, then, are we? We are first of all *radicals*—because (a) we go to the root of things, we construct fundamental principle, and follow truth wherever it leads; and (b) we therefore advocate fundamental change from our present political structure. And we are *libertarians* because we believe in individual liberty. I used to think that we were "true liberals," but I have recently come to the conclusion that it is better not to be identified with the old liberals of the 19th century. Despite their merits, they were (a) great advocates of democracy and majority rule, and (b) adherents of the public school

system, and (c) anti-clerical to the extent of banishing Jesuits, etc. Best to start afresh with the "libertarian" appellation, which, for once, we have seized from the leftists instead of *vice versa*.[181]

He had his radical cadre but no mass movement. The best Rothbard could manage was a committee of correspondence of sorts, making sure that libertarians had an epistolary lifeline with others who didn't think they were crazy or evil. He tried to keep up correspondence with everyone he could find and send the Volker Fund in the right direction to help those whom it could help.

These scattered libertarian individualists across America differed widely in their preconceptions and the direction they figured a stateless (or very limited state) society would or should go. Still, they all could see the family resemblance in their various faces, handsome, scarred, twisted, Roman, however they appeared to the world or to each other. They tended to gravitate toward each other in these dark days for individualism, antennae honed to an unbearable fineness from a lifetime underground, sensing each other through reams of warmongering, through mountains of welfare state equivocating. The simple bond of being fellow libertarians created fascinating unities and connections between and among people of very different outlooks and ways of life.

Contemplate, for example, Mildred Loomis, who was running a rural intentional community in Ohio based on the principles of Ralph Borsodi (a back-to-nature guru who thought the only thing a state should do is collect land rent à la Henry George and boycott munitions). From this rural commune, the sort that would attract thousands of younger seekers in the 1960s and 1970s, she was corresponding with FEE's Edmund Opitz and attending Robert LeFevre's libertarian Freedom School in Colorado. She had hung out with Gerald Heard on one of his earliest visits to America in the late 1930s. Despite her lifestyle, which differed from that of the other libertarian thinkers she palled around with, she was an active and respected member of the libertarian community of correspondence, which was open to nearly anyone who shared an interest in these recondite and mostly despised ideas. Because they shared libertarianism, even Jasper Crane, major industrialist, researcher, and manufacturer of poison gases for DuPont, spent some of his spare time pouring over Loomis's mimeographed newsletter of rural decentralist back-to-the-land whole food anarchists.

These strange pulls of otherwise inexplicable attraction are what make a movement—especially a movement as varied and colorful as the libertarian one. As Hayekians, they had to love the spontaneousness of it all, the strange and far-flung paths that varied libertarians walked on their attempt to reach a promised land of liberty. By 1958, former Cornell economist Baldy Harper, one of the few libertarians no one seemed to bad-mouth, was free at last from what he saw as the smothering of Leonard Read and now working with the Volker Fund operation in California. He looked out on the delicious and varied chaos and thought there should be a group to at least guide libertarian progress, if not organize it.

Toward that goal, by 1961, Harper had finally convinced Harold Luhnow, chief of the Volker Fund, to finance his dream: a libertarian academy of sorts, an institute modeled after Princeton's Institute for Advanced Studies in which hard-core libertarian scholars, free of day-to-day worries about teaching, academic politics, disciplinary boundaries, and publishing schedules, could indulge in the high-level, in-depth study and research on the principles of liberty that the movement needed to grow—solving hard problems, finding new arguments, extending the science of liberty to fresh areas. Rothbard and Liggio—who each could have used such an institute as a home—brainstormed the project with Harper and George Resch, Harper's assistant.

In preparation for the launch of this new project, to be called the Institute for Humane Studies, Harper wanted to figure out the best ways, and identify the best people, to inculcate and explore libertarianism. He polled his libertarian friends, asking them who they thought were the most effective educators for liberty. His use of the term "educators" is revealing about the ambitions and intentions of libertarians then, at a time when brethren on the right were beginning to hitch their star to Barry Goldwater, the cowboy senator from Arizona, the jut-jawed, steely-eyed hero who could stare down bureaucrats and communists alike and never blink. Although many of them found Goldwater encouraging (and some did not), libertarians of the early 1960s were not, in the main, advocating direct action in the political arena; they didn't really talk of making a free world but of educating people as to the benefits of *having* a free world. Then individual will and initiative would take care of the rest.

It made sense, given some of their intellectual forebears and immediate inspirations and guides. Etienne de la Boétie, the sixteenth-century proto-libertarian thinker beloved of Rothbard, taught that all government is ultimately based on consent, that we were slaves in our minds and our understandings before any mere government could make us slaves in fact. Leonard Read, attracting more and more money by his artful method of not asking for it, knew that the best a libertarian could do is make himself a better libertarian. As his understanding of the principles of freedom and how to apply them deepened, his consciousness expanded, his light shone brighter, he became then a personal light unto the nations—or at least to other individuals.

The answers Harper got from his libertarian committees of correspondence in late 1961 are a fascinating window into where libertarians had gotten by the early 1960s, and what they thought of where they had been. Pierre Goodrich was a wealthy Indiana businessman involved in banking and other concerns (not from the tire company). At the same time Harper asked him these questions, he was conceptualizing his own vision of a libertarian educational institution for the ages, which exists today as Liberty Fund. Goodrich noted that more individualists were disciples of Mises than of any other master. Robert LeFevre, who had launched his own academy of libertarian education for young and old, the Freedom School, in the Colorado mountains, adored R. C. Hoiles "in spite of his flag waving." Another of Harper's correspondents asks, "Who had put more people in touch with the pure libertarian gospel than Hoiles?" (Still, the regional nature of Hoiles's Freedom Newspaper chain prevented it from being a widespread national influence among professional libertarians.)

Here are the top 10 most valuable teachers of the principle of liberty, circa 1961, as chosen by Baldy Harper's twenty-five friends and colleagues, with number of votes in parentheses (votes for people who were full-time staffers at the Volker Fund were not counted): Mises (19), Hayek (17), Hazlitt (15), Read (15), Chodorov (13), Lane (10), LeFevre (10), Jim Rogers (the Ingersoll Milling Machine company's in-house libertarian guru) (9), Friedman (8), and Rand (8). Rothbard, though he had not yet published his first book, got five votes—tied with Buckley, John Chamberlain, Garrett, Goldwater, Nock, Sylvester Petro (an NYU law professor and friend of Mises's who wrote the classic antiunion account of the 1950s most famous labor unrest, the Kohler strike), and Frederick Nymeyer (who ran a small libertarian publishing house and a journal of Calvinist–libertarian economics).[182]

Rothbard was delighted at the thought that Harper would actually get the institute off the ground and wrote him a long memo in January 1961 explaining what he thought it ought to concentrate on, what questions it might be able to answer. Rothbard thought economics was where libertarians had gotten the farthest. Between *Human Action* and his own *Man, Economy, and State*, he thought the world had about as much libertarian economic understanding as it needed. He now saw philosophy as most important, and indeed that became one of his two big projects for the next decade—working up a fully libertarian science of ethics based on natural rights.

Tricky questions involving the application of libertarian principles remained, questions that Harper's institute could perhaps help resolve. Libertarians knew that property was the key to liberty and social peace, but there were areas—the sea, the air, matters of pollution, ideas, reputations—where it was often hard to tell exactly how property could, or should, be defined or protected. And libertarians needed a more sophisticated legal philosophy, examining, for example, theories of just punishment, and the sort of court systems that might or could exist in a fully libertarian world. And then metaquestions of scholarship and business were important, such as how best to do research or develop a better theory of organization (e.g., can organizations coerce without violence, as in a kibbutz?).

The hard sciences had some things to add to the understanding of libertarianism as well, Rothbard thought, so the institute shouldn't leave them out of the picture. What can examining human biology, for example, tell us about natural law ethics as it reveals new information about the nature of man? The arts are also an open field for libertarian thinking. How do free markets affect aesthetics and culture? Is modern art helping push bad modern politics? Libertarians also needed to work on a more rigorous understanding and theory of foreign policy, on relations between states. Libertarian-minded analyses of history were in order, both general and explaining specific incidents. They also needed histories of meeting government-dependent needs in libertarian ways, such as private canals and medieval fairs, to more fully grasp direct historical evidence that human social needs can and have been met without a state. Explorations of the history of libertarian thought that dig deeper than just Bastiat, Spencer, and Sumner were also in order.

And strategy! How do we make this all work? Is there a libertarian technique for social change—a theory of conversation, say, that could illuminate how best to convert people? Is political action useful to the libertarian? Rothbard couldn't have known it, but this memo to Harper pretty much set out the agenda that self-consciously libertarian institutions and thinkers would follow from that time to this.[183]

Rothbard's head spun as he contemplated everything libertarians had to do—things they might be *able* to do with the Volker Fund's financing of Harper's dream. The late 1950s doldrums were over for the libertarian movement.

But not everyone was as optimistic or forward-looking. Four years after the stunning body blow to collectivism and altruism of *Atlas Shrugged*, fourteen years after the gathering of the high-brow brain power of the Mont Pelerin Society, fifteen years into FEE's mission of patiently and calmly explaining the benefits and glories of anything that's peaceful, seventeen years after Hayek proved to a huge mass audience that state planning was the *Road to Serfdom*, eighteen years after the startling one-two-three punch of Rand, Paterson, and Lane's bracing lessons on the glories of unbridled human energy and uncompromised free human creativity, Virgil Jordan, retired from his post as chief of the National Industrial Conference Board (former home to Garet Garrett, Leonard Read, and Alan Greenspan), replied to Baldy Harper with a comment that could only ring with a chilly truth as the 1940s and 1950s consensus of government economic management and arms races and regulation and regimentation turned more solid, more impenetrable, more omnipresent: "I am sure only that education for the cause of human liberty in this country has gotten nowhere and nobody has accomplished anything in it."[184]

6

THE GOLDWATER MOVEMENT, THE OBJECTIVIST CRACKUP, AND THE HIPPIES OF THE RIGHT

"The power I have may enter even Khrushchev. The step is to tune in on this power and let it work." This curious announcement, among other curious announcements, was made at the beginning of February 1962 by Harold Luhnow, chief of the Volker Fund, to a gathering of the libertarian elite assembled at his invitation in a California hotel to discuss the mission and program of Baldy Harper's proposed Institute for Humane Studies. It was officially to be its own organization, doing things that the Volker Fund had not been doing, and this cabal of leading freedom fighting intellectuals was to figure out what this institute could do for liberty.[1]

"ONE WITH GOD IS A MAJORITY."

Throughout 1961 Luhnow had seemed thrilled by the institute project, asking Harper, Harper's assistant George Resch, and fellow Volker employee Ivan Bierly to develop lists of students it might support or bring on as fellows, possible full-time staffers (with Rothbard topping the list), and mull over long-range strategies and tactics to spread the ideas of liberty. (Like Baldy, Bierly was a veteran of both Cornell

University and FEE, but most of the other Volker Fund staff at the time didn't get along with him.) Baldy's years as an advocate for libertarianism, from Cornell in the 1940s to FEE in the late 1940s and early 1950s to his Volker time from 1958 on, had made his a name to conjure with among scattered libertarians. Many of them responded to the invitation and the challenge with great interest.

F. A. Hayek, because of the reputation of *Road to Serfdom,* his founding of the Mont Pelerin Society, and the more recent *Constitution of Liberty,* was a first among equals at any such gathering and had a lot to say. With his eyes as usual on the top of the pyramid of social and intellectual influence, he doubted that aiming the institute's efforts on students was the best use of its resources. While more conservative-leaning student groups, such as Chodorov's ISI and the Buckley-inspired Young Americans for Freedom, were growing in membership on colleges across America by 1962, Hayek hadn't been impressed with what he'd seen of them. Louis Spadaro was also at the meeting. He was an economist who'd received his Ph.D. under Mises at NYU and would later be president of the Institute for Humane Studies for a while in the 1970s. Spadaro was even more dismissive of such student groups. He found that campus "freedom movements" of the right attracted many unstable kids and thought the best you could do for them was to give them good literature and hope they'd go away.

Libertarian arguments were not yet well developed enough to convert top-level intellectuals, Hayek insisted; the fledgling Institute for Humane Studies needed to advance libertarian ideas on the deepest, most profound levels. You can't do that by assigning tasks; great scholars must be supported to do whatever they find necessary to do. Hayek noted that, had such an institute been available for his old mentor Mises when he'd arrived in America, it would have been a beautiful and helpful thing. Now at least they had the chance to make sure it existed for a possible future Mises.

Hayek advised them to start small at first, perhaps just Baldy Harper and one other scholar. He had further specific advice: Philosophy and even psychology needed to be added to the libertarian movement's arsenal. Further, libertarians must not fear or elide differences and divisions within the movement; such differences must be celebrated and accepted as necessary for further intellectual progress. Serious disagreement ought not be driven out of the movement through tedious heresy hunting or schisming. But most of all, it was important to keep the structure and strategy for the institute loose. Its mission should be to support fine minds and see what happens. Any short-term plan for "success" would only guarantee failure.

Bruno Leoni, an Italian legal scholar who wrote a Volker-supported and very influential (among libertarians) book, *Freedom and the Law* (1961), on the common law and its historical importance to liberty, understandably suggested that the institute needed to concentrate more on the law. He insisted that in actual human practice, freedom is more of a legal concept than a philosophical or economic one.[2] John Sparks, a businessman on FEE's board, thought that questions surrounding liberty and authority in the business context—where most of us spend most of our time—had been neglected by libertarians.

Luhnow, however, was the boss, and he set the tone. And the tone was disconcerting. Luhnow's contributions to the meeting were erratic, as the man himself had been for a while. He had in the past year seemed a little unstable to his employees, changing his mind on important questions weekly; vowing to concentrate all Volker's resources first in one area, then another very different one; praising the Institute for Humane Studies concept as what he'd been waiting for all his life, then sneering that he didn't buy it, and never had. He was spending more and more time with Ivan Bierly and less with anyone else, seeming to trust only Bierly, demanding that secrets be kept between and among his high-level staff.

Among the bon mots Luhnow dropped on his libertarian employees and colleagues at this meeting: That William Volker had told him to keep running the fund as long as he was still interested, but not a day longer; that "I want some dividends for my time—that is my price"; that students and college campuses were his main interest now, but that "if we can get control of the U.S. Senate, we have it made"; that "we have just a short time" and "we already know enough." He made it clear that he was still The Man: "I can set up anything I want to do without the support of anybody" and—hard to argue with this one— "One with God is a majority." Then there was that queer observation about Khrushchev.[3]

Perhaps after his strange performance at that meeting, it should not have been much of a surprise to anyone that Luhnow, less than two months after summoning more than ten of the highest-level libertarians in the world to spend a weekend hashing over the Institute for Humane Studies's future, issued a memo on March 15, 1962, tersely declaring that the William Volker Fund "is terminating its activities" and that the assets would be distributed "according to the founder's very specific instructions."[4]

He had adopted shifting pretences that Volker had ordered the fund to be liquidated back in 1958, and he was only now getting around to remembering that or telling anyone—and offered no proof of it other than his own apparently recovered memory. The standard story, contained in the Luhnow-sponsored William Volker biography by Herbert Cornuelle, and repeated by Luhnow to his employees, is that Volker decreed a lifespan of thirty years after his death on the fund, which should keep the fund alive until 1977. But on different occasions Luhnow would say the fund would die with him or die anytime he chose to kill it (which is how it turned out).

No one seems sure why Luhnow made this decision. Ivan Bierly at the fund, one of Luhnow's closest confidantes, had, some insisted, been converted to the radical Christian philosophy of Reverend Rousas J. Rushdoony—a philosophy that became institutionalized under the rubric "reconstructionism." It calls for a return to a strict interpretation of Old Testament rules as a proper constitution for civil government.[5] This would result in a bizarre political program of no interference with economic activity combined with dutiful stoning of adulterers and homosexuals. In Murray Rothbard's judgment, "Bierly managed to convince the increasingly senile Luhnow that the Volker Fund (especially [F. A.] Harper, [Kenneth] Templeton, [George] Resch, Rothbard) had fallen into the hands of a dangerous anarchist, pacifist, atheist clique out to subvert the Volker Fund's Christian mission."[6]

Neither Templeton nor Cornuelle, both working for the fund in its last days, remembers a move toward reconstructionism as a prime motivator in the Volker Fund's death. (Luhnow had shown some interest, of a somewhat peculiar nature, in God. He told another Volker staffer in early 1962 that he had received direct and specific communication from God, and also expressed the opinion that he thought Baldy Harper would someday receive a similar courtesy call from the Lord.) Some said Luhnow had never been the same since his old consigliere Loren "Red" Miller died. Kenneth Templeton, who accompanied Luhnow to Miller's funeral in 1958, says it was the one and only time he saw the usually teetotaling Baptist resort to a snort of scotch.[7] George Resch remembers Bierly's constant emphasis on Christianity, and the lack of it among other staffers and intellectuals associated with the fund, in his talking with Luhnow.[8]

For whatever reason, the anarcho-libertarian cadre had lost its major—in many cases only—source of cash, support, and organization. Harper was forced to scrape together some semblance of his Institute for Humane Studies dream without Volker money, and he struggled with it through most of the 1960s. (The institute got rolling in earnest by the late 1960s.) George Resch, Harper's right-hand man, had to go back to college. Rothbard still had enough Ayn Rand in him to talk with a bitterness somewhat mock and somewhat real of how they might all have to "take jobs 'at the quarry'" à la Howard Roark.[9]

In the later days of the Volker Fund, Dick Cornuelle had run a program called the Foundation for Voluntary Welfare under its aegis. The roots of the idea had arisen from Garet Garrett, the old *Saturday Evening Post* protolibertarian and friend to Rose Wilder Lane, with whom Cornuelle had worked at the National Industrial Conference Board's *American Affairs* magazine. Garrett had been annoyed at Cornuelle's youthful doctrinaire devil-take-the-hindmost capitalism. He advised Cornuelle to visit some of the ex-coal miners who, Cornuelle had blithely suggested, ought to disappear in a free market if the mine was no longer efficient. Cornuelle's conscience was troubled by seeing the human costs of the dynamic changes inherent in market capitalism, of how losing jobs could affect families and communities. This inspired in him the notion that communal help programs had to be integrated more solidly into the libertarian project, that libertarians needed to show how those disadvantaged by free markets could be helped through nongovernmental means. Thus the Foundation for Voluntary Welfare was dedicated to promoting private sector provision of public charitable needs. He could no longer abide by the Randian idea that no one owed anything to those who couldn't succeed under capitalism. Cornuelle thought there was no way for libertarian ideas to win out unless people could see that a free market wouldn't mean widespread, unaided destitution, that the state wasn't needed to make sure those in need of help got help.

Cornuelle kept up similar activities after the Volker collapse through an organization called United Student Aid Funds (which, instead of displacing government efforts in this area, became a tiny adjunct to a much larger and more expensive federal effort in the same field).[10] Cornuelle became a minor policy celebrity in the mid-1960s by pushing the cause of political change via the private sector attempting activities the public sector was trying to arrogate for itself, from student financial aid to job training. (United Student Aid Funds, as per its name, found private money to provide low-interest loans to students otherwise unable to afford college.)

Cornuelle spent time during the 1960s as a vice president at the National Association of Manufacturers. He made some headway with his idea of the voluntary sector meeting public needs. He wrote a well-received 1965 book about it called *Reclaiming the American Dream,* after an article in *Look* magazine popularized this "new conservative" idea.[11]

While his model never came to dominate conventional philanthropy, he did inspire action in its direction during the Nixon administration. A task force he headed on the matter was credited with inspiring Nixon to launch a program to encourage and coordinate private sector initiatives to solve social problems ranging from unemployment to lonely old ladies.[12] Cornuelle hoped this program would ultimately squeeze out government action in charitable areas entirely, though it didn't work out that way. He started a Center for Independent Action to work on demonstration projects of private solutions to public problems.

His old friend Rothbard, who had been especially proud of Cornuelle—in Rothbard's own estimation, his first recruit to anarcho-capitalism—groused at seeing him win press attention and praise for his new dispensation while he denigrated the libertarian movement from which he arose for its heartlessness regarding human misery. He thought Cornuelle was taking the easiest, most establishment-friendly path possible, to go from "right anarchism" (as Cornuelle characterized his previous stance to an adoring reporter from *Look* in late 1964) to advocating an expanded, better organized private charity as an answer to social ills.[13]

Kenneth Templeton of the Volker Fund ended up handling educational grants for the Lilly Foundation. He helped obtain funding from the Foundation for Foreign Affairs for Rothbard and Leonard Liggio regarding their projected libertarian exposition on American history.[14]

Other programs that depended on Volker largess, such as Mises's position at NYU, were left hanging. Volker kept up its support for Mises until 1964. Then Leonard Read, Henry Hazlitt, and Lawrence Fertig (a friend of Mises's on the NYU board), who had taken responsibility for Mises's well-being, scrambled to find four other foundations to cover what Volker had been doing alone.[15] They succeeded.

"I THOUGHT I WAS GOING BACK TO SOME FUNDAMENTALS RATHER THAN CREATING ANYTHING NEW."

Milton Friedman's days as an economic guru to governments around the world left, right, and center, and as the most controversial figure ever to win a Nobel in economics, were mostly in the future. But his most enduring contribution to popular libertarianism was already in place by 1962: his book *Capitalism and Freedom*. Friedman was no stranger to the libertarian movement. He had co-authored the controversial *Roofs or Ceilings?* pamphlet in FEE's first year. He was a founding member of the Mont Pelerin Society and regularly attended conferences sponsored by the Volker Fund in the 1950s. Friedman spoke on the necessity of an unrestricted market economy for true liberty and the larger social good in the mid- to late 1950s at Volker-sponsored seminars at Wabash College, Claremont College, the University of North Carolina, and Oklahoma State University. His wife Rose helped assemble speaking notes from those presentations into the book.

What has never been controversial about Friedman is his status as one of the most accomplished and influential technical economists of his era, as well as one of the most effective proselytizers for the political philosophy of extremely limited government—libertarianism. Friedman's success at influencing and appealing to mainstream conservative thought has inspired conservatives to embrace him as their own—an embrace Friedman has often struggled to escape.[16]

Friedman was born in Brooklyn on July 31, 1912, the child of Jeno Saul Friedman and Sarah Ethel Friedman, née Landau, two Jewish immigrants from Carpatho-Ruthenia, then a part of Austro-Hungary, and since then parts of Czechoslovakia, the Soviet Union, and now the Ukraine. Though his parents emigrated from the same area, they didn't meet and marry until arriving in the United States.

His parents lived a typical American immigrant existence, with his mother working first as a seamstress in what enemies of capitalism call "sweatshops," but which the likes of Friedman would recognize as often rough, but often necessary, steps to economic betterment for both individuals and the nation at large. Both his parents worked as dry goods merchants when they moved to Rahway, New Jersey, shortly after Milton was born. Friedman was raised there and graduated at age sixteen from Rahway High School in 1928, going on to undergraduate education at Rutgers in New Jersey (paid for, in one of those ironies that bedevil a libertarian in a statist world, by a scholarship from the state of New Jersey).

Friedman started out his studies intending to be a mathematician and later an actuary. At Rutgers, though, he studied under two professors who imbued him with a passion for economics: Arthur Burns (a long-time friend of Friedman's who later became chairman of Friedman's bête noire, the Federal Reserve, and who also served on Murray Rothbard's doctoral dissertation committee) and Homer Jones, who was pursuing a doctorate at the University of Chicago while teaching at Rutgers. (Jones also later worked as a vice president for research at the Federal Reserve Bank of St. Louis. It's not hard to see where Friedman's interests in monetary policy came from.) Jones helped Friedman win a graduate scholarship from Chicago in economics, which Friedman chose over a scholarship offer from Brown in mathematics. It was a fateful choice, inspired by the ongoing Depression and his belief that understanding economics could be key to solving its dilemmas. Friedman's reputation and career would be forever intertwined with the University of Chicago, the colleagues he met there, and the intellectual tradition it represented.[17]

Friedman started at Chicago in fall of 1932, where he met his future wife and writing partner Rose Director in a class taught by Chicago's Jacob Viner. (Friedman and Director were married in 1938 and had two children, Janet and David. David became an economist and a leading advocate of anarcho-capitalism.) Friedman took a year off from

Chicago to accept a fellowship at Columbia University, where influential statistician Harold Hotelling gave him a grounding in that discipline. Friedman returned to Chicago the next year, where he befriended the remaining two members of the trio (Rose was the first) he credits with most influencing his intellectual evolution: George Stigler (later a fellow Nobel laureate and Chicago professor) and W. Allen Wallis (later dean of Chicago's business school and undersecretary of state for economic affairs).[18]

Friedman summed up the effects of the two elements of his graduate education: "The combination of influences stemming from Chicago and Columbia—the one heavy on theory, the other heavy on statistical and empirical evidence—has shaped my scientific work, essentially all of which has been characterized by a mixture of theory and fact—of theory and attempts to test the implications of the theory."[19]

Friedman returned to Columbia to finish his dissertation over the course of a decade while working professionally. Friedman labored at the Industrial Section of the Natural Resources Committee, doing what he describes as "work on the New Deal . . . but we were just technical statisticians and economists, not anything that had any policy role."[20] In 1937, he began his long affiliation with the National Bureau of Economic Research (NBER), an organization "founded by Wesley Clair Mitchell and others in 1920 as a private, nonprofit institution to establish the main facts about the structure and operation of the American economy."[21]

There Friedman began research that connected with his doctoral dissertation and led to the first of many controversies over coming to conclusions too libertarian for certain colleagues. Working with future Nobel laureate and national income statistics pioneer Simon Kuznets, Friedman produced a study that bothered a supervisor at NBER, who delayed publication of the work because of its uncharitable assertion that professional licensing, particularly that supporting the American Medical Association, might be used to restrict entry and thus raise income for licensed doctors.[22]

These days, whether or not one advocates eliminating professional licensing (as Friedman always has, and strenuously), that simple economic conclusion doesn't come as much of a shock. Much of what Friedman has written doesn't these days. That is due more to his success in shifting the boundaries of intellectual acceptability than to any mildness in his libertarianism. He has been remarkably successful at making the radical almost mainstream.

World War II, as it did for most men of his generation, disrupted what might have been Friedman's normal career pattern. After a year teaching at the University of Wisconsin, Friedman worked in the U.S. Treasury's tax research division. There he was partially responsible for a policy decision that to this day his libertarian wife, as well as other libertarians, excoriates him for: developing the withholding system for the income tax. "They wanted," Friedman said, "to raise as much in taxes as they could, a larger fraction of the expenditures. You could not do that in wartime or in peacetime without withholding. And so people at the Treasury tax research department where I was working investigated various methods of withholding; I was one of the very small technical group that worked on developing it."[23]

Friedman also learned viscerally from this experience a feature of bureaucracies that became a central theme decades later in his popular 1984 book, *The Tyranny of the Status Quo*: Bureaucracies are loath to change. The IRS, Friedman says, was the biggest opponent of the new idea, insisting there was no way it could work. "We were paying almost no attention to the postwar consequences of anything we did," Friedman admits now. "We were just asking ourselves: What can we do to win the war? I have no apologies for it, but I really wish we hadn't found it necessary to do that and I wish there were some way of abolishing withholding now."[24] (Libertarians think paycheck withholding makes it easy for citizens to not notice how much they are paying for the privilege of being governed. Millions actually feel grateful come April when some of the money taken from them is returned. This lowers the political costs to government of taxing, a result libertarians lament.)

For the remainder of the war, Friedman worked on statistics as associate director of the Division of War Research at Columbia. He and his coworkers, including old friend Allen Wallis and old teacher Harold Hotelling, came up with a sampling technique, sequential sampling, that "became the standard analysis of quality control inspection. Like many of Friedman's contributions, in retrospect it seems remarkably simple and obvious to apply basic economic ideas to quality control; that however is a measure of his genius."[25]

After the war, he took a one-year teaching stint at the University of Minnesota before returning to Chicago in 1946 (to a position that his friend Stigler failed to get; Stigler puckishly calls this his greatest contribution to Chicago).[26] Friedman made full professor in 1948 and remained there, with a year or quarter off here and there visiting at other universities, till 1976.[27]

Friedman's side career as an adviser—sometimes formal, sometimes informal—to governments across the globe began in 1950, when former students invited him to work with a Marshall Plan agency; while there he made a serious proposal, which went nowhere at the time, for Germany to float its exchange rate, another cause Friedman became famously associated with arguing for, and another case where what he argued for became reality, as of 1973.[28] ("Floating exchange rates" means applying the basic free market logic about price controls to international currencies—that governments should not attempt to dictate what their currencies sell for in terms of other currencies, but allow the conversion price to be set freely by market forces.)[29]

But *Capitalism and Freedom* came early in his career, and before most of his fame. He traces the intellectual roots of the book—a sustained, evenhanded assessment of how, where, and why government fails and private markets are better, both morally and practically—to attending the first Mont Pelerin Society meeting and being exposed to the give-and-take, support, and sense of community among international libertarian scholars and advocates. (His presence at the first Pelerin meeting was also due to Volker Fund largess.)

Friedman also thanks the group of students who gathered around Hayek during his stint at Chicago's Committee on Social Thought during the 1950s and 1960s for creating a pleasingly libertarian atmosphere around Chicago. (This gang, spearheaded by Circle Bastiat mainstays Ralph Raico and Ronald Hamowy, produced the *New Individualist Review*, an early and well-respected libertarian college magazine that Friedman advised.)[30]

Capitalism and Freedom is published by the University of Chicago Press and has sold over a half million copies, has been translated into eighteen languages, and was a favorite samizdat publication in the Soviet Union. The book was both a great teacher and a great symbol of respectability—issuing as it did from a successful and largely respected academic and later journalist—to the generation of young libertarians coming of age in the 1960s (even though some who had already been dedicated to the libertarian cause considered it soft on the state in parts).[31]

The book was a reasonably comprehensive exposition of the libertarian position, one that did not try to begin with rigorously establishing philosophic principles from the ground up. "I thought I was going back to some fundamentals rather than creating anything new," Friedman says.[32] His reasons for advocating individual liberty seem hopelessly wan compared to, say, Rand's airtight philosophizing from first principles. He starts "from a belief in the idea that nobody can be sure that what he believes is right, is *really* right."[33]

Friedman has never shown much interest in arguing basic questions of "why liberty?" He simply assumes that men of good will favor the same things—peace and prosperity—and patiently explains why freedom will bring them, in the most efficient way possible. He has a similar belief in regard to the fundamentals in economics where, contrary to popular opinion, he insists arguments among economists rarely hinge on values, but more typically on arguments about what the actual effects of certain policies might be.[34]

Capitalism and Freedom still opens young libertarians' eyes to the proper role of government. It contains almost all of the themes and ideas Friedman would continue to advocate over the course of his career as a columnist, author, and speaker on public policy issues. Friedman grants the government responsibility for more than the two functions libertarians traditionally assigned it of defense and domestic peace, protecting us from enemies internal and external. He credits it also with responsibility for "foster[ing] competitive markets" and "enabl[ing] us at times to accomplish jointly what we would find it more difficult or expensive to accomplish severally."[35] (He grants this area is fraught with danger.)

He also emphasizes the principle of decentralizing and localizing government power as much as possible, declares fealty to the term *liberalism* (which he still prefers), and explains how it was corrupted over time. He adumbrates the necessary connection between economic and political freedom in the early 1960s when so-called liberals were wont to forget it, explaining why the then prevalent (and still not entirely dead) dream of democratic socialism was impossible.

For the rest of the book, he delivers argument after argument that has seeped through the loam of intellectual culture to become bromides in the op-eds of libertarian-leaning free market scriveners and talk show hosts from college newspapers to the halls of Congress, though they were not hoary clichés when Friedman wrote them.

Friedman explains how markets permit unanimity without conformity—we can all get our desires for products and services met in a free market, even if what we want is not the same as what the majority wants, which provides an effective proportional representation that mere democracy never can. He gives more credence to the danger of monopolies than do "Austrian" libertarians (Rothbardians, remember, think the only possible monopolies are those created or enforced by the state), but still thinks an unregulated private monopoly is a lesser evil than government attempts to regulate it. Certain market actions, he admits, might have neighborhood effects—things that spill over to the detriment of those not involved in the transaction, such as pollution, that warrant government action—but he advises that the initial presumption must always be against such action.

He lists government functions and programs that he argues ought to go (all but one still exist): price supports, tariffs, licensing, minimum wages, Social Security, housing subsidies, the draft, post office, and national parks. The one on that list that has passed away, the draft, was Friedman's pet issue. Here he succeeded. He is popularly credited with a key role in ending it through his role on Nixon's commission on an all-volunteer army. This is the policy victory of which he is most proud (more on which later).[36]

Much of the rest of *Capitalism and Freedom* focuses on Friedman's particular concerns as a monetary economist. He spends chapters arguing against commodity standards (the notion that money ought to be only gold or other metals—his rejection of the gold standard is another aspect of Friedman that pisses off Austrian libertarians, who think that only gold prevents government from manipulating the money supply easily to its own advantage), but also discusses the failures of the Federal Reserve and calls for strict rules defining a set rate of growth in the money supply from year to year to help curb inflation. Another chapter discusses foreign reserve imbalances and calls for another of his polemical successes: floating exchange rates between national fiat currencies, which became a reality by 1973.

Friedman also attacks the basics of Keynesianism, debunking the notion of the magic multiplier that allegedly makes government spending more efficacious than private spending. (Keynes believed that any amount of increased government spending and investment would multiply itself in terms of real income in the economy. Friedman demonstrated that this is only true under extremely unlikely circumstances.)[37] He floats the now popular idea of vouchers for education financing instead of government-run schools. More radical libertarians hate the voucher idea, since it still leaves the state funding schools through taxation, even if they aren't necessarily running them. Libertarians have argued that, in practice, there will be no way to create a truly free market in schooling even with vouchers, since the government will undoubtedly insist on controlling how the schools that take voucher money are run.[38] He explains how unions help cartelize industry to the consumer's detriment (antiunion sentiment is almost universal among libertarian intellectuals); attacks the idea of corporate responsibility (he thinks that a corporation's responsibility to its shareholders is simply to make profits; individual shareholders should be able to decide for themselves how much of their money they want going to other causes, not have that decision made for them by corporate executives) and corporate taxes; explains how professional licensure is just a tool to allow professionals to block competition and neither ensures quality nor helps consumers; advocates the flat tax and defends the fact that free markets will necessarily lead to inequality of income; accepts the need for government income floors but advocates a negative income tax—a set stipend that you could spend as you wished in a free market—as a replacement for all current social welfare programs as the cheapest, least bureaucratic, and most economically efficient way to help the poor. This idea entered the serious debate over poverty programs before the decade ended, another sign of Friedman's influence above and beyond the limits of the libertarian movement, where libertarians seemed to be talking to themselves for so long.[39]

In the end, Friedman concludes that by the early 1960s America has had sufficient experience with big government so that arguments about the state can be cast in terms of actual government performance versus actual market performance, rather than simply assuming that whatever the government tried to achieve, it could achieve, as the socialists of the early twentieth century were wont to do. After such sober consideration of actual government results versus their promise, Friedman believed the regnant ideology would turn from a statist to a market direction. After forty-five years, his optimism is tempered; but events since then, thanks in no small part to his efforts and those of his fellow libertarians, have at least tentatively borne out some of his optimism.

Part of Friedman's joy at Chicago in the early 1960s, remember, was the presence of *New Individualist Review.* Two Circle Bastiat members, Raico and Hamowy, won admission to Chicago's Committee on Social Thought and studied under Hayek in the late 1950s and early 1960s, and with some initial financial support from the Chodorov-founded Intercollegiate Studies Institute launched a serious, printed and bound journal of classical liberal, libertarian, and conservative thought called *New Individualist Review.*[40] The circle members used it as a launching pad to establish their unique intellectual tradition (particularly in articles by Raico on Benjamin Constant[41] and Wilhelm von Humboldt[42]) and to bash their ideological enemies, an opportunity to clear and claim their unique libertarian ground.

Hamowy took aim at *National Review's* warmongering in the pages of *New Individualist Review,* declaring that Buckley-style conservatism was not "the conservatism of the heroic band of libertarians who founded the anti–New Deal Right, but the traditional conservatism that has always been the enemy of true liberalism; the conservatism of Pharonic Egypt, of Medieval Europe, of the Inquisition; the conservatism of Metternich and the Tsar, of James II and Louis XVI, of the rack, the thumbscrew, the whip, and the firing squad."[43] He earned an amusingly snide set of replies from William Buckley, who felt he had to at least mind these youngsters' complaints, even if he didn't quite take them seriously. He referred to "Contributing Torturer [Russell] Kirk" and "Senior Warmonger Frank Meyer" and "Contributing Executioner John Chamberlain" and then, more seriously, insisted that "we must not, if we are to pass for sane in this tormented world, equate as problems of equal urgency, the repeal of the social security law, and the containment of the Soviet threat."[44]

Hamowy also took aim at his own beloved professor, Hayek, in an analysis of the unlibertarian nature of Hayek's definition of coercion. Hamowy thought it allowed for too much state action by declaring that any state restriction that was preannounced and applied equally to all did not qualify as coercion. Hayek took no offense and noted that

Hamowy's critique was "so far the only one I felt I had to reply to," and indeed he changed how he conceptualized the idea of coercion later.[45]

The libertarians at *New Individualist Review* seemed to be baiting the conservatives among them. Ed Facey, a Mises student from NYU, admitted that libertarians only talked about the Constitution tactically, as an aid in their Fabianism-in-reverse (the socialist Fabians of England took over the institutions of government without necessarily stating their end goals; the libertarians hoped to do the same to move back from socialism to liberty) to shrink the U.S. government.[46] The libertarian editors ran further right-wing baiting pieces, such as those by old World War II revisionist Harry Elmer Barnes, praising A. J. P. Taylor's controversial history of the war, which argued that it wasn't really all Hitler's fault;[47] specific attacks on Russell Kirk[48] and victimless crime laws;[49] former old right congressman Howard Buffett on how the GOP should sink its teeth into abolishing the draft as its major issue, saying it was the moral equivalent of the slavery the Republican Party was born to combat—"an issue of actual physical freedom, as vital and fundamental as the infamous Negro slavery, exists in America today. Its abolition awaits a political party courageous enough to champion liberty as the Republicans did a century ago. I refer, of course, to the Old World evil of conscription, carried out here under the soothing label of Selective Service."[50] In a later issue dedicated to draft elimination that included a contribution from Friedman, Joe Cobb stands up for classic draft dodging by pointing out that you can always avoid the draft by emigrating.[51]

New Individualist Review featured more standard Chicago School free market economics as well, including attacks on antitrust law[52] and most regulatory agencies,[53] and discussion of the dire effects of unions and minimum wage laws on efficiency in wages.[54] While clearly skewed toward its founding editors' radical vision, it was on balance the closest thing the libertarian or conservative world ever got to a high-quality intellectual magazine that tried to actuate the "fusionism" between libertarianism and conservatism that *National Review*'s Frank Meyer advocated—and did it with hints of an intellectual *Mad* magazine about it, with absurdist fake ads in which international leaders praise the magazine. For example, Charles de Gaulle: "I congratulate you for having published, and I congratulate myself for having read, the Winter issue. . . . Your discussion of whether or not David Hume was a whig or a tory was charming but quite needlessly prolonged. He was a tory."

While Chicago students were presenting an intellectually radical libertarianism in academia under the smiling eyes of Hayek and Friedman, the world of presidential politics was also offering something for libertarians—young libertarians especially—to get excited about.

"GOLDWATER AND THE CONSERVATIVE MOVEMENT ARE NOT ONLY NOT LIBERTARIAN, BUT THE PREEMINENT ENEMIES OF LIBERTY OF OUR TIME."

The 1964 Goldwater presidential campaign was a revivifying moment for the modern libertarian movement, unwittingly fomenting new energy and new recruits for a political tendency more radical than the Arizona senator himself, and ultimately radical in different directions. Almost every future libertarian movement activist between the ages of ten and twenty in 1964 was thrilled and inspired by the image of Goldwater the seemingly radical outsider. His campaign and his pronouncements about how he came to Washington to repeal laws, not to make them, helped many a young libertarian think that he or she had a place in the real political world, and a real-life hero who fought for unpopular political principles with a stern gaze and a no-nonsense directness.

Despite having been an Eisenhower delegate at the 1952 GOP convention and riding into the Senate that year on his coattails (to the extent that libertarians still cared about the GOP then, they were far more likely to be Taftites), Goldwater sold himself as a very libertarian figure: anti–farm subsidies, anti–welfare state, anti–New Deal regulations and giveaways. His 1960 jeremiad *Conscience of a Conservative,* which sold over 3 million copies, cemented nascent antigovernment feelings in many bright young protolibertarians. The book launched him to national prominence, making him simultaneously hero and devil to huge segments of the American public.

But those who loved him, *really* loved him. Here at last was a public figure speaking against big government who, however derided, was at least being *heard*. Opposition to the post–New Deal welfare-managerial state was now in the papers and on the news thanks to Goldwater, even if only to be bashed and mocked. Many youngsters coming of intellectual age in Kennedy's New Frontier could only assume their thoughts and beliefs had no place in the modern world. As Rick Perlstein, a liberal journalist who wrote the best study of the Goldwater movement, *Before the Storm*, wrote, what the Goldwaterites were fighting against wasn't seen as some alternate, arguable ideology—it was *reality*.[55]

Goldwater showed that another reality could exist. Something *could* be said—maybe even *done*—about modern liberalism; the cause of small government advocacy had some sort of future, as long as Barry was flying high. Some were so dazzled that they saw him as the walking, breathing embodiment of everything Ayn Rand stood for, John Galt in a fighter plane; even Rand herself was a measured supporter.[56] Sam Husbands, a San Francisco investment professional who served on the boards of both FEE and later the Cato Institute, thought a victory for Goldwater would be a victory for FEE values. Another FEE supporter told Leonard Read he was confident that Read's efforts spreading the freedom gospel were the true ideological bedrock underlying Goldwater's nomination victory. A treasurer with the Republican National Committee assured Read that the Goldwater movement was at heart a libertarian one, "incorporating the ideals of Ludwig von Mises, Hayek, Hazlitt, and some of the other greats who helped form the intellectual base for this movement."[57] (He at least knew the right names to drop.)

Radical libertarianism was shot through the Goldwater movement, but with small-caliber ammo. Through his friendship with American Enterprise Institute chief Bill Baroody, leader of Barry Goldwater's brain trust, Milton Friedman became an economic adviser to the Goldwater campaign, no doubt providing him with advice that helped cement Goldwater's reputation as a dangerous radical (and attract many young libertarians to Goldwater's cause). The public attention this brought, along with *Capitalism and Freedom*, made Friedman a sought-after lecturer and led to the polemical job that brought him to the attention of the most people for the longest time: his tri-weekly column in *Newsweek* magazine, beginning in 1966, where he pushed reasonably hard-core libertarianism on matters both economic and personal to the largest audience of American readers that would ever see them, for nearly twenty years. And rag ends of the libertarian remnant had attached themselves to Goldwater. One Goldwater delegate from Nebraska, Butler Shaffer, later an active movement libertarian, was once doing a home visit to some local Republicans and stumbled across three earnest young men in a back room eagerly talking over the economic doctrines of strange characters like Hayek and Rothbard.[58]

The Goldwater story (inspirational for ideological political outsiders of any stripe) of how a squad of activists with no power center in a major party, lacking even the wholehearted support of their supposed standard-bearer, catapulted their man to a presidential nomination, suffered a crushing defeat, and then saw their ideas percolate and grow and eventually win the presidency sixteen years later with Ronald Reagan, has been told elsewhere. And it is not, despite some of Goldwater's rhetoric, and despite the effect that he undoubtedly had on many young libertarians, a strictly libertarian story. Not for nothing was his book called *Conscience of a Conservative*, and none of the inner circle of the draft Goldwater movement, nor many of his inner circle of advisers (except Friedman) were libertarians at the time, though one prominent convert, Karl Hess (about whom more later), would arise from the very bosom of Goldwaterism. Goldwater won the hearts of many prominent libertarians for being the only major political figure who even seemed to think (at times, at least) that the New Deal needed to be rolled back—even though he was not across the board reliable even on this.

Goldwater was ultimately on the other side of the conservative/ libertarian divide in his belief that the United States has to remain eternally active overseas so long as the Great Soviet Bear still stalks the woods. And despite his (sophistic) declaration that he never, never, never called for a nuclear war against the Soviets, even the most charitable of readers would find it difficult to figure out whatever he might have meant in *Conscience* about the commies if he *didn't* mean that.[59]

Some hard-core libertarians understood that, regardless of how solid a libertarian they thought he was, placing great value on a Goldwater electoral victory was misreading the libertarian's situation in modern America. Politicians, as Leonard Read always argued, are lagging indicators, not leading ones. Once the libertarian educational missions had progressed enough, then the politicians would naturally fall in line. Benjamin Rogge, a libertarian economics professor at Wabash College (and Read's choice to succeed him at FEE) noted that "the great mistake was made, not during the campaign, but precisely when those conservatives who pride themselves on being activists and on 'knowing how to get things done,' decided that conservatism could be brought to America by what would amount to a political coup . . . *Goldwater's campaign could not build on any solid foundation of widely accepted ideas on society, economics, and the state.*"[60]

Former *National Review* writer Garry Wills, who had by 1970 made a turn to the left, analyzed the connection between the Goldwaterite right and the libertarians interestingly, starting with a consideration of libertarian Friedman's links with Republican politics: "The logistics of competition within the two-party system made Friedman, in his effort to defend Market fundamentalism, ally himself with the mishmash of Right-Wing forces behind Barry Goldwater in 1964. This was an alliance that had no true theoretical bond at all."[61] The libertarians, in his reading, needed the Republicans to have any nexus with the world of effective politics; but what the Republicans needed from the libertarians was the only respectable intellectual theory the right could rely on: free market economics. "The Right could formulate no basic philosophy of politics," Wills wrote. "The best-articulated scrap of theory available to them, one that almost everyone could find some use for, was the free-market economy. Other components of Right-Wing theory were often mere instincts, prejudices, unformulated preferences. Only the economists marinated a respectable academic base and an intellectual tradition of any rigor."[62] From then on, much of what the right has had to offer in terms of interesting theory—and it nearly always remained theory in Republican practice—has derived from free market libertarianism.

But Rothbard, ever contrary, could not be satisfied by the occasional rhetorical sops that Republican politicians throw toward libertarian ideas. He was appalled by widespread libertarian enthusiasm for Goldwater. (Rothbard had supported Stevenson over Eisenhower in 1956 because he thought him less bellicose about the Soviets. When Adlai failed to win the Democratic nomination in 1960, Rothbard became an active worker—answering phones in the office and all—of a group urging Kennedy to make Adlai secretary of state.)[63] When a writer in one of the first libertarian zines, the *Innovator,* praised Goldwater as a libertarian choice, Rothbard responded with a lengthy letter that sums up where Rothbard saw himself, intellectually and politically, in relation to the conservative movement.

"I simply cannot understand how you can regard Goldwater as a libertarian or genuine liberal in any sense," he wrote.

> I would like, in fact, for you to point to one *specific* mainstay of the current statist system that Goldwater proposes to repeal. It has become clear that Goldwater does *not* propose to eliminate even the graduated features of the income tax (let alone repeal the income tax altogether) . . . he does *not* propose to make Social Security voluntary or to sell TVA to private enterprise. . . . On the union side, Goldwater shows no signs of calling for repeal of the Wagner-Taft-Hartley Act structure; instead he wants to add more statist oppression on labor relations by subjecting unions to anti-trust laws and passing 'right-to-work' laws which prohibit employers from making, voluntarily, closed shop agreements with unions. . . . Goldwater's choice of economic advisers makes it clear that he would support a Keynesian fiscal policy of greater government spending in recessions. . . . I conclude, then, that Goldwater's supposed pro-libertarian views are meaningless political rhetoric cut off from any specific application. . . . Goldwater and the Conservative Movement are not only not libertarian, but the preeminent enemies of liberty of our time. For the Goldwaterites are, first, aggressive and ardent champions of American imperialism and intervention in political and military affairs all over the globe; and, second and most important, are eager advocates of nuclear war against the Soviet Union. . . . The threat and the reality of nuclear annihilation is the great threat—far more intensely and widely than domestic statism—to the lives and liberties of Americans and indeed of the human race itself. . . . Those libertarians who believe in taking part in the political process should bend their every effort to defeat Barry Goldwater and all Goldwaterites candidates in November.[64]

National Review—whose Buckley, Bozell, and Rusher were deliberately kept out of a close position of counsel in the Goldwater campaign, and which recognized that he had no chance of winning and worried what such a drubbing might mean for public perceptions of any conservative resurgence—was still the natural place where eager young individualist intellectuals who got excited by Goldwater would go to seek intellectual and emotional ammunition for the long march against FDR's legacy. The ones who would later become active libertarians began to wonder what the hell old European traditionalists, such as Thomas Molnar or Joseph de Maistre, often printed or lauded in that magazine, had to do with American liberty anyway.

"IT'S SORT OF A DANGEROUS THERAPY, BUT IT SEEMS TO BE WORKING PRETTY WELL."

One of the most important libertarian institutions of the 1960s was a school known originally as the Freedom School, and later Rampart College. It was founded and run by a former radio announcer, actor, traveling salesman, and one-time acolyte to ancient Ascended Masters suffused with direct pure-light wisdom beamed from the noggin of the living but ethereal St. Germain. The Freedom School's master was blessed with the mellifluous name of Robert LeFevre.

LeFevre was born in 1911 in Idaho, did some acting in Hollywood's 1930s golden age, and hit the Great Depression showman road with a family troupe, in between working with his father and solo on some minor door-to-door salesman cons.[65] Most interestingly, he had spent four exciting months, months that would affect the rest of his life, in 1939–1940 on stages in auditoriums across America working for the cult of the Mighty "I AM," to which he had been introduced by a friend at a radio station where he'd been working. LeFevre became briefly a key cog in a traveling inner circle of acolytes, wishing down the spectral blue lightning of vengeance on America's enemies while standing beneath flags with gold stripes in place of red (red being a spiritually bad color in "I AM" doctrine), aiding and abetting avatars of a religio-politico-wacko machine run by Guy Ballard (who channeled his eternal wisdom under the name Godfre Ray King). Ballard claimed to be the reincarnation of George Washington, and a being—who can call him a mere man?—with the clout to get Jesus Christ himself to show up and hold still for a multihour portrait sitting. Hey, it was a living.[66]

LeFevre was a tall man with a silver voice, a jack-of-all-trades in the early days of radio, the veteran of vicious fights with unions that were thuggishly trying to shut down his stations. The bogus spiritualism thing with the Mighty "I AM" was short-lived (though LeFevre insisted he was a genuine believer, hearing eerie disembodied voices in his head and all—this wasn't just another con to him). This cult in which he was a votary began to fray after beloved leader Ballard, despite the promises he transmitted via the secret masters, died the tawdry death of a mortal. With the assistance of a fellow cult priestess he was mad for, LeFevre had begun transmitting his own messages from ascended masters. He decided that Mama Ballard, Guy's widow and the new leader of "I AM," seemed more fraud than medium.

Helping push the sensible out the door of the Mighty "I AM" was the mail fraud prosecution, which made it all the way to the Supreme Court. It led to an important decision in which the court declared that the U.S. government can't be in the business of deciding whether the claims of a given religion or cult are *true* or not. But it can rightly be called upon to judge whether its high priest and priestess *believed it was true* in judging a fraud prosecution. (Promised but undelivered healings could be judged by the standard of man's law, not God's.)[67]

LeFevre ran away from the Mighty "I AM" and to the Mighty U.S. army during World War II. There he met a USO songbird named Loy Leuling and married her. After the war LeFevre, reunited with some of his old "I AM" friends (the female ones), first succeeded and then failed in the apartment and hotel business. Along the way he ran into some local regulatory graft that planted seeds of suspicion about how wonderful things were in America in this formerly very Yankee doodle soldier. (Fanatical patriotism was an "I AM" tenet.) He and his friends bought Rudy Valentino's old Falcon Lair in L.A. and were accused in the press of running a "love cult."

LeFevre had caught the anticommunist bug, and in the early 1950s became a prominent professional anticommie and antiunion lecturer under various ad hoc committee names. He failed in a run for Congress from the Los Angeles area. Later he expressed shame for not calling for an end to public education (as he had for Social Security), since

he *knew* that was the right stand. He was afraid, though, that his potential constituents weren't ready for it (not that they were ready for him
anyway). One of his girls from the "I AM" days began working with
Spiritual Mobilization, and handed Bob a copy of Rose Wilder Lane's
The Discovery of Freedom. He learned there was more to liberty than
just being antiunion and anti-Soviet.[68]

With a new sense of mission, he moved to Florida where he worked
as news director at a Fort Lauderdale TV station, and became a cause
célèbre by condemning the Girl Scout handbook for praising the
U.N. Universal Declaration of Human Rights.[69] By 1954, he was
known as a right-wing jack-of-all-trades, and was hired on briefly by
Merwin Hart at the National Economic Council, the free market advocacy outfit whose book review newsletter Albert Jay Nock and
Rose Wilder Lane wrote in the 1940s. LeFevre found Hart's linking of
socialism, communism, and other world ills with the Jews distasteful
and got out quick.[70] For a short while LeFevre became executive director of the Congress for Freedom, a national right-wing organization he hoped he could turn into an intelligent, capable, and genuinely
pro-liberty movement, something more sophisticated and libertarian
than the right-populism of the McCarthy era. But a 1955 Congress
for Freedom national convention in San Francisco dedicated to "getting the U.S. out of the U.N." demonstrated that the mass movement
types were more dedicated to hating commies and preserving a fantasy
of America as a strictly Christian nation than to understanding and
acting on the principles of liberty. LeFevre's fellow Congress of Freedom director and fellow anarcho-libertarian, Thaddeus Ashby, then an
editor at Spiritual Mobilization's *Faith and Freedom* magazine, wrote
that "if [Congress of Freedom] could be boiled down to a single type,
we would be a little lady, aged 55 to 70, vigorous, vocal, sometimes
self-righteous, with flowers on our hat."[71]

But professional libertarians were rare. What institutions existed had
to pick from a small, often interlocked band of qualified workers.
LeFevre replaced Thaddeus Ashby (who had made his own intramove-
ment shift to work for *Faith and Freedom*), working directly under R.
C. Hoiles's younger son Harry on the editorial page of the *Colorado
Springs Gazette Telegraph*.

While working there, he discovered the Palmer Range and bought 320 acres of land where Plum Creek crossed the mountains, a wooded fir and pine paradise, 7,000 feet above sea level. LeFevre was on top of the world, up in these mountains; he knew this was *the place*, far from madding crowds and creeping socialism, to root his dream for a full-time educational institution for inculcating his version of libertarianism. Not just an institution to publish pamphlets and books and magazines for strangers to read, but one that directly, face-to-face and soul-to-soul, contemplated and inculcated the eternal verities of human freedom.

Most of the land he bought was mountainous and tree clogged, and the cabins on the site were mostly uninhabitable. So LeFevre, wife Loy, and the trio of women from the "I AM" days who were still following him hunkered down and, before and after his day job writing controversial editorials for Harry Hoiles at the *Gazette-Telegraph,* built log cabins for lodging and teaching, and bought horses to add to the rustic charm and give the students something to do between lectures on, in the great LeFevre style, the universal law that if you trespass on someone's property, you'll make him mad, and you wouldn't want that, would you? (LeFevre's philosophy, however convincing when delivered in person, lacked rigorous reasons for *why* one oughtn't trespass on another's property, but this sort of folksy Golden Ruleism—you wouldn't want someone doing it to *you,* would you?—had its charm.)

LeFevre first hoped this fresh-minted Freedom School would be a place for the inculcation of Baldy Harper's version of libertarianism. They had been friends and correspondents, as all libertarians were wont to be (at least the latter) in those lonely days. LeFevre was convinced that Harper had the firmest grasp of libertarian principles as he saw them, and the best gentle, Socratic guiding techniques to lead the young to grasp them as their own.

This was 1956, and Baldy was still working at FEE. Although more than ready to leave an institution where he felt increasingly stifled by Leonard Read, and increasingly certain Read was micromanaging the operation into the ground (he was expressing this viewpoint to FEE board members and anyone else who would accept a letter from him),

Baldy didn't think that the Palmer Range and LeFevre was the right next step. They liked old LeFevre well enough, most of his ideological colleagues did, including Harper. But one had to admit he was a queer duck, with a lot of strangely shaped baggage carted around with him, one being his relationship with these three woman helpmeets/employees/roommates/partners who had been following him since the "I AM" days, *besides* his wife. That was just a trifle too risqué for an old Cornell man like Baldy. Now LeFevre 'til the day he died—and Loy 'til years after—insisted that the situation was nothing like what the filthy minded might think.[72] But there it was; LeFevre was too genuinely bohemian in his way for this libertarian movement made up, at the time, mostly of old-line businessmen and college professors.[73]

His ideas, though on the surface within the libertarian mainstream (the anarchist eddy at least), took some curious turns that ultimately consigned LeFevre to the role, from today's perspective, of mostly forgotten influence. But his direct disciples include some of the most important and influential figures in the libertarian movement's future, from Roy Childs (1970s editor of the magazine *Libertarian Review*) to free market environmentalism pioneer R. J. Smith to Charles and David Koch, a pair of brothers who became the biggest source of funding for libertarian causes in the 1970s and beyond. LeFevre's heresy was his conclusion that retaliatory force was just as morally problematic as any other kind of force. LeFevre preached a thoroughgoing pacifism that held it to be an impermissible violation of the property rights of an assailant to destroy the ropes he'd tied you up with (just so long as they were his ropes) and just as bad to take a necklace back from a blackguard who stole it from you as it was for the blackguard to take it from you in the first place.

Our moral obligation—and our only practical hope for a properly propertarian future—is to defend our property *before* it gets taken from us. LeFevre believed the market had, and would continue to, come up with newer and better techniques to defend yourself and your things without relying on the moral crime of retaliation.[74] He liked to make the point in his presentations that in reality, no state, no outside organization, *could* protect you but yourself. All those entities could do was try to seek vengeance or restitution after you had been violated. (And with modern states, vengeance is all you *can* get. You get nothing back when a thief who has stolen from you is arrested—in fact, it takes *more* from you, in the form of the taxes that pay for his trial and imprisonment.) LeFevre was once in the middle of a lecture to a group of execs and would-be execs from the textile company Deering-Milliken— LeFevrite training was de rigueur in that company for over a decade, though its chief Roger Milliken, also a one-time FEE board member, later became, and remains, an arch-protectionist in the interests of his textile business—making that point about the futility of government "protection" when someone ran in to tell the class that President Kennedy had been shot. The class thought LeFevre was using tastelessly shocking means to make his damn point.

LeFevre started the Freedom School small. Many over the years had tried to start libertarian colleges or postgraduate teaching institutions, including Leonard Read at FEE for a few years in the early 1960s and Mises student Hans Sennholz, who tried through the late 1950s and early 1960s to get enough money from J. Howard Pew and other libertarian financiers to start the American School of Economics, which would teach pure Misesianism and would have its own New York City campus. (That idea fizzled into a short-lived series of lectures in rented halls.) The first graduating class of Freedom School in 1957 was four people—a minister, a college kid, a rancher, and a staffer's mom.

It was slow, getting this Freedom School going, though even in the beginning LeFevre succeeding in getting the greatest stars in the libertarian sky to come out to the Colorado mountains and shine; Leonard Read and Rose Wilder Lane and Frank Chodorov and Gordon Tullock (pioneer, along with future Nobel winner James Buchanan, in the "public choice" school of economics, which analyzed government actions as if they were as self-interested as market actions) were early guest lecturers. Rose Lane thought LeFevre's mission was so vital that she became his first financial angel before Roger Milliken's LeFevre obsession kept Freedom School financially stable for the rest of his teaching career. Chodorov made his last public stand there in the Colorado mountains, suffering a stroke on the podium in front of a Freedom School class. LeFevre, sure it would be what he wanted, guided the babbling Chodorov to a chair—after prying his clutched fingers from the lectern—and gave the lecture, which he'd heard many times before, himself.[75]

Word of what LeFevre was doing, and how well it often seemed to work, spread among the scattered freedom devotees who were sure socialist influence had ruined standard education. LeFevre ultimately succeeded longer than anyone else at this strange idea of a purely libertarian school. He was like catnip to a certain class of businessman, perhaps because the school's short sessions gave off a pleasing feel of "all you need to know about social science and philosophy in a week." LeFevre would be flown out by his wealthy and influential fans to speak to local business organizations or schools, or sent to educate their underlings in the importance of the freest possible enterprise. In addition to Milliken, a group of Milwaukee-based free market businessmen assembled as the Employers Association of Milwaukee were big early supporters of LeFevre.[76]

He delivered LeFevrianism in all its peculiarity straight—no one ever accused old Bob of holding back for popularity.[77] Wichita was another center of LeFevrian action, and he once treated the local Lions Club to a presentation called "Prelude to Hell" in which he brought his best pacifist libertarianism to bear. The speech was a brutal presentation of what it might be like for a typical American city—say, Wichita, Kansas—to be nuked as a result of those mighty, terrible, pointless conflicts that the modern state inevitably creates. The school's eccentricities attracted its share of eccentrics in return—including the blond-haired, blue-eyed scion of a wealthy old Virginia family who became an enthusiastic "freedom nazi" openly plotting the dictatorship he'd establish in order to force LeFevrianism on the world.[78]

As to what it was like to be taught by LeFevre, well, I've read the books that arose from his lectures and it just doesn't come across, whatever magic that made multimillionaires—people with not much but time left to economize—go through it all more than once, which some did. As LeFevre once explained in a school newsletter, "The impact of the course is deeply personal and involved a series of developments in logical thinking not readily communicable to the casual inquirer."[79]

Textile king Roger Milliken's obsession with LeFevre confused (and frankly aggravated) some other libertarians who might have thought his money better spent on *them*. In a letter to Leonard Read, a management consultant who worked with Milliken said, "I have to admit that Bob has, in his one week and two week sessions, gotten through to a lot of men I have been unable to touch over the years. With rare exceptions they hold back enough acceptance of Bob to end up where you and I would like to see them [i.e., libertarians but not anarchists]. I think that with these men, Bob had telescoped your process by quite a few years. It's sort of a dangerous therapy, but it seems to be working pretty well."[80]

Milliken got hooked on LeFevre when a cadre of his top execs went to the Freedom School without him, and more or less threatened to quit if Milliken didn't go see for himself what this wizard had to say. (After one exposure to LeFevre, Milliken gave him $100,000.)[81] LeFevre had such charismatic power; the libertarian movement was full of oversize eccentrics in those days, all recruiting for their own army and forging their own path.

LeFevre, a true Midwestern Wizard of Oz character, struck you as either the most direct, sincere, courtly, amiable, kindly yet intellectually brave man you'd ever met, or a suspiciously oleaginous snake oil pusher clearly out to sell you some bill of goods for mysterious reasons of his own. He was, though, capable of facing down angry lieutenant colonels, who raged at his pacifistic refusal to fight for the flag, and explaining his theory of human rights so patiently, so guilelessly, that in the end the crusty colonel had to admit that LeFevre was right to stand his ground. He may not have been for everyone, but those who loved Robert LeFevre, loved him passionately. One Boeing exec said that everyone he knew who took the course (more than a thousand passed through, in small batches, over the school's decade plus in business) considered it the most profound intellectual experience of their lives. Graduates could see his ideas spreading from person to person through chains of personal connection, infecting many who had never heard the name LeFevre.

Robert Smith, who spent some time at the school, sums it up: "LeFevre was a convincing cross of a professor, a father figure, and a religious—not quite a charlatan, but a *spellbinder.* I remember him telling the story of union goons busting into a radio station he worked at. And he just fell flat on the ground and lay there. They were so nonplussed they walked out without beating the shit out of him. That convinced him of the principles of nonviolence."[82]

Some found that sort of moral education through storytelling charming and convincing, and some didn't. LeFevre reports with some humor on the student who lived in LeFevre's ideological world for a week and then shouted loudly about how "anything I was for, he was against. Anything I was against, he was for it" and ran from the classroom and away from the mountain stronghold.[83]

Some found his approach to libertarian education so eccentric and dangerous that he simply had to be *stopped*. In January 1964, Dean Russell of FEE declared public war on LeFevre, trying to get the Curran Foundation (Jasper Crane of DuPont's operation, on whose board Russell also sat) to stop funding the Freedom School. Russell had somehow just noticed LeFevre was an anarchist and declared— both in private letters and in a *Freeman* article—that anarchists were positive enemies of human freedom, whether they knew it or not.[84] This contretemps launched another of the movement's oceans of correspondence flowing east to west and back again, with LeFevre's fellow "100 percent voluntaryists" appalled at Russell's vindictiveness, and detecting behind it the controlling hand of Boss Read.[85]

Read was jealous, went the gossip, that LeFevre was overtaking him as homiletic king of libertarian education. FEE had launched in the early 1960s its own short-lived summer School of Political Economy in competition with LeFevre, in which Russell taught economics and Reverend Edmund Opitz taught politics, using the works of Rothbard and Hayek as texts.[86] Rose Wilder Lane sharply upbraided her old friend Jasper Crane when he seemed to be vacillating in Russell's direction. She pointed out they both always knew where LeFevre stood and *agreed with it*; what could be more pure than LeFevre's technique of avoiding political action, refusing to use political power or rely on government services, and merely acting independently and morally in a market setting?[87] Still, LeFevre hated the term "anarchism." He thought it meant actively destroying existing institutions. He certainly did not believe any state had any moral authority or ought to exist, but he preferred the portmanteau term "autarchy" for his system.

For youngsters, the Freedom School tended to spit them out after a week or two cocksure that they knew everything they needed to know about liberty; alternately, they'd decide, given the chance for a bit of independent thought after they'd descended from the thin mountain air, that they'd been taken for a ride by a slick, though slow-talking, charlatan. That sort of negative reaction from a couple of high school teachers caused LeFevre some trouble. Another of LeFevre's major corporate supporters was the Rockford, Illinois–based Ingersoll Milling Machine Company. The Rockford chamber of commerce, under Ingersoll persuasion, sent a group of local high school teachers to Freedom School. They came out unconverted and reported back to the Rockford chamber that LeFevre was running a racket and running down state and religion to boot: "We do not believe that the Chamber wants us to teach that there should be no government."[88]

Baldy Harper summed up the often peculiar vibe at Freedom School during one of his guest lecturing stints as "some ski resort where some teen-agers were snowed in for the winter . . . a strong overtone . . . evident in all sorts of ways, a near rebellion against something there."[89] One young anarchist—with the help of a renegade staffer—ran up the black flag of anarchy on the day a potentially big donor of businesslike sensibilities arrived; the money didn't come through.[90]

In 1965, LeFevre launched the first semischolarly journal dedicated to modern anarchist libertarianism, the *Rampart Journal of Individualist Thought*. It featured, among other interesting examples of mid-1960s libertariana, Roy Childs's first public explanation of why Objectivism necessarily implied anarchism;[91] an early version of what became a remarkably popular tool for retailing libertarianism, now known as the "Nolan chart"—a two-dimensional grid of political ideology, beyond just left and right, in which libertarianism seemed to have a place;[92] and one of those explorations, beloved by libertarians, into obscure human communities that lacked the sort of government we have and yet still survived, in this case Pashtun tribes in Afghanistan.[93]

One summer day in 1965, the rains came to the Palmer Range and stayed; 14 inches soaked into the ground of the hills and ranges above the headquarters of what LeFevre was now calling Rampart College. The ground began to buckle and slide and soon most of the cabins and classrooms were filled halfway to the roof with mud. The students insisted on staying to help clean up; muddy library books were sold in a "dirty books from the Freedom School" sale. The LeFevrites, who proudly used no public services whatsoever in their mountain stronghold, noted that they began taking care of their own problems immediately, while in the lowland towns with city managers hit by floods, the folks waited for someone to come take charge. The school was only insured for direct rain and hail damage, not mudslides, and got only $3,500 in coverage on $150,000 in damage.

LeFevre mortgaged the place even more to keep going, consumed with realizing grander ambitions than merely giving one- and two-week classes to youngsters and corporate executives. Despite having no formal academic credentials, he tried to reshape the Freedom School as Rampart College, an actual accredited degree-granting graduate school. He recruited libertarian-leaning economist W. H. Hutt from South Africa and anarchist historian and war revisionist James Martin to head their respective departments.

Both scholars quickly ran into conflicts of personality and ideology with LeFevre, and began to suspect they'd been sold a bill of goods regarding the respectability and stability of Rampart College as a long-term career move. Hutt decided that his reputation would be damaged by association with LeFevre and Rampart, and he gently accused LeFevre's version of libertarianism of being based more on faith than evidence. Hutt pointed out that "all technically trained 'libertarian' economists perceived the need, in any free society, for some collective action" and listed such areas as eminent domain, antitrust, public goods, and patents as places where LeFevre was outlibertarianing the libertarians.[94] In September 1967, the dream of a graduate school at Rampart was abandoned.

The college never recovered from the mudslide, and LeFevre's heart broke—he couldn't bear to even drive by the site in later years. (He sold it to the Mennonites to use as a mountain retreat for troubled boys.)[95] In 1968, he moved to Orange County in California, where Rampart College lived on, after a fashion. But it was a very different libertarian movement by then.

"I'M AFRAID I CANNOT TELL YOU."

Imagine you paid for a series of lectures on liberty. You were afraid they might be a little dull, but you found yourself electrified by an entirely new way of seeing life, of conceptualizing the human social order and how to make it work best for everyone. You were mostly interested in science and engineering, and never knew that political, social, and moral sciences could be so rigorous, so well organized, so convincing and deductively solid. You were excited, burning to tell your associates and friends what was so special about this particular lecturer, a man of the physical sciences like yourself, a man who really got to the core of why liberty was vital and what its diligent pursuit really implied. He was a former astrophysicist by the name of Andrew Joseph Galambos, teaching in Southern California under the rubric of the Free Enterprise Institute.

But you couldn't. You couldn't say a word. Because if one of the very interesting new ideas that Galambos had convinced you of was true, you had to honor his "primary property"—his ideas—to the extent that you were not free to share them with someone who hadn't paid Galambos for them. You couldn't even share *why* you couldn't explain it. It could lead to some awkward conversations. As libertarianism's comic historian Jerome Tuccille presented his meeting with a Galambosian:

> "There are five legitimate functions of government," said the Galambosian.
>
> "No kidding. What are they?"
>
> "I am not at liberty to say. The theory was originated by Andy Galambos and it is his primary property."
>
> The Galambosian also informed me that Andy had been introduced to Ayn Rand several years before, and that after five minutes of conversation they had pronounced each other insane.
>
> "Of course it is Miss Rand who is really insane," said the Galambosian.
>
> "Why is that?"
>
> "I'm afraid I cannot tell you. The reasoning behind that theory belongs to Andy."
>
> "If the rest of us were free to discuss his ideas," said the Galambosian, "there is no question in my mind that Galambosianism would spread throughout the world like wildfire."[96]

In the small world of libertarianism in the early 1960s, everyone had met everyone else. It was a small pond then, and jumping into any part of it meant you'd splash all the other occupants. Despite his madden-ing eccentricities, Galambos became the leading libertarian teacher and guru in Southern California after starting his Free Enterprise In-stitute in 1961, in a community primed by the *Register*'s R. C. Hoiles and a general cultural atmosphere in which antigovernment extrem-ism seemed as natural as an orange grove. Galambos was a rare success-ful libertarian ideological entrepreneur, depending not on donations but actually making a living selling libertarian ideas. He was, like many in Southern California, an aerospace fanatic; his interest in liberty arose from his belief that only a truly free society would ever create the means to get to outer space and back in a truly big way.

Galambos kept his overhead and advertising costs low. His students' comfort meant little to him and word of mouth seemed to guarantee a steady supply of people intrigued by what they could only learn di-rectly from him. You had to sign a form explaining that all you were buying with your tuition was the right to be aware of the ideas—not to use them or reveal them to outsiders. Harry Browne, later a leading investment guru and two-time Libertarian Party presidential candidate who worked with Galambos for a while in the mid-1960s, com-plained that the form was so incoherent the students couldn't under-stand what they were agreeing to. That was okay, Galambos insisted. After taking the course, they would understand enough so that they *would* agree with it.[97]

He was a terrible lecturer—incoherent, rambling, sucking on ice while he talked—but the strength and peculiarity of his ideas got him across. There was little in him (besides the ideas as primary property stuff) that wasn't also in Rothbard or LeFevre, but their thoughts were not yet widely published. You'd only know about them if you were lucky enough to be one of their correspondents, or if you'd at-tended LeFevre's Freedom School in Colorado. Many hundreds of people paid Galambos $500 (in mid-1960s dollars) for his wisdom.

Leonard Read of FEE and Baldy Harper of the Institute for Humane Studies found Galambos sound enough when they encountered him, and the East Coast libertarian crew credited him with creating in the Southern California area the largest and most hard-core bunch of non-professional protoactivists the libertarian movement had yet seen. John Rousselot, a Birchite California congressman, got flooded with letters wondering if this Galambos guy they'd heard some good things about was free of the communist conspiracy; he was quite the sensation in Southern California then. His disciples tended to be accomplished people from scientific or engineering backgrounds, most of whom went on to successful careers in their chosen endeavors.

Part of Galambos's routine was extreme optimism about the imminence of a rational and free America. He had to believe this, as he was eager to get to outer space on a free market rocket. He generally taught a relatively straight mix of the standard libertarian catechism of the time as "volitional science," starting from property as inviolable and building from there to the idea of "the free market as true democracy," larded with his special astrophysicist blend of references to Newton and Maxwell, and explaining how justice and defense could be sold and delivered by private insurance companies. "Primary property" was his one unusual innovation, and that's all anyone remembers about him now.[98]

Rothbard found Galambos congenial at first, but when he found out about the primary property business, he could only shake his head. He noted that if libertarians thought they had trouble *now* with people thinking libertarianism was inherently antipoor, what would critics say when they learned about the libertarian who thought poor people shouldn't even be able to *talk* to each other without paying off whoever "owned" whatever ideas or concepts they discussed?

Though little remembered, from the Galambos movement grew an entire industry, one that generated great interest, great profit, and some small amount of panic in America in the 1970s: the hard money movement, that squad of writers of newsletters and best-sellers, purveyors of advice on how to stock up on survival food and old metal coins to ride out the economic catastrophe that government mismanagement of the economy was about to create. Many of the early, successful entrepreneurs in the silver and coin industry, and especially those whose ideological fervor and ability as publicists turned hard money (its advocates became known, somewhat pejoratively, as "goldbugs") from just a business to a cause, were Galambosians, most prominently Harry Browne, the hard money promoter of the early 1970s who wrote the best-selling *How You Can Profit from the Coming Devaluation* (1970).

As the 1960s progressed, some of Galambos's brighter acolytes were being driven away by his pounding on the primary property idea. Though Galambos was around and teaching his courses for many more years he quickly washed himself away into an eddy of the movement, from which no fresh water would issue, and little could flow in. Still, Browne remembers, "he had a way of changing almost all his students' lives. And I never heard of a Galambos graduate regressing to his former ways."[99]

"HEY, MAN—I'VE GOT BAD NEWS FOR YOU! YOU'RE PARANOID."

Out of the early 1960s Galambosian ferment in Southern California arose the tradition of strictly libertarian zines, self-published and distributed almost entirely via mail and word-of-mouth, with tiny but dedicated audiences, starting with the *Innovator* (which began life in February 1964 as *Liberal Innovator*). Bill Bradford, then a young libertarian in Michigan, later a major coin dealer and editor and publisher of the movement journal *Liberty*, recalled how thrilled he was to finally find a hip, engaged magazine—not a *Freeman*-like journal that strove so mightily to stay above the fray it could seem too empyrean to touch—that forged a unique identity for people who thought as he did, who didn't see libertarianism as some weird subset of conservatism.

The *Innovator* defined its audience as "the libertarian, the truly radical rightist, [who] seeks complete freedom to live his life for his own sake—complete freedom from initiated violence or threat of violence by government bodies. In this respect, the libertarian is an extremist and properly so. A political 'moderate' is one who entertains the notion that a little slavery is a good thing!"[100]

The zine was begun by Tom Marshall, an engineer/nerd type from Los Angeles and one of the earliest libertarians to theorize about and plan for the creation of new libertarian countries, including, he hoped, ones on a platform floating in the ocean. He became discouraged at the increasingly obvious practical difficulties of the scheme, and by its rejection from his hero Ayn Rand. Along with his new country project, which he pursued under the name Preform, he also started the *In-novator* to discuss and explore the ideas and applications that Preform-style purely libertarian life would require.

The zine's goal was to focus on "long-range strategies for acquiring greater freedom; techniques of government having future applicability; reports on experimental community development; news of private companies that provide what have traditionally been governmental services; innovations in personal relationships and child development; and analyses of international aspects of freedom."[101] The magazine was a playground and gathering place for a fresh generation applying liber-tarian thought to the world. Unlike Objectivists opposed on principle to the current culture, the magazine looked for, and was delighted to find, libertarian themes in everything from science fiction stories to Lesley Gore songs to pirate radio to soft-core porn novels. They didn't want—at least at the start—to run away from the world or cram them-selves into some barricaded corner of it.

The Innovator contained prescient little lucubrations on matters such as a coming leftist war on advertising as a front in the war on capital-ism (attacking advertising meant—Objectivism was, as always, a big part of the ecumenical libertarian mix—an attack on the notion of man as a rational being). It worried that the masses might rush to lib-ertarianism before the libertarian vanguard had fully worked out the meanings and implications of libertarian social theory.[102] The *Innovator* was talking about enterprise zones—areas that could be made free from regulation and taxation to create an economic boom—a decade before better-connected right-wing foundations managed to make them a live policy option. They suggested a startling way for America to get out of the Vietnam mess: Just buy the whole damn country. It celebrated private fire departments, private roads, Ralph Borsodi's back-to-the-land School for Living, "sexual liberty," and the Taxis pri-vate mail system around which Thomas Pynchon built his novel *The Crying of Lot 49*. They were already questioning the libertarian value of Friedman-style school vouchers on the grounds they'd just import state control into private education. The magazine never reached more than 1,000 readers but later became the Velvet Underground of political zines, with a surprising number of its readers eventually starting their own libertarian political zine.

Innovator took an increasingly cranky tone as the decade wore on. What had once been merely one of its interests became the dominant one by 1968. It arose from Marshall's Preform project. The actual plan to create the island nation faded soon enough, but the ideology— which came to be known as libertarian Zionism—remained: the idea that the only way to find freedom in this unfree world was to hide from or physically escape the eyes of the state. A libertarian is almost by definition an eccentric; these guys pushed the boundaries of mental utopianism with articles on designing a new, more rational alphabet.

Some of the magazine's eccentricities can be understood by contemplating an eccentric who briefly edited *Innovator*. A graduate of LeFevre's Freedom School named Kerry Thornley had moved back to Southern California and hooked up with Tom Marshall, eventually editing the zine. In the late 1950s in dull suburban Southern California, Thornley had helped his high school buddy Greg Hill invent the comedic religion of Discordianism. It was dedicated to the worship of Eris, the Greek goddess of chaos. Its flavor can be gleaned from this bit of powerful magick, the Turkey Curse, from its holy book, the *Principia Discordia*:

> Face . . . towards the direction of the negative aneristic vibration that you wish to neutralize. Begin waving your arms in any elaborate manner and make motions with your hands as though you were Mandrake feeling up a sexy giantess. Chant, loudly and clearly: GOBBLE, GOBBLE, GOBBLE, GOBBLE, GOBBLE! The results will be instantly apparent.

Discordianism became the heart of the most influential libertarian novel since *Atlas Shrugged*, though its libertarianism is not always recognized by more economistic libertarian movement types: Robert Shea and Robert Anton Wilson's *Illuminatus!* trilogy.

Thornley had a storied past before hooking up with Marshall and the *Innovator*. He had joined the marines in 1959, where one of his buddies at the El Toro marine base outside Santa Ana, California, was Private Lee Harvey Oswald, an openly communist "outfit eight ball" known as "Oswaldskovitch" to his fellow grunts. Thornley began writing a novel based on his disillusioning experience in the marines. After hearing that Oswaldskovitch really meant it with all that commie talk—he actually defected to the Soviet Union—Thornley transformed the novel, called *The Idle Warriors*, into a roman à clef about Oswald—making Thornley the only person to write a book about Lee Oswald *before* he finally made good that fateful fall day in Dallas.

Thornley was living in New Orleans when Kennedy was killed and hanging out, in his own recollections (which some friends suspect might be largely invented), with a curious cast of characters, including some unfortunates caught in New Orleans district attorney Jim Garrison's feckless late 1960s investigation into the supposed JFK murder conspiracy.

It is definitely not Thornley's imagination that he was dragged into the public "Who killed Kennedy?" melodrama—testifying before the Warren Commission and targeted himself by Garrison, who decided Thornley might have been part of the conspiracy as a "second Oswald," since the two old marine buddies allegedly looked frightfully similar (as well as because of a weird series of coincidences apparently linking them).[103]

While working with *Innovator,* Thornley also became an advocate of early free love cult Kerista, which neopagan historian Margot Adler credits as "the true beginnings of the neopagan movement in contemporary culture."[104] He was simultaneously hanging around with ultra-right anticommie quasi-revolutionaries the Minutemen.

Through the 1970s and 1980s, the phony order of insanely elaborated conspiracy theories won Thornley's heart away from Eris, losing him most of his old friends. No one wants to hang with someone who takes you for a government agent, part of a baroque conspiracy against him. Thornley had decided that District Attorney Garrison was right after all, that he *was* a CIA mind control slave, that a mysterious pal in New Orleans was really E. Howard Hunt, and finally that he had been a Manchurian candidate from birth, with his parents undercover Nazi spies.

He spent the last decade or so of his life (he died in 1998) occasionally washing dishes for a living and skulking about in storm drains, hanging out as a neighborhood eccentric in Atlanta's Little Five Points neighborhood. A pathetic fate, perhaps, but Thornley still had his eristic fun. When the Super Bowl was held in Atlanta in 1994, he put up flyers urging: "Boycott the illegal weapons amnesty program: Don't bring your illegal weapons to the Super Bowl in exchange for tickets!"

Innovator founder Tom Marshall's fate was similar, in its way. He became the patron saint of what would be condemned by Murray Rothbard as the libertarian deviation of "retreatism"—the idea that the
state was irredeemably corrupt and more or less impossible to fight, so
the only option for liberty is to escape all the entrapping accoutrements of statist life—homes or apartments, jobs, streets and post offices and tax men and traffic cops—and retreat to the woods or even
caves. This became widely enough talked about in the movement—if
not actually practiced—that the would-be cave dweller had a widely
understood name: "trog" (for troglodyte).

In its last years before it disappeared at the end of the 1960s, the *Innovator* was more or less inventing the fad of survivalism, with stories
about, for milder and more nervous escapists, "van nomadism" (living
in civilization, but in your car), and then for the more serious and dedicated, pure living off the land. The magazine would advise its readers
on what plants you could safely eat in nature, unoccupied land where
the federales were not apt to find you, how to bury your money and
your food stores safely, and the like. The headline story in its final issue
in 1969 was "America: Loathe It and Leave It." That seemed to say it
all, and with that the zine folded.

When it came to the survivalism/retreatism of the later *Innovator*,
Thornley seemed like the normal one on the team. Even though he
was one of the founding fathers of retreatism with his *Innovator* articles
on libertarians retreating to the high seas on giant ships to escape the
state, Thornley later took to mocking Marshall's eccentricities. He
joked that in Marshall's vision, the freest person was the one who
locked himself up alone in his dungeon; after all, no one could interfere with his choices and actions from that point on. Marshall's favorite
kind of article, Thornley said, was one "that instructed the reader how
to enjoy freedom from the State here and now—usually by means of
acquiring such an array of unique skills and equipment or by employing such complex stratagems that it almost always wound up sounding
to most people like more effort than it was worth."[105]

Marshall ultimately embraced an even more radical and individualistic version of the Preform idea, which he dubbed Vonu—an invented
word meaning a life outside the reach of any who could oppress you.
In practice, it meant hiding in the woods in Oregon, where he man-

aged to disappear from the sight or knowledge of anyone who ever knew him—his ultimate fate is unknown. Until 1972 or so, he communicated via mail from a P.O. box in Oregon, and occasionally trained others in Vonu living—arranging meetings through code words and whistles at the rendezvous spot.

He had a female partner and a permanent base camp out in public woods in Oregon, lots of stored food, and a growing impatience with all other human beings, libertarian or no. He always was annoyed at how all-talk-no-action the rest of the movement was. We can only imagine how, or whether, he enjoyed his life in the woods—however long it ultimately lasted. One man who went through a week of Vonu training with Marshall reports that Marshall, when prodded about the beauty of outdoor life, announced that "it's not that great."[106]

Thornley had a story about Marshall's later days he liked to tell. Seems that Marshall was living in a hole dug in the ground where he'd built a sturdy room of sorts. Some hippie friends of friends wrote to him at his P.O. box wondering if they could meet while they passed through the area. Marshall carefully arranged a meeting in a public place and told them he'd love to take them back to his place, but would they mind if he blindfolded them?

Okay, man. The hippies found themselves in a "modestly furnished, man-made, underground cavern. A gracious host, Marshall then got out his stash of grass and commenced to roll a joint." Not knowing of his retreatist philosophy—they only knew he was a groovy buddy of one of their buddies—they concluded all this subterfuge was strictly to avoid the prying eyes of marijuana-mad cops. One hippie said to Marshall, "Hey, man—I've got bad news for you! You're paranoid."[107]

"IF YOU HAVE AN OUNCE OF MORALITY LEFT IN YOU . . . YOU'LL BE IMPOTENT FOR THE NEXT TWENTY YEARS!"

The Objectivist movement, in contrast, was meant to be an island of peerless rationality that guaranteed happiness. Rand intended to call her forever-unwritten treatise on Objectivism "a philosophy for life on earth." Yet she admitted that its "best representative" was John Galt, a fictional character.[108] Leonard Peikoff, her intellectual heir, years later wrote that "any standard of morality other than Objectivism's can have only one ultimate result. 'Since life requires a specific course of action,' Ayn Rand observes, 'any other course will destroy it.' To support her point, we have more than the evidence of theory. We also have the sobering spectacle of all the countries and centuries that tried some version of 'non-life' as their standard. They got what they asked for."[109]

In other words, no one has ever followed our philosophy (capitalism, remember, is "the unknown ideal")—which is the only possible one for human life—and everyone died. While libertarianism beyond the tight strictures of Objectivism held out hope for a continual movement toward human political liberty—something that, in an American context, we used to have more of, in some respects—the more totalistic Objectivist system saw all human history as in essence an inhuman charnel house. To escape it required an entire change in culture and philosophy, from ontology on up. The hard-core Objectivist could conclude, with despair (or sometimes gloating satisfaction), that no human had ever been fully moral, fully happy, no culture genuinely healthy. Rand pointed to herself and her close associates as the exception.

Students of Objectivism everywhere were rudely awakened from their dream of a happy clan of Objectivist heroes in 1968 by a mysterious set of inexplicable actions from their goddesses and gods, disguised revelations about fatally flawed human experiments in practicing the Objectivist theory of romantic love.

Rand had put her love affair with Branden in abeyance during her post-*Atlas* depression, but as she tried to resume it in the mid-1960s, Branden, not willing to go back there, admits he began to try to please Rand in other ways—with his ruthless moral condemnations of others. Objectivism, which spat on the Christian imperative to "judge not lest ye be judged" in favor of "judge, and be prepared to be judged," expected and demanded constant scanning of everyone and everything for any falling short of full moral righteousness, any failures in total adherence to Objectivist principle. The moral goal was complete purity at all times. Although Objectivism was officially an atheistic philosophy with no explicit room for sin, irrationality and moral failings were treated like sins.[110]

But for years Rand missed the most irrational moral failing of all on the part of her chief enforcer. Branden kept putting off Rand's demands for a more thorough resumption of the happy sexual affair they had once reveled in. He was certain disaster would strike if he told her that he had begun an affair with a young Objectivist, a budding actress named Patrecia who had adopted the Randian surname of Wynand. Nathaniel and Barbara had officially separated after many unhappy years, and Nathaniel let slip to Barbara news of his affair with Patrecia. Branden believed Rand was so irrational on the subject of age and sex that she could never understand or permit Branden to end their sexual relationship without destroying all that the two of them had built to promote Objectivism.

Barbara was appalled and frightened; she knew Nathaniel and Rand's relationship—a relationship of *any* sort—would not survive Rand's learning of this affair. While positing herself as the most rational person who ever lived, who understood and controlled every emotion and could trace it clearly to the roots in objective reality that caused them, Rand was still a woman, still had vanity, and would not take well to hearing she was being sexually rejected for a beautiful woman decades her junior.[111]

Nathaniel finally told Ayn that he was no longer, and could never again be, her lover. He did not mention Patrecia. Ayn was outraged but struggled to maintain a professional relationship, to keep NBI and the larger Objectivist movement afloat. NBI, flush with success, had just taken out a long-term lease on office space in the Empire State Building—the greatest of great skyscrapers, to Rand the mightiest symbol of man's glory and achievement.

Rand expunged Nathaniel from her will and told Barbara that she was now Rand's sole heir. Barbara rebelled at keeping Nathaniel's confidence any longer, deciding she could not in good conscience continue to deceive Ayn under those circumstances.

When Ayn learned the whole truth about why, and for whom, she was being abandoned by her young protégé and lover, she was both devastated and enraged. She summoned Nathaniel to her presence, forcing him to sit in her foyer; he was no longer to be permitted the intimacy of her living room. There she administered a final condemnation, a ferocious performance that ended with her thundering at him that, "If you have an ounce of morality left in you, an ounce of psychological health—you'll be impotent for the next twenty years!"[112] She slapped him three times, and it was over. The sound of her hand on Nathaniel's face heralded the end of the Nathaniel Branden Institute, and the end of any significant attempts to expand Objectivism's public impact.

Rand continued, desultorily, to issue the *Objectivist* magazine, giving it up in 1971 in favor of the *Ayn Rand Letter*, consisting of four-page personal essays by Rand, mostly commenting sourly on current events. She got further and further behind schedule and finally gave up entirely in 1976. Her productive life was over. She talked for years about writing a complete book-length summation of Objectivism and made some notes toward this project, but it was never finished.[113]

The Rand/Branden split also splintered the Objectivist movement.[114] Rand and Branden were perceived as radiant, rational, heroic mother/father figures to Objectivists, the living example, as Rand would often tout them, of the fact that real heroes of the sort she wrote about could and did exist. The break shattered that belief and tossed a bolt of irrationality and mystery—a call for belief based on that quality previously anathema among Objectivists, faith—into their lives, because Rand's public condemnation of both Brandens in the pages of the *Objectivist* refused to name the true reason for the break.

Rand couched the story instead in phrases such as "gradual departure from the principles of Objectivism" and "a tendency toward non-intellectual concerns." Of Nathaniel's refusal to resume their affair, she wrote that he had given her "a written statement which was so irrational and so offensive to me that I had to break my personal association with him."[115] She accused him of financial mismanagement regarding NBI and the *Objectivist* (two separate business ventures, NBI being solely owned by Branden, and the magazine a partnership between him and Rand). The other NBI lecturers, including Nathaniel's cousin Allan Blumenthal and Barbara's cousin Leonard Peikoff, signed a statement that they "condemn and repudiate [the Brandens] irrevocably, and have terminated all association with them and with Nathaniel Branden Institute."[116]

Defensively, the Brandens wrote and mailed to the *Objectivist* mailing list their own version of what had caused the break. At the end, Nathaniel wrote, "In writing [her statement about his written message

to her], Miss Rand has given me the right to name that which I infinitely would have preferred to leave unnamed, out of respect for her
privacy. I am obliged to report what was in that written paper of mine,
in the name of justice and of self-defense. . . . It was a tortured, awkward, excruciatingly embarrassed attempt to make clear to her why I
felt that an age distance between us of 25 years constituted an insuperable barrier, for me, to a romantic relationship."[117]

The break, with its charges and countercharges, created enormous
confusion among the Objectivist faithful. "The scene in the offices [of
NBI] was of total hysteria," Barbara Branden wrote in her Rand biography. "Students kept arriving from New York and from cities dotted
around the country, upset, depressed, angry, crying, confused, stunned
by the news of Ayn's break with Nathaniel and me and by the closing
of NBI. Some of the students had come to denounce me; I had become a pariah along with Nathaniel, as the rumors continued to
spread. . . . The hysteria never completely died away. Even today, almost 18 years after 'the break,' as it became known among Objectivists, the pain of disillusionment and indignation still is present in
some of NBI's former students. They have never been told the truth. It
has not ceased to be a living issue to them."[118]

Rand, according to Barbara, insisted on "unquestioning loyalty from
both friends and students" on this matter; suddenly the Brandens were
persona non grata among all their colleagues and friends of the past
decade. Among Objectivists across the country, "friend turned against
friend, families split into warring factions, husband raged at wife and
young people at parents. . . . Those who attempted to question Ayn's
demand for loyalty in the absence of knowledge, or who refused to
take sides, were denounced."[119]

Joan Kennedy Taylor remembers a phone call, after the break but
before Rand's statement about it had been published, from Rand's
lawyer Henry Holzer, who was also handling Taylor's father's estate.
"He said, 'You may have heard there has been a split between Nathan
and Ayn and I'm calling to ask you, which side are you on? You understand that if you are on the wrong side I can no longer represent
you.' I said I don't know what you mean by the wrong side, Henry,
but I understand Ayn is writing something in the *Objectivist* that will
put forth her position and I'm looking forward to finding out what
it's all about.

"And he said,'Then you understand I can no longer represent you.'"[120]

Ayn and Nathaniel had shared agents and publishers; she tried to get both of them to dump Nathaniel and his forthcoming work of Objectivist psychology, *The Psychology of Self-Esteem*. She succeeded in getting the publisher to cancel the book contract on the pretext that the book was delivered slightly late, which doesn't customarily result in contract cancellation.

Rand failed in foiling Branden's career. He has since become a successful therapist and author of popular psychology books, mostly centered around his theories of self-esteem.[121] Branden gave equal emphasis to paying attention to one's emotions—not using them as tools of cognition or orders to act, but noticing them, not repressing them, and trying always to understand their rational or experiential roots. Branden moved to Los Angeles, where he still lives, and became therapist to many libertarian activists. He still speaks regularly to libertarian groups, and to the extent that a libertarian society requires self-realized, self-responsible people—which he believes it does—Branden considers his work in psychology to be an extension of his interest in political liberty.[122]

Rand's lawyer and Barbara, before Rand banned her as well, had written up a business plan to continue an NBI-type operation without Nathaniel. Rand had had enough of liars, moochers, those who tried to use her work and effort for their own ends. As Barbara relates, "Ayn glanced at our plan for only a moment. And then she exploded. 'I don't want it! I won't hand my endorsement and my reputation to anyone, for any reason! . . . I can't run a business and I can't let anyone else run it when it carries my name!'" At that moment, "the philosophical movement that had spanned ten years and several continents, was dead."[123]

"A LEFT/RIGHT ALLIANCE IN FAVOR OF BRAINS AGAINST STUPIDITY."

While Rand's Objectivist movement was growing and then imploding throughout the 1960s, Rothbard, already estranged from her, found himself estranged even from his beloved Mises and his circle over disagreements on foreign policy and imperialism. From that estrangement he tried to forge his own distinct libertarian intellectual/activist movement.[124]

The libertarian movement, after the death of the Volker Fund, seemed almost fatally weakened to Rothbard; with FEE's retreat, in his mind, from intellectual action, sticking instead to constant repetitions in the *Freeman* of basic homiletic truths about markets; Rand building a limited cult and supporting *Goldwater*; Hayek having left the University of Chicago and the United States in 1962 and having failed to build any kind of cadre of Hayekians;[125] Baldy Harper floundering with the Institute for Humane Studies without the Volker largess he'd planned on; Robert LeFevre too far away and too limited in his vision to provide the libertarians he created with anything they could *do* to further the cause of liberty; Rothbard worried that no one realized that scattered libertarian intellectuals and activists and pamphleteers had to *build a movement,* that structures had to be in place so some day bright libertarians could actually pursue the advocacy of libertarianism as a career, a paying profession.

He, along with old Circle Bastiat pal and historian Leonard Liggio, thought they'd found a way to do ideologically entrepreneurial outreach that might help build such a movement: find common cause with the rising antiwar left of the mid-1960s and possibly find new libertarian allies there. In 1965, the two started a new libertarian journal meant to bridge the gap between antiwar forces of all political stripes, called *Left and Right.*[126]

In his introductory essay in the first issue, Rothbard went public, and tough, with his total abandonment of conservatism and the right. They were "the party of reaction, the party that longed to restore the hierarchy, statism, theocracy, serfdom, and class exploitation of the Old Order."[127] He admitted that the new left had not yet "worked out a systematic ideology, a coherent vision of the society it wishes to bring into being" but praised it for "what it *doesn't* like, what it totally opposes in our present society, even if its vision of the ultimate future is a bit cloudy. . . . After generations of inculcation of the virus of positivism and utilitarianism, a virus that helped atrophy the moral fervor of each successive generation, it is magnificent to see morality once again used to pass swift and final judgment upon American institutions."[128]

Left and Right was a place for Rothbard and crew to write encomiums to communist guerrilla Che Guevara upon his death (not for his communism, but for being "the living embodiment of the principle of Revolution");[129] to praise Black Power leader H. Rap Brown; to tie a right-wing anti-interventionist tradition in with the leftist one represented by historians such as William Appleman Williams and Ronald Radosh; to print long articles by revisionist historian Harry Elmer Barnes; and for Liggio to write on the collapse of the Taft anti-intervention wing of the Republican Party. The cachet of *Left and Right* gave Liggio entrée into various free universities run by new left groups for education outside the corruption of big institutions, and to antiwar teach-ins. In the academic atmosphere of that time, Liggio remembers, "people on the right and people on the left were the only ones interested in my ideas—or any ideas—whether they agreed with them or not. It was the bureaucratic center who were opposed to *any* ideas. They were really mindless, but they tended to run the academic departments. So there was kind of a left/right alliance in favor of brains against stupidity, which was the center."[130]

Ronald Hamowy joined his old Circle Bastiat pals in this reach to the left, and sold the *New Republic* an article hyping this new right/left fusion. "What is most surprising and welcome . . . about the New Left as a political and intellectual movement," Hamowy wrote, "is that it, today, almost alone, stands emotionally as the heir of what is left of 19th-century liberal thought, classically the intellectual background of the American Right."[131] Thanks to friends made and associations formed around *Left and Right*, Rothbard coedited an anthology with Ronald Radosh (who later wrote a book on the right-wing anti-interventionist tradition, *Prophets on the Right*, then turned to the neocon right in the 1990s), *A New History of Leviathan* (1972). The book's essays presented a revisionist history of the role of big business in the rise of the twentieth-century American megastate, with contributions from both leftists and libertarians. It contained Rothbard essays on the fascist-collective nature of the American economy during World War I, and a return to the theme of his *America's Great Depression* with an essay attempting to debunk Herbert Hoover's reputation as a stern practitioner of laissez-faire.

Left and Right was filled with historical revisionism regarding America's role in various wars and imperialisms, the kind of writing exemplified by Harry Elmer Barnes. Barnes's last article, a revisionist look at Pearl Harbor, filled the entire last issue of *Left and Right* in 1968. Rothbard and Liggio were the major conduits of this historical revisionism, which had been much admired by many standard conservatives as well in the 1940s and 1950s, into the modern libertarian movement—though by the 1980s no libertarian institution still concentrated on such matters. Revisionism, Rothbard insisted, inculcated a historical understanding that was of great importance to a larger libertarian understanding of the state.[132]

Using a proper understanding of history to buttress libertarian understanding became a recurring theme in Rothbard's writing, and it went beyond foreign policy. Naming the real actors who make bad things happen leaves you open to being called names yourself, such as "conspiracy theorist." Rothbard preferred calling such scholarship and polemic "power elite analysis." As a Misesian praxeologist, Rothbard naturally preferred to study the state's growth in terms of specific human actions, not just "historical forces."[133]

"But now I'm mature, and working for a realistic goal: 'anarchist revolution.'"

By 1966, Rothbard's grant to write his American history project was running out. The book, however, was still unfinished and still growing. (Liggio, as thorough a researcher as you'll find, tended to come back with one hundred pages of material and analysis for Rothbard when he asked for one.) Rothbard reentered the job market somewhat frantically and got his first steady college berth, teaching economics at an undistinguished school for engineers in Brooklyn, the Polytechnic Institute of New York. (He became a full professor there in 1970.)

Thanks to *Left and Right*, 1966 was also the heyday of Rothbard's— delightful and exciting to him—actual, street-level dealing with the leading antiwar forces in New York City. Many of them, of course, were communist fronts. Liggio was working with the May 2 Movement, an antiwar group that was essentially a front for the Progressive Labor Party, though he was purged eventually, apparently for insufficient party discipline—being too much anti-imperialist and not enough pro-socialist. Rothbard enjoyed some old-fashioned Circle Bastiat japery in a 1966 letter to Hamowy: "Can you imagine, Ronald? The excitement of it? Did any of us ever think that *we . . .* would get involved in Communist faction fights? To see with our own eyes, vicious Communist tactics, caucusing, back-stabbing, etc., things which we had only read about in the musty red-baiting tomes of John Chamberlain, Frank Meyer, and all the rest? When those old guys from the '30s talk about the vicious Commie tactics on TIME in 1938, *we* can now counter with the vicious PL-Commie tactics in 1966!!!! Wowie!"[134]

But were they advancing libertarianism while reveling in the dark comedy of mad communist faction fights and treachery? "It's hard to say," Rothbard told Hamowy, "since the atmosphere runs more to activism than to theoretical discussions; there's not much interest here in whether it is aggression for a guy to be hurled by a monkey through a plate glass window. . . . We hand everybody LEFT AND RIGHT, a diligent reading of which would divine our position, but few of these guys read; they are more bent on activism." Rothbard was gleaning what small pleasure he could from face-to-face dealings with the likes of Tuli Kupferberg of the East Village freak comedy-shock-rock act the Fugs, all the talk of "fuck- and suck-ins" for peace in Vietnam, and endless coordinating committee meetings (Oscar Wilde did warn of how socialism could eat up one's evenings), which Rothbard found lively human dramedy.[135] Anarcho-left theorist Murray Bookchin became an occasional visitor to the famous Rothbard living room—until Rothbard one day angrily kicked him out of the house.[136] Noam Chomsky was a penpal for a while; Paul Goodman would occasionally join the gang in the Rothbard living room, as did Joan Didion at least once.

Still, his outreach to the left did find some prominent converts, including former Students for a Democratic Society head Carl Oglesby, who found *Left and Right* "the most useful magazine I've seen and I wish there were a hundred back issues I could buy." Upon discovering the Rothbard/Liggio synthesis, he knew that "many of those now on the right ought to be on the left; vice versa. The issue becomes neither capitalism vs. socialism nor Americans vs. Russians but rather the big centralized state vs. people. People in the New Left are immediately open to this idea. . . . We are able to wonder now if one Bob

Taft might not be much more useful in the current situation than a dozen RFKs." Oglesby—already a working adult, not a mere uppity kid feeling his oats away from parental supervision when he joined SDS—still had some reservations about the dangers of monopoly capitalism, and the threat to humanity from the automation that the free market energized. But still, "right libertarianism makes a lot of emotional or intuitional sense to us, and we want to know—this is almost desperate—what you have to say."[137] In an age of cybernetic liberalism, of a system for every social problem and everyone in their system, the messy chaotic decentralization of Rothbardian anarcholibertarianism held out promise to certain new left minds.[138]

The left/right Rothbardian synthesis was also pulling in youngsters from the Objectivist right, some of whom retained a mordant self-deprecating humor about the whole thing: "A couple of years ago," one said, "when I was an immature kid, I was organizing and raising money for the Randian movement. But now I'm mature, and working for a realistic goal: 'anarchist revolution.'"[139] Rothbard got scattered letters from young Republican types across the country who stumbled across *Left and Right* and were turned on a dime from "Victory in Vietnam now!" to "Get us out!"

In 1968, Rothbard's stature within the leftist movement rose when the leading lefty magazine *Ramparts* ran his lengthy declaration of old right solidarity with the new left, "Confessions of a Right-Wing Liberal": "Twenty years ago I was an extreme right-wing Republican, a young and lone 'Neanderthal' (as the liberals used to call us) who believed . . . that 'Senator Taft has sold out to the socialists.' Today, I am most likely to be called an extreme leftist, since I favor immediate withdrawal from Vietnam, denounce U.S. imperialism, advocate Black Power and have just joined the new Peace and Freedom Party. And yet my basic political views have not changed by a single iota in these two decades!"[140]

In the *Ramparts* article, Rothbard limned how the right had changed so as to make him feel a stranger there; most of the rot, of course, lay at the feet of his old friend Bill Buckley's *National Review* and its circle of former communists-turned-conservatives. "A new, younger generation of rightists, of 'conservatives,' began to emerge, who thought that the real problem of the modern world was nothing

so ideological as the state vs. individual liberty or government intervention vs. the free market; the real problem, they declared, was the
preservation of tradition, order, Christianity and good manners against
the modern sins of reason, license, atheism and boorishness."[141]

"We have allowed ourselves," Rothbard concluded, "to sacrifice the
American ideals of peace and freedom and anti-colonialism on the altar of a crusade to kill communists throughout the world; we have surrendered the libertarian birthright into the hands of those who yearn
to restore the Golden Age of the Holy Inquisition. It is about time that
we wake up and rise up to restore our heritage."[142]

The right wing's general sententious pining for supposedly better
days gone by sent the modern–urban Rothbard into conniptions. "I
am getting annoyed at all the charges of the haters of the Industrial
Revolution, now continued by the New Conservatives of our day, that
people don't enjoy themselves now, that they don't enjoy their work. .
. . [and] in some earlier century (13th, 17th or whatever, depending on
the crochet of the particular social philosopher) everyone was happy.
'Was you there, Charlie?' seems to be adequate answer to that. . . . on
what insufferable presumption do these people ground their dogmatic
assertions . . . that some poverty-stricken shoemaker of the 17th century was *truly* happier than I am, either when working, or when looking at (someone else's) statue, in contrast to my watching a Sydney
Greenstreet movie."[143]

Rothbard was also running as far and as fast as he could from the
Randite/National Association of Manufacturers heritage of painting
big business as necessarily heroic, or excusing its obvious playing along
with, and even active encouragement of, statist shenanigans as merely
unwillingly giving in to government pressure, or as an unwitting result
of brainwashing by leftist intellectuals. Rather, following in the tradition of, most famously, leftist historian Gabriel Kolko, Rothbard and
Liggio studied and spoke of how many regulations were in fact ginned
up and supported by the very businesses they were meant to be regulating.[144] "I am . . . convinced that one of the really big reasons that
libertarianism is not making much headway among intellectuals is precisely this huge blindspot toward big business in which most of our
libertarians indulge. The intellectuals see this, and therefore they cannot be much blamed for rejecting the whole thing as a front for big

business. . . . There are many young lads of the 'New Left' . . . who are enormously susceptible to libertarian ideas, who are in reality libertarians and not socialists as most people believe, but who, not knowing economics and seeing supposed free-marketeers engaging in apologies for big business, flounder around with no sense of direction."[145]

Rothbard leapt into the nascent Peace and Freedom Party in 1968 and ended up in a tactical alliance with the Maoist Progressive Labor Party (PLP) for complicated interparty faction fighting reasons. (His comrade, economist Walter Block, remembers their involvement in these things as more for their amusement than serious attempts to effect change—along the lines of a college prank, an ideological panty raid of sorts.) With PLP help, Rothbard and his libertarian cohorts managed to inject some hard-core libertarianism into the party platform, mostly because they showed up at all the meetings.[146]

As Rothbard recalled, they got a Peace and Freedom platform "more laissez-faire than anything since Andrew Jackson, total freedom in trade . . . drastic reduction in taxes. Gold standard. The only thing [the Progressive Labor people] balked at, they refused to go along with abolition of rent control. . . . They were organizing tenants, they couldn't go along with that. [Rothbard's Progressive Labor leader friend] was driving this thing through the caucus, [and] it comes to the plank about total freedom of trade and abolition of all subsidies . . . this fantastic laissez-faire plank. So one of these PL [Progressive Labor] characters says, hey, what's this, this looks like bourgeois free trade, and [the leader] says, no, no this is an antimonopoly coalition."[147]

Rothbard became more and more excited about the rising student antiwar left as the 1960s wore on. Even their apparent attacks on property delighted him: "the libertarian must cheer any attempt to return stolen, governmental property to the private sector: whether it be in the cry, 'The streets belong to the people', or 'the parks belong to the people', or 'The schools belong to those who use them,' i.e. the students and faculty."[148] Slogans such as "Death to the state" and "Power to the people" sounded right on to him.

In the Leninist jargon, it seemed as if objective and subjective conditions for a libertarian revolution might be merging. Rothbard had begun conceptualizing a fully "revolutionary" strategy for libertarianism. In early 1969, he published a strategy memo in the libertarian amateur press association publication, *Libertarian Connection*.[149] In it he analyzed four libertarian movement strategies he found wanting: (1) mere "educationism" of the FEE variety; (2) "quick buck" thinking where libertarians, to insulate themselves from statism, merely tried to do well for themselves financially (this attitude, still young in the movement, would grow into the libertarian hard money/goldbug movement that had its heyday in the 1970s); (3) "retreatism," looking for new countries, hidden places in the woods, and so on, where libertarians would live only for and with themselves (as per the strategy that Tom Marshall had championed with Preform and Vonu); and (4) pure new left–style cultural rebellion against the status quo.

Rothbard advocated instead an inchoately sketched revolutionary style, Lenin-inspired in method though not in eventual goal, with a professional cadre pursuing a two-pronged strategy: a public outreach organization and an internal pure-cadre gang to ensure the hard-core remained hard. No use educating publicly for libertarianism, after all, if you couldn't ensure that what the professional libertarians taught was proper libertarianism. Rothbard was a student of, and now enthusiastic participant in, the hallowed Western radical tradition of tiny, united but fractious gangs self-consciously conspiring to change the world.[150]

But he knew that libertarians, still small in number, needed to leverage the greater power of those already making headlines and a suitably world-shaking noise: the new left. After any toppling of the government—were it to occur—as in Russia in 1917, the revolutionary factions would turn on each other, and who knew what might happen then if the libertarian ideological cadre were strong enough, smart enough, dedicated enough? Some libertarians countered with the idea that Leninist strategy is only appropriate in commandeering an existing state—that the same strategy wouldn't work for what must ultimately be an ideological war against statism in general, not just the current American state. If the proper mass educational groundwork had not been laid, as per the FEE strategy, carefully, with the light of libertarian wisdom shining from individual to individual, then having a revolutionary cadre of libertarians here, there, or anywhere when a state collapsed wouldn't do a damn bit of good, because a new state would surely arise to replace it.

While to a middle American parent watching all this 1960s student rebellion ferment on TV all the kids might have seemed the same, the politicos and the freaks, Rothbard knew the difference. It wasn't the hippies or freaks he thought worth targeting. Nor did he object to them coming along, though he refused to downplay his strong aversion to the drug culture to help win them over. "You keep stressing the fact that hippies make good candidates for conversion to libertarianism," he wrote to friends trying to get him to see the benefits of psychedelic culture for libertarianism. "I think you're right, but I really don't give much of a damn. The idea is not simply to make converts, but to make converts who in turn will exert leverage on the society. Hippies, having dropped out, exert no leverage whatsoever."[151] Radical ideas needed respectable advocates or at least student activists who were playing the game of political change as it is traditionally practiced, not just sitting on the sidelines and jeering or looking the other way.

Left and Right folded from lack of money in 1968, and Rothbard launched a less ambitious, less scholarly small newsletter to keep track of and comment on all the swift changes in the libertarian and larger radical movement, with the support of his friend Joseph Peden. *Libertarian Forum* was Rothbard's major outlet for his short commentaries on politics and the growing libertarian movement through 1984, when he ceased publication. It was a monthly when Rothbard could get around to it, but it came out most consistently during the late 1960s and early 1970s when it seemed burningly probable that America might be on the cusp of a mass breakthrough of libertarian movement consciousness. Rothbard had an important new ally by then as well: former Goldwater speechwriter Karl Hess, a fresh recruit to hard-core anarcho-libertarianism, was by his side in this endeavor. For a short while, at least.

"The field marshal of the revolution."

Karl Hess was a paradigmatic movement libertarian, more important ultimately for his image and actions as an activist and public figure than for contributions as a thinker or philosopher. He was vital to the nascent libertarian movement's growth to an actual (though still small) mass movement in the late 1960s and early 1970s, and not just because his charisma and style were perfectly suited to the anti-authoritarian and anti-status-quo spirit of that time. The way he thought, wrote, and comported himself attracted a different type of devotee than did other libertarian leaders, influences, or institutions. Karl was not merely smart; in the context of the student revolution against not just the state but against the whole repressive style of life that the young thought staid, uptight American death culture represented, Karl Hess was *hip*. The bow tie–wearing college professor Rothbard, or the student rebellion–cursing Russian novelist Ayn Rand, or the *Newsweek* columnist Milton Friedman calmly and squarely talking economic sense, weren't quite.

Critics—of whom Hess had a few—thought his role in the libertarian movement was a triumph of style over substance.[152] But Hess did contribute a particular emphasis that has been largely ignored—too much ignored, some say—in the libertarian movement since his death: a commonsense Yankee emphasis on the vital importance of individuals and small communities doing things for themselves, so that they need not depend on a faraway central government to do things for them. (This was similar, in Hess's wild-eyed antisystem way, to Richard Cornuelle's quieter, establishment emphasis on the private sector taking up government charitable functions as a means to wither the state.) Decentralism linked Hess to the line of American libertarian thought stretching back to nineteenth-century individualist anarchists such as Josiah Warren and Stephen Pearl Andrews.[153]

Though Hess dabbled in Rand-sounding rights language in some of his writings (he had a restless intellect, not one to settle on and doggedly stick to definite answers), his libertarianism came down to an aesthetic love of liberty and an appreciation of the power of technology and tools over ideologies. Even Jesus Christ, said Hess, paled as an influence on human history before the humblest maker of tools.[154]

Hess was born on May 25, 1923, the son of a philandering millionaire of Philippine descent named Carl Hess and his wife Amelia. Hess was born in the United States but was taken to the Philippines, where his father's family lived. His mother soon tired of her husband's tomcatting and took young Carl Jr. back to Washington, D.C. She accepted no alimony and struggled along as a switchboard operator and then apartment manager. Hess, unhappy with his absentee father, later changed the spelling of his first name to "Karl" to distance himself.

Still, though, the windmill-tilting romantic Karl liked to tell the story of how his father was beheaded during the Japanese occupation for refusing a Japanese soldier's order to interrupt a card game.[155]

Young Karl's mother taught him to trust himself and his own mental and spiritual resources. She encouraged in him a skill and love for reading and research by refusing to answer any question for which he could find the answer through a printed source, as well as a passion for making his own way in life regardless of the opinions of others. When walking ill clothed through a fancy hotel as a kid, obviously embarrassed, his mother publicly lectured him on the unimportance of what other people think.[156]

Hess worked various newspaper and magazine jobs through the 1940s, including stints as a reporter at the *Washington Times Herald* and the *Washington News*, and editing jobs at *Aviation News* and *Pathfinder* (where he was religion editor).[157] By the end of the 1940s, he had become active in Republican Party circles. His boss at *Pathfinder* introduced him to some old right thinking, particularly the writings of Felix Morley. The dangers to individualism, to the liberty he had learned to love from his mother, from these Soviet bastards seemed palpable. Anticommunism became Karl Hess's passion. He did ghostwriting gigs for politicians during those years as well, and then for mobsters. He'd been dabbling in speechwriting for the Republican National Committee (RNC) since Thomas Dewey's 1944 presidential run. Through a friend at the RNC who had been national affairs editor at *Newsweek*, Hess was hired at the magazine in 1950 as press editor, in charge of covering print journalism from around the world.[158]

At *Newsweek* Hess, often with the collusion of his fellow anticommunist *Newsweek*er Ralph de Toledano, indulged in his radical enthusiasm for action over ideology. He collected both guns and napalm (given him gratis by Dow when he flashed his *Newsweek* credentials and claimed he was conducting gardening experiments) to contribute to a pre-Castro attempt by Carlos Hevia, a former president of Cuba, to overthrow Batista. Hess even flew a plane over Havana to drop anti-Batista pamphlets but forgot to unwrap the bundle of paper. While the coup attempt was squashed by the U.S. State Department and Hevia was arrested, Hess was not prosecuted, though he heard through his friend Whittaker Chambers's FBI connections that the

FBI knew full well what he was up to.[159] Hess and Toledano also tried
to recruit the Mafia into the war against domestic communism. They
met with Frank Costello's lawyer to encourage him to talk the mob
boss into using Family muscle to hijack Soviet cash payoffs to American communists.[160]

Hess's enthusiasm for Joseph McCarthy and radical anticommunism
was his undoing at *Newsweek*. He signed a public ad supporting Mc-
Carthy with his *Newsweek* affiliation listed, and was fired as a result in
1954.[161] Hess then floated about the anticommunist right wing, hung
out with Buckley in the pre- and early *National Review* days, contributed anticommunist writings to various publications, and became
an editor for the anticommunist newsletter *Counterattack*. Hess writes
in his autobiography *Mostly on the Edge* of the incestuous connections
between right-wing anticommunist journalists and the FBI in those
days. Many of his scoops came directly from G-men. He was briefly
employed by colorful right-wing Texas multimillionaire and hard-core
anticommunist H. L. Hunt.[162] Some ugly old attitudes were still relatively uncontroversial among parts of the anticommunist right back
then. Once when Hunt was introducing the famous anticommunist
Hess to some of his right-wing pals, he referred to him casually (and
quite mistakenly) as "the well-known anti-Semite from New York."[163]

By the end of the 1950s, Hess was working in public relations at
Champion Papers and Fibre in Ohio.[164] Champion's president was a
good friend of President Eisenhower's, and he helped Hess get a gig
working on the Republican Party platform in 1960. That in turn led
to a stint at the American Enterprise Institute, a mostly free market research institute of appeal to Republican politicians. Hess remained a
GOP platform writer in 1964. Through AEI president William Baroody, a trusted adviser to Barry Goldwater, Hess became a speechwriter and an important ideological spark plug for Goldwater's 1964
campaign, which kindled the imaginations of so many young libertarians and gave Hess his first important influence on the nascent libertarian movement. Within the movement Hess was widely assumed to
have written one of Goldwater's most famously radical lines, in his acceptance speech at the 1964 Republican Convention: "Extremism in
the defense of liberty is no vice; moderation in the pursuit of justice is
no virtue." While Hess was involved in deciding what to include in the

speech, the sentence was in fact provided by another Goldwater speechwriter, the Straussian political science professor Harry Jaffa.[165]

Hess, ever the romantic, claims to have been the only inner circle member who steadfastly believed Goldwater would win until all the poll results were in that sad day in early November 1964. But after that day, Goldwaterites were mud in GOP circles. Hess continued working with Goldwater, even past the days when Hess no longer considered himself a right-winger, ghosting newspaper columns for him and continuing to contribute the occasional speech. In 1967, Hess published *In a Cause That Will Triumph*, a book that still flew the banner of Goldwaterism. Hess blamed his man's defeat on continual media misrepresentation of what Goldwater really thought and believed.

In the aftermath of the Goldwater defeat, Hess was out of sorts, out of place, not particularly employable in his chosen bailiwick because of the stink of his boss's failure, recently divorced, and generally finding the life of the middle-class Washington political worker disappointing and stultifying. In line with his praise of tools over ideology, the end of bourgeois right-wing Karl's life began when he bought a motorcycle in 1966. Hess learned how to weld, both to earn a living and as a means of artistic expression. He found a hippie girlfriend and began living on a houseboat near the Anacostia area of Washington, D.C. Having left AEI and the Republican Party behind, Hess began working at the Institute for Policy Studies, a left-wing think tank. And, most significantly for the libertarian movement, he read Murray Rothbard's article in *Ramparts* magazine and discovered that he wasn't crazy and he wasn't alone—that there *was* a real link between the right-wing spirit of his old ideological home and the new left he was increasingly attracted to.[166]

Unlike the staid, culturally conservative Rothbard, Hess went all the way with the new left—not just ideologically but organizationally and sartorially as well. He began sporting a Castroesque beard and field jacket and came across, as Jerome Tuccille put it in his satirical look at the early libertarian movement, like "the field marshal of the revolution." Hess became the favored libertarian guru for students wanting to be part of the whole experiential revolution of their times. To many of them, reading Mises seemed less exciting and valuable than getting whacked over the head by riot cops at some antiwar protest, and Hess was the man to lead them. Some of his libertarian colleagues who didn't make the full leap into activism didn't appreciate what they recall of his bloody-minded revolutionary rhetoric.[167] Hess ran the full gamut of 1960s revolutionary fervor, wearing a ring made of metal from an American plane shot down by the Viet Cong (something he later regretted) and even briefly embracing a Marxian labor theory of value.[168]

Hess's combination of left and right even managed to convert a U.S. government informant sent to spy on SDS and the youth radical movements. Don Meinshausen, a young Republican, a member of Young Americans for Freedom (the conservative student group launched from Bill Buckley's Sharon, Connecticut, estate in 1960), had been charged with reporting back to the House Internal Security Committee (HISC) on the likes of Hess, but was converted to libertarianism by him instead.

Meinshausen had started out as a young Goldwaterite from New Jersey appalled by what he saw as the potentially Stalinist excesses of the new left. When he met members of local Red Squads and then HISC through YAF circles around Rutgers University, he became a freelance government spy on SDS and the left. He believed in freedom, even then. But these left radicals, he was sure, were Stalinists who menaced all human liberties everywhere. He remained active in YAF during his time spying on SDS and even after his conversion to libertarianism, sometimes bedeviling the trads (as the traditionalists in YAF were known—the opposite of the "rads"—the more radical libertarians) by introducing resolutions firmly supporting all consensual sexual activities among adults. "And we didn't leave out a one, bestiality, any kind of fetish, orgies, just grossing out the trads."[169]

The freshly libertarian Meinshausen began to feel as if Hess and Rothbard were guides to this uncharted ideological valley, very fertile, connected by visible trails to everything that Meinshausen valued, both unbridled personal freedom *and* private property, a revolution against the modal American values of the day that was still deeply rooted in the classic virtues America was supposed to stand for. He admired both men and hung out with both, but ultimately "I somehow felt much closer to Karl because Karl was living it while Murray was just thinking it."[170]

He eventually confessed to his new buddy Karl that he was spying on SDS but realized it wasn't right. Hess convinced Meinshausen he should make one more report to HISC, a public testimony in which he announced he was recanting his services. He borrowed Hess's typewriter to compose a statement saying that "during my membership in SDS I learned of a much more dangerous organization which has seized and destroyed more lives and property than SDS ever could—I am speaking about the United States government." He said his new philosophy came not from Marx but "the revolutionary American tradition of liberty expressed by Jefferson, Webster, Thoreau, Josiah Warren, Benjamin Tucker, Lysander Spooner, Twain and others."[171]

When Meinshausen's HISC handler saw he had brought Karl Hess to the hearing, Meinshausen's testimony was canceled, and he had to give it in a press conference solo later.[172] "And that's how I got on Cronkite. Friends told me it was better that way, because if I'd embarrassed the Committee during public testimony and then they asked me questions I refused to answer, they could have indicted me."[173]

This public turning of a government spy—covered in the *New York Times,* no less—was a triumph, and Hess's radicalism grew more intense. He became a public tax protestor in 1969, enclosing with his 1040 form a letter reading, in part, "The Federal government of the United States of America today is guilty of exactly every sort of infringement, abuse, and denial stated as intolerable by the Declaration of Independence. I cannot, in conscience, sanction that government by the payment of taxes."[174] For the rest of his life Hess was unable to earn any legal income or own property in his own name. "Refusing to pay taxes is not a laughing matter," he noted in his second autobiography. "It has cost me a mint of money, left me pretty much destitute, and caused a terrible amount of trouble for my family and for other friends."[175]

In March 1969, Hess scored a major coup in publicizing libertarianism by placing his long essay "The Death of Politics" in the pages of *Playboy*. (*Playboy* was a small-scale anarchist playground in those days, with future author of *Illuminatus!* Robert Anton Wilson working as an editor on the "Playboy Forum" section and slipping in Lysander Spooner references. Hugh Hefner's mellow live-and-let-live good life

Epicureanism always had a very libertarian streak, although in his search for a huge audience he never explicitly identified the Playboy philosophy with the marginal political term "libertarianism." Hef was rumored to be a big Rand fan as well.) Hess's essay defined and defended anarcho-capitalism, exposing that curious idea to its widest public readership yet, explained how the death of the nation-state could help solve the problems of drugs, monopoly, civil rights and civil unrest, and war. It also explained how every dominant tendency in America, from left to right to hippie to patriot, rejected libertarianism's tenets.[176]

Despite this victory for publicizing the libertarian cause, Hess's ideological peccadilloes and passion for counterculture living and protesting as adjuncts to antistate philosophizing precipitated a break with Rothbard. Hess was one of Rothbard's partners in early issues of the *Libertarian Forum*; he was "Washington editor." The split over Rothbard's growing enmity toward the new left student movement—particularly over Rothbard's public criticisms of the Black Panthers—came so abruptly that Hess's name had to be blotted out by hand on the May 1, 1970, issue. The two most prominent public faces of the activist libertarian underground were never again united.[177]

Hess's countercultural activism, especially noteworthy when contrasted with his prominent GOP and anticommunist past, earned him press attention as the colorful avatar of the new libertarian revolution. He was profiled at length and respectfully in both the *New York Times* and *Washington Post* Sunday magazines—on the same day. Hess told the *New York Times Sunday Magazine* writer that in an unlibertarian America, "We have the illusion of freedom only because so few ever try to exercise it. Try it sometime. Try to save your home from the highway crowd, or to work a trade without the approval of the goons, or to open a little business without a permit, or to grow a crop without a quota, or to educate your child the way you want to, or to not have a child. We all have the freedom of a balloon floating in a pin factory."[178]

Hess told the *Post* that Goldwater was still the man he most liked to spend time with, and that "I don't know anybody who would make a better Weatherman" than the GOP senator.[179] Goldwater, for his part, was perfectly friendly to his prodigal son when, during a 1969 war protest outside the capital, he stumbled upon Hess. "Karl, where the hell have you been? I haven't seen you for months." Karl told him he figured that his staff wouldn't be thrilled to have the bearded anarchist war protestor showing his face around the Senate office. "Piss on them," Goldwater snapped. "You're my friend. Give me a call as soon as you're free."[180]

The *Post* writer recognized that "after switching from Old Right to New Left, from business suits to Levis, Hess is still the same man—dead-set on his same libertarian cause—the old Karl Hess and the new Karl Hess are one and the same."[181]

"KILL THE LAZY FAIRIES!"

It began, perhaps, with Ayn Rand, or Leonard Read, or Barry Goldwater, or even with the daring and eccentric Murray Rothbard or Karl Hess. But mostly it began with a questioning kid—more often than not a child of parents with some right-leaning or anti-authoritarian stances—and a set of books and magazines and ideas that helped make sense of the world and of an inchoate sense of right and wrong, of the way things should be. And it ended—or began again—with a bunch of slavering, violent traditional rightists screaming, shoving, throwing punches, and shouting threats to "kill the lazy fairies!"

Such was campus politics among the young and excitable, 1969. Unlike the Weathermen (the final evolution of Students for a Democratic Society), none of the fractious, angry attendees at the Young Americans for Freedom's 1969 Labor Day weekend national convention in St. Louis were within a year blowing themselves into small, hard-to-identify chunks.

YAF had grown to be the largest and most significant student group for right-leaning students, with substantial factions both "trad" (more tradition-minded conservatives) and "rad" (more libertarian and friendly to the counterculture). The road to that 1969 YAF floor fight in St. Louis stretched back a ways. Joseph Peden and Rothbard had begun sponsoring a series of dinner meetings of libertarians in New York in 1968 as the number of interested attendees became too large to fit into Rothbard's living room—the legendary birthing place of the modern movement.[182] Other local libertarians, such as Gary Greenberg, who drifted into anarcho-capitalism from a Randian orbit and the Metropolitan Young Republican Club (an Objectivist group, despite the name, run by Rand inner circle member Joan Kennedy Taylor and her husband), also began sponsoring specifically anarcho-libertarian conferences in New York City around this time.[183]

But most of the quasi-mass libertarian activism in the last years of the 1960s was conducted under the aegis of Young Americans for Freedom. Though dedicated to a Buckleyan kill-the-commies conservatism and engendered by a very unlibertarian fight for loyalty oaths, YAF attracted in the wake of Goldwater many liberty-loving individualists, among them many Randians, who found themselves leaning more libertarian than conservative.

But YAF wasn't where *all* the action was. Berkeley's Alliance of Libertarian Activists (ALA) was already around by 1965, making it one of the earliest college groups adopting the term "libertarian." ALA pamphlets proudly announced its "nonendorsers," ranging from Robert Welch to Gus Hall, from Ho Chi Minh to Robert Strange McNamara, from George Lincoln Rockwell to Martin Luther King. ALA leader Danny Rosenthal was once arrested for his involvement in the free/filthy speech movement at Berkeley in 1964, and his arrest radicalized his girlfriend Sharon Presley. The two of them spearheaded the ALA, which was successful enough for a time to have its own rented office space. Presley remembers the street address to this day because it was the same number the protagonist in Rand's dystopian novella *Anthem* was assigned by his totalitarian state; the office was filled with a hundred-plus volume library of libertarian books.

ALA worked both ends of the ideological street with its button business. The same people behind ALA were also behind "Cal Conservatives for Political Action," selling trad buttons and stickers such as "Support Your Local Police" and "Nietzsche Is Dead—God" and "Ronald Reagan for President." At the bottom of that same button solicitation was a small come-on, like a sign alluding to the backroom at a seedy yet superficially respectable magazine shop whispering, "Libertarian conservatives: we have access to a limited supply of unusual libertarian-oriented buttons. Send for listing."

That listing contained not only gold dollar signs on a black back-ground—the flag of Objectivist anarchy—but "End the Selective Slav-ery System," "Keep California Green—Legalize Grass" and even "Legalize Spiritual Discovery." (Picture buttons of Milton Friedman were kept on that libertarian list; when it came to where Friedman really belonged, the conservatives might not know, but the libertarians understood.)

At the University of Kansas, many YAFers of a libertarian bent real-ized they had much in common with SDS and shifted bodily from one group to the other.[184] Libertarians began to dominate certain YAF chapters and dreamed of taking over the group nationally. A poll of YAF leadership published in the January 1970 issue of their magazine *New Guard* showed 22 percent of them thought of themselves as liber-tarian, and named Rand and Mises as chief influences.[185]

YAF had a libertarian caucus going into its 1969 convention in St. Louis, led by Don Ernsberger from Pennsylvania. Ernsberger's group was independent of the New York Rothbardians, and openly repudi-ated the message of Rothbard's article "Listen, YAF" that had just ap-peared in *Libertarian Forum*—an open call for all libertarians to leave YAF forthwith: "Get out, form your own organization, breathe the clean air of freedom and then take your stand, proudly and squarely, not with the despotism of the power elite and the government of the United States, but with the rising movement in opposition to that government."[186] Going into St. Louis, the libertarian caucus simply wanted more libertarians in the national YAF organization, and for YAF to consider stronger positions on ending the drug war and sup-porting draft resistance—not merely opposing the draft, which YAF had always done.

Walter Block and other Rothbardians, Hess and his son Karl Hess IV, and others from the anarchist caucus (only a third or so as large as Ernsberger's less confrontational libertarian caucus) all descended on St. Louis, many in a manic and fondly remembered bus ride from New York City. Hess, denied a place on the official program for the conven-tion, gave a midnight speech under the St. Louis arch calling for YAFers to truly embrace the freedom in their name and abandon the conservatism that dominated them. About a quarter of the 1,200 YAF delegates marched to the arch to listen to Hess. The libertarian caucus tried running its own slate of candidates for national office, even as the national office was purging libertarian-dominated delegations left and right, continuing a pattern begun earlier that summer. The blood flowing between the trads and the rads was bad and getting worse. A couple of California libertarian crazies were going around the St. Louis convention playing deliberate mindfuck games, dressing and comporting themselves as grotty hippies while being ideologically as staunchly and purely free market as possible, out-righting the righties.[187]

The anarchist caucus came in with its *Tranquil* Statement, named after hippie Hess's houseboat, written by Hess's son, Karl Hess IV (now writing professionally as Karl Hess Jr.), which tried to recast YAF's foundational Sharon Statement in more explicitly antistate terms. This caught the attention of convention keynote speaker Buckley, perhaps possessive of the original statement of purpose, which had after all been written at his Sharon, Connecticut, family estate. Buckley's speech, as Hess Jr. recalls, was obsessed with nothing so much as debunking his little anarchist caucus declaration. "He said that our ideas were linked with the battle against communism, and that this was a battle 'til the end of time and the end of the world, using very flowery but apocalyptic terms, that this was an armageddon and we represent the other side leading down the same path that Lenin and Stalin had led the people of Russia down. He was adamant in his opposition and anger—all he spoke to was our *Tranquil* statement." (Hess Jr. also recalls *Man from U.N.C.L.E.* actor Robert Vaughn following them around suspiciously all weekend.) Buckley refused an invitation to debate the senior Karl Hess, while the young Hess began his nominating speech for the anarchist caucus's YAF chair candidate by introducing him proudly as "an enemy of the state."[188]

Then a symbolic, flamboyant gesture was made on the convention floor that many who were energized by it mark as the beginning of the modern libertarian movement. Indeed, some drama-minded characters saw it as the moment when light first broke through the black iron prison and liberty began to peek, however tentatively, through. A *Rashomon* of memories surrounds this highly charged event; here's a synthesis.

Four different people are said to have had a hand in the provocation. At the urging of Don Meinshausen, pagan-minded and conscious of the need for some sort of magickal summoning action, David Schumacher got a facsimile of a draft card (burning it wasn't illegal yet) from a California libertarian operating in the underground by the name Skye D'Aureous, editor of the major libertarian amateur press association, *Libertarian Connection*. (D'Aureous, now operating under the name Durk Pearson, became a best-selling author and creator of a cultural and business revolution of sorts in the early 1980s, in partnership with fellow libertarian Sandy Shaw, with their book *Life Extension: A Practical Approach*.) The lighter was provided by Jarret Wollstein, then running an Objectivist/libertarian organization called the Society for Rational Individualism. "The symbol of YAF is the torch of liberty," Meinshausen recalled. "Dave became that symbol by lighting that draft card."[189]

And then the oppression inherent in the YAF system manifested itself—in roars, shouts, shoving, waving fists, a rushing mass of bodies eager to smash in lazy fairy noses. ("Lazy fairies" had become the trads' favorite childish insult to the rads.) Hess Jr. and some of his anarchist comrades formed a protective phalanx for Schumacher as they pushed their way out, through corridors and out the building, and decided, shades of Oswald, to slip into a movie theater until the heat eased up. The movie showing was, as Hess Jr. recalls, one with both anarchist and nihilist overturns, an allegory about an authoritarian English boarding school, whose climax involves students shooting from the parapets of their old school down at a graduation ceremony. Hess Jr. thought it a propitious movie for this strange moment of metaphorically shooting from the parapets at authoritarian institutions.[190]

By the time the anarchist cabal got back to the convention hotel, angry YAFers were still running down halls shouting for lazy fairy blood. According to Tuccille's account, a mob of libertarians did some countermob angry stalking down hotel corridors. The conference theme was "sock it to the left," whereas the libertarians and anarchists wanted to "sock it to the state." By the time it was over, as far as the modal YAF member was concerned, libertarians and anarchists *were* the left. Any YAFer who was also a member of SDS was expelled.[191] Before the convention was over, all the libertarian factions, the libertarian caucus and anarchist caucus and the California crew, had met and exchanged addresses and committed to remaining in contact.[192]

Political chaos ran through these years in the world at large—as above, so below, the mystic-minded Meinshausen might have said, comparing the libertarian movement's upheaval with that of the larger political cosmos. With Columbia University burning, France almost toppled by barricade-manning student ideologues, radical bombings in the homeland more common than spooked post–9/11 Americans seem to remember, many young libertarians felt their blood quicken at the sight of the bombs and mobs, saw through the smoke of revolutionary fires the dimly lit vision of a glorious liberated future ahead as this whole statist system seemed on the verge of being torn down piece by piece by angry kids. All the libertarians had to do was get these kids (some not so young) to understand what they *really* were— or really *should be*—angry about. Unlike the stultifying liberal consensus of the 1950s and early 1960s which insisted that a managerial welfare state could sensibly and intelligently manage the world, indeed that it really was already doing so, the younger generation was creating a revolutionary situation unspooling daily in occupations, fires, bombs, mobs, and a burning desire to see quick and severe social and political change, *now*.

Something—maybe everything—seemed to be over; the dawning of the age of Aquarius, the death of consensus, the greening of America, and all that. Libertarians couldn't let commies be the only ones out there explaining the roots of American misery and degradation—or the only ones having all the fun shouting and toppling things in the street.

In attitude, appearance, and style, many of this post-YAF libertarian generation, some following Hess explicitly, some merely reflecting the zeitgeist on college campuses, loved the glamour of belonging to an outlaw radical underground. Many were adopting revolutionary pseudonyms, whether out of genuine fear or for their own amusement, and imagining FBI tails wherever they looked. As if summoned by the magickal symbolism of Schumacher's bogus draft card burning—guerrilla theater and sleight of hand merged, and it couldn't have worked better—many moments of synchronistic symbolism were offered up, like strange gifts from Fate to goggle-eyed young libertarians.

Meinshausen, especially sensitive to such revelations, remembers a huge patriotic rally around the Washington Monument back in those days, starring Bob Hope and featuring a gaggle of fresh-faced American kids reciting the Declaration of Independence. He felt a strange frisson, seeing the flower of American youth reading centuries-old lines about "when it becomes necessary to dissolve these bonds" while in front of him, in front of those chanters bringing back the spirit of a dead revolutionary past, cops were smacking protesting American citizens with billy clubs in a chaotic scrum. How long could this kind of ridiculous, inspired madness go on? "For several years, I thought the revolution would come the next day," Meinshausen confesses. He was not alone—a combination of youth, the atmosphere of chaos and revolt, the crystal burning clarity of the social order of perfect liberty they had gotten from Rand, or Rothbard, or LeFevre, or Hess, or just from a sloppy mimeo sheet written by someone who had read those people, all combined to make many a libertarian under twenty-five think that *it really might be falling apart*, and that *we might really have a chance to put it back together—and correctly this time!*

"This horseshit is precisely why the anarchists lost out in 1917 to the Bolsheviks."

While the YAF ferment was bubbling and then boiling over, with a madcap confidence possessing many in the newest generation of young libertarians, Rothbard was still gathering—as he had been through much of the 1960s—a new circle of potential cadres. Leonard Liggio was still around, working with *Left and Right* and collaborating with antiwar leftists in the streets and in free universities. Old friends like Robert Hessen and George Reisman had broken with Rothbard to ally themselves with Rand, and Ralph Raico and Ronald Hamowy were both teaching outside of New York City after their stints studying under Hayek and running *New Individualist Review* at the University of Chicago.

Newer faces on the Rothbard scene included Roy Childs, a brilliant autodidact from Buffalo. At age nineteen, Childs had lectured at
LeFevre's Rampart College in its last days (though he later turned violently against LeFevre for his Gandhian lack of belief in even retaliatory force), and had won notoriety in the buzzing community of
small libertarian zines by having the nerve to write an open letter to
Ayn Rand telling her she was mistaken about government—that Objectivism necessarily implied anarchism, since a state could not deny
competing private defense agencies the liberty to operate without violating what under Objectivist ethics were supposedly inviolable individual rights.[193]

Father James Sadowsky, a Jesuit philosopher from Fordham University who had been converted to a strong interest in free market economics by reading Rothbard's *America's Great Depression*, called its
author and got converted forthwith to anarcho-capitalism. Walter
Grinder was a student of Hans Sennholz's at Grove City College who
hooked up with Rothbard and Liggio in the early 1960s, and was an
enthusiastic supporter of the turn toward SDS and the Peace and Freedom Party. The war was always his prime concern, and he had been
tear-gassed many a time fighting against it. Still, Grinder always believed that a scholarly cadre was vital if street activism were to have
any long-lasting positive effect. Robert J. Smith was another veteran of
LeFevre's school and a student of Mises's at NYU who went on to become one of the founding fathers of free market environmentalism.

Walter Block was in the economics graduate program at Columbia
when a classmate, Lawrence Moss, also later a professional Austrian
school economist, discovered Block's free market views. (Block was already attending New York NBI/Objectivist meetings with some regu-
larity.) After his first party at Rothbard's in 1965 or 1966, "It was like
the ugly duckling coming home," Block recalls. "This is where I belong, this is my gang."[194]

Rothbard, though, surprised him. "When I first met Murray, after
reading some of his stuff, I pictured a guy like Huey Newton with a
matching gun and spear. And here he was, this little fat guy who kept
giggling maniacally."[195] The network of libertarian zines and student
organizations got thicker before and after the YAF break, but it was still

small enough that every time one libertarian found another, it was a cause for great encouragement and joy (even if it led to schisms and excommunications).

The Rothbard crowd began its own official organization—the Radical Libertarian Alliance. (Its slogan: "War is murder. Taxation is theft. Conscription is slavery. Government is chaos.") Hess was executive director at the beginning, and Roy Childs, corresponding secretary, tried to keep in touch with young anarcho-capitalists across the country. Childs worked hard to get Rand to admit that Objectivism implied anarchism. For his troubles, Rand's lawyer canceled his subscription to the *Objectivist* and informed him that Miss Rand would be seeing no more correspondence from Roy Childs.

In October 1969, mere months after the St. Louis YAF break, Joseph Peden and Rothbard put together the first Libertarian Conference over a three-day Columbus Day weekend at New York's Hotel Diplomat. Over two hundred people attended—more than twice the number Rothbard expected—from all over the United States, some traveling via bus and some even hitchhiking from North Manitoba. The speakers included Rothbard, Hess, Peden, Liggio, Childs, young journalist Jerome Tuccille, and young economists Block, Moss, and Mario Rizzo. Panel topics included libertarian economics, foreign policy, relationships with special groups, and campus organizing. Hess, whose attraction to new leftism was becoming too all-encompassing for Rothbard's taste, enraged Rothbard by leading more than half the crowd away from the conference and to direct street action, joining a student left–antiwar march on Fort Dix.

Jerome Tuccille was a former *Wall Street Journal* writer and budding novelist, one of the libertarian children of the Goldwater campaign. During the libertarian movement's miniboom in the early 1970s, Tuccille published a fictionalized comic opera memoir of an individualist Everyman (mostly himself) moving through the libertarian movement's 1960s history, with stops at Goldwater, Buckley, YAF, Objectivism, Rothbard, Hess, and beyond. *It Usually Begins with Ayn Rand* is kept in print today by libertarian bookseller Laissez-Faire Books as a movement classic, although everyone portrayed in it emphasizes that Tuccille took liberties with the truth, usually for humorous effect. (It is a very funny book, though libertarians deeply concerned with their dignity could be excused for disagreeing.)

Tuccille's book features vivid reminiscences about that Columbus Day conference and explains the hopes it raised in libertarian hearts. Tuccille imagined the glory of "a giant Left-Right libertarian coalition: left-wing anarchists and acid-dropping love children; middle-class tax resisters and blue-collar hardhats; right-wing free traders and intransigent individualists. We had to make them know each other and respect each other. Love, maybe even understanding, was too much to hope for. So long as they respected one another and agreed to leave everybody else alone. That was the ticket. Anything else was doomed to failure."[196]

As Tuccille tells it and most of those present remember it, failure is what they got. At first it seemed promising, Tuccille wrote, with "business executives from the Midwest whose vest pockets bulged with bank accounts and credit cards" chatting amiably with "real live love children with beads and sleeping bags and a serene gentility glazing their eyes."[197] Rothbard was pleased with the intellectual quality of the presenters, though he feared there were too many of them, of too heavy an intellectual heft, for the crowd to absorb in such a short time.

Then Hess arose in his "field marshal of the revolution" outfit—combat boots, khakis, and a Fidel Castro fatigue cap. "The matrons from Georgia and business executives from Kansas just stood around self-consciously, shifting from foot to foot," at the sight, Tuccille wrote. "Was this the same, was this really the same gentleman who used to write speeches for Barry Goldwater?"[198]

Yes it was, and he wanted to keep his thumbprint solidly on this rising libertarian activist movement. At the first evening of the convention, Tuccille reported, "It was Hess's turn. The Field Marshal of the Revolution poured forth a message to match his attire. Strike! Assault! Direct action against the state!

> How could you keep up with a guy like this? His swing from the Goldwater Right to the Left was breaking the ideological sound barrier. The matrons and business executives were riveted to their chairs, too dumbfounded to move. . . . "Which side of the barricades will you be on when the chips are down?" Hess asked hard-

eyed from the podium, menacing the profit mavens and other right-wing libertarians in the audience. He had perfected a way of asking questions so that they sounded like threats. "There is no neutral ground in a revolution," Hess continued . . . "You're either on one side of the barricade or the other," he said, cleverly paraphrasing Eldridge Cleaver's "You're either part of the problem or part of the solution" ultimatum.

At that precise moment the polarization was complete. Mary [an angry Randian as Tuccille portrayed her, though Mary Frohman, the Ann Arbor former Wobbly left-libertarian Tuccille was writing about, found the portrayal so ridiculous and wrong she contemplated suing] and her friends were joined by the love children, left-wing anarchists and adventurers, and other cultural New Leftists, all of whom were on their feet shrieking!

"To the barricades! Shoulder to shoulder with our brothers and sisters of the revolution! To Fort Dix tomorrow morning!" This last representing a spontaneous collective decision by the Leftists to join the war-protest march on Fort Dix the following day.

The other half of the crowd remained in its seats. The division was clean down the middle. The right-wing anarchists, moderate Objectivists, and business types sat in stone-faced opposition to the radicals singing and chanting maniacally around them. The emotional release was almost sexual. The revolution was here and now, you could feel it all around you. Tension! Violence![199]

Hess led off half of the convention's audience—into tear gas, always a possibility in those days when you marched on federal military property. Rothbard's left-right fusion was dissolving in clouds of acrid smoke from the agents of Their Enemy, The State.

Rothbard worried about this miasma of street-fighting fever infecting his scholarly conference even before his friend Karl and his radical left street-fighting buddies took off with a huge chunk of his audience. A call on the part of poorly disciplined young turks for less structured academic paper giving and more open-ended rapping exposed the huge fault lines between the varied types attracted to a libertarian message. (Rothbard also noted that they had been supplying free beer, which doubtless didn't improve anyone's judgment when it came to the assault on Fort Dix.) He tried to talk his intimate cadre into not marching away from the conference: "This horseshit is precisely why the anarchists lost out in 1917 to the Bolsheviks—the propensity always of anarchists to be ultra-left adventurists, to be whim worshipers, and to listen as some guy says 'Seize the street', or 'Charge the cops', and everyone rushes out and does it and gets their heads beaten in— and exit both them and the revolution."[200]

On the evening of the march, Rothbard and some friends were heading back to the convention hotel after dinner. They were stopped by fellow conventioneers warning them that the place was now crawling with undercover cops. The fuzz might be waiting for Hess or planning to arrest all of them on some cockamamie anti-anarchist gathering or conspiracy statutes left over from Palmer raid days, or any number of potential crimes related to the Fort Dix goings-on. "We all felt that we had plunged right into the middle of a corny World War II–Nazi spy thriller," Rothbard remembered. "All of a sudden there seemed to be cops everywhere. . . . Some guy, who looked familiar, whom various people said he was a cop, but *could* be just another Times Square freak, lurched up to us and started asking us curious questions. Like: 'Are you people connected with that affair at the Hotel Diplomat?' 'Affair, what affair?' 'You know, that anarchist convention up the street.' 'What convention? We're just friends.'

"By this time we started melting away, like in a spy movie, in twos and threes. . . . Joey was left on the corner with Art Carol . . . a sympathizer who teaches eco[nomics] at Poly . . . Art is a little, scrawny guy. The quasi-cop asks: 'What kind of friends are you?' Arthur answers: 'intimate friends.' The cop presses on: 'How intimate?' Arthur rebuts brilliantly: 'I daren't say.'" Exhilarated by fright, these academics and Mises readers began talking of plans to create safehouses and fake identities. Rothbard joked that he figured it was about time to hit the archives for some deep research into interest rates. The Rothbards were horrified to discover that Hess, who had been staying with them, and his friends had left bags filled with pot and guns in their apartment.[201]

Rothbard's disenchantment with his new left allies was complete when Columbus Day weekend was over. They were in the main far too flaky for him to deal with, too adventurist, not really convertible to the live-and-let-live yet system-smashing possibilities of strict propertarian anarcho-capitalism. Potential cadre such as Joe Cobb from the

University of Chicago, the final editor of *New Individualist Review*, were busy writing about how, come the revolution, libertarian property rights were going to be meaningless without constant control and protection. The Tuckerite dream of no absentee ownership would be a reality, and intellectual property, inheritance, even keeping control of your factories without keeping your workers happy every second of the day, would all be a dream of a hated bourgeois past.[202] Jerome Tuccille dramatized the situation—and his own hope for an ecumenical, forgiving approach that could actually hold together a multifront libertarian alliance—in *It Usually Begins with Ayn Rand*:

> "What are we going to do with these motherlovers, these morons, these cretins?" Professor Murray Rothbard was practically vibrating in his armchair, his bow tie on an angle.
>
> "To know them is to hate them," offered Walter Block.
>
> "They're deviationist creeps!" Rothbard continued.
>
> Oh no! Not again. I heard enough of that crap when I was an Objectivist. I didn't deviate from conservatism to start denouncing other people for deviationism!
>
> "Not deviationism," I said lamely.
>
> "The right-wing deviationists are walking around with their goddamn dollar signs plastered all over the goddamn place, and the left-wing deviationists are destroying what's left of their brains with acid and pot."
>
> Let them. Let them do anything they want so long as they don't hurt anybody else. Let's not start the bullshit all over again. There's room for everybody who's nonaggressive, who's nonviolent: the weak, the insane, the lame, the strong; those with square jaws and receding jaws, with no jaws at all—even those with two jaws; those with dollar signs on their foreheads and gold-plated pricks; those who blew their minds on acid six times a day.
>
> "We're too small to start worrying about deviationists," said Block.
>
> "We aim for quality, not quantity." Rothbard's mind was made up. "We can't accept all the shit that walks in off the street."[203]

However much libertarians were trying to look, talk, and act left back then, Meinshausen remembers that the libertarian activists didn't really fit into the zeitgeist. They tended to be nerdier, less in the mode of effortless long-haired hipster cool, than the student radicals they tried to swim amongst. A lot of what being an active libertarian means, Meinshausen figures, is being an odd person more into reading philosophy and economics than socializing, and while it isn't universally true, it's fair to say it is widely true. Partially for that reason (and probably more for simple and well-understood intellectual divergence) Meinshausen notes that left culture never really opened up to the libertarians. For the most part such organs as the *Nation* and *Village Voice* didn't accept them as part of any viable coalition, or even as in the same intellectual and political universe.

Some young libertarians tried to remedy this and succeeded at least partially. Charles Hamilton, a young student of left-anarchist Paul Avrich, was drawn into the Rothbardian synthesis after a youthful attraction to FEE (he was impressed at receiving serious, well-considered personal responses from Leonard Read to questions he wrote as a green teenager), and started an academic-leaning libertarian zine called *Libertarian Analysis* in the early 1970s. In 1972, he started a publishing imprint called Free Life Editions that tried to bridge the left-right anarchist gap, publishing both Albert Jay Nock and Murray Bookchin, John Flynn and Charles Dolgoff, Etienne de la Boétie and Wobbly history, often earning reviews for his publications in the *Nation* as well as in the libertarian zines.

One reason that young libertarians failed to make significant inroads into the larger world of youth radicalism at the time, theorizes political historian Jonathan Schoenwald, was that the overwhelmingly white, male movement had little interest in or understanding of *specifically* black or female concerns, judging from the contents of most of its periodicals at the time. However, libertarians would insist their brand of illegitimate-hierarchy-toppling economic and personal freedom was all blacks or woman really needed.[204]

Looking back, Rothbard wrote, "The first sign I had that a certain element of emotional stability was lacking in the new youthful libertarian adherents was a message sent from the University of Kansas libertarian group, which has shifted from YAF to SDS, proclaiming me as 'God.'"[205] In assessing his own failure of strategic vision vis-à-vis the new left move, he wrote, "I think my error was two-fold: (a) gravely overestimating the emotional stability, and the knowledge of economics, of these fledgling libertarians and as a corollary, (b) gravely underestimating the significance of the fact that these cadre were weak and isolated, that there was no libertarian *movement* to speak of, and therefore that hurling these youngsters into an alliance with a far more numerous and powerful group [the new left] was bound to lead to a high incidence of defections. In New York and Washington, the defection was led . . . by Karl Hess who, after a few short months as an anarcho-capitalist, hurtled into real leftism of the left-wing-anarchist-Maoist-syndicalist variety. . . . [ultimately leading to] ideological defection to leftism and/or . . . self-destructive, ultra-adventurist street-fight tactics against the State."[206]

Leonard Liggio thinks that many misunderstood Rothbard's intent in the late 1960s, both then and in writing about it later. He didn't want to turn the libertarian movement into a movement of the left. "Murray was of course speaking to various groups . . . including left-wing groups," Liggio recalls. "I think Tuccille saw that as the strategy itself. I think it was more that Murray was trying to create a center of people who understood and accepted his ideas, and he tried to go different places to present it. It was neither left nor right—it was libertarian ideas and he was presenting them to see who would respond to them. He wasn't trying to catch the radical left or the Nixon right—he just wanted to present his views. The strategy was merely to find people who understood."[207]

Rothbard's intent was not fully understood by many of his old comrades from the 1950s, some who followed his late 1960s rhetoric with much head shaking and tut-tutting. When *Barron's* ran an article about a socialist scholars conference at which Rothbard and Liggio spoke, it made many of Rothbard's old comrades pray for his soul, and left Liggio the only future president of the Mont Pelerin Society to be accused in that financial newspaper's pages of being part of a dedicated socialist conspiracy to "overthrow . . . our form of government by Socialist seizure of state power."[208]

Rothbard always stressed that the libertarian should not *become* a leftist, even as he ought to cheer leftists when they battled the state. In the context of political activist upheaval of the day, Rothbard thought libertarians would have an advantage in appealing to the middle class, since libertarians, unlike leftists, believed in private property and thus ought to shun "lifestyle" leftism, which offended that middle class. Going clean for anarchy, then, was the wisest course for a young libertarian revolutionary.[209] By early 1970, he called off any explicit libertarian alliance with other political organizations of any stripe. "What we must do," he wrote, "is to attract the myriad of unorganized individuals, on the Left or the Right, who are instinctively libertarian, and who are groping for libertarian guidance and fellowship."[210] By March 1970, Rothbard declared the new left dead.

But that didn't mean all his disciples, real or potential, were listening. A young libertarian studying at Stanford University, Williamson "Bill" Evers, had seen Ronald Hamowy's *New Republic* article in 1966 on the nascent old right/new left fusion. He approached Hamowy, who was a lecturer at Stanford at the time, and asked to be hooked up with this libertarian movement. "What libertarian movement?" the acid Hamowy replied, which merely redoubled Evers's will to create one out there. By 1970, he was involved with the Stanford branch of the Radical Libertarian Alliance, which was described in a Stanford campus radical guidebook as "part of a nation-wide network of anarchists who are working to end the Indochina war and destroy the United States government. As radical decentralists, they seek to abolish the state and put all social organizations on the basis of voluntary associations."[211] This was no longer Leonard Read's libertarian movement, quiet, pious, based on economics and above the scrum of day-to-day politics.

"THE NEW RIGHT CREDO: LIBERTARIANISM."

Even after the Hess/Rothbard split and the failure to effectively yoke libertarian ideas to new left activism, the early 1970s were still heady times for the libertarian movement, featuring breakthroughs in public attention that would have seemed miraculous a decade earlier.

Publications from *Newsweek* to the *Nation* took wondering notice of this new anarchist strain on the right. Karl Hess, as noted, was lengthily, respectfully profiled in the *New York Times* and *Washington Post* Sunday magazine sections. Two young student radicals from Columbia University, Stan Lehr and Louis Rossetto, associated with the Radical Libertarian Alliance journal the *Abolitionist,* wrote a cover story in January 1971 on the burgeoning libertarian movement for the *New York Times* Sunday magazine, with themselves photographed on the cover, called "The New Right Credo: Libertarianism."[212] (Decades later Rossetto would launch a different kind of revolution, when he started *Wired* magazine.) They cut a fine Hessian figure, right-wing radical chic, hip without being threatening, and managed to outleft the left by pointing out how the state, not the market, is to blame for air pollution and the overuse of the automobile, and called for a return to a tort liability system to prevent pollution, rather than the current system whereby polluters can harm you with as much filth as they want so long as the government says it's okay.

The cover of the *New York Times* Sunday magazine! "The movement is made!" Rothbard crowed. Indeed, it had this bracing effect on plenty of politically homeless youth who saw that article—from Heinlein fans to ex-Goldwaterites who knew in their hearts that Richard Nixon was not, in any way, shape, or form, the one, to Rand fans not fully enmeshed in the occasional lunacies of the official Objectivist movement—they could read it and finally know who they were. For many of them, it also let them know that they should try, somehow, to do something about it.

Even William Buckley was not *totally* opposed to this new development. In a column commenting on the *NYT* magazine article, he called Rothbard an "affable and talented absolutist." Granted, "the absolutization of freedom by these gentlemen is the oldest and most tempting heresy," but still, "the radical libertarians have a great deal to contribute." He then wondered aloud why Nixon hadn't seen the freedom light on matters such as the draft, agricultural subsidies, and union monopoly.[213]

Tuccille was first of the new libertarians to break into the promised land of American journalistic commentary, the *New York Times* op-ed page, in January 1971 "because I was attacking Bill Buckley on the draft and Vietnam. Anytime we were attacking conservatives, the liberal press was only too happy to give us a lot of space. They asked me after that who else they could invite from my perspective, and I got Murray down there."[214] In 1971, Rothbard was invited to write occasionally about this growing "radical right wing" for the *New York Times* op-ed page, and to condemn Nixon's turn to fascism with his wage and price controls. Rothbard and Tuccille coedited, for the *New York Times's* Arno Press, a thirty-eight-volume series on the right-wing individualist tradition in America, issued in late 1971.[215]

In 1970 (slightly prematurely, as the big media blitz didn't happen until 1971), Tuccille wrote a quick manifesto for the Radical Libertarian Alliance side of the movement, *Radical Libertarianism*, and sold it to an editor at Bobbs-Merrill (the original publishers of Rand's *Fountainhead*), who happened to be a friend of Leonard Liggio's. He then sold *It Usually Begins with Ayn Rand,* his comic movement history, to another respectable New York trade publisher, Stein & Day.

"We knew we had to reach the middle class," Tuccille remembers, "and we saw the media as a synecdoche for the middle class. We thought if we got all this media attention, then we were reaching the middle class. But it turned out not to be true. The media was just out there looking for the sexy new story of the moment, and then you are trash in the dustbin."[216] The middle class, Tuccille realized—then and now—is too comfortably entrenched in the state system to be a reliable source of revolutionary libertarian fervor.

Media attention didn't necessarily translate to bodies in the streets or on libertarian newsletter subscription lists. J. Neil Schulman had read the Lehr and Rossetto *New York Times* article and felt it hit him with the force of revelation, of self-understanding. At last he knew what he was, and started doing things about it. (He later became a professional author of libertarian-themed science fiction.) He and some young libertarian compatriots tried to pull off a Boston tea party reenactment, thinking it would win them great publicity. "But while we were on this little tugboat in Boston harbor there were 50 thousand screaming antiwar protestors on the shore. That was the libertarian movement then. It seemed no matter what we did—the only rally we were ever able to do where you didn't have 50 thousand screaming leftist surrounding us was our April 15 anti-IRS rallies— and that we managed to get 10 people out for. So I never had the experience of libertarianism being a mass movement, never had any illusion that it had any sort of mass popular support. It was always— libertarians? Yeah, I think I've heard of that."[217]

That may have been all media attention was worth in terms of bodies in the street. But beyond that attention, and ultimately beyond those bodies in the street, libertarian thinkers were vital in one of the apotheoses of 1960s consciousness, though not widely credited for it. When the draft ended in 1973, it was the final step in a push whose respectable roots were with University of Chicago economists and advocates—young libertarian Jim Powell from *New Individualist Review* who toured the country speaking out against the draft, a four-day conference in December 1966 of policy intellectuals and students about conscription at the University of Chicago, including Milton Friedman; former Rand insider Martin Anderson, a Nixon adviser in 1968 who helped convince candidate Nixon draft elimination was a great idea. As an aftereffect of Anderson's urging, upon Nixon's taking office a fifteen-member advisory commission, with Milton Friedman as a member, was named to contemplate the future of the draft—with the idea that they would come up with a realistic plan to replace it with an all-volunteer army.

Coming in, they were ostensibly split three even ways—five opposed to the draft, five in favor, five undecided. In less than a year of meetings, and with Friedman's argumentative power and moral force, the commission, known as the Gates Commission after chairman Thomas Gates, a former secretary of defense, unanimously recommended ending the draft. Friedman turned his polemical star power on full—Vietnam troop commander William Westmoreland gruffly announced that he was not interested in leading an army of *mercenaries.* Friedman coolly replied, "Would you rather command an army of slaves?" Westmoreland bristled. "I don't like to hear our patriotic draftees referred to as slaves."

"I don't like to hear our patriotic volunteers referred to as mercenaries," Friedman snapped back. He pointed out that if they were mercenaries, then in this market economy in which we rightly count on freely offered monetary incentives to inspire our professional actions, he was a mercenary professor, Westmoreland a mercenary general, and so on. In an age of recasting the taunts of your enemies as a badge of pride, Friedman reclaimed mercenary power as the mark of the free man. His logic and passion won over the commission and then the administration—though with Martin Anderson's thumb on the scales from the beginning. It is widely understood that the commission was intended to come up with a workable and realistic plan for shifting to an all-volunteer force from the beginning, one that would give Nixon the cover he needed for a decision he already intended to make.[218] Nixon instantly announced his agreement with the general shape of the Gates Commission's plans, though he didn't move as quickly as Friedman would have wanted, nor did he raise the salaries of enlisted men as much as Friedman thought necessary.

This is not to discount the value of the political pressure of street activism and youth unrest in the decision to end the draft, which had been a constituent and barely questioned part of postwar American life since 1951. But Nixon himself said that "what really tipped the balance in my decision to support the voluntary army was the unrest over the draft because of the Vietnam war. But I would not have followed through after the election had I not become convinced that a voluntary army was economically feasible and militarily acceptable."[219] And that achievement was to a large degree the result of Milton Friedman's intelligence, dedication, and persuasive power.

Even after the major media attention faded, a thread of life did twine out from the radical student ferment that helped spread libertarian thinking to young Americans, soon to be enjoying some of the liberty that Milton Friedman helped attain for them.

"LYSANDER SPOONER DIED FOR YOUR SINS."

The libertarians expelled from YAF after St. Louis, as well as the ones who left in disgust, merged with Jarret Wollstein's Society of Rational Individualism (funded by Objectivist Frank Bond) to form the Society for Individual Liberty (SIL), which was born as SDS was dying. Within a year, SDS would blow itself to bits as the Weathermen exploded the Greenwich Village safe house where they had been making bombs. From the perspective of his congressional office in D.C., with a not entirely unwistful nostalgia, Dana Rohrabacher says that they dreamed SIL would be their SDS, take up where it left off, but with the proper set of ideas and no excess of mad revolutionary madness. It tapped into a pent-up demand for a neither left nor right student activist organization; within a year there were 103 campus SIL chapters.[220]

The story of SIL ultimately lacked the drama, and of course the impact, of SDS. No communist party sought to take it over; no gang of bomb makers or armed robbers arose from it. It is ex-SDSers, not ex-SILers, who have achieved public and political prominence. With the exception of Steve Symms (a former senator whose anarcho-libertarianism dissolved after he took office, though he was one of the prominent supporters for relegalization of gold ownership) and Rohrabacher, none of them achieved obvious political power.

At its beginnings, though, they had both grand dreams and grand fears. SIL claimed 2,500 members from the start, insisted its forces would be resourceful enough to survive and thrive even under complete totalitarianism, and stated "with epistemological certainty that in the years to come, SIL will effectively be *the* responsible libertarian movement in the United States and perhaps the world."[221] By spring 1971, SIL wasn't sure that America would see another spring in which intellectual agitation for liberty would be possible, or useful.[222]

Still, SIL produced its magazine, the *Individualist,* for a few years and produced and mailed out tens of thousands of small foldover pamphlets explaining libertarian ideas and positions. It supplied advice and literature to help people start their own campus branches, and for a decade issued a monthly newsletter charting the actions and comings and goings of libertarian organizations and rallies, polling their readers and members, and watching the number of active college chapters plummet. From 1970 until the mid-1980s, SIL's newsletter, though relatively colorless, presented a non–ax grinding look at what was happening in the libertarian movement.[223] But SIL's drama was the individual drama of thousands of young minds bold enough to grapple with ideas that marked them as strange; however, they pursued these ideas with a burning moral and intellectual passion.

SIL was biggest on the East Coast. Out west a California Libertarian Alliance (CLA), with Dana Rohrabacher and Shawn Steel (later a Republican Party chairman in California) as chief organizers, often in cooperation with Robert LeFevre (freshly relocated there), ran huge mass meetings and conferences with names, such as the Left/Right Festival of Mind Liberation, and featuring speakers ranging from Mises to Hess, from LeFevre to ex-SDSer Carl Oglesby.

This ecumenical spirit, along with the smelly revolutionaries with unwashed hair that it attracted, alarmed some former Rothbardians. Gary North, an acolyte and son-in-law of Christian Reconstructionist theoretician R. J. Rushdoony, yet for all that a big fan of Baldy Harper and Rothbard and an early player in the world of ideologues and salesmen who forged (influenced by libertarian economists all the way) the hard money movement, attended one of these CLA/LeFevre festivals at Cal State–Long Beach. And he saw the dark smoke of hell rising all around him.

Mises was speaking, and North thought he could get the great man to condemn his prodigal son by asking him publicly if he could abide Rothbard's anarchism and seemingly lefty turn. The moderator refused to pass on the question to the hard-of-hearing Mises. Free markets were fine for some things, but not for sins, such as drugs, North believed. Secular libertarianism, North had come to believe, was suicidal. Left-right unity, sure: "The unity of the tower of Babel, with no agreement other than on the issue that the free market has replaced Jehovah as lord of *man's* creation. If the fusion takes place, it will be the death of the young conservative movement." North saw intellectual chaos, not fusion. He was appalled by the black flag of anarchism adorned with the gold dollar sign of Objectivism flying everywhere. And then, on a classroom blackboard, he saw the ultimate blasphemy: "Lysander Spooner died for your sins."[224]

As many libertarians as enjoyed gatherings like the one that shocked Gary North, many more just liked to sit by themselves and read and write. The late 1960s and early 1970s saw an explosion of small, independently produced libertarian zines, hardly any of which lasted until the mid-1970s, but many of which were of high quality or at least pleasing quirkiness. There was *Efficacy*, *Rights by Right*, *Focus: A Monthly Journal of Issues and Ideas*, *Bull$heet*, the *Torch*, *Invictu$*, the *New Radical*, *Living Free*, *Libertarian American*, and more, which even their editors likely don't remember now.

It was a thrilling time to be a young libertarian, though, as strange and unformed and in flux as it all was, recalls Tom Palmer, now of the

Cato Institute. "There was a real evolutionary ferment, where all sorts of mutations get tossed out and—fortunately!—most didn't survive. I remember the *New Banner,* picturing a crumbling capital dome with a black flag behind it. Intellectual life on campus in general was quite bizarre then. I remember a zine picturing a big lizard cracking a whip saying 'onward to the tribal anarchist convention' and one of Mao and Nixon playing chess, and a 19th century anarchist figure with a black hat and bomb and the caption—'the choice is anarchy or chaos!!' as the chessboard is being overthrown. The 'Social Revolutionary Anarchist Federation' with a 'U.S. Out' over a map of North America. That sort of thing, receiving this weird 'Laissez-Faire Books' catalog—it made you feel that you were part of a secret movement in a way."[225]

The three most accomplished and interesting participants in this zine explosion, and the only three that lasted beyond a year or so, were the *Abolitionist* (later *Outlook*), the *Individualist* (the magazine of SIL, which also had a newsletter that lasted over a decade), and a more Randian, less countercultural one—*Reason.* The magazines were trying to deal with a libertarian audience still split by some 1960s holdover schisms of style, culture, and attitude. *The Abolitionist* was the most lefty, featuring Steve Halbrook's eccentric attempts to cast Lenin and Mao as libertarian heroes. These types made some inroads on lefty strongholds like New York radio station WBAI, with editorial staffers Walter Block and Ralph Fucetola (a New Jersey ex-YAFite) interviewing libertarian activists and intellectuals on the air.

A defining characteristic of the new generation of young libertarians—something you certainly couldn't say about the Leonard Read generation or the Objectivists—was a mordantly amused absurdism about their own ridiculous, often seemingly hopeless position in the ideological and political universe. Gary Greenberg, on taking over editorship of *Outlook* in 1973 and surveying the movement's growth and progress, noted that "the libertarian movement has turned from fifty libertarians selling books to each other to fifty libertarians exchanging magazine subscriptions with each other." This sort of tone was the young libertarian's best defense against witless fanaticism or maddening depression, in the era of Nixon, wage and price controls, continuing war, and a growing regulatory state, when reality rarely gave libertarian revolutionaries much cause for hope.

These small journals tended to fold into each other, with *Outlook* picking up *Individualist's* subscription list and obligations when it folded, then *Reason* doing the same for *Outlook*. *Reason* was the sole survivor of this zine explosion, and is still around today (and employs this author as a senior editor).

Reason was launched by Objectivist Boston University student Lanny Friedlander in 1968. By 1970, he had sold the magazine to a couple of fans and contributors in California: Bob Poole, a Heinlein and Rand man, a Goldwater kid, an engineer from MIT, and a total aviation geek with a father working for Eastern (ironically a casualty of the more competitive, less-regulated environment in the airline industry the young Poole helped engender). Poole wrote one of the first *Reason* pieces to garner the world's attention (after being reprinted in the *Freeman)*, a cover story calling for privatization of the air traffic system. Poole has been pushing the issue ever since, and now explains the benefits of private air traffic control directly to Congress instead of in small-circulation mimeographed magazines.

Poole's partner in *Reason* was Tibor Machan, a philosopher, a refugee from communist Hungary, and a tenacious Rand fan, who turned out to be the most prolific libertarian philosophy writer around, with dozens of books written or edited to his credit, mostly exploring various aspects of libertarian rights theory, which he approached from an Objectivist perspective. Poole and Machan recruited an L.A.-based lawyer, Manuel Klausner, whom they discovered giving libertarian-themed commentary on a Southern California Pacifica radio station. Klausner had been briefly a part of Rothbard's New York crew in the early 1960s while studying under union-fighting Sylvester Petro at NYU.

Reason's first big circulation boost, from 400 to 4,000, came in 1972, when they nabbed the first major interview with Nathaniel Branden, post-Rand break (the full details of the sex scandal behind the break, though rumored, were not made fully public until Barbara Branden's Rand biography in 1986) and hit his mailing list with direct mail solicitations. A similar rental of Bob LeFevre's mailing list, around the same time, almost killed them. They made the amateur mistake of hitting the entire list at once rather than testing a portion first. It contained scads of bad addresses and inspired numerous people to send colorful hate mail upon receiving a subscription solicitation from a young libertarian magazine. Through the 1970s, *Reason* found lists from libertarian-inspired taxpayer activist group National Taxpayers Union and various hard money newsletter lists helpful in building up circulation.[226] The magazine shifted in the late 1970s from specifically intramovement concerns to mainstream public policy and culture debates that happened to be of a libertarian bent, rather than a magazine for, and covering, the libertarian movement, and is still the most widely read libertarian periodical.

LeFevre had also retreated to Southern California by the early 1970s, unable to recover from the flood and mudslide at the old Rampart College. Zoning laws in California scuttled his plan to run another Rampart-like operation from a nice spread he bought to live on with his wife Loy, so the rump of Rampart retreated to an office building in Santa Ana, near the headquarters of his old patron R. C. Hoiles at the *Register.*

He had already recruited former NBI man Sy Leon, and decided, as antihippie as LeFevre had been, to try some of this "outreach to the radical young" thing. A young folk-singing Rampart graduate named Dana Rohrabacher—one of the libertarian YAFers purged in St. Louis, and a man well acquainted with the rituals and mores of the radical young, say those who knew him when—was sent out on a shoestring budget to sing his anarcho-LeFevrian folk songs at college campuses across the nation to help turn right-wingers into LeFevre-style libertarians.[227] Rohrabacher is known today to the residents of Orange County as their congressman.

LeFevre added his own contribution to the pile of libertarian magazines, this one with the strange scent of someone who doesn't quite get it bending over backward to pander. The magazine started as *Pine Tree* but quickly morphed to *Rap* with a so-mired-in-its-times-it's-a-timeless-classic psychedelic-unreadable design, and containing a profile of some ex-YAF chick who became forgiving and groovy and gave up on right-wing power trips, man. The article ended with the fetching lady, consumed with deep concern for honesty and a true, nonpolitical liberation dancing and prancing with the awed and charmed author along a California beach.

When libertarians weren't reading magazines, they were attending meetings—supper clubs, which popped up in most major cities, where fifty to a hundred libertarians would gather to eat, debate, and hear speeches on matters libertarian—and bigger conferences for all-day or all-weekend slates of libertarian talk and debate. The Society for Individual Liberty in November 1971, probably at the high point of its draw, threw conferences in Chicago, New York, and Los Angeles, drawing nearly five hundred in Chicago, slightly fewer at the others. (Milton Friedman appeared at two of them.)

John Muller started a libertarian bookstore in 1972 in Greenwich Village with Sharon Presley, one of the founders of the Berkeley Alliance for Libertarian Action. As Muller told Andrea Rich, who later bought the operation from him and turned it into a successful mail-order business that's still around today (though no longer run by Rich), "It was either that or pick up a gun." (Libertarians have always been more likely to head to a bookstore than an armory, which some think is half the problem.) The store became an important social center for the movement in America's biggest city, a place for any traveling libertarian to stop for company and succor and to find congenial drinking companions, and a source of aggravation for European anarchists who heard tales of New York City's anarchist bookstore and found its political economy selection infested with right deviationists such as Murray Rothbard; a place for signings and parties when significant new libertarian books were issued (the grand opening featured Rothbard and Tuccille signing); and showings of *The Prisoner* and other libertarian entertainments. At last the movement had a clubhouse outside of Rothbard's living room.

"THIS KIND OF ABSURD ANSWER TO THE PROBLEM OF SOCIAL PROTECTION AND DEFENSE."

Not that interesting things weren't still arising from that room. During this popular ferment for libertarianism Rothbard won his first—and only—major contract from a New York trade publisher, to write a book explaining the libertarian philosophy. The result, published in 1973 (with a revised edition in 1978) was *For a New Liberty*. This book strove to synthesize, in condensed form, the economic, historical, philosophical, and policy elements of Rothbard's vision in the post-

Watergate context when, Murray thought, the "subjective conditions," as the Marxists put it, were more propitious than ever for the rise of a movement to eliminate government. Watergate, oil crises, tax rebellion, stagflation—by the time he revised the book in 1978, the ever optimistic Rothbard thought the movement's time was nigh. As the ultimate statement of Rothbard's applied political thinking, and thus in many respects the ultimate statement of libertarian movement thinking in the 1970s, the book warrants extended attention.

Rothbard started by contextualizing libertarian philosophy as a vital—indeed, defining—part of the American political tradition. He traces the waxing and waning of the libertarian spirit in American history, from our Lockean revolution through the conservative counterrevolution against industrial laissez-faire, as he characterized the Progressive movement. The result of that was "a right-wing collectivism based on war, militarism, protectionism, and the compulsory cartelization of business and industry—a giant network of controls, regulations, subsidies, and privileges which forged a great partnership of Big Government with certain favored elements in big business and industry."[228]

The book was meant as both primer and manifesto, so Rothbard crammed in as much of his overall theory of liberty as he could. He began with what he considers the axiomatic moral basis of libertarianism: the nonaggression axiom, the idea that "no man or group of men may aggress against the person or property of anyone else."[229] The libertarian's primary educational mission, Rothbard says, is to expose the state as an exploiter, to hammer home a libertarian vision of class warfare between exploiting rulers and exploited ruled.

He lays out his propertarian foundations clearly, grounding his political ethics in the idea that man owns himself, is capable of owning portions of the world through homesteading, and thus establishes rights over person and property that no one, and no collective, has the right to usurp or invade. "The right of self-ownership and the right to homestead," writes Rothbard, "establish the complete set of principles of the libertarian system. The entire libertarian doctrine then becomes the spinning out and the application of all the implications of this central doctrine."[230] Belief in an unrestricted free market follows. If we own ourselves and are free to own other things, we must be free to trade or give away such ownership—and no one has any right to interfere in such trades.

This propertarian ethical vision leads to a bill of particulars against the state. Rothbard tries to cast the golden idol of democracy into the dust, pointing out that all states are inevitably run by oligarchies, never "the people," no matter their populist pretensions. He quotes Lysander Spooner's portrayal of the state as nothing more, morally, than a bandit gang. How, then, have the people been cowed and enslaved by this monstrous invention, the state? Through the complicity of the intellectuals, who supply most people with their ideas. According to sixteenth-century French political philosopher Etienne de la Boétie, we are all in essence "voluntary" slaves. Force alone could never keep a whole populace enslaved. Thus the state co-opts a culture's thought leaders and controls the educational system to inculcate the idea that we ought to obey the state—that civilized life would be well-nigh impossible without it.

Rothbard presents a thought experiment to show how absurd the state's pretensions would seem if we hadn't been saturated in an intellectual atmosphere—in most cases through schools run by the state—in which it received the benefit of every doubt:

> Suppose that we were all starting completely from scratch, and that millions of us had been dropped down upon the Earth, fully grown and developed, from some other planet. Debate begins as to how protection (police and judicial services) will be provided. Someone says: "Let's give all of our weapons to Joe Jones over there, and to his relatives. And let Jones and his family decide all disputes among us. In that way, the Joneses will be able to protect all of us from any aggression or fraud that anyone else may commit. With all the power and all the ability to make ultimate decisions on disputes in the hand of Jones, we will all be protected from one another. And then let us allow the Joneses to obtain their income from this great service by using their weapons, and by exacting as much revenue by coercion as they shall desire." Surely in that sort of situation, no one would treat this proposal with anything but ridicule. For it would be starkly evident that there would be no way, in that case, for any of us to protect ourselves from the aggressions, or the depredations, of the

Joneses themselves. . . . It is only because we have become accus-
tomed over thousands of years to the existence of the State that we
now give precisely this kind of absurd answer to the problem of social protection and defense.[231]

The bulk of *For a New Liberty* tries to convince a typical concerned
citizen of the United States in the 1970s how libertarian ideas and
their application can solve the pressing political and social problems of
the day. From taxes to crime to traffic to war to pollution to bad public services to stagflation to Watergate, government is everywhere presented as the cause of problems and crises—private action and the
death of the state everywhere the solution. Rothbard supplies what
have in most cases become (or already were) standard libertarian briefs
against state education, drug laws, conscription, taxation, licensing,
welfare, and inflation. He explains why someone is more apt to get
what he or she wants from a service in a free market than from one
run by a monopoly government and financed by taxation.

Rothbard emphasizes how government programs tend to especially
hurt the very people they are intended to help—the poor, the disadvantaged, minorities. This sort of unintended consequences argument—drilling home that merely because the government claims
good intentions doesn't mean it achieves good results—has become
the central weapon in the libertarian armory in popular policy arguments over government's benefits—summed up as a slogan by 1990s
Libertarian Party presidential candidate Harry Browne as "government doesn't work."

Rothbard hits the harder anarcho-capitalism stuff, but slips it in so
smoothly that many readers might not notice that this "libertarian
manifesto" promotes anarchism.[232] He gives a detailed speculative description of how streets and roads could be owned and operated by private neighborhood associations (and how historically roads have often
been built privately); and how even police protection and courts could,
and in many historical cases have been, provided by private markets. He
credits Gustave de Molinari as the first theoretician of how protection
could be treated as a private good on the market, just like any other
good. He explains why a world of competing private defense agencies
would not be apt to descend into constant warfare. That would be bad

for business for everyone, and rogue agencies would most likely be shut down by more honest ones forthwith. He relies on the scholarship of his *Libertarian Forum* publisher Joe Peden to describe how ancient Celtic Ireland survived with a system of completely private courts, unconnected with any particular political leader.[233]

Providing detailed blueprints for a libertarian utopia is something of a mug's game, Rothbard recognized. While Hayekian "spontaneous order" was not one of his favorite tropes—he was too much the Misesian rationalist for that—he did know that people in free markets often come up with solutions we cannot foresee beforehand.[234] The point of the anarchistic arguments is not to show exactly how the anarchistic utopia will solve every problem with the utmost efficiency and no rights violations. He merely wanted to show that there's no reason to believe that trying to solve the problems of defense and adjudication without a single monopoly source of force would result in a situation any *worse* than what we have now—and probably better. Rothbard wasn't assuming that everyone would suddenly start behaving themselves if there were no state; market anarchists are often accused of relying on such a foolishly Pollyannaish view of human nature. Not so for Rothbard: "The 'better' that people will be, of course, the better *any* social system will work, in particular the less work *any* police or courts will have to do. But libertarians make no such assumption. What we assert is that, given any particular degree of 'goodness' or 'badness' among men, the purely libertarian society will be at once the most moral and the most efficient, the least criminal and the most secure of person or property."[235]

Not one to settle for a small fight when a big one is tantalizingly near, Rothbard doesn't slough over the ultimate anarchist bugaboo: national defense. He argues that invading a nation that lacked a central government would be hopeless. With no capital to defeat, no state apparatus to staff with foreign conquerors, how would such an invasion ever pay off? An attempt to conquer an anarcho-libertarian North America would be an endless guerrilla war, with every hamlet and homestead a separate site to conquer.[236]

On the environment, Rothbard the pure propertarian takes a tougher stance against pollution than does all but the most fanatical environmentalist. He admits an inescapable conclusion of his own theories of property rights and invasion: that pollution of any sort is always a rights violation, one for which the victim should be able to sue for damages and cessation in a libertarian court. The state, Rothbard asserts, has blocked us from doing this by in most cases deciding that the causes of pollution are public goods and we just have to suck up whatever they put out.

Such a hard-core propertarian line on pollution might seem to mean the end of industrial civilization. Rothbard thinks that even raising that concern is a monstrous moral dodge. "The argument that such an injunctive prohibition against pollution would add to the costs of industrial production is as reprehensible as the pre–Civil War argument that the abolition of slavery would add to the costs of growing cotton, and that therefore abolition, however morally correct, was 'impractical.' For this means that the polluters are able to impose all of the high costs of pollution upon those whose lungs and property rights they have been allowed to invade with impunity."[237] A court regime properly tough on pollution, he maintains, would spur the invention of new pollution control technologies far more efficiently than do government ukases. "The only remedy is to force the polluting invaders to stop their invasion, and thereby to redirect technology into nonpolluting or even antipolluting channels."[238]

The closing chapter of *For a New Liberty* exemplifies why Rothbard was considered such an enemy by the cold war right, and even by such old Circle Bastiat comrades as George Reisman.[239] In the Us Versus Them game of postwar foreign policy gamesmanship, Rothbard says *we* were the bad guys. The Soviets, he argues, were concerned not with conquering the world for the glory of the party and international communism, but rather with the old-fashioned Russian game of desperately trying to ensure its own survival.[240]

He ends with a stirring call for disarmament, contrasting this libertarian stance with a Buckleyite, stop-the-Soviets-at-all-costs mentality. "Anyone who wishes," Rothbard writes, "is entitled to make the personal decision of 'better dead than Red' or 'give me liberty or give me death.' What he is *not* entitled to do is to make these decisions *for* others, as the prowar policy of conservatism would do. What conservatives are really saying is: 'Better *them* dead than Red,' and 'give me liberty or give *them* death'—which are the battle cries not of noble heroes but of mass murderers."[241]

Rothbard, mindful of his audience, realizes that speculations about civilization functioning smoothly without a state will strike many as absurdly fanciful, utopian in the worst sense of the word—it could happen nowhere. Assuming at least that his typical reader doesn't believe in a reinless megastate, he notes that "the idea of a strictly limited constitutional State was a noble experiment that failed, even under the most favorable and propitious circumstances. If it failed then, why should a similar experiment fare any better now? No, it is the conservative laissez-fairist, the man who puts all the guns and all the decision-making power into the hands of the central government and *then* says, 'Limit yourself'; it is *he* who is truly the impractical utopian."[242]

Anarchism was the craze in libertarian thinking in the early 1970s, and not just from the Austrian/natural rights Rothbard or Objectivist-anarchists like Roy Childs. The first big anarchist tome to hit the movement—beating Rothbard's *Power and Market* (which had been written a decade or more earlier) to print by a year—was *The Market for Liberty* by Morris and Linda Tannehill, a pair who dropped out of the movement and then dropped out of society. Their book gives a detailed picture of how a moral stateless society might work. Their thinking was in a similar Randian vein to Childs's.

The Institute for Humane Studies was by the late 1960s the one survivor, barely, of the old Volker Fund dream, though it took years for Baldy Harper to get it active on more than a paper level after the 1962 Volker collapse. Rejoined in 1966 by Kenneth Templeton from the old Volker days, Harper eventually launched a program of seminars, conferences, financial aid to researchers, and a small publication program—mostly dedicated to the quietly anarchist end of libertarianism. IHS never became the anarchist Center for Advanced Studies he envisioned. Since his death it has mostly given scholarships to graduate students with libertarian bona fides and provided seminar-style introductions to libertarianism to undergrads—whom the institute mostly ignored for its first couple of decades.

Harper was another beloved movement eccentric, though lacking the qualities that made LeFevre and Read turn some people off. I've never heard a bad word about Harper.[243] His pet pair of almost forgotten anarchistic libertarian thinkers was Spencer Heath and his grandson and intellectual successor Spencer Heath MacCallum. They were struck with the realization that hotels approximated pure anarcho-capitalism. After all, they provide, for a fee, a community offering the "governmental" services of utilities and waste removal, public spaces, private spaces, defense (the hotel dick), and many of the other accoutrements of community life such as meeting spaces, recreation opportunities, restaurants, and so on. Consequently they merit extended study as examples of a private government of sorts that maintains a workable social harmony.

Heath and MacCallum promoted the proprietary community—hotels and shopping centers as prime examples—as the proper anarchist solution in Heath's book *Citadel, Market, and Altar.* The Institute for Humane Studies published *The Art of Community* by MacCallum.[244] That book came out in 1970, the same year the institute issued Rothbard's anarchistic *Power and Market.*

Milton Friedman's son, David Friedman, a former columnist for YAF's *New Guard,* approached anarchism from a different direction, using the classic Friedmanite/Chicago School economic analysis of utility, mindful of empirical evidence, with rights left out of the picture entirely.[245] Friedman too sold his radical anarchic vision to a major New York publisher in 1973, which was published as *The Machinery of Freedom.*

As the son of Milton, David grew up a small-state classical liberal with a yen for Goldwater.[246] Then a friend explained how private streets could work. Then his science fiction hero Robert Heinlein showed in his 1966 novel *The Moon Is a Harsh Mistress* (with its avuncular friendly old anarchist professor, based on Heinlein's Colorado pal Robert LeFevre) how an anarchist society might work. Beginning as Rothbard did with property, Friedman proceeded to show his readers (many of whom he seemed to assume were groovy kids) that everything they wanted would come to them in greater abundance with private property and free markets, and that this range of wealth and options could be theirs without exploiting anyone.

He turned to Chicago School law and economics tools to examine how promised government benefits regarding areas such as private business monopoly were not benefits at all. In reality Standard Oil did *not* thrive by running competitors out of business predatorily, and in economic logic no company of whatever size really *could* get away with such a strategy.[247] He showed how theft creates a deadweight efficiency loss to society as a whole (the thief only gains what you lose; you lose what you lose plus the expenses of trying to protect yourself against theft)[248] and how private anarchist law would undoubtedly evolve in a libertarian direction because unlibertarian laws are the kind of public goods that the market can't provide well.[249]

He takes on the hard cases as well, imagining a system of justice largely based on tort law where courts only come into play when someone has been harmed—and where the purpose of the court tends toward restitution to the victim, not punishment for the benefit of a state. Various free market anarchist thinkers have tried to deal with the problem of restitution for murder. Obviously (and, it should be noted, punishment faces the same intellectual problem) there is an inevitable arbitrariness in deciding what constitutes proper restitution for murder, and of course the recipient of the restitution would not be you but a next of kin, or anyone to whom you had sold off your right of restitution, in a matter similar to the way you can sell off the right to collect on your life insurance policy to someone else for cash today.

In tackling the tricky (for anarchists) problem of national (or large group) defense and the free rider problem that paying for it voluntarily creates, Friedman points out the intriguing datum that tipping in taxi cabs—almost purely a situation of paying for a public good because of social expectations—is widespread and amounts to over $100 million a year. This indicates to Friedman that most people in reality don't get carried away with the economic benefits of free riding and neglect public goods when a developed social rule dictates that we should do the right thing.[250]

Friedman insists that hitching his ideas to a mass movement is not his concern and should not be the reader's concern; the only thing the reader needs to know about the number of libertarians is that, if the reader is convinced, it has increased by one.[251]

He was staking out the usual position of the intellectual libertarian revolutionary. Whether Friedman knew it or not, he was right in the main of Leonard Read thinking, educating people one at a time in libertarian truths through the written word, the way the movement had progressed from Read's founding of FEE in 1946 to these days in the early 1970s, when four major New York publishers were buying up books pushing this charming, radical, hot new thing: anarcho-capitalism.

But there are other potential ways to spread libertarianism beyond educating one mind at a time. There is also political action. Out west in Colorado, as David Friedman was conceptualizing this book, a fellow ex-YAFer survived the rubble of the revolutionary 1960s, stared Nixon in his baleful, dark eyes, and knew that libertarianism needed something new, something beyond a magazine, a book, or even a street demonstration. It was time for a Libertarian Party.

Libertarian Zionism, the Koch Bubble, and America's Third Largest Political Party

That goddamn Nixon had finally done it: appeared on TV on August 15, 1971, with his dark, shifty mug—no face that Ayn Rand or Robert Heinlein would ever glorify—and announced he was going to dictate to all Americans how much they could charge for things they wanted to sell, and how much they could be paid for the work they did. And while he was at it, he was going to take the dollar completely off the gold basis—the American dollar would henceforth be nothing but a piece of paper, redeemable in nothing. It was an act of economic tyranny so sinister that it was worthy of the craven national leader in *Atlas Shrugged*.

Although David Nolan had spent most of the past decade as a Republican, that was *it*. Nolan was one of many young libertarians first attracted to political liberty through their reading of science fiction novelist Robert Heinlein, author of a series of adolescent science fiction novels as well as more mature works such as *Stranger in a Strange Land* and *Starship Troopers*. Heinlein was not an across-the-board doctrinaire movement libertarian, but his novels frequently had hyper-individualist messages combined with an intelligent and critical sniffing at hidebound traditions. (He was personal friends with Robert LeFevre, to boot, and based a character in his influential libertarian-revolution-on-the-moon novel *The Moon Is a Harsh Mistress* on him.)

Nolan was an MIT graduate in addition to being a science fiction fan, and his first political action as a very apolitical young man was making and wearing a buttom that read "Heinlein for President" during the 1960 campaign. He was also a multiyear road veteran of the Liberty Amendment campaign (a far-rightist, in culture and feel, campaign to amend the Constitution so that Congress could only do things that the Constitution specifically allows it to do—a bit redundant, perhaps, but to such extremes had post–New Deal government led). Nolan was a former YAFer, and was pals with the old libertarian caucus crew now doing business as the Society for Individual Liberty. Though libertarian in philosophy, this former head of the most successful Students for Goldwater group in New England during his MIT days had remained a Republican in practice.

But Nixon was never what Nolan meant by Republican. In 1971, he was working for an ad agency in Denver and happened to have a handful of libertarian-minded friends over that day when Nixon hit the airwaves with his wage and price controls announcement. They all agreed: It was time for a third party, a libertarian party, a Libertarian Party.[1]

Nolan had shared pre–St. Louis libertarian disenchantment within YAF and had tried, and failed, to get YAF to sign on to the Liberty Amendment. He remembers late at the 1967 YAF national convention a gathering of disenchanted Objectivists and libertarians complaining about feeling shut out. The trads were already scared of the rads, and were already beginning the slow purge that would come to a head in 1969—not because the rads "had any real muscle or money, but the trads were afraid we'd take this vehicle they spent seven years and countless millions creating and subvert it into something they never intended." YAF really existed for the entertainment of its funders, not for the students themselves, and those old businessmen had no patience for youthful libertarian radicalism. So while the libertarian YAF members were sitting around commiserating, "someone sent around a piece of paper and said 'sign up on this list'—as far as I know it was the first comprehensive list of self-styled libertarians consciously trying to create a network of contacts." There were eighty-eight signatories, he recalls.[2]

Nolan, his wife Susan, and their Denver friends began contacting libertarians they knew around the country in the second half of 1971. Nolan had a head start from the libertarian button business he had been running—he already had a mailing list of dedicated libertarians. The first place Nolan floated the Libertarian Party idea before a national audience was in an article in the SIL magazine *Individualist*. Subsequently they advertised it in the little libertarian magazines of the day. He pointed out that most extant libertarian strategies—still the usual, from education to Fabianism (the slow takeover of major institutions and turning them subtly in a libertarian direction, as per the English Fabian socialists) to hiding in the woods—ignored the realities of how political events tend to be shaped by, well, the political process.

He made no grandiose promises for what a Libertarian Party might achieve. He suggested that it could lead to increased media attention for libertarian ideas, which might bring more latent libertarians out from hiding, create a permanent institution to spur those libertarians into action for their beliefs, and help further a breakdown between the traditional right and left by providing a new home, seriously proliberty and anti-state, to the forces on either end of the standard political spectrum that ought not feel comfortable with the rest of their coalition. He pointed specifically to, on the left, the Institute for the Study of Nonviolence, and on the right to the Birchers and the Liberty Amendment Committee (his own former far-right home).

The earliest group of LP activists, reported *SIL News*, consisted of 75 percent former Republicans, 36 percent Objectivists and 16 percent who embraced Heinlein as their major ideological influence, 23 percent Misesians, and 17 percent anarchists. (Nolan recalls a far higher Objectivist percentage.) Their hopes and dreams for a libertarian presidential candidate ran a wide, perplexing gamut, from Rand insider, Nixon adviser, and *Federal Bulldozer* (a libertarian classic on the dire motives and effects of urban renewal) author Martin Anderson to tax rebel Vivien Kellems (a woman from Vermont who in the late 1940s refused to withhold income taxes from the employees at her cable grip company, got away with it for a while, and became a national heroine among antitax forces for it)[3]; from Karl Hess to Senator Sam Ervin.

But number one was Murray Rothbard. When Nolan called him, Rothbard scoffed at the idea and declined.[4]

The opening announcement of the LP's formation got quite a bit of press; quite possibly more than for anything the LP has done since. Even the *New York Times* gave the party's official debut, in Denver on January 31, 1972, respectful coverage. Its story noted such LP principles as repeal of victimless crime laws, draft amnesty, death to the Federal Communications Commission, no commitment of troops without Senate approval, withdrawal from Vietnam, and even recognition of the right of secession. Isn't that anarchy, Mr. Nolan? His cryptic reply: "Anarchy is simply Libertarianism carried to an unworkable extreme."[5]

In June 1972, the fledgling party first met in convention assembled at a Radisson Hotel in Denver, with eighty-nine delegates present. Naturally for a libertarian party—and to the exact degree that it would seem impossibly eccentric, bordering on ridiculous, for a major party—they drafted analytical philosopher John Hospers as their first presidential candidate. He had published a comprehensive guide to libertarian ideas the year before, called *Libertarianism*; he had a respectable academic berth at the University of Southern California; he had an Objectivist background, having once been a philosophical associate of Rand's. He was eventually kicked off her team, of course, after hosting her at a presentation on aesthetics at a philosophy conference. She insisted that her friend Hospers be the designated commenter on her presentation. But when he dared to go beyond fulsome praise in the comment, their friendship was over.[6] Rand's reaction to her old friend running for president? She told a questioner at one of her speeches, "If, at a time like this, John Hospers takes ten votes away from Nixon (which I doubt he'll do), it would be a moral crime."[7]

Tonie Nathan, a TV producer from Oregon with a left-liberal and then (after being converted by her son, home from the navy with a fresh yen for Rand) Objectivist background, showed up to cover the convention. Because of some well-phrased comments from the floor during debates over the platform and statement of principles that impressed the rest of the delegation, she left as a candidate for vice president of the United States.

The Hospers/Nathan ticket was on the ballot in only two states, Washington and Colorado. Still, it made electoral history, thanks to the late Rose Wilder Lane. Lane's young protégé and heir, former Vermont state legislator Roger MacBride, was a Republican elector in Virginia that year. He could not maintain his self-respect if he were in any way responsible for returning the horrid Richard Nixon to the presidency. The Republican Party could have seen this coming. MacBride had written a book on the Electoral College in 1953 praising the ability and right of electors to vote their conscience. And as Rose Wilder Lane's adopted grandson, he could be expected to make grand gestures in defense of libertarian principles.[8]

Using the rarely exercised yet often feared power of the elector in the Electoral College system to ignore the voice of the *demos,* on December 18, 1972, MacBride cast one electoral vote for John Hospers and Tonie Nathan. This made Nathan the first woman to receive an electoral vote in U.S. history, an achievement little noted nor long remembered by conventional American feminism. (It also put the Hospers/Nathan ticket a mere sixteen electoral votes behind the Democrats' McGovern/Shriver one.)

MacBride had given courtesy announcements of his intentions to LP higher-ups, including an unexpected call to Tonie Nathan while she was watching the evening news (she *hated* to be interrupted then). This serious voice was telling her that he intended to vote for her for vice president. She assumed she was talking to someone a bit tetched in the head—didn't he know the election was over? It was *too late* to vote for her now.[9]

MacBride had alerted the media beforehand of his intentions, under a strict embargo. For the first time in its history, the room where Virginia's electors met was flooded with klieg lights as most of the electors passed in their preprinted ballots with Nixon's name on them. MacBride crossed out the president's name and wrote in Hospers's. When the vote count for vice president was announced, Theodora Nathan (her legal name) had become, to the puzzled man reading the results, "Theodore." TV cameras zoomed in close on this moment, as the moving hand wrote the first electoral vote for a woman in American history. While his fellow electors were cool to hostile, citizens back in his home county congratulated him heartily in the street for standing up in opposition to Nixon.[10]

"UNTIL I WALKED INTO THAT CONVENTION HALL, I HAD NO IDEA HOW MANY ALTERNATIVES THERE WERE."

At that first LP convention in Denver was a California-based investment professional named Edward Crane III. His was a traditional young libertarian story—turned on to political ideas by Goldwater, which led to Rand and some Nathaniel Branden Institute lectures and subscriptions to all the little libertarian newsletters and zines. He became a Goldwater precinct captain for two precincts in Berkeley in 1964 (where he had attended college and ran for student government on a platform of abolishing student government). Goldwater got seven votes in one precinct and six in the other. Crane knew the names of every single one of those voters.

The Goldwater campaign radicalized him in a way the GOP standard-bearer didn't intend. Crane was disillusioned with how quickly Goldwater ran away from the issue of privatizing Social Security. And he did seem gratuitously hawkish on Vietnam. Reading Russell Kirk's *Conservative Mind*, as it so often does, provided a final conversion experience for Crane—away from conservatism. "I just assumed I was through with politics, because I was a libertarian and there was no libertarian alternative. But then one of those underground newsletters notified me in June of the 1972 meeting at the Radisson Hotel in Denver. I knew as a libertarian that it was imperative to be tolerant of alternative lifestyles. Until I walked into that convention hall, I had no idea how many alternatives there were."[11]

Crane found goldbugs, left-anarchists, hidebound Objectivists, and even to his surprise a fair number of free-market rightists disillusioned by Nixon on wage and price controls, but still foursquare for fighting Vietnam to certain victory. (Because of this, the first LP platform didn't explicitly commit the LP to withdrawal from Vietnam. There was serious disagreement over this among the delegates at the first convention, and the first platform insisted in a Randian manner that "while we recognize the existence of totalitarian governments, we do not recognize them as legitimate governments. We will grant them no moral sanction. We will not deal with them as if they were proper governments.") Crane was part of a team of eight or so sitting in a room with Hospers writing the party's statement of principles—a statement still in effect, with the controversial line (some LP candidates complain it makes them sound like kooks) about how libertarians "oppose the cult of the omnipotent State." Crane took on the purely nominal title of campaign manager for Tonie Nathan but worked hard on building up the party in California, finding people to chair twelve different districts, and taking advantage of statist tools like FCC equal time requirements to spread the libertarian word in editorial rebuttals on television.

MacBride became an LP folk hero for his Electoral College apostasy and befriended Crane. Seeing more real-world acumen and energy in Crane than in most other LPers, MacBride encouraged him to take over the national party and help him (MacBride) run for president in 1976. The Libertarian Party's official phone rang for a while at Ed Crane's desk at Scudder Stevens in San Francisco.

Crane won the national chairmanship in 1974 at the LP's national convention held near Dallas and expanded the *LP News* from a members-only premium to a tabloid sent to every libertarian mailing list he could dredge up. At Dallas, with a fresh influx of anarcho-Rothbardians in the party, the platform was radicalized and the unofficial "Dallas accord" arose from late-night platform debates—establishing the principle that anarchists and minarchists must vow to exclude from the platform anything that alienated either of them. This meant in effect that the LP platform must never specify any particular thing the state *should* do.

Crane repeated his efforts at finding California district chairs on the national level—or, as he put it, he was "wandering around the country trying to find people whose eyes tracked and convince them to run state parties." He was exasperated that many so-called state parties were not even a step above the supper clubs that had dominated libertarian social organizing in the years preceding the party's founding, showing little concern and exerting even less effort toward actually running candidates or building a party apparatus. "I still have enemies to this day in most states in the union," he says, because of his tough love party-building efforts in the mid-1970s.[12]

The LP began to take up more and more of his time, and Crane found himself at a competitive disadvantage in the investment world. He left his job and took an 80 percent pay cut to run the LP full-time, moving it to a Washington office in 1975.

It wasn't all dire on the state level for the LP between 1972 and 1976, although a lot of political energy went into wan stunts like celebrating the two-hundredth anniversary of the Boston Tea Party by mailing tea bags to politicians and milling around in front of IRS offices on April 15. But Jerome Tuccille's 1974 gubernatorial campaign in New York won national publicity in *Newsweek* through stunts such as riding a woman wearing a beige body stocking through the streets of New York on horseback in a Lady Godiva–inspired consciousness-raising about tax rates. However, they soon realized that even that kind of major media attention doesn't translate into votes, or even into people remembering a minor party candidate's name. Tuccille's goal was to win the 50,000 votes that would have guaranteed the LP permanent ballot status in New York. He failed. Tuccille recalls secret backroom advice from a sympathetic New York City GOP kingmaker, Art Finkelstein, who told them—correctly, as it turned out—that they could expect one vote for every six bucks they spent.

Reason magazine editor and L.A.-based lawyer Manuel Klausner was another early LP candidate, running as a write-in for U.S. Congress from California in 1972, dubbing himself "the candidate of principle for the thinking person." He didn't pay the filing fees that would guarantee his votes would be counted, and thus he can proudly state that "countless numbers of people voted for me for Congress." While defending libertarianism in a campaign context, he realized he could no longer rationally defend coercive taxation. In his case the LP, rather than watering down his hard-core libertarianism in the difficult electoral arena as some radical anti-party libertarians feared it might tend to do, radicalized him.[13]

The party was still so small and ragtag that when Crane noticed that his letters from MacBride were on *embossed stationery*, he thought, yes, it was as MacBride said—*this* guy has to be our next presidential candidate. And so it was. They'd advertise as a premium for campaign donations that with a grand you'd get an autographed copy of MacBride's campaign book; if you sent in $50, you'd get one anyway. You could show up for the first time to a national convention without knowing anyone, instantly become a delegate, and walk out a member of the governing national committee. It was a small-time operation, to be sure.

MacBride, more conservative/traditional in his manner and back- ground than many of the younger LP firebrands, let it be known at the 1975 nominating convention for the 1976 race, held in New York, that he would not accept a couple of the likely vice presidential candidates who had wide delegate support: John Vernon, because he was gay, and Jim Trotter, who was known to have committed the very libertarian crime of owning gold when it was still illegal for private citizens to do so.

As a compromise, David Bergland, a California lawyer (and former LP candidate for state attorney general there) was called back west and dispatched immediately on a redeye flight to New York to seek and win the VP nomination. The candidate's tasks at that point involved going to state LP conventions and talking to radio and newspaper re- porters. Bergland was suitably hard-core for the rank and file, even if more conventionally bourgeois than the modal party member—or, most importantly, than Vernon or Trotter. When running for California attorney general, Bergland publicly debated the Democrat and Peace and Freedom candidates. It was the year of Patty Hearst, the heiress kidnapped by the nihilist-leftist Symbionese Liberation Army. (She then became their apparently willing ally.) The SLA made the unusual ransom demand of publicly financed handouts for the poor. Bergland announced that as attorney general, he'd have no compunctions about prosecuting for receiving stolen property any poor Californian who took advantage of this Symbionese generosity. "The moderator's jaw dropped and he couldn't talk for 10 seconds," Bergland recalls.[14]

MacBride flew himself around the nation campaigning on his per- sonal jet, cheekily dubbed No Force One, and garnered a smattering of press attention that mostly stressed the zany hopelessness of the LP candidate's task. He did end up pushing the party up field quite a bit— he got on the ballot in thirty-two states and earned 173,000 votes.

But soon after the LP's founding the state struck a powerful blow against it. Ed Crane now says he should have known that the LP would be hopeless as a serious, effective vehicle for winning elections as early as 1974, as soon as the post–Watergate Federal Elections Campaign Act (FECA) was passed. Its limits on donations to politicians made it impossible for a small circle of wealthy individuals to support unpopular candidates, which was the lifeblood, for example, of such Democratic campaigns as Gene McCarthy's or George McGovern's, who each had the six-figure support of General Motors scion Stewart Mott.

FECA survived a court challenge in *Buckley v. Valeo*—a case in which the LP was a party trying to eliminate these new campaign-funding restrictions. When Crane was deposed in the case and asked if the LP was intimately connected to any predecessor organization, he replied, but of course, "The American revolution." FECA, Crane mordantly notes, is "the only law that ever did exactly what it was intended to do: cement the two-party system in an impregnable fortress of cash from which no challenger could ever evict them."[15]

"BELIEVING WE'D BE ABLE TO . . . ENGINEER A LIBERTARIAN REVOLT WITHOUT MASSIVE EXTERNAL BACKING WAS VERY NAIVE."

Not everyone in the movement was thrilled with the arrival and rise of the LP. To this day, some blame it for bringing the disparate and multileveled energy of the post–*New York Times* Sunday magazine cover days to a dull, bureaucratic, in-fighting halt. Louis Rossetto called the party the "booby prize" that the movement won for all the attention and progress and growth of the early 1970s. Freelance libertarian philosopher George Smith, an old-fashioned "voting is a crime" libertarian (voting, after all, means participating in and implicitly agreeing to the outcome of a political game whereby other people's lives and property are considered up for grabs) was disgusted by what he saw as extreme cynicism on the part of friends who became LP insiders. One old friend of his, an LP advocate until after the 1980 Ed Clark presidential campaign, told Smith that the LP represented no opportunity costs to the libertarian movement, since most of the party rank and file were so unintellectual and otherwise unskilled in the social change game that if they weren't out on street corners petitioning for ballot access, they wouldn't have anything to contribute to the movement.[16]

The LP's most sincere, loudest, and most tenacious enemy was an anarchist science fiction fan named Sam Konkin, who styled himself the true center and conscience of the movement. For him, said one old friend, the libertarian split from YAF in St. Louis in 1969 was Luther nailing the theses to the church door and the light of revelation entering through a crack in the phenomenal universe all in one; the beginning of true revolution and the quintessence of all things. Konkin joined the New York branch of the LP in 1973 as a spoiler. From then on he raged against "partyarchy"[17] and the corruption of his pure market anarchism with the stain of party politics.

Throughout the 1970s, Konkin was the most thorough chronicler of the movement's ups and downs with his *New Libertarian Notes*, a newsletter of philosophical controversies, reviews of science fiction magazines, and non-party-centered discussion of the world of libertarian gatherings, supper clubs, books, and magazines. He issued it weekly for a few years in the mid-1970s, then sporadically in the 1980s and 1990s, usually under subtly shifting names, all with the words "New Libertarian" in there somewhere.

To him, the heart and soul of libertarianism (he called his variant "agorism" after *agora*, the Greek word for market) was the thousands of libertarians he knew were out there participating in "countereconomics," creating institutions and markets hidden from the eyes of authorities and tax collectors—indulging in unregulated businesses that paid no taxes. These black free marketeers, he asserted, not those running for office with the LP or issuing ameliorist policy papers from the libertarian think tanks that arose later, or writing milquetoast journalism about municipal privatization from *Reason*, were what the libertarian movement was really all about.[18]

Konkin's agorism was a more daring and disreputable version of the Richard Cornuelle vision, and parts of the Robert LeFevre one—that libertarians needed to show-not-tell how markets and liberty made the world a better place, that they didn't need to wait for the state to go away, or even convince lots of people that it *ought* to go away, to start "living liberty," as the movement saying goes, right now. Reading

Austrian economists, adoring Ayn Rand and trying to remember that A is A, merely thinking and believing the proper political line—what availed any of it if you remained an aboveground tax slave? Konkin insisted that at least 10,000 peaceful guerrillas for liberty, inspired by him directly or secondhand, had entered the brave taxless world of black market countereconomics. By the nature of the phenomenon, it is difficult to confirm Konkin's assertion.

Some libertarians were even more radical than Konkin. They weren't content to hide and scuttle around, trying to live and profit unnoticed, in a statist America. They thought it was time to start over. Just as the LP activists realized there was no room for libertarians in the American two-party system, some libertarians went one step further, deciding there was no real place for them in America—or any other existing country.

I've discovered bits and pieces of evidence of at least idle plans to create an entirely new libertarian nation dating back to the late 1950s. It was surely Rand and *Atlas Shrugged* and Galt's Gulch that started it all. Ever since Rand vividly imagined that self-sufficient, regulator-free paradise people have periodically popped up to sell the idea that the only sure path to liberty is for libertarians to gather together in close proximity. Then no one would mooch or rob or force paper fiat money on their fellows. Freely minted gold coins would clink on the counters of brothels and, if you please, opium dens. And the weasels who in a statist world would be telling brave producers what they had to make or what they had to pay their employees would need to find new work—perhaps as tort lawyers, since lawsuits for proven harms would replace the regulatory state, or as toll booth operators on private roads.

The 1960s zine *Innovator*, recall, arose out of the short-lived Preform movement, which mused on the possibilities and places for creating a new libertarian nation, including retreating to the high seas, but never seemed to get past talking and writing about it. Probably the first to make a concerted attempt to create an ocean-based libertarian society, not just write about it, was a wealthy pharmaceutical firm owner named Werner Stiefel. In 1968, under the name Operation Atlantis (and several other names that all had "Atlantis" in them somewhere), he began recruiting eager young libertarians to move into an old mo-

tel in Saugerties, New York. From that humble base they would eventually obtain sovereignty over some island—the Prickly Pear Cays in
the British West Indies were an initial target—and turn it into a fresh
country. Under that new country's flag, Stiefel and his freebooters
could sail ships that would build artificial platforms in the ocean,
which would become the *real* new nation. They coined their own silver money, the deca, and earned a brief mention in *Esquire* in September 1970. "Operation Atlantis is a real mind-blower," *Esquire* said.
"They're not just interested in a floating community, but an honest-
to-God independent *country*. . . . How are they going to do it? They're
going to build an island, baby, in the middle of the ocean."[19] The Atlantis Project newsletter shifted in 1971 from being priced at 24
American cents to 32 "deca-cents."

In the early 1970s, Stiefel and his crew built from scratch a rebar-
and-cement boat inside a geodesic dome in Saugerties. With many difficulties along the way, including getting the boat stuck on its side in
the Hudson River and catching fire (short-lived thanks to its being
made of cement), they managed to sail the homemade vessel down to
the Silver Shoals area, near the Bahamas. There the boat sank in a hurricane, but Stiefel and his Atlanteans had in the meantime gotten control of some land on Tortuga Island. His efforts eventually ran afoul of
Haiti's Duvalier, who had designs of his own for the area Stiefel tried
to nation-build in. (Sunken Spanish galleons with unclaimed treasure
were known to be in the area.) Stiefel and his crew were driven out of
competition for the area, and that dream died.[20]

But not for everyone. Simultaneously Mike Oliver, a Lithuanian-
born concentration camp survivor, coin dealer, and land developer
from Nevada, with Galambos and NBI in his background, was inflam-
ing libertarian minds with his 1968 book, *A New Constitution for a New
Country*.[21] In it he presented a model constitution for a nation whose
(extremely limited) government would be financed voluntarily. You
could free-ride on national defense, he had to admit, but could only
use the courts and depend on the police if you were paid up. Oliver
did more than just write constitutions for sand castles in the sky and
imagine ocean-bound libertarian strongholds—he actually gathered
teams and money to build them. (Who would actually *inhabit* them always seemed an afterthought.)

A team of Oliver supporters first supervised the sea kingdom of Minerva in 1972, built on a south Pacific reef dry only at low tide. This was after lots of air miles expended in ultimately fruitless negotiations with over a dozen other countries to see if they could buy off sovereignty in some portion of the nation. Oliver noted, ironically, that the only chance of this approach succeeding—not that it ever did—was if you were dealing with dictators. They can actually make things happen. Still, all your progress could disappear on the dictator's whim. It's impossible to even get started on the new country idea in democracies.

Oliver's team claimed possession of two small coral atolls 400 miles south of Fiji in January, and in May an engineering crew was brought down to dredge and build seawalls, creating dry land they could sell in quarter acre lots to libertarians seeking freedom. The engineering crew quickly discovered that dredging wasn't creating enough potentially dry land fast enough, and the plan was shifted to building a sea city floating on pilings.

This Minerva project was breaking apart over personal squabbling—three members of the governing/owning council were trying to vote out the other one, and Oliver was washing his hands of the whole thing—when the whole matter was settled for them. The nascent nation of Minerva was conquered—in one spasm and with one gunboat—by the king of Tonga.[22]

Oliver and his circle, which eventually included John Hospers, the first LP presidential candidate, in the mid-'70s tried to make common cause with a separatist movement in the Bahamian island of Abaco, but that fizzled out as well, with no gunboats at all. Hospers so angered the socialist Progressive Liberal Party (then running the Bahamas after England had pulled out) by giving pro-independence speeches in Abaco that the next time he tried landing on Bahamian territory, they wouldn't let him off the plane and shipped the troublemaking philosopher back to Miami.[23]

But Oliver had realized that trying to get existing separatist movements to adopt something like his libertarian constitution was a more likely tack to take than creating a sovereign nation from scratch. Oliver's most serious, yet ultimately most comic-opera, reach for libertopia came on the south Pacific island of Vanuatu in the New Hebrides.

Representatives of Oliver's Phoenix Foundation (which for a while had *Reason* editor Robert Poole on its board of directors—that magazine throughout the 1970s was also the best news source on Oliver's various new country schemes) supplied advice and some technical skill, including radio operators and some hand-to-hand combat training, to the separatist movement on Vanuatu known as Na-Griamel, led by Jimmy Moly Stevens.[24] The tribal traditions there, some Phoenix Foundation types swore, were very respectful of private property. Soon libertarian entrepreneurs were selling gold Na-Griamel coins with "Individual rights for all" emblazoned on them. This was at the cusp of when the French and British, who had a peculiar dual protectorate system over the islands, were pulling out. While some questioned Stevens's libertarian bona fides, the world never got a chance to find out.

This nascent new libernation, to be called Vemerana, was strangled in its crib. At least this time it took more than one Tongan gunboat. Stevens and his movement had been a thorn in the side of the local socialist party, which was waiting to take over the New Hebrides from the French and British; the conflict had led to a series of skirmishes, takeovers of small areas repelled by counterattacks, appeals to the United Nations, and general unrest since 1975.[25] In 1980, after the U.S. government announced that it would only recognize the socialist government, led by a priest, Father Walter Lini (who also had the enthusiastic support of the World Council of Churches), Stevens's crew took over government offices in the city of Santo. Troops from both Papua New Guinea and Australia, in service of Lini's socialist government, helped suppress Stevens's rebellion.

Stevens was captured and his son, killed. He spent a decade in jail and the Phoenix Foundation caught the eye of the feds, who briefly considered possible prosecution of the parties involved for violations of the Logan Act (which prohibits private citizens from interfering in national relations with foreign powers) and the Arms Export Control Act. Everyone associated with the Phoenix Foundation (which along the way suffered a typical libertarian movement schism and relocated to Amsterdam with Oliver no longer involved) or mentioned in the *Reason* 1980 cover feature on Na-Griamel were barred from the island by the new socialist government.

Oliver's last foray into libertarian nation-building—sobered, perhaps, by the potential for violence in latching onto postcolonial separatism—returned to the classic idea of starting from scratch with artificial ocean cites. Thus he launched a mid-1990s bid for investors and builders for Oceania, using the nostalgic name Atlantis Project. It is memorialized now only by its old website, oceania.org, still online, but glumly reading, "The Atlantis Project, which proposed the creation of a floating sea city named Oceania, began in February '93, receiving nationwide publicity from *The Art Bell Show*, *Details* Magazine, *The Miami Herald*, *Boating* Magazine, and worldwide publicity in Canada, New Zealand, Hong Kong, England, and Belgium. The project ended due to lack of interest in April of 1994." How many people want to live in a floating artificial city-state anyway, however low the taxes and absent the regulations?[26]

With the perspective of three decades, *Reason*'s Poole now says, "Believing we'd be able to steal away with something that appeared to be unclaimed or engineer a libertarian revolt without massive external backing was very naive."[27] Erwin Strauss, who for more than a decade edited the libertarian amateur press association zine *Libertarian Connection* and is author of the only book-length account of new country ventures, has a realpolitik view on what libertarian new nation builders must do: "Holding onto sovereignty would require control of weapons of mass destruction. If other groups would realize [this], they could avoid a lot of wasted effort, by either settling down to the business of making or otherwise getting such weapons, or (more plausibly) by redirecting their efforts into shipboard communities under flags of convenience or into clandestine wilderness communities."[28]

"LET'S CALL KOCH'S BLUFF!"

The LP had been Ed Crane's party through most of the 1970s. Crane was an accomplished man with a professional vision for the LP who wasn't charmed for long by the peccadilloes and amateurism of many in the party—and he wasn't shy about letting them know it. He didn't worry about seeming imperious or damaging people's feelings while trying to realize his vision for what the party could accomplish. Even David Bergland, later on the opposite side of heated internal LP fights, grants that during the 1970s in the LP, "Everyone would say, 'Ed, what do we do next?' And they'd do it, and it would work out well."[29]

Crane was in retrospect unhappy with MacBride as presidential candidate in 1976. While MacBride was solid on libertarian principle, he didn't seem willing to master or talk about the policy minutia of the day that dominated campaign coverage. Although MacBride wanted to run again in 1980, by the end of 1978 he was aware that Crane and all Crane's supporters within the party, including by now Murray Rothbard, were against him. MacBride dropped out and threw his support behind a friend of his, New Hampshire state LP chair Bill Hunscher, an early computer industry worker.

The Crane team—soon to be known (and condemned) as the Crane Machine by their opponents in the party—had its own man ready: Ed Clark, a lawyer for the oil company Arco in Los Angeles. Clark was already a proven success in LP terms, one of the two superstars of 1978 for the six-year-old LP. The other was Alaskan Dick Randolph, who that year won the LP its first state congressional seat. Given Alaska's small population, Randolph was able to win with fewer than 6,000 votes. Alaska would see two other Libertarian Party state legislators in the 1980s, Ken Fanning and Andre Marrou. It has had none in that state since the 1980s.

The year 1978 was propitious for libertarians, especially in California. It was the year of Proposition 13, which succeeded in holding down state property taxes, and a general burgeoning middle-class tax revolt, a libertarian issue if ever there was one, though most of the prime movers in the Proposition 13 campaign were standard antitax populist right-wingers. The libertarian movement never figured out a way to attach themselves to the Prop. 13 movement successfully or even, as some hoped, pull an old-school communist-style takeover where they'd inject themselves into a mass movement they hadn't really assembled, one dedicated to separate goals, and subtly dominate it from the highest levels to shift the entire movement in their direction. They did join in it of course; as Roy Childs celebrated in his *Libertarian Review*, "here was a cause that [libertarianism] has *worked* for, a *libertarian* cause that had *won*. [Libertarians] had written and passed out leaflets, appeared at meetings, debated, asked questions in the public debates of others, came to rallies, spoken out on radio and television, manned literature tables, and campaigned for 13 in the streets."[30]

All that was true, but alert and cynical libertarians, through their glee, might have noticed that libertarians by no means dominated the coalition. The Clark gubernatorial campaign that year attempted the me-tooism of "Libertarians for Prop. 13" bumper stickers, and Prop. 13–inspired agitation on people's minds that year about overweening, overthieving government must have contributed to Clark's unprecedented (and so far unrepeated) win of over 5 percent of the California gubernatorial vote. In this off-year election, with the party only six years old, LP candidates won 1.2 million votes nationwide—and that's with twenty states having no LP candidates on the ballot at all.

Crane had cajoled Ed Clark, an early member of the New York LP who had relocated to California, into running for governor. Crane was pleased with the results. Even though Clark was not technically a Libertarian on the ballot—he was listed as an independent, for ballot access law reasons, but ran as a proud Libertarian—the LP had proven one of its boys could control the balance of power in one of America's biggest and most important states. They felt they were on a roll, possibly unstoppable. Crane was certain that 1980 was going to be a make-or-break year for the party.

Even before the Clark campaign, prospects for Crane and the LP had been buoyed by a portentous event, for them and the entire libertarian movement. MacBride had befriended a former LeFevre student at a Mont Pelerin Society meeting, a Kansas oil (and other things) baron named Charles Koch, of the Wichita Koch family. Father Fred had launched the family business, now known as Koch Industries, in 1927, developed techniques for squeezing more gasoline out of the oil refining process, and gotten involved in bitter patent wars with some of his domestic competitors. He went into business in Stalin's Russia for a while, where he built refineries, and was understandably shook up by what he learned about communism in practice. Fred Koch's translator was an old Bolshevik from prerevolutionary days who told the American businessman confidently that Soviet communism was the inevitable wave of the future, for the whole planet. Fred Koch knew he couldn't let that happen. He came back to America a fervent anticommunist and became a founding member of the John Birch Society and author of *A Businessman Looks at Communism*.[31]

Fred Koch raised his four boys in the catechism. "He was constantly speaking to us children about what was wrong with government and government policy," remembers David Koch. "It's something I grew up with—a fundamental point of view that big government was bad, and imposition of government controls on our lives and economic fortunes was not good."[32] The youngest Koch boys, the twins David and William, studied together at MIT in the early 1960s. They once threw an anti-Castro frat party/rally there, hanging a Castro effigy in military fatigues with a dagger thrust in its chest through the emblem: "Yankee sí, Castro no." With the exuberance of drunken Boston youth, it turned into a full-scale anticop riot, fires and all, when the police came by to brutally break it up.

David learned about more sophisticated ways of stopping communism than hanging Castro in effigy with the guidance of his older brother Charles, who became chairman of the family company. At Charles's insistence the brothers attended Robert LeFevre's Freedom School in the Colorado mountains in the mid-1960s. While Charles Koch's entrée into radical libertarian thought was through LeFevre, he has remained, one longtime associate says, intellectually curious and always searching for newer, better ways to understand, use, and spread libertarian ideas. Baldy Harper and the Institute for Humane Studies approach of supporting high-level scholarly research became his next obsession, and Charles Koch briefly became president of IHS when Baldy died from a heart attack in 1973, a week after a jarring car accident. Charles Koch remained the institute's prime financial mover throughout the 1970s and beyond.[33]

While dabbling in libertarian philanthropy through the Institute for Humane Studies, Charles was also growing the family company, turning it from a $250 million a year operation to a nearly $80 billion one. As of this writing it is the most valuable privately held company in America, after the company bought out Georgia Pacific in late 2005.[34] Charles and David are together at number 45 on the Forbes 400 for 2005, with a joint net value of $4.5 billion.

The LeFevre/Rampart College separatist approach—which dictated that a libertarian had nothing to do except try to ignore and avoid the state (but never fight it, not even through the ballot!)—no longer appealed to Charles. He began to support the Libertarian Party, though he says "I didn't have much illusion about the LP being a political force. But I didn't see any mechanism to get these ideas out in the political discussion; I didn't see anybody trying to apply them to deal with real policy issues. But I could see the LP *trying* to do that and I thought that was a worthwhile experiment."[35]

With the guidance of his ideological lieutenant through the 1970s, George Pearson, Koch money began financing and creating other experiments in libertarian education, including, most prominently, centers of Austrian economics education at mainstream universities, such as a program at NYU run by Israel Kirzner, who had received his Ph.D. under Mises.

Academic research and agitation for libertarianism was moving in the mid-1970s from other directions as well. Walter Grinder, an ally of Rothbard's, had with Walter Block been running a series of Libertarian Scholars Conferences where academics delivered papers of interdisciplinary libertarian-leaning scholarship. These conferences evolved into the Center for Libertarian Studies, an academic support organization launched in 1976 that gave research scholarships, continued the Libertarian Scholars Conferences series, and launched a Rothbard-edited *Journal of Libertarian Studies* as, among other things, a home to publish the papers delivered at the conferences.

A Grinder student and economics professor from Rutgers named Richard Fink, with Koch's support, launched an Austrian program that came to be called the Center for Study of Market Processes. It began at Rutgers and in 1980 relocated to George Mason University, where it has since evolved into the Mercatus Center. The Institute for Humane Studies itself relocated from California to George Mason in 1985, where it remains today.

It could doubtless be psychologically somewhat like leaping into a shark pit for Charles Koch, landing in the movement with his pockets so full and with some willingness to empty them, moving among these starving, eager ideological activists, most of whom thought they knew exactly how to turn Koch's billions (or at least the millions they *knew* he could spare) into a libertarian revolution. At an early Center for Libertarian Studies meeting, discussion of Koch's $10,000 offer of support degenerated into a hysterical bidding-up of the absent billionaire's support. "Let's call Koch's bluff!" one young economist gleefully hooted. It could seem almost comic, this sudden injection of enormous wealth into a small movement, this bizarre gravitational shifting as Planet Koch adjusted everyone's orbits, inclining them toward Wichita and then San Francisco which, with Ed Crane as Charles's new libertarian activism majordomo, became the center of Kochian libertarianism by the late 1970s.

Roy Childs, himself a recipient of Koch largess at *Libertarian Review* (a slick-covered, professional magazine of libertarian grappling with current events and culture that they funded and Childs edited in the late 1970s and early 1980s), noted that many in the movement came to treat Charles Koch as a walking wallet, to Koch's undoubted discomfort.[36] Charles Hamilton, founder of the left-libertarian publishing house Free Life Editions, who was briefly publisher of *Libertarian Review*, recalls that at his first meeting of that magazine's board, including Koch, they ate at McDonald's—and went Dutch. "It was a wonderful and no doubt conscious decision."[37]

The Kochs don't discuss their ideological giving too often or too deeply in public. In discussing how Koch philanthropy has jumped in and pulled out from various institutions and projects over the years, David Koch told me that "If we're going to give a lot of money, we'll make darn sure they spend it in a way that goes along with our intent. And if they make a wrong turn and start doing things we don't agree with, we withdraw funding. We do exert that kind of control."[38] They try to be conscious of effectiveness—admitting the difficulty of measuring effectiveness in a potentially centuries-long war of ideas.

"A failing of the libertarian movement," Charles Koch tells me from the perspective of three decades of pouring tens of millions of his dollars into it, "is that a lot of it has been slogans and unproven theories and hasn't been tested." This gap he hopes to fill with the rigorous development of an inchoate "science of liberty" that will develop answers as to what strategy is best to both sell and actuate liberty, the personal and institutional values that best comport with a free society, and the best means to make a transition from statism to freedom while causing minimal disruption and pain (some of which seems inevitable as systems that people have come to rely on begin to disappear).

Koch decided libertarians

> need an integrated strategy, vertically and horizontally integrated,
> to bring about social change, from idea creation to policy develop-
> ment to education to grassroots organizations to lobbying to litiga-
> tion to political action. The limit was talent—finding somebody
> who could take on some piece [of the overall strategy] and have
> some confidence they would make something of it. This is true in
> business as well—there will be more failures than successes and
> that's part of business. The best business philosophy is one of exper-
> imental discovery. We don't mind [failures]. It's just that when you
> have something that's not working, you have to cut your losses.[39]

In the late 1970s, the Koch largess, and the concentrated strategy
that was apparently behind its distribution, led to condemnation
(mostly from people not getting any of it) of what Sam Konkin
dubbed "the Kochtopus"—a supposedly strangling, controlling mon-
ster of multiple limbs. During the waning years of the 1970s, the new
libertarian policy think tank the Cato Institute, the Libertarian Party,
Students for a Libertarian Society, *Inquiry* magazine, and *Libertarian Review* were all largely Koch financed and/or "controlled" by people
who were.

One longtime Koch lieutenant characterized the overall strategy of
Koch's libertarian funding over the years with both a theatrical metaphor and an Austrian capital theory one: Politicians, ultimately, are just
actors playing out a script. The idea is, one gets better and quicker results aiming not at the actors but at the scriptwriters, to help supply
the themes and words for the scripts—to try to influence the areas
where policy ideas percolate from: academia and think tanks.[40] Ideas,
then, are the capital goods that go into building policy as a finished
product—and there are insufficient libertarian capital goods at the top
of the structure of production to build the policies libertarians demand. Support that the Kochs have given to, for example, a think tank
such as the Cato Institute or an organization that finds and supports
young academics, such as the Institute for Humane Studies, is a means
to increase the amount of libertarian capital goods in order to create
more of the ultimate political consumer good of libertarian policy.

"WE MANAGED TO ALIENATE A BUNCH OF PEOPLE ON THE RIGHT UNNECESSARILY."

After the MacBride campaign, a discouraged and going-broke Crane had initially planned on leaving the LP and returning to a full-time investment gig in his beloved San Francisco. Charles Koch, Crane recalls, asked him what it would take to keep him doing libertarian movement work full-time. While not yet completely discouraged by the LP, Crane thought the libertarian movement needed alternate institutions, if only as suppliers and marketers of ideas for the political party. He suggested to Koch that a full-service libertarian think tank would be a grand idea—not an above-the-political-fray educational institute such as Leonard Read's FEE, but an in-the-debate public policy house. He suggested it be located in San Francisco, partially for libertarian symbolism (this was not to be a traditional think tank scratching the belly of the Washington beast) and partially because that's where Crane wanted to live. The think tank was named, at Murray Rothbard's urging, the Cato Institute, after the series of early-eighteenth-century British pamphlets popular among American revolutionaries, known as "Cato's Letters," which advocated a strictly limited, natural rights–respecting government. The Cato Institute began operations in early 1977.

Cato in its earliest days had a mixed personality; it tried to unify under one institutional roof Koch's academic interests, Crane's public policy interests, and the interest of Rothbard's latest ideological best friend Williamson "Bill" Evers (a former libertarian student radical at Stanford in the late 1960s and early 1970s and former editor of *LP News*) in a libertarian intellectual magazine that could appeal to the left, while still working around Crane's continuing preoccupation with the LP up to and through the 1980 presidential election.

Bill Evers helped convince Koch and Crane that ideological magazines were vital in spreading unusual ideas and injecting them into the general intellectual conversation. Where would modern liberalism be without the *New Republic*, or conservatism without *National Review*? *Reason* was then the only prominent national libertarian magazine, but it was outside Cato control; they wanted their own magazine to play with. Koch made a play at buying the *Nation*, with Leonard Liggio supplying a proposal stressing the magazine's nineteenth-century

classical liberal heritage. Contemplating their benefactors' amazing resources, some joked around the Cato complex: Why didn't Koch just
buy *the nation*—that is, the whole country.

Evers became founding editor of the magazine Cato launched instead, *Inquiry*. It was meant to appeal to leftists and progressives who
might be amenable to libertarian thinking if they weren't slapped in
the face with words such as *capitalism* and *libertarianism*. Evers was optimistic: "We actually thought that somehow out of the breakdown of
legitimacy in government in Vietnam and Watergate, and that young
people seemed to be sympathetic to some libertarian basics, plus the
fact that our ideals were compatible with industrial civilization and
American political traditions, that we had a good shot at shaping the
future of the country."[41]

With Ralph Raico editing the back of the book, and no flag-waving
for the term *libertarian*, the magazine for a few years was an attractive
and well-written collection of pro-peace, pro–civil liberties, yet also
pro-market reporting and commentary that achieved Evers's goal in at
least one sense—it was meant not so much to seem leftist, but to be the
sort of publication "a liberal intellectual could pick up and not feel like,
'I can't even relate to the world these people are in.'"[42] It succeeded at
this, attracting regular contributions from the likes of Anthony Burgess
(in the book review section) and Noam Chomsky.

In retrospect, Crane is no longer confident that this deliberate outreach to liberals and the left was the right move for the libertarian
movement. (Though he thought so at the time—in 1978 he said that
"if libertarianism is going to succeed as a political movement in this
country . . . we're going to have to attract support from the left. . . . I
view that leftward drift of the movement as very helpful."[43]) But with
Inquiry, he now concludes, "We managed to alienate a bunch of people
on the right unnecessarily. But it helped create a distinctive image for
libertarianism."[44]

That they succeeded in distancing Cato from the right is exhibited
vividly by the publicity given this young think tank and the libertarian
movement it was rapidly seen as central to in a 1979 cover story in
Buckley's *National Review,* playing its usual role as enforcer of ideological orthodoxy, patrolling the acceptable borders of limiting the state.
Using Rothbard as a stick with which to beat Cato and the libertarian

movement, a cover story by Ernest van den Haag and Lawrence Cott slammed them as a gaggle of soft-on-communism antinomian rebels who'd as soon tear down the pillars of Western civilization around all of our heads as read a book by Mises or Hazlitt.[45] Libertarians were apt to respond that they have no problem with tradition, as long as it isn't propped up by the violence of the state.

Crane still has a framed copy of that issue of *National Review*, with its Cato mailing address, hanging in his office.

"We at the Kochtopus have been too purist, narrow, and dogmatic."

Within a couple of years, the Cato Institute would shed the influence that caused *National Review*'s intemperate attack.

Rothbard, his nose ever sniffing out the stink of softness in his comrades' libertarian hard-core, became disenchanted with his new allies and supporters, Crane and Koch. They had brought Rothbard out to San Francisco, paid him to write a history of the Progressive movement from a libertarian perspective, and provided a home for his shorter writings in both *Inquiry* and *Libertarian Review* (not technically a Cato publication, but the Libertarian Review Foundation was another Koch-funded operation, working out of offices down the street from Cato's and *Inquiry*'s in San Francisco, a hub of professional libertarian activity and tomfoolery remembered fondly and wistfully by the young libertarians who got the chance to work in it). Cato in the beginning was pushing Rothbardian libertarianism, including an interest, which went away quickly, in war revisionism. They were Austrians, they were war revisionists, they provided an institutional home for anarchists. Though not officially and institutionally across-the-board anarchist, it was certainly a warm home for Rothbard and Rothbardians.

The first major danger sign Rothbard detected at Cato was the hiring of an economist who was not a 100 percent Austrian, but rather a Chicago School libertarian, David Henderson, later editor of the *Fortune Encyclopedia of Economics*. As sympathetic to the Austrian approach as Crane was, he found them wanting as policy analysts. "They are so a priori, they aren't into learning facts. They can be great scholars, but aren't so good at public policy because that stuff bores them to tears. Chicago guys are curious" about government policy and number manipulations. "Austrians don't believe in it, and I don't for the most part either, but it works."[46]

Crane had seemed the sort of man Rothbard had always dreamed would come along. For the past twenty years Rothbard had tried to create a vibrant libertarian movement to ensure that such a man would have a cadre to work with and a set of well-articulated ideas to embrace: a competent, energetic, accomplished hard-core libertarian with real-world business success and acumen, capable of building and maintaining libertarian institutions. Whatever the facts about the rest of Crane's qualities, Rothbard decided that the "hard-core" part was sadly no longer true.[47]

The Clark for president campaign in 1980 fractured the mighty Kochtopus. It was going so well at first. The campaign season started with a professional convention in 1979 built around the theme "toward a three-party system." Crane and Rothbard beat back through intraparty machinations the wishes of many of the LP's National Committee—the "space cadet" faction, Rothbard and Crane dubbed them—to dedicate most of the programming to popular libertarian preoccupations with science fiction and futurism. The Crane team thought it would be a crippling PR blow if that were the image the LP presented to the national media that they prayed would be paying attention.[48] Liberal columnist Nicholas Von Hoffman of the *Washington Post* was an enthusiastic Clark fan, and Clark's press clips were piling up triple and more what MacBride's campaign had achieved. The LP's distinctive neither-left-nor-right policy mix, with some of the best elements of both, seemed zesty, attractive, and worth noting to many columnists.

The Clark campaign was also buoyed by the tactically brilliant move of making an end run around FECA by naming David Koch the vice presidential candidate; this allowed him to spend unlimited amounts of his immense personal wealth on his own campaign, and this made for the best-financed LP presidential campaign ever, with $3.5 million spent (over $2 million of it David Koch's money). Clark even played in Peoria, with an endorsement from the *Peoria Journal Star.*

The establishment *Washington Post* wrote admiringly of his noninterventionist foreign policy: Clark "thought through foreign policy and fitted ends . . . to means. . . . Not for him the asserting of ambitious purposes that the country cannot in fact uphold, nor the spending of resources for which no reasonable policy goal can be framed. This is a model of discipline that ought to be demanded of all the candidates."

But in the spring of 1980, the momentum and enthusiasm regarding Clark's chances ended for those watching the augurs with a realistic and balanced eye, even if some uplifting news kept trickling in. Centrist Republican John Anderson offered himself up as a lightning rod for the dissatisfaction with the two major party options that had been clouding and sparking the political culture, dissatisfaction Clark might otherwise have benefited from. "It wasn't so much that we thought Anderson would steal our voters, but he did steal any cultural or media cachet or steam as the only other serious option on all fifty ballots," recalls David Boaz, currently executive vice president at Cato, who was then a former editor of YAF's *New Guard* magazine writing position papers and campaign books for the Clark campaign, and accompanying the candidate on the road.

Still, Clark did extraordinarily well for a third-party candidate with a radical ideology, though Rothbard and his friends in the LP's radical caucus thought that an attempt to make Clark seem more understandable and palatable to the masses by framing his libertarianism as "low-tax liberalism" was a grotesque sellout of libertarian principles. Clark won 921,000 votes, over 1 percent of the total, more than any LP candidate before—or since. Except for investment guru and former Galambosian Harry Browne, who in 1996 got a smidgen more than half that, it was more than *twice* as well as the LP ever did before or since. But despite the hot vote total, Clark's performance on the campaign trail left many longtime libertarian activists cold. For example, what radical could cheer Clark's *Nightline* appearance in which he said, "We want to get back immediately to the kind of government that President Kennedy had back in the early 1960s, which I think was much more benevolent . . . had much lower inflation, much higher growth rates, much lower levels of taxes."[49]

Rothbard was detecting what he perceived as the stench of deviationism around the Koch properties even before Clark's perceived perfidy. Roy Childs at *Libertarian Review* and Milton Mueller, of the Koch-financed campus group Students for a Libertarian Society (SLS), thought it would be a good idea for the libertarian movement to be explicitly antinuclear, in the year of the Three Mile Island scare and the film *The China Syndrome*. It was a properly libertarian stance, they insisted, since nuclear power wouldn't exist without state subsidies. Rothbard thought this a daft outreach to a rabidly antitechnology, anticapitalist left.[50]

Many other libertarians thought Rothbard was indulging in counterproductive sectarian sniping at his Kochtopus associates. Rothbard's constant heresy hunting, combined with a libertianism so radical it alienated many of the people and institutions that self-identified as libertarian, made him a controversial and much-condemned figure as his centrality to the movement waned. For his part, he claimed his pugnaciousness was a defense of principles, insisting that the Koch-funded groups and the Clark campaign were selling out libertarian purity in their attempt to appeal to a wider constituency. Rothbard had written as early as May 1979 to an LP comrade:

> I've concluded that what is happening is a paradigm shift in all parts of the "Kochtopus" . . . although they of course would put the same content in different value-laden terms. The basic paradigm shift—supported by Koch, Crane, and Childs, though who thought it up first is difficult to know—runs as follows: that we at the Kochtopus have been too purist, narrow, and dogmatic, and therefore have been alienating and turning away various forms of support, from people and votes to business contributions of money. What should be done instead is to broaden our base, include non-purists . . . to soft-soap our opposition, gain control of the bureaucracy, and do what we want. Koch explicitly wants to run the movement like a corporation, where orders are given, dissidents are fired, etc. Crane ditto.

To Rothbard, this was all "sliding down the slippery slope to opportunism and sellout of libertarian principle."[51]

And Rothbard's Lenin-inspired devotion to the importance of cadre in a revolutionary idological movement—a devotion not much shared among contemporary libertarian institutions—led him to object to growth in party membership if it outpaced cadre education. "For if . . . cadre . . . principled and knowledgeable activists—is not fostered, nourished, and intensified, then that cadre will inevitably be spread more and more thin in proportion to the growing number of LP members, voters, and sympathizers. In short, as their number of voters and members grows, and the cadre gets weaker and certainly not larger, the vital cadre/member or cadre/voter ratio will inevitably fall—which will spell disaster for the LP as an instrument for the achievement of liberty."[52]

Rothbard thought Crane's strategy was to soft-pedal the more radical implications of libertarianism just to win a wider range of allies and voters. Rothbard insisted, contrarily, that the LP "must have the principle and the courage to be *radical*—to hold high the banner of libertarian principle, to urge the principles as well as the detailed political applications in our great platform, to call for dramatic and radical advances toward these principles, and . . . to state our case boldly, clearly, and dramatically."[53] The war between these two approaches has continued in the LP to this day.

After tense months of backroom feuding Rothbard finally declared open war on his funders and coworkers. He dedicated an entire issue of his *Libertarian Forum* to delineating what he saw as Clark/Crane sellouts of libertarian principle on everything from taxes to welfare to the draft to immigration (where Rothbard attacked Clark for taking a position he later took himself, against open-border immigration). The pugnacious Rothbard was especially incensed that "in the Clark campaign there *were no* Bad Guys. . . . There will be no pain for anyone, not even briefly, as we all march into the new dawn. . . . But of course that is all pap and nonsense. The advent of liberty will immeasurably benefit most Americans. But some will lose—those who have been exploiting us and feeding at the public trough. And these special interests and ruling elites will not surrender their ill-gotten gains so readily. They will fight like hell to keep it. Libertarianism is not a message of treacle and Camelot; it is a message of struggle."[54]

Rothbard's fulminations against the Kochtopus increased after he was fired from Cato in March 1981, and his shares as a founder of the Institute taken from him (illegally, he insisted).[55] He declared rhetorical war on the Koch/Crane axis, mostly in the pages of his own *Libertarian Forum* and in the LP radical caucus newsletter *Libertarian Vanguard*.

The radical caucus was mostly an alliance between Rothbard and Evers and some younger firebrands from the LP/Students for a Libertarian Society complex, Eric Garris and Justin Raimondo. Raimondo adored flamboyant radical gestures, including his gay rights pamphlet *In Praise of Outlaws* that featured burning police cars on the cover and argued in very strong terms that the state is always and everywhere the enemy of gays, using the short sentence Dan White received for the murder of fellow city official, the openly gay Harvey Milk, in San Francisco as a hook. "We did some pretty absurd things, ultra-left things," in those days, some "I won't even go into out of fear of being terminally embarrassed," Raimondo now says.[56]

Students for a Libertarian Society, the stern Raimondo, mindful of revolutionary discipline, tut-tutted, was drunk on the easy Koch money, printing thousands of copies of newspapers without considering who wanted them, dumping entire bundles on campuses for uncaring audiences. And that wasn't their only bourgeois excess: "They'd have catered food at meetings," Raimondo frowns. "I thought, 'Catered food? *Comrades!*'"[57]

"NEVER AGAIN CLARK. NEVER AGAIN CRANE."

Although the LP was coming off an extraordinary success by its own standards, the four years after 1980 saw it suffering a hangover from the debt the expensive campaign left it in, despite the influx of David Koch money, and it was roiled by fights between a coalition of everyone else versus the "Crane machine."

The reasons why everyone ganged up on the Crane crew, who had gotten the LP on the ballot in all fifty states and won it a vote total twice as high as the party would ever again earn, even while fighting against a well-known third-party candidate and a Republican candidate, Ronald Reagan, whose rhetoric was as libertarian as any Republican's during the LP's existence, seem difficult to discern with twenty-five years hindsight. LP founder David Nolan recalls feeling like the Crane crew treated anyone outside their immediate circle with great disrespect, alienating the rank and file and leading them to mistrust Crane and his team.

Rothbard managed to get various other forces within the LP, including Nolan and *Reason* editor Robert Poole, to join a "coalition for a party of principle." Its principle? "Never again Clark. Never again Crane." As with many tempests in teapots among small, contentious, ideologically charged groups with a sense of millennial mission, it is hard for outsiders with the perspective of time to figure out what they were thinking, and why, and everyone involved can only remember that their side was right, and the other side wrong, with the most uncharitable possible spin put on the whole contretemps.

The Crane machine was painted as the arrogant central controller selling out libertarian principle; its opponents were painted as whiners and obstructers driven by an irrational desire to tear down, destroy, or stymie the doers from accomplishing anything.[58] One Crane machiner had a sympathetic explanation for his enemies' attitudes:"Ed, in his career as essentially a political organizer, of great talent I must say, had of course alienated a lot of people. He tends to be quick-tempered and, in a way, authoritarian in his own style. And so he had cast some people out into the outer darkness, and they never forgave him. Really, when you think about it, why should they?"[59]

A Crane machine associate, Eric O'Keefe, became national director of the LP in 1981, after a potential competitor, Gale Norton, who later became secretary of the interior under President George W. Bush, dropped out of the race."I'm sure she's pretty happy with her choice," O'Keefe says."Don't know if I'd say the same."[60]

Even the Clarks turned on their former close associate Crane.[61] Clark's wife Alicia, the LP's national chair from 1981 to 1983, fired O'Keefe with no warning in the middle of a National Committee meeting in 1982 (she already had her proposed replacement changing the locks back in D.C. while the unsuspecting O'Keefe attended the NatCom meeting) and moved the LP's national headquarters from D.C., the center of Crane influence as the new home of his Cato Institute (which he had reluctantly moved from San Francisco for practical reasons), to Houston, where her handpicked new national director, Honey Lanham, lived. (The party's headquarters moved back to D.C. in the late 1980s.)

Gearing up for the presidential nominating convention for the 1984 election, a libertarian radio talk show host from Orlando, Gene Burns, was the only announced candidate whom all factions seemed willing to countenance. However, the more Burns learned about the actual resources and capabilities of the party, the less thrilled he was at the thought of throwing away a year of his life and dropped out of the race only weeks before the convention.[62]

All factions leapt into the scrum. Two candidates rolled into the convention with juice behind them. From the Crane machine was Earl Ravenal of the Cato board of directors, a foreign policy intellectual of real-world heft—a former Robert McNamara golden boy. Finally! A candidate with genuine establishment cred, if not candidate polish; Ravenal was hard of hearing and tended to stammer. Lacking much hard-core movement background, he was sniffed at by many LPers as a blank slate who couldn't be counted on to take the hard-core line enthusiastically. The Crane machine took advantage of loose delegation seating requirements to cram the convention floor with ringers; women who had never seen snow were suddenly delegates from Alaska, and Austrian economist Mario Rizzo showed a sudden interest in the LP he never had before, or since.

Rothbard and his coalition for a party of principle determined that the most vital strategic imperative was defeating anyone Crane backed. They unified behind old-time LPer David Bergland, MacBride's vice presidential candidate in 1976 and LP national chair from 1977 to 1981. More conspiratorial-minded libertarians were concerned that Ravenal's Council on Foreign Relations membership signaled a possible Rockefeller wedge into the libertarian movement. But it's just a *professional* organization, Ravenal insisted.

The Crane faction scoffed at Bergland—just a party apparatchik lightweight, no equal to the respectable Georgetown professor and foreign policy establishment player Ravenal. During a candidate debate, one old Crane machiner remembers, Ravenal revealed a weakness that alarmed the party's hard-core: He *endorsed* compulsory vaccination.

Bergland won the nomination, getting a bare majority by one vote. Along the way, in a moment of bitter betrayal that reportedly drew tears from Bill Evers, Justin Raimondo and Eric Garris of the radical caucus, which was supposed to be united behind Bergland and against the Crane machine, allowed themselves to be bowled over by Ravenal's foreign policy acumen and potential for respect from D.C. insiders and voted for him. The radical caucus was rent asunder.

More fateful for the LP was the fact that Crane and his crew, along with the Kochs and all their money, departed the LP after their candidate lost, never to return. Despite an earlier all-factions accord for postnomination solidarity, party unity was an instant corpse. Most of the Crane machine leaders and hard-core rank and file walked out as soon as the nomination was over, not even sticking around for the postelection banquet. (Ravenal, known as "Earl the Pearl" to fans and doubters alike, politely stayed.)

Sore losers, Bergland sneered. The Crane crew always thought they were a lot smarter than the LP rank and file. "So if they lost, it couldn't be because they weren't as smart as they think they are, but because most libertarian are stupid bastards," Bergland figures the thinking went. Bergland recalls passions against him from the Crane faction so severe that a Crane machine woman at a party shortly after he won the nomination got so angry and upset at the sight of Bergland that she retreated to the bathroom to vomit in rage.

That wasn't the only slight. Roger MacBride, Bergland recalls, wrote to the archivist at the University of Virginia to whom he had entrusted his LP-related papers and advised him to throw it all away; the party was a dead letter with Bergland at the helm.[63] Crane and his pals tried briefly to make common cause with John Anderson, their nemesis from the last election. Because of his 1980 run, he could technically be considered a political party and had millions in potential federal funds waiting if he chose to launch another campaign. Crane recalls that they had almost talked him into bringing the anti-Bergland LPers on board for a "national unity" run, "but his advisers talked him out of it at the last minute."[64]

Not even knowing he was going to seek the nomination until a week earlier, Bergland didn't have much in the way of a team or a plan or money lined up. Lacking Koch money, the campaign lived down to its detractors' grimmest fears, throttling down any post-Clark momentum for the LP and ending up with 228,000 votes. (Still, it *was* the first year that the LP candidate actually came in third.) However, 1984 was a year for outclassed political underdogs, which Bergland would point out to reporters who asked the traditional third-party candidate question—why run when you must know you have no chance to win? "Why don't you ask Mondale that?"

The party was feeling the ill effects of the faction fights that followed the Clark campaign. As one Crane machiner put it acidly, "The Clark campaign, *we* ran without *them*. The Bergland campaign, *they* ran without *us*. The results are some evidence of the difference."

The post-Bergland hangover led to a few dispiriting years for the party, with convention attendance low, debts high, a revolving door for national chairs, the *LP News* not appearing for months at a time, and a general malaise that Rothbard characteristically analyzed in Austrian economic terms: Koch money created an inflationary bubble in the LP's fortunes, and they were living through the inevitable recession that follows inflationary booms.

"THERE IS ONLY ONE POSITION IN THE UNITED STATES WHERE WE ARE WANTED, AND YOU GOT IT."

The Austrian school of economics approach that informed that metaphor remained a central inspiration and spine for libertarian understanding of the dangers of state interventionism. It too was expanding in influence and support during the 1970s. Mises had died in 1973. His three most prominent American acolytes were Murray Rothbard (never an official student at NYU, merely a seminar attendee), Hans Sennholz, and Israel Kirzner. When it came to extending the Misesian tradition, Sennholz served as apostle to generations of eager undergrads at a good Christian college. Rothbard's colorful career as a political activist and polemicist took him in different directions, as the apostle to the libertarians (and the new left, and eventually the paleoconservatives, who rejected his counsel). But the quiet, scholarly Israel Kirzner was the apostle to the professional economists, and he built up the first respected stronghold for the Austrian tradition within American academia, at Mises's NYU itself.

Sennholz, after a year teaching at Iona College in New Rochelle, New York, had impressed FEE board member J. Howard Pew, who in 1956 granted him chairmanship of the Economics Department at Grove City College in Pennsylvania, of which Pew was chairman of the board and a major funder.

"I'd go to Mises and complain of being stuck in the hinterlands of Pennsylvania," Sennholz recalls. "When I'd express my unhappiness, he always told me, 'Be happy, be satisfied. There is only one position in the United States where we are wanted, and you got it.'"[65]

While Sennholz made no great theoretical or scholarly contributions to the Austrian cause, he was the teacher who directly influenced the largest number of students toward a passion for Austrian economics and libertarianism, and the connection between the two. Many dozens of them have some role in libertarian or conservative activism or promotion or scholarship now. Most who dealt with him have a Hans Sennholz story to tell, often with a head-shaking combination of admiration and exasperation. One former student, who now works for a libertarian legal defense foundation, recalls how his students often asked Sennholz why, with his strongly held political views and obvious love of expounding upon them, he never chose to run for office. "Oh sure," he would say in his thick German accent, "I can see some United States veteran with an injured or missing arm come to me at a speech crying, 'Did you do this? Did you do this?!'"

Peter Boettke, an Austrian economics professor at George Mason University and editor of the most thorough guidebook to modern Austrian economics, *The Elgar Companion to Austrian Economics*, was a Sennholz student almost by accident (all Boettke really cared about was basketball), but Sennholz's fervor changed his life.

"Sennholz could get you hyped up on your ability to walk through fire for the truth," Boettke remembers. "He doesn't reach you with the technical aspects, but with the ideological aspects. Sennholz explained the welfare state as this giant circle with all of our hands in our neighbors' pockets. This lecture was 15 years ago and I can still remember it.

How many people with one lecture 15 years ago can make you still remember that lecture? That's the kind of guy Sennholz is."[66]

Israel Kirzner was born in England in 1930, moving at age ten to South Africa where he studied at the University of Capetown. He moved to the United States and got his bachelor's from Brooklyn College, and went on to NYU with the intention of getting an MBA and becoming an accountant. He knew nothing about Mises, except that he seemed to be one of the better published faculty members, and that made him attend Mises's courses and seminar. He became enamored of the old Austrian and his style of economics, and eventually pursued his Ph.D. under Mises. Kirzner nabbed a tenure track faculty position with NYU in September 1957, and continued attending Mises's seminar and serving as his assistant.

For years, Kirzner was the lone Misesian at NYU. He was teaching standard courses, not Austrianism, though "I would inject points where I disagreed with mainstream approaches and theory, and in those courses a handful of people interested in Austrian economics would join me."

Right after Mises's death in 1973, "the idea came up of trying to develop some [larger program] for Austrians. I'd get occasional correspondence, students would write me and I'd have to write back and say there was no place really where one could study Austrian economics, certainly not on the graduate level. But as interest grew, I was able to find enough funding to bring Ludwig Lachmann in as a visiting research professor. We got one or two students in a graduate program. Walter Grinder, a Sennholz student, came and took some courses with me. Gradually, in that fashion, it came to be felt there might be potential at NYU for some sort of program."[67]

Ludwig Lachmann went way back with Austrianism. He had been a colleague of Hayek's at the London School of Economics in the 1930s during the great debates with Keynes. (See Chapter 2.) Lachmann wrote a major book extending Austrian capital theory in 1956, *Capital and Its Structure*. He was the most heterodox of the major Austrian figures, politically and methodologically. He became enamored of the work of neo-Keynesian G. L. S. Shackle, who emphasized the subjectivity of expectations—that humans do not have enough knowledge of the future to have anything close to a defined set of expectations, or even probable expectations, about it from which to choose. Lachmann, who found subjectivism the most attractive aspect of Austrianism, considered this the next important step after the early Austrian subjectivization of value.

His belief in subjectivity of expectations led Lachmann to see the free market process as even more chaotic than did the staunchly antiequilibrium standard Misesians, who at least believed that a tendency toward a final equilibrium could be assumed. But if varying human expectations can never be expected to match, this made the market process even more "kaleidic"—a favorite term of Lachmann's, connoting the constantly shifting chaos of a kaleidoscope. Austrians tended to emphasize market processes (to the extent that use of the phrase "market process" became a code word of sorts for Austrianism) versus the equilibrium structures that so fascinate mainstream mathematical economics. Austrians stressed the fact that the circumstances and facts and values that shape the economy are constantly changing and can't be profitably analyzed as if they had achieved, or could be expected to actually achieve, an equilibrium state of completed perfection. Austrians in the Misesian tradition tend to occupy a middle ground between the neoclassical conception of markets that are, or ought to be, always in equilibrium and the Shacklean notion that they are always kaleidic—a chaotic mess of sorts.[68]

Kirzner's economics focuses on the entrepreneur, who can be any and all of us trying to make the world conform to our hopes and expectations. Humans look for opportunities for profit, places where people haven't yet realized they can buy low and sell high. The market's endless grindings tend toward the elimination of profit; one person's profiting alerts others to the fact that they can do the same. Eventually, through competition, profit disappears.

In theory, that is. In reality the world is changing so much, so rapidly, that profit never fully disappears. New opportunities for entrepreneurs to make money by noticing things that others haven't noticed always come along. In profiting, as per Adam Smith's invisible hand and Bastiat's notion of "social harmonies," the entrepreneurs not only satisfy themselves but also help bring other people what they want. In economists' lingo, entrepreneurs help the world move toward an equilibrium where everyone has what they want and no one need trade any more.

The entrepreneur in the free market acts to bring the economy toward that equilibrium, Kirzner theorized, while recognizing that the process doesn't ever reach an end. Lachmann tends to be skeptical that equilibrium is even approached. He emphasized entrepreneurial *error*—entrepreneurs can be and, Lachmann maintains, are apt to be mistaken in their decisions about what to make, do, and sell to make a profit. They might, through their screw-ups, be as apt to divert the market process away from equilibrium as to lead to it.

That's why Lachmann is the least libertarian of Austrians. In the face of human ignorance and mistakes, he sees no inherent problem with a government agency attempting—though he knows full well the attempt can't work perfectly—to coordinate and spread useful information through the industrial economy.[69] In the face of the almost nihilistic uncertainty about economic knowledge that Lachmann toys with, one of the many things we can no longer be sure of is that the free market will lead to outcomes that are necessarily preferable to government intervention.[70]

Still, even the Lachmannian kaleidic vision of the economy has its libertarian implications, as Lachmann recognized: "The extreme complexity of such a world . . . defies all facile generalizations. What chances of success . . . all attempts at 'social planning' that are based on such facile generalizations are likely to have is one of the melancholy reflections . . . the student of economics cannot eschew."[71]

Kirzner similarly has never been a political firebrand, eschewing political activism and any writing on particularly political issues. Still, his emphasis on the entrepreneur's role in discovering relevant and useful information has its libertarian political implications. Kirzner's entrepreneur is most effective at finding profit opportunities (which are ultimately opportunities to satisfy others) through chance learning in a free economy, of a sort that by its very nature could not be figured out in advance by government planners who think they could "rationalize" the process of economic progress. Free markets thus generate the greatest quantity of profit generating and consumer-satisfying entrepreneurial action.[72]

"IN YOUR FACE WITH THE AUSTRIAN ECONOMICS."

Before Kirzner, with Lachmann, could begin a new, vibrant Austrian program at NYU in the late 1970s, the founding event of the modern Austrian revival occurred: a conference dedicated to Austrianism at South Royalton, Vermont, put together under the auspices of the Institute for Humane Studies, using money supplied by the Kochs.

Kirzner, Lachmann, and Rothbard were the leaders. Kirzner, who helped IHS man and Koch lieutenant George Pearson put the conference together, recalls that there was some debate whether to use the term "Austrian economics" for the conference. "Ex post, the name given to it had a great deal to do with the subsequent resurgence. But if you think back to the early 1970s, it's not at all clear that there was still an Austrian economics in existence. Most historians would have said it petered out decades earlier. It wasn't clear that calling it 'Austrian' was the best marketing move."[73]

Karen Vaughn, in her history of the Austrian economics movement in America, isn't very charitable to the spirit of Royalton, though she grants its historical importance. The problem at the conference, as she saw it, was "a widespread attitude . . . that Austrian economics was a completed project that had to be learned from the masters, taught to students, and communicated, it was hoped, to a misguided economics profession. For a large subset of the participants at South Royalton, the relevant question for discussion was not so much 'What does all this imply that we don't yet understand?' as it was, 'What did Mises say about this?'"[74] Vaughn also looks askance at the lack of respect and attention showed to Hayek at the conference, which she blames on Rothbard's influence. (Hayek had previous responsibilities in Europe that prevented him from attending.) Milton Friedman, who summered nearby, showed up at the conference, where he dropped a famous Chicago School v. Austrian School epigram on the assembled Austrians: "There is no Austrian economics—only good economics and bad economics."[75]

The Royalton conference is remembered fondly and wistfully, but also somewhat incredulously. The location, as Richard Ebeling remembers it, was a strange sort of ghost town, with bizarre accommodations.

The room I'm in, the floor has a slant in it, the bed is under the window, and I virtually had to hold on to the frame of the bed so as not to roll out the window every night. Sudha Shenoy came down and said that something horrific had happened in the shower, but it could not be repeated in mixed company. After a certain hour of the day, in the evening, the telephones didn't work. You could not call out. Rothbard tried to persuade us all that this was some type of a plot, so that all these Austro-libertarians could not escape. And at night, if you went beyond a certain perimeter of the town, you'd hear barking dogs, like guard dogs to keep you in. One evening when Murray was waxing eloquent on this conspiracy theory of the concentration camp for all the Austro-libertarians here, Steve Pejovich came down the next morning, and someone asked, "Well, how'd you sleep last night?" He says, "Well, I lived under the Nazis. I endured the Communists," since he'd lived in Yugoslavia. "Last night, for the first time in my life, I slept with a light on."[76]

South Royalton was only the beginning of the modern Austrian revival. Over the next two years IHS sponsored more conferences, out of which arose more books; and more voices beyond those of Rothbard, Kirzner, and Lachmann were added to the Austrian choir. By 1982, the Federal Reserve Bank branch in Atlanta was asking Kirzner at NYU to help them find an Austrian economist to hire as an analyst.

By 1983, the previously skeptical Hayek told Kirzner that, as Kirzner recalled, "once [Hayek] had asserted that a continuation of the Austrian school was neither necessary nor possible. It was not needed because the mainstream had absorbed so much Austrian Economics; it was not possible because there was no one to carry on the Austrian school. Now, Hayek continued, he wished to publicly retract the earlier statement. He was, he said, no longer as optimistic about mainstream economics, nor as pessimistic about the Austrian school. In fact, he continued, the Austrian School is today 'alive and kicking,' it is 'domiciled in the United States.'"[77]

A second collection of Austrian conference papers, *New Directions in Austrian Economics,* edited by Louis Spadaro (another of Mises's small set of Ph.D. students), set forth a challenge for Austrians that has still not been fully met. Spadaro accused his colleagues of spending too much time correcting what they saw as errors in the mainstream neo-classical consensus, and not enough time extending their own approach in new directions. In laying out a challenge for more focus on the way business organizations actually run, and on helping students through academia, his essay set the agenda for the approach taken by various Koch-funded libertarian organizations in the 1980s, particularly IHS and the Center for the Study of Market Processes, now called the Mercatus Center.[78]

By 1978, Kirzner with Lachmann felt he had carved a distinctly Austrian niche at NYU, one bigger than just the two of them. They added a third Austrian faculty member, Mario Rizzo, out of the University of Chicago's graduate program. Rizzo remains the only other Austrian besides Kirzner at NYU who ever managed to win tenure.

Rizzo was first attracted to NYU with a postdoctoral fellowship offer from Kirzner in 1976, as Kirzner was beginning to gather funds, mostly from the Kochs, to expand the Austrian presence at NYU.[79] Rizzo nabbed an assistant professorship there in 1978. Other young Austrians, such as Gerald O'Driscoll, Lawrence White, and Peter Boettke, also came to teach at NYU but failed to get tenure. Nearly thirty years after Kirzner began his attempt to fashion an Austrian stronghold at NYU, only he and Rizzo have firm positions. (Kirzner has now retired from active teaching.)

Austrianism's fate at NYU, its first institutional home in America, is a reflection of its marginalization within the economics profession at large. Rizzo thinks that the Department of Economics "is positively hostile to the Austrian presence. They've always been hostile. Why I got tenure I'm not sure. In the early '80s perhaps the school recognized we did something that got them some attention that was valuable, so they were more ambivalent then. Now the hostility has strengthened since the department has become so highly ranked along conventional lines that they see no need to indulge us. Back then, while they didn't like us, they didn't want to screw the program entirely. That's probably why I got tenure. Now there's no interest in what we are doing at all. The only reason we're here is, we're here."[80]

Random Austrians teach at various colleges, and more all the time, but not in significant concentrations. West Virginia University and San Jose State in California are two schools with a newer active Austrian presence. Auburn University is home of the Rothbard-centric Ludwig von Mises Institute, though it has few Austrian economists actually on its faculty. (Its summer seminars gather students from all over the country interested in Austrianism for independent teaching, study, and research, a valuable service to many newer young professors teaching in the Austrian tradition.) George Mason University, home of various Koch-financed operations such as the Institute for Humane Studies and the Mercatus Center, has the most consciously and radically free market economics department in the country; it had in the past been chaired by black libertarian economist and political columnist (and sometimes guest host for Rush Limbaugh) Walter Williams, and is now run by another Austrian, Donald Boudreaux, who briefly ran FEE in the late 1990s and is conscious of keeping the program free-market solid.

Peter Boettke was a product of the Koch/George Mason machine in the 1980s, as were many other young Austrians such as Tyler Cowen (who now runs Mercatus and writes a monthly economics column for the *New York Times*), David Prychitko, and Roy Cordato. Boettke remembers those days fondly. Richard Fink, who had been running the Center for the Study of Market Processes at its initial home at Rutgers, advised Boettke (after he had graduated from Sennholz and Grove City) to try George Mason.[81] Fink helped bring in a band of young Austrians to George Mason in the 1980s. "He was an amazingly dynamic leader," Boettke remembers.

> He gave an orientation to the first-year grad students. He said every student here is going to do three things besides pass classes and do their dissertation. 1) They will present a paper at a professional meeting. 2) They will teach a course on their own. 3) They will publish a paper in a professional journal. He used an analogy with the civil rights movement: Before we just wanted to be let on the bus and not raise a ruckus. Now we're gonna be like Malcolm X, Austrian and proud. In your face with the Austrian economics.
>
> Rich would get you hyped up about this stuff. We were coming from a non-top-ranked school and had this [Austrian] label on our heads, so we had to outcompete other people. When I was a kid I wasn't intellectual, but as a basketball player I was competi-

tive. Sennholz and Fink made these appeals that fed into my psyche: We'll form this team and go out and beat 'em![82]

As a result of achieving what Fink expected of him, Boettke "entered the job market out of this backwater school with three formal job offers." The first week at his first job, he got a call from Leonard Liggio, then an officer at IHS, asking how he was doing. "GMU was that way for all the grad students."[83]

Boettke is amazed at how far Austrian economics has come since South Royalton. "[Karen] Vaughn wrote this book on the history of Austrian economics, and one of the leading academic publishers in the world, Cambridge, published it. That's phenomenal. Go back to the mid-1970s, and realize the only publisher that will do the Dolan collection is a Catholic devotional publisher that Koch underwrites, that he'll pay the whole expense for the book to be published. Fast forward to 1994 and leading academic publishers are publishing these books. I publish with Routledge and Kluwer, and it's not at all subsidized. They pay me."[84]

"THESE FLAWS REPRESENT VERY SERIOUS DISTORTIONS . . . IN THE UNDERSTANDING OF MARKET PROCESS IN CAPITALIST ECONOMIES."

Despite a renaissance since 1974, Austrianism qua Austrianism is still a misunderstood minority in the economics profession at large, its centers of influence small and scattered. Its biggest problems, to its detractors, include its methodological heresies and its ideological connection with libertarianism.

Its biggest problem is also what defines it. The Austrian tradition approaches economics with a different style, different concerns, and different preconceptions than the standard neoclassical consensus. In the 1930s, though, Mises didn't recognize the Mengerian tradition as necessarily distinct from, or in opposition to, the rest of neoclassical economics. It differed from the Lausanne and Anglo-American schools, he thought, "only in their mode of expressing the same fundamental idea [of subjective marginal value] . . . they are divided more by their terminology and by peculiarities of presentation than by the substance of their teachings."[85]

Kirzner outlined modern Austrianism's differences with the neoclassical mainstream in a contribution to an early 1980s book, *The Crisis in Economic Theory*, which surveyed a discipline that seemed in some ways up for grabs, with certain aspects of the mainstream consensus breaking down, in a manner such that Austrianism might have been able to carve a larger place.

> Modern mainstream economics displays a number of related features which, for Austrians, appear as serious flaws. These features include especially: a) an excessive preoccupation with the state of *equilibrium*; b) an unfortunate perspective on the nature and role of *competition* in markets; c) grossly insufficient attention to the role (and subjective character) of *knowledge*, *expectations*, and *learning* in market processes; and d) a normative approach heavily dependent on questionable *aggregation* concepts and thus insensitive to the idea of *plan coordination* among market participants. Together these flaws represent very serious distortions, at best, in the understanding of market process in capitalist economies which modern neoclassical economics is able to provide.[86]

Other Austrians have written more detailed attacks on aspects of modern neoclassical economics, particularly its obsession with mathematical method at the expense of causality[87] and its price-adjustment models that ignore the motives and behaviors of the real individuals who make up the economy.[88] Lachmann thinks that neoclassical theory is inadequate because of "the significance of the elements from which one must abstract: in macroeconomics one abstracts from the human actions and plans that underlie all economic phenomena, while in microeconomics these actions and plans appear all too often as an idealized distortion ('perfect competition')."[89] Neoclassical models give economic science the appearance of certainty and precision; to Lachmann, precision is less important than understanding, when the phenomenon one wishes to understand cannot be expressed precisely.

The Austrian rejection of neoclassical-type models, which attempt to emulate the methods of the physical sciences, can be traced to Mises. Economics is concerned with human behavior, Mises insisted, which is not predictable and modelable in the way that the physical world is. The nature of the experimentation possible in the worlds of physical sciences and human behavior is different. Mises and his fellow Austrians have always seen economics as a science of process and change, not of static models of constrained maximization within given, ordered, and stable preferences and resources.

Methodological differences between Austrians and the economics mainstream affect the policy implications that give Austrianism its libertarian tinge. The Austrians don't have much use for aggregative measures. Thus they question most government economic macropolicy, which attempts to jigger with macroeconomic magnitudes such as price levels, unemployment rates, and gross national products. To the Austrians, the neoclassical perfect competition model that assumes everyone knows everything they need to know and that everyone is a price taker (accepts whatever price is given), not a price maker (able to, through actions and choices, affect or change market prices), makes everything that actually comprises real competition in a real market seem like imperfections that need fixing, often by government action. Other Austrian tenets, like the incomparability of utility across persons, while shared by neoclassicals, are usually carried to extremes by Austrians, leading to death blows to the heart of any welfare economics calculations that decide government actions can increase social welfare.[90]

Gerald O'Driscoll, an Austrian economist who spent much of his career working at the Federal Reserve Bank of Dallas, sees the difference between the Austrians and neoclassicals this way: The Austrians have stayed true to the original insight of classical economic science, as best expressed in Adam Smith—that spontaneous order arises from freely acting market forces. Modern economics, particularly under the influence of Keynes, often denies that free markets coalesce into such a workable order; the Mengerian/Misesian/Hayekian/Kirznerian tries to explain how they can and do.[91]

Kirzner thinks the future of Austrianism is uncertain, as all good Austrians must. "It's very difficult to forecast academic trends. What's going on in the economics profession today is that it's moving so much in so many different directions that the development of Austrian economics over the past twenty years is irreversible. Not that we'll take over the profession, but that historians of thought will always be able to point out a body of thought developed from the 1970s on rebelling against an overemphasis on equilibrium that has characterized the mainstream."[92]

"You get involved in it and you're like in the X-Files of academics."

Austrian economics often suffers from being seen as merely a faux-scientific masquerade for libertarianism, to a degree that some young Austrian scholars are sometimes advised even by some fellow libertarian institutions trying to further their careers to downplay, or even not list, certain of their more specifically Austrian or libertarian world publications.[93] One Marxist critic claims that "the main objective of neo-Austrian theory is to abolish the state's ability to implement any form of economic policy."[94] Even Robert Nozick, the superstar Harvard libertarian political philosopher, suggested, in a study on Mises's methodology, that ideology might explain some of his choices: "Why does Mises think it so important to argue that the structure of preferences cannot be irrational? Perhaps because he doesn't want anyone interfering with choices on the grounds that they arise from irrationally structured preferences."[95]

The libertarian/Austrian association is obvious for many reasons. Three of the leading Austrian-tradition economists of the twentieth century—Mises, Hayek, and Rothbard—were also political philosophers and advocates of either an extremely minimal state or, in Rothbard's case, outright anarchism. Mises's economics treatise *Human Action*, the first grand treatise on all of economics since World War I, was read and praised mostly by businessmen and right-wing and libertarian intellectuals, not his fellow economists.

While Boettke is firm in his belief that Austrian economics is, or at least can and should be, as staunchly *wertfrei* (value-free) as Mises insisted it must be, he understands the sociological realities that created a connection between the Austrian economic approach and libertarian political philosophy. "Not being mainstream, it's going to take something special to convince people to have an interest in Austrian economics," he says.

> And what's the most likely way to find out? Through libertarianism. If you get excited about that, and go to grad school, you have two forms of roughly libertarian academic economics to pursue: the Chicago style—that has outposts, successful economists have done this. They're at Rochester, UCLA, Virginia. You can go anywhere that way, have a nice career.
>
> Or you can go the Austrian route, and you see Rothbard in a broom closet at Brooklyn Polytechnic, Kirzner one guy out of thirty-five at NYU, Sennholz at Grove City, these little outback places. The only reason you'd have to continue is that you are *so* convinced of the argument. What argument is that? It tends to be philosophical, methodological. You say, "I'm not like Milton Friedman; I'm not a Popperian." So you end up just doing methodology, and where are the economic methodologists, as opposed to monetary theorists, industrial organization people, whatever? They are one out of thirty-five, in a broom closet, or in little colleges across the country! You won't get a good job, *whatever* your methodology, as a methodologist. Austrians are interested in the history of economic thought. That's not valued as a field. Comparative systems isn't valued as a field. *The things that Austrians care about aren't valued.*
>
> It's hard to find talk of public finance in Austrian economics. The majority of Austrians don't like talking about technical public economics issues. Because of our libertarianism, it's like having a fascination with studying the books of the Mafia. For a normal economist, there's no normative revulsion against studying public finance. But to someone who comes up through libertarianism, the idea of doing these things—bean counting for the Mafia—why would I want to do that? I'd rather talk about philosophy. Which means I have a limited professional audience.[96]

Boettke admits that

> there are some non-normative, analytical reasons that Austrians
> end up advocating certain institutional configurations which hap-
> pen to be consistent with classical liberalism. But the issue about
> libertarianism in general is multifaceted. Austrians have an unusu-
> ally large, for an economic doctrine, lay audience, even though it's
> an obscure school of thought. Why people often get interested is
> they found Rothbard was such a powerful writer for libertarian-
> ism that they became converted to libertarianism through Roth-
> bard. And he tried to demonstrate a causal connection with
> Austrian economics, and they buy into that. Rand also recom-
> mended the works of Mises over other advocates of capitalism.
> She didn't say go read Smith, she said go read Mises.
>
> But Austrian economics is not libertarian in the sense of there
> being some direct connection. It can be an important input into
> someone who adopts libertarian values, but it doesn't necessarily
> imply it.
>
> The lay audiences don't always understand the questions that
> gave rise to the Austrian economics philosophy. They know it says
> don't use math, and laymen are happy because they don't under-
> stand complicated math either. But it's not at all true that Austri-
> ans don't do math because they are mathematically illiterate.
> Rothbard was an undergraduate math major. [Roger] Garrison
> and Kirzner are engineers. Anyone who gets a Ph.D. in econom-
> ics has to have a general competence in math, because that's what
> goes on in economics graduate schools.
>
> But Austrian economics cares about philosophy, so those into
> Rand and the analytic/synthetic dichotomy can also read about it
> in Austrian economics. But what's *really* interesting in Austrian
> economics is capital theory, relative price movements, knowledge
> arguments, and in my view lay audiences don't see those as im-
> portant issues. So people start to think Austrian economics is easy,
> which it's not. They think they can read a body of work in four
> months and have a deep appreciation of what Austrians are up to,
> which I don't think is right. And they also think that Austrian
> economics is political, which isn't accurate either. They think it's

easy, and political, and that there's a giant conspiracy keeping it out of the mainstream. Therefore, you get involved in it and you're like in the *X-Files* of academics. You think "I can be part of this non-conspiratorial approach against these silly academic pigs."

The problem is, it builds into the idea that the world is divided into stupid people, evil people, and people who agree with me. The first thing you have to learn is that there are lots of brilliant, kind-hearted people who just disagree with you.[97]

Boettke's evolution from Sennholz-inspired hard-core libertarian to a more nuanced, scientific perspective isn't uncommon among young Austrians going through their professional evolution. Other of Boettke's mid-1980s George Mason colleagues, such as Tyler Cowen and Daniel Klein, have gone through similar evolutions, and there are many young professional economists who consider themselves ex-Austrians. Boettke says he can detect the smell of Austrianism even in the work of many who have officially abandoned it. "The typical young IHS turk in the 1980s believed in the three A's: anarchism, Austrianism, and atheism."[98] But as they age, go through the grad school grind, and learn more about different perspectives, many find themselves broadening out from that filter.

That's as it should be, Boettke thinks. "All I care about is if I'm learning something, being given something new to think about. I learn tremendous things from people who don't call themselves Austrian. It would be a mistake to shut yourself off, to say, 'Hey, you don't publish in the *Review of Austrian Economics* so I won't read you.'"[99]

Nowadays, there is a noticeable disjoint—in terms of where they write, where they lecture, the conferences they attend—between populist-leaning and explicitly libertarian avatars of Austrianism centered around the Mises Institute at Auburn (though they still emphasize training and fellowship support for young academics) and the more academic ones in the NYU/GMU orbit. Sennholz would sometimes crankily note that these more academic Austrians tend to concentrate on abstruse issues of process and coordination and interpretation and histories of Soviet economic development and avoid using economic thinking as an explicit tool to attack state interventionism. The more academic ones counter that their loyalty must be to economic science as a learning and teaching enterprise, not as a tool for winning points in political arguments.

Even if Austrianism loses its intimate connection with libertarian political philosophy and activism, as Sennholz fears, the Mises connection will remain. His influence, ideas, and style, through his books and through those he influenced such as Hayek, Rothbard, and Rand, are cornerstones of the modern libertarian edifice. And if what is called Austrian economics evolves further from a recognizably Misesian line, it will retain traces of Mises's method, his approach to process, his vision of the entrepreneur's role, his theories of interest and business cycles, and his notions of the importance of constant change, the passing of time, and man's limited knowledge for economic analysis—and of the implications of those ideas for the futility and inappropriateness of state intervention in the economy.

"THE EXACT OPPOSITE OF MY VIEWS."

As the libertarian movement grew through the 1970s, Ayn Rand alternately ignored and attacked it, not acknowledging that it advanced the same political ideas she stood for. Apparently believing that the notion of a strictly limited government was her own invention, she alternately declared that libertarians "plagiarize the Objectivist theory of politics"[100] and that libertarians believe "the exact opposite of my views."[101] Rand was past elaborating her thoughts by the 1970s, and the Brandens today are perplexed by her ferocity on the subject of the libertarian movement, a ferocity that has only grown hotter in the official Objectivist movement after her death.[102]

A marvelously scabrous essay by Objectivist Peter Schwartz, published in the Objectivist journal *Intellectual Activist* after Rand's death and then reprinted in one of Rand's posthumous collections, sums up the split between official Objectivists and official libertarians (though in reality, many people who think of themselves as Objectivists have no problem thinking of themselves as libertarians as well). Schwartz violently objected to various statements and judgments made by mostly

Libertarian Party–related libertarians, mostly in the late 1970s. He couldn't abide libertarian noninterventionism. Rand's successors enthusiastically perpetuated her hawkish anticommunism and desire for the U.S. government to destroy the world's evils (although they do not tend to mention that Rand opposed U.S. entry into World War II). The anarchist streak (or actual anarchism) of many libertarians drove Schwartz to decide that it was not love of liberty but hatred of the state that motivated libertarians. (To Rand, rational liberty was impossible without a minimal state that enforced a singular set of just laws and prevented what she thought would be the chaotic warfare of competing private defense agencies. But she did think such a state could and would be supported voluntarily.)

Schwartz, as an Objectivist, was enraged by the theoretical eclecticism of the libertarian movement. Openness on important basic philosophical questions strikes many Objectivists as the equivalent of abandoning philosophy and ethics altogether. A common front of people with different core beliefs but common goals? Irrational, antilife madness to Schwartz, although Rand herself approved of it during the Goldwater campaign in 1964, when she wrote that "if [a political figure] advocates the right political principles for the wrong metaphysical reasons, the contradiction is *his* problem, not ours."[103]

Anything any libertarian ever said or wrote was dragged in by Schwartz as evidence to put libertarianism in the dock; for example, one member of the LP's radical caucus suggests that power cannot be wished away, and suddenly "libertarianism" is all about armed violent revolution.[104] The revisionist history Rothbardian libertarians advocate that emphasizes the sometimes villainous role of the United States drives the extrapatriotic Objectivist to apoplexy; libertarianism "provides the grotesque, nauseating spectacle of a movement claiming to support individual liberty—and reviling America as the world's most immoral nation."[105]

Their lack of a firm philosophic base makes libertarians nihilists; Schwartz insists libertarians want to destroy all values, particularly all moral values, to which they are unremittingly hostile. Schwartz sees no distinction between being free to achieve anything one happens to value—the libertarian notion that liberty is the precondition and background for achieving any, and all, personally chosen values—and the notion of liberty to "achieve nothing in particular. But the zealous, belligerent, purposeless pursuit of nothing is in fact the pursuit of . . . destruction" (ellipsis in original).[106] Note the sudden switching of "nothing in particular" to just plain "nothing."

Schwartz's Objectivist indictment of mainstream libertarianism ends with a nightmarish vision of life in a Rothbardian world, with raucous, violent street parties celebrating the PLO's victory over Israel, a war-painted Indian evicting you from your home, Jesse Jackson taking the earnings of everyone making over $20,000 a year, your seven-year-old daughter encountering heroin dealers on the school playground, newspapers accusing you of helping Mengele torture babies—and you with no legal recourse to sue for libel! All the while government welfare expenditures, for some reason, are steadily increasing. It ends, naturally, with the Kremlin conquering the United States.[107]

Nathaniel Branden thinks that Rand, if she had bothered to fight through her prejudices, might have come to different conclusions about modern libertarians. Through her unpleasant dealings with Rothbard, "Ayn Rand somehow drew the false inference that the majority of libertarians were anarchists."

> She didn't know that the vast majority of libertarians believed in limited constitutional government and in fact more people had come to that viewpoint through her writings than [through] any other figure, certainly incomparably more than [through] Murray Rothbard. So there was a simple lack of information on her part. Also, since she had such an integrated mind, for her political philosophy has to be part of an overall philosophy. Yet with libertarians, you find some of them are natural rights theorists, some believe rights come from God, some were utilitarian, so she felt that without Objectivist foundations libertarianism is floating in space.
>
> My answer to that would be, that's no more true of libertarianism than of any other political movement where people come together. If the defining characteristic of the libertarian movement was noninitiation of physical force with all the implications of that, and if politically they are not advocating anything that contradicts our wider philosophic viewpoint, then it's completely

unreasonable to require them all to be Objectivists. But I also think that if she weren't so turned off by Murray Rothbard personally, and if she weren't turned off by the anarchist wing, she might have come to a very different perspective with a bit of time on the whole thing.

Libertarianism has come to be understood as the political theory which holds to a minimalist view of the proper function of government, and to that extent Objectivists are libertarians! You can say we're Objectivist libertarians, we're not Catholic libertarians, we're not anarchist libertarians, fine, but we're libertarians.[108]

Even when libertarians tried to pay her respect, Rand sometimes didn't want to hear it. Libertarian science fiction author J. Neil Schulman remembers a long phone conversation with Rand that ended with her barking, "I despise all libertarians, including you!" and hanging up.[109] She threatened *Reason* magazine with a lawsuit when it used her likeness on a cover of an issue filled with stories about her. Manuel Klausner, a lawyer and then one of *Reason's* editors, rather hoped the suit would go forward (it didn't) because he was sure they'd win, first of all. And he couldn't help mordantly relishing a case on the record in a U.S. court called *Rand v. Reason.*[110]

"THE FABIANS ARE YET TO COME . . . WE HAVE TO BE THE HARD-CORE ONES."

Reason, the longest-lasting and most central to the movement of the libertarian journals, had gathered a panel of ten of the movement's heavy hitters circa 1978, on the occasion of the magazine's tenth anniversary. They discussed where the libertarian movement had been, where it was, and where it might or should go.

It was a summit meeting of all factions of the movement. From the Kochtopus they had Charles himself (in a rare public discussion of his libertarian strategic thinking), Ed Crane (at the time running both Cato and, in essence, the LP), and Roy Childs (then editing the Koch-funded *Libertarian Review*); from the activist side, LP founder

Dave Nolan, Don Ernsberger and Dave Walter (the founders of Society for Individual Liberty), and Joe Cobb, the final editor of *New Individualist Review* at the University of Chicago. From the *Reason* crew were Bob Poole, Manny Klausner, and Mark Frazier (then working with Poole on a side business consulting with local governments on how to work more efficiently, often through privatizing and contracting out services; this strategy was the root of the Reason Foundation, the think tank Poole launched that year and which now publishes the magazine).

They all felt an electric sense of peering over an edge into what might be something like victory, or at any rate a libertarian world bigger, surprisingly bigger, than the one they had all helped forge. In the past decade they had seen the audience for their magazines, their party, their books and pamphlets grow and continue to grow. There seemed every reason to believe that that rate of growth would only continue. It was the year of Proposition 13, four years after Watergate; never before had middle-class resentment and mistrust of the state seemed stronger, more widespread.

They recognized, as Rothbard had been complaining since the 1950s, that the movement needed more institutions that provided opportunities to be *professional* libertarians. That, of course, meant more money, and one can't help but assume they were all staring at Charles Koch when *that* topic came up. All of them, at the time, considered the LP to be an important, nearly constitutive part of the movement, the nexus between theory and practice.[111]

Some of them, like Childs, thought that marshaling libertarian ideas with skilled communication techniques and ideological entrepreneurship would make the world theirs; others, like Bob Poole, thought that at best libertarianism might see sporadic victories on certain policy issues, but very likely no imminent sea change in political ideology or practice across the board.

Koch, interestingly, insisted that libertarians must remain uncompromisingly radical: "Our greatest strength is that our philosophy is a consistent world view and will appeal to the brightest, most enthusiastic, most capable people, particularly young people. But to realize that strength, we have to state it in a radical, pure form."

The temptation to temporize is strong "because the other side of that is our greatest weakness: that is, because we have a radical philosophy, we don't appeal to people who are in positions of influence, people with status or wealth. . . . So the temptation is, let's compromise . . . let's be much more gradual than we should be. As a result, we could destroy the appeal to the comers of the world, and therefore we destroy the movement."[112] Koch called out Milton Friedman and Alan Greenspan specifically as sellouts to the system, merely trying to make government work more efficiently when the true libertarian should be tearing it out at the root.

The key question that the great minds and planners of libertarianism assembled needed to answer was, as Joe Cobb put it, Is the libertarian movement in the late 1970s to play the role of the Marxists—the hard-core fire-breathing theoreticians—or the Fabians—the gradualists who try to effect some version of the radical goals within the system?

Cobb said that "the Fabians are yet to come and that we have to be the hard-core ones." None of them knew that, thanks to Ronald Reagan, a man who had told *Reason* magazine a few years earlier that "I believe the very heart and soul of conservatism is libertarianism," that question would become more relevant than they could have then guessed.[113] The answers they came up with in three years would be quite different from what they might have expected them to be in 1978. Cobb himself, along with the rest of the libertarian movement, would soon have to decide, as the Reagan 1980s dawned, whether they would rather try to be Marxists or Fabians.

A MAINSTREAMED
RADICALISM

The 1980s was a decade of mainstreaming and growth for the libertarian movement, building on foundations of influence built up over the past decade in areas as diverse as economics, academic philosophy, psychiatry, and science fiction. The movement's story became more diverse, multifaceted, complicated, less a straight line of intellectual and institutional influence in which every professional libertarian was connected intimately with every other.

The most obvious manifestation of apparent libertarian success was the election of Ronald Reagan, a president who, rhetorically at least, was a libertarian dream, a man who could declare with apparent sincerity in his first inaugural address that "government is not the solution to the problem, government *is* the problem."

Ronald Reagan was famously a reader of the *Freeman,* as per an iconic shot of Nancy's head on his shoulder as they snuggle on an airplane while he peruses Leonard Read's magazine, taken the day after his election in 1980. His economic policy advisory team was peppered with movement figures, including Milton Friedman and friend of Rand Alan Greenspan. Former Robert Lefevrite troubadour—and, as many press reports on him noted, past illegal drug user—Dana Rohrabacher was writing speeches for the president.[1] Rohrabacher once crowed, quoting Bernard Shaw, that the U.S. Constitution was essentially a charter not of government but of insurance that the American people would barely be governed at all, and this was the true spirit of Reaganism.[2] Reagan excited many libertarians and libertarian sympathizers. Nathaniel Branden, for one, adored the man, although "I did not expect him to be John Galt. I did not expect him to be Ayn Rand. I expected him to be a hell of a lot better than everyone else, and he was. I believe he was a man of principle very devoted to certain principles I shared, and that he did his damndest to bring them into reality. What more can you ask for?"[3]

Some action, maybe. The Cato Institute had relocated itelf to Ronald Reagan's Washington in the early 1980s, realizing that the dream of creating a viable, respected public policy house in San Francisco wasn't apt to come true. By the summer of 1982, Cato's Ed Crane had already written the president off in a *Washington Post* op-ed, fingering him as a rudderless, ideology-less "good government" type surrounding himself with "experienced" and "competent" aides and driving the serious small-government ideologues from his service.[4]

In the end, most libertarians were sorely disappointed in Reagan and, given his libertarianoid pretensions, almost enraged at times. Sheldon Richman mocked him in *Inquiry* for telling columnist Rowland Evans that his favorite thinkers were Mises, Hayek, Cobden, Bright, and Bastiat. Richman notes, "Judging from Reagan's performance in office so far, you might deduce that they were firm believers in the strongest possible military force, a globe-girdling foreign policy, a government oriented toward big business, and a generally Rotarian approach to the administration of public affairs."[5]

Despite his professed love for Bastiat, Cobden, and Bright, radical free traders all, Reagan raised tariffs and imposed import quotas left and right, increased farm subsidies and quotas, and ramped up the drug war. His tax cuts were overbalanced by tax raises through inflationary bracket creep and "loophole closing." With the help of Rand's pal Alan Greenspan, also written off as a sellout by many libertarians, he "saved" Social Security through raising payroll taxes. The important deregulatory moves of the era were brought about, or begun, by Jimmy Carter, not Reagan: abolition of the Civil Aeronautics Board (which regulated the airlines' prices and schedules), oil and gas deregulation (which Reagan did speed up), and trucking deregulation. Reagan talked of abolishing useless federal agencies but the energy and education departments continued their mission, and still do.

Despite the gaps between rhetoric and reality, libertarians could notice that the interesting parts of the Reagan revolution as it applied to most Americans' lives were ideas more properly libertarian than conservative—cutting taxes and eliminating regulatory agencies. What did conservative notions of traditionalism and order have to say about that? Regulation sounds like order, right? But libertarians knew that order is spontaneous and arises from liberty; conservative thinking is often running on libertarian fumes.

Murray Rothbard, representing the most virulent libertarian disdain for Reagan (of the type that led many fellow libertarians to accuse him of making the perfect the enemy of the good), concluded that "the historic function of Ronald Reagan was to co-opt, eviscerate, and ultimately destroy the substantial wave of antigovernmental, and quasi-libertarian, sentiment that erupted in the U.S. during the 1970s."[6] Nowadays, mainstream libertarians are more apt to laud Reagan as a president who was at least an eloquent spokesman for libertarian principles and for furthering an ideological sea change in which marginal tax rates are not apt to ever break 50 percent, and in which even a Democrat such as Bill Clinton feels obligated to declare that "the era of big government is over," even if it really isn't.

"Wearing an Adam Smith tie and arguing for subsidies."

The first few months of the Reagan administration were a heady time for the former outsiders, with an administration that knew part of its mandate involved a rejection of Democratic big government. Certain libertarians were feted, even hired, if only so the administration could say, hey, look at the libertarians around us. A frisson of daring glamour surrounded libertarians, for once. They hoped they could function as an id of sorts to the Reagan administration, theoretically standing for its true antistate desires, not a superego constantly criticizing it. Roy Childs and Joan Kennedy Taylor of the *Libertarian Review* staff, also moved from San Francisco to Washington, were enjoying *The Little Foxes* at the Kennedy Center in the presidential box thanks to their new connections with White House staffers.

Former Rand Circler Martin Anderson, author of *The Federal Bulldozer*, a classic work on the nightmares caused by government attempts to help the poor through urban renewal and thus a libertarian favorite, was a policy adviser to Reagan.[7] He in turn brought on young libertarian journalist Doug Bandow as a fellow assistant to the president for policy development. Bandow had been a pal of Bill Evers at Stanford, and knew the whole Cato/Crane/Koch crowd. He worked on a plan to eliminate draft registration, which Carter had reinstated—a libertarian policy change that Reagan had claimed enthusiastic support for. The report they worked on setting forth the hows and whys of ending draft registration landed on Reagan's desk, Bandow recalls, the same week that the Polish communist government cracked down on the independent Solidarity union.

Ardent cold warrior Reagan wasn't about to do anything that could be interpreted as a lack of fervent military resolve in the face of this commie provocation, and that was that for ending draft registration. Bandow saw the Department of Education still operating and found himself attending frustrating meetings with people "wearing an Adam Smith tie and arguing for subsidies," people who didn't understand the huge chasm between being pro-business and being pro–free enterprise. He decided, in a synecdoche of libertarian hopes for the Reagan era, that "I had better things to do than stick around just so I could ride around in government cars."[8]

Bandow jumped ship to the Cato Institute, which was delighted to provide a home for a libertarian Reagan White House renegade. He edited *Inquiry* during what proved to be its dying days. (*Inquiry* had been spun off from Cato proper by then, but Bandow became a Cato senior fellow as well.) Joe Cobb, a former *New Individualist Review* editor from the University of Chicago, ended up getting the Bandow position in the administration; he could tell it was thought of as a designated "libertarian" slot, meaning that his libertarian background got him the job.

The Kochs' libertarian magazine miniempire didn't survive the first Reagan term. The business end was chaotic, and lack of direct mail investment led them on a vicious spiral toward extinction. As Roy Childs tried to explain to his funders, you *can* grow circulation for a magazine merely by throwing money at it through relentless barrages of direct mail. A reasonably predictable science tells you how many pieces you have to mail out to earn so many new subscribers. One former recipient of Koch largess thinks the Kochs didn't seem to fully grasp that "what we're trying to do is sell the world something that they don't want," so losing money on projects, even ones with a purchase price, is inevitable for a while—probably a very long while.

Libertarian Review never managed to break much above 10,000 in circulation. Childs had brought in Joan Kennedy Taylor from the 1960s Rand Circle to assist him in the late 1970s; she later wrote books reconciling feminism with libertarian individualism. Childs had already hired on Jeff Riggenbach, a young broadcast journalist who had gone through the classic FEE/Rand background common to libertarians of his era, but who never saw himself as part of any revolutionary cadre: "A lot of the people [around the Koch operations in the late 1970s] did seem to think that this was the revolution, that what we were doing here is changing the world. *I* thought what we were doing was putting out a magazine, surrounded by people who had read and loved the same obscure things I had read, and were interested in the same ideas I was, in a congenial atmosphere."[9]

Childs's pet *Libertarian Review* died in the aftermath of the Koch-funded operations move from San Francisco, and was theoretically folded into the Cato-owned *Inquiry,* which was spun off from Cato and renamed *Inquiry: A Libertarian Review* (though *Inquiry* in its original conception studiously avoided the "libertarian" label as part of its outreach to the left strategy). While Childs had tried to gently explain that these sorts of ideological political magazines *never* make money, that every single one of them is supported either by foundations or wealthy sugar daddies such as the Kochs, that *National Review* could not have had the success it had in building a viable conservative movement without tenaciously continuing a long sail through year after continuing year of red-ink oceans, Koch frowned on the magazines' inability to get themselves independently above water. These journalists, Koch thought, in the judgment of one late-period *Inquiry* staffer, were simply not taking his money very seriously. *Inquiry* had sunk to below 10,000 circulation before the end. Koch was, some say, mindful of opportunity cost: If the magazines were meant as outreach to a wider world and the wider world wasn't buying it, then it was better to do something else with his money.

Childs, from his berth at *Libertarian Review* and his LP activism, had been the most consistent personal inspiration and support to a rising generation of young libertarians, and is remembered fondly by all of them. He was the sort of man whose presence put smiles on people's faces, the sort of figure all ideological movements need, playing a role like Leonard Liggio's: the tireless networker, letter writer, phone caller, dedicated to a larger vision of a long-term libertarian project that extended beyond whatever work he happened to be doing, as dedicated to promoting and connecting other libertarian comrades as producing specific tangible work of his own. After the magazine went, though, he had no steady outlet for his work. Long-planned book projects were never finished, and he began writing detailed and erudite reviews for the monthly catalog of libertarian mail-order bookseller Laissez Faire Books.

Ultimately, Cato chieftain Crane also decided that good ideological magazines don't fit well under the aegis of think tanks. Magazines require a certain level of entertaining pugnaciousness, while think tanks work best if they maintain a sober, civilized tone in relations with policymakers and thought leaders. In the years since Robert Poole started his Reason Foundation think tank, *Reason* has managed to keep a sturdy wall of separation between the magazine and the policy house, keeping the work of one division from overly influencing the tone or reputation of the other. With *Inquiry*'s passing, *Reason* was once again the only libertarian-run policy magazine of any significant circulation.[10]

While never unreservedly for Reagan qua Reagan, *Reason,* then edited by Robert Poole, fit in better with the pugnacious Reagan-era anticommunism. Poole never bought the Rothbardian line on the cold war and considered defense against possible Russian aggression a legitimate state function, and the Soviets the villains on the world scene. *Reason* during the Reagan years ran a series of articles by Jack Wheeler, the anticommunist Indiana Jones. Wheeler started a career of youthful adventurism early, being one of the first white men (at age seventeen) to befriend a group of Jivaro Indian headhunters in the Amazon. Then for an encore he decided to swim the Hellespont naked. He was an old friend of Dana Rohrabacher's, and Dana helped turn him on to the 1980s greatest adventure: partying down and blowing shit up with anticommunist rebels from Nicaragua to Angola to Afghanistan.

Wheeler loved every minute of it and sent colorful reports back to *Reason*, which helped fund his adventures. As he told Sidney Blumenthal at the *Washington Post*: "Well, we had a great time . . . I mean it was night . . . and the Soviets started firing these rockets and recoilless rifles, and finally they hit the power station, and it was just like a movie, a war movie, the tracer bullets and explosions and bombs. . . . But they were missing and we were racing around, all down these alleys, and mortars were exploding and we're all laughing and doubled over laughing and tears were pouring down our faces. We were embracing each other and laughing so hard we could hardly run . . . it was quite a time, quite a time."[11]

The early 1980s, with both Cato and *Reason* feeling their oats and growing in influence and effectiveness, opened a golden age for libertarian movement gossip mongers. Even the modern blog age has not reproduced the level of snide public infighting among libertarian institutions to establish the supremacy of their take on movement personalities, actions, internal policy and personnel shifts. In addition to Rothbard's personal *Libertarian Forum,* both the Cato crowd and *Reason* got into the gossip newsletter game as well. The Cato crowd's was called *Update*; *Reason*'s, *Frontlines* (which had evolved from a section in *Reason* magazine, spun off as the magazine segued out of this sort of intramovement focus in the late 1970s). Every twist and turn in Libertarian Party firings and hirings, Cato Institute controversies, new books and new conferences received coverage, with an essential cheekiness and side taking under a thin veneer of reportorial objectivity.

By the mid-1980s, the gossip newsletters were gone, and nothing similar has replaced them. Crane looks back on them as a relic of the movement's lack of maturity, creating enemies and bad feelings where there should have been allies: "It wasn't taking seriously the responsibility of trying to change the world."[12] Bob Poole agrees, mostly: "I miss it a little, it *was* fun, but the libertarian movement was

too self-referential then, and small, and reveling in being radical outsiders. As we've grown and gotten more serious and done more effective work, we're still outsiders to a certain extent but we *are* listened to
in the halls of power. We are making an impact, and getting some
things changed, and picking up fans on network TV news, so it became more satisfying to do those things then score points off Murray
Rothbard in this self-contained world."[13]

"BARELY INSIDE THE FENCE OF RESPECTABILITY."

Cato had moved to D.C. and was mostly welcomed there as the "yuppie think tank." It briefly pushed the ideas of political scientists
William S. Maddox and Stuart Lilie, who thought they had detected a
sea change in American politics—the rise of a generation of yuppies
who would be socially liberal and fiscally conservative. That was the
basic libertarian mix, even if the attitude was expressed in language
that evaded the underlying reason why one might hold those views: a
dedication to freedom or rights. Cato launched a national radio commentary program aimed at this imagined new constituency, called *Byline*, managed by old *Libertarian Review* hand and radio pro Jeff
Riggenbach, and aired by 150 stations at its height.[14] The program did
not survive the 1980s as Cato became more narrowly focused on being a policy paper and book house. *Reason* also moved into, and out of,
the field of syndicated radio commentary in the 1980s.

In 1985, Cato won new respect in Washington by getting William
Niskanen to come on board as chairman. Niskanen was a veteran of
Reagan's Council of Economic Advisers, was a respected economist in
his own right, and had a reputation for integrity from quitting as chief
economist for Ford Motors over disagreement about their embrace of
trade protectionism. Now they had an actual political insider onboard;
and besides, the bulk of Cato's policy thinking was not terribly out of
place in the Reagan 1980s, even if Reagan didn't actuate all of it, or
even much of it. Even the most antigovernment of Gipperites weren't

ready to turn their back on the war on drugs, as Cato urged, but program cutting, regulation bashing, these sorts of things were right in the main. Even so, standard conservative policy houses such as the Heritage Foundation that expressed those ideas with personnel, and based in a culture, that meshed better with the Reagan right, got most of the reputational juice, and cash, from this brief renaissance in government cutting in D.C. And the Cato vision for foreign policy and defense, well, that was right out.

Ted Galen Carpenter was running Cato's foreign policy department by the end of the 1980s, and still is. He came from a working-class YAF background and wrote his doctoral thesis on the old right noninterventionist politicians and publicists Rothbard loved so much.

The Carpenter/Cato vision, which has remained a dominant part of the Cato ethos to this day, doesn't come across as animated by a particular moral passion. Even the Vietnam War, which he opposed, seemed to Carpenter more a blunder than a crime. Looking for hidden motives is not part of the Cato intellectual arsenal either. From the cold war to the war on terror, Carpenter is willing to assume that what policymakers say their motives are, whether saving the world from communist domination or from Islamist terrorism, genuinely represents their motives. He just disagrees that the U.S. government's professed foreign policy goals can be safely or affordably reached.

Cato in the waning days of the cold war supported getting intermediate-range missiles out of Europe, cast warnings about the nature of the people we were supporting in Afghanistan, and discouraged the United States from propping up dictators in pursuit of foreign policy goals. Unlike conservatives who insisted almost to the day before the Berlin Wall fell that the Soviets were ten feet tall and on the march to Western capitals, and that we needed to spend to our last penny to crush them, Cato recognized that it wasn't necessary for the United States to play every chess move in every obscure corner of the globe just to ensure the Soviets weren't getting their way. We could, and ought to, download certain military responsibilities on allies such as Europe and Japan who had been free-riding on us for decades. In the Washington foreign policy community, Carpenter's views in the cold war days were "barely inside the fence of respectability." These days he isn't the only person at any given conference of foreign policy mavens taking roughly his realist noninterventionist stance.

With the 1991 Gulf War Cato ran afoul of the essential differences between the standard libertarian and standard conservative foreign policy position. Cato was solidly against the war. However, some of its funders, such as the right-wing Olin Foundation, which supported many free market and economics-oriented libertarian causes over the years, were solidly for it. William E. Simon, Olin's then-president, former Treasury secretary under Nixon, and author of one of the huge bestsellers that marked the late 1970s as an era of resurgent free market thought, *A Time for Truth,* told Crane that "you cannot imagine how astonished I was—indeed 'outraged' would be a better word—to read in your memorandum your description of the recent war in the Gulf as a conflict in which 'the world's most advanced military power laid waste to a Third world nation' . . . and your lament that 'It really is a tragedy that so many good free-market conservatives have signed off on the Gulf War.'" Simon told Crane he would recommend the foundation cut off Cato. Cato did lose nearly $1 million in funding over its stance against the Gulf War.[15]

"Onward and upward with central banking. Hail to its high priest from Chicago."

Helping underlie and give intellectual heft to the vogue in free market thinking that buoyed both libertarianism and Reaganism in the early 1980s was the fact that two libertarian economists and advocates received the Nobel Prize in economics in quick succession: Hayek in 1974 and Milton Friedman in 1976.

Hayek was the first libertarian hero to have his brow kissed by the Swedish monarchy (in an award with the same name as, but not established by, dynamite magnate Alfred Nobel's prizes). However, Hayek's public heyday as a polemicist and philosopher of liberty occurred decades earlier, and his stature was not nearly as high as Friedman's at the time.[16]

Friedman needed bodyguards on his trip to Stockholm, where he stepped forward on Thursday, December 10, 1976, to receive his laurels from the king of Sweden. The moment was marred by a mob of hecklers and protesters outside, condemning Friedman's alleged complicity in the crimes of the Pinochet regime ruling Chile. It was a telling, if not typical, moment in the University of Chicago economist's controversial career.

Friedman's ideological enemies, including many more sophisticated than the mob outside the Nobel hall whose brethren haunted Friedman for a couple of years thereafter (Friedman believes the protests were "orchestrated by the international communist apparatus"), maintained that his victory was more political than scientific.[17] One made the patently ludicrous claim in the *Washington Post* that Friedman only won because the economics Nobel, rather than being one of the original prizes established in Nobel's will, was a later addition financed by the Swedish Central Bank, and central banks love Friedman.[18] Friedman, of course, is well-known for gleefully supporting the abolition of the Federal Reserve of the United States, the world's mightiest central bank.

Such political commentary journals as the *New Republic* and the *Nation* unsheathed their claws more readily and viciously on Friedman than they did on Hayek, doubtless because they and their readers were more familiar with Friedman. Hayek's award got no reaction from them; Friedman's occasioned the *Nation*, with characteristically blunt and unamusing irony and an incomprehension of Friedman's actual stances similar to the *Post's*, to cheer, "Onward and upward with central banking. Hail to its high priest from Chicago."[19] (The *Nation* has no principled opposition to the concept of central banking and is not known for advocating private competing currencies. Such a stance would move it beyond its statist/progressive orbit and into libertarianism. Unsubstantiated smears make strange bedfellows.)

The *New Republic* of 1976 was even more vicious, likening a Friedman economics Nobel to a peace prize for Idi Amin, or a literature prize for Spiro Agnew. While acknowledging that no economist was surprised or appalled at Friedman's laurel, it claimed that "much of the world" bridled at the prize. But it went on to sum up handily what

Friedman stood for in the public mind—such as the millions who read Friedman's triweekly column of political and economic commentary in *Newsweek* from 1966 to 1984:

> Friedman is best known as a tireless, peppery advocate of liberalism *in the 19th century European sense*, perhaps the nation's outstanding intellectual exponent of laissez-faire. In short, in the 20th century American sense, he is a hyperactive extremist of the right. He opposes government activity of practically all kinds, and especially economic interventions. He would abolish virtually all regulations on industry, working conditions, and the professions. He would turn over to private industry the nation's schools, highways, federal parks, the post office and all other publicly operated services like water supply, local buses and subways. He would scrap Social Security, the entire welfare system and the progressive income tax schedule. Few, if any, measures to protect the environment or the consumer would win his approval. He would terminate all government efforts to stabilize the economy through fiscal and monetary policies, public works or other means. He would leave presidential candidates, and I suppose all other candidates for public office, with nothing to talk about. In other words, all economic decisions would be left to what Friedman conceives as a perfectly competitive private market system populated by firms, workers and consumers with perfect knowledge.[20]

Though the description comes from an enemy, it's a fine summation of the public reputation Friedman had developed in the years since *Capitalism and Freedom*. Despite that list of anti-government bona fides, Friedman is still judged skeptically among radical segments of the libertarian movement. Libertarian economists from the Austrian tradition often attack him because he works within a traditional neoclassical framework, and sometimes for just not being sufficiently radical in his libertarianism—a complaint that limns the peculiarity of the libertarian ideological world compared to the standard intellectual zeitgeist. But there has been a long-lasting tension between economists of the Misesian/Austrian School and those of Friedman's Chicago School.

Although many of them have done theoretical or empirical work that buttresses libertarian conclusions about the necessity (or lack of necessity) of state action, most of the major Chicago School economists, besides Friedman and his wife and writing partner Rose, have not become public polemicists for libertarian ideas. However, as one analyst of the school has noted, "The Chicago school was, nevertheless, an important influence in giving the newly libertarian value system a powerful symbolic representation (providing better 'scientific' metaphors) and in seeking to translate the libertarian ethos into concrete plans for political and social change."[21]

Even though most of them were not libertarian activists in the Friedman or Rothbard sense, the arguments of other libertarian analysts, think tanks, and polemicists would be sadly lacking without backing from the technical work of the likes of Chicago School economists Harold Demsetz on antitrust and industrial concentration, Sam Peltzman on the efficacy and rationality of government regulatory agencies (and of Yale Brozen, who served on FEE's board of trustees, on both those issues), or Gary Becker on why racial discrimination was economically irrational and thus could be expected to be ultimately competed away in a free market without government intervention.[22] (For decades, the Economics Department at UCLA was dominated by libertarian-leaning Chicago School economists, including Demsetz and leading property rights theorist Armen Alchian. The Austrian libertarians are not quite so comfortable with the Chicagoites who, policy concerns and similarities aside, embrace the empirical and mathematical equilibrium analysis and assumption of perfect information techniques of mainstream neoclassical economics.)[23]

In 1976, the same year he won the Nobel, Friedman retired from active teaching to become a senior fellow at the Hoover Institution at Stanford University, a position he still holds as of this writing as he continues his popular and occasional technical writing and speaking on economics and public policy. His major polemical energy these days is dedicated to school vouchers, the major project of the Milton and Rose Friedman Foundation, and an idea for which he was one of the first major advocates.

The central economic insight for which Friedman is known is dubbed "monetarism." Friedman led a revival of the quantity theory of money, which reached its modern form in the work of early twentieth-century American economist Irving Fisher but dates back to David Hume in the eighteenth century. Friedman wrote an influential article called "The Quantity Theory of Money: A Restatement" as an introduction to a collection he edited in 1956, *Studies in the Quantity Theory of Money*. He concentrated on the topic in later books, all written under the aegis of the National Bureau of Economic Research and in collaboration with Anna J. Schwartz: *A Monetary History of the United States, 1867–1960* (1963), *Monetary Statistics of the United States* (1970), and *Monetary Trends in the United States and the United Kingdom* (1982). In those books he and Schwartz assemble data to prove the central contention of monetarism: Money supply changes are the cause of inflation and the workings of the business cycle.

Eventually Friedman's ideas triumphed over the Keynesian notion that fiscal policy is more effective than monetary policy in smoothing or managing changes in economic aggregates.[24] Friedman argued that government fiscal policy could have no strong real effects on the economy. If the government taxed to spend more, the citizens from whom the money was taken would have that much less to spend. If the government borrowed to spend more, that much less money would be available for private borrowers. Similarly, if the government tries the reverse fiscal policies, spending less by cutting either taxes or borrowing, it just leaves more for private citizens to spend. Thus government attempts to manipulate "aggregate demand" are generally useless.

Of course, as befits his positivist methodology, which considered empirical evidence more important than theory, Friedman didn't depend only on that sort of logical argument to make his point. He and Schwartz spent years accruing data showing, in as close to controlled experiments as history allows, how monetary changes usually showed far greater effect on nominal income, prices, and output than did fiscal changes. Friedman doesn't think that singular dramatic examples utterly prove a point; he insists on the slow, painstaking formation of theories and testing of those theories against reality in a continuous feedback loop.

As Friedman would be the first to emphasize, this collection of reasonably clear cause-and-effect cases does not mean that monetary policy provides a magic wand for fine-tuning the economy. That is the juicy libertarian implication of Friedman's dry and scientific work on money. Government stabilization policy attempts, whether through fiscal *or* monetary policy, are bound to fail, since the effects of money on the economy work only through a lag that is both long and variable.

Thus any attempt to respond to an economic ailment for which Federal Reserve wizards decide more or less money might be a remedy is apt to be too little, too late, or too much, too soon. Fed jiggering with the money supply is as apt to exacerbate problems as solve them. Friedman thus thinks we should remove the Fed's ability to make such decisions. He advocates abolishing the central bank and setting money growth on automatic pilot: 3–5 percent growth a year, to keep up, in Friedman's calculations, with growth in population and production.[25]

That monetary lag is important not just because of the grit it throws in the machine of government economic management. It is also key to winning the debate that did the most to cement Friedman's reputation for victory over the Keynesians: the debate over the Phillips curve (why it didn't hold true) and stagflation (how it occurred). These two phenomena relate to another of Friedman's famous ideas: the natural rate of unemployment. (Friedman is unusual among economists in having so many well-known, successful theories and observations to his credit. His significance as an economist is hard to overrate.)

The Phillips curve supposedly showed that government economic managers could manipulate a trade-off between unemployment and inflation: more inflation reduced unemployment. Friedman's notions of how monetary lags worked explained why this might sometimes appear to be so, and also why in the long term it was *not* so.

The first effects of new money in the economy can make businesses mistakenly identify a greater demand for their specific product, possibly leading them to increase production and hire more people. This is the initial positive jolt that makes inflation an irresistible drug to politicians. But like many drugs, it has a downside. After a while, people realize that there was no real increased demand for their product in relation to all other products—that the apparent extra demand was merely a result of more money in people's hands—and the holders of the extra money begin to bid up all prices and soon realize their overall purchasing power is falling. They then try to spend more, faster, which makes nominal incomes increase more than the amount of inflation.

The eventual adjustment process in Friedman's model involves successive fluctuations up and down in income and prices until a new equilibrium is reached. That causes the relation between money growth and business cycles that Friedman and Schwartz observed. (The lag for nominal income is usually six to nine months, while the lag for price rises is twelve to eighteen months.) Unlike the Austrians, Friedman downplays the possible real effects of inflation on the economy—its tendency, in the Misesian/Hayekian business cycle theory, for inflation to cause bad investments whose eventual collapse has real effects on the economy. He mostly thinks inflation's effect is on nominal quantities.

Only with constantly accelerating *rates* of inflation can the initial Phillips curve jolt that increased employment keep working; and that path can end only in reducing the currency to uselessness. The stagflation of the 1970s showed there was no long-term value in inflating to cut unemployment—we could suffer both simultaneously. Friedman maintained that in the long run the economy tends to have a natural rate of unemployment that cannot be flouted through monetary manipulations. This rate is not really "natural" per se, as it depends on the institutional environment. Greater availability and use of unemployment insurance, for example, would tend to make the "natural rate" higher than otherwise, since people would be more willing to remain unemployed.

Nowadays, at least among economists, Friedman's basic battle about stabilization policy and the Phillips curve is almost entirely won. Successive editions of Paul Samuelson's famous college economics text give more and more weight to money.[26] Nonetheless, politicians continue to make noises about tiny tax breaks to achieve some sort of immediate economic stimulus, another idea beloved of Keynesians, and another idea Friedman demolished, in what he considers his greatest achievement as an economist, his 1957 book *The Theory of the Consumption Function*.[27] In it, he postulated another notion that proved a tremendous success within the economics profession and created a new model for research and tweaking in an academic discipline that loves a good model above all else (even more, the Austrians argue, than accurate and truthful reasoning).

Friedman challenged the Keynesian notion that people make consumption decisions based on their immediate circumstances—on how much money is available to them at any given moment. He showed that people's consumption decisions instead are made based on a theoretical construct Friedman called "permanent income." People make calculations based on some notion of their entire life income. Thus sudden and immediate changes in their circumstances, either for better or for worse, don't affect their consumption decisions as much as Keynes thought they might.

If they gain a sudden windfall, they aren't apt to spend it all immediately; if they suffer a sudden loss, they aren't apt to suddenly cut their consumption by the amount of that loss. They smooth out gains and losses based on a vision of lifetime income, though not literally managing to spend their last dollar with their last breath—nor necessarily, in Friedman's methodology, with actually making such calculations. All that mattered to Friedman was that people seemed to behave *as if* they make such calculations. As long as that holds true, whether they actually do or not is irrelevant.[28]

The consumption function notion should seem intuitively plausible to anyone who gets paid with a staggered paycheck (almost all of us). We don't spend an entire paycheck within days of getting it and then remain destitute until the next payday. Friedman, playing the game of his profession masterfully, proves his point with sophisticated and difficult-to-follow mathematical models. Like any good economizer, he understands what means to use toward given ends.

This leads his friendly intellectual opponent Paul Samuelson (author of the most famous neo-Keynesian college economics text) to suggest, uncharitably, "if you are a yokel, Milton will give you a hokum answer."[29] Friedman is a master of both the conversational polemical style that made his *Free to Choose* one of the best-selling nonfiction books of 1980, and the mathematical language of economics that made him respected and heeded by his profession. Whatever Samuelson alleges, no argument cast in the vernacular could change the way economists look at the world.

Someone who loved the lucid explainer of *Capitalism and Freedom*, Friedman's first polemical classic, and then attempted to tackle, say, his technical explanations of how income differentiation in society reflects people's own choices and not just some inherent unfairness or exploitation in capitalism, would doubtless hit a wall. Unlike the works of the Austrian libertarian economists, Friedman's economic work is not necessarily understandable by an educated layman willing to think through things yet untrained in the profession. It might be a pity to that reader, but it has been responsible for building Friedman's substantial influence within his profession.

"MILTON FRIEDMAN IS THE ESTABLISHMENT'S COURT LIBERTARIAN."

Some of Friedman's most discussed work was not a contribution to economics per se but an attempt to explain how economics is done. Friedman tired of the game of commenting and arguing about methodology early, and assumes that this helped embolden others to comment on it endlessly.[30] The game of arguing over positivism in economics that Friedman started spawns books and articles to this day.

The essay that started it all was called "The Methodology of Positive Economics," first published in Friedman's 1953 collection *Essays in Positive Economics*. Friedman wasn't obsessed with the philosophy of science per se. He was foremost an economist, not a philosopher, and he wanted to explain what he thought economists ought to try to do: predict. Thus, he thought, economists need not be overly concerned with whether or not theoretical assumptions were "realistic." Friedman was attempting to defend, within a historical milieu in which it was under attack, the standard models of neoclassical economics, particularly perfect competition as refined by Alfred Marshall.[31] Friedman pointed out how the physical sciences, just as economics did, use unrealistic assumptions to good effect in making predictions.[32]

Friedman was *not* a Popperian falsificationist, as some interpret him. Popper famously believed that the definition of a scientific theory is that empirical evidence exists that can contradict it and prove it mistaken. Friedman is not looking for single instances to falsify theories; he is looking for ways to confirm them through their ability to predict. His monetarist concepts, suffused as they are with variable lags and a willingness to assume that sometimes unknown effects overpower the effects he's trying to test, show clearly that he is not ready to throw out a useful theoretical edifice because of a duff prediction or two, though some of his enemies certainly are.[33]

The bulk of the evidence he and Schwartz collected clearly show, to him, the overall correctness of monetarism. An Austrian might question the necessity of a man of Friedman's brilliance taking years of his life cobbling statistics to prove the point that more money causes price inflation, a point that praxeological reasoning can get you to in a few minutes reflection. However, arguments against that simple proposition abounded before Friedman and Schwartz did their work, and they are less loud now—though never silenced, as Friedman notes.[34]

The basic ideas that money matters (not, as detractors say, that money is *all* that matters) and that gross monetary fluctuation can cause inflation and business cycles are widely accepted. Friedman's methodology, while not necessarily embraced, is still argued over (as much of a success as most academicians can hope for; Friedman's actual influence on the world makes him like unto a god among intellectual scriveners). His consumption function thesis was an unqualified success, breeding new research and refinements to this day. As an economist, Friedman has been an almost unqualified success.

Friedman has mirrored that success as a polemicist for libertarianism, though his views are often mistakenly characterized as conservative. His ideas and his relentless writing and talking about them have won policy victories from the volunteer army to floating exchange rates to the elimination of legal ceilings on interest rates. (As per Friedman's own understanding about how libertarian ideas tend to win public acceptance, in each case these changes resulted when the existing systems faced near-crisis situations.)[35] Friedman is certainly the most widely read libertarian polemicist of his time, mostly thanks to his *Newsweek* column. In 1966, *Newsweek* editor Osbourne Elliot invited him to become one of a triumvirate taking over an economics column that had been manned by libertarian Henry Hazlitt since 1946. Friedman joined liberal Paul Samuelson and moderate Henry Wallich in rotation on the column; Friedman was meant to flank them both on the right. Friedman wrote the column tirelessly, eventually ending up with only one opposite number, Lester Thurow, until it was ended at *Newsweek*'s suggestion in 1984.[36]

In his columns, Friedman explained to millions of readers, in the context of commenting on current events, the basics of monetarism (plenty of Fed watching filled the column); wage and price controls; and his principle, now taken very seriously among fiscal conservatives, that since governments always spend what they tax plus some more, one should *never* raise taxes in an attempt to eliminate deficit spending. He advocated school vouchers and a volunteer army; he attacked the minimum wage, urban renewal, rent control, and usury laws. His was the loudest and most prevalent voice for market freedom in American journalism for two decades. The effect of his advocacy journalism, particularly in the context of a newsweekly, not just a segregated movement journal, cannot be measured; neither should it be underrated.

Friedman's next public splash as a libertarian polemicist was his TV series and book *Free to Choose*, which sold 400,000 copies in hardcover. The TV series idea was initiated by Robert Chitester, the president of an Erie, Pennsylvania, public TV station, WQLN. Friedman had just retired from the University of Chicago when Chitester approached him in 1977. The initial idea was to tape Friedman giving a series of lectures, but it soon turned into a full-fledged documentary series.[37] The series was shot from 1978 to 1979, and Chitester got PBS to air it nationally in 1980. Friedman suspects, since Chitester had little luck with previous or future attempts to sell PBS on free market documentaries, that it was because the year before they had shown John Kenneth Galbraith's series, *An Age of Uncertainty*.[38] Friedman and his wife Rose wrote a book covering much of the same ground as *Capitalism and Freedom*, structured into ten chapters analogous to the ten episodes of the TV series, and based on "more nuts and bolts, less theoretical framework" than *Capitalism and Freedom*.[39]

The TV show brought Friedman and his curious ideas about freedom to an even larger audience than the *Newsweek* column, making him a household name. Still, though, the middlebrow intelligentsia couldn't take him quite seriously with all those sweeping statements about liberty. Friedman's fellow Nobel winner Kenneth Arrow, reviewing the book in the *New Republic*, thought Friedman callously ignored wealth inequities and overstated his case for freedom; the book suffered, Arrow said, from "lack of guiding principles, the casual recommendation of sweeping changes without consideration of their systematic effects, and the one-sided selection of evidence."[40]

Friedman's political advocacy has not been aimed only at the public. He was an economics adviser to Goldwater's 1964 presidential campaign, and while refusing to take an official position within the administration, he was an also an informal adviser to Nixon during the early years of his presidency until Nixon imposed wage and price controls. (Except on the matter of the draft, there's little evidence Nixon was much of one to take Friedman's advice.) He was also part of an economics brain trust surrounding Reagan during his campaign, and was a member of Reagan's Presidential Economic Policy Advisory Board. One critic of both men saw such strong similarities between their economic philosophies that he claimed Reagan's *Economic Report from the President* reads like excerpts from *Capitalism and Freedom*.[41] Friedman has also given advice to government officials in nations from Israel to England, China to Yugoslavia. His face-to-face persuasive technique, ably described by Martin Anderson, who worked with him during the Reagan administration, worked like this: "At first he listens quietly, intensely. As long as he totally agrees he listens, but that usually isn't for long. At the first sign of the slightest break in your logic, or your facts, he pounces with a bewildering array of questions, statements, and relentless logic. And it's all done in such a friendly, earnest way that even the intellectually shredded thoroughly enjoy the encounter."[42]

Friedman's most controversial dallying with governments was in Chile during the early days of the Pinochet regime. Pinochet's economic advisers were all University of Chicago-trained, and thus known semicontemptuously as the "Chicago boys" and presumed to be blank transmitters of commands from their master, Friedman. Friedman was perhaps too quick to praise what happened in Chile under Pinochet as an economic miracle, even during the 1980s when it had not yet matched its own record in terms of inflation and unemployment during the 1960s, and when it pursued exchange rate policies Friedman generally opposed. Protesters who attempted to smear him with moral complicity in the Pinochet regime's political crimes, however, showed a gross misunderstanding of Friedman's actual political stances, and his evenhanded advising of governments from all ends of the political spectrum when his advice was sought.[43]

Friedman's Nobel, his prominent opinion columns, his closeness to Republican politicians, and his popular TV shows and books have won ideological victories for a radical libertarianism that no strictly libertarian movement ideologue has matched—not that the movement ideologues have always loved him for it. Rothbard wrote in 1971 that "Milton Friedman is the Establishment's Court Libertarian, and it is high time that libertarians awaken to this fact of life. . . . It is high time to identify Milton Friedman for what he really is; it is high time to call a spade a spade, and a statist a statist."[44] Surely Rothbard must have been rankled to read in a widely used college macroeconomics text, "We might as well treat Friedman as the spokesman for all libertarian economists, for that is more or less what he is."[45]

The hard-core Austrian or anarcho-libertarian could detect many sins in Friedman. He's too tolerant of statist evils through his advocacy of such programs as education vouchers and a negative income tax, which don't move all the way to the ultimate libertarian end immediately. Rothbard complained that Friedman, while professing to value freedom, "in practice allows a myriad of damaging exceptions, exceptions which serve to vitiate the principle almost completely, notably in the fields of police and military affairs, education, taxation, welfare, 'neighborhood effects,' antitrust laws, and money and banking,"[46] making Friedman, in Rothbard's judgment, "fundamentally and basically mistaken and wrongheaded."[47] When I interviewed Friedman within weeks of Rothbard's death, his rankling over how Rothbard treated him was apparent. He accused Rothbard of not recognizing the value of steps in the direction of where he wanted to go, even if they fail to leap the chasm from statism to liberty entirely in one bound, and credited some of his distance from the libertarian movement qua movement to distaste over Rothbard's vicious treatment of him and his ideas.[48]

Friedman's disdain for the gold standard exasperates Austrian-leaning libertarians as well—though Friedman in his later career considered more radical ideas about money. He used to think the gold standard was unwise because of the costs involved in mining and storing it compared to paper. But he's ultimately granted that the social costs of paper fiat money (because of all the complicated institutions for hedging in financial markets that absorb resources) might balance out those costs of the gold standard. Friedman has become much more willing to entertain the more radical libertarian notion that government should have no role in currency at all.[49]

Friedman saw economics as an experimental and mathematical science, also anathema to the Misesian catechism. Mises himself was known to refer to Friedman (along with Paul Samuelson) as one of the two most dangerous men in America. Mises confidante Bettina Bien Greaves, who remembers this remark that Mises never publicly wrote, says this was because Mises felt Friedman was an inflationist who didn't understand prices, since Friedman insisted on considering only aggregate price levels in his monetarist theory, ignoring the effects of different relative individual prices, which were all that mattered to Mises. All the while Friedman masqueraded as the preeminent defender of market freedom. At base, Mises didn't think Friedman understood economics.[50]

When Austrians tell Friedman he's wrong in paying so much attention to macroaggregates and price levels and ignoring specific imbalances and relative prices, the positivistic Friedman replies that he'll believe in such effects when evidence demonstrates them, not just because logic says they must exist.[51]

Insults between Friedman and other libertarian luminaries have run both ways. Friedman likes to finger Mises and Rand in particular for their intolerance, though Rothbard couldn't have been far from his mind as well. In a speech before the Future of Freedom Conference in 1990, reprinted in the movement journal *Liberty*, Friedman slams both Mises the man and his praxeological (purely logical, nonempirical) economic method as intolerant of difference of opinion. Ralph Raico, who knew both Mises and Friedman and says the impression of Mises given by the anecdotes Friedman likes to tell don't capture the man entire, argues that Friedman's attack on praxeology falls apart on Friedman's own grounds of predictive accuracy. Friedman likes to say that the praxeological method, because it is based on pure reason, leaves no room for appeal to empirical evidence to settle differences, and thus must necessarily leave only fighting as a means of settling differences. If this were so, Raico said, the same should apply to logic and mathematics, which similarly allow for no recourse to empirical observation to settle differences; and no such "incessant bloody brawling" can be seen in those disciplines.[52]

In the same 1990 speech, Friedman decries the utopian strain in libertarians that makes them disdain the half steps in the direction of less government that Friedman spends much of his polemical energy advocating.[53] However, Friedman is sometimes too timid even on his own terms. While he has written that "I have been inclined myself to give little weight to political feasibility—in the sense of the prospect that any proposal will be quickly or readily enacted," he often makes policy proposals that are short of his own professed final goals in consideration of political reality—education vouchers, for example, when he would ultimately like to see an end to compulsory state-financed schooling.[54] His son David, anarcho-capitalist author of *The Machinery of Freedom*, thinks this is merely because his father's thinking is geared toward immediate results, while his own anarchism is geared more toward long-term goals.[55]

Milton Friedman ruefully admits that he would "like to be a zero-government libertarian," but can't get over what he sees as the insurmountable problems of national defense and enforcing public peace.[56] (Friedman's arguments with anarchism sound honed against the arguments of his anarchist son, and David Friedman acknowledges this is probably so.)[57] Friedman did, and does, consider himself a radical; he once praised Adam Smith as "a radical and a revolutionary in his time—just as those of us who preach laissez-faire are in our times."[58]

That Friedman is the most argued-with libertarian of his time—from the left as well as from fellow libertarians and the standard right—is just one more facet of his success. His claiming the libertarian mantle has done more to make more people understand and respect the general tenets and thrust of libertarian ideas than have the efforts of any other libertarian advocate.[59] Friedman died at age ninety-four in November 2006, just as this book went to press.

"HOW CAN INDIVIDUALS LIVE IN SOCIAL ORDER WHILE PRESERVING THEIR OWN LIBERTIES?"

Friedman's Nobel was not the end of victories for libertarian-leaning economics in that rarified realm, or in the realm of general academic and intellectual success. In 1986, James Buchanan—then part of the Austrian-centric George Mason University economics department— earned the laurel. Buchanan's fascination with constitutional rules and procedures, and his apparent belief that any result that comes from them, if they themselves are fairly and properly set up, is normatively acceptable, often makes him seem less than fully libertarian, but he in his own mind had an intellectual project with a moral aspect that inclined him toward respect for the individual and limitation of the power of the state.[60]

Although one could argue over his specific libertarian bona fides, he and his old partner Gordon Tullock, with whom he did the early foundational work in the school of economics that has come to be known as Public Choice, have unquestionably given libertarians a valuable intellectual and ideological tool. Buchanan and Tullock helped build a professional consensus and a rigorous scholarly apparatus around the notion that—despite what many economic professionals used to assume—the behavior of government agents can fruitfully be modeled the same way we model individual behavior in markets; that is, as largely motivated by maximizing the personal utility of the government worker or politician, not by some empyrean concept of the "public good" or an overall "social welfare function" that a technical economist could calculate.

As Tullock explains it, "the different attitude toward government that arises from public choice does have major effects on our views on what policies government should undertake or can carry out. In particular, it makes us much less ambitious about relying on government to provide certain services. No student of public choice would feel that the establishment of a national health service in the United States would mean that the doctors would work devotedly to improve the health of the citizens."[61]

Tullock and other economists associated with the Public Choice School also pioneered economic research in the concept of "rent seeking," a powerful weapon in the contemporary libertarian intellectual arsenal. This is the idea that seeking special privileges through government that impose costs on others has harms and costs beyond the matter of whether it is morally wrong, as rights-based libertarians would argue it is. Though some economists used to see such activity as having no net social costs, since the taxpayers' loss was the special interests' gain, the "rent seeking" idea posits net social losses because the resources expended on the part of the special interest in getting the advantage from government amount to costs above and beyond the taxpayers' loss.[62]

The Buchanan/Tullock Public Choice approach also came to be known as the Virginia School of political economy because of Buchanan's formative years teaching at the University of Virginia. (Buchanan had been, unsurprisingly, an economics student at the University of Chicago.) The Volker Fund was one of the early supporters of the Thomas Jefferson Center for Studies in Political Economy and Social Philosophy that Buchanan ran there, and helped them bring in other libertarian thinkers such as Hayek and Italian legal scholar Bruno Leoni for half-year stints. Buchanan sums up the libertarian implications of his research program: "The Virginia emphasis was, from the outset, on the limits of political process rather than on any schemes to use politics to correct for market failures."[63]

The unorthodoxy of the Buchanan/Tullock approach created problems with the university administration, and the public choicers were pushed out of the University of Virginia. The movement regrouped in the 1970s at Virginia Polytechnic University. By 1983, Buchanan and what was now called the Center for the Study of Public Choice had landed at George Mason University, where it remains (along with major centers of other such libertarian-leaning approaches as the Austrian and law and economics schools).

In 1986, Buchanan won the Nobel Prize. As with Friedman and Hayek, many were upset that someone with his unpopular libertarian ideology had won it. Buchanan understands why his ideological adversaries might object to the "moral passion" at the heart of his political economy—his program "has advanced our scientific understanding of social interaction, but the science has been consistently applied to the normatively chosen question: How can individuals live in social order while preserving their own liberties?"[64] While their insights point in a libertarian direction, most Public Choice economists, in line with Buchanan and Tullock, and unlike, say, Friedman or Rothbard, eschew public talk or agitation about public policy and thus have not become an active part of the libertarian ideological movement.

Another superstar economist of libertarian leanings, though he's avoided the label publicly, is Thomas Sowell, a man who has done sophisticated work in the Hayekian field of institutional effects on the efficient use of knowledge. He is usually described—to his great consternation—as a "black conservative" and was offered the positions of secretary of education and secretary of labor in the Reagan administration, which he declined.[65] His 1982 book *Knowledge and Decisions* is perhaps the greatest work of popular libertarian economic thinking of the past thirty years. It presents an insightful and sophisticated explanation of how the institutions of the free market, from private property to market prices to corporations, help craft incentives and utilize knowledge in ways that create the greatest overall social wealth and the least overall social cost. He analyzes how government planning is generally based in a presumption that individuals are bad at choosing and pursuing their own interests and defends the proposition that letting people pursue their own interests is the only way to ensure knowledge and incentives are best brought to bear in a manner that enriches everyone.[66]

In 1987, Objectivist libertarian Alan Greenspan achieved the highest position of power and influence that any movement libertarian ever had—chairmanship of the Federal Reserve Board, where he resided for nearly twenty years and racked up a reputation as the greatest wizard of finance the world had ever known. To the consternation of his libertarian fans, however, that reputation had little basis in anything specifically libertarian. Ayn Rand told the *New York Times* when he first went to D.C. as a member of Gerald Ford's Council of Economic Advisers that "Alan is my disciple, philosophically. He is an advocate of laissez-faire capitalism. But neither he nor I would expect it over night."[67] Indeed, it has yet to arrive. He would have no problem saying on *Meet the Press* that he didn't really cotton to antitrust laws or letting libertarian Republican Congressman Ron Paul, when Paul teased him about it, know that he still believed every word of an essay he wrote for Rand's *Objectivist Newsletter* about the beauty and utility of the gold standard. However, he didn't go out of his way to stress such points as a moral imperative in the manner of a Howard Roark. While some angry Objectivists saw him as a sellout, it might be more apt to see him as a professional who tried to do the job he was hired to do the best way he knew how. Occasionally he sent a signal to the libertarian faithful, such as telling a Senate committee that, though he would probably be the only member of the Federal Open Market Committee (the Fed board that controlled interest rates and money supply changes) to support a return to the gold standard, there would be at least one vote for it on the committee—his.[68]

While many said the American economy was better for his having been Fed chief—largely because he had incorporated a basic Milton Friedman–style understanding of the bad effects of willy-nilly increases in the money supply—it would not be true that he made the American economy any freer than he found it or seemed particularly concerned with doing so. He was a quiet, hardworking man and a remarkably skilled politician, which doubtless explains how he not only got through nineteen years at the Fed with sterling reputation largely intact, but also remained friends with the imperious and difficult Rand until the end of her life.

"A FAIRLY LARGE MARKET FOR FREE MARKET IDEAS."

While not respectable economics in the Nobel Prize–winning sense, another fertile field of pop economic advice in the 1970s and early

1980s was unabashedly libertarian dominated: a once hugely popular arena of investment advice, the hard money subdivision pejoratively known as the goldbugs. These were financial advisers influenced by the Austrian economic theorizing of Mises and Rothbard who were confident that government mismanagement of money and the economy was leading to an inflationary collapse in which only gold or other hard assets held any hope of protecting investments and wealth. Libertarians dominated this *very* popular movement to warn people to flee government paper and preserve their wealth, their property, their *life* from the social agony and convulsion that were the inevitable result of the predictable failures of government economic interventionism.

To a large degree because of hard money's popularity, the early 1980s were a propitious time for libertarian ideas and thinkers in the public realm. Doug Casey is an adventurer who was converted to anarcho-capitalism by reading Morris and Linda Tannehill's 1969 classic *The Market for Liberty* at the behest of Jarret Wollstein. Casey wrote one of the best-selling books of 1980 with *Crisis Investing*.

The last third of *Crisis Investing* is a detailed fantasia inspired by the Tannehills about how a stateless society would work. Because of the book's months on the *New York Times* best-seller list, Casey got anarcho-capitalist thoughts into the hands and heads of an unprecedented number of Americans.

The economic breakdown the goldbugs foresaw never came—or *hasn't yet come*, as some insist to this day. Still, Harry Browne, another best-selling goldbug writer, author of *How You Can Profit from the Coming Devaluation* (1970) and similar books, the former follower of 1960s Southern California libertarian guru Andrew Galambos (who, as noted, didn't permit anyone to explain his theories but himself) and future LP presidential candidate, wasn't embarrassed. He figured that with inflation the way it was going and gold prices as high as they got, you could have done better in the market in the 1970s and early 1980s with a mistaken belief in that imminent collapse than with a more accurate assessment of the facts—*if* you got out of gold at the right time.

Doug Casey was a huge Harry Browne fan and considers him a pioneering genius. But Casey also realized that lots of goldbugs and Austrian economics devotees knew what Browne knew. "I thought goddamn it, I could have done [what Browne did]—and ten years later I did. [*Crisis Investing*] was really just a redux [of Browne] in many ways; just the title was different."[69]

Browne and Casey, both best-selling avatars of this significant, though ill-remembered by social historians, American movement, were both hard-core radical libertarians, marinated in the analyses of Mises and Rothbard, often filtered through the likes of Galambos. From Galambos rose several of the early figures in hard money sales and advocacy, including silver dealer Lou Carabini (who had Berkeley Alliance for Libertarian Action activist Dan Rosenthal writing copy for him) and popular investment newsletter and book writers Jerome Smith and Jack Pugsley.

Ironically for those contemplating the rise and fall of the goldbugs in libertarian terms, the judicious application by Federal Reserve Chairman Paul Volcker of another popular libertarian's prescriptions, Milton Friedman's monetarism, helped avert the apocalypse that Casey and Browne and others predicted so vividly. Gold maxed out at a bit over $800 an ounce in 1980, and has never again been as valuable.

The whole goldbug phenomenon showed that libertarians, when selling what seemed like practical advice and not waving the libertarian flag, could be remarkably successful—without effecting much real policy change. Harry Browne was selling out Carnegie Hall with lectures in the mid-1970s. Casey's best-sellerdom got him an hour on the *Phil Donahue Show* the week of the 1980 elections, in which he gave all the anarchist reasons why he didn't vote at all. Browne once said, "There has always been a fairly large market for free market ideas—as long as they are presented in a way by which the customer believes he can profit from them."[70]

Libertarian goldbugs did more than just top best-seller lists with historically discredited scare tactics; one of them, James U. Blanchard, a Rand fan who through her discovered Mises and Hayek and was converted to hard money economics, achieved notoriety by calling out Milton Friedman in an open letter for not advocating gold as the key to monetary stability. That letter was published in Harry Schultz's hard money newsletter, and from the correspondents Blanchard gained through that open letter, he formed in the late 1960s the National Committee to Legalize Gold, a citizen's pressure group. They forged effective congressional alliances with the likes of Phil Crane, Steve

Symms, and Jesse Helms, pulled off PR stunts such as appearing publicly with illegal Canadian gold bullion and daring the feds to arrest them, and buzzed Nixon's second inaugural with a plane trailing a banner emblazoned, "Legalize Gold."

Their efforts were successful, for gold ownership was legal again in 1975.[71] This paved the way for other libertarian goldbugs to sell books and advice about how everyone needed to buy it as a hedge against the looming collapse of Western civilization. The gold obsession was intimately connected with survivalism, another 1970s American fad that the libertarians of the 1960s *Innovator* zine were ahead of the curve on. If an idea involved assuming that government was going to screw everything up so much that we'd all need canned foods and remote hideaways to survive, you can bet libertarians will be on its cutting edge.

I interviewed the athletic, thoughtful Doug Casey at the 2005 meeting of his Eris Society—an invitation-only gathering of mostly libertarians with an interest in exotic thinking and the cutting edges of science, politics, and the applications of extreme personal liberty. He was cheerfully sanguine about his apparent failures as a prophet. *Crisis Investing* made very little money for him since he sold the hardback rights to another best-selling libertarian author and investment adviser, Robert Ringer, for a nominal fee in order to get Ringer's promotional might and mailing lists on his side. Ringer's hard-core libertarian bestsellers almost never use the word "libertarian," and they include *Looking Out for Number One* (1977) and *Winning Through Intimidation* (1974), both enormous successes and major cultural phenomena. Their Randian *epater le bourgeois* titles hid a perfectly respectable, nonviolent and noncoercive but self-assured libertarianism similar to what Harry Browne pushed in another huge libertarian best-seller and "me generation" classic, which also didn't push the term "libertarian," *How to Find Freedom in an Unfree World*.

Casey became fabulously wealthy anyway, through a series of hundred-to-one market wins. His success is an interesting case study in the Austrian theory of kaleidic chaotic markets, as opposed to the Chicagoite vision of ceaselessly rational ones based on perfect information. He became a hugely successful author selling advice that turned out to be wrong in its big picture. He gladly admits he missed the timing of the collapse in *Crisis Investing*, and also admits, hey, crisis, shmises, he had a great time, both in life and in money, even in those bad old days of 15 percent interest rates. Casey delights in the fact that his social position as a very rich man allows him access to places where he can pointedly refuse to shake Dick Cheney's hand and tell him to his face that it's because "I hold you and everything you stand for in contempt." He can get up in front of thousands of hard money businessmen and customers and excoriate them for their slavish devotion to criminal politicians.

He still believes, though, that the crisis caused by government fiscal and monetary mismanagement—one that might be even worse than he used to imagine—is on the horizon. He's perversely proud of being one of the few people still saying it in his investment advice newsletter. (In an interesting irony for someone who made his fame selling advice that was supposed to help you flourish in the worst sort of downturn, the 1987 crash devastated his holdings, though he's since recovered.) He is perfectly willing to delight in the chaos and unpredictability of semifree markets that he's surfed. He did remarkably well in the 1990s but characterizes his three biggest investment successes that decade as due not to any brilliant perspicacity or studious application of his socioeconomic thinking; frankly, he says, "One was an accident, one was a fraud [not on his part], and one was a psychotic break."[72]

His speculating successes have allowed him the luxury of pursuing the old libertarian dream of creating a new anarcho-nation. His wealth gave him entrée to meetings with actual third world dictators, whom he tried to sell on the notion of converting their countries into private companies and distributing the shares to all their citizens. He's tried this in the Dominican Republic, Surinam, Ciskei, and Haiti among other places, though the idea never got much traction beyond a few meetings with this strange American multimillionaire.

Casey is disgusted with prominent libertarians for never being willing to help on these nation-building missions, even when he assured them that showing their faces and helping him craft publicity campaigns in one third world hellhole or another could actually get the idea percolating among the kleptocrats.

"'Oh gee, isn't this going to be dangerous?' 'Oh my, I can't take the two weeks off from the university.' I told them, look, we can *do some-*

thing of world-historical importance!" Casey figured if he put up the money for a big ad campaign and they had the right serious, credentialed idea people on the ground, he would have gotten the masses into the streets, demanding to be stockholders in their nation's wealth, not merely victims mulcted by taxes and regulations to support their "leaders." He thought the timing might have really been right in Surinam, for a while there, but no, it didn't happen. Now he's beyond being eager or hopeful about any of it. He still dabbles in the occasional dinner with a dictator or bull session with some international mercenary for his own amusement and for delicious cocktail party stories.

"The conservatives had the money, and the libertarians had the ideas."

One particularly fruitful model for libertarian institution building that helped bring the insights of libertarian economists to policymakers and general lay public awareness was brought to America by a Brit, Antony Fisher. As with that other distinctly American underground phenomenon turned mainstream, punk rock, Fisher was bringing back home a flame of inspiration originally kindled in America.

Fisher, a former British fighter pilot, was dazzled by the early work of Leonard Read's FEE, after being turned on to libertarian ideas by the *Reader's Digest* version of Hayek's *Road to Serfdom*. He once told Read that if FEE had existed at the beginning of the twentieth century, the world wars of this century would not have happened.[73] Inspired by the Read/FEE model, but ultimately aiming for a more scholarly and less folksy tone in its work, Fisher founded the Institute for Economic Affairs (IEA) in Britain, under the leadership of Arthur Seldon and Ralph Harris. IEA, founded and funded by Fisher's fabulously successful chicken farms, laid down the loam from which the Margaret Thatcher revolution sprouted, becoming the major pushers in England of Hayek's general anti–central economic control notions, and the ideas of privatizing sclerotic British industries.

After IEA was rolling, Fisher went on to apply libertarian thinking in another business venture, an early experiment in free market environmentalism in practice. He began trying to mass-produce green sea turtles, an endangered species. By farming them, he could both increase their total numbers on earth and profit from selling their meat for soup and their penises for the delectation of superstitious Asians. This was the mid-1970s, and that sort of free market environmental thinking had even less traction among environmentalists and conservationists than it does now. A concerted campaign against the selling of turtle parts, even if the end result was more turtles on the face of the earth rather than fewer, drove Fisher out of turtle farming.[74]

Fisher then turned to franchising the IEA model of free market think tanks in America and around the world. His money, connections, and organizational efforts launched the ICEPS, which later became the Manhattan Institute. The institute grew to prominence under the stewardship of William Hammett, former head of the Center for Libertarian Studies. Manhattan's first big splash came with sponsoring libertarian Charles Murray's *Losing Ground*. Joan Kennedy Taylor, who worked with Hammett at Manhattan in the 1980s and shepherded that project to completion, says he told her to no longer identify herself publicly with her membership in the Association of Libertarian Feminists because their donors despised both libertarians and feminists. (She thinks Hammett saw his CLS past as something to live down in the Manhattan Institute context, since they were trying to reach out to a standard conservative donor base.)

Fisher also helped launch the Pacific Research Institute, initially helmed by David Theroux, a young libertarian from the University of Chicago who had been part of Ed Crane's early team at Cato, though fired for his part in a failed coup against Crane. (Theroux went on to run the staunchly libertarian and antiwar Independent Institute in Oakland.) Theroux recalls that Fisher impressed American donors by waving Margaret Thatcher like a talisman. IEA provided the intellectual firepower that brought her to power in England and perhaps could do the same here. It was a successful pitch.

Fisher eventually institutionalized this free market institute building energy in the Atlas Foundation, launched in 1981, which advises and aids the formation of free market think tanks around the world. It has experienced remarkable success in Latin America, where chance attraction to the works of Mises and FEE had already laid fertile ground and created ready libertarian entrepreneurs for such organizations.

Successful think tanks launched or substantially aided by Fisher or Atlas include state-based market think tanks such as Pennsylvania's Allegheny Institute, Arizona's Goldwater Institute, Ohio's Buckeye Institute, Florida's James Madison Institute, North Carolina's John Locke Foundation, Utah's Sutherland Institute, and Oregon's Cascade Policy Institute. Specialty houses applying free market thinking to specific policy areas or audiences include the Institute for Energy Research, the Acton Institute (selling free market economics to the American religious community), and the Minaret of Freedom Foundation (discussing liberty in terms of Islamic thought).

The groups funded by Fisher (and those inspired by them), while often run by people who self-identify as libertarian rather than conservative, generally focus on free market and privatization issues that don't create skirmishes on the DMZ between libertarianism and conservatism; more about tax cuts than military cuts; more about introducing market incentives into health care delivery than ending prescription drug laws. They also tend to be localized, focusing their attention on policy battles within their states that national policy houses like Cato or Heritage don't have time for.

By the same token, the Fisher/Atlas progeny aren't generally out there talking up Christian virtue or fighting against abortion or gay marriage, or for a tougher push on the war on drugs, or for American military intervention overseas. They represent an amalgam between libertarian and merely free market thinking that avoids the controversial areas on the nonoverlapping parts of the libertarian/conservative Venn diagram. They could, depending on one's feelings toward temporizing in the rush toward complete liberty, be seen as representing either the libertarianizing of conservative activism or the conservativization of libertarian activism—or just a rich arena for public policy advocacy and development that manages to successfully split the difference.

Not all state and local libertarian think tanks arose from Fisher activism. Chicago's Heartland Institute arose in the early 1980s from a group of local libertarian businessmen, gathered by one-time Center for Libertarian Studies and Cato board member David Padden as the

Loop Libertarian League. They financed local young libertarian Joseph Bast, then publishing one of the last holdovers of small-circulation libertarian zines, *Nomos*. Staunchly libertarian Bast realized that to succeed in the funding marketplace with a local focus, he would have to be studiedly fusionist, concentrating on those free market issues where most conservatives and libertarians could agree. "The conservatives had the money, and the libertarians had the ideas," he said. After some Illinois success Bast became an Antony Fisher II, creating branch offices throughout the Midwest with funding support from right-wing foundations such as Scaife.

Other foundations from which Bast sought funding were leery of the franchising notion, thinking high-level academics were needed to run a free market think tank. Bast disagreed. "My motto is, you need to find a used car salesman who's a libertarian—an aggressive, articulate guy who wants to build an organization. Academics are in fact almost uniquely *not* fit to head a think tank. They don't have management or financial skills."[75] Lack of foundation belief in the affiliate idea made Heartland eventually retreat back to Chicago, where it now works as a set of virtual sinews uniting the policy work of dozens of other local and national market-oriented policy organizations, and circulating that work out to state legislators around the nation in order to maximize the impact of the smaller policy groups.

The disjunction between being pro–free market and being pro-business has in the past stymied Heartland's relations with the Illinois business community, especially when Illinois had big-spending Republican governors. Heartland's inevitable attacks on Republican policies would scare off businessmen who needed cordial relationships with the state Republican power structure.

"I was told I'd discredit myself as a person."

Antony Fisher's attempts to franchise the British IEA model achieved its first and strongest effect on American politics via the Manhattan Institute. Next to Milton Friedman, think tank sociologist Charles Murray is the libertarian intellectual who has had the most direct effect on a vital policy debate. His 1984 book *Losing Ground*—commissioned and shepherded to completion by ex-Rand inner circle member and *Libertarian Review* staffer Joan Kennedy Taylor (who Murray says was "the equivalent of the person discovering me sitting on the stool at Schwab's Drug Store"), under the aegis of the Manhattan Institute, run by former Center for Libertarian Studies chief William Hammett— quickly elbowed its way to the center of the serious debate about welfare policy.[76] Four years after it came out, I was assigned to read it in two separate political science courses in a not particularly libertarian state university, and by the mid-1990s the ideas it injected into the debate animated Clinton-era welfare reforms.

In *Losing Ground,* Murray tries to demonstrate that by most available measures, the late 1960s wave of income transfer programs— such as greatly liberalized Aid to Families with Dependent Children standards, job training, funding for disadvantaged elementary and secondary school students—did not improve the lives of the poor, and in most cases made them worse off. He uses trendline analyses to show that any improvement in the lives of the poor that happened after the programs went into effect was merely a continuation of progress that had begun long before the federal effort did—and that the progress in most cases stopped as the 1970s began and the program's effects became clear. Crime and unemployment went up for the poor as the welfare state grew in the 1960s; income and educational achievement went down.

Murray does not rely on the "welfare cheat" rhetoric that welfare supporters think characterized the antiwelfare stance of the Reagan years. Murray thinks liberals found *Losing Ground* exasperating because he took a different tone and approach to the free market assault on welfare, speaking in a voice clearly concerned with the fate of the poor and blacks, about incentives and productivity and self-respect. He stepped outside his assigned role of curmudgeonly basher of welfare queens. He used thought experiments to show how the incentives for the rational poor created by the modern welfare state made it more likely that children would be born illegitimate and less likely that men would feel the need to work or provide for their children. His policy recommendation to improve the lot of America's poor was to eliminate all racial preference programs, institute educational vouchers, and

eliminate all income transfer programs, later reinstating short-term unemployment insurance.

Murray used the ideological think tank, an institution that the libertarian movement helped popularize because of its necessary separation
from existing centers of policy power, whether academic or governmental, to effect policy. The think tank is a place for people to do
scholarship and policy advocacy without having to teach or deal with
academic and faculty politics. Murray also credits new technology for
helping him succeed: computers, which allow non-university affiliated
scholars to crunch data without needing an army of indentured grad
students. His next project after *Losing Ground* was more explicitly libertarian: *In Pursuit of Happiness and Good Government* (1988), in which
he argued that a mostly libertarian independent Jeffersonian republic
infused people with virtue and purpose. He began to see "little platoons" (his term for local communities acting to meet their social
needs themselves) as necessary for the rigorous development of important human virtues and human flourishing, and saw that government
social programs stunted the formation of such platoons. This realization turned him into a full-on libertarian. *In Pursuit* ends by asking
that "we take more seriously the proposition that Jefferson's was a vision suitable not only for a struggling agricultural nation at the outset
of the nineteenth century but also for a wealthy postindustrial nation
at the close of the twentieth."[77]

His next book, *The Bell Curve* (1994), consumed the social capital he
had built from *Losing Ground*'s success in the welfare debate. Iconoclasm, sometimes dangerous iconoclasm, is par for the course for libertarians. But *The Bell Curve*, which delved into the dangerous grounds
of race-based differences in intelligence, was so extreme that many
ideological allies, including Cato and the Manhattan Institute, dis-
tanced themselves from it. The basic science in the book had nothing
to do with Murray's ideological interest in libertarianism. It discussed
differences in social outcomes related to IQ and suggested that blacks'
IQ distribution was on average lower than whites', which were in turn
lower than Asians'.

Murray maintains his inspiration for *Bell Curve* was purely intellectual
curiosity over an issue in which he detected an enormous chasm between most accepted opinion and what the experts understood and be-

lieved. He does, though, think that libertarian sociopolitical implications can be found in *The Bell Curve*. If we recognize, as *The Bell Curve* argues, that humans are not completely malleable and can't necessarily achieve on an equal level, we'll be more skeptical about the effectiveness of government social engineering. *The Bell Curve* thesis implies that, because of inherent differences in human intelligence and ability, we will continually see inequalities in social outcomes that no amount of remaking institutions and redistributing incomes will ever eliminate. "Lots of my friends were upset I was doing this book," he notes, including some of his ideological comrades at the libertarian Cato Institute. "I was told I'd discredit myself as a person, that all the work I did on *Losing Ground* will be lost, people will just look at me and say, oh, we know about *him*. And to some extent that has happened."[78]

But he notes optimistically that most of *Losing Ground*'s major contentions have gone from heresy to conventional wisdom since the Clinton welfare reforms. He is confident that the same will happen to *The Bell Curve* within twenty years. After the furor about that book subsided somewhat, he returned to libertarian thinking, with *What It Means to Be a Libertarian* (1997)—a standard libertarian primer on how markets could solve social problems most people think we need government for.

Murray thanks his post–*Bell Curve* pariah status for one thing. He no longer gets asked to testify before Congress, which he found frustrating and unpleasant.

"CAPITALISM *IS* THE BEST SYSTEM, BUT ONLY BAD PEOPLE WOULD THINK SO."

The Reagan era glorification of antigovernment rhetoric created a golden age for libertarianism. But these victories—even if mostly only in terms of rhetoric and visibility—in the political realm did not arise from nowhere. Groundwork had been laid by the incursion of libertarian thinking in the 1970s in realms from academic philosophy to popular literature to psychiatry to such crazes as survivalism and life extension.

In 1974, for example, libertarian political philosophy won its greatest professional success of the postwar era with the publication of the National Book Award–winning *Anarchy, State, and Utopia*. For many movement libertarians, for whom Rand was the most important philosopher and the standard bastions of political and intellectual culture implacable enemies, that victory came from an unlikely source— Robert Nozick, a young philosophy professor from Harvard University.

This brilliant Nozick, only thirty-six when the book appeared, shook up the academic world with his tangled and sophisticated arguments in favor of libertarian political positions that most academics found repellent. Many movement libertarians were similarly impressed and similarly not convinced.

Nozick was born in Brooklyn on November 16, 1938, son of Max Nozick, a Russian immigrant and small businessman, and Sophie Cohen Nozick. He obtained a doctorate in philosophy from Princeton in 1963 and became a full professor at Harvard in 1969. His work has been the touchstone for academic philosophical grappling with the libertarian project from the time he burst on the scene with *Anarchy*, his first book. As libertarian scholar Tom Palmer has noted, "Nozick's book has come to enjoy canonical status among academics, who normally assign it to students as 'the' libertarian book, with little appreciation of the broader tradition of libertarian thinking and scholarship within which Nozick's work took shape."[79]

Although Nozick was snugly ensconced at the pinnacle of academe, which had barely deigned to acknowledge the existence of the libertarian intellectual tendency, he was also enmeshed in aspects of the self-conscious libertarian movement that few nonlibertarian academics would countenance. As Nozick remarked in the introduction to *Anarchy*, "It was a long conversation about six years ago with Murray Rothbard that stimulated my interest in individualist anarchist theory."[80] Nozick was introduced to Rothbard's ideas through Bruce Goldberg, who had been a member of Rothbard's Circle Bastiat, and also a philosophy graduate student with Nozick at Princeton.

Goldberg's friend Ralph Raico remembers that Goldberg

> pressed his libertarianism on Bob [Nozick], who, ever intellectually omnivorous, quickly absorbed Mises, Hazlitt, Hayek, and

other thinkers. Soon Nozick was radically questioning his social-democratic orientation, picked up pretty much by accident from his New York Jewish environment. As Bruce told me the story, one time Bob went back to his pals at *Dissent* magazine and confronted them. If the minimum wage is so good, why not set it at, say, $10 an hour? They had no answer to the question. . . . Then one evening, it must have been in the early '60s, Bruce brought Bob to a gathering of the Circle Bastiat at the Rothbards' apartment on West 88th Street. It turned out to be a historic moment. If Nozick hadn't been impressed by the Rothbardian synthesis before then, he was at that meeting. This was the genesis of his celebrated book.[81]

Nozick's transition from social democrat to libertarian was not seamless or easy. During his undergraduate years at Columbia he was, as he once said, "convinced by socialist arguments. . . . At Columbia . . . I founded a socialist group, the local chapter of it, that is: the Student League for Industrial Democracy" which later morphed into Students for a Democratic Society. "I was a social democrat. I never actually encountered principled arguments for capitalism. I encountered arguments that said, well, there will be higher productivity under capitalism, which I think is true, but nothing that spoke to certain moral concerns that one might have about whether it was a legitimate system." After he encountered Goldberg and Rothbard, "I thought that they couldn't be correct and I set out to find out what was wrong with them. The more I explored the arguments, the more convincing they looked. For a while, I thought: 'Well, yes, the arguments are right, capitalism *is* the best system, but only bad people would think so.' Then, at some point, my mind and heart were in unison." Nozick soon learned that his ignorance of the arguments in favor of capitalism was not unique. "When I have a course on socialism and capitalism, most of the students—and it's quite striking, many of them are children of people in influential positions—had never heard principled arguments in defense of a free-enterprise system."[82]

Nozick did not stay ensconced in his ivory tower. His defense of libertarianism in an unsympathetic milieu—upper-level academic philosophy—earned him a certain reputation for dashing verve and daring, but it did not make his social existence smooth. "There was a time . . . in the aftermath of *Anarchy, State, and Utopia*," Nozick later reminisced, "when it was probably the case that my social life was somewhat curtailed. There may have been many parties I wasn't getting invited to because people despised the views in my book."[83]

In a way, Nozick might understand why. After all, in *Anarchy*'s preface he wrote, undoubtedly thinking of right-wingers he might be lumped in with because he defended capitalism, that "since many of the people who take a similar position [to the one he takes in *Anarchy*] are narrow and rigid, and filled, paradoxically, with resentment at other freer ways of being, my now having natural responses which fit the theory puts me in some bad company."[84]

Social problems with his colleagues paled in relation to the annoyance some Harvard students felt toward his ideas, particularly during the ferment of late 1960s and early 1970s student radicalism. He was teaching a course on capitalism before *Anarchy* came out and was approached by a grad student who told him, "We don't know if you're going to be able to give this course."

"And I said, 'What do you mean?'" Nozick recalled. "He mumbled something, 'there may be interruptions or demonstrations in class.' And I said—I was then, you have to remember, 30 years old—I said, 'If you disrupt my course, I'm going to kick the shit out of you. . . . It's my course, if you want to pass out leaflets outside the classroom door, and tell people that they shouldn't come in and take the course, that's fine. I won't allow you to do things inside the classroom.' He said, 'Yes, well, we may pass out leaflets.' Time went by and nothing happened. . . . So I saw him in the hallway and asked, 'Where are the leaflets?' He said, 'Well, you know, we're very busy, we have a lot of things to do these days.' I said, 'I called my mother living in Florida and told her that I was going to be leafleted, now come on!' But nothing ever happened."[85]

While he firmly resisted becoming pigeonholed as "that libertarian guy," Nozick did not shy away from the grittier aspects of the political/philosophical movement he had become a leading defender of. He even attended the Libertarian Party convention in 1975 as a delegate from Massachusetts. Nozick proposed from the convention floor a platform plank emulating the Ninth Amendment, a favorite of libertarians, in saying that "Our silence about any particular government law, regulation, ordinance, directive, edict, control, regulatory agency, activity, or machination should not be construed to imply approval."[86]

While he did not convert his profession (that wasn't even his goal), Nozick did bring libertarian ideas to the center of the academic philosophical argument and, as a fellow philosopher whose conversion to a libertarian outlook was launched by Nozick wrote, "woke a number of us from our dogmatic slumbers."[87]

Because of his background in the individualist anarchist tradition via Rothbard, Nozick didn't take the existence and propriety of the state for granted. All too often, as libertarian philosopher Loren Lomasky has written, "liberal theorists . . . respond to the anarchist challenge by ignoring it. . . . One who does not, who is the conspicuous defender for our time of a liberal politics against the anarchist challenge, is Robert Nozick."[88] The first segment of *Anarchy, State, and Utopia* defends the proposition that a morally permissible state could arise from a starting point of Rothbardian anarchy.

In the broadest strokes (and bearing in mind that Nozick is a nuanced and complicated writer), Nozick's argument for how a state could morally arise from anarchy went like this: In a world of private competing defense agencies (which would surely arise to meet people's natural needs for protection and adjudication in a stateless world), violent conflicts would inevitably break out between those agencies. And it seems most likely that through economies of scale— and victories in conflicts—one such agency would naturally grow much larger than the others. For that very reason, it would be more attractive to other customers, trapping competing defense agencies in a vicious spiral to irrelevancy and penury.[89]

At that point we would have one mostly dominant private protection agency in any given geographical area. But this agency would still fall short of being a state because it does not claim a monopoly on the use of force in its area—yet.

Nozick then summoned a new principle, one not usually included in the anarcho-libertarian vision of rights: the notion that even in a perfectly libertarian world it is appropriate to prohibit actions if they pose an undue risk to cause harm to others—even before the harm is actually done. However, if you enforce a prohibition on someone before any harm is committed, you owe him compensation.[90]

Nozick then posits a further principle formerly unknown to standard anarcho-libertarian theory: procedural rights—a right to have conflicts adjudicated by the procedure known to be least likely to make mistakes.[91] The dominant protection agency would thus have a right to ensure that its clients enjoy this procedural right, which means they must be free from fear of suffering adjudication through less than optimal procedures.

This means that the dominant protection agency would have the right to prohibit any competing agency from using these illegitimate procedures on its clients. At this point, we have what Nozick calls an ultraminimal state, one that *does* try to enforce a monopoly on the use of force, without anyone's rights being violated.

From the anarchist perspective, this protective agency/ultraminimal state is injuring those it prohibits from using defensive services that agency/state has deemed too risky. But it's okay, in Nozick's view, for the ultraminimal state to impose on the smaller agencies and their customers this cost of having a more preferred adjudication system prohibited, just so long as appropriate compensation is given. And if the dominant agency provided defensive services to everyone else, for free if necessary, that would be appropriate compensation and the ultraminimal state would be harming no one.[92]

When the ultraminimal state, using the principle of procedural rights to squash competing defense agencies, decides to compensate anyone aggrieved by this squashing by providing a free defense, we have a minimal libertarian state that arose, in Nozick's view, without any rights violations. Nozick acknowledged that no actual state arose this way, but he thought it sufficient to show that in theory a minimal libertarian state could, contra the anarchists, arise without rights violations.

As Roy Childs, one of the many anarchist libertarian theorists who rose to Nozick's challenge, put it, "What is [Nozick] willing to offer us as *compensation* for being so prohibited? He is generous to a fault. He will give us nothing less than *the state*. Should one wish to reject this admittedly generous offer, it would be responded that he *cannot* reject it."[93]

This was Nozick's titular transition from anarchy to state. Having conjured a morally permissible state, Nozick then proceeded to the arguments that most shocked the liberal intelligentsia: proving that this state could not permissibly do anything other than provide defense services without violating rights. This is where he grappled with John Rawls, whose *Theory of Justice* (1971) was the most popular defense of a modern liberal welfare state at the time and remains powerfully influential today. Rawls declared that "all social values—liberty, opportunity, income and wealth and the bases of self-respect—are to be distributed equally unless an unequal distribution is to everyone's advantage."[94]

Rawls believed that justice demands maximizing a single quality—equality. Nozick did not believe justice has to manifest itself in such a given pattern. In fact, he argued, attempting to impose such a pattern will lead to injustice, if we believe in rights. Nozick posited what he called an entitlement theory of rights—we deserve any unowned thing we can get from a state of nature (as per Locke) and any previously owned thing we receive in mutually agreed trade, or as a gift. Nozick argued that in a world of private property, *even if you don't own any yourself,* you are still apt to be better off than in a world without it.[95]

Nozick used basketball player Wilt Chamberlain as an example of how we would need a constantly activist state to maintain any system of property distribution dedicated to equality above other considerations. We might start in a position of complete equality; but if millions of people freely spend a quarter each to see Chamberlain play, Chamberlain will then end up, through a process that Nozick says should be morally unproblematic, an unequally wealthy man.[96]

Nozick also attacked Rawls's view that we are not entitled to our own natural attributes; that we haven't legitimately earned anything we get just because we were born with a talent. Nothing of moral significance, Rawls believed, can arise from something as arbitrary as a natural talent. In a touch Rand might have appreciated, Nozick pointed out that this principle would condemn the very process by which human beings exist, since "each existing person is the product of a process wherein the one sperm cell which succeeds is no more deserving than the millions that fail. Should we wish that process had been 'fairer' as judged by Rawls' standards. . . . We should be apprehensive about any principle that would condemn morally the very sort of process that brought us to be, a principle that would therefore undercut the legitimacy of our very existing."[97]

Nozick built no impregnable barriers against any conceivable forced redistribution of wealth. Since all entitlements, to be just, must be the end result of a series of just exchanges going back to the original acquisition from nature, Nozick recognizes that historical injustices underlie many current property titles, undercutting their legitimacy. Sure, such injustices are far too tangled for him to neatly untie with some theoretical innovation. But he cautions defenders of the market status quo that "one *cannot* use the analysis and theory presented here to condemn any particular scheme of transfer payments, unless it is clear that no considerations of rectification of injustice could apply to justify it. Although to introduce socialism as the punishment for our sins would go too far, past injustices might be so great as to make necessary in the short run a more extensive state in order to rectify them."[98]

The utopia part of Nozick's work has been neglected, but it provides one of the more inspiring arguments for a libertarian world, one with the potential to make sense to those for whom neither economic arguments based on efficiency and wealth creation nor philosophical arguments based on side constraints and boundary crossings resonate. The libertarian minimal state may be the closest we can come to utopia. Not a utopia with one central vision of the good life that all must love or else, but rather a multivariate, cornucopic world where people can freely choose communities to meet their needs without being ordered around by a managing state. "Utopia is a framework for utopias," Nozick concluded, "a place where people are at liberty to join together voluntarily to pursue and attempt to realize their own vision of the good life in the ideal community but where no one can *impose* his own utopian vision upon others . . . utopia is meta-utopia: the environment in which utopian experiments may be tried out; the environment in which people are free to do their own thing."[99] A libertarian minimal state, Nozick posited, is that utopia.[100]

"The most important attempt in this century to rebut anarchism . . . fails totally and in each of its parts."

Most academic criticism of Nozick aimed at his entitlement theory of justice. But the libertarian movement—at least its then-dominant anarchist wing—was also highly critical, even though outsiders might assume Nozick was its academic champion. Anarcho-libertarians were aghast at Nozick's "invisible hand" explanation of how a morally permissible state could arise from anarchy. Early issues of the *Journal of Libertarian Studies* featured dissections of this Nozickian argument from Rothbard, Childs, and others. There was a bit of the notorious narcissism of small differences in these attacks, the notion that a heretic is more to be excoriated than an infidel. But the anarcho-libertarians showed Nozick respect even as they tried to tear down his arguments. This spirit is best summed up in Rothbard's jibe regarding *Anarchy*: "The most important attempt in this century to rebut anarchism and to justify the state fails totally and in each of its parts."[101]

Childs pointed out that there is an equally plausible invisible hand argument to explain why Nozick's minimal state would fall back into first an ultraminimal one and then merely one more protection agency among others.[102]

In a world with a minimal state, Childs posited, another protection agency might arise that uses the same procedures as that state. That state could not then stifle the new competing agency on the grounds that its procedures are too risky for its clients, and would morally have to leave it unmolested. Since this new defense agency has not taken upon itself the minimal-state responsibilities of providing free compensatory protection to others, it would doubtless be able to provide its defense services at a lower cost than Nozick's minimal state.

Since this minimal state's commitment to providing free defense as compensation for those it inconveniences (by banning, remember, their preferred methods of law enforcement) is merely moral, it would probably find itself abandoning that principle in the face of this new competitive pressure. It would then retreat from Nozick's minimal state back to an ultraminimal one.

With further competitive pressure, especially given that the former ultraminimal state has taken upon itself the responsibility of spying on the procedures of all the other ones (to make sure those procedures aren't so risky that they violate its clients' procedural rights), it would likely find its market share shrinking in the face of rising competitive pressure to merely one-among-many defense agencies again in an anarchistic world of private defense. Nozick's state—in a process that also violates no one's rights—disappears.

The anarcho-capitalists thought that Nozick failed to make his case in other areas as well. Rothbard, for example, pointed out that Nozick's notion that private agencies would likely consolidate into one because of constant conflicts and division of labor ignores the enormous variations possible and probable in a real market for defense and adjudication.[103] Rothbard noted the historical record showing that many different such authorities used to overlap peacefully, such as the various different legal institutions in the old market fairs of Europe and in ancient Ireland. He also noted that Nozick illegitimately presumed that any agreement on third-party conflict resolution among varying defense agencies makes them essentially one unified agency.

Regarding Nozick's vital notion of the moral propriety of risk prevention, Rothbard argues that Nozick misunderstands where the greatest risk lies. However risky the adjudication methods of any agency may seem, such that a more dominant one would take upon itself the right to prohibit it, surely the risks involved in having one monopoly state are higher: "The grisly annals of crimes and murders of the state throughout history give one very little confidence in the non-risky nature of *its* activities."[104]

From his Austrian economics perspective Rothbard finds the entire Nozickian concept of compensation for boundary crossings incoherent. To the Austrians, the inherently shifting and incommensurate nature of people's values makes the notion of compensating them in any meaningful way beyond a freely chosen market price impossible. "What about the dedicated anarchists in the anarchistic state of nature?" Rothbard asks. "What about their trauma at seeing the . . . emergence of the state? The existence of only one fervent anarchist who could not be compensated for the psychic trauma inflicted on him by the emergence of the state is enough by itself to scuttle Nozick's allegedly non-invasive model for the origin of the minimal state. For that absolutist anarchist, no amount of compensation would suffice to assuage his grief."[105]

Many nonlibertarians also noticed that Nozick's arguments were often too weak to establish unassailable libertarian conclusions. Many academic journal articles attempt to prove how, on Nozick's own terms, his philosophy leaves room for a state far more activist than the minimal state he thinks he is defending.[106]

Some nonlibertarians thought the ideas in *Anarchy* were too evil to countenance. Characteristic of this attitude was Brian Barry's review of the book in the journal *Political Theory*. Barry refers to Nozick's sometimes playful style as "quite indecent in someone who, from the lofty heights of a professional chair, is proposing to starve or humiliate ten percent or so of his fellow citizens." He also maintains that Nozick represents "the prejudices of the average owner of a filling station in a small town in the Midwest who enjoys grousing about paying taxes and having to contribute to 'welfare scroungers.'"[107]

Nozick refused to be sucked into the maelstrom of debate that *Anarchy* generated in both the anarchist and liberal philosophical communities. He eschewed academic bluster and warfare, fearing that his intellectual career might be consumed by an ongoing debate over the ideas in his first and most talked-about work. So he never seriously returned to the political issues in *Anarchy* or grappled with his critics.

While Nozick was no longer writing about political matters, except for some short articles through the 1970s (in libertarian movement journals like *Reason*), he was still seen as part of the libertarian team, despite a brief tempest in a teapot when he sued his landlord, *Love Story* author Erich Segal, during a dispute regarding Nozick's rent-controlled apartment. Nozick later said, "I knew at the time that when I let my intense irritation with the representatives of Erich Segal lead me to invoke against him rent control laws that I opposed and disapproved of, that I would later come to regret it."[108]

He wrote extended critiques of alternate approaches to libertarianism, Rand's Objectivism and Mises's Austrian economics, that were published in philosophical journals.[109] Throughout his career he would cite the works of such thinkers as Israel Kirzner and Julian Simon, little lauded outside the libertarian world. While his intellectual and political activism on libertarian matters was done, his status as the leading libertarian academic was secure. But with the release of Nozick's first purely popular work in 1989, *The Examined Life*, the libertarians' elation in their Harvard champion collapsed.[110]

The Examined Life contained a rather sharp—and not particularly well explained—recanting of the central political ideas in *Anarchy*.

"The libertarian position I once propounded now seems to me seriously inadequate," Nozick wrote, "in part because it did not fully knit the humane considerations and joint cooperative activities it left room for more closely into its fabric. It neglected the symbolic importance of an official political concern with issues or problems, as a way of marking their importance or urgency."[111]

Sometimes, Nozick now maintained, society needs to speak in everyone's name. Something is wrong with a libertarianism that "prevent[s] the majority from jointly and publicly affirming its values."[112] Once solicitously protective of the "side constraints" that prohibited anyone from using another human being as a means and not an end, Nozick now thinks that "no principle draws that line" of when you stop expressing public values—in other words, forcing other people to adjust to majority values.[113] Even antidiscrimination law now passes muster, for this former defender of what he called any "capitalist act between consenting adults."

Many libertarians read him out of the movement after *Examined Life* came out, not that Nozick was concerned with what "team" anyone thought he was on. But in his final interview in the libertarian world, included on the Laissez-Faire Books website accompanying the publication of his final book, Nozick insisted that he still considered himself a libertarian, if not a hard-core one.[114] He did not, however, try to reconcile this statement with what he wrote about politics in *The Examined Life* or disown those statements.

But swaying people to his beliefs, whether philosophical or political, was not Nozick's goal. "I never wanted to force people to believe things," he once said. "I wanted to help them understand things better. Therefore, I thought that it would be better to structure the enterprise of philosophy around the activity of understanding, rather than the interpersonal activity of argument, which didn't fit my motivation for coming to philosophy. . . . [*Anarchy*] was very anti-coercive in the political realm. Perhaps there was a natural outgrowth in continuity, and I came to be anti-coercive in the philosophical realm."[115]

Nozick is still identified with his most political work, which remains powerfully influential. As Jonathan Wolff, author of a book on Nozick, wrote, "I first read Nozick as an undergraduate in 1980. At that time philosophy students usually reacted to *Anarchy, State, and Utopia* in one of two ways. Either they thought its conclusions so repugnant that it should not be taken seriously as political philosophy at all, or they thought its conclusions so repugnant that it was vital . . . to show how it fails." Yet in 1990, Wolff wrote as a professor that he "fairly often . . . encounter[s] a third [view]: that, broadly speaking, Nozick is right."[116]

Other academic philosophers have arisen in Nozick's wake to defend libertarianism; some from the Randian realm, including Tibor Machan (whose work preceded Nozick's), Douglas Den Uyl, and Douglas Rasmussen; some in more standard academic philosophical styles, such as Jan Narveson and Loren Lomasky. In *The Libertarian Idea* Narveson attempts to establish a rough libertarianism on contractarian grounds (the idea that if everyone got together and rationally agreed to a political order, it would likely be a libertarian one), grounded in the thinking of David Gauthier. Narveson argues that "if we accept that libertarianism does not have some of the more extravagant implications popularly attributed to it, then the prospect for getting from contractarianism to libertarianism seems to be fairly promising."[117] He notes that good arguments for libertarianism of the sort that would win universal consent in a contractarian manner are neither purely utilitarian nor purely deontological—dueling philosophical categories of justification, the first about results, the second about rights considerations that precede any concern about results, things that are right just because they are *right*.

> Are arguments concerning [the real-world bad] effects [of government] to be *contrasted* with arguments "in principle"? . . . The defenders of libertarianism I have in mind do not think that the considerations leading us . . . to the conclusion that the benefits of the State are illusions are just accidental. The use of force or fraud, in their view, does not just "happen" to lead to worse results but, rather, guarantees it. . . . They agree that the contemporary State thinks it is being benevolent, would dearly love to be so, and spends a good deal of your and my money trying to get us to swallow the view that it is so. The claim is that the despotism of the State is ineradicable so long as it remains a State, and systematically, necessarily,

undermines its benevolence. This would seem to be argument from principle, yet with empirical ramifications. But that is the way good theories should be."[118]

Narveson's is a deeply academic book, largely concerned with grappling with antilibertarian arguments from other political philosophers. He grew into his libertarianism from unique roots, not showing fealty to any previously popular approach to the topic. He knows his Nozick (who helped nudge him in the libertarian direction) and Rothbard and the Tannehills (authors of the early market–anarchist underground classic *The Market for Liberty*), though not his Hayek and Mises and Rand; yet he's a disciple of none of them. Narveson thus represents a new branch of the libertarian evolutionary tree, one that so far has no known offspring.

Narveson laments one effect of Nozick's prominence on other libertarian philosophers. "Nozick is regarded by all other philosophers who aren't libertarians as the bible of libertarianism," he says. "They don't know anything else. Few have heard of my book, even though I disagree with Nozick about several things—we are not all the same! He is always referred to when it comes to philosophical libertarianism, and that's had somewhat deleterious consequences. It has very much narrowed the ambit of discussion [about libertarianism]."[119] Narveson identifies Randy Barnett and Anthony de Jasay as libertarian thinkers who are neglected in philosophical academe.[120]

Barnett was drawn into the libertarian orbit during the mid-1970s Center for Libertarian Studies days, crediting people around that organization—Walter Grinder, Leonard Liggio, and Rothbard—with helping keep this young Spooner fan, law student, prosecutor, then law professor, in the larger libertarian orbit. In the 1990s, he wrote the most comprehensive philosophical defense of anarchism of the decade, though his preferred phrase for the society he envisions is one with "polycentric legal systems." He's managed to do well in standard academia—he's currently at Georgetown University—with some very nonstandard ideas, though he's become expert at making anarchism sound mild.

Barnett suggests only *two tiny changes* in the way the world currently works: (1) you can't make your customers pay for your services by force and (2) you can't drive your competitors out of business by force. Those two changes—which sound perfectly reasonable and just to most people, when put that way—would lead to, Barnett thinks, a functioning anarchism of competing legal codes and defense agencies.[121]

Unusual for this apostle of Spooner, Barnett also came to a separate peace with the U.S. Constitution in a book that has made him newly popular with the conservative legal scholars around the Federalist Society: *Restoring the Lost Constitution* (2004), which defends the Constitution not on the grounds of consent, which he admits is nonsense, but on the grounds that a Constitution that only requires or allows for just laws—laws that "are both necessary to protect the rights of others and proper insofar as they do not violate the rights of the persons whose freedom they restrict"—does indeed require obedience and argues for an interpretation of the U.S. Constitution which says that, properly interpreted, it does only allow these just laws.[122]

De Jasay is a deeply academic-philosopher-style thinker, with no set academic affiliation, playing his profession's games of consent, contract, Pareto improvements (a technical term meaning something that benefits at least one person and makes no one else worse off) and prisoner's dilemmas, in order to prove that every justification for the state offered by contemporary philosophers fails. He's a thinker of great complexity and subtlety who cannot be fully and accurately summed up here. In his work he sets out to explain why no contractual agreement to create the state could be said to hold up by pointing out that if states are needed for a workable binding social agreement, which nonanarchists argue, then a state can't develop contractually in the first place; and if an institution such as the state can develop contractually, then we don't need states in order to come to workable social agreements anyway.[123] De Jasay similarly notes the contradiction in the belief that we need a state as a final enforcer to solve the problem of not being able to trust people in social agreements to do what they say they will do and to behave justly, because there is no way in logic to ensure that the state does not present the same problem, and plenty of evidence in practice that it does. The state is not apt to restrain itself once we've handed over to it access to our property and the privilege to be final defender of our rights.[124]

An academic journal arose in the 1980s to draw libertarian ideas into the larger academic discussions on political philosophy and political science. In 1987, former Students for a Libertarian Society leader Jeffrey Friedman, a one-time true believer for whom the most thrilling day of the month was the day *LP News* showed up in his mailbox, had grown disillusioned with the level of sophistication and willingness to grapple with other ideas of academic thinking in the libertarian world. He also realized that a full and unnuanced attachment to classic Rothbardianism would make human life a continuous rights violation, since any photon or molecule of air pollution that one human imposed on another without consent could be interpreted as a libertarian crime.[125] Friedman thus launched an academic political and philosophical journal, *Critical Review*, dedicated in large part to critiquing libertarianism in favor of what Friedman called "postlibertarianism."

Despite the journal's often pointed critiques of standard libertarian arguments, Friedman found early funding from the Kochs and got libertarian activist and financier of Laissez-Faire Books and term limits efforts, Howie Rich, to be his publisher. Later on, old Mises disciple and Volker Funder Richard Cornuelle, ultimately disillusioned by the small-scale success of his efforts in private charity to offset state welfare, reappeared to help out Friedman. Toward the late 1990s, Friedman—who finds it suspicious that libertarians find that their rights arguments and their empirical arguments all dovetail to the same libertarian conclusion—turned *Critical Review*'s attention to attacking the rationality of democracy. He still thinks that libertarians have many good arguments going for them in economics, and that they should rely more on historical-economic empiricism and less on rights language. He thinks what the libertarian movement needs most in order to achieve greater academic respectability and impact are high-level books of academic rigor that can authoritatively argue such points as that capitalism did *not* cause the Great Depression, that the Robber Barons were not despoiling America and creating ruthless economic royalties, and that poverty can be as much the result of state policies as it is of market failures. He thinks the movement does *not* need further explorations in an ultimately failed quest to find the trumping philosophical/moral rights argument that will turn the world libertarian.

"PSYCHIATRIC TRAINING IS . . . A RITUALIZED INDOCTRINATION INTO THE THEORY AND PRACTICE OF PSYCHIATRIC VIOLENCE."

Most major libertarian thinkers, writers, and activists worked in the fields of philosophy, politics, and economics. But one postwar libertarian, Thomas Szasz reached a large popular audience and made a name for himself, achieving both prominence and infamy, in a seemingly distinct field. Szasz, though, would insist that his radical stance in psychiatry is firmly rooted in those three disciplines, including what he learned from Mises and Hayek about the vital importance of both freedom and responsibility in crafting a humane and successful social order.

Szasz's libertarian agitation resulted in decades of writing and speaking for liberty on behalf of society's most scorned and abused figures: the mentally ill. From a tenured faculty position, this renegade psychiatrist argued that the central contention of his field was an ugly lie, told to prop up a system of tyrannical social control.

Szasz insists there is no such thing as a "mental illness" (understood as neurochemical lesions or imbalances in the brain) that relieves, or ought to relieve, a person of both liberty and responsibility. "The psychiatrist's two most important social functions," Szasz wrote, are "incarcerating innocent persons in mental hospitals and freeing guilty persons from prison" through the insanity defense.[126] Szasz dedicated his life to stopping those practices through a long series of books, speeches, and even court testimony.

Szasz, now an emeritus professor of psychiatry at the State University of New York Health Science Center in Syracuse, was born in 1920 in Budapest, Hungary, of nominally Jewish but nonobservant parents.[127]

During childhood (Szasz and his brother George were mostly raised by a beloved governess) he internalized a lesson that influenced his later understanding of certain so-called mental illnesses as malingering. He was frequently ill as a child. "My illnesses taught me some valuable lessons," he recalled. "One was a clear realization of the advantages of being ill: I enjoyed the languorous passivity of lying in bed and dozing, the anxious concern of my parents and governess, the visits of the kindly pediatrician, the choice of whatever food I wanted . . . the opportunity to occupy myself with drawing, coloring, assembling puzzles. . . . I disliked being away from home, being separated from [his governess]. So I had a powerful motive to malinger. I learned not only how to lie about feeling ill, but how to cough, how to vomit, and how to have a fever. . . . I was well aware of the difference between being ill and occupying the sick role decades before encountering these terms."[128]

Thus Szasz saw possible strategic purposes behind illnesses or dysfunctions that have no apparent physical cause; Freud himself was willing to admit that, for example, electroshock was a "pretense treatment" for a disease—hysteria—that was more acting than anything else.[129] The innovation—or semantic trick, as Szasz would have it—of classical psychoanalysis was to turn *faking* an illness into an illness in and of itself. The human capacity for deception is central to Szasz's intellectual program. Human beings lie; and many a so-called insane delusion, such as voices in the head advising one to commit heinous acts, are, Szasz maintained, best understood as lies—often strategic ones.

In response to the rise of Hitler and the obvious threat of war on the Continent, the Szasz family immigrated to the United States in October 1938. Despite knowing not a word of English when he left Hungary, Szasz started at the University of Cincinnati four months after arriving in the United States. Szasz thought that, being Jewish, his chances of getting into American medical schools were slim, but he was eventually admitted to the University of Cincinnati College of Medicine, starting in August 1941.[130] He graduated in June 1944 but hated his medical residency. "I didn't like the idea of practicing medicine. It seemed boring. Sitting in an office seeing patients with hypertension and diabetes, it seemed like chopping wood day after day. I was interested in how people live."[131]

In 1946, Szasz switched to a psychiatric residency at the University of Chicago. The program there was psychoanalytically oriented, with no "psycho ward." A new supervisor took over and demanded that Szasz leave the pleasant, easygoing atmosphere of the university hospital for a county hospital, since Szasz was getting no experience "with treating seriously ill patients."

Szasz, who believed in keeping his eccentricities under his sleeve early in his career, recalls that "I was not about to tell him that the persons he called 'seriously ill patients' I regarded as persons deprived of liberty by psychiatrists."[132] So he quit. He later wrote that "psychiatric training is, above all else, a ritualized indoctrination into the theory and practice of psychiatric violence. The disastrous effects of this process on the patients are obvious enough; though less evident, its consequences for the physician are often equally tragic."[133]

Szasz was simultaneously attending the Chicago Institute for Psychoanalysis. Analysis appealed to him as the only area of psychiatry where doctor-patient relations were voluntary. To Szasz, psychoanalysis proper had nothing to do with medicine. It was conversation, with one person paying the other. "The psychiatrist has only one duty: to keep his mouth shut outside the room and maintain total confidentiality. It has nothing to do with disease. It has to do with human problems."[134]

Szasz took a position in the Psychiatry Department at the State University of New York College of Medicine in 1956 and waited until he had tenure to drop his bombshell on the psychiatric profession, his 1961 book *The Myth of Mental Illness*. "If I hadn't had tenure, I would have been fired," Szasz says. "They called me paranoid, crazy, unfit to teach. It was total war."[135]

He had begun playing with some of the dangerous ideas in *Myth* in journal and magazine articles before the book came out. "When I began to publish on the civil rights of mental patients, some of this hit the papers, the *New York Times*. I began to get invitations from patients and lawyers—'I have this client locked up for 10 years and he hasn't done anything. He's been in long enough. Can you get him out?'" Szasz began testifying on behalf of imprisoned mental patients—some alternately hilarious and harrowing transcripts from those court cases are in his book *Psychiatric Justice* (1965)—though he rarely succeeded in winning freedom for anyone. He'd find himself, he recalled, "in the courtroom in front of some very nice judge who said something like, 'Szasz, how can you say that he should be out when six of his doctors say he should be in?' I said, 'Your honor, those are not his doctors. Those are his adversaries. He wants his freedom. I am the one that he calls his doctor.'"[136]

Szasz's open opposition to the dominant theories and practices of his profession caused a tense battle of academic freedom versus state intervention, with the New York State commissioner of mental hygiene ordering the school to get rid of Szasz for his violently heterodox views. Szasz went through "endless tribunals, all of which ended up vindicating me. I hadn't done anything to be fired over. I published a book with Harper! What do they want? My relations at the medical school were fine. I was well thought of there. They just saw it as stupid psychiatrists fighting. Most medical doctors have no interest in psychiatry except as a means to get rid of patients."[137]

There is very little that is specifically political in *Myth*. Despite its primacy and legendary status in Szasz's corpus, it is not the best place to understand his mature, fully detailed argument against the theories and practices of psychiatry, especially its libertarian aspects. For that, see the later summation of his thinking in *Insanity: The Idea and Its Consequences* (1987). *Myth* was written to speak to his profession and stresses the notion of mental illness as a sign-laden communication method—a language of its own—that psychiatrists need to understand, not just label. Keeping *Myth* rooted in a Freudianism that was far more prominent in psychiatry when the book was written than it is now, Szasz uses hysteria as a synecdoche for mental illness generally. He comes to the conclusion that—as he learned in childhood—a lot of "mentally ill" behavior can profitably be seen as someone deliberately choosing to take on the patient role in the human medical game for reasons of their own. While *Myth* does not emphasize the unlibertarian nature of involuntary commitment—which became vital to Szasz's later political–ethical critique of psychiatry—he does in its conclusion complain that "the concept of mental illness . . . undermines the principle of personal responsibility, the ground on which all free political institutions rest."[138]

Szasz was now seen within his profession, as one reporter noted, mostly as "a fanatic, troublemaker, and extremist."[139] But he considers his heterodox positions pure common sense, marred by the power-grabbing pretensions of psychiatrists and the government-psychiatry establishment. Those pretensions have been embraced by a credulous populace all too ready to believe that people should be relieved of both responsibility and liberty whenever it became convenient for either the state or any relative or caretaker troubled by the so-called mentally ill. From the very beginning, Szasz recognized that psychiatry isn't really about what it purports to be about.

"What is *the thing itself* that psychiatrists describe, debate, diagnose, and treat?" Szasz asks. "The psychiatrist says it is *mental illness*, which, he now quickly adds, is the name of *neurochemical lesions* of the brain. I say it is conflict and coercion and the rules that regulate the psychiatrist's power and privileges and the patient's rights and responsibilities. The former perspective leads to an analysis of psychiatry in terms of illness and treatment, medical theory and therapeutic practice, while [my] perspective leads to an analysis in terms of coercion and contract, the exercise of power and the efforts to limit it, in short, political theory and legal practice."[140] He believes that psychiatry is more properly conceived as an ethical and political field—the arena of human troubles, communication, and conflict—than as a medical science. Psychiatry is rife with "hidden agendas of domination and submission concealed by a rhetoric of disease and treatment."[141]

"Even the Marxist sociologists I've met respect Szasz."

Szasz's view of psychiatry is rooted in his early intellectual development. French liberals such as Voltaire and American iconoclast Mark Twain were favorites of his, and Mencken became an influence shortly after Szasz arrived in America. Sometime in the 1950s—he does not precisely remember where or how—he fell under the influence of Mises and Hayek.[142]

The burgeoning counterculture of the 1960s made liberatory attacks against major institutions of American life briefly au courant, and Szasz became a minor culture hero.[143] While defending the rights of mental patients not to be treated or imprisoned against their will, Szasz was dismissive of the "antipsychiatry" movement and its figurehead R. D. Laing, with whom Szasz was often mistakenly conflated in the late 1960s and early 1970s. Szasz had little sympathy with the Laingian view that saw the so-called insane as victims of an insane society—or going through an understandable reaction to that insane society—or vision-aries taking a valuable "journey through madness."

"I insist," Szasz wrote, "that schizophrenia is no more a journey through madness than it is a disease of the brain. Both of these state-ments assert literalized metaphors. Of course schizophrenia may be said to be *like* a journey or *like* a disease; but it is also *like* many other conditions or situations; for example, being childish, aimless, useless, and homeless, or being angry, obstreperous, conceited, or selfish."[144]

Laingian assessments of the so-called insane, then, were in most cases higher than Szasz's, who is above all a moralist, not a groovy admirer of alternative lifestyles. (A student skit at his university joked about the "Szasz diagnostic manual" which has two categories: "crook" and "bum.") The antipsychiatrists, to Szasz, were just as paternalistic and anti-individualist as their opponents, merely in the opposite direction. Szasz did not want to *ban* psychiatry, mental wards, or even shock treatment. He merely wanted to make sure that only those who vol-untarily choose to subject themselves to such disciplines or treatments are subjected to them. In the political-ethical argument, he thought it irrelevant to base the debate on whether certain specific psychiatric treatments, like lobotomies and electroshock therapy, are harmful. All that mattered was whether those subjected to them consent freely: "Without informed and uncoerced consent by the patient, no medical or psychiatric intervention is justified, while with consent every such intervention is justified, even if there is no illness and even if the inter-vention is considered to be harmful by its critics."[145]

Szasz stresses the responsibility side of society's relationship with the mentally ill, not merely the liberty side.[146] He opposes the insanity defense as well as forced institutionalization. He recognizes that many of the behaviors of the so-called insane are criminal and need to be punished as such. He also recognizes that many of the so-called insane are simply irresponsible annoyances to others.

Still, he grants an individualist respect to the so-called insane that most don't. He realizes that actions that seem unmotivated or simply mad to many have, if granted respectful consideration, clearly under-standable, if often unpleasant, motives. A couple of Szaszian epigrams sum this up: "The point of the berserk lunatic's behavior is perfectly obvious, often painfully so: its sense lies, and may be inferred from, its aim or consequence, in exactly the same way as we ascertain the sense of a normal person's behavior. For example, a berserk lunatic may claim to be Jesus or kill his wife. The point of such a person's behavior, I dare say, is to be revered like Jesus or be rid of his wife. (Why a person chooses such ends and means is another question, the answer to which is often easily obtained by asking him.)"[147] "The patient's delusion is a *problem* to the patient's family, employer, and friends; to the patient it is a *solution* to the problem of the meaning(lessness) of his life."[148]

By the early 1970s, Szasz was appearing on the *Dick Cavett Show* and was the subject of a mostly flattering *New York Times* Sunday magazine profile.[149] But as the 1970s wore on, his moment of trendy popularity waned. By the 1980s, his appearances in major periodicals, such as the *New Republic* and the *Washington Post* (where he had frequently appeared, usually commenting on and mocking the latest pretensions of the insanity defense and forensic psychiatry in such high-profile trials as Patty Hearst's, Dan White's, and John Hinckley's), became fewer and farther between.[150] His books ceased being published by major New York trade houses.

Szasz had, in the meantime, extended his libertarian arguments beyond the legal and scientific practices of psychiatry, most extensively with his 1974 book *Ceremonial Chemistry: The Ritual Persecution of Drugs, Addicts, and Pushers*, which assails the history of quasireligious suppression of users of forbidden chemicals. This established him as the major libertarian thinker on the subject of illegal drugs—what came to be known in public policy as the war on drugs. Szasz's ideas on drug laws, like his ideas on mental illness, are thorough, radical, and uncompromising. If a human being owns himself—a basic tenet of liberalism and a political axiom to Szasz—then he has the right to ingest any substance he wants.

Because of his fully developed critique of medical-legal abuse of power—spelled out most thoroughly in his book *Pharmacracy: Medicine and Politics in America* (2001)—Szasz despises the quasi-libertarian "medicalization" approach to drug law reform that, thanks to such financiers as George Soros and such advocates as Ethan Nadelmann, dominates the antidrug war debate today. Turning illegal drugs into prescription drugs would be no improvement, Szasz maintains. Many thinkers and institutions in the libertarian movement still haven't caught up with Szasz's bracing radicalism on this question.

Although he radically defends the right to use drugs, Szasz has never advocated or even approved of illegal drug use. Libertarian psychologist and LSD advocate Timothy Leary considered *Myth of Mental Illness* "the most important book in the history of psychiatry—great in so many ways—scholarship, clinical insight, political savvy, common sense, historical sweep, human concern—and most of all for its compassionate, shattering honesty" and Szasz a personal hero. However, Szasz strongly disapproves of the transvaluation of values approach to illegal drugs that sees them as a positive, "consciousness-expanding" good.[151] But he is a libertarian who believes that a free adult must have the right to be wrong.

Szasz sees himself as more radical than most of the libertarian movement on his pet issues of the mentally ill, drugs, and the medical-legal establishment but sees a role for state action in areas where many libertarians would not. He is far from an anarchist and has expressed measured support for antitrust laws, recognizing that institutions other than the state can create situations in which citizens could be seen as unfree.[152] One of these areas involves the greatest public controversy surrounding Szasz: the accusations that he is the key ideologue responsible for the deinstitutionalization of mental patients.[153]

This practice has, according to its critics, dumped tens of thousands of damaged humans, unable to care for themselves, onto the streets. There they have become an ongoing quality of life problem for others, and their lot in life has not improved, contra those who agitated for their "freedom" from "psychiatric tyranny." Szasz, looking at the complicated system of enforced drugging, "outpatient therapy," nursing homes, and prisons that has replaced the traditional mental hospital, questions how real "deinstitutionalization" has been.[154]

Although Szasz denies any responsibility for deinstitutionalization in practice, he agrees with the standard bill of indictment against it. "The forcible eviction of desocialized patients from mental hospitals is a moral scandal on par with the forcible involuntary mental hospitalization of persons who are not desocialized. The responsibility for both rests squarely on the shoulders of psychiatrists," he wrote.[155] A hard-core libertarian would argue that if the patients can't afford to pay for the asylum, then no one has any obligation to store them gratis.

Szasz thinks that such libertarians have a blinkered view of the human condition. "Libertarians don't want to look at the issue of dependency," Szasz says. "That's what I don't like about Ayn Rand. There are no children in her world, and no old people. But it's a fact of life." Still, he stresses, "there is a difference between taking care of people and coercing them. You should always be able to escape from your caretaker."[156] But Szasz does believe in an obligation to care for such people—though that obligation should follow a principle of subsidiarity, falling first on the family, then if that fails on religious organizations, and only then on the state.[157]

In his own eyes, then, Szasz is an outsider's outsider. He is, of course, a psychiatrist bitterly opposed to his profession. Szasz has also come to feel out of place in the libertarian movement and with major libertarian thinkers, even ones he mostly admires. He quoted Mises and Hayek in his works on psychiatry from the beginning; in the 1970s, Szasz was drawn into the orbit of the libertarian movement proper, befriended Roy Childs and Ralph Raico, and began appearing in libertarian magazines and at libertarian events and Libertarian Party conventions. Because of his popularity and his defense of the liberties of some of society's most despised, Szasz had a cachet with the late 1960s and early 1970s counterculture radical movements that most other libertarians lacked. In a 1973 letter from *Reason* magazine's Lynn Kinsky with advice for libertarian activists, she wrote that "*the* most effective and influential libertarian for both gays and PU [Prisoners Union] members is Thomas Szasz—he carries a clout that Rand, Rothbard, et al. just don't have (even the Marxist sociologists I've met respect Szasz.)"[158] Szasz continues to be a regular guest at libertarian conferences. His byline regularly appeared in libertarian magazines for decades, and the Center for Independent Thought, a foundation run by libertarians, grants a yearly award in his name honoring individuals who advance civil liberties.

Despite the respect and accolades he receives from fellow libertarians, Szasz thinks that organized libertarianism doesn't take the issues of mental health, mental illness, and the rights of those damned as insane as seriously as it might.[159] Szasz's position within his profession is similarly, to use a colloquialism he would surely disapprove of, schizophrenic. He is well known within it, though frequently as a bogeyman. Not only his ideas, but also the political affiliations that they were seen as burdening him with, affected his reputation. Szasz is variously charged by his many intellectual opponents with holding an overly restrictive and inaccurate definition of "disease"; of not understanding that not all human actions should be considered chosen and responsible; for failing to keep up with new advances in brain chemistry and drug treatments that to their minds prove the chemical nature of certain mental illnesses; for not recognizing that the agonies of the mentally ill, whatever you want to call them, cry out for treatment, and that the sufferers may not recognize their own best interests.[160]

Still, his ideas have made a lasting mark within the profession. My own college psychology text, used in the early 1990s, cites Szasz as saying, in a decent enough simplification, that "terms such as *mental illness* . . . are really value judgments. They are used to talk about persons whose values, thoughts, and actions simply differ from those of most other people."[161] Guidebooks for psychology graduate programs still consider knowledge of Szasz essential for passing entrance exams, although they inaccurately conflate his stances with Laing's.[162] Karl Menninger, the most prominent psychiatrist of the postwar generation, wrote Szasz in 1988 to admit that Szasz had a point: "I think I understand better what has disturbed you all these years and, in fact, it disturbs me too now. We don't like the situation that prevails whereby a fellow human being is put aside, outcast as it were, ignored, labeled, and said to be 'sick in his mind.'" Menninger then apologized for not being more open to discussion with Szasz when he first floated his ideas.[163]

Szasz is perplexed that any part of the psychiatric industry sees him as anything other than a bitter enemy. He speculates that those of his colleagues who accept him as a friendly and welcome addition to the scholarly debate "just don't give serious enough thought to this to either agree or dismiss it and dismiss me as completely wrong. They just write me off as 'interesting.'"[164]

Szasz's status within the libertarian movement is similarly nuanced and complicated. He makes scientific-philosophical arguments regarding the relative importance of brain chemicals versus self-responsibility in human behavior that can't be reduced to libertarian first principles. Yet the standard-bearers for Szasz's reputation tend to be libertarians. There are obvious reasons why Szaszian arguments in defense of radical drug rights and rigorous defenses of human self-responsibility and liberty in contradiction to an industry that paints us all as in thrall to chemicals coursing through our brains would appeal to a libertarian mind-set. However, libertarian magazines—because he is taken most seriously there—are also the most likely place to find articles attacking Szasz's positions on mental illness.[165]

Szasz has a message of great importance to the libertarian project, although many libertarian thinkers and activists are not quick to embrace it. Szasz points out that many people loathe and fear liberty, and not just for others—that tyrannical impulse is easy enough to recognize—but even for themselves. Many of these people, shedding the difficult responsibility of making something valuable and lovely out of their lives, take on the social role of "mentally ill." Building a competent human life is not something to be taken for granted, Szasz insists; it is difficult and onerous, and many of the supposedly mentally ill have failed or given up on that task. In critiquing both the Laingians and standard psychiatry, Szasz writes that both perspectives "obscure . . . the simplest and most ancient of human truths; namely, that life is an arduous and tragic struggle; that what we call 'sanity'—what we mean by 'not being schizophrenic'—has a great deal to do with competence, earned by struggling for excellence." He has analogized a sane human life to a statue carved out of marble. Although we may all metaphorically have a chunk of marble at birth, we don't all automatically have the statue, as standard mental health professionals seem to think we ought; nor does the lack of a statue mean a repressive culture has smashed ours. It means we haven't done the work to sculpt it.[166] Szasz is the libertarian movement's most stoic exponent, hoping for a fully free and responsible culture but painfully mindful that it may be impossible—for reasons that don't necessarily have to do with the outward tyranny of the state.

"MY GOAL ISN'T TO GO TO JAIL FOR MY CAUSE. MY GOAL IS TO BE FREE."

Most libertarian thinkers and activists of public prominence achieved it through things they wrote, thought, or said. The early 1980s return of draft registration—though not, thank Friedman, an actual draft— brought notoriety for one longtime LP and movement activist for acts of public libertarian civil disobedience.

Paul Jacob first learned about the iniquities of the electoral system in a mock election in grade school in the 1970s, when he was physically prevented from casting a ballot for Libertarian Party candidate Roger MacBride. He thought, I can't *wait* to get out of high school and vote for whomever I want. He learned long, expensive, arduous lessons about exactly how true to electoral reality his grade school experience was when he ran ballot access for the LP in the late 1980s.

But he'd seen even worse out of the government by then. In the early 1980s, the young libertarian Paul Jacob became an outlaw folk hero, in the libertarian movement and outside it, as the first public fugitive resister to this new wave of draft registration.

Opposition to draft registration had been the main concern of Students for a Libertarian Society, a Koch-funded college group that had a brief heyday from 1979 to 1982 before collapsing in acrimony. Paul's sister, Kathleen Jacob, had been its last chair. SLS failed to win its campaign, obviously, but Paul Jacob—who was in Florida working for the Ed Clark campaign when he saw Jimmy Carter on TV announcing the revival of the hated program—took antidraft activism into his own hands. He had done more conventional protesting against the draft in his hometown of Little Rock, Arkansas. In front of local news cameras there he declared that not only was he not going to register, but also that no one *else* should either. His father knew that couldn't have been a good idea. He told fiery young Paul that the draft board wasn't apt to let that slide. "It's the only time I can remember that my dad was right."[167]

By July 1981, he had received the last in a series of letters from his draft board, this one informing him that he was being turned over to the Justice Department for prosecution. Naturally he decided to go on a national tour of libertarian activism, working clandestinely out of SLS's D.C. office and attending the LP convention that year in Denver. He didn't want to be a martyr. "My goal isn't to go to jail for my cause," he'd say. "My goal is to be free." He spent the next year or so on the road and on the run, making a living doing petitioning work for the LP and talking up draft resistance to *Village Voice* reporters under a pseudonym. He was officially indicted in September 1982, and began living, traveling, and working under assumed names—much easier to do in an age, not so long ago and yet so far away, when showing ID wasn't a requirement for everything from getting on an airplane to renting a private post office box.

After more than a year on the run, with his relationship with his girlfriend and family strained, he returned to Little Rock and decided to resume a normal life and wait to see how long it took them to find him. He was finally arrested in his home the evening of December 6, 1984—he figures that was so news of it would hit on Pearl Harbor Day, not a good PR day for draft resistors. Jacob became a heavily quoted national agitator against draft registration, pointing out that the only people the government ever tried to prosecute were those who, like him, made a public show of defiance. He was not really being prosecuted for refusing to register for the draft, he argued, which thousands did without being indicted. He was being prosecuted for speaking out against it publicly.

He found the reaction from the libertarian community when he was an underground fugitive heartwarming and movement-affirming. His comrades took care of him in his travels, and men who had something to lose, such as corporate lawyer Ed Clark (the LP's 1980 presidential candidate) and Congressman Ron Paul (who later became the LP's 1988 presidential candidate), traveled to Little Rock to testify for him in his trial. One old libertarian movement hand even wrote to apologize for the fact that in paying taxes he was in essence supporting Jacob's jailers. The rest of the American public, though, he found less understanding. He'd do talk radio to make his case, and caller number one would want to know: Paul Jacob, why are you such a yellowbellied commie coward? And he'd explain, patiently, that he was a staunch libertarian, no communist and no pacifist; that he was perfectly willing

to fight for his freedom or his home, but he was not willing to be enslaved. And then on to caller number two, who would want to know:
Paul Jacob, why are you such a yellowbellied commie coward?

Jacob had never registered for the draft, but he had registered to
vote. And on his voter registration card he had scrawled, as young libertarian firebrands liked to do, "smash the state." Republican congressman Ron Paul from Texas, traveling on his own dime to testify, was
asked to explain this. Well, the congressman said, he might not use
those exact terms, but he certainly understood the sentiment.

Although Jacob was sent to jail for five and a half months, he was
pleased that he forced the director of Selective Service to come down
to Arkansas for the trial. Jacob tried a First Amendment defense, but it
didn't go anywhere. The government swore to prosecute lots of people
for not registering, not just protestors like Jacob, but it never did. After
serving his time in jail, Jacob served as ballot access chief for the LP in
the late 1980s, and after that did field organizing work for various term
limit campaigns, mostly funded and managed by old libertarian hands
such as the Kochs, Howie Rich, and Eric O'Keefe.

After head banging in libertarian electoral causes for years, Jacob
thinks the movement isn't properly appreciative of the wonders of initiatives and the opportunity they afford to cherry-pick libertarian issues
without having to defend every farthest extrapolation of the noninitiation of force principle to skeptical voters. The term limits crusaders got
a firsthand reality check on how hazardous linking a specific cause to
the larger libertarian message could be, when their Washington State
campaign in 1992 was derailed by the press's discovery that those fanatical libertarian Koch brothers were the secret paymasters behind the
term limits initiative. Suddenly the fight was not about the wisdom of
term limits, but the probity of eliminating drug laws and Social Security. Term limits, which had been generally successful electorally in the
1990s with real voters, if not with the Supreme Court and Congress,
lost that one.

Ballot access laws—Jacob's bailiwick in the LP in the late 1980s—are
the weapon major parties use to destroy the will and empty the coffers
of challengers. The LP has done yeoman's work in taking the punishment, though, actually managing to get itself on all fifty state ballots for

the presidential race three times in its history. It was the only third party to do so in two consecutive elections (1992 and 1996).[168]

The story of any third party becomes, tediously, maddeningly, a story of collecting signatures for ballot access, 100,000 clipboards proffered, oceans of ballpoint pen ink. Young LP supporters spend entire summers thrusting petitions in hostile strangers' faces outside supermarkets, on campus quads, at state fairs (contrary to what you might think, the popularity of the petitioners' cause has little effect on the ease of getting signatures, petitioning experts insist; it's always just a matter of asking, asking, asking in some place with lots of opportunities to ask); other libertarians put up with them crashing on their couches or floors for weeks at a time; experts need to master arcane legal demands, fifty different sets of them (at least).

The LP's ballot access mavens would hire attractive young women to hit California beaches during the summer; sometimes they'd hire stoned college kids who clearly just sat down at the kitchen table and sloppily signed names from the phone book, and cross their fingers and submit them because in some states a competitor has to challenge your petition submission for it to fail and sometimes they don't even bother. One prankish young libertarian candidate, Stephanie Sailor, once got on the ballot with the name "Stephanie 'vs. the Machine' Sailor" and then in a later congressional race against Jesse Jackson's son made her own completely groundless appeal to a liberal political dynasty by getting on the ballot with the phony name "Stephanie Kennedy Sailor." In that election, she submitted an official state ballot application with just one signature—her own—but squeaked through because she filed close to the last minute and no one bothered to challenge her.[169]

Ballot access laws are constantly changing, often in response to lawsuits or lobbying from the LP or coalitions of the LP and other third parties. The LP's ballot access guru, Richard Winger, editor of *Ballot Access News*, has been involved in nearly seventy different legal challenges to ballot access law. Most of them are devoted to the three major stumbling blocks: (1) deadlines for application, (2) number of signatures required for access, and (3) what is required to automatically stay on the ballot once you get there, so you don't have to go through all the expensive headaches again the next time. No one seems sure of exactly how much ballot access consumes, but Winger estimates always more than a half a million bucks per election year. Beyond cash, its strain on the mental energies and sanity of LP volunteers is immeasurable, as I know from a long, hot Florida summer in which my roommate and best pal invited a trio of traveling ballot access volunteers to crash in our house, in which I was already sleeping in the living room.[170]

"I TALKED TO BLACKS, I TALKED TO PUERTO RICANS, I TALKED TO ALL KINDS OF FRIGHTENING PEOPLE."

Because most Americans only pay attention to politics when it involves elections, the Libertarian Party remained one of the libertarian movement's most prominent public faces through the 1980s and 1990s, whether in campaign pamphlets or information tables at county fairs. Despite the LP's poor fortunes rolling out of David Bergland's dismal vote totals in 1984, two reputable party outsiders were still eager to fight for the hand of this tattered damsel when its 1987 nominating convention rolled around. Their reputations, however, could scarcely have been more divergent. Together they presented an almost perfect metaphor for a bifurcation running through the LP's ethos and the image that various factions hoped the party would put forward.

One was Russell Means, the Oglala Lakota Sioux rebel, cofounder of the American Indian Movement, with a colorful past that included firefights with feds at Wounded Knee. Means, still an Indian rights activist at heart, expressed his highest possible praise for the LP thusly: "There is nothing in the LP Platform that isn't Indian."[171]

The second contender for the LP crown was Ron Paul, a former Republican congressman from mid-Texas, an obstetrician and goldbug. Means was said to be a great outreach for the LP to the disenfranchised and, well, anyone who likes the idea of voting for a presidential candidate who'd been involved in a firefight with federal agents, and hobnobbed gladly with Libyan dictator and supporter of revolutionary movements Moammar Gadhafi and Nation of Islam firebrand Louis

Farrakhan, as Means did. Unbelievably to more sober-minded political outsiders, the outcome was by no means a foregone conclusion. Ron Paul was for anyone who liked the idea of voting for a former Republican congressman and family man, who had personally delivered thousands of babies; and there weren't that many of that type of person in the LP at the time. Still, Paul did win the necessary majority on the first ballot—by only three votes.

Some old party hands such as Bergland thought Ron Paul ended up a carpetbagger, moving in on the LP merely to expand the mailing list and donor base for his investment advice business. The party didn't get the hoped-for influx of members and cash from Ron Paul's hard money hard right. Paul did better than Bergland, almost twice as well, with 432,000 votes, but less than half as well as Clark—and this with Paul facing no significant other third-party challenge, himself the first (and still only) LP presidential candidate with actual federal political experience, and up against a Republican, George Bush, with zero libertarian credentials.

In 1992, Ron Paul's running mate, Andre Marrou, who had served in Alaska's state legislature as a Libertarian, won the presidential nomination, with the party's second female vice presidential candidate, Nancy Lord. Marrou sailed on with some old-time party regulars on his campaign team and scored a PR coup in Dixville Notch—the New Hampshire town that counts its votes first in the nation during the New Hampshire primary. Marrou won eleven votes to George Bush's nine.

It was all downhill from there. Marrou had lost key parts of his campaign team by the summer. They resigned after sending a long memo, along with piles of documentation, to the LP's National Committee begging to have Marrou stripped of the nomination. It seems he hadn't informed the party of some unpaid child support obligations that made it impossible for him to enter Massachusetts without risking arrest on outstanding contempt of court charges; for some reason, he claimed to have only been married twice, when in fact he'd been wed four times; that outstanding investigations into campaign improprieties hung over his head in Alaska; and that he was running up unpaid credit card bills in a campaign PAC's name without telling the other officers of the PAC, and was to boot habitually months late in house payments.

His erstwhile campaign team decided these facts were in and of themselves alarming or would disgrace the party were the media to make hay of them. The National Committee chose to sit tight with Marrou—doubtless figuring, as has often been the case, that when it comes to national media, the LP's very obscurity can cover a multitude of sins.[172]

The party's biggest media notice of the 1990s came when notorious radio shock jock Howard Stern, with his enormous national audience, chose the LP as target for a 1994 performance art run for governor of New York. Some LP members and Stern fans who had been feeding the mercurial host party information and propaganda insisted that he was sincerely libertarian, but from the outside it seemed as if the LP merely functioned as a vehicle to add verisimilitude for his "Howard as politician" stunt. The LP was a known quantity with staff and activists Stern could take advantage of to get on the ballot. And with the party's usual loose requirement for seating delegates, it was easy for Stern to game the system so he'd win at the state gubernatorial nominating convention.

Stern delighted in parodying the sententious E Pluribus Unum blathering of politicians. During a stump speech, he stressed that he was a unifier: "I talked to blacks, I talked to Puerto Ricans, I talked to all kinds of frightening people." While speaking in Saugerties, he assured its citizens that Saugerties had always been his favorite philosopher.[173]

His platform—more Sternite than Libertarian—had three planks: reinstating the death penalty, filling in potholes at night, and staggering toll collection to make his drive into the city easier. Even some serious party faithful were willing to overlook whether or not Stern had a libertarian bone in his body, as well as his naming a Democratic politician as his running mate (a choice the delegates blithely rubber-stamped). They were confident it would all be worth it when Stern won the 50,000 votes the LP needed to have automatic ballot access next time around, and then a *real* libertarian could take advantage of what Stern wrought.

Stern's formal nomination was performed by a fan whose gavel was a huge dildo. After winning the nomination—shipping in dozens of his fans, cronies, strippers, cripples with speech impediments and the like as ringers—Stern stopped returning phone calls from the party and offered no help in collecting ballot-access signatures. The Stern crew's contempt for their new allies had never been well hidden; his producer Gary "Baba Booey" Dell'Abate announced mock-apologetically at the convention that "we're ruining their chess club meeting."[174]

Stern then bridled at campaign finance laws that required him to disclose his income and leave New York media markets for the duration of the campaign; his own radio show would be tantamount to a huge campaign contribution under the law. He quit the race, to the relief of those who found him an embarrassment to the party. (For perspective on what's embarrassing to the LP, at the 1993 national LP convention, a fourteen-year-old girl lost her bid for the LP's national chair by only twenty-three votes.)

In the late 1990s, the LP did something it had never done before: nominated the same presidential candidate twice. (Roger MacBride was the only candidate who ever expressed such an interest in repeating the experience, even for a while.) In both 1996 and 2000, the standard-bearer was Harry Browne, former assistant to Joseph Galambos (the Southern California libertarian educator who didn't grant his students the right to talk about his ideas) and author of libertarian best-sellers in the 1970s on hard money and on the necessity of escaping social traps—including morality and politics—to find true personal liberty. Browne became a guru of sorts, but one genuinely advocating that you had to do your own thing to find happiness. He would answer letters to a reader requesting advice with one sentence: "Do whatever you think is best."

Browne was the closest thing to a celebrity the LP had captured, though his heyday was two decades past by then. Browne was a key element in the ferment of best-sellers that made the 1970s the "Me Decade," and the last significant libertarian thinker anyone would have expected to run for president. Browne's version of libertarianism, learned from Galambos, had been antipolitical to the core. His name had become an adjective within the movement in the 1970s, usually

used pejoratively: "Browneing out" meant leaving political or ideological activism behind and seeking freedom in an unfree world (the title
of one of his best-sellers) by yourself, for yourself, in your private
realm, not in the public scrum of ideas or politics.

Still, the hard money movement had been on the wane along with
the price of gold since its 1980 peak. The coming devaluation and crisis
Browne had been warning readers of had still not arrived, and his wife
had told him to stop bitching about the president to the TV set and do
something about it, and longtime party insider Michael Emerling
Cloud helped guide him through the minefield of internal LP politics.
So Harry Browne decided the time was ripe to find freedom through
politics.[175] He launched a largely talk radio–based campaign (some
within the LP criticized him for doing very little real retail campaigning on the road) with a characteristically nonmoral approach,
summed up by the title of his books, *Why Government Doesn't Work*
(full disclosure: I was a paid research assistant on that book) and *The
Great Libertarian Offer.*

If libertarians want people to listen to them, Browne figures, they
need to prove to that audience that limiting government will benefit
them directly. Contra Rand, he wasn't too sure that convincing people
limiting government was the "right" thing to do would be enough.
The "great libertarian offer" was to have *you* give up your favorite
government program in return for the promise that you'd never have
to pay income tax again. For whatever reason, the vast majority of voters chose not to take the offer.

"TANSTAAFL!"

Libertarianism is still not widely reflected in popular culture, despite
its inroads in many areas of the American landscape. But libertarian
ideas have always had a home in the world of American science fiction. Science fiction, as much as some libertarians have no use for it
and regret the association of someone *else's* geeky enthusiasm with
their geeky enthusiasm, has long and intimate connections with libertarianism. Some libertarians have argued that the genre's reliance on

imagined radical change, actuated by acts of individual genius and gumption, make it inherently libertarian in principle.

Some of the links between the two worlds are accidental. Such leading libertarian publishers and publicists as Robert Poole of *Reason* and Sam Konkin of the *New Libertarian* were serious science fiction fans and covered the science fiction world in their publications for many years. Many major science fiction writers, including Robert Heinlein and Poul Anderson, were libertarians and infused libertarian themes in their work.

Heinlein is a particular favorite and inspiration among libertarians for his American revolution on Luna novel *The Moon Is a Harsh Mistress* (1967). That book features a character based on avuncular libertarian educator Robert LeFevre, and its revolutionaries use the Friedmanite phrase "There ain't no such thing as a free lunch" as an acronymed slogan, TANSTAAFL, which mocks the notion that government can give people things it hasn't taken from them in the first place. That appealed to the tough, patriotic economic and political liberty side of the movement; he also had a classic for the more groovy, libertine, "living liberty" end of the movement, his highly influential (inside and outside the libertarian movement) 1961 novel *Stranger in a Strange Land*. It featured a human raised by Martians who returns to earth and starts a religious-social movement that demolishes restrictive conservative shibboleths about sex and religion, showing them the way to truly "live liberty." A youthful love for Heinlein's tales of rugged individualists often lies in the past of dedicated libertarian activists (including this author).

Modern movement libertarians have written a fair amount of popular science fiction, including longtime Sam Konkin friend and roommate J. Neil Schulman (with his portrayal of an overregulated, overinflated urban dystopia in *Alongside Night*) and Colorado-based sometime LP candidate L. Neil Smith's fictional histories, such as *The Gallatin Divergence,* of an alternate America in which the more radically libertarian Founding Fathers defined the nation's direction, not statist sellouts like Alexander Hamilton, and established a nation truly built on unanimous consent.

The intellectual affinity between science fiction and libertarianism is obvious on some levels. Libertarianism, especially its anarcho-capitalist variant, *is* political science fiction of a sort, imagining a social world very different from the one we've known. A strong streak of optimistic techno-visionary utopianism has been an integral part of the post-1960s libertarian movement as well. Libertarians tend to believe in the opportunities and possibilities and potential glory of unfettered human reason and imagination, an idea both Randian and simply capitalist.

Not long after writing his two early 1970s books on radical libertarianism, Jerome Tuccille wrote a pioneering book on the wonders of cryogenics—freezing the human body in order to preserve it for longer life in a more scientifically advanced future. Notorious LSD guru and former Harvard psychologist Timothy Leary made a public shift to political libertarianism along with his new obsessions with space travel, immortality, and intelligence increase after he got out of prison in the late 1970s. He even hosted a fund-raising party in his Beverly Hills home for straightlaced LP candidate Ron Paul in 1988. The most outré livers of, and agitators for, an unimaginably different future of nanotech, alt-energy, and DNA modification, who called themselves the Extropians—radical culture heroes to the wilder edges of the mid-1990s *Wired* generation of Silicon Valley visionary techno-geeks—were hard-core anarcho capitalists. Libertarian magazines are still the place one is most likely—or only likely—to see stories celebrating such weird sciences as cryogenics and radical gene splicing technology, and the like. *Reason's* current science correspondent, Ronald Bailey, is the loudest public voice celebrating the anything-goes future of biotech while giving little credence to tut-tutting traditionalist fears of "things mankind was not meant to know/do."[176]

One libertarian science fiction novelist and popular philosopher, Robert Anton Wilson, coauthor of *Illuminatus*, was one of the last of the pure Benjamin Tuckerites. Wilson discovered nineteenth-century individualist anarchists independent of Murray Rothbard or the mainstream libertarian movement. He lived for a while in the early 1960s at the School for Living in Brookville, Ohio. The school was designed around the back-to-the-earth, stateless communal living ideas of Ralph Borsodi, and run by Mildred Loomis, a dedicated student of decentralized, intentional alternative living arrangements, especially ones influenced by Josiah Warren and his ideological children. The Borsodi system, as Wilson characterizes it, was classically American, a Jeffersonian vision of families outside the wage system, living on their own independent freeholds and forging their own strength and character. F. A. Hayek, who saw clearly the interconnected ideological and political problems caused by the dependent mentality of the employee, should have understood.

Wilson's libertarianism represents a unique strain within the modern movement, a libertarian house in which there are many more mansions than there were in the 1940s to 1970s. Libertarian scholar Chris Sciabarra believes libertarianism needs to become a more "dialectical" philosophy, subsuming more about human life and culture than just politics. He should appreciate the Wilsonian style of having libertarian values inform not just politics but a vision of a life entire. Mildred Loomis recognized the links between Borsodism and the more political libertarian movement. She was a penpal of FEE's resident Nockian, Edmund Opitz, and had visited Robert LeFevre's Freedom School. Wilson edited the School of Living's journal, which had been called *Balanced Living* and which he renamed *A Way Out*—a way out of a way of life, state, church, and culture that seemed a trap. He scandalized the more puritan among their vegetarian clean living readers in the early 1960s with articles celebrating Wilhelm Reich, sexual liberty, and Ezra Pound, and running poems by Norman Mailer.

Wilson and his family left the rural experimental utopia for the fleshpots of Chicago and an editing gig at *Playboy* in the late 1960s, where Wilson became a fan of libertarian zines, discovering a world of ideas he found "simultaneously very close and very different" to his own. He loved liberty but held fast to Tuckerite ideas that modern corporate capitalism and banking just wasn't any kind of liberty he valued. The libertarian obsession with Austrian economics and what he saw, frankly, as disdain for the poor, turned him off.[177] He saw in libertarian writing stress on such matters as poor people receiving unearned benefits from the government. That was just basic mammalian pecking order stuff, Wilson thought, just masking a cowardly desire to fight those below us more avidly than those above us. As a scientific observer of mammalian behavior, Wilson understands it but doesn't dig it. *Playboy* during Wilson's era was an avatar of an unrecognized cultural libertarianism—people liberated from old-fashioned moralistic strictures, freely expressing themselves, with a natural live-and-let-live streak that occasionally became more explicitly political, as when Hugh Hefner ran Karl Hess's anarcho-capitalist declaration "The Death of Politics" in *Playboy* in 1969.

Wilson made a friend in the libertarian movement who shaped his novels: former *Innovator* editor Kerry Thornley (see Chapter 6). Thornley's Discordianism and plumping for libertarians to retreat to floating ocean utopias caught Wilson's fancy and fed into the plot of a phantasmagoric novel he wrote in collaboration with fellow libertarian *Playboy* editor Robert Shea. That novel is the most powerful and widely read libertarian artistic statement of the past thirty years. *Illuminatus!*, while deliberately multivariate in its ideas, stars some heroic libertarian role models fighting all sorts of repression—both external and internal. Some sympathetic characters, in the manner of a good old rightist, identify FDR's New Deal as fascism, but the novel opens up on intellectual and sexual worlds larger than Ayn Rand's.

The general plot-gimmick involves treating as true every far-right and far-left conspiracy theory around, navigated by truth-seeking hippies, machine-gun wielding tough chicks, and a Sicilian anarchist submarine captain fighting the world's oldest and most successful conspiracy.

Rand is parodied in *Illuminatus!* as Atlanta Bliss, the author of *Telemachus Sneezed*, a blockbuster philosophical novel based not on neo-Aristotelianism but neo-Herecleitianism. In it, a gaggle of seemingly innocent people meet dreadful deaths, which can be traced to the evil error they made in denying that everything is really made of fire.[178] Wilson made libertarian anarchism—both political and epistemological, even ontological—seem open-hearted, fascinating, with a mysterious and energetic history, something that could win hearts and minds against any number of competing means of modeling human social reality. Never has the notion of spontaneous order's ability to meet human needs been more colorfully presented than in the scene (as in Rand, there is a fair amount of characters lecturing each other in *Illuminatus!*) in which a beautiful woman explains to a stoned man, in a metaphor for how human orders can, will, and must develop without some Big Boss ordering everyone around, that, if there were no chairs, we'd sit on our asses—or we'd build some.[179]

Wilson was a grand recruiter for libertarianism, both through *Illuminatus!* and his series of optimistic, futuristic, epistemological anarchistic essays and nonfiction works, which stress the glories of no human limits, physical, spiritual, or political. This is true despite his separation from most aspects of the standard movement, and despite the fact that his work appeals on so many levels that one can become a Wilson Head without reaching his libertarianism. Through Wilson's influence one might become an Aleister Crowleyan, a Wilhelm Reichian, an old-fashioned Tuckerite, a techno-future-optimist in the manner of Buckminster Fuller or Timothy Leary. It is an aspect of the growing health of libertarian ideas that it is no longer the small pond it was up until the late 1970s, where it could be assumed that knowledge of or involvement in any aspect of the movement means you almost certainly were quite familiar with, and probably intimately involved with, all the other parts. Until the 1980s, it was not only easy, but even likely, that you might meet or correspond with every other American pursuing libertarian intellectual or political activism. Even if you disagreed on points of doctrine, you were at least part of the same intellectual universe.

Thanks to, among other thinkers and forces (including simply the gradual spread of libertarian books and magazines to more and more people), Wilson, Leary, and the Extropians, libertarian political ideas are opening out to, even coming close to dominating, social and intellectual movements that overlap, but are not coterminous with, the conventional "libertarian movement" as it has been defined and explained in this book. (One progressive commentator wrote an entire book lamenting what she sees as the libertarian takeover of Silicon Valley culture in the 1990s.)[180] If any politics defines those on the cutting edges of bio- and computer research, it is libertarianism, even if a libertarianism not necessarily rooted in deep immersion in Mises, Rand, or Rothbard—more likely Hayek, whose ideas about the spontaneous natural orders at the heart of human economies and societies were recreated (independently discovered, author Michael Rothschild insisted) under the rubric of bionomics, a brief fad in Silicon Valley in the 1990s.[181]

"WHERE WERE WE TO FIND THESE PERFECT SOCIAL CONTROL WIZARDS?"

Libertarian thinkers and institutions were generally concerned, by their nature, with issues of government acting where it didn't belong. This made libertarians and libertarian ideas—for reasons that go beyond their general cultural peculiarity and outsider status from at least the 1940s to late 1970s—far from major players in some of the biggest arenas of sociopolitical ferment of the 1960s and 1970s: the women's rights, civil rights, and black rights movements. There were always some women libertarians (including, of course, major movement founders and influences such as Rand, Paterson, and Lane) and black libertarians, but really, not all that many, either in the highest ranks or the rank and file.

Two major black economists and polemicists, Thomas Sowell and Walter Williams, are mostly libertarian, and for a while Williams ran the George Mason University Economics Department (and turned down various offers from LP people to run for president) and served on the board of the Reason Foundation. They wrote frequently on issues involving the status of blacks and other ethnic minorities, but they, and other libertarians who wrote on civil rights and affirmative action issues, generally took a firm libertarian position that put them outside the pale of the standard conversation on certain matters: that government should relate to all citizens as individuals, not as members of any racial or ethnic collective; and that the principle of equal protection does not support affirmative action but works against it. Libertarian economic analysis indicates that in a free market discrimination is costly and is apt to eventually disappear if not propped up by the state (if you can make a mutually enriching deal with someone but refuse because of irrational prejudice, you are hurting yourself), and libertarian historical analysis points out that it was the state, and often labor unions in collaboration with the state, that proved the most formidable enemy to black economic and civic advancement.[182]

Similarly, in the 1970s the Association of Libertarian Feminists was dedicated to bringing feminist messages to the libertarian movement and individualist and/or libertarian messages to the feminist movement. Ideologically, of course, libertarianism opposes legal barriers against women doing or being whatever they want, as well as government efforts to ameliorate wrongs against women such as unequal wages. Let the market sort that out, libertarians would say, again pointing out that economic logic would imply that businesses could clean up by bidding qualified women away from other companies by offering them a little more than the alleged unequal wages they were receiving elsewhere. Female libertarians such as Wendy McElroy, Sharon Presley, and Joan Kennedy Taylor wrote and researched along such feminist libertarian lines as reviving and anthologizing forgotten women anarchist thinkers like Voltairine De Cleyre and explaining why a complete and true feminism must be individualistic—treating all humans as equal socially and politically, regardless of gender.[183]

The movement even had a prominent black woman sociologist, Anne Wortham, supported through personal patronage by old Mises associate George Koether and then institutionally by the Institute for Humane Studies. Wortham felt the pains of possible triple and mixed discrimination in the academy, with her greatest difficulty coming from being both black and female as well as bringing to bear a set of ideas that were unwelcome in the academy and especially unwelcome from a black female sociologist. Working in an era before the easy access to computer power we now have, Wortham began an ambitious and as yet unfinished sociological investigation, based on hundreds of survey forms with answers to thousands of questions, into the status and attitude of libertarian and right-leaning young intellectuals and activists in the 1970s and 1980s. Wortham also wrote an individualist take on the meaning of being black in America, *The Other Side of Racism*, advising American blacks to avoid identifying racially and instead live and struggle as individuals.

The libertarian take on blacks and women's rights has not succeeded intellectually or politically nearly as well as its take on economic matters.

A third big sociopolitical movement that rose to prominence in America in the 1970s, environmentalism, drew a more varied and successful libertarian response. A bevy of economists, policy entrepreneurs, and think tanks have arisen to extend the libertarian fascination with property rights to environmental problems, a growing public concern since the first Earth Day and founding of the Environmental Protection Agency in 1970.

The approach was launched after two young Montana economists, John Baden and Richard Stroup, happened to attend a speech by Milton Friedman. In response to a question, Friedman mentioned that eliminating the U.S. Forest Service and selling off its property would probably be a good thing. Baden and Stroup weren't sure at first but researched and thought over the matter. Eventually they concluded that Friedman was probably right. They launched an organization called the Political Economy Research Center (since renamed the Property and Environment Research Center) in 1980 to promote and support further research and education along these lines. Baden has since left and runs his own similar group, the Foundation for Research on Economics and the Environment. The early days of PERC and general new resource economics research received copious financial and intellectual help from various libertarian movement financiers including the Liberty Fund, which sponsored many of the early conferences where economists and environmentalists met and hashed out ideas. Some of their seminal early journalism on the topic appeared in *Reason* and the now defunct Cato/IHS project, *Literature of Liberty*.

Baden's revelation was rooted in ideas from Public Choice and Chicago School economics and a general understanding of the value of individual property rights to encourage people to make decisions that reflect the long-term value of resources to everyone and to discourage rampant pollution that damages other people's property. He began to realize that "the best way to ensure environmental quality and sound land use is to appeal to self-interest . . . reduce or eliminate the emphasis on bureaucratic management of natural resources, and reverse financial incentives so that environmental protection becomes a source of profit rather than penalty. . . . Legislated pollution control has largely been a colossal failure; that the public lands have been poorly managed no matter who has staffed the federal agencies."[184]

Like the Law and Economics School out of Chicago, which was nurtured in its early days by the Volker Fund, the Institute for Humane Studies, and the Liberty Fund, free market environmentalism stresses that incentives matter and that private ownership gives the greatest incentives to preserve the values of any resource, natural or otherwise. Free market environmentalist thinkers and organizations perform and publicize critiques of expensive and destructive excesses of existing government environmental management of water and forest resources. That we are wealthy enough to begin valuing environmental amenities—to see a forest as something of inherent or recreational value rather than a source for housing or fuel—is a victory of free markets. In the resource-use field, market pressures lead manufacturers to constantly seek to do more with less, finding new ways to make production processes cheaper. (Lynn Scarlett, a free market environmentalist thinker with the Reason Foundation in the 1980s and 1990s, would demonstrate this point by exhibiting how much easier it is to crush a new soda can than one from 30 years ago.) Libertarian free market environmentalists point out how government mandates on recycling often cost more in resources' than they save, and in general how government projects have wreaked more environmental havoc—with huge water projects in the American West and subsidized, costly timber sales in national forests being big examples—than private industry ever could afford to.[185]

Using insights from Buchanan's Public Choice school of economics, libertarians argue that government managers are motivated by what makes their lives easier, not by what might be best for the environment. In fact, a private owner, held accountable for imposing costs such as pollution on others and able to capture the long-term value of any environmental amenities under his control, can be expected to be more environmentally conscious than a typical bureaucrat. If we can have transferable property rights in, say, fish before they are caught, the problem of overfishing can be dealt with. Free market environmentalists have led in conceptualizing and pushing for such solutions to the famous "tragedy of the commons" (how commonly owned resources are doomed to depletion) through legal devices such as individual fishing quotas that allow individuals to benefit from *not* catching fish, without worrying that someone else will.

The free market price system, by spreading in its Hayekian manner information about relative resource scarcity, is the best conservation mechanism we can imagine. The environmental degradation in the Soviet Union shows what can happen when all environmental values are subsumed to one state purpose, and America's own record with its forest and water management has its own horror stories. Hayekian principles also tell us that environmental conditions and needs are too complex and situation-dependent to be successfully modeled and managed from Washington. Free market environmental ideas have had remarkably quick real-world application and success. For example, reductions in sulfur dioxide emissions have been dealt with for over a decade through creating tradable emission rights, thus encouraging industry to figure out the cheapest way to reduce emissions rather than being forced to do the one thing government decides is best.[186] That old system is dismissively known in free market environmental circles as "command and control." And on the personnel front, George W. Bush's Department of the Interior was run for years by Gale Norton, a former LP member, and former Reason Foundation president Lynn Scarlett is currently deputy secretary of the department.

One D.C. think tank that promotes free market environmental ideas, the Competitive Enterprise Institute (CEI), isn't encouraged by either of those apparent victories for its cause. CEI chief Fred Smith condemns tradable permit schemes as market socialism, since government still manages and defines the end goals within which the market must work. He thinks Scarlett has been too timid in introducing real market reforms at Interior. In surveying some of the other leading figures in the free market environmentalism field, a general sense of disappointment with how much progress Scarlett, only one person in a huge bureaucratic machine, has been able to make in effecting market reforms makes for an interesting case study in how merely getting the "right people in power" can be less effective than ideologues might hope, if the old-fashioned Leonard Read–style changing of the intellectual zeitgeist through individual education hasn't been done.

Until a Lynn Scarlett, or any other libertarian figure who achieves political power, can move in an intellectual and bureaucratic culture that understands and appreciates the free market environmentalist perspective, it is naive to expect radical policy change pleasing to the libertarian intellectual community to arise from positioning movement figures in political power, not that such positioning isn't a necessary early step and a pleasing sign of how much more seriously libertarian ideas are being taken in corridors of power now than twenty years ago. But in general, as John Baden said when asked how much real-world policy success free market environmentalist ideas have had so far, many of their ideas work against special interests, both bureaucratic and otherwise, and when it comes to resource management (many private businesses get many benefits, for example, out of government's below-market sale of resources such as timber and water), so far their major constituency is intellectual.

Scarlett has begun to doubt that the most hard-core FME solution of "make everything private property" is an achievable or proper approach: "I find because there is such a focus solely on the property rights and tort liability side in free market environmentalism, there is a disinclination to look out there at some budding decisionmaking arrangements that may have some public sector underpinning but really are emergent models of voluntary cooperation among voluntary individuals."[187] Environmental issues, she has come to think, especially ones involving air and water, inherently involve interrelation and interdependence across private property lines. Thus institutions to coordinate and deal with environmental harms—going beyond the original Rothbardian approach of "treat pollution as a tort rather than regulate it, and let people sue if it harms them" approach, which has gotten nowhere in the policy world—will have qualities that are inherently more like public institutions than private ones. The trickiness of applying property in market amenities and special interest opposition to major changes in current resource management schemes mean free market environmentalism in its purest form will be facing an uphill climb no matter who is running the Interior Department.

CEI's chief Fred Smith thinks he's learned a lot about actuating change in public attitude and public policy in his years toiling in trenches both bureaucratic and movement. He started in the libertarian movement as an analyst with the Koch-funded Council for a Competitive Economy (CCE) in the early 1980s. "The CCE idea," Charles Koch recalls, "was to get business people to oppose subsidies and regulations even when doing so was not in their short-term financial interest. You can imagine how well that went over."[188]

Before his futile CCE stint, Fred Smith was a young liberal from Louisiana, where in the early 1960s if you weren't a racist, you were attracted to liberal or socialist communities. He read and admired Rand but saw that embracing Rand meant rejecting socialism, which he wasn't yet ready to do. He remembers being annoyed with fellow socialists who claimed to be big Rand fans.

He ended up working at EPA in the early 1970s, trying to apply a mechanistic liberal social fine-tuning approach to recycling, emboldened

by moral fervor. Working in a federal bureaucracy cost him his innocent belief in its possible efficacy. One day he was talking with some of
his fellow true-believer comrades at EPA about how they could somehow solve the solid waste problem in America: design this program,
compose these regulations . . . but then who would ensure it all
worked as planned? Well, not our division at EPA, they all realized,
since in their estimation their bosses were idiots. "Where were we to
find these perfect social control wizards?" Smith wondered. "That became the dilemma."[189]

He began thinking more on these matters, reading Hayek, and becoming a libertarian. While Smith was working at CCE, his colleague
Sheldon Richman became his personal guru in libertarian truths. CEI
deliberately took the tack, an idea picked up from CCE days, of being
what some might call corporate shills—making arguments (that they
sincerely believed in) for corporations and their rights against government actions for times when it wasn't best, for PR purposes, that corporations make them on their own behalf. As Smith puts it, "GM are
not the best people to make the argument that what's good for GM is
good for America."[190]

Big businessmen, in Smith's estimation, are insecure about their position in society, and sucking up to the left offers them more in the
way of security and emoluments and feelgoodism than libertarians
can offer, even though it is libertarians who often stand up for their
interests (though also, when fighting corporate welfare, giveaways,
tariffs, and subsidies, often stand against corporate interests). Corporate leaders get no respect for being openly pro-market or pro-
prosperity. The left can offer corporations accolades, Hollywood, and
an aura of moral respectability beyond just making a good living and
providing jobs and wealth.

Smith has thought a lot about the various roadblocks on the way to
a wider libertarian understanding on the part of the general public.
"People aren't stupid because they are stupid" when it comes to public policy, he insists, drawing on Chicagoite economic arguments
about rational ignorance. Given how much any citizen can affect
public policy—very little—it just doesn't pay for most people to expend their resources into learning much about it. Thus "people are
stupid because they are smart." It doesn't, then, always pay for libertar-

ians to try to win arguments based on sophisticated policy analysis. For example, in discussing environmental health problems such as lead paint, Smith recommends not so much referencing scientific studies that indicate that the problem isn't as severe as the panicked claim, but instead arguing that poverty is the real problem underlying the lead paint issue, and stressing how libertarianism can help with inner city poverty through reforms such as educational vouchers, drug legalization, and enterprise zones.

In practice, the libertarian approach to environmentalism has been linked to many in the lay public, and among libertarianism's ideological enemies on the environmentalist left, almost exclusively with the debunking of supposed environmental crises. The Cato Institute has produced a series of books doing this with global warming, for example, and CEI frequently stresses such risk debunking.

From the early 1980s on, Julian Simon, a researcher dedicated to showing how human ingenuity in regard to the environment and immigration tends to make all resources cheaper and more abundant rather than more scarce and expensive, became a libertarian hero. His greatest moment of glory came when he won a bet about resource scarcity with environmental and population doom monger Paul Ehrlich over whether a set of resources of Ehrlich's choice would be cheaper or more expensive a decade down the line.[191] The message of Simon's research is that most resource and environmental problems were getting better rather than worse. In general the human race was healthier and the things we need to live were getting cheaper and more abundant.[192]

The possibility of running out of resources or space or killing ourselves via pollution or global warming is a scientific issue, not a political one. But politics is important in deciding how we are most efficiently and justly to deal with them if problems they prove to be. Policy advocacy and research do not occur in a vacuum. It is natural, given libertarianism's temperamental inclination and ideological need to cast doubt on the need for big government—and given how environmental crises are almost always used as a reason for big government intervention—that libertarians would tend to be sponsors and advocates of attempts to show that environmental scare stories are based on exaggerated "junk science." This can make it seem to the uncharitable as if it's a libertarian principle that nothing done for a profit ever hurts anyone, which is not the case. The real central message of free market environmental thinking remains the core libertarian insight into the value, in terms of incentives to preserve values and not harm others, of spreading information about the true value of resources through the price system and the justice of extending private property rights and the responsibilities that come with them to aspects of environmental policy, where government management and command have mostly reigned.

"You know they're gonna sell out, they're not gonna make any real changes."

The greatest example of the mainstreaming of libertarian ideas came with the Gingrich revolution of 1994, when Republicans unexpectedly and dramatically retook Congress under the aegis of the Contract with America, reputed to be (though not actually) an impressively antigovernment document. That victory was seen at the time, in media ranging from *USA Today* to the *Wall Street Journal* to *Rolling Stone,* as representing an unprecedented upswing of libertarian sentiment and libertarian political influence. *USA Today* boldly announced that "what liberalism was to the '60s and conservatism was to the '80s, libertarianism may be to the youth of the 1990s."[193] The *Wall Street Journal* noted that "because of their growing disdain for government, more and more Americans appear to be drifting—often unwittingly—toward a libertarian philosophy."[194] Famed Washington watcher E. J. Dionne was seeing libertarianism as "the *latent and unconscious* ideology of millions of new voters."[195]

What did all this attention and punditry avail the libertarian cause? Certainly many of the promises of Gingrich's Contract with America, if enacted, would have warmed libertarian hearts. For example, the contract committed congressmen to vote to consider term limiting themselves. Term limits had become practically a libertarian monopoly in the early 1990s, with Cato's Ed Crane one of its primary theoreticians, ex-LP ballot access whiz Howie Rich (whose wife Andrea ran libertarian mail-order house Laissez-Faire Books) and ex-LP national director Eric O'Keefe as its field managers, and the Koch brothers one of the term limit movement's prime financiers (until bad publicity and a threat of backlash from politicians caused them to ramp down their funding of the cause).[196]

Some libertarians felt like they'd sat through this movie before as Gingrichmania spread through Washington, and the ending was just as disappointing as the first time, when Ronald Reagan raised many libertarians' hopes only to dash them. Doug Bandow, remembering his brief disillusioning stint in the Reagan White House, listened to a libertarian-leaning Republican friend call election day in 1994 "the happiest day of my life."

"This is a guy who's married with kids. I'm glad his wife didn't hear that! I told him, 'You know they're gonna sell out, they're not gonna make any real changes.' He said, 'Shut up and leave me alone, I want to enjoy this.'" In the Reagan years, Bandow recalled, the mantra to explain why Reagan's small-government rhetoric so rarely led to small-government action was, hey, the president can't do it all; we've got to control Congress. Then they did control Congress, though they lost it in 2006. More than a decade after the "Gingrich revolution," we see federal discretionary spending rising at historic rates, federal involvement in and control of education increasing, Medicare entitlements expanding to bankruptcy levels, abortion rights in danger, overseas adventurism continuing apace, Social Security still unprivatized, and federal criminal justice policies a continuing libertarian nightmare.

But some movement libertarians hold significant power in D.C. now; we've already met Lynn Scarlett and noted how she has disappointed many of the hard-core in the libertarian think tank world by not instantly enacting a plan to sell off all federal land controlled by the Department of the Interior.

Grover Norquist, leader of Americans for Tax Reform, major Washington player and the man regularly dragged out by the mainstream press as the secret mastermind behind all Republican activism, was once the hardest of hard-core libertarians; he is even accused in one book by a *Washington Post* reporter of having driven wildly around D.C., belting old Circle Bastiat songs out the window: "Tis time to right the great wrong done/Ten thousand years ago/The state conceived in blood and hate/Remains our only foe. . . . Come meet thy fate, destroy the state/And Raise black banners high."[197] Norquist tells me it isn't true, but he does know the lyrics to the song.

Even now, he positions the GOP message in a libertarian way as the "Leave Us Alone" coalition and talks colorful quasi-anarchist talk about getting the state small enough to drown in the bathtub. Yet still, actual GOP practice is more entitlements, more war, and more corporate welfare than real diminution in government power. This doesn't discourage Norquist, who hates the libertarian game of positing ideological purity as the defining characteristic of success: "A lot of libertarians seem to relish losing, because it proves how pure they are. They think they are winning, if you get into a conversation and get more radical in your position to the point where no one else in the room can agree with you. Then I win! Win what? 'Most Pure Person in Room' award? A cookie?"

While insisting he is not a whit less dedicated to limiting government because of whatever might (or might not) be happening with the Republican Party at any given moment, he insists libertarians need to remember that there is no point trying to go farther politically than a voting majority of the American people are ready to go along with (which brings us back to Leonard Read and the ongoing mission of libertarian ideological education). In his day-to-day work with Republican operatives, he insists, he finds that many more of them are across-the-board libertarian than most movement libertarians would expect—they just don't constantly stress the full antistate package because they have their own issue they are working on, whether it be guns or taxes or trade. Despite his positioning as a Republican operative par excellence, Norquist likes to tweak those who would call him a sellout for his D.C. success by winkingly saying things like, "I like the libertarians—I just think they overstate the case for central government."[198]

Sitting now in the House of Representatives is 1988 Libertarian Party presidential candidate Ron Paul, doing so well in his fifth term since returning to the House from Texas as a Republican that in 2004 no one bothered running against him. He holds his seat as an absolute maverick, refusing to vote for anything he doesn't think is explicitly authorized by the Constitution, proposing libertarian bills that never make it out of committee, working in general obscurity with GOP colleagues who admire his principles yet refuse to learn any lessons from him.

They treat him as some sort of inexplicable mystery and never imagine his success means they could, if they wished, be more consistently antigovernment than they are. The Republican Party apparatus finds him frustrating and can't count on party discipline from him. When he first tried to come back to Congress in 1996 the entire GOP power structure threw their weight behind a primary challenger, a turncoat Democrat.

"This week on a national television show I explained why government flood insurance was bad," Paul told me in his Hill office in the summer of 2005, adorned with congratulatory plaques from Milton Friedman and copies of Mises's books. "And I have 180 miles of coastline in [my district in] Texas, but I was explaining to Sam Donaldson why subsidized insurance makes that problem much worse. I don't know if [I get away with it] because people just believe what I'm saying, or that I'm not here for special interests. I think that's what gets me by more than anything. Then again, the freedom philosophy shouldn't be challenging to too many people, when you emphasize that all I want to do is leave you alone. That's not the kind of threat like an authoritarian coming in and trying to make you believe it."[199]

Dana Rohrabacher, from California's Orange County, is the other sitting congressman with a libertarian past—and a far wilder such past than Ron Paul's. Paul came from the more staid hard money side of libertarianism; Rohrabacher was a California Libertarian Alliance founder, a YAF libertarian renegade, and the hippiest of libertarian hippies, singing libertarian-themed folk songs around the country and spreading the gospel of Robert LeFevre to college kids across the land in the late 1960s and early 1970s.

By the 1980s, a calmer Rohrabacher was a Reagan speechwriter, and pure anticommunism seemed to be motivating him more than his old-school libertarianism. Still, he hasn't turned his back on his past. He showed up at "agorist" libertarian undergrounder Sam Konkin's memorial service in the black jeans and black turtleneck of anarchy; one of his top aides in the House is Society for Individual Liberty founder Don Ernsberger, still a long-haired libertarian radical.

What happened? Rohrabacher, his office filled with memorabilia relating him to friends and heroes from Ronald Reagan to former Van Halen vocalist Sammy Hagar, tells me that "we did what young people always do: carried our ideals out to the very farthest logical extension. Once you push abstract theory out too far in reality it becomes un-workable. So right now I've drawn back a whole lot to what I think is practical, but still pushing to maximize human liberty and justice.

"You have to compromise. Real-life politics is compromise. There are some things I have not advocated because I know they are irrele-vant and they can't possibly be achieved."

What might some of those things be? I ask. I was fishing to see if Congressman Rohrabacher would admit to a lingering attraction to LeFevre's anarchism.

"No politician would ever tell you!" Then, after a while, he offers, "There are lots of things I no longer advocate. I used to advocate no government. I wasn't a limited-government Randist. I was a no-government hippie-dippie and that's what I believed we should go for, no government. And of course it doesn't take you long to realize that's not going to be too much a part of the public debate."[200]

9

THE TWILIGHT OF THE LIBERTARIAN GODS

The 1980s and 1990s saw the passing of the founders and the founding influences of modern American libertarianism. Many had taken intellectual or institutional paths that removed them from the mainstream of the movement that their work and influence had built. Libertarianism never became so institutionalized that its major thinkers became trapped in their own pasts or their own success; separate from real political or even academic power, they could and did follow their own intellectual and personal whims.

"LEONARD WON THE TONTINE."

Ayn Rand's life through the 1970s was uneventful. She stayed ensconced in her New York apartment with her husband Frank, working desultorily on the *Ayn Rand Letter* through the mid-1970s and then working on not much at all. Frank died in 1979, and most of Rand's friends and associates gradually drifted, or were driven, away. Joan and Allan Blumenthal were driven away by Rand's continued hectoring over issues of art, by Blumenthal's gradual realization that Objectivist psychotherapy tended to inculcate crippling moral guilt, and by

Rand's insistence that they have no personal life apart from her.[1] The-atrical director Philip Smith and his wife, novelist Kay Nolte Smith, put on a production of Rand's play *The Night of January 16th* and al-lowed an actor to change a line to suit his preference. Kay confessed this to Rand and was banished. Just before Rand's death, Robert Hes-sen, operating an Objectivist-approved book service, decided his audi-ence would be interested in one of Kay Smith's novels. He carried it despite Rand's orders and left her circle.[2] Rand brought her sister Nora—her only surviving immediate family member—to New York from Russia. The two feuded so violently that Nora returned to the Soviet Union.[3]

Part of the tragedy of Rand's waning years, says Barbara Branden, is that she never had any idea of her cultural impact, of how many people deeply loved her. Branden recalls seeing videotapes of Rand's final public appearance at Jim Blanchard's 1981 annual hard money goldbug conference in New Orleans (he transported her to the event on a private train car; the author of *Atlas Shrugged* couldn't resist that gesture), packed to the rafters with libertarian Rand lovers, admirers of the woman who wrote of the potential holiness of the dollar sign. She saw astonishment in Rand's eyes at the waves of enthusiastic ap-plause from all the financial wizards, brokers, and economists.[4]

Upon Rand's death in 1982, she was working on a screen adapta-tion of *Atlas Shrugged*, which has never been completed. Of her old circle of friends and followers, only philosopher Leonard Peikoff was left, and he became her sole heir.[5] "Leonard won the tontine," Robert Hessen wearily puts it, emphasizing that during the NBI heyday Leonard was way down the line of succession.[6] (A tontine is an agree-ment among a group of people to pass on full possession of a prop-erty from which they had all profited to the last surviving member of the group.) Peikoff has kept the Randian machine alive not only through the Ayn Rand Institute but also through reissues and publica-tions of volumes of Rand ephemera.[7] His group has not maintained a monopoly on Objectivist intellectual activism, however. Philosopher David Kelley, a Vassar professor and author of *The Evidence of the Senses*, a book of Objectivist epistemology, disagreed with official Objectivism about the inherent evils of Barbara Branden's Rand biography. Kelley dared to speak before libertarian supper clubs and further dared to *publicly defend on principle* the notion of Objectivists talking to libertarians.

After being booted from the official Objectivist world, he pulled together funding from Objectivists tired of the Peikoff gang's intolerance to found the Institute for Objectivist Studies, now known as the Atlas Society (and no longer actively run by Kelley), in 1991. It's a public advocacy organization not oriented toward academia (where the Objectivist cause is still bleak, except for a forty-member Ayn Rand Society within the American Philosophical Association) but toward public intellectuals, people interested in spreading ideas outside a university context, through the usual full-service think tank means such as conferences, student seminars, op-eds, media appearances, and its own specialty magazine, the *New Individualist*. Kelley even had the temerity to invite Nathaniel Branden to speak to Objectivist audiences.

"ONCE AN INDIVIDUAL BECOMES MENTALLY ABERRATED . . . HE GETS INTENSELY ATTRACTED TO OBJECTIVISM."

Rand's radical opposition to the morality and thinking of the prevailing culture made her a consistent target of often cruel public criticism. As Mimi Reisel Gladstein, author of a book on Rand, said, "If she is not held in awe, she is usually despised."[8] This is a case of tit for tat in the sense that Rand was rarely fair in any scholarly sense to her intellectual foes. She felt it perfectly appropriate, for example, to write lengthy critiques of books she hadn't read, and she declared that one should "defeat collectivists and altruists by the single method of contempt. Take away their aura of holiness. Look at them for what they are—parasites."[9] Rand had declared cultural and philosophic war, and she got, if not as good as she gave, at least in like manner.

The serious secondary literature on Rand is growing in the early twenty-first century. As a purely literary figure, she has received almost no commentary, except for one book in the Twayne American Authors series, featuring factual errors on almost every page and a seemingly willful inability to understand what Rand was getting at.[10] Her only serious biographers so far have been the Brandens. Her philosophical tradition is carried on by the likes of Tibor Machan (a former editor of the libertarian magazine *Reason*, now teaching at Chapman University and working as an ideological conscience of sorts for the Hoiles family–owned Freedom Communications chain, still dedicated to the libertarian principles of its founder), Douglas Rasmussen (a professor at St. Johns University in New York), and Douglas Den Uyl (now with the Liberty Fund). Chris Sciabarra, author of one of the first serious, nonhostile attempts to integrate Rand within a larger philosophical tradition, *Ayn Rand: The Russian Radical*, edits an academic journal devoted to her, the *Journal of Ayn Rand Studies*. Generally, though, the criticisms of Rand from the world of academic philosophy have been heated; one professional philosopher called her "the worst philosopher in the history of Western Civilization."

Rand was not erudite; most of her education in contemporary philosophy came from things she was told by philosopher friends, like Peikoff or John Hospers (before he was banished). Modern culture, except for her beloved detective and adventure novels, drove her to fits. She didn't read much, and most of what she knew about the world in the last decades of her life came from the *New York Times*. Her library, Hessen recalls, consisted largely of "books autographed and sent to her from other Random House authors, like Dr. Seuss or whatever, and books from research done in connection with railroads or architecture and steel. She never went to bookstores."[11]

Rarely do other philosophers comment on her without hostility or incomprehension. The first instance of educated, measured criticism was an edited volume by Den Uyl and Rasmussen with critiques and commentary on Rand by a variety of scholars, most of them disagreeing with her conclusions or methods. But the book at least treats her as a fellow player in the philosophy game. Barbara Branden says that she knew NBI's main goal had been achieved when Rand's *New York Times* obituary called her a "novelist and philosopher." It is not an honor that many professional philosophers would grant Rand.[12]

Den Uyl and Rasmussen found many who did. J. Charles King challenged Rand's contention that only a being whose choices involved life and death, existence or nonexistence, could have or could need values. Even an indestructible immortal could have preferences, things he enjoyed and wanted to pursue more than others, and surely that means he is "pursuing values."[13]

Eric Mack questions the seemingly Kantian stream in Rand's conclusions about what is right for an individual to do. Rand, supposedly an individualist, ignores the fact that the things mankind as a group cannot do and survive—like live always and only as parasites on the productivity of others—are things that individual men can and in fact do all the time. Rand fails to prove, as a necessary fact of existence, that every *individual* man needs to practice the virtue of productivity; at best, productivity provides a good general strategy, not an unbreakable command.[14]

The most thorough and imaginative scholarly take on Rand is Chris Sciabarra's book, which connects Rand with the dialectical method that she is presumed to have marinated in during her early Russian education. Sciabarra argues for thinking of Rand as a dialectical thinker—one who transcends and/or combines apparent opposites—because "she both accepted and rejected significant principles within each of the polar traditions which she analyzed. Consequently, by abstracting particular aspects from the totality of her thought, one can see elements of rationalism *and* empiricism, idealism *and* materialism, liberalism *and* conservatism."[15]

Rand also has a history of being victimized by random drive-by shootings masquerading as books. Rational–emotivist psychologist Albert Ellis, after a series of frustrating public debates with Nathaniel Branden, wrote *Is Objectivism a Religion?*, a farrago of mostly ignorant and uncomprehending critiques, largely on politics and economics; in the book's own introduction Ellis admits his ignorance in those areas and vows not to dwell on them. The book contains such clever ripostes as summing up Rand's argument about how man establishes property rights in objects—the standard Lockean one, for the most part—with the unelaborated critique that it is "pretty crummy thinking."[16] Ellis the therapist claims that "once an individual becomes mentally aberrated, and in particular very hostile, he gets intensely attracted to Objectivism."[17]

For books like Ellis's, Nathaniel Branden had a response: Rarely do Rand's attackers deign "publicly to name the essential ideas of *Atlas Shrugged* and to attempt to refute them. No one has been willing to declare: 'Ayn Rand holds that man must choose his values and actions exclusively by reason, that man has the right to exist for his own sake, that no one has the right to seek values from others by physical force—and I consider such ideas wrong, evil and socially dangerous.'"[18]

"A COMMAND TO FUNCTION AT ONE'S BEST, TO BE THE MOST THAT ONE COULD BE."

Ayn Rand's work vibrates with unresolved tension between glorifying man qua man, the greatness possible in man, and glorifying only the Great Man. This was left over from the earlier Nietzscheism that she officially disavowed and even tried to purge from *We the Living*, an attitude that led to a seemingly hateful contempt for the nongreat. Both tendencies can be found in her work, from her very first attempt at a novel, never completed, in 1928, *The Little Street*, where she wrote of the "one and only horror—*the horror of mediocrity*" and how she wanted her book to show that the typical common man's life "can't be tolerated, for all their life is a rotten swamp, a sewer, a dumping place for more filth than they can ever realize."[19]

Rand was uncharitable. She didn't believe that other people's need or suffering constituted any claim on her life or anyone else's—unless people chose to take on the burden because the happiness of the helped person was specifically valuable to them. In her notes for *Atlas*, she was passionate on this point: "*God damn it, I must put an end to the idea of misfortune as an all-embracing pass-key and a first mortgage on all life! That's what I must blast.*"[20]

To Rand, contemporary irrationalism was destroying human minds—the most heinous crime imaginable. In a long essay, almost a monograph, she condemns modern educational methods as anticognitive and anticonceptual, failing to help the young mind think rationally. Here Rand's contempt for her foes reaches a true, exalted moral fervor. It also functions as smart, far-seeing social criticism. She even concludes that some victims of progressive education might not be able to bootstrap themselves up solely by their own efforts, a real concession for Rand.[21]

Critics who hear only hatefulness and heartlessness in Rand are tone-deaf to peals of glory. As Barbara Branden wrote in her Rand biography (and Branden had intimate exposure to the worst Rand had to offer), "In Ayn's presence, and in her work, one felt that command: a command to function at one's best, to be the most that one could be, to drive oneself constantly harder, never to disappoint one's highest ideals."[22] As Rand herself put it, the "essence of life is the achievement of joy, not the escape from pain."[23] *Fountainhead* lovers don't just want to hiss at Toohey—they want to *be* Roark. And despite cavils about his "unrealism" or "inhumanity," a man of consummate skill, bursting creativity, and unyielding integrity is a man eminently worth being.

This is the positive side to the libertarian's emphasis on what he's against—illegitimate government. It's a valuable and important addition to the libertarian movement's "sense of life." Rand identified and in some ways defined the world of libertarian enmities. Only someone of libertarian heart could fully understand and appreciate the scene in *Atlas* where Cheryl Taggart, the unskilled but good-souled admirer of the great who mistakenly marries Jim Taggart (not realizing his sister is the true hero of the railroad), throws herself in the river and drowns rather than submit to the tender mercies of a social worker who is *only out to help her.*

Rand's passionate belief in the possibility of individual glory and greatness, as well as her burning admiration for it, is central to her appeal, the reason why many intelligent, capable people bound themselves to her, often under psychologically difficult circumstances, for so long; the reason why she has millions of devoted fans and readers.

Although some write her off as a clumsy political-ideological novelist, Rand appeals more broadly to what conservative movement founder Russell Kirk, echoing Edmund Burke, calls "the moral imagination." While conservatives of the Kirk ilk found little to admire in Rand—and vice versa—she, more than most conservative intellectuals, actually lived out in her work the idea that the human soul must be fed by more than just politics and policy and economizing; that literary art can focus the human soul on greater aspirations.

Rand went out of her way to speak to intelligent young people who feel alienated in a culture that doesn't respect their achievements, their possibilities, that—especially in a high school or college context—seems afraid of those who rise above the herd, of those who are different in the way Roark and Galt and Dagny Taggart are different—not the kind of people who would be fun at a kegger, not the kind to flow along in a typical dorm room bull session.

Many may identify themselves with Roark and Galt without the real stuff to back it up, which is the root of popular disdain for the Randroid; a Roark type who isn't actually an accomplished genius can be insufferable. Rand writes almost tenderly understanding paeans to the plight, both emotional and practical, of the above average in an average world.[24] As Peikoff put it, "Ayn Rand offered people something they could not get elsewhere, and in return they gave her love, awe, wealth."[25]

Barbara Branden's statement about the unyielding command to rise that Rand represents contains the reason for another common phenomenon among Rand readers. The political and ethical message of her novels is hard to mistake and in *Atlas*, nearly impossible. (Though many readers "skip the speeches.") Rand has had tens of millions of readers, but few have internalized and lived out her message. People commonly refer to "outgrowing" an affection or admiration for Rand. Barbara Branden speculates that "people figured out how unpopular her ideas were, and maybe they didn't outgrow anything, maybe they were just afraid to admit to it publicly because the wrath of God would descend on them from people they knew."[26]

In a passage later cut from the twenty-fifth anniversary edition introduction to *The Fountainhead*, Rand wrote,

> The instances of men who paid me extravagant, unsolicited compliments at private gatherings, but never stated it in print or on public occasion, are too numerous to count. I do not mean the usual sort of gushers. These men were prominent literary or professional figures who had no reason to flatter me; in many cases, they did not even say it to me, but to others, without knowing

that I would ever hear about it. If such were their views, they had
no reason to be afraid of expressing them publicly. Yet they kept
silent.

The final clue was provided by a very perceptive friend of
mine. He said he had observed a strange quality in many people's
enthusiasm for *The Fountainhead*: It was a furtive, secretive, subjective quality, almost like the reluctant confession of a guilty love.
"They talk as an unhappily married man would talk about his secret mistress," he said. "Their marriage is to the Establishment, to
conventional values and the 'accepted' intellectual positions. But
The Fountainhead is their passion."[27]

Objectivism is a jealous God, demanding obedience to a strict code
and the forsaking of all others. Certainly Rand hated as passionately as
she loved. Still, critics such as Whittaker Chambers (and many other
Rand critics share this view) who hear in Rand's writings a stern voice
commanding, "To a gas chamber—go!" are themselves revealing a
crabbed sensibility. True, Rand was frequently unfair to her intellectual
opponents, seeing moral corruption where there was only honest intellectual disagreement. As libertarians from Milton Friedman to Roy
Childs have suggested, one got more positive value from Rand the
thinker the farther one stayed from Rand the person. Most accounts of
the Randian inner circle emphasize damage and repression that resulted
from intimate exposure to her over time. But as they all say, no one held
a gun to their head; the warmth of her genius and the jolt of feeling
close to an epoch-making mind compensated, for a while at least, for
the heat of her ceaseless demands and the shock of her wrath.[28]

Personal unpleasantness and peccadilloes aside, Rand's fiction energized millions, including a majority of the significant figures in the
American libertarian movement. Her books continue to sell hundreds
of thousands of copies a year and will continue to enthrall future generations—and continue to lead a certain savvy percentage to appreciate the necessity of personal liberty and limited government.
Libertarianism may not "usually" begin with Ayn Rand anymore. And
Rand herself might have thought her epistemology more important
than her ethics and politics. But her systematic approach and her
burning moral passion will remain a powerful introduction to the idea

that a man's life belongs to him, not to the state or the collective, and to the rich and complex series of conclusions about the proper nature and mission of government which follow from that idea.

"ASHAMED EVER AGAIN TO USE THE TERM 'SOCIAL JUSTICE.'"

While Ayn Rand remained the most popular of libertarian influences, F. A. Hayek has in the past decades grown into one of the most sophisticated and respectable ones. Shortly after *The Constitution of Liberty* was published in 1960, Hayek left Chicago for the University of Freiburg in Germany, but not for scholarly or romantic reasons. Chicago's early retirement age and niggardly pension prompted Hayek to follow the lure of better provision for his and his wife's old age and take the professorship at Freiburg in 1962, where he concentrated on teaching economic policy rather than theory, since the professional zeitgeist in regard to theory had largely left him behind.

He taught there for eight years and worked on a restatement and amplification of *Constitution*, which was eventually published in three installments from 1973 to 1979 under the umbrella title *Law, Legislation, and Liberty*.

He focused more on modern democracy and its discontents but retained the overarching themes in *Constitution*: spontaneous order, rule following, the price system, the limits of reason. Hayek summed up the book's intention concisely: "The thesis of this book is that a condition of liberty in which all are allowed to use their knowledge for their purposes, restrained only by rules of just conduct for universal application, is likely to produce for them the best conditions for achieving their aims; and that such a system is likely to be achieved and maintained only if all authority, including that of the majority of the people, is limited to the exercise of coercive power by general principles to which the community has committed itself."[29]

The book's major impetus was demolishing the concept of "social justice," a task of which Hayek wrote, "I have come to feel strongly that the greatest service I can still render to my fellow men would be that I could make the speakers and writers among them thoroughly ashamed ever again to employ the term 'social justice.'"[30] Social justice had come to its prominence in modern Western thought, Hayek maintains, as intellectual and ethical cover for power and resource grabs by an untethered legislature.

Thus his slashing attack on social justice—the central feature of volume 2 of the trilogy—is in the service of the work's significant innovation, which Hayek lays out in great detail in volume 3: a curiously constructivist scheme for restructuring the legislatures of Western democracies in order to curb their tendency to overstep the bounds of the rule of law and manipulate the market order to reward constituents, using social justice as an excuse.

The problem, as Hayek sees it, is that legislatures in the West have come unmoored from their historic intention, which is making *real* law, or "rules of just conduct" in Hayek's terminology. They have become administrative bodies that deal not just with crafting abstract rules that apply to everyone, everywhere, equally, with no respect to person, status, or the specifics of individual situation, but with the day-to-day business of government itself. Only the former deserves the sacred rubric of law to Hayek. Such rules of just conduct are what Hayek supposed underlay "common law," or judge-made law, in the English tradition, and such laws didn't necessarily require a legislative body at all. They could and did develop through spontaneous evolution, from the scattered experience of thousands of people and many generations, as expressed in the decisions of judges. That is the law Hayek respects and venerates.

Once legislatures burst the confines of lawmaking in the old-fashioned sense and claim the power to pass laws that treat citizens differently and grant special favors to some at the expense of others, the only ideological rein on government expansion is gone. Suddenly politicians stop thinking of any common good and merely act to carry out their constituents' demands, since voters control the politicians' access to the privileges and emoluments of office. Individual self-interest can benefit everyone in free markets, Hayek believed; but organized group interests tend to be inherently antisocial, frequently demanding special favors from government for themselves at the expense of everyone else.

To combat this trend, Hayek proposes dividing legislative responsibilities among two houses: one to consider only changes in the overall abstract rules of just conduct and another to deal with the day-to-day operations of government, including fiscal policy. The "lower" house would have to operate within the abstract rules set by the "upper" house.[31]

Hayek was in despair both for himself and for the future of Western civilization while he wrote these volumes.[32] It's understandable that he would find it hard to be sanguine about the prospects for the market order he champions. He believes both reason (which thinks it can outsmart traditional rules) and instinct (which wants to overturn the abstract order of the modern market for the atavistic tribal order of our past) are fighting against some of the rules on which that order depends, most significantly the tradition of private property. In Hayek's reading it evolved without most people understanding its central role in creating and extending prosperity, yet it has allowed more humans to survive and thrive than any system of central control or ownership ever could. "Man will have to recognize that it is neither his inborn instincts nor his intelligence on which his future chiefly depends." It is rather the institution of private property and markets, which helps groups and societies thrive even though they don't understand why.[33]

While the three volumes of *Law, Legislation, and Liberty* were trickling out, Hayek won the Nobel Prize in economics in 1974. This award delivered great financial benefits as well as an unparalleled prestige boost. It helped ease his depression and stimulated a burst of intellectual and career energy if not joy.

The scamps in Stockholm diluted the value of the prize by rewarding it jointly that year to Hayek and socialist economist Gunnar Myrdal, of whom Hayek once said, "I don't think he has ever been a good economist."[34] The *Washington Post* managed to confuse the point of the Nobel committee's pairing of Hayek and Myrdal by declaring that while Myrdal was both economist and political philosopher, Hayek was mostly an economist.[35] Officially it was because both men had done work that combined economics with larger social and institutional phenomena, but it is widely understood that it was a deliberate act of ideological balancing of left and right to avoid the complaints that would result from giving it to local Swedish favorite Myrdal alone.

For the thirty years prior to winning the Nobel, Hayek had done practically no economic work and had built a body of social, political, legal, and scientific philosophy on which his current (and doubtless future) reputation soundly rests. At a time when the chickens of the Keynesian inflation were coming home to roost, Hayek felt compelled to tell his colleagues, as he received his profession's paramount honor, exactly where they had gone wrong.

"We have indeed at the moment little cause for pride," Hayek declared in his acceptance speech. "As a profession we have made a mess of things."[36] He went on to criticize economists' addiction to cobbling together measurable magnitudes such as price levels and gross domestic products at all costs, even when their measurements had no theoretical or practical value; their hubristic attempts to predict precisely when only generalized predictions of likely patterns are possible; and their belief that their understanding of social processes gives them the power to manipulate them to achieve desired ends.

Hayek summed up the most libertarian aspect of his message to the uncomprehending crowd at the Nobel acceptance ceremony: "There is danger in the exuberant feeling of ever growing power which the advance of the physical sciences has engendered and which tempts man to try . . . to subject not only our natural but also our human environment to the control of a human will. The recognition of the insuperable limits to his knowledge ought indeed to teach the student of society a lesson in humility which should guard against him becoming an accomplice in men's fatal striving to control society—a striving which makes him not only a tyrant over his fellows, but which may make him the destroyer of a civilization which no brain has designed but which has grown from the free efforts of millions of individuals."[37]

Hayek returned to his native Austria in 1969 to take a professorship at the University of Salzburg. He returned to Freiburg in 1977 (though not to active teaching) and remained there until his death in 1992.

Hayek made many visits and lecture tours, and spent summers pursuing research in America under the aegis of libertarian organizations such as the Institute for Humane Studies and Liberty Fund. The Cato Institute paid for a secretary to keep the grand old libertarian on top of his business and free some of his time for further scholarly work. At the

Institute for Humane Studies in the mid-1970s Hayek would be hounded by radical young acolytes eager to convert him to "anarcho-Hayekianism" and pumping him for every anecdote and observation about the Austrian and libertarian movement past they could glean. While the grand old man could have written off these eager youngsters as pests, they all remember his patience and old-world graciousness.

During his later years, Hayek grew obsessed with publicly and finally refuting socialism in the eyes of the world. His thoughts about his intellectual opponents became less charitable.[38] He decided the time was ripe for a grand public debate between a gang of Mont Pelerin Society members and a gang of socialists to prove to the world once and for all who was right and who was wrong. "This proved to be impractical," Hayek told a gathering at the American Enterprise Institute in February 1978. "An affair like this, on the scale on which I had contemplated, is very expensive, and our effort to raise funds from the capitalists was a failure. Evidently, the capitalists did not have an interest in the intellectual defense of capitalism."[39] (Libertarian intellectuals have always made similar complaints and will doubtless continue to do so.)

In the 1980s, Hayek produced his last major work, *The Fatal Conceit,* another tome exploring his life's work and featuring what he hoped would be the final intellectual refutation of socialism. He again mined, with clipped brevity, his ideas about spontaneous order, rules, the limits of reason, and the importance of property. Hayek agreed with Hume and Locke that property, along with the rules defining it and how it could be legitimately transferred, is the base of civilization.

In this final work Hayek focuses on the unguided evolution of moral rules as the key to a "group selection" that employs variation, adaptation, and competition in regard to moral and social orders that allowed certain groups or societies to survive and thrive while others failed. The book was published in 1988 as the first volume in the University of Chicago's ongoing series, the *Collected Works of F. A. Hayek.* More recently, Hayek scholars have mostly agreed that *The Fatal Conceit* was heavily edited and perhaps essentially more or less written by Hayek's would-be biographer W. W. Bartley, his intellectual companion during Hayek's fading years.[40]

"A successful free society will always . . . be a tradition-bound society."

Despite his high reputation as an advocate for human liberty and against state control, Hayek's arguments in some ways provide more room for state power and less for individual autonomy than did those of his fellow libertarian giants. Though Hayek often advocates the private sphere as the key to preserving the extended order of human cooperation that allows us to thrive, he leaves a lot of room for state interference within that sphere—and does so with intellectual justifications that, some critics argue, aren't always coherent.

Hayek's definition of coercion has been questioned by libertarians ranging from Rothbard to Ronald Hamowy, Hayek's student, who took him on in *New Individualist Review*. Hamowy points out that merely requiring rules to be applied equally to all in society, as in Hayek's original definition of coercion, allows far too much state action. Indeed, Hayek's focus on the abstract nature of law, the necessity of law not respecting persons or noticing particular circumstances, does seem to satisfy a certain version of what is fair (as a child will complain that any unequal treatment is "not fair"), but it seems a thin definition of justice in a wider sense. Most people's sense of justice, which operates by unarticulated and perhaps unarticulatable principles, as Hayek knows, would recognize that all sorts of state acts, even if applied with scrupulous fairness in the sense that all are treated equally, are or could be considered unjust.

Hamowy uses the example of conscription, which, as long as it follows an abstract rule, is acceptable to Hayek as per *Constitution of Liberty*.[41] To Hamowy, and many other libertarians, forcing all young men to provide the state with years of essentially unlimited and hazardous service is definitely unjust, even if done scrupulously by preannounced rules. Hayek later revised his definition of coercion so that it has to involve abstract rules, not respecting persons, that affect your conduct *toward other people*, not merely imposing any rule on you willy-nilly.[42]

But to posit preventing state intervention in people's lives as the primary political goal is to flirt with anarchism, and Hayek is no anarchist. Those who take a "rigid position" against such matters as a government role in social insurance, education, or even subsidizing "certain experimental developments," he insists, are taking a "position which is defensible but has little to do with freedom."[43] Freedom, to Hayek, exists only under law.

Some of his libertarian critics said that Hayek tended to be loose in his acceptance of various state actions. He believed the state has to provide certain public goods without addressing the arguments against that necessity, and did the same for state wealth redistribution. Hayek usually ignored the implications of, for example, permitting a welfare state in his schema. He thought that following unfettered markets makes sense most of the time for rule–utilitarian reasons (i.e., following the rule of free markets would in general create the largest economic pie for all), though some would suffer hardship, and a minimal welfare state would be a way to solve this problem. But there are practical difficulties associated with a welfare state, which have arisen clearly in the decades since Hayek first endorsed it. Hayek surely would have been alarmed by, for example, the rise of the underclass, the poverty bureaucracy, and the various state power and taxing apparatuses that have arisen around it—the same reasons libertarian Charles Murray attacked the welfare state in *Losing Ground*.

Attacking these aspects of the modern welfare state has become one of the cottage industries of modern libertarianism, but Hayek's thought has been of no real help. The empirical results of the welfare state since the 1960s might have made Hayek change his mind, but he never did so publicly. Considering the high level of abstraction Hayek tended to rely on, rarely supplying real-world examples that support his argument or illustrate his meaning, this is not surprising.[44]

Much of Hayek's work, abstract and suggestive as it is, begs for further clarification and exploration from future scholars. The number of books devoted to his work and life has increased steadily in the years since his death in 1992. The evolutionary theory of his later years has the most blanks that need filling in. Hayek admitted that his evolutionary social theory is largely speculative and boldly asserted that *"mind and culture developed concurrently and not successively"* (italics original). He admitted that "we find that we know so little about precisely how this development took place, of which we have so few recognizable fossils, that we are reduced to reconstruct it as a sort of conjectural history in the sense of the Scottish moral philosophers of the eighteenth century. The facts about which we know almost nothing are the evolution of those rules of conduct which governed the structure and functioning of the various small groups of men in which the race developed. . . . The most important part of cultural evolution . . . was completed before recorded history began."[45]

Austrian movement economist and intellectual historian Karen Vaughn has pointed out that Hayek "certainly does not *in practice* rely on the long sweep of evolution to bring about the optimal rules of a just order. . . . For all his emphasis on tradition, Hayek's programme has been revolutionary."[46] His apparent insistence that this evolutionary process must be blind, that intelligence can have nothing to do with it, further riles some Misesian libertarians. Hayek's abandoning of the purely a priori Austrian method of economics in favor of the Popperian notion of social science as capable of "pattern predictions" is considered a betrayal by many of the Austrians surrounding the Mises Institute, such as Rothbard and Hans-Hermann Hoppe. They find Hayek's abandonment of the Misesian notion of man's rationality dictating his choices absurd.[47]

To most Misesians, you don't need blind accident or evolution to explain why men adopted private property and the institutions of a market order. Just as economists can figure out the advantages of these institutions, so can intelligent, purposive man adopt them because he recognizes their advantages, not because he is blindly following social group evolution.[48]

Hayek's reliance on evolution made his later writings sound more conservative than libertarian in some ways, despite his denying the "conservative" label. Hayek claimed that a presumptive reliance on traditional ways and morality (since they embodied the collective wisdom and evolutionary success of the ages, above the feeble workings of any single rational mind) was the only way for society to thrive. Consequently it's easy to see how he could be mistakenly identified as conservative for statements such as, in *Fatal Conceit*, "Virtually all the benefits of civilisation, and indeed our very existence, rest, I believe, on our continuing willingness to shoulder the burden of tradition. These benefits in no way 'justify' the burden. But the alternative is poverty and famine."[49]

Hayek-the-traditionalist argued that too much personal quirkiness may be bad for society[50] and claimed that "a successful free society will always in a large measure be a tradition-bound society."[51] He even had a kind word for social regulation of religion under circumstances where everyone *believes* that God will punish all for the sins of some.[52]

Yet his social philosophy also allows for maximal evolution and change. He straddles a line between the conservative and the radical, in the end reconciling them with the belief that a progressive rallies forward best from a solid, trustworthy home in the received wisdom of generations as carried down to us in custom, particularly the custom that allowed for the creation of the mostly unrestricted market order. Figuring out the boundaries—where man can and should adjust his rules—is not clear-cut in Hayek. He admits that spontaneous orders can sometimes lead to results that require positive legislation to change.[53]

Hayek's social philosophy and intellectual project are not meant to provide the final, authoritative answer.[54] It is fitting that Hayek's project was unfinished. More than anything else, Hayek taught humility. Human beings don't know as much as we think we do, can't do everything we may wish to do, and rely more than we may wish on achievements and collected wisdom and habits that we had no part in making and don't fully understand.

In his book *Counter-Revolution of Science*, at the end of an account of the intellectual (and practical) evil that flowed from the well of Saint-Simon, Hayek wrote,

> We are still, largely without knowing it, under the influence of ideas which have almost imperceptibly crept into modern thought . . . we are to a great extent still guided by ideas which are at least a century old, just as the nineteenth century was mainly guided by the ideas of the eighteenth. But whereas the ideas of Hume and Voltaire, of Adam Smith and Kant, produced the liberalism of the nineteenth century, those of Hegel and Comte, of Feuerbach and Marx, have produced the totalitarianism of the

twentieth. . . . I doubt whether it is possible to overestimate the influence which ideas have in the long run. . . . It is our special duty to recognize the currents of thought which still operate in public opinion, to examine their significance, and, if necessary, to refute them.[55]

Hayek lived his intellectual life by that credo and changed the world. Mont Pelerin's and Hayek's personal influence on such think tankers as Antony Fisher of Britain's Institute for Economic Affairs, and through them on politicians such as Margaret Thatcher and dozens of other classical liberal intellectual institutes the world over, has had and is having a decisive influence on what Hayek called the secondhand dealers in ideas, the intellectuals, that makes him (despite his occasional doctrinal looseness when it comes to purist antistatism) a prime engine of modern libertarianism. The twenty-first century could still turn out to be the century of Hayek and the loosely associated thinkers who fall under the rubric libertarian.

"THE COLLECTIVE POLITICAL WISDOM OF THE AGES WAS NOT WORTH A GOOD SET OF FORGED-STEEL HAND TOOLS."

In 1986, the Libertarian Party brought back a blast from the movement's past to edit the *LP News*. Since the mid-1970s, Karl Hess had become a public spokesman for a community-based liberty rooted in self-sufficiency and technologies manageable on a small community scale.[56] He left the revolutionary battle and returned to his love for neighborhoods, technology, and self-sufficiency. He and Therese Machotka, whom he married in 1971, tried to turn their Adams-Morgan neighborhood in Washington, D.C., into a functioning experiment in local technological and agricultural self-sufficiency. Hydroponic gardens sprouted on rooftops, machine shops were opened to the neighborhood kids, trout were breeding in tanks in rowhouse basements. Years later, Hess wrote a book summing up the experiment and what he learned, *Community Technology* (1979). After numerous break-ins to his home and too many kids who wanted "a job" (read: a paycheck) rather than meaningful work to do, he abandoned the neighborhood and the city in 1976. He and Therese relocated to a solar-powered home they built themselves on the Opequon River near Kearneysville, West Virginia, where they lived for the rest of his life.

As they prepared to leave D.C., Hess experienced a perfect epiphany regarding the value of words versus the value of tools:

> We had, of course, several thousand books, institute-type books mostly on political science which look terribly impressive on walls but which few people, including myself, ever read in their entirety. We decided to offer them in trade for books that might actually be of use to us in West Virginia. We didn't get a single nibble on our offer. So, we then offered to swap them for tools. We advertised on bulletin boards and in the local newspaper our desire to trade a set of politically correct books for a good set of socket wrenches. Nothing. The market had made its decision: The collective political wisdom of the ages was not worth a good set of forged-steel hand tools.[57]

In 1975, Hess published the first of two autobiographies, *Dear America*. The book is an interesting study of a man teetering on the edge between libertarianism and antiproperty leftism. He still believes that freedom is a great value; he's still contrary enough to think FDR was pushing "social fascism."[58] But he's no longer a full private property Rothbardian. He thinks corporations owe something to their communities and should not be free to just up and leave if doing so would harm those communities.[59] He has kind words for Fidel Castro.[60] He worries as much about concentrated corporate and business power as he does about state power.[61] The book's arguments mostly stand on the three legs of the Hessian stool: local freedom, workplace democracy, and technology as a tool of personal empowerment.

Hess edited a newsletter on self-sufficiency called *Survival Tomorrow* from 1981 to 1985, published by Robert Kephart, a former publisher of the right-wing *Human Events* who was converted by Hess and

Rothbard to a more anarchistic libertarianism and became a longtime funder of libertarian causes. Hess and Therese made cash under the table (he was still under the watchful eye of the IRS for past tax protests and legally earned income was snatched) selling hand-refinished furniture at D.C.'s Eastern Market. He took occasional one-year stints as both artist in residence and "radical in residence" at small colleges.

Hess was still a folk hero among libertarians, and he ran the *LP News* until 1989, aggravating some by making it a more wide-ranging movement organ not strictly devoted to party news and hype. He began having heart trouble in the late 1980s, and in August 1992 he had a heart transplant operation. During his waning years, he befriended a West Virginian neighbor and fellow libertarian writer, Charles Murray. They were introduced by former Rand insider and libertarian feminist Joan Kennedy Taylor, who had shepherded his antiwelfare state classic *Losing Ground* to completion while she worked at the Manhattan Institute in the early 1980s.

Murray, the staid policy analyst, had a lot in common intellectually with the welding anarchist-localist, with their shared interest in forging the good life in small communities free from outside interference. But personal charisma was always key to Hess's influence, and Murray became personally enchanted by him. "What I learned from Karl is as much from example as from anything he wrote," Murray recalled.[62] Karl Hess died in April 1994, the same week as Richard Nixon and Russell Kirk.[63]

The libertarian movement has been, largely, a movement of ideologues and activists inspired by ideologues. Hess was resolutely anti-ideological. "What really changes our world and the way we live in it are devices and innovations," he wrote. "If you want to know what is happening in a society at any point, look at the tools—not the rhetoric, not the books, not the philosophy. If a tool is available you can bet somebody is going to use it, and if it works well you can be certain the world will never be the same again. The free market, for example, is such a tool. Wherever there is unfettered commerce, ordinary people thrive."[64] Although his writings are mostly out of print, Hess has retained valuable currency in the libertarian movement through the friends he made and the people he influenced.[65]

"WHAT *HUMANS* . . . HAVE THE RIGHT TO BE COERCIVE PARASITES WITHIN THE BODY OF AN UNWILLING HUMAN HOST?"

Having left (with some pushing) the family of Koch operations by 1981, Murray Rothbard settled in a new institutional berth in 1982, one that met all his needs for unrepentant Rothbardian radicalism and gave him his head in whatever direction he wished to go. The Ludwig von Mises Institute, named for Rothbard's beloved mentor, was launched by Lew Rockwell Jr. Rockwell was a traditionalist libertarian who arose from the conservative movement. He had been an editor at Arlington House, a publisher devoted to conservative books on politics and culture, which had published Rothbard's *Conceived in Liberty* series on American colonial history, and published or reprinted many Mises and Hazlitt books as well. Rockwell had also worked at the traditionalist Hillsdale College (which refuses to accept government aid) under former FEE man George Roche, and as an aide to Ron Paul during his first stint in Congress.[66]

The Mises Institute publishes a monthly pamphlet with short articles that apply free market thinking to current problems, called the *Free Market*; runs a series of summer seminars teaching Austrian economics to college students; publishes an academic journal, the *Review of Austrian Economics*, initially edited by Rothbard and Walter Block (now retitled *Quarterly Journal of Austrian Economics*); and grants graduate fellowships and research residencies for students in the Misesian tradition.[67] Rothbard was thrilled to have an institute dedicated to promoting the pure Misesian—and Rothbardian—line. Walter Block delighted in writing journal articles showing the antilibertarian implications of the works of many reputedly libertarian economists, including those of the Chicago School and even Hayek. It's worthwhile, he thinks, as well as more challenging: "Lashing out at Marx and Galbraith becomes like shooting fish in a barrel."[68]

Rothbard finally published *The Ethics of Liberty* in 1982, a book two decades in the making. Ivan Bierly at the Volker Fund had originally suggested it to Rothbard as a book "bringing natural rights to libertarians and liberty to conservatives."[69] Rothbard here presented the fullest explanation of the ethical philosophy behind his property-based

anarcho-capitalism—and lets some of his truest radicalism shine
through. For example, he says that a libertarian mustn't stand for merely
protecting any existing distribution of property; rather, he is interested
in defending *justly held* property. When we can authoritatively say that a
current property holding is not based in an unbroken line of just possession, and can find a victim or an heir of the victim from whom the
property was taken, then that victim or heir must take possession.

Rothbard is fully prepared, then, to throw current society into tu-
mult in an attempt to rectify past injustice, since a "give America back
to the Indians and Mexicans" platform can be inferred from Rothbard's argument. As he once wrote, "'Land reform' is a portmanteau
concept that covers a lot of sins and virtues, and so is a virtually meaningless term. What we favor, here as always, is justice and property
rights, and we favor the return of stolen property to its rightful owners. In many areas of the world, arable land was stolen by conquest and
government expropriation from the peasants and handed to favored
groups of 'feudal' landlords, and we consider it not only just but essential to restore this property to its rightful peasant owners."[70] In practice, he thinks that because most lines of possession are so muddled
that as a second-best option we should treat current legal property as
homesteaded. This land reform issue was brought up in magazine articles in the 1970s by then Rothbard disciple Roy Childs, editing *Libertarian Review*. Barely a word has been breathed about it from any
libertarian publication or institution since.

Rothbard takes care in *Ethics* to define the limited range in which
libertarian law can justifiably use force. Mere threats, for example, are
not a just pretext for violent intervention. This notion of the strict
limits of legal force leads him to further radical conclusions. A libertarian cop, for example, should be fully liable for anything he does to
anyone who was not an invader of someone's property or person.
This means you can't force people to testify in court proceedings or
serve on juries, and no one can be justly held prisoner or required to
pay bail until after being convicted of an invasive crime.

In a libertarian court system, only the victim could press charges.
With no state, the only crimes are those against individuals. If a victim
chooses not to prosecute a crime against himself, then no prosecution
will occur. A murder victim's heirs must press charges, or the victim

himself must state clearly in a will how he'd like his murderer punished, or provide for a "crime insurance company" to find and prosecute his murderer.[71] Since the criminal's debt is not to society but to the victim, pure restitution is the proper punishment. Rothbard shows how historically this has been a typical principle of human law, gone moribund because the state has taken up the burden of justice enforcement as its own monopoly. "The ideal situation, then, puts the criminal frankly into a state of *enslavement* to his victim, the criminal continuing in that condition of just slavery until he has redressed the grievance of the man he has wronged."[72]

The most controversial positions in *Ethics* regard children's rights. Rothbard is perfectly willing to posit that a fetus is a full-fledged human, with all the rights of a human being—*but no more*. And in his libertarian defense of abortion rights he asks, "What *humans* . . . have the right to be coercive parasites within the body of an unwilling human host? Clearly, no *born* humans have such a right, and therefore . . . the fetus can have no such right either."[73] In arguments based on the writings of his then lieutenant, Williamson Evers (and relying also on a scholarly journal article by the lawyer then known as Hillary Rodham against the child's supposed "right to be wanted," which Rothbard rejected), he presents a theory of full parental ownership of children, ending only when the child chooses to leave home and support himself, at whatever age that might be. One of the more extraordinary conclusions of the Evers/Rothbard child rights theory is the parent's absolute right to let the child starve to death, though not to actively aggress against him in any way. Taking his logic to the farthest reaches, far beyond most people's inchoate moral convictions, is a characteristic Rothbard shared with his nineteenth-century individualist anarchist hero Benjamin Tucker, who drove allies away from his magazine and movement with a similar insistence on absolute parental rights over children.[74]

Rothbard delights in defending the shocking conclusions to which his pure property rights libertarianism leads. He insists, for example, that libel cannot be a crime. Crimes require attacks on person or property, but libel damages only someone's reputation. Since your reputation consists of thoughts in other people's heads, it is not your property. Rothbard insists there's no particular right to immigrate or move anywhere, in a world of strict private property. Any such freedom of movement requires crossing other people's property, and one needs permission to do that. Because libertarians want justice and they want it now, to Rothbard a libertarian should always and everywhere advocate immediate abolition of any injustice—anything done by the state. He summons to his side the ghost of William Lloyd Garrison and the abolitionists' moral fervor toward ending slavery. Rothbard does admit that the libertarian will often have to settle for transitional steps toward the ultimate goal of abolishing the state. That's fine, so long as the libertarian is "*always* holding up the ultimate goal of liberty as the desired end of the transitional process."[75]

"CONSERVATIVES HAVE ALWAYS ARGUED THAT POLITICAL FREEDOM IS A NECESSARY BUT NOT SUFFICIENT CONDITION FOR THE GOOD SOCIETY, AND THEY'RE RIGHT."

Rothbard had stopped publishing *Libertarian Forum* in 1984. He ceased writing for *Reason* after its editor Robert Poole rejected two of his columns in quick succession in 1983: one lauding tax resister Gordon Kahl, who had killed a federal agent, and one suggesting the United States did not have clean hands in the furor over the Soviet shootdown of Korean Air Flight 007.[76] From 1987 to 1989, he served as founding editor and frequent contributor to the new libertarian movement journal *Liberty*, published by coin dealer R. W. Bradford. But through most of the 1980s his contributions to libertarian periodicals were meager in comparison to the 1960s and 1970s, and mostly concentrated on Mises Institute publications.

In 1985, Rothbard became the S. J. Hall Distinguished Professor of Economics at the University of Nevada–Las Vegas, where he taught economics and economic intellectual history. Rothbard's largest project through the 1980s and 1990s, which he left uncompleted at the end of his life, was a history of economic thought from an Austrian perspective. The project was started under the impetus of and with financial support from libertarian economist and investment advisor Mark Skousen. Rothbard's central contention in the work is that the standard Whig history of economic thought—positing that Adam Smith created economic science full-blown and that it has been rising steadily upward in insight and accomplishment since then—is wrong. Smith, Murray claimed, was more villain than hero in the history of economic science, and many pre-Smith thinkers got closer to the truth about such vital matters as subjective value and marginal utility than Smith did.

The twists and turns in the historical and theological debates over such matters as usury and just price get plenty of attention in the book. Grand Rothbardian characters such as Juan de Mariana, a Spanish scholastic of the sixteenth and seventeenth centuries who justified tyrannicide for such crimes as taxing without consent or preventing a meeting of a representative parliament, are rescued from history's dark closets.[77]

Ever the iconoclast (his enemies, as well as some exasperated friends, characterize it as an almost willful truculence), Rothbard applied his iconoclasm to the libertarian movement itself in 1989. He decided he'd had enough of every aspect of the movement not controlled by his friends Rockwell or Burt Blumert (a coin dealer from California who had taken upon himself the otherwise moribund Center for Libertarian Studies, whose sole activity for most of the 1980s and 1990s was publishing the *Journal of Libertarian Studies*). In the aftermath of the 1988 Ron Paul presidential campaign, Rothbard was repulsed by LP members who hated Paul's GOP past, straight-laced demeanor, and anti-abortion stance. Rothbard thought the Libertarian Party had been taken over by what he characterized as *luftmenschen*, a Yiddish term for "people of the air," people of no fixed means whose method of earthly survival is mysterious. Rothbard, with Rockwell, began insulting these counterculture types in the pages of *Liberty*. Rockwell threw down the gauntlet with a controversial essay defending "paleolibertarianism"—libertarian politics combined with cultural conservatism.

"Conservatives have always argued that political freedom is a necessary but not sufficient condition for the good society, and they're right," Rockwell wrote. "Neither is it sufficient for the free society. We also need social institutions and standards that encourage public virtue, and protect the individual from the state."[78] He attacked the "Woodstockian flavor of the movement. *Hair* may have left Broadway long ago, but the age of Aquarius survives in the LP."[79] Rockwell and Rothbard had given up on the LP but hoped to revive a libertarian movement of middle-class, middle American appeal through a ten-point program, positing "Objective standards of morality, especially as found in the Judeo-Christian tradition, as essential to the free and civilized social order" and "social authority—as embodied in the family, church, community, and other intermediating institutions—as helping protect the individual from the State and as necessary for a free and virtuous society."[80]

Rothbard enthusiastically agreed that outreach to a culturally traditionalist right was the proper strategic move for libertarians. With Soviet communism gone, he thought, the old cold war divisions that separated him from the right should crumble with the Berlin Wall. The Rothbardians formed an organization called the John Randolph Club with the similarly old-fashioned end of the conservative movement, the paleoconservatives centered around the Rockford Institute and its magazine, *Chronicles*.

This "paleolibertarian turn" was not out of the blue for Rothbard. Even when singing the praises of the 1960s student movement, he always pledged fealty to old bourgeois cultural values. He loved pre–big band New Orleans jazz and old-fashioned narrative movies with heroes or broad comedies.[81] He'd regularly rag libertarians' concern with what he saw as faddish nonsense like humanistic psychology and science fiction visions of the future. In his history of economic thought, and elsewhere, he praised Christianity as the bedrock of almost all that was valuable in the Western philosophic tradition. While other libertarians talked of "living liberty" (a phrase Rothbard detested) through daring experiments in unique and sometimes bizarre social arrangements, Rothbard declared even in the early 1970s that "the Christian ethic is . . . a Rock of Ages, and it is at least incumbent on an individual to think long and hard before he abandons that Rock lest he sink into the quagmire of the capricious and the bizarre."[82]

This emphasis on the need for a conservative, traditionalist cultural context for libertarianism in his later years—and the way he turned venomously on every part of the libertarian movement not under the paleo tent in the pages of the newsletter he and Rockwell launched in 1990, the *Rothbard/Rockwell Report*—lost Rothbard many of his old fans and friends in the movement. Scattered among Rothbard's commentary on current events in the pages of *RRR* were jaundiced looks and often mean-spirited gossip about other libertarian organizations, publications, and individuals. He mostly attacked them (including this author) for being tools of the leftist egalitarianism that he decided was an enemy as great as the state.

After leaving the LP, Rothbard plumped eagerly for Pat Buchanan (in support of his foreign policy stance; Rothbard and Rockwell tried but failed to disabuse him of his rampant trade protectionism) in the 1992 Republican primary, then drifted to a brief flirtation with populist outsider Ross Perot before publicly endorsing George H.W. Bush in a *Los Angeles Times* column. He thought that the rising Buchananite movement—if not Buchanan himself—and the 1994 Republican congressional victory (though he was no fan of Newt Gingrich) represented the rising of Middle America against Leviathan that he had long hoped for.[83] Some old comrades thought Rothbard just liked to move into new ideological communities where he had some chance of being a minded, respected influence. "I can't imagine a more noxious set of political beliefs reposing in one human being" than Buchanan, said Rothbard's old pal from the early 1970s New York City days of libertarian ferment, Jerome Tuccille. "Yet Murray found some way to break bread with this guy, because at that stage Buchanan paid attention to Murray and lots of other people didn't."[84]

On January 7, 1995, Rothbard collapsed and died of a heart attack while visiting his optometrist in New York City. His old friend and nemesis William Buckley wrote an ill-tempered attack obituary, in which he repeated an unsupported canard that Rothbard stood in the street and cheered Khrushchev during his 1959 visit to the United States. Buckley, while thanking Rothbard for supplying the economics research that underlay Buckley's *Up from Liberalism*, concluded that Rothbard died "with about as many disciples as David Koresh had in his little redoubt in Waco. Yes, Murray Rothbard believed in freedom, and yes, David Koresh believed in God."[85]

"KNOWING HIM WAS THE MOST REWARDING EXPERIENCE OF MY LIFE, AND HIS LOSS WAS MY GREATEST LOSS."

Since his death, Rothbard's stature within the larger libertarian movement has declined. *Reason* magazine, to which he had been a contributing editor from 1973 to 1983, didn't even note his passing. He is still, even in death, the linchpin of the Ludwig von Mises Institute. In its concerns, focus, and tone, that institute is more spreading Rothbardianism than pure Misesianism. Because he is still alive as a human being—often a contentious one—in many libertarians' memories, Rothbard's reputation is still tied up in his personality and people's assessments of it. Delight with infighting and sniffing out heresy was certainly part of Rothbard's style.[86] Gary Greenberg, a New York LP leader who worked with Rothbard, recalls,

> I tried to stay close to Murray, but he's a very difficult character. Murray has two features that are related. One is to trash and destroy anyone who publicly disagrees with him or criticizes him, resulting in constant alienation of people, both among economists and conservatives, and he thus tended to isolate himself. But on the other hand, he's extremely magnanimous and generous to people who look to him for guidance and are friendly to him.[87]

His old Circle Bastiat comrade Ronald Hamowy had a different perspective, although he had no sympathy for Rothbard's paleo turn:

> There was no falling out. But believe me, it was extremely difficult to tread that course. You had to watch your step. But it wasn't like seeing Murray was like seeing someone who you could only stand for 15 minutes. We'd spend an enormous amount of time

together. But you learned what to avoid. After a while, you could take some liberties.

I wouldn't call what Murray had "wrath." He was more like a little kid. He'd get upset and take it out on whoever he was angry about. On ideological things, he was very touchy about certain issues. He didn't want to have to defend himself ideologically all the time around those he felt closest to. That was important to him, so you'd know not to enter into arguments with him. If you wanted something explained, you put it in these terms—"How does one answer people who say . . . ?"

For some reason he allowed me a lot more leeway to laugh at his craziness than other people. I didn't have patience for the whole social conservative thing in his last days. I'm more a product of the left socially and psychologically about those things. It doesn't bother me that *Heather Has Two Mommies* is being taught in school or anything. I'm more annoyed at the right's tack on social issues than I am the left. So it took effort to be a friend of Murray's. But I'll tell you, after 40 years it was worth every effort I put in. Knowing him was the most rewarding experience of my life, and his loss was my greatest loss.[88]

Where some saw flightiness, personal animosities that overwhelmed his intellectual sense, and a constant desire to burn bridges in Rothbard (some old associates suspecting that if the world were to turn libertarian, Rothbard would become a statist just to be contrary), his biographer and old LP radical caucus comrade, Justin Raimondo, saw "ideological entrepreneurship," a constant search for the most fruitful ground on which to cultivate support for what Rothbard always saw as the most important political issue: war and peace. This idea, Raimondo posits, makes coherent sense of Rothbard's initial flight from the right to the new left and his later move toward Pat Buchanan: the search for the most politically potent anti-intervention force. Rothbard himself once wrote that "my ideological and political activism has been focused on opposition to America's wars, first because I have believed our waging them to be unjust, and second, because war, in the penetrating phrase of the libertarian Randolph Bourne . . . has always been 'the health of the state,' an instrument of the aggrandizement of state power over the health, the lives, and the property of their subject citizens and social institutions."[89]

Robert Poole sums up the most charitable current assessment of Rothbard in most mainstream libertarian institutions outside the Mises Institute circles, in which he is still revered as Mr. Libertarian (a title frequently granted Rothbard from the early 1970s on):

> Rothbard was very important, particularly in the 1970s. He was the first to really popularize the term libertarian—to help get scattered people who thought this way to become a self-conscious movement. He helped instigate the split of the libertarian faction from YAF. He was a continual rabble-rouser and pusher of the envelope and a great rhetorician in terms of shaping radical views. He'd switch tactical allies from one year to the next, but you had to respect his energy, his intellect, his skill with words, and some aspects of his vision. But still, in many ways I thought then and thought more as time went on that he was a very divisive figure and a negative influence.[90]

In the movement journal *Liberty*, editor R. W. Bradford argues that Rothbard's rights-based libertarian project is being eclipsed by economistic–utilitarian arguments redolent of Milton Friedman or Mises. Bradford is especially caustic in questioning the polemical value of Rothbard's foundational "nonaggression axiom," which states that the core political–ethical principle is that one should not initiate aggression against anyone else's person or property: "Invoking the non-aggression imperative in argument with other libertarians very often wins arguments with those who agree with it," Bradford wrote. "But unfortunately, as those of us who have cited it in discussions with non-libertarians are well aware, a lot of people find it unconvincing. I understate: when we cite the non-aggression imperative in a discussion of a political issue, a lot of people just shake their heads and walk away thinking we're nuts."[91] Many libertarians who find Rothbard's influence on the movement baleful complain that he was an ideologue in the worst sense—one who dedicated his reasoning and research not toward the fullest and fairest possible picture of the truth about the phenomena he wrote about, but merely toward scoring argumentative points that aimed toward the conclusion he wanted to reach: total liberty.

"I know there are a lot of people around in the libertarian movement who say Rothbard is nothing," says Chris Sciabarra, author of the first scholarly assessment of Rothbard, *Total Freedom: Toward a Dialectical Libertarianism.*

> But I'm telling you, by virtue of them feeling it necessary to say that, he's something. For better or worse, he's probably influenced more scholars in libertarianism than anyone else I know. When you consider the number of young libertarians, and others, who came through his living room and literally sat at his knee learning and interacting with him and with the others he gathered around him. . . . There were lots of squabbles as the years went on and lots of personal difficulties and people going their separate ways. But if you are going to think about libertarianism, you have to grapple with Rothbard.[92]

Old friends who became bitter foes, such as Cato Institute president Ed Crane, acknowledge that, at least through the 1970s, "you can't write about the libertarian movement without Rothbard being central."[93] Even libertarian thinkers as different in approach, style, and conclusions from Rothbard as Robert Nozick were guided down the path of libertarian ideas by him.[94]

Randy Barnett, a Georgetown University law professor and former big city prosecutor, who has argued medical marijuana cases before the Supreme Court, is an anarcho-legal theorist and Lysander Spooner promoter who in recent years has been embraced by conservative forces in the Federalist Society for his reinterpretation of the Constitution. While he arose from the Center for Libertarian Studies scene in the mid-1970s, he has riled some of his old anarcho-friends by his public support of the Iraq war. Barnett emphasized to me his continued fealty to the Rothbardianism that formed him—and in a very Rothbard style, insisted I note that he was exactly as radical as he ever was. Rothbard "had a model of thought that I definitely bought into, and still operate within. I used to be 100 percent within it, now maybe 90 or 80 percent within it. The key part is reducing everything to property rights. I still operate within that property rights framework." His anarchist tome *Structure of Liberty* "is not necessarily Rothbardian in arguments, but it is in conclusions—there are limits to Rothbard's methods of justification, but that thing I'm trying to justify is still Rothbardian."[95]

Putting aside the personal animosity he engendered and his self-imposed exile from what he saw as culturally destructive elements in the libertarian movement, Rothbard still embodies the purest form of the libertarian political philosophy—particularly the radical elements that distinguish it from the limited-government wing of the GOP. As Norman Barry, a historian and critic of classical liberalism, wrote, "Rothbard's social thought, quite unjustifiably neglected in the contemporary teaching of social science, represents a remarkable synthesis of economics, politics, jurisprudence, and the philosophy of social science, directed entirely at the problems, and indeed prospects, of a free society. His work constitutes perhaps the most powerful and sophisticated case for individualist anarchism."[96]

"Our nation and her people have been vastly enriched by his devotion to the cause of freedom."

In his quiet and serious and relentless way, Leonard Read continued running the first modern libertarian institution, the Foundation for Economic Education. But as the 1960s became the 1970s became the 1980s, FEE and its central project, *Freeman* magazine, was more and more in its own alternate-dimension path running alongside the mainstream libertarian world, only occasionally impacting it, mostly by sending some eager young soul from the FEE world to the larger libertarian one. In a post-Goldwater world where many right-wingers tried at least rhetorically to embrace a more thoroughgoing free market position and where FEE remained uninfected by anarchism, third-party politics, or epatering le bourgeois, FEE was more and more feeding young minds into the conservative movement's free market wing as well. Read's operation remained a favorite of the young, who were discovering these strange and powerful libertarian ideas, and the old, who had grown up with Leonard Read and had never seen their libertarianism get more radical, those whose businesses or families remained long-term supporters.

In May 1983, after a typically long day at his office and the week before a meeting of FEE's board of trustees, Read died in his home on the grounds behind the FEE manse. The board meeting went on as scheduled; what Leonard would have wanted, you know. President Reagan, a longtime *Freeman* fan, sent a telegram of condolence, writing that "our nation and her people have been vastly enriched by his devotion to the cause of freedom."[97]

Upon his death, a FEE trustee summoned G. K. Chesterton's admonition that all Western men are living statues to the Romans to declare that all libertarians are statues in tribute to Leonard Read. There is truth in that. Certainly Read is no more than one link away in the chain of influence on any libertarian, at least through the 1980s.

FEE lost its way for a while without its founder and guiding spirit. An ugly succession battle ensued, with the senior staff rebelling over plans to name a younger president who, the board hoped, might bring a youthful spirit to an institution that had begun to smell of camphor and old candy. A string of compromise, short-term presidencies followed, more than one ending in miniscandals and lawsuit threats, which started FEE on a downward spiral through the rest of the 1980s and most of the 1990s. From Read's death to 1992, FEE spent $5.2 million more than it took in.[98]

Some blamed Leonard's refusal to do anything about succession, especially after economics professor Ben Rogge of Wabash College in Indiana, understood to be his favorite, died before him. One former trustee complained, "Leonard always bragged: 'I'll ride my bicycle until I fall off.' He forgot: it wasn't his bicycle. He ran it into a wall. Its front wheel is still bent. You have to unbend it and get the bicycle moving forward again."[99]

Hans Sennholz, a crusty old Misesian retired from imbuing undergrads with a passion for free markets and justice at Grove City College, took over in the early 1990s and instituted a set of un-Readian practices in an attempt to raise the foundation's aging head above a sea of crimson ink. For one thing, FEE was no longer giving away the

Freeman or other publications to anyone who asked. This move cut the magazine's circulation by tens of thousands but stanched the cash hemorrhage, at least for a while. For two years in the mid-1990s Sennholz got the annual finances in balance, but then they began to sink again.

Donald Boudreaux, an American Austrian economist who went on to chair the Economics Department at George Mason University, and then Mark Skousen, an economist and investment adviser who arose from the hard money world, had short reigns at FEE in the late 1990s as well. Skousen lost the faith of his board, and large portions of the libertarian hard-core in his audience, by inviting Rudolph Giuliani to speak at a FEE banquet. Rudy may have been the hero of 9/11 to most Americans, but to many libertarians he would always be the bastard who hounded various stock traders and businessmen for the bullshit crime of "insider trading."

Austrian economist Richard Ebeling now runs FEE, with longtime movement journalist Sheldon Richman, who had previous stints with Citizens for a Competitive Economy, the Institute for Humane Studies, the LP, and Cato, editing the *Freeman*. Both foundation and magazine are respected and stable in the early twenty-first century, still explaining the basics of the freedom philosophy in day seminars in cities across the country, in summer minischools, through lectures, and through a website that is a popular source of pro-market information and analysis for homeschoolers.

Nearly sixty years after Leonard Read founded FEE, there are still (believe it or not!) people out there who are not properly educated in the freedom philosophy. The libertarian remnant is larger and more varied; technology and wealth seem more liberating than reading and contemplating the rightness of allowing people to do anything that's peaceful. Leonard Read was the first American to make libertarian education in the modern sense his life's work. The state continues to wage nondefensive war, tax for the private benefits of others, and interfere in the economic and personal decisionmaking of its citizens. Leonard Read's mission continues.

AN ETERNAL REVOLUTION

By 2006, it was obvious that Social Security privatization, whether the Cato Institute's plan or some milder version, was not going to begin that year or the next, or most likely during George W. Bush's administration at all. Many reasons for the failure were floated from the libertarian side (unwilling to grant that maybe the American people just don't want responsibility for their own retirements or perhaps fear the stock market more than government mismanagement): Bush didn't do the proper full-court press prelobbying with Congress; Bush didn't get the right charismatic, powerful person to front for reform within the administration; the megastate interventions of his first term, starting with the budget-busting prescription drug benefit, lost him any credibility with the free market Republicans he'd need to be passionately on its side; by focusing on the minutia of payout amounts and bankruptcy years and variable assumptions about economic growth, Bush lost the moral edge that would have gotten people excited: choice, personal possession, the idea that your money has been freed from serving politicians' needs for short-term gain.

Perhaps Bush flubbed the politics. Perhaps ugly partisanship killed the chances for reform in the direction of privatization or (as it came to be called when the administration realized the term "privatization" was still political poison) "personal accounts." For whatever reason, Social Security privatization fizzled.

Libertarians had foreseen the crisis, prepared the ground, come up with a solution that ought to have resonated with a basic American instinct for choice and self-control—and even private benefit. The Cato plan promised retirees greater cash returns via private accounts than they can expect from the Social Security status quo. They even offered a cautious path out of Social Security without killing it instantly. Still, it wasn't a solution the country or the politicians were ready for. Libertarians were still radicals in a country grown comfortable for the most part with the way things are, dominated by a massive middle class doing just fine, for now at least, with the defining elements of American big government such as Social Security.

The failure of Social Security privatization, as well as many other issues, makes it easy for a libertarian to despair in the midst of George W. Bush's second term. By plumbline libertarian standards, the world is not getting freer. What the government takes, what it presumes it can regulate, has been getting larger, not smaller; the powers in foreign policy and secret investigations and arrests that the executive branch has chosen to arrogate to itself are getting wider, not narrower. We are, on the whole, taxed more, regulated more, asked for our papers more than ever before.

And yet, especially if you are a relatively well-off Westerner, it's hard not to see a world that is well worth celebrating—perhaps even reveling in—to the extent that it runs on approximately libertarian principles, with a general belief in property rights and the benefits of liberty. This is the "neoliberal" world that has been seen by pundits and politicians all over the West as dominant since the death of communism. For most people living under it, it's doing a pretty good job of delivering the "pursuit of happiness" part of the Declaration of Independence, at least.

There is a continuing tension in modern libertarian thought. Libertarians tend to celebrate the wonders brought to bear and widely spread by markets and the free human mind using reason to control the world through technology; yet they also recognize that our markets and technologies are embedded in a system that violates core libertarian principles of self-ownership and property rights every day of the week and twice on Sunday. No Ayn Rand–inspired moral revulsion against the state has yet swept America. Still, on the twentieth anniversary of *Reason* magazine in 1988, Robert Poole Jr. found a lot for libertarians to celebrate.

In an article titled "Things Are a Lot Groovier Now," Poole noted that when the magazine was founded in 1968, Americans lacked such market and personal freedoms as attaching answering machines to phones (or choosing from phone companies); being able to withdraw cash from a bank out of state or after hours; earning a free market rate on certificates of deposit; owning gold; enjoying price competition in air fare; staying in hotels as unmarried couples or having legal access to contraceptives or home access to porn. And we faced the draft, 70 percent marginal income tax rates, a level of socially acceptable discrimination against blacks and women that seem relics of two hundred years ago, not just twenty; bans on advertising for doctors and lawyers. The cold war was raging, most of Southeast Asia was still Third World and socialism was the governing philosophy in Europe. Whatever troubles we still face from the state, libertarians—and all Americans—can and should thank both the power and the philosophy of "free minds and free markets," the magazine's slogan and a fair description of the larger libertarian message, for making life better.

Thus some people on the libertarian team have begun to wonder whether those hard-core standards make much sense in the stunningly rich, cornucopian modernity of the twenty-first century. Ninth Circuit Court of Appeals Judge Alex Kozinski, both celebrated and denounced as the most libertarian-minded jurist in America today, recently wrote on the Cato Institute's website, in reaction to minimal-state constitutional amendments suggested by public choice pioneer and Nobel Prize–winning economist James Buchanan:

> There is . . . a lingering nostalgia for the vision of the minimalist state as a purer form of government, one that advances everyone's economic well-being while maximizing personal freedom. While I have a romantic attachment to this vision, I'm far from convinced that it would achieve the goals set for it—that we'd be living in a better world today if only we repudiated the New Deal, or had never adopted it in the first place. Whenever I try to

imagine what such a world would look like, I look at the world
we do live in and recognize that we don't have it so bad at all. We
have the world's strongest economy by far; we are the only super-
power, having managed to bury the Evil Empire; and we have
more freedom than any other people anytime in history. We must
be doing something right.

One thing I'm pretty sure of, though, is that Dr. Buchanan's vision is not shared by most of the American public. While nearly
everyone has some beef with government at its many levels, there
are very few who would, had they the power, fundamentally
change the relationship between the government and the governed. . . . Thus, unless we assume that his three proposed constitutional amendments are to be imposed by some power outside
the American democratic process—by a Philosopher King, as it
were—we have to imagine a very different world, and a very different popular attitude toward what the government is expected
to accomplish.[1]

As Nathaniel Branden once told me, given libertarians' beliefs about
markets and their rich benefits, the intellectual and activist energy
necessary to achieve a fully libertarian world may never arise. "When
we get halfway there, life will be so good that people won't give a
damn about politics anymore; there won't be any energy left to fight
for the last stages."[2]

In regard to the old distinction between positive and negative liberty, "freedom to" versus "freedom from," libertarians have traditionally been on the side of the negative—the freedom that merely
requires other people to not actively interfere with you. Lately some
libertarians, *Reason* magazine's current editor Nick Gillespie the most
prominent, have stressed that technological advances and even the
constrained market freedom we now enjoy have created a range of
positive freedoms worth celebrating, freedoms that make the lack of
certain paper negative freedoms easier to ignore. In an essay on *Reason*'s website, he floats the heresy that the places rated best to live based
on calculations of economic regulation levels by free market think
tank Pacific Research Institute (founded by Antony Fisher) aren't the

places most people really want to live in. "The economic freedom metric may be pretty far down the list, if not quite irrelevant, to what drives most people's—and businesses'—decisions about where to hang out," he concluded. "Yes, regulations are always and everywhere too high. . . . On the margins, higher taxes are a bad thing. But the margins aren't the whole ball of wax. . . . And the folks at . . . the Pacific Research Institute are unlikely to be trekking en masse to Kansas [which came in number one in its economic freedom index] anytime soon. Why is that? Because most of the time, economic freedom's just another word for nothing else to do."[3]

It's a constitutive part of the modern libertarian mind-set to celebrate the glories of choice, and it's hard to ignore that in terms of wealth and lifestyle, our range of choices, even given a state that takes 31 percent of our income in taxes, is still impressively huge and worth celebrating. Despite the megastate, life for most in the West is grand and in most ways getting better.[4]

That's easy to say if you aren't trying to run your own business; you don't deal in or consume substances the government says can't be sold or consumed; your property hasn't been claimed by eminent domain; you are not being investigated by the IRS; you are not an Iraqi, Branch Davidian, or other victim of U.S. bombs or bullets.

Still, American blacks or women, Americans who like reading odd and unpopular things or who want to marry outside their race or within their gender might find libertarian complaints about government growth silly. Most of them certainly feel freer in many important ways than they would have in the nineteenth century, regardless of the size of their tax burden or the existence of the Americans with Disabilities Act or banking secrecy regulations. Libertarians risk losing credibility with a substantial audience by not recognizing that some types of highly valued liberty are flourishing outside the movement's primary concerns with the size and activities of government and by pretending everything is horrible and on a steady decline when it comes to our freedoms.

The latest attempt to achieve a libertarian Zion—gathering libertarians together in one place to build a libertarian polity—is known as the Free State Project. Project organizers decided that 20,000 libertarian

political activists could turn New Hampshire into a libertarian paradise if they moved en masse but have hit a wall of about 7,300 interested parties after a few years of proselytizing in the libertarian
community, most effectively on the Web. This is likely because modern
American libertarians' complaints about the state are, for the most
part, more ideological and principled than based in experienced
tyranny in their day-to-day lives.[5]

"YOU LIBERTARIANS ARE THE TYPES THAT WOULD ALLOW FORNICATION IN PUBLIC PARKS!" "WHAT DO YOU MEAN, *PUBLIC* PARKS?"

Libertarians have other reasons for optimism besides increasing wealth
and options for those living in the modern, semifree West. The movement qua movement has never been richer, healthier, or more varied.

A libertarian in these early days of the twenty-first century can attend weekend or weeklong conferences full of libertarian speakers,
lecturers, and socializing sponsored by the Reason Foundation, the
Cato Institute, *Liberty* magazine, or other freelance event organizers.
Far from the days when libertarian magazines were short-lived and
subterranean in circulation, libertarianism has both a standard public
policy and culture journal pushing its ideas (*Reason,* now at around
40,000 print circulation and with over a million Web readers monthly)
and a more standard movement journal, *Liberty,* at around 5,000 circulation. The Web is filled with more libertarian pundits, professional and
amateur, than you could read if you spent all day doing it (and to judge
by the comment threads in various libertarian blogs, it seems that
some in their audience do just that). Pop culture celebrities from Kurt
Russell to Drew Carey, from Penn Jillette to *South Park* creators Trey
Parker and Matt Stone, have publicly linked themselves to libertarian
causes and organizations.

Libertarian scholars, often financed and guided through their graduate programs by the Institute for Humane Studies, can find university
appointments without fear that their ideology will blackball them.
Once in their professional positions, they can—by invitation only—

meet to discuss the great ideas of the Western world and of modern political philosophy under the aegis of the Liberty Fund. It's the wealthiest
libertarian organization around, spending the collected wealth (worth
about $350 million these days but spent at a rate that guarantees the
continuation of the endowment) of early FEE supporter Pierre
Goodrich on these sorts of meetings—the modern apotheosis of the
original Leonard Read idea of spreading the light of liberty one to one,
face to face, all reasoning together in intellectual comity. Liberty Fund
also pursues an ambitious publication program of inexpensive collections of the greatest books of free market, libertarian, conservative, and
constitutionalist thought ever written, and a rich searchable Web
archive of same. Despite its resources, in keeping with its founder's intent, it is a staid, gentlemanly, old-fashioned group, not interested in
policy struggles or publicity seeking.

Libertarians can also read an endless and continuous stream of libertarian books, both from specialty presses and the biggest New York
houses; they can listen to self-identified libertarian voices such as Larry
Elder and Neal Boortz on their talk radio stations and read in the
pages of the *New York Times*(!) a regular column on the op-ed page by
the highly libertarian John Tierney (at least until the end of 2006
when he quit his op-ed column) and a monthly one in the business
section from Tyler Cowen, who arose from the George Mason University, Koch-funded, Austrian economics program, and is currently
president of the Mercatus Center. (Cowen's predecessor in that *New
York Times* slot was former *Reason* editor Virginia Postrel, who has
gone on to be a contributing editor to the *Atlantic*.) By 1997, a survey
of D.C. congressional staff and journalists found the Cato Institute a
more relied-on think tank source than the venerable, more right-wing
American Enterprise Institute.[6] It's a world of ideological and institutional success that would doubtless make Leonard Read swell with
pride and possibly amazement.

More money is flowing into the libertarian movement, more
people are making their living in professional libertarian activism, and
more academic research is being done in libertarian directions all the
time. Even ABC News has a hard-core libertarian reporter, John Stossel, a man converted by reading *Reason* during his days as a liberal
consumer reporter. He's out and proud with his libertarianism, and

has been given carte blanche to produce an ongoing series of polemical hour-long prime time specials. He's featured Roy Childs explaining how being morbidly obese (Childs died because of it in 1992) does not obligate others to grant him special treatment; Objectivist philosopher David Kelley explaining why greed can be good, since it encourages economic progress that grows the pie for everyone; economist Walter Williams of George Mason University explaining why using the state to freeload is both wrong and inefficient, for individuals and corporations.

Stossel tries to have at least one former *Reason* intern or Institute for Humane Studies alum on his staff to make sure someone around him understands where he's coming from. Despite his berth at the top of America's media food chain, Stossel remains glum about the prospects for libertarian ideas in America. Even around ABC, he laments, many colleagues still don't respect or understand him.

> I think my success has made them friendlier. The late Peter Jennings was the most hostile. He'd jerk his head away from facing me if we passed each other in the hall, as if I had betrayed the objectivity canon.
>
> I think to myself, bullshit, they have opinions too and they are leaking out in their work all the time. They just don't know it. And I had a point of view when I was a consumer reporter bashing individual businesses too. I only started to piss people off when the point of view became that government regulation could be a problem. Then suddenly I'm not objective. I had won nineteen Emmys [as a pro-regulation consumer reporter] and haven't won one since. Not even nominated since.[7]

He assumes that even if he's reaching 10 million people on national TV with a highly libertarian message, that 9.9 million or more of them aren't really getting it.

Popular radio talk show hosts such as Neal Boortz and Larry Elder call themselves libertarians and reach millions across the country with a solidly libertarian line most of the time. And if you are a libertarian—there are plenty such—who thinks the Iraq War is properly libertarian, then you'd find them solidly libertarian pretty much all of the time. Boortz had a decade as a conservative talk show host behind him when he found certain elements of the philosophy bothering him. A reader sent him Rand's *Atlas Shrugged* and it "completely changed me," he says. From then on "I have a default position on almost every issue, and that default position is freedom, and I'm going to stand up for individual freedom on basically anything unless someone can show me someone's rights are being violated by the exercise of that freedom."[8] Fed up with some GOP depredation or another, Boortz switched his party affiliation to the LP on the air in the mid-1990s. He credits his ratings success in the Orlando area with a statistically disproportionate number of Harry Browne votes there in 2000, votes that were noted skeptically on the air by Peter Jennings. Boortz wonders, with a bit of nervousness, what he would have felt if he'd encouraged enough would-have-been Bush voters to switch to the LP to swing the state to Al Gore.[9]

Rush Limbaugh, the apotheosis of modern talk radio, has for years occasionally chosen Walter Williams, the libertarian former chairman of George Mason University's Austrian- and public choice–centered economics department, as a guest host. On Limbaugh's show Williams, who is black, has tried to make headway on a very conservative audience by applying radical libertarianism about free trade and private property rights to the sale of organs and illegal drugs.

Academics continue research of vital interest to libertarians into the nature of private property and how dispute resolution and law have not historically needed a monopoly state to function, and how prisoner's dilemma and game theory show that intelligent humans can reach a workable, ordered social equilibrium without outside compulsion.[10] Nobel Prize–winning economists continue to arise from the libertarian world, linked with libertarian support organizations. Ronald Coase, a 1991 Nobel winner, thinks that even the so-called problems of externalities in markets would be solved through mutually agreed trades in free markets, if the proper institutions and rules to minimize transaction costs could be developed. His ideas guide the field of law and economics in trying to figure out how to design rules so as to create the greatest efficiency and wealth for all. Recent Nobel winner Vernon Smith of George Mason (stop rolling over in your grave, Ludwig von Mises!) uses empirical lab experiments to discover how and why and where markets can develop to efficiently solve human problems.[11]

The set of institutions getting money from the Koch brothers alone is a full-service intellectual movement, covering every aspect of the production and spread of ideas. The Institute for Humane Studies works the classic top of the Hayekian pyramid of intellectual influence, training and supporting young academics (and sometimes journalists and screenwriters) with a demonstrated interest in libertarian ideas. Americans for Prosperity Foundation, the successor of the earlier Citizens for a Sound Economy, works on ginning up grassroots agitation mostly on the state level—where the Kochs have decided it's more likely to succeed—for libertarian leaning policies, mostly regarding taxing and spending. The Mercatus Center, formerly the Center for the Study of Market Processes, based at George Mason University, targets congressional staffs and committees with cutting-edge libertarian economic and policy ideas that arise from academia; the Cato Institute works on both high-level media and congressional staff with a full-service, $22-million-a-year operation covering every policy issue under the sun through books, policy studies, op-eds, media appearances, speeches, and congressional testimony, with full-time policy chiefs issuing and organizing libertarian policy ideas about taxes, regulation, criminal justice, international trade and aid, entitlement programs, monetary policy, natural resources, and education—among other issues.

On the grassroots level, there are effusions of libertarian energy to appeal to every personality and every level of ideological advancement. A couple, among many, include the Advocates for Self-Government, an almost Amway-style group for grassroots personal libertarian conversion and salesmanship, and Bureaucrash, a gang of libertarian college kids who prank leftists at major international events by taking the implications of their policies to absurd extremes, which the lefties tend not to even notice. Bureaucrash created a fake group it called "Progressives Against Progress" whose symbol was a caveman with a club. You can if you wish expend your libertarian energy in rebellion against taxes (while by no means coterminous with libertarianism or implied by it, there's some overlap between libertarians and those who believe, for a dizzying variety of weird technical reasons, that we have no legal obligation to pay the income tax).[12] Or you can also, as per the radical militia-leaning author who rose to popularity in the 1990s among a certain segment of the libertarian world, Claire Wolfe, revive old Vonu-style ideas and take to the deep woods, your liberty intact from controllers and prying busybodies. These are the types who don't give a damn about influencing public policy—they just want to, in that old Karl Hess style, *live liberty*, by any means necessary. Such libertarians tend to emphasize self-sufficiency in weapons as well as in food. They tend to be fans of defunct bookseller Loompanics, from whom you could order Henry Hazlitt along with advice on picking locks, purveyor of libertariana and forbidden advice on making weapons, drugs, fake ID, and other experiential edginess—a sort of *Whole Earth Catalog* for the daring (or deranged). The ways to be libertarian have multiplied, delivering the abundance that free markets always promise.

Institutions that leading libertarians used to muse about in correspondence as a dream for the future exist now, such as the Institute for Justice, launched in 1991 with Koch seed money. It's a libertarian ACLU, a public interest law firm defending economic liberties and property rights, fighting for school choice and against eminent domain, restrictive occupational licensing laws that prevent the poor and unconnected from running their own businesses, and campaign finance laws that restrict political speech, among other libertarian causes. In its first fifteen years of operation, the institute actually succeeded on occasion at reviving the libertarian dream of getting American courts to once again, post–New Deal, take economic liberties seriously.

The institute has already won two cases at the U.S. Supreme Court: *Zelman v. Simmons-Harris* (2002), in which a Cleveland voucher program was upheld by the Supreme Court against charges of unconstitutionality, and *Swedenburg v. Kelly* (2005), which overturned a New York state ban on interstate wine shipment. IJ has also lost one at the Supreme Court, in the *Kelo v. New London* (2005) case, but a loss that created a public outcry against eminent domain for the benefit of private developers that may well lead to an eventual victory on the issue, at least through legislative changes on the state level.[13] The *Kelo* decision also inspired a well-publicized bit of ideological guerrilla theater, as Objectivist libertarian Logan Darrow Clements launched a public campaign to take Supreme Court Justice David Souter's New Hampshire home through eminent domain in order to build the "Lost Liberty Hotel."

Also in the realm of legal practice and philosophy, the Federalist Society, while still on balance more conservative than libertarian, has a significant and influential libertarian contingent. From most accounts, promising for the libertarian future, the younger members tend to skew more libertarian. And University of Chicago legal scholar Richard Epstein has been a prominent defender of libertarian principles, both in general and applied rigorously to such specific topics as takings law, health care policy, and antidiscrimination law. Supreme Court Justice Clarence Thomas was challenged by Senator Joe Biden during Thomas's 1991 confirmation hearing over having expressed a fondness for Epstein's libertarian thinking. Biden even waved a copy of Epstein's book *Takings: Private Property and the Power of Eminent Domain* in the air, questioning the probity of any legal thinker who could support Epstein's belief that when government actions take away or diminish the value of private property, the government has to pay for it—even if the taking is through regulation, not outright confiscation.

While this book has focused on the American movement and its American concerns, libertarians have remained true to the one world liberalism aspects of Hayek and Mises, the dream that the libertarian movement must be a worldwide one, that peace and liberty will succeed only if they girdle the globe. Longtime libertarian movement hand Tom Palmer, who over the years has worked with Students for a Libertarian Society, the Institute for Humane Studies, and currently the Cato Institute, spent much of the late 1980s smuggling printers, copiers, and forbidden libertarian literature into Eastern Europe. American libertarian institutions have feted and promoted the likes of Hernando de Soto, the Peruvian theorist who stresses the vital importance of defined and legally enforceable private property rights to make the Third World flourish,[14] and African thinkers and activists such as George Ayittey and June Arunga, who promote markets and property rights, not foreign aid, as key to their continent's healthy future.[15]

The most substantial success for the movement, on the surface, is that every longtime movement hand tells of more and more people who not only know what libertarianism means but also profess to *be* libertarian— without it being either their profession or a major hobby or obsession.

Because of this, the definition of "libertarian" may be evolving or, as some old hard-cores types fear, being polluted or sullied. The late Bill Bradford, founder of *Liberty* magazine, insisted that old-style rights-based libertarianism of the Rand/Rothbard variety is losing importance within the movement. A number of people calling themselves libertarians, especially among college students and the blogging world, have a vision of the proper size of the state far larger than the modal libertarian leaders of the 1950s, your Baldy Harpers and Robert LeFevres—or even your Leonard Reads. More dominant is the Hayekian style of a general belief in leaving people be, combined with some faith in the coordinative power of free markets that doesn't end up in a totalist vision of eliminating government from human interactions.

Look at it this way: You're young, you're intelligent, you have a rough sense that people ought to be free to do whatever the hell they want, mostly, as long as they aren't hurting anyone else—a simple, honest, live-and-let-live moral sense. You grew up after the fall of the Berlin Wall, so you have some sense that central economic planning, as Hayek said (even if, as is likely, you're not quite sure who Hayek is, beyond perhaps a name you've heard), leads to an ugly situation, a poor, decrepit mess that people are willing to risk being shot to escape. So you have a basic appreciation for free markets, an idea associated in American politics with the GOP.

But you are young, and you don't want to order people around regarding things that you know are their business, and theirs alone. You certainly don't want to be on any team that's obsessed with locking people up for what they smoke, or treating people differently under the law because they're gay. And people like Rush Limbaugh seem awfully small-minded and petty, and George W. Bush an obvious weasel waging a war based on lies, so your superego and sense of social positioning lean against self-identifying Republican.

So what are you? You might start thinking of yourself as a libertarian. Even in right-wing circles, libertarianism has maintained a mostly admirable cred that pivots between edgy and geeky. Libertarians do enjoy their badboy reputation, especially among conservative ranks, for taking this personal liberty thing as far as it can go. As an old movement joke goes, "You libertarians are the types that would allow fornication in public parks!" "What do you mean, *public* parks?"

But this hypothetical young libertarian may think that certain regulatory agencies, such as the FDA and the Justice Department's antitrust division, ought to exist, even if they are overly active and not always overly smart. Just as those who remained true to liberal principles of the nineteenth century had to change their name to adjust to changing fashions in the meaning of the term "liberal," so might libertarians of the Rothbard variety have to reconstitute themselves as "classical libertarians" in the twenty-first century.

The movement whose history I've told in this volume may be losing its monopoly on the term *libertarian*. The general approach to politics that can be loosely defined, as LPers and Cato types sometimes do when explaining themselves to nonideologically savvy audiences, as "socially liberal and fiscally conservative" has hit the big time. As libertarian scholar Tom Palmer of the Cato Institute noted, it is not unusual that in conversations with strangers at the gym, if politics or occupation comes up, he'll be informed that, hey, *I'm* a libertarian too!

If that person actually read Mises, Rothbard, or Friedman and came to understand that a consistent and full libertarian view means disbelief in antitrust law or the FDA, he might reconsider that self-identification.

R. J. Smith notes that "it used to be if you met a fellow libertarian, they were truly libertarian. They had read everything and knew everything—and now everybody's a libertarian and no one reads anything. It's just astounding—ask them the most basic book, they've never read it—'I'm just a libertarian.'"[16]

This may make them seem poseurs to old-school warriors like Smith, with his memories of Rothbard's living room, LeFevre's Freedom School, the sitting room at FEE's Irvington mansion, working at Cato's first D.C. rowhouse headquarters, and helping develop the early theory and practice of resource and species conservation through private property. But it's a victory for the movement—from a term that no one understood or trusted to an acceptable, sometimes even glamorous option for identity even among people who may not vote LP (more likely they don't vote at all) or read *Reason* or give to Cato, or may never have heard of those institutions.

Even radical left icon Michel Foucault was advising students to read Mises and Hayek in his later years.[17] More and more people, then, are roughly familiar with what it means to be a libertarian and think it applies to their live-and-let-live vision of politics. Not all, or even most, of those people will become activists. But all libertarianism needs for political victories is to effect this zeitgeist change regarding acceptable options. (Tyler Cowen has argued convincingly that many big changes in the direction of more markets and less state control around the globe happen because a small number of important decisionmakers are cognizant of market benefits and push for them, not because of popular demand for, or even understanding of, the reforms.)[18] In that case, though, what wins might not even be understood as a victory for this gang of strange scholars, ideologues, and activists whose story I've told here. It will be the conventional wisdom—the wind, as CEI's Fred Smith puts it, filling the empty socks that are politicians—which is always and ever right, even when it is different from what it was ten years ago. As libertarian activist Michael Holmes noted, you don't hear so much about the antimonarchist movement anymore. We are all antimonarchists now, and there's no need to single out or honor those who were correct on that issue ahead of their time.

"Now they say, hey, we are promoting free markets—so give us more money."

The libertarian movement's major victory has been taking an idea that was once considered hateful and crazy—or nonexistent—and making it an understood part of a larger political–social debate. Since the days of Newt Gingrich and the press that contextualized him and his grab bag of programs as the new dominance of libertarian ideas in the GOP coalition, libertarianism is an understood—if often derided or even feared—part of the political landscape.

Certain leftist writers, including Thomas Frank, the most popular left intellectual of his generation, pretend that their side has been routed by libertarian thinking in the battle of ideas and politics; that government no longer meaningfully stands between rapacious global capitalism and its hapless victims—you, me, all of us; that laissez-faire reigns supreme,

leaving anyone who thinks the state ought to have any power whatsoever to tax, regulate, or redistribute scattered in small cells in hidden
safe houses, Jacobites of progressive politics.

Some opponents of what they call "neoliberalism"—the rough
post-Thatcher, post-Reagan consensus that for the most part it is better for countries to have lower taxes, a public sector they can afford
without confiscatory taxation or endless borrowing, and openness to
flows of foreign capital and trade—pretend that it is a laissez-faire vision and that it rules the world. But neoliberalism is an ideology of
planning, still an ideology of cronyism, still a world where national
goals and national interests and the interests that international business
can take care of through international political institutions rule the
day—a world of crony capitalism, not true libertarian laissez-faire.[19]

Libertarians are acutely aware that a lot of seeming libertarian
progress has been more ideological or even rhetorical than actual. In
the field of international development, for example, former Cato Institute senior fellow and syndicated columnist Doug Bandow (he resigned in late 2005 when it was revealed he accepted money from
lobbyist Jack Abramoff to write columns that furthered the interests of
Abramoff's clients), who writes often on that topic, notes that the libertarian insights of the likes of Lord Peter Bauer (winner of the first
Milton Friedman Prize, instituted in 2003 to honor and support libertarian heroes by giving them $500,000) about how foreign aid tends
to support quasi-criminal governments more than it helps development efforts for the average citizen, and that instituting free market reforms will be more beneficial to the average person than pure foreign
aid, have made headway, rhetorically at least. But that rhetorical headway hasn't slowed the juggernaut of the IMF or the World Bank.
Would-be recipients of international aid "used to say, give us money to
promote development. Now they say, hey, we are promoting free markets—so give us more money."[20]

It has always been one of libertarianism's insights (one that the likes
of Tom Frank get close to, but can never seem to make that final step)
that massive concentrations of government power are more likely to
be used to benefit other huge concentrations of wealth and power
rather than help the needy or downtrodden. The insights professional-

ized by public choice economists such as James Buchanan and Gordon Tullock about concentrated benefits versus diffused costs show why government is never apt to be a curb on other centers of social or economic power, but merely another weapon for them to use. The powerful few who benefit from government action are more highly motivated to work the mechanisms of democracy to their benefit than are the masses who all pay just a little—often too little in each specific case to feel it worth fighting, or even knowing about—and thus win in the democratic game of shifting property and wealth from one person, or group, to another.

If government were restricted to its libertarian minimums of protecting citizens' life and property from force and fraud, all a corporation could do is try to sell us something, and we could decide whether or not to buy. It couldn't tax us for its benefit, raise tariffs on its competitors to make their products more expensive, subsidize bad loans or overseas expansion, or take formerly private property on the grounds that it will make more lucrative use of it than would the original owner. Libertarianism could be a very powerful weapon for the anti-corporate left, as soon as it abandons the fantasy of a perfectly fair government that can be empowered to do only the good progressive things the left wants it to do. An end to what libertarians attack as "corporate welfare" would go a long way toward equalizing, as progressives wish to do, the citizen and the corporation.

"I'LL BE WORKING ON SO OFFENDING YOU THAT YOU'RE GOING TO LEAVE TOO."

Until the Libertarian Party and the Cato Institute and the Reason Foundation came along in the 1970s, no libertarian institution dreamed of achieving actual policy change in a libertarian direction. FEE, the Freedom School, the Institute for Humane Studies, various libertarian magazines and student groups were all about education, about spreading the word, about *making libertarians,* or about extending libertarians' own understanding of history, philosophy, the warp and woof of what liberty could mean. As to how that understanding would lead to real-world policy change, well, that strategy hadn't been worked out.

And it didn't seem too important. Their faith in liberty's manifest benefits and rightness seemed to imply either that with understanding its actuality would come, or that given the realities of power, maybe it never *would* come—that the tug-of-war between the state and the individual would go on forever. The libertarian's job, then, was to give intellectual succor and support to the side of liberty, to maintain a cadre of people who would be be monkish "keepers of the books" in that old Remnant style derived from Nock and extended by Read. That was enough.

Having characters like Read, LeFevre, and Baldy Harper as the gods of your movement, with their belief in one-to-one education, and Ayn Rand as its goddess, who believed when it came to cultural and political change that "it's earlier than you think"—that reforming people's irrational metaphysics has to come before policy change—was not conducive to short-term optimism about a libertarian victory. In fact, it made short-term optimism unnecessary.

On that Leonard Read level of lighting the candle of liberty, the movement has been an extraordinary success. People by the hundreds of thousands *have* received economic education. They *have* learned, say, that minimum wage laws are more apt to hurt lower-wage workers by pricing them out of the market entirely than help them; that the incentives of the welfare state are apt to hinder, not help, people in becoming self-sufficient; that any benefit to American industry that seems to arise from protectionism is destroyed by the damage to the mass of citizens not being able to get the things they want in the inexpensive abundance that's possible; that having poorer countries enter into the system of international trade more unrestrictedly will help them grow rich, not impoverish them; that we can't lower unemployment in the long term by increasing inflation; that enforcing drug laws drives up the prices and increases property crimes and makes what would just be a problem to the user a problem for everyone. The libertarian candles shining now couldn't help but make Leonard feel proud. Rose Wilder Lane's highest hope for success for her intellectual movement was that "at the end of this century there will be a higher percentage of people believing in liberty than ever before," and by that standard, everything has succeeded wonderfully.[21]

But even advances for libertarianism can be bittersweet. Bandow has written mostly about foreign policy in his books and columns, arguing against entangling alliances and military interventions. Those ideas are definitely taken more seriously in more reputable venues than they were twenty-five years ago. His articles, as well as those by Cato's Ted Galen Carpenter, appear in bigger and more respectable foreign policy journals more frequently. Officials from the Japanese embassy now invite him over to hear what he has to say. "But there's a disjunction between being taken seriously in those ways, and affecting policy," Bandow notes. "We [libertarians] can write in well-read publications now about why we shouldn't bomb Kosovo. But we're still going to go off and bomb Kosovo."[22]

"Opposing the state has become an industry," says Richard Cornuelle, of the old Volker Fund, an entrepreneur at the very beginning of that industry.

> And it failed. The state is doing fine. I remember the American Enterprise Institute when it was Bill Baroody in one office on the dumpy side of Washington. I went over to meet Charles Murray and the goddamn AEI is fifteen stories high, everyone looking very prosperous, and you realize what a big business the unsuccessful effort to retard the growth of the state in the U.S. has been. [He could have said the same about the lovely glass-encased tower that the $22-million-a-year Cato Institute now inhabits on Massachusetts Avenue.] If you want to measure it by, did it preserve the point of view through a dark time? It did that. But did it slow down the growth of the state? I don't see any evidence of that. Murray [Rothbard] and I used to talk about blowing up the UN. Now the table talk at these free market foundations is about fringe benefits.[23]

The sort of short-term policy successes, or near successes, that the likes of Cato had with Social Security or the Reason Foundation has had with municipal privatization and influencing transportation policy and becoming serious players in state and local government reform strike some radical libertarians as barely worth celebrating. Some still see the libertarian movement as something meant to be uncompromising to such a degree that mass popularity is out of the question. Jacob "Bumper" Hornberger, a Texas lawyer who had a revelation after stumbling across some old *Freeman* reprint essays in a public library, worked a stint at FEE during its chaotic late 1980s and launched his own libertarian institution, the Future of Freedom Foundation, in the 1990s. He hired Richard Ebeling, then a professor teaching Austrian economics at Hillsdale College, a school famous for accepting no government money, even in the form of loans to students. "We prided ourselves," Ebeling remembers, "on making a point of focusing on every challenging and cutting-edge issue, and to be so principled and uncompromising that we eventually would drive away every conceivable reader. And I looked at Bumper and said, 'I'll be working on so offending you that you're going to leave too.'" Ebeling was kidding, but only kind of.[24]

Some, though, like the rare libertarian syndicated opinion columnist Steve Chapman (*Reason* magazine's Jacob Sullum and Walter Williams are a couple of others) are excited by smaller victories than the ultimate conversion of the masses. "It's very encouraging where we are today compared to when I got into Washington back in the mid-'70s," Chapman tells me. "Lots of things were taken seriously then—price controls and deficit spending to ensure economic growth and things like that—and people basically know that they are bogus, and windfall profit taxes are not going to go anywhere these days. China in the mid-'70s was one big North Korea. Now look, it's the most dynamic economy on the planet because they adopted market reforms. So I'd have to say that the world had moved in our direction in the past thirty years."[25]

"THERE IS NO MASS CONSTITUENCY FOR SEVEN-YEAR-OLD HEROIN DEALERS TO BE ABLE TO BUY TANKS WITH THEIR PROFITS FROM PROSTITUTION."

The Libertarian Party's status in the larger libertarian intellectual and activist movement has become a sidestream (though some LP devotees would say the *rest* of the movement is the insignificant sideshow). Many LP activists and candidates are far more likely than in the party's beginnings to know only the LP side of the larger libertarian movement. LP advocates could point to the fact that the LP has received far more votes than any libertarian magazine has had readers, or think tank has had donors or customers. Still, the days when major libertarian academic intellectuals such as Szasz and Nozick would show up at LP conventions merely as interested parties, delegates, or platform members are over; a fresh purely political class has dominated the LP since the 1990s. A huge disjunction often exists between them and the intellectual books, think tanks, and magazines part of the movement, spurred by a general sense of embarrassment from many of those who see themselves as the serious professional libertarians about the LP. LPers can often sense that contempt, so resentment often runs back.

Some have argued that the party merely pulls political activist energy out of the two major parties that might better be used to turn the major parties in a more libertarian direction. Thus the LP's existence may be making the major parties—the only ones with any chance of winning in our nonproportional representation, first-past-the-post system—marginally *less* libertarian than they would otherwise be. The Republican Liberty Caucus since the late 1980s has supported and encouraged more libertarian candidates within the GOP. Ron Paul, who has been as radical a libertarian as one could hope for as a politician, despite being titularly a Republican, is a poster boy for this approach.

Libertarian Party politicos often scoff at endless policy papers and conferences and argue that real victories for libertarian causes, such as the protolibertarian free trade advocates Cobden and Bright's overthrowing of Britain's Corn Laws (tariffs on imported grains) in the nineteenth century, came only when libertarian ideas were combined with political action.

It's an irresistible temptation for libertarians, who should know better, to centrally plan the larger movement or be uncharitable to those who pick strategies, techniques, and audiences for their libertarian activism that seem foolish or counterproductive or hopeless. David Bergland, the 1984 LP presidential candidate who returned to chair the LP National Committee in the late 1990s, has harsh words for fellow libertarians who question the efficacy (or even the sanity) of LP activism as a major outlet for world-changing effort: "If I'm told I have the burden of proving to you that I'm not wasting my time, well, fuck you. You can quote me on that."[26]

The Libertarian Party may have reached an impasse of sorts. It has never again approached Ed Clark's near million votes on the presidential level in 1980, and it holds no federal or state congressional seats (after a heyday in New Hampshire in the mid-1990s when there were four Libertarians in the state house). In 2004, it ran an unemployed computer programmer for president, Michael Badnarik, a man who believes driver's licenses are unconstitutional, who spent months driving around the country to local and state party meetings and lecturing about the Constitution. Despite his lack of experience and his eccentricities, though, he managed to get a vote total slightly better than former best-selling author Harry Browne earned in his second run for president in 2000—approximately 397,000 to Browne's 384,000. Still, the LP has proven remarkably tenacious for an American third party, and the numbers, while never enough to win major offices, would have heartened an early movement libertarian insistent that they were a lonely remnant. In 2000, for example, 1.7 million votes nationally were cast for 255 LP candidates for the U.S. House of Representatives. Hell, even the number of *candidates* is larger than some libertarians in the mid-1940s thought the number of serious libertarians in the whole nation might be.[27]

A few old party activists think that seeing the LP as something meant to win office inherently sells out libertarian principle. Gary Greenberg, one of the founders of the New York State LP and its 1978 gubernatorial candidate, thinks that "the very idea of worrying about the LP becoming a major force is essentially selling out, because hardcore libertarianism *has no mass constituency*. And if you are constantly covering it up, you are just playing games. There is no mass constituency for seven-year-old heroin dealers to be able to buy tanks with their profits from prostitution, and once you face that the LP has to decide: Are they compromising their principles for votes, or are they running candidates for the opportunity to educate people?"[28]

Some forces in the LP, acting now as the "Libertarian reform caucus," insist to the contrary that the LP can run candidates who fit anywhere within the top quadrant of the Nolan chart—a two-dimensional grid popularized as "the world's smallest political quiz" and often used as a device to catch people's attention at LP or Advocates for Self-Government booths at county fairs and the like. The quiz asks ten questions covering both personal and economic liberties and places the test taker, based on his answers, at a point on a two-dimensional grid as either libertarian (strong on both), conservative (strong on economic liberties, weak on personal ones), liberal (strong on personal liberties, weak on economic), or populist (bad on both). The LP needn't, and shouldn't, the Reform Caucus types argue, insist on the sort of Rothbardian anarcho-purity that Greenberg summoned. Others in the party think that there's no point in having an LP that doesn't stand staunchly for a pure libertarian position—that the other two parties have plenty of room for people who mostly believe in freedom, except for this, or that, or what about that? By that line of thinking, if the LP becomes just Republican-lite, why should anyone bother voting for it, since the Republican Party already exists?

The LP as an organizer of libertarian forces in politics can and has been effective, just not necessarily at electing candidates (except at the local and county board level, mostly, or for nonpartisan offices). For example, a squad of LPers in California wrote the official opposition to a state bond initiative—the state issues pamphlets with pro and con arguments about ballot measures. Despite both major parties and most of the media being for the initiative, it was defeated. Was the LP's written attack responsible? It's impossible to know. But it did provide a readily available set of reasons not to vote for it, as well as alternative solutions to the problem the bond issue was supposed to solve.[29]

The LP's most prominent role today is as a spoiler—a concept based on the notion that every vote *really* belongs to a Republican or a Democrat. (Ryan Sager argues in his 2006 book *The Elephant in the Room* that the GOP is ignoring the needs of its libertarian-leaning wing in favor of its religious right wing at peril of its electoral future—especially in the mountain West, which Sager posits, with some evidence, is far more libertarian leaning than traditionally right or left wing.) Thus when a libertarian gets more votes than the vote difference between the two major party candidates—allied with the presumption that most libertarian voters would have *really* preferred the GOP candidate to the Democrat—then the LP candidate is assumed to have cost the Republicans the election. By that standard, in 2006 a widely ridiculed Montana libertarian candidate, Stan Jones, notorious for turning his skin blue by overuse of the quack therapy "colloidal silver," cost the GOP control of the Senate by beating the spread between the winning Democrat and the losing GOP incumbent. The Republicans haven't done anything about it except accuse libertarians of ruining everything with their childish bullshit.[30]

"SINCE CRIME WE HAVE ALWAYS HAD WITH US AND THE STATE IS JUST ORGANIZED CRIME, WE'LL ALWAYS HAVE THE STATE."

The history of libertarian movement strategy is one of alternate, often conflicting, strategic imperatives delivered with oracular assurance. Even within the larger divisions, such as ideas versus politics and radicalism versus gradualism, there are finer gradations. Must the libertarian revolution be a middle class one? Or, since the middle class has it made in this complex round-robin system of state theft and giveaway, must libertarians aim at the disaffected and hurt: inner-city residents whose lives are torn apart by drug laws and zoning laws and occupational licensing laws and every little barrier in the way of personal bootstrap lifting; drug users; gun owners fearing further registration requirements and ownership restrictions. Could such a coalition of single issues where people have reason to embrace the libertarian message of less government be turned into a coherent mass movement? Or are the likes of gun rightsers and drug legalizers too dug into their own personal trenches to see the larger principles that should unite them?

Longtime movement hand Jeff Riggenbach told me, "The reason libertarians don't succeed as a revolutionary political movement is that they are pushing abstract ideas to a world of people who *don't get* abstract ideas. No abstract ideas ever win—the communists won through a coup d'état. There *is* a growing fuck-off-and-leave-me-alone strain in American culture and that's great, but since crime we have always had with us and the state is just organized crime, we'll always have the state. People will always be tempted to use the easiest, quickest route to what they want."[31]

Chris Sciabarra, the dialectical libertarian philosopher, thinks Hayek's most valuable idea is that government interventionism shifts the psychology of the culture toward an unlovely dependence. He thinks libertarians need to embrace a more holistic view of the dangers of statism, prove they are willing to link libertarian ideas with larger questions about what makes a worthwhile, livable culture, and avoid seeming like atomists out for number one or obsessed with mere freedom to buy and sell.

Whole Foods grocery chain founder John Mackey, a libertarian and a successful entrepreneur inspired by Mises, Hayek, and former *Reason* editor Virginia Postrel, has pursued a similar line of thinking with an organization he founded called FLOW (Freedom Lights Our World), which tries to frame free trade and free markets as a progressive cause, the key to raising the Third World out of poverty in a sustainable way, rooted in self-actualization through personal responsibility and control over health care, education, and retirement.

"What I love most about the freedom movement," Mackey told the crowd at a libertarian conference in 2004, "are the ideas of voluntary cooperation and spontaneous order when channeled through free markets, leading to the continuous evolution and progress of humanity." He told them that from his perspective as a successful entrepreneur, the movement is doing an awful branding job trying to sell its inherently excellent product.

He particularly blamed the Randian "virtue of selfishness" strain and Milton Friedman's insistence that the only obligation a corporation has is to its shareholders for making libertarianism seem to be a doctrine of crabbed atomistic greed rather than of peace and plenty. Mackey insists corporations also have an obligation to their community, and indeed the entire world community. Libertarianism can be sold as an idea that grounds liberty and prosperity in a full, inspirational vision of human life and society that aims toward the top of psychologist Abraham Maslow's famous hierarchy of needs, toward self-actualization.[32] The FLOW approach, still new, has been exciting some old-timers looking for a fresh way to explain libertarianism's benefits to an audience that might not be ready to buy the full property rights libertarian paradigm delivered in the traditional way.

Many libertarians have become excited about pursuing insights from the larger libertarian intellectual project into areas beyond politics per se (see the discussion below of the Koch brothers' fascination and efforts on behalf of market-based management). Richard Cornuelle agrees that freedom can extend to relationships within organizations and families, not just relationships in markets. "Many of the great lions of libertarianism thought there was no alternative to regimentation in the internal affairs of government, firms, and families. I think they are dead wrong about that. There *is* a better alternative, and a theoretical basis for knowing that more libertarian internal structures will get better results." A realization of the dangers that authoritarian structures create even outside government—particularly the danger that free and open communication gets stifled, as people strive to tell the boss only what they think he wants to hear—has animated libertarian thinkers from Liberty Fund founder Pierre Goodrich to science fiction writer Robert Anton Wilson.

Cornuelle and others believe that the gap in the thinking of many libertarians—command-and-control institutions such as firms and families existing in a world of freedom—can and ought to be closed. And firms can move toward a potential new, more libertarian management style, without having the theory fully worked out. After all, free markets existed before Adam Smith wrote *Wealth of Nations*. Cornuelle remembers something he learned from Wilhelm Röpke during the old Mont Pelerin days: Many of the problems with early industrial society that people thought the state needed to combat were merely ephemeral matters in the transition to industrial modernity and were not permanent no matter what the state did or didn't do. That whole Marx/Charlie Chaplin vision of industrial worker hell is no longer the dominant reality in the wealthy West. It may be the same with the modern *Dilbert* version of a working man's hell—that a more libertarian approach to internal management within the firm could help create a richer cultural context for political libertarianism.

"YOU TEACH THEM BY EXAMPLE."

New libertarian movement strategies and areas of interest developed in the 1970s and came to fruition in the 1990s. Libertarians had always been opposed to state schooling. Libertarian magazines had always shown a great interest and enthusiasm in alternative education, Montessori schooling, and the "unschooling" and antischooling ideas of popular writers not always identified with libertarianism per se, such as John Holt and Ivan Illich. Those ideas and the ideological entrepreneurial work of Milton Friedman, who made school vouchers his pet issue in the 1990s, have seen fruit in mass movements for both homeschooling and vouchers—movements that are not completely dominated by libertarians but show how libertarian ideas can achieve mass constituencies when separated from the entire package.[33] Homeschooling goes back to Etienne de la Boétie and his theories of how the state must have ideological obedience or else it cannot impose its will by force. As radical libertarian education theorist Joel Spring wrote, "Any successful radical change in society partly depends upon changes in the character structure and attitudes of the population."[34] This doesn't mean the creation of some Leninist new libertarian man. The instincts and abilities for liberty, a libertarian has to believe, are innate: an ability to fend for ourselves in the Randian sense and to form spontaneous orders of fellowship and cooperation in the Hayekian sense. But it would help if a squad of experts from the government with a whole different set of ideas weren't socializing most children.

From one of the most personal of state interventions in life, education, to some of the most apparently abstract, public services, the libertarian movement is covering the waterfront. "Privatization" is another movement that has ramped up in the past two decades, rooted in radical libertarianism but actuated through gradualist steps. Robert Poole of *Reason* magazine began a side business doing consulting on local government privatization issues, in collaboration with the National Taxpayers Union, in the mid-1970s, and became the first nationally known prophet of municipal privatization—taking services previously provided by government and letting private enterprise take over, or at least inserting competition into the process of contracting. Poole edited a series of books laying the basic groundwork for severe cutbacks or privatization in municipal services, regulation, and defense—more based on economic efficiency, as befits Poole's engineering background, than a rights-based libertarian radicalism.

In 1978, Poole launched the nonprofit Reason Foundation to pursue these interests. The foundation took ownership of the magazine, though *Reason* retained a separate identity and function from the think tank activities. The foundation's bailiwick became a national approach to local policy, with policy papers and consultations on how to introduce more choice, competition, and market discipline in urban policy areas from education to solid waste and air pollution to road congestion, forging close relationships along the way with various reform-minded mayors and governors. The foundation is now run by David Nott, who ran the Institute for Humane Studies in the 1990s.

Reason magazine has continued its own way, shedding the internal movement focus and aiming to be the libertarian version of *Harpers* or *Atlantic* that Poole envisioned when he and his partners took over the magazine in the early 1970s. It was edited in the 1980s by Marty Zupan (currently president of the Institute for Humane Studies), through the 1990s by Virginia Postrel (who since leaving *Reason* was for a time a *New York Times* business columnist and is now a staff writer for *Atlantic* and author of *The Future and Its Enemies* and *The Substance of Style*) and current editor in chief Nick Gillespie (under whom this author works as a senior editor at *Reason*).

With the Civil Aeronautics Board eliminated by Jimmy Carter, Poole remains the most listened-to national voice on privatizing airports, air traffic control, and, especially post–9/11, airport security. The Reason Foundation's leadership on municipal privatization of services has won it friends, allies, and supporters in mayor's and governor's offices from California to Florida. On transportation policy, one of its central concerns, the idea of high-occupancy toll roads (to introduce market incentives to road-building and road-using decisions), which Reason pioneered, is grabbing the imagination of urban transportation planners across the country. Reason staff agitation against a universal preschool ballot measure in California in 2006, slamming it as a new entitlement mostly for the benefit of the middle-class and wealthy, was a vital spur to a media blitz that helped defeat it, despite huge spending by its proponents and teachers union support. To taxation-is-theft libertarians, the small victories and steady progress on municipal privatization of services isn't very exciting. Some even condemn it as counterproductive, as more like governmentizing private business than the reverse. The ready insult that any libertarian has for *Reason*, when they want to jab at it, is some reference to its (long mythical) obsession with such boring minutia as private fire services.

In spirit, though, what Poole has been up to since the mid-1970s is an essential, if not always sexy or headline-making, part of the libertarian project: convincing both the state and the business world that all the things people in the twentieth century thought the state must or ought to do, from garbage collection to road building to prison operation, don't need the state—and that segueing from a governmental to a competitive or private approach can benefit businesses and even government officials (by allowing them to do more with less and slough off some headaches) as well as taxpayers.

Even if change through privatization and the long debate over whether certain things government does ought to be done by *anyone* (attacking such only-the-government-could-afford-to-try-it fiscal disasters as light rail is another part of the Reason Foundation project) is slow and incomplete from a hard-core perspective, Poole defends the radical implications of his incremental approach:

> Most average people, who aren't intellectuals, learn not from textbooks and from theory; they learn by everyday observation. If somebody sees that a private company does a better job of putting out fires than a government bureaucracy, that's the way they learn . . . a lesson about the advantages of the private enterprise system versus the disadvantages of government. And if they see enough examples like that, eventually, with a little coaching from the side, from journals of opinion and think tank studies, they may start learning general lessons. . . . I don't think you effectively make significant change by teaching the general public the theory and expecting them to say, "Oh, now I see.". . . You teach them by example, by building up enough practical cases where they can walk down the street and see things being done in a better way.[35]

"HE HAS A STRATEGY THAT PROBABLY
WE ARE UNAWARE OF."

The empire of Koch-funded libertarian organizations saw some up-heaval in the early 1990s, as Koch tried to develop in both his business and philanthropies what he dubbed "market-based management." While this concept and its operations remain opaque to many, it is an attempt to incorporate calculations of internal markets of sorts, apply-ing principles of competition, knowledge, and discovery within the firm. Ideally it involves as much quantifying of internal values added as possible with, for example, employees earning "decision rights" within the company in an analogous manner to how one wins property rights in the outside market: through a more intelligent and resourceful use of their "local knowledge" in the Hayekian lingo. Market-based man-agement strives to base internal company decisionmaking on proven arenas of local knowledge within the firm—the person who has proven himself to be in the best position to know, not necessarily "the boss." Charles Koch admits the entire MBM project is still, in the Aus-trian economics style, ongoing and experimental, not a set grab bag of obvious tenets and tricks; its implications and possibilities have not yet been set in cement.

In the brouhaha over applying some of these ideas to the organiza-tions he funded, Charles Koch eventually cut down his support of Cato and left the board of the think tank he helped found. The Insti-tute for Humane Studies saw the old-school libertarian guard of Leonard Liggio and Walter Grinder move on. The institute attempted for a time to increase the number of students at its seminars in an at-tempt to create quantifiably larger results. One old lecturer com-plained that clever foreign students began seeing the institute as a cash source they could manipulate to get free trips to the United States. One suspicious sign was listing as major personal influences such clas-sic but little read libertarian forebears as seventeenth-century legal theorists Samuel Pufendorf and Hugo Grotius.

Grinder, for one, thought this all added up to quantity over quality, and after fighting an internal rearguard action against the new dispen-sation, he was gone. Kochology is the kremlinology of the libertarian movement, mostly because Charles and David rarely discuss publicly the reasons for the funding decisions they make or don't make, or stop making. Grinder for his part perceives a sudden change in Charles's time preference, a desire to somehow speed up the whole process of ideological and cultural change along with a feeling that whatever his organizations had been doing, it didn't seem to be working. The quest for quantification led to ideological questionnaires for students before and after the weeklong student seminars. Some old-time IHSers noted that especially bright kids are bound to resent that sort of thing, and are very likely to write down anything whimsically, or precisely what they think you don't want to hear.

Dave Padden, a libertarian businessman from Chicago who has served on boards of libertarian organizations with Koch, says when it comes to apparent back-and-forth on Koch's part, the rest of the world should just sit back and let the master do his thing. "I would never attempt to second-guess whatever he's doing in the interest of making this a free country. He has a strategy that probably we are unaware of. He's so smart and so successful that I'm just going to await the outcome."[36] Similarly, Charles's longtime assistant and ideological majordomo George Pearson (who no longer works for Koch) says Koch has been "as strategic and patient and probably as effective [in his ideological investments] as in his investments in business. He's produced great results."[37] As far as many are concerned, you could never say that Charles Koch has let the libertarian movement down; if there has been any letting down, it has been in the opposite direction.

As for what happened between Cato's Ed Crane and his longtime biggest supporter, Crane himself insists "I don't know what happened. I'll go to my grave not understanding what happened."[38] Some movement watchers think it had to do with Crane's resistance to the imposition of "market-based management" techniques at Cato; some think that Koch had been convinced by others in his orbit that Cato was saying or doing things that weren't libertarian; some think that Koch's fascination with the writings of Michael Polanyi led him to distrust the more old-fashioned ideological approach to politics that he saw Cato and other parts of the movement as representing. (Memos I've seen from the early 1990s period of upheaval at the Institute for Humane

Studies indicate a Polanyi influence on the changes contemplated and actuated there as well, an attempt at developing a more flexible and less dogmatic approach to research and advocacy. Of course, to many libertarians, one man's dogma is another man's belief in liberty and rights.) For his part, Charles Koch decided at a certain point that "my involvement [with Cato] was counterproductive. I have strong ideas, I want to see things go in certain direction, and Crane has strong ideas. I concluded, why argue with Ed? Rather than try to modify his strategy, just go do my own thing and wish him well. I had to get out to let them reach their potential, and I think it worked out to their benefit."[39]

Pearson, a longtime Koch lieutenant (originally introduced to Charles by Hans Sennholz, Pearson's economics professor at Grove City), says that "Charles doesn't like to spend money on things where he doesn't see results." But as anyone in ideological activism could (and they do, they do) argue, it's hard to quantify results when selling a product that people don't want. Libertarianism is a set of ideas that are *not popular*, explaining why you need a dedicated ideological movement to try to sell them.

Koch philanthropy in the past decade or so, as both Koch brothers and Richard Fink, who has decades of experience working with and for the Kochs in their ideological giving, tell me, is concerned with developing meaningful metrics to quantify its effectiveness. While none would say they've mastered this art of quantifying the effectiveness of what could be a centuries-long struggle, Fink tells me he has learned one thing that is *not* a good measure of effectiveness and value for libertarian work: how closely someone hews to the total hard-core libertarian vision. Fink would rather see real-world impact, even incremental, than celebrate ideological purity. "There were these purity indexes, where people were promoted, judged, and ranked and rated based on the purity of their ideas. To me [libertarianism] is a toolbox to advance social progress, which is very, very different from saying, 'This is a set of ideas for sainthood that if you were consistent with them and agreed with them, that you were somehow a star.' The idea is to *do something* with it."[40]

Which is not to say that the moral passion of the hard-core approach (as Richard Ebeling told me, echoing many a purist libertarian, no one ever went to the barricades to eliminate a milk subsidy) isn't necessary to inspire people to pursue the nuts-and-bolts methods of effecting change.

Cornuelle recognizes that some of the criticisms their enemies threw at him and his fellow libertarians in the old days were valid— they *were* ideologues. Still, he credits his old gang around the Volker Fund in the 1950s as for that very reason serving a vital purpose. "That emphasis on doctrinal purity was needed for one very important task: keeping that tradition alive and well during a period when it was in danger of extinction. If you are going to preserve something for the ages, you must preserve it in its purest form."[41]

For Poole of the Reason Foundation, in his work to convince city managers and mayors and city councils and state transportation agencies and airports to get government out of certain businesses, or at least make them compete with private services, or introduce more market discipline to their activities, he realized purely ideological approaches are positively detrimental. You won't convince any agency to change the way they do airport screening by talking about the illegitimacy of taking one's income from taxpayers at the point of a gun. But where the ideological passion is important, Poole realizes, is in inspiring people to do the research and thinking that will convince the nonideological to come along. Utterly disinterested policy analysis is a myth, but libertarian think tanks provide a context for the ideologically motivated to do objective, pragmatic research that, it is hoped, will sell libertarian solutions even to people who reject libertarian moral premises.

But reality, and thus ideological movements attempting to grasp reality and turn it, has many sides. Certain prominent sociopolitical movements *have* used pure moral passion to build mass constituencies that completely upend the Hayekian notion of starting from the top of the intellectual pyramid. The Christian right and the anti-abortion movements, for example, did not start with high-level academic intellectuals and then trickle down to journalists and high school teachers. They went straight to the masses. For such a strategy to work for libertarianism would require that the masses agree not just with the most generic "life, liberty, and pursuit of happiness" version of libertarianism. Most Americans show lots of support for libertarian ideas on the abstract level, which can delude libertarian politicos into thinking the American people are more primed for libertarian policy change than they really are. To go straight to the masses with libertarianism also requires mass agreement with libertarianism's harder applications, such as ending public education and almost all weapons regulations.[42]

It was a principle of Leonard Read's, embodied in one of his colorful homiletic essays and speeches, that if there were a button in front of him that would end all illegitimate state actions, ones that unjustly violate people's rights to life, liberty, and property, then as the creative spirit of the universe is his witness, he'd push that button! Charles Koch's reaction to this idea, given the influence his vision has had in shaping modern libertarian institutions, is worth contemplating: "I like to consider policy change in terms of the test: Does this change in laws or institutions lead us toward a more prosperous and progressive and civil society?'" Koch tells me. "And each step needs to be tested along the way. I mean, if we did away with government tomorrow . . . I'd have said to Leonard, no, I wouldn't push the button! That approach scared me to death. We'd have mass chaos. I want to go just as fast and as far as we continue to get better results but we must do it in a way that the change demonstrates that people will be better off. I don't see how we'll get far down the road if we take steps that make people worse off."[43]

When considering libertarian ideological philanthropy and its strategies and impact, it is worth contemplating that one of the most important events for the spreading of libertarian ideas and shaping the libertarian mind and movement was Rand's *Atlas Shrugged*. As one libertarian market intellectual—one not affiliated with any of the institutions that suck up most libertarian philanthropy—commented to me, "Imagine Rand trying to get a grant from libertarian funders. Announcing that she's a novelist, it will take her fourteen years to get it done, and she won't even have any faculty berth while doing it! Of what *possible* use to the movement could it be to fund this, would be the response." (I've discovered no small amount of resentment toward libertarian funding sources from those who have chosen to take a path other than institutional think tankery or academia for their libertarian work.)[44]

"LIBERTARIANS WHO COULD CARE LESS ABOUT THE MASS MURDER OF IRAQIS. . . ."

To talk about "the" libertarian movement is a bit misleading. The days when they all were working with something recognizably connected to the original Leonard Read vision are over. This is all the better for the overall health of the fight to inculcate libertarian ideas; since there are many differences among the American people, it only makes sense for there to be differences in attempts to influence their ideas.

These differences make the libertarian movement contentious, with intramural ideological wars waged over differences in style, approach, tone, and emphasis. As CEI chief Fred Smith says with some regret (since he wishes for better coordination of efforts in the movement), collectivists make better collectivists than libertarians do. Some organizations and figures who consider themselves fighting for libertarianism are ready to declare war on others. A particular example of this schisming over personality and persona can be seen in conflict between elements within the Cato Institute and the Ludwig von Mises Institute, best expressed in lively warfare on the website of Cato's Tom Palmer. In Palmer's estimation, Mises Institute president Rockwell's personal website, LewRockwell.com, is overbrimming with pro-Confederacy, anti-American material (mostly in the context of polemics against the U.S. war efforts in Iraq), as well as writings by people who (in other venues) are unacceptably racist or so traditionally Christian they call for stoning of sinners according to Old Testament rules. People in the Mises Institute orbit have a tendency to push ideas that would offend the hell out of the typical *New York Times* reader. The Cato approach can be summed up by something Crane once wrote: "We need less of a bunker mentality and more of a sense that the vast majority of humanity favors peace and prosperity and that they can be convinced of a rational but radical alternative."[45]

The Mises Institute approach is similarly populist, but unlike Cato it pretty much writes off the necessity or even the possibility of meaningful dialogue with the existing power structure in government and media that has become Cato's stock-in-trade. The Mises crowd still represents an occasionally chip-on-shoulder outsider brand of libertarianism, proud of its own radicalism and oppositional stance. This distinction can be seen in differences between libertarians more apt to see the "uncompromising" Mises as a hero versus the hedging Hayek. While both Mises and Hayek had their faculty berths in America paid for by the Volker Fund, only the Mises fans tended to revel in that detail and embrace its underdoggedness and implications about how stupid American academia was to not see the greatness of Mises. Hardly any discussion of Mises by his current fans fails to stress that.

Hayek's devotees, however, tend to embed him in a standard academic dialogue rather than highlight his principled separation from it, and they barely mention his being funded by Volker. They do not use it as proof of his purity or the stupidity of American academia. The Mises Institute crowd delights in being outsiders, speaking a purist truth that needs to be kept alive, whereas the Cato types value their place at the Washington policy table and try to leverage libertarian ideas and policy changes where they see them as most effective: in mainstream politics and media. Both approaches appeal to their own audiences, and both are necessary to a movement that needs to reach a variety of audiences.

While both institutions officially opposed the 2003 invasion of Iraq, differences exist in the larger libertarian movement over the appropriate government responses to 9/11 and post-9/11 realities. In the 1990s, some libertarians were giddy at the thought that the end of the apparent threat of Soviet communism meant a purist antistate coalition, including cold warriors with otherwise strong antistate instincts, could and would rise again. (This inspired Rothbard's later move toward paleolibertarianism.) Justin Raimondo from the LP's early 1980s radical caucus—who is now the chief voice at the libertarian antiwar website, antiwar.com—followed through the 1980s what he saw as Rothbardian strategic maneuvers against imperialism. He joined with his old comrades Eric Garris and Colin Hunter to run a mostly paper organization called the Libertarian Republican Organizing Committee, following a Maddox/Lilie–inspired path of trying to appeal to middle-class yuppie moderates in the GOP and predicting the end of the cold war in newsletters they passed out at GOP conventions. When the end really happened, Raimondo got a phone call from an old libertarian pal in Dana Rohrabacher's office gleefully announcing that they could all be together, one unified antistate movement, now that the question of what to do about the Soviet Union no longer divided them. With the fall of the Berlin Wall should come the fall of the right-wing/libertarian wall.

Even during the cold war, there was no monolithic libertarian consensus. Particularly for those into Rand or Heinlein, a robust sense that world communism needed a strong counterforce was shot through the movement; in the LP in the 1980s *Reason*'s Bob Poole and others ran a Libertarian defense caucus promoting a pro-defense stance (though not advocating an unprovoked aggressive war on the commies), one that saw the value of helping anti-Soviet proxy warriors and keeping up a cutting-edge nuclear deterrent. Some libertarians had that old Leonard Read/Rose Wilder Lane faith that a command economy was too weak to pose a real threat. Ed Crane visited the Soviet Union in the early 1980s and recognized it for the decrepit, collapsing failure that it proved to be. He wrote that it would collapse and be gone within two decades; he swears his first inclination was to say "one decade" but checked himself, thinking it too crazily optimistic.

Ted Carpenter, the Cato Institute's foreign policy chief, realized that the foreign policy consensus toward military buildup and imperial overstretch would not change overnight just because we'd lost the enemy that occasioned it. The end of the cold war did help Cato-style critiques become a more prominent part of the intellectual conversation on foreign policy, and allowed Carpenter's articles to be published more often in prominent mandarin foreign policy magazines such as *Foreign Affairs*.

The difference between Cato's Carpenter and the more radical antiwar libertarians such as Raimondo and his antiwar.com crew—who delight in poking at Cato for not being emphatic enough about a radically libertarian consistent pro-peace stance—can be limned by something Carpenter said about the neocon world-changing vision that Raimondo excoriates weekly. The super-Wilsonian vision of Bush's second inaugural address, Carpenter says, is "not wrong, it's just impractical. You're not going, in the foreseeable future, to convert a region like the Middle East into a Muslim version of Iowa. It ignores the cost in blood and treasure. It's a dangerous policy. But yes, they are right, if the whole world were liberal, democratic, capitalist, it would be a more peaceful place."[46]

Shorn of the moral fervor of a Raimondo, the Cato vision can be ensconced within the neorealist tradition in foreign policy, best exemplified by the journal *National Interest*, which generally looks askance at grand world-changing visions of the sort that animate the George W. Bush administration. Carpenter calls his position "cosmopolitan realism." It is not completely value-neutral when it comes to war or peace. It recognizes a strong presumption in favor of peace that must be overcome before force is brought to bear overseas—before people begin to be killed en masse for U.S. foreign policy goals. Unlike the Raimondo approach, it tends to assume that the crafters of American foreign policy are well-meaning but mistaken about ends and means.

The Cato foreign policy vision is anti–United Nations but not in a fanatical or panicked way (getting out of the United Nations would be fine, is the idea, but it isn't some horrible threat to our sovereignty), and anti–foreign aid largely in the tradition of libertarian-hero economist Lord Peter Bauer, who argued that foreign aid has done more to prop up corrupt governments than prod development. The necessary ingredients for development are not giveaways from richer countries, but market institutions and trade.[47]

America has faced a fresh set of foreign policy questions and crises since the end of the cold war. Long before 9/11, libertarians stressed the hazards of empire and the threat of radical Islamic blowback. An aware libertarian could react to 9/11 not with a shocked, "How could this happen?" but with a knowing, "Damn, it finally happened." If libertarians were challenged—as they were—with "How does your doctrinaire noninterventionism deal with this?" the libertarian could reply, with some justice, that his doctrinaire noninterventionism, if followed, would have meant that this would never have happened in the first place; that one of noninterventionism's major virtues is to prevent the rising resentments and enmities and complicated power politics that caused 9/11.

Nowadays, Carpenter and Cato have no use for the more radical conclusions of a thoroughgoing anarcho-libertarian foreign policy. "To talk about privatizing national defense, I regard that as idiotic. Not only would it be a bad idea substantively, but the minute one voices that kind of policy option, you don't just marginalize yourself—you take yourself out of the debate entirely."

What does Cato's responsible, in-the-debate foreign policy vision advise in regard to the most pressing foreign policy problem facing the United States in 2006—the occupation of Iraq? Pack up and go, Carpenter advises. And yes, the forces of radical Islam will spin that as a victory. "But that's what happens when you engage in stupid, unnecessary, unwinnable military interventions," Carpenter notes. "You can't back out cost-free."[48] But better now than after another thousand, two thousand, many thousands of American dead.

Many libertarians—especially the Mises Institute crowd, Justin Raimondo's antiwar.com, and David Theroux's Independent Institute—have also maintained the hard-core libertarian nonintervention tradition, based on the notion that Iraq was no direct and proven threat to America, often with more polemical and moral fervor and pugnaciousness than is the typical Cato style. (Libertarian luminaries have often questioned the strategic appropriateness of stressing a full-on noninterventionism when a smaller argument was on the table. Milton Friedman, for example, once advised Students for a Libertarian Society leader Milton Mueller, in the late 1970s debate over the revival of draft registration, to definitely *not* link the draft argument to any larger libertarian noninterventionist vision.[49])

While Cato's foreign policy division has steadfastly opposed the war, other Cato scholars have publicly supported it. And some others who were against the invasion have been, in the eyes of the radically antiwar libertarians, not sufficiently forceful or overly equivocating on the matter of getting out immediately. (My own institutional home, *Reason* magazine, has been ecumenical on this matter, with splits among staff members and those who have written about Iraq in its pages.)

Some libertarians, with a more expansive vision of national interest or even a neocon-inspired belief that loving liberty means extending it around the globe by any means necessary (see, for example, history professor R. J. Rummel, who has started calling himself a "freedomist" rather than a libertarian because he is aggravated over what he sees as libertarian pusillanimity on the importance of fighting for global liberty) saw the U.S. invasion of Iraq as the right thing to do. Justin Raimondo of antiwar.com has no patience for "libertarian" pro-war thought. He condemns "libertarians who could care less about the mass murder of Iraqis as long as they can read the latest novel by Heinlein or whoever. That's *their* moral priorities."[50] The pro-war libertarians, many of them enmeshed in a Republican-dominated world of discourse, think the antiwar ones are further marginalizing libertarianism as an unrealistic and defeatist ideology, unequipped to deal with the serious challenges of foreign policy, and bloodily opposed to America in a hysterical and offputting way. In the ugly lingo of blogger debate, they fear that libertarian antiwar sentiment, too heartily expressed, brands libertarians as "moonbats." Antiwar libertarians for their part think pro-war ones are selling out the basics of the liberal heritage of peace for a soupçon of Beltway respectability.

It is in the nature of ideologues to squabble, so expecting a united libertarian movement is foolish, when you consider human differences and the division of labor, both key tenets of how free markets make us so rich. The lack of unity hasn't kept the movement down. People of power and influence who take the phone calls of a Bob Poole or an Ed Crane and know what they stand for and know that their work can be trusted and used, have infiltrated corridors of political and economic power in a way hardly dreamed about in the 1970s.

Not that libertarians have been able to leverage that to the extent they'd like. Despite having billionaires like the Kochs on their side for decades, despite the presence through the years on Cato's board of such heavyweights as Rupert Murdoch and Fred Smith (the founder and president of Federal Express), the libertarian movement is among the most underfunded ideological tendencies in America, with no more than $125 million total given to or spent annually on the work of explicitly libertarian ideological think tanks, advocacy groups, political parties, or publications. (The Liberty Fund uses Pierre Goodrich's immense wealth to support endeavors that are intentionally below the radar and not meant to impact the public directly, except through book sales.)

It frustrates Crane, who says that if *he* were a billionaire and saw an opportunity, for example, to help privatize Social Security, he'd unhesitatingly sink $50 million into it. "I'm blaming myself at this stage.

I'm not sure why I can't get seven figures" from some of Cato's wealthier supporters.

It may not have all the money it wants, but Cato has an enviable presence on Capitol Hill these days, with a full-time government relations executive, almost weekly Hill testimonies, and a yearly guide to policy that is, says Cato's David Boaz, treated like forbidden pornography by Republican staffers, who imagine how deliciously *wonderful* it might be to actually *do* all that, but no, no, no, they just *couldn't dare*. Despite these signs of being enmeshed in the unlovely business-as-usual of governance, Crane assures me he maintains a healthy libertarian distaste for the whole sorry business, the same feeling that made him want to keep Cato in San Francisco. "I feel like I have to take a shower after I meet with some of these guys. It's very unpleasant what this power thing does. People who want to be congressmen are creepy people."[51]

"IT'S NOT SURPRISING THAT CONTRARIANS END UP BEING THE DRIVERS OF CHANGE."

If it hasn't been obvious through this entire book, libertarians as a class tend to be peculiar people—though getting less so as new generations are presented with a prebuilt movement they can slot into, not uncharted territory for the brave, foolhardy, and powerfully self-assured to slash through and build their own unique settlements in. One of the glories of ideological movements and why they are needed—as opposed to scattered thinkers and activists—is tied in to something Milton Friedman told me about the early days of the Mont Pelerin Society: It is bracing and affirming and empowering to discover that, however peculiar the rest of the world thinks you are, you are not alone, that other people of quality and intelligence are toiling in the same fields. Nowadays a libertarian is just a mouse click from another libertarian and can usually find others nearby in the physical world as well.

Especially in the old days, a libertarian ideologue is also embedded in a libertarian social world; to the more young and raffish, this manifests itself in wild communal homes such as the "anarcho-village," an apartment building in Long Beach, California, inhabited by Sam Konkin, libertarian science fiction writer J. Neil Schulman, and a shifting group of young, hungry libertarians. And in Austin, Texas, there was in the 1970s a nudist libertarian apartment commune (that one made it onto *Donahue*). For others, libertarian togetherness is the intellectual and affirming camaraderie of life around the office of a libertarian think tank or magazine. Of course no one is better equipped to complain about how annoying libertarians can be than another libertarian. Arising as I did from a self-consciously absurdist clique of punk rock libertarians at the University of Florida in Gainesville in the late 1980s, I've come to appreciate as one of the movement's most salubrious qualities its lack of a deadening self-seriousness and self-aggrandizement in the face of libertarians' difficult and eternal mission, sailing on seas of opposition and indifference with an often bizarre and difficult bunch of shipmates. Old movement hand Ralph Raico was known to sigh, at news of the latest absurdity or strategic misfire or failure on the part of a fellow libertarian, echoing the *Godfather*, "This is the movement we have chosen." But hardly a libertarian I spoke to doesn't also have some other libertarian's kindness, support, or belief to credit for whatever they've accomplished professionally. If it hasn't changed the world, at least the movement has sustained its members in fellowship and an always interesting ride through changing circumstances.

This shifting group of radical misfits has managed some interesting accomplishments along the way, and there is reason to believe that history in the twenty-first century is on their side. Jeff Riggenbach has argued convincingly that the personal liberation and empowerment movements of the 1960s and 1970s, as represented in such phenomena as the *Whole Earth Catalog* and the "Aquarian age" of personal growth and taking control of your own life—from your tools to your food to your education to your living and sexual arrangements—were libertarian in character, and it is true that they are. It is also true that most of the people following along in these traditions have not swallowed libertarianism whole or been systematic enough in their ideological and political thinking to even realize that they might want to be.[52]

But sometimes the forces of history can be bigger than all of us. Classical liberalism and classical free market economics, Marxists argued, were merely intellectual justification for a world that had already changed, a world of bourgeois accumulation. The forces of material production, they believed, come ahead of ideas. Perhaps, then, libertarian theorists are particularly farseeing, ginning up an ideological superstructure to defend a class interest that has yet to come to dominance—the class that will dominate a world to come where everyone recognizes the gains arising from free commerce and the unrestricted free play of human will and human desire, a class who will not tolerate any interference with what they want to say, do, make, build, consume, study, travel, buy, sell, marry. This class recognizes, as Hayek taught, that the benefits of liberty, in minds or markets, come not just from the already-known things that we can see governments interfering with. The most important benefits come from the unpredictable ways of bettering, enriching, making more delightful human life that come from giving people their head to make, trade, and behave as they wish. They recognize the unexpected *fertility* of freedom and the virtuous cycle of power and knowledge and wealth it creates.

Such a class began to appear in the intellectual and cultural forces that in the 1990s came to be known as the digerati, when their market wealth made them the looming wave of the future—the technicians and businessmen and ideologues who saw in a digital high-tech future a world in which government had little or no place. As libertarian John Perry Barlow, a lyricist for the Grateful Dead and a leading cyberintellectual, declared in a famous cyberworld manifesto:

> Governments of the Industrial World, you weary giants of flesh and steel, I come from Cyberspace, the new home of Mind. On behalf of the future, I ask you of the past to leave us alone. You are not welcome among us. You have no sovereignty where we gather. We have no elected government, nor are we likely to have one, so I address you with no greater authority than that with which liberty itself always speaks. I declare the global social space we are building to be naturally independent of the tyrannies you seek to impose on

us. You have no moral right to rule us nor do you possess any methods of enforcement we have true reason to fear.[53]

Libertarians have often had a strong futurist–optimist streak to go
with their peculiar streak (perhaps from some dynamic inherent in the
nature of their beliefs about the benefits and glories of unbridled human imagination and wealth). The popular avatars of life extension,
Durk Pearson and Sandy Shaw, authors of the early 1980s megabest-
seller *Life Extension,* used to be known within the libertarian movement as Skye D'Aureous and Natalee Hall. They are living examples of
making end runs around guild and status because they have made their
careers as freelance research scientists, using themselves as experimental subjects, without medical degrees or licenses (though they are both
trained scientists in other fields).

They are pure old-school movement libertarians, former editors of
Libertarian Connection, contributing editors of *Liberty* magazine, former columnists for *Reason,* and have pursued their activism not just in
far reaches of life extension speculation but in legal-political actions,
such as winning a lawsuit against the government over the ability to
make truthful health benefit claims about the supplements they make
and sell.

The most extreme movement advocating a richer, freer, more powerful human future, the Extropians, are a product of the libertarian
movement; their ideas about liberated humans warping their minds
and bodies through technologies of all varieties, living forever, blasting
off to the stars, or downloading themselves to computers, first presaged
in the 1970s writings of the libertarian and former acid guru Timothy
Leary. Leonard Read used to define the core of the libertarian message
as "anything that's peaceful." Modern libertarians of extropian-futurist
leanings have extended that to *everything* that's peaceful—whatever
humanity can invent the technology to do, let's go for it. Like our classical liberal forebears von Humboldt and Mill, let's celebrate the wild
abundance of experiments in living that a liberated human being
might choose to indulge in. And with these abilities come means of
doing things that we used to think we needed governments for, ways
to protect ourselves, ways to exchange our goods, ways to relate in
mutually beneficial ways with our neighbors both next door and

across the globe, that promise increasing ineffectiveness and perhaps eventual irrelevance for government as we have known it. As libertarian economist Tyler Cowen says, old measures such as "the government's share of gross domestic product" are "misleading" when it comes to judging our "economic freedom. If we focus on this measure we will conclude that societies are less free when in fact they are freer . . . . As long as the absolute size of the market sector [the world of freely chosen, wealth-improving exchanges] is increasing, people are . . . enjoying more economic freedom."[54]

The leftists of the Tom Frank variety are right in the sense that the twentieth-century leftist dream of centralized control of the human future *is* over. Libertarianism can be seen as the inevitable result of history in the sense that its opposite dominated twentieth-century world politics to a degree that the old socialist dreams of central management of the world to better humankind has been thoroughly debunked.[55]

In the 1970s, the L-5 Society was a libertarian-driven group dedicated to imagining and figuring out ways to actualize human communities in orbit. And as Robert Heinlein and other science fiction visionaries have shown, the possibilities for liberty are rich in such environments. And now, in the early twenty-first century, libertarian movement supporter Burt Rutan has achieved the dream that lay at the heart of Heinlein's libertarian future fantasies. He's built a privately funded spacecraft that can leave the planet and return. The era of private escape from the planet has officially begun. It may turn out to be the most important thing that has ever happened for libertarianism. The new way of governing human beings that happened in America—whose promise was so inspiring to so many modern libertarians—happened in a land that, given the technologies of the day, was the equivalent of a space colony. New places and new technologies give rise to new ideas and new possibilities.

The 1990s thought leader for libertarian computer entrepreneurs and businessmen, a chief guider and chronicler of those new ideas and new possibilities, to close a circle or two, was none other than Louis Rossetto, founder of *Wired* magazine and one of the young anarcho-libertarians who helped break the movement big with his 1971 cover story in the *New York Times* Sunday magazine. He spent the 1970s and 1980s abroad, working on the film *Caligula,* making documentaries with mujahideen in Afghanistan, living in squats in Amsterdam. He no longer felt committed to ideology, finding it more important to live out liberty in his day-to-day life, finding and occupying the spaces where he didn't have to care what government was doing or trying to do. As Rossetto sees it, the liberating advances in technology of the dawn of the twenty-first century are a technological and historical reality that make full human liberation inevitable, regardless of politics.

Making visible headway in Washington political circles for libertarian ideas is "not the right way to think about it," he says. "It's like wondering how to restructure the horseshoe industry to fit with the arrival of the automobile. Their era is not the new era. We still have these constructs in our minds that are historical rather than forward-looking and have yet to fully disabuse ourselves of them. But we must and we will."

We are moving, Rossetto thinks, because of our growing ability to manipulate both matter and computer processing, to levels of ability and practical liberty that will make the governmental and ideological structures that turned the twentieth century into such a bloody series of tragedies irrelevant and pointless.

> And the things we will imagine, and are imagining, and the discussions we have that help shape the mind that these new technological mediums create, have been formulated and originated by this collection of misfits over the last half a century.
>
> It's not surprising that contrarians end up being the drivers of change. Conventional wisdom, middle of the road people, that's not where the action is. Things happen on the margin, whether you are making a decision about stocks or cultural change. The place where decisions happen is at the edge. And out there laboring in obscurity, if not in derision, have been these people who have been able to keep a pretty pure idea going, and adapting it to circumstances and watching it be validated by the march of history.[56]

"Quintessentially and metaphysically," Murray Rothbard once wrote, the libertarian "should remain of good cheer. The eventual victory of liberty is inevitable, because only liberty is functional for modern man. There is no need, therefore, for libertarians to thirst maniacally for Instant Action and Instant Victory, and then to fall into bleak despair when that Instant Victory is not forthcoming. Reality, and therefore history, *is* on our side."[57]

NOTES

INTRODUCTION

1. Milton and Rose Friedman, *Two Lucky People: Memoirs* (Chicago: University of Chicago Press, 1998), 220.

2. Murray Rothbard, *For a New Liberty*, rev. ed. (New York: Collier, 1978), 298.

3. David Boaz, *Libertarianism: A Primer* (New York: Free Press, 1997), 134.

4. Rand's attitude toward Mises was wildly ambivalent. Rand's longtime disciple and lover, Nathaniel Branden, writes that she was "friendly, respectful, admiring . . . almost girlish in the way she complimented him on his momentous achievements." Yet she also disagreed heatedly with certain aspects of his extraeconomic philosophy, and wrote disparaging comments in the margins of her copy of *Human Action*, his magnum opus. Branden relates Rand's delight when Mises referred to her as "the most courageous man in America." See Nathaniel Branden, *Judgment Day: My Years with Ayn Rand* (Boston: Houghton Mifflin, 1989), 136–137. In Rand's letters, she refers to Mises both as "the great economist" and "the kind of 'almost' I would tolerate." See Michael S. Berliner, ed., *The Letters of Ayn Rand* (New York: Dutton), 582, 308.

A collection of Rand's marginalia features many of her heated critiques of Mises. See John Hospers, "Leaving a Margin for Error," *Liberty*, September 1997, 67. Still, Mises's student Hans Sennholz credits Rand with being "she, more than anyone else, [who] introduced Misesian economics" to American youth. See Hans Sennholz, "Postscript," in Ludwig von Mises, *Ludwig von Mises: Notes and Recollections* (Spring Mills, PA: Libertarian Press, 1978), 173. One old associate of Rand's says she can't recall Rand privately referring to Mises as anything other than "that old fool."

5. Many conservatives noticed Mises's lack of fit in the right-wing consensus. He is the subject of a catty and substanceless sharing of insults in the collected letters of *National Review* contributor Ralph de Toledano and *National Review* saint Whittaker Chambers. Chambers called Mises's brief 1956 tome *The Anti-Capitalist Mentality* "one of the most pernicious pieces of writing that the Right has produced" and reveals his ignorance of Mises by claiming that Mises (and the economics profession) have nothing to say on economic crises, one of Mises's central theoretical interests. De Toledano upped the ante by saying he read the book "with horror—appalled first by its sheer German stupidity and vulgarity and second by the utter ignorance it exhibited," concluding with snotty references to its "bad politics. . . shoddy history, and the watery regurgitation of Irvington-on-Hudson philosophy. . . oy vey." From Ralph de Toledano, ed., *Notes from the Underground: The Whittaker Chambers–Ralph de Toledano Letters* (Washington, DC: Regnery, 1997), 279, 282.

6. Murray N. Rothbard, "The Laissez-Faire Radical: A Quest for the Historical Mises," *Journal of Libertarian Studies*, Summer 1981, 250–251. Still, upon his death in 1973 at the age of ninety-two, Mises was eulogized in the right-wing press. *National Review* ran a tribute that was entered into the *Congressional Record* by a young ex-football player and congressman from New York named Jack Kemp. Over a decade later, Kemp would teasingly sign his name "Ludwig von Kemp" in notes to Cato Institute president Ed Crane.

7. "Inside Ronald Reagan: A Reason Interview," *Reason*, July 1975, 16.

8. Gerald Frost, *Antony Fisher: Champion of Liberty* (London: Profile, 2002), 107.

9. In the late 1990s, Chris Whitten ran a libertarian nerve center on the Internet called free-market.net with links to dozens of other libertarian-oriented sites. Whitten is certain that Internet exposures and searches are how most people lock on to libertarian ideas today.

10. Chris Matthew Sciabarra, *Ayn Rand: The Russian Radical* (University Park: University of Pennsylvania Press, 1995), 1.

11. Berliner, ed., *Letters of Ayn Rand*, 664.

12. Ayn Rand, "To the Readers of *The Objectivist Forum*," *Objectivist Forum*, February 1980, 1.

13. Upon Rand's death, an associate of her heir's released this restriction. Harry Binswanger, "From the Editor," *Objectivist Forum*, February 1983, 16.

14. One of the more substantial takes on this criticism can be found in William F. O'Neill, *With Charity Toward None: An Analysis of Ayn Rand's Philosophy* (Totowa, NJ: Littlefield, Adams, 1972), 22.

15. Murray Rothbard, *The Ethics of Liberty* (1982; New York: New York University Press, 1998), xlvii.

16. Rothbard once told Rand that she "introduced me to the whole field of natural rights and natural law philosophy, which I did not know existed." Quoted in Justin Raimondo, *An Enemy of the State* (Amherst, NY: Prometheus, 2000), 133.

17. Alan Walters, "Friedman, Milton," in John Eatwell et al., eds., *The New Palgrave: A Dictionary of Economics* (New York: Stockton, 1987), 2:427.

18. Benjamin A. Rogge, "New Conservatives and Old Liberals," *New Individualist Review*, Autumn 1962, 33.

CHAPTER 1

1. English barrister John Lind pointed out, with some justice, that the American Declaration of Independence was a formula for anarchy, since every government violated the inalienable rights it listed in some manner. Quoted in Murray Rothbard, *Conceived in Liberty*, vol. 4, *The Revolutionary War, 1775–1784* (1979; Auburn, AL: Ludwig von Mises Institute, 1999), 184.

2. For a good discussion of the antifederalists' libertarian case against the Constitution, see Bernard Bailyn, *The Ideological Origins of the American Revolution*, enl. ed. (1967; Cambridge, MA: Belknap, 1992), 331–351; and Jack N. Rakove, *Original Meanings: Politics and Ideas in the Making of the Constitution* (New York: Vintage, 1997), 142–160.

3. A libertarian-themed popular discussion of how lack of private property harmed the early American colonies at Jamestown and Plymouth can be found in Tom Bethell, *The Noblest Triumph: Property and Prosperity Through the Ages* (New York: St. Martin's, 1998), chap. 3.

4. Quoted in Herbert J. Muller, *Freedom in the Ancient World*, paperback ed. (New York: Bantam, 1961), 121.

5. Contemporary conservative M. Stanton Evans tries to make the case from this fact that far from any eternal conflict between religion and liberty, as many modern liberals and freethinkers aver, Western liberty is fully derived from, and meaningless outside of, this Judeo-Christian heritage, which he posits also made medieval times the true ancestors of

American liberty, not the megastate-building monarchies of post-Enlightenment times. This might seem convincing, as long as you focus solely on the most abstract sense of the nature of government, and not on what people were in actuality free to do, move, read, buy, sell, and so on. See M. Stanton Evans, *The Theme Is Freedom* (Washington, DC: Regnery, 1994). For another discussion that touches on the pre-Enlightenment, classical, and medieval roots of the Western notion of a higher law that restricts government power, see Edward S. Corwin, *The "Higher Law" Background of American Constitutionalism* (1928; Ithaca, NY: Cornell University Press, 1961).

In contemplating the religious roots of Western liberty, consider Herbert Muller's observation that "men entrenched themselves behind the Bible to fight against almost every major cause in the history of Western freedom—freedom of conscience, democratic government, civil liberties, the abolition of slavery, equal rights for women." Muller, *Freedom in the Ancient World*, 143.

6. For a discussion of the natural law and natural rights tradition in an explicitly modern libertarian context, see Rothbard, *Ethics of Liberty*, chaps. 1–4.

7. Mario Attilio Levi, *Political Power in the Ancient World* (1955; New York: Mentor, 1968), 134.

8. For an interesting discussion of what Greek playwrights had to say about questions of higher justice in the context of Western ideas of freedom, see Muller, *Freedom in the Ancient World*, 199–209.

9. Levi, *Political Power*, 9.

10. A modern edition with a libertarian-centered introduction by Charles Hamilton is Franz Oppenheimer, *The State* (1914; New York: Free Life Editions, 1975).

11. The writing of specifically and explicitly libertarian takes on history has been one of the movement's biggest lacuna, lamented by many libertarians. Two works of history that libertarians rely on heavily in telling and interpreting the story of how markets and capitalism were key to Western wealth, and how the industrial revolution was boon, not bane, to the millions it supposedly immiserated are Nathan Rosenberg and L. E. Birdzell Jr., *How The West Grew Rich: The Economic Transformation of the Industrial World* (New York: Basic, 1986); and F. A. Hayek, ed., *Capitalism and the Historians* (Chicago: University of Chicago Press, 1954).

12. Gordon S. Wood, *The Radicalism of the American Revolution* (New York: Vintage, 1991), 13.

13. A modern edition of Trenchard and Gordon's *Cato's Letters* with an informative scholarly apparatus edited by a modern anarcho-libertarian is Ronald Hamowy, ed., *Cato's Letters, or Essays on Liberty, Civil and Religious, and Other Important Subjects, Four Volumes in Two, by John Trenchard and Thomas Gordon* (Indianapolis: LibertyFund, 1995). Among their many protolibertarian insights, the pair of pamphleteers presaged the public choice theory for which James Buchanan won the Nobel Prize in 1986: "[Politicians] all professed to have in view only the publick good; yet every one shewed he only meant his own" (118); and the importance of term limits: "A rotation, therefore, in power and magistracy, is essentially necessary to a free government: It is indeed the thing itself; and constitutes, animates, and informs it, as much as the soul constitutes the man" (423).

14. Quoted in Wood, *Radicalism*, 191.

15. Pauline Maier, in her history of the Declaration of Independence, argues that the text of the various state declarations of independence casts doubt on the extent to which Paine's historical radicalism inspired the move to independence (though he was undoubtedly widely read in the colonies). "State and local resolutions on Independence said nothing about the flaws of the British constitution, or the future of mankind, or the birthday of a new world. . . . the argument for separation from Britain among Americans turned, as it always had, on what the Mother Country did, who was responsible for its actions, and

what implications those considerations carried for the American future." Pauline Maier, *American Scripture: Making the Declaration of Independence* (New York: Knopf, 1997), 90–91.

Paine, unlike most modern libertarians, did not believe in absolutely unrestricted private property ownership. He was upset by income imbalances caused by what he saw as imbalances in occupancy rights on land. While he did not develop a theory of what caused this, he may well have been attracted to the theories of the Benjamin Tuckerites on occupancy as the only measure of ownership; he thought there should be a large-scale inheritance tax to help equalize income. This was not in the way of establishing socialism, but rather, in Paine's mind, of preserving a system of private property ownership by eliminating the tension that system created in allowing income inequalities that could be seen as gross and intolerable. See John Keane, *Tom Paine: A Political Life* (Boston: Little, Brown, 1995), 426–427.

16. Rakove, *Original Meanings*, 293.

17. Quoted in Rakove, *Original Meanings*, 326.

18. A founder of this tradition often looked back on fondly by modern libertarians is John Lilbourne and his Leveller movement. He challenged the power of Parliament's star chambers, thus making himself a popular pamphleteer for liberty from behind bars, and became one of the most popular men in England for his fight against the tyranny of both the House of Lords and Cromwell. For a libertarian reading of the Leveller story, see Jim Powell, *The Triumph of Liberty* (New York: Free Press, 2000), 11–18; and Carl Watner, "'Come What, Come Will!' Richard Overton, Libertarian Leveller," *Journal of Libertarian Studies*, Fall 1980. Watner calls the Levellers "the first modern political movement to embrace the principles of individual liberty to any great extent" (405) and stresses their belief in self-ownership and total religious tolerance.

19. "Jefferson's assertion of the right of revolution summarized succinctly ideas defended and explained at greater length by a long list of seventeenth-century writers that included such prominent figures as John Milton, Algernon Sidney, and John Locke, as well as a host of others, English and Scottish, familiar and obscure, who continued and, in some measure, developed that 'Whig' tradition in the eighteenth century. By the time of the Revolution, those ideas had become, in the generalized form captured by Jefferson, a political orthodoxy whose basic principles colonists could pick up from sermons or newspapers or even schoolbooks without ever reading a systematic work of political theory. The sentiments Jefferson eloquently expressed were, in short, absolutely conventional among Americans of the time." Maier, *American Scripture*, 135.

20. Wood, *Radicalism*, 217. In his history of colonial America, Murray Rothbard discovered an obscure time in Pennsylvania history when, as he interprets it, there was no functioning government at all. As far as he could tell, few complained. See Murray Rothbard, *Conceived in Liberty*, vol. 1, *A New Land, a New People: The American Colonies in the Seventeenth Century* (1975; Auburn, AL: Ludwig von Mises Institute, 1999), 402–411. For an alternate take on dominant beliefs about liberty in American revolutionary times stressing how those steeped in British/American political–legal traditions of the time feared the anarchy of "natural liberty," see John Philip Reid, *The Concept of Liberty in the Age of the American Revolution* (Chicago: University of Chicago Press, 1988), particularly chapters 3–4.

21. While these histories are by no means comprehensive, this author is quite fond of Arthur A. Ekirch Jr., *The Decline of American Liberalism* (1955; New York: Athaneum, 1967); and Robert Higgs, *Crisis and Leviathan: Critical Episodes in the Growth of American Government* (New York: Oxford University Press, 1987), two volumes that libertarians rely on in regard to the decay and downfall of American liberty, including its hows and whys.

22. The most thorough assault on Lincoln's political reputation lately comes from a libertarian economist associated with the Ludwig von Mises Institute, Thomas DiLorenzo, *The Real Lincoln* (New York: Three Rivers, 2003). While not arguing that Lincoln—who suspended habeas corpus and arrested opposition newspaper editors—was any kind of lib-

ertarian hero, other libertarians think that, whatever complicated issues are tied up in the Civil War, it is strategically idiotic for modern libertarians to seem, for whatever reason, to be within miles of showing sympathy for the Confederacy that fought for human slavery as well as state's rights. The complicated issues involve interpretation of rights of secession, the paper merits of the Confederate constitution, and Lincoln's tyrannical means or true motives.

23. For contemporary libertarians celebrating Justice Field, see David Friedman, "Earl Warren in a White Hat," *Liberty,* September 1998; and Damon W. Root, "Unleash the Judges: The Libertarian Case for Judicial Activism," *Reason,* July 2005.

24. Root, "Unleash the Judges," 37.

25. Quoted in D. Friedman, "Earl Warren in a White Hat," 52. The quote is from Justice Field's dissent in the *Munn v. Illinois* (1877) case. Friedman links Field's philosophy not so much with Spencer and Adam Smith as with Andrew Jackson and his fight against special privilege, with the best protection against such privilege being to keep government small and decentralized. For a negative assessment of Field's philosophy and role in late-nineteenth-century jurisprudence, see Robert Green McCloskey, *American Conservatism in the Age of Enterprise, 1865–1910* (1951; New York: Harper Torchbook, 1964), 72–103. When Field summoned the concept of substantive due process, "the Court took the steps that brought the Constitution into line with the new social gospel and remedied the misfortune that the founding fathers had lived too soon to read either Malthus, Ricardo, or William Graham Sumner. Economic liberty, unsheltered by the original document, was granted the protection its apostles demanded" (77).

26. Quoted in Bobby Taylor, "Anti-Imperialism on the Right," *Liberty,* May 1989, 38.

27. Quoted in Taylor, "Anti-Imperialism," 39.

28. Quoted in Taylor, "Anti-Imperialism," 38.

29. Libertarian-leaning economists and historians have taken stabs at the robber baron story as well, painting the histories of such figures as Rockefeller and Carnegie in a more nuanced and positive manner than does the standard high school history version. For examinations of the nature of the robber barons that strive to *not* make it seem as if federal action to curb them was necessary, see Burton W. Folsom Jr., *The Myth of the Robber Barons: A New Look at the Rise of Big Business in America* (Herndon, VA: Young America's Foundation, 1991); and Thomas DiLorenzo, *How Capitalism Saved America* (New York: Crown Forum, 2004).

30. See Paul Johnson, *A History of the American People* (New York: HarperCollins, 1997), 368–369; and Sidney Fine, *Laissez Faire and the General-Welfare State* (1956; Ann Arbor: University of Michigan Press, 1964), 21–23, for details on the states' experience with internal improvements in the early nineteenth century.

31. See Jonathan R. T. Hughes, *The Governmental Habit: Economic Controls from Colonial Time to the Present* (New York: Basic, 1977), for a history of nineteenth-century violations of laissez-faire principles in America.

32. Fine, *Laissez Faire,* 23.

33. Fine, *Laissez Faire,* 96.

34. Ekirch, *Decline of American Liberalism,* 149. Chapter 10 gives more background details on America's post–Civil War turn from laissez-faire to a government that actively helps big business.

35. Kenneth Templeton to Murray Rothbard, March 12, 1958, Murray Rothbard Archive, Ludwig von Mises Institute.

36. Murray Rothbard to Kenneth Templeton, March 25, 1958, MRA, LVMI.

37. For a rare work by an explicitly libertarian historian on the threats to liberty connected with the Civil War, see Jeffrey Rogers Hummel, *Emancipating Slaves, Enslaving Free Men* (Peru, IL: Open Court, 1996).

38. Ralph Raico, "Benjamin Constant," *New Individualist Review* 3, no. 2 (n.d.): 50.

39. Raico, "Benjamin Constant," 47.

40. Raico, "Benjamin Constant," 54.

41. Comte and de Tracy quotes are from Tom Palmer, "The Classical Liberal Theory of Class Conflict" (manuscript in the author's possession), 8. This discussion of the early nineteenth-century French liberal economists as seen by modern libertarians relies on that essay, Leonard P. Liggio, "Charles Dunoyer and French Classical Liberalism," *Journal of Libertarian Studies,* Summer 1977; and Mark Weinburg, "The Social Analysis of Three Early 19th Century French Liberals: Say, Comte, and Dunoyer," *Journal of Libertarian Studies,* Winter 1978. Destutt de Tracy was a favorite thinker of Thomas Jefferson's; see Joyce Appleby, "What Is Still American in the Political Philosophy of Thomas Jefferson?" *William and Mary Quarterly,* April 1982.

42. For the cross-influence of Bastiat and Cobden and Bright, as well as the failures of the French free trade movement in the 1840s, see Dean Russell, *Frederic Bastiat: Ideas and Influence* (Irvington-on-Hudson, NY: Foundation for Economic Education, 1969), chaps. 6–8. For a modern libertarian take on the Cobden/Bright movement, see Powell, *Triumph of Liberty,* 123–130.

43. A classic collection of such parodic writings (along with other types) by Bastiat, brought out by libertarian publisher R. C. Hoiles and with an introduction by Rose Wilder Lane, is Frederic Bastiat, *Social Fallacies (Economic Sophisms)* (Santa Ana, CA: Register, 1944).

44. Quoted in Murray Rothbard, "On Gustave de Molinari," undated, unpublished memo to Volker Fund (from 1950s), 3, 8, MRA, LVMI.

45. Humboldt's political career did not stay true to his radical libertarianism. In 1809, he became director of Germany's Section for Public Worship and Education. He also helped reorganize the nation's public education system and founded the University of Berlin. He *was* later dismissed from his government post for objecting to Metternich's censorship policies. Details on Humboldt's life and career from J. W. Burrow, "Editor's Introduction," in Wilhelm von Humboldt, *The Limits of State Action,* ed. J. W. Burrow (Cambridge: Cambridge University Press, 1969); and Ralph Raico, "Wilhelm von Humboldt," *New Individualist Review,* April 1961.

46. Raico, "Wilhelm von Humboldt," 20.

47. Fine, *Laissez Faire,* 41.

48. Details on Spencer's career from Powell, *Triumph of Liberty,* 268–273; quotes from 272.

49. W. H. Greenleaf, *The British Political Tradition,* vol. 2, *The Ideological Heritage* (London: Methuen, 1983), 48.

50. Auberon Herbert, *The Right and Wrong of Compulsion by the State, and Other Essays,* ed. Eric Mack (Indianapolis: LibertyClassic, 1978), 129.

51. Herbert, *Right and Wrong of Compulsion by the State,* 157 n.

52. Details on Auberon Herbert's thought and career from Eric Mack, introduction to Herbert, *Right and Wrong of Compulsion by the State.* One of Herbert's acolytes, J. Greevz Fisher, is thought by Rothbard to have written the first extended theoretical and practical discussion of the market–anarchist concept of voluntary taxation, which was also Ayn Rand's preferred method of funding government's necessary functions. J. Greevz Fisher, *Voluntary Taxation* (London: Liberty and Property Defence League, 1889).

53. So did many original American revolutionaries themselves. See Bailyn, *Ideological Origins of the American Revolution,* 331: "The antifederalists emerge as the ones who *kept* the faith—the ancient faith so fundamental a part of the ideological origins of the Revolution from which, they argued, the Constitution departed."

54. One writer on modern libertarianism calls the individualist anarchists the "true culture heroes" of modern libertarians. Stephen Newman, *Liberalism at Wit's End: The Libertar-*

ian Revolt Against the Modern State (Ithaca, NY: Cornell University Press, 1984), 24. But David DeLeon, "The American as Anarchist: Social Criticism in the 1960s," *American Quarterly*, December 1973, 529, notes with some validity that modern libertarians are more likely to *mention* these figures than *understand* them, much less be influenced by them directly. The farther one gets in space and time from Murray Rothbard—the major conduit of these individualist anarchists to modern libertarianism—the less likely an early twenty-first-century self-identified libertarian is to have even heard much about them, much less embrace them as ancestors. Even to the extent that modern libertarians do appreciate and honor them, they discover them in a fit of intellectual archaeology, dredging for a usable radical past, after already becoming fascinated with or converted by the modern libertarian synthesis; they were not converted to libertarianism by them.

55. One of the longest modern works on the nineteenth-century individualist anarchists, *Partisans of Freedom* by William O. Reichert, though published in 1976, doesn't discuss their influence on modern anarcho-capitalists like Rothbard. The other standard texts on the individualist anarchists, Eunice Minette Schuster's *Native American Anarchism* (1931) and James J. Martin's *Men Against the State* (1953), were written before the authors could know that the tradition, in however attenuated or evolved a form, would continue. Martin's book became the canonical text for modern libertarian understanding of this part of their intellectual heritage. Martin later became more active in libertarian and historical revisionist causes, and he briefly became head of the History Department at Robert LeFevre's libertarian Rampart College.

56. Proudhon was an interesting thinker who made subtle distinctions between legitimate property, which he considered the root of liberty, and property that is the result of oppression or theft. He thought in the nineteenth-century context that the privileges of kings and classes meant that most existing property is, as his famous saying goes, theft. As a founding father of anarchism of a leftist variety, his and his movement's thought and experiences have some relevance for modern anarcho-capitalists. For the most part, though, the reasons and conclusions of his brand of European communist and syndicalist anarchism are so different from those that play a major role in the American libertarian tradition, and are so often complicated and contradictory, that we will let them pass by here. Peter Marshall has written a thorough book mostly about the Proudhonian tradition, both before and after the man himself, that does glancingly situate the American libertarian anarcho-capitalists in *that* context, and it is worth consulting. See Peter Marshall, *Demanding the Impossible: A History of Anarchism* (London: Fontana, 1993). For the anarcho-capitalists specifically, see 559–565.

57. For a detailed discussion of Puritan antinomianism in an anarchist context, see Eunice Minette Schuster, *Native American Anarchism* (Port Townsend, WA: Loompanics, [1933]), 13–35; David DeLeon, *The American as Anarchist: Reflections on Indigenous Radicalism* (Baltimore: Johns Hopkins University Press, 1978), chap. 1.

58. For more on Noyes and perfectionism, see Schuster, *Native American Anarchism*, 51–58. She notes the prevalent connection in the nineteenth-century context between anarchist and quasi-anarchist politics and the other social ferments of the time, such as "peace, slavery, capital punishment, temperance, and women's rights" (58).

59. For more on the Non-Resistance League, see Schuster, *Native American Anarchism*, 58–86.

60. American anarchist historian James Martin disagreed with Schuster's and DeLeon's (before DeLeon published) tracing of the American anarchist tradition back to these Puritan heretics. "It now appears that the assumption that American anarchism stemmed from Puritan Antinomianism and was associated with the peculiar variety of resistance to the state found in the non-resistant and 'no-government' sentiments of the Garrison school of 'Christian Anarchist' abolitionists is untenable. It is more probable that, rather than being a

derivative of native American conditions, the real source of the anti-statist evidences observed in Antinomianism and other varieties of early colonial dissidence and unrest can be discovered in the radicalism, both religious and socio-economic, already developing in England before the times of Charles I, and which found expression through lower class spokesman at the time of the English Civil War . . . it can be argued quite effectively that the designation 'Christian Anarchist' is really a contradiction in terms, and that religious rebellion along individualist lines can be interpreted as anarchism only under highly specialized circumstances." James J. Martin, *Men Against the State: The Expositors of Individualist Anarchism in America, 1827–1908* (1953; Colorado Springs: Ralph Myles, 1970), viii–ix.

61. For a modern libertarian survey of Garrison's work and career, see Powell, *Triumph of Liberty,* 45–52.

62. For Warren's experience and conclusions about Owen and New Harmony, see Martin, *Men Against the State,* 6–13. See also William O. Reichert, *Partisans of Freedom: A Study in American Anarchism* (Bowling Green, OH: Bowling Green University Popular Press, 1976), 66.

63. In a crude labor theory of value, he identified the time it took to make an object or perform a service as its true cost, and thought that time should more or less trade with time. He asked to be paid in labor notes, where the giver promised to give equal labor to Warren to compensate him for the cost of the item, his labor, plus a 7 percent markup for overhead and shipping. He closed that first Time Store in May 1830, though he thought it had been a perfect success. See Martin, *Men Against the State,* 16–22, for a full account of the first Time Store experiment. Warren also ran a second Time Store during his return to New Harmony in 1842–1844. For details on that Time Store, see 42–45. With the New Harmony Time Store, trying to be a bit more sophisticated in his economics, Warren added consideration for "repugnance" of labor as well as time. See Schuster, *Native American Anarchism,* 97.

64. Quoted in Reichert, *Partisans,* 72.

65. Reichert, *Partisans,* 65.

66. Wm. Gary Kline, *The Individualist Anarchists: A Critique of Liberalism* (Lanham, MD: University Press of America, 1987), 12.

67. Reichert, *Partisans,* 66.

68. It was still active as late as 1875, though the community was now called Smith's Landing. James J. Martin reported that "occasional reports indicated that some of the business transacted by residents continued to be done on the labor exchange principle, and that despite the serious depression then prevailing in the nation at large, labor notes based on corn continued to be honored with little fluctuation from the first estimates made almost thirty years before." Martin, *Men Against the State,* 64. Warren himself, though he never visited Utopia after 1856, declared that as an experiment it "worked to our satisfaction." Quoted in 64. See 56–64 for a full account of the Utopia experiment.

69. Martin, *Men Against the State,* 54–55.

70. See Madeleine B. Stern, *The Pantarch: A Biography of Stephen Pearl Andrews* (Austin: University of Texas Press, 1968), 34–38, for details on Andrews's early Texas days.

71. See Stern, *Pantarch,* 36–51, for the whole saga of Andrews's attempt to sell Texas to Great Britain in the name of abolitionism.

72. Quoted in Reichert, *Partisans,* 82.

73. See Reichert, *Partisans,* 86, for a discussion of Andrews's views on market competition.

74. The intersection of nineteenth-century anarchism and other outré—not to say cranky—beliefs is interesting. Spiritualism was as common as pro-suffrage, pro-free thought attitudes among many of them. In 1879, Andrews and Ezra Heywood helped form a multifront Union Reform League uniting adherents of every form of radical social

thought of the day, including Andrews's bugaboo of adopting a new, simpler language. See Martin, *Men Against the State*, 164–165.

75. Quoted in Reichert, *Partisans*, 75.

76. Comte himself was not surprised by Edgar's failure to find recruits at Modern Times. As he wrote to his disciple, "Conversions will be rare in your anarchical village. You should devote your attention above all to conservatives, who are . . . the most likely converts to positivism." Quoted in Martin, *Men Against the State*, 79.

77. See Martin, *Men Against the State*, 65–87, for a detailed history of the Modern Times experiment.

78. Stern, *Pantarch*, 149. Modern historians of anarchy like Schuster, Martin, and Reichert mostly slough over these more entertaining details of Andrews's checkered career. For a sense of the full range of peculiarities of Andrews's life and career, and such curious details as speculations about the "abnormally large" size of his "bump of amativeness" (83), one must go to Stern. Details on Universology and the Pantarchy in Stern, *Pantarch*, chaps. 8–10.

79. Reichert, *Partisans*, 96. See also Stern, *Pantarch*, 114–115 for a discussion of the First International's alarmed reaction to the Universologists in their midst.

80. Martin, *Men Against the State*, 100.

81. Quoted in Charles H. Hamilton, "The Evolution of a Subversive Tradition," in Michael E. Coughlin, Charles H. Hamilton, and Mark A. Sullivan, eds., *Benjamin R. Tucker and the Champions of Liberty* (St. Paul, Minn.: Michael E. Coughlin and Mark Sullivan, n.d.), 6.

82. Martin, *Men Against the State*, 114.

83. See Martin Blatt, "Ezra Heywood and Benjamin R. Tucker," in Coughlin et al., eds., *Benjamin R. Tucker*, 36–41, for a good detailing of Heywood's various Comstock prosecutions. In a later Comstock prosecution, Heywood indulged in a grand proto-Randian gesture: defending himself in court with a four-and-a-half-hour speech. Like Roark in *The Fountainhead*, he won his acquittal.

84. Reichert, *Partisans*, 143.

85. Martin, *Men Against the State*, 269.

86. A collection of de Cleyre's writings edited by a modern libertarian feminist is Sharon Presley and Crispin Sartwell, eds., *Exquisite Rebel: The Essays of Voltairine de Cleyre: Feminist, Anarchist, Genius* (Albany: State University of New York Press, 2005). Presley wrote of de Cleyre for an explicitly modern libertarian audience in "Liberty's Heritage: Voltairine De Cleyre," *Libertarian Review*, March 1979.

87. Rothbard revived this Tuckerism for his column in the late 1970s in *Libertarian Review*, "The Plumb Line."

88. "Anarchism knew in him its bitterest enemy," Tucker wrote in his Marx eulogy, "and yet every anarchist must hold his memory in respect. Strangely mixed feelings of admiration and abhorrence are simultaneously inspired in us by contemplation of this great man's career. . . . Intense as was his love of equality, no less so was his hatred of liberty." Benjamin Tucker, "Karl Marx as Friend and Foe," in Frank H. Brooks, ed., *The Individualist Anarchists: An Anthology of Liberty (1881–1908)* (New Brunswick, NJ: Transaction, 1994), 96–97.

89. Brooks, ed., *Individualist Anarchists*, 76.

90. Quoted in Martin, *Men Against the State*, 224.

91. The Haymarket incident and its aftermath have been the most studied and written about aspect of American anarchism. For a discussion of it in the context of the individualist anarchist tradition discussed here, see Reichert, *Partisans*, 216–230.

92. Tucker once wrote, "I would use dynamite if I thought that thereby I could best help the cause of freedom." Elsewhere he wrote that "violence, like every other policy, is

advisable when it will accomplish the desired end and inadvisable when it will not."
Quoted in Reichert, *Partisans*, 155.

93. Joshua K. Ingalls, another Massachusetts man and general-interest reformer also into
temperance and Samuel Graham's curious dietary theories, was the most influential individualist anarchist author on land issues. He contended that occupancy and use constituted the only legitimate claim for land ownership. He wrote on such matters in Tucker's
publications, and his beliefs dominated individualist anarchist thinking on land. See Martin, *Men Against the State*, 139–152, for a full explication of Ingalls's life and thought. See
also Reichert, *Partisans*, 509–511, on Ingalls.

94. For expositions on William B. Greene's banking theories, see Reichert, *Partisans*,
109–114; Schuster, 128–135; and Martin, 125–138.

95. "A greater equality than is compatible with liberty is undesirable," Tucker wrote.
"The moment we invade liberty to secure equality we enter upon a road which knows no
stopping-place short of the annihilation of all that is best in the human race. If absolute
equality is the ideal; if no man must have the slightest advantage over another, then the
man who achieves greater results through superiority of muscle or skill or brain must not
be allowed to enjoy them. All that he produces in excess of that which the weakest and
stupidest produce must be taken from him and distributed among his fellows. The economic rent, not of land only, but of strength and skill and intellect and superiority of every
kind, must be confiscated. And a beautiful world it would be when absolute equality had
been thus achieved! Who would live in it? Certainly no freeman. . . . Liberty will ultimately make all men rich; it will not make all men equally rich." Quoted in Brooks, ed.,
Individualist Anarchists, 156–157.

96. Benjamin Tucker, "State Socialism and Anarchism: How Far They Agree, and
Wherein They Differ," in Brooks, ed., *Individualist Anarchists*, 86.

97. Schuster, *Native American Anarchism*, 88.

98. Quoted in Schuster, *Native American Anarchism*, 31.

99. See Benjamin Tucker, "The Sin of Herbert Spencer," in Brooks, ed., *Individualist Anarchists*, 45, for Tucker's critique of Spencer. For a good discussion of all the English individualists and *Liberty*, see Carl Watner, "The English Individualists As They Appear in
Liberty," in Coughlin et al., eds., *Benjamin R. Tucker*. For another account of how and why
the writers of *Liberty* began rejecting Spencer, see Martin, *Men Against the State*, 238–241.

100. Quoted in Charles T. Sprading, ed., *Liberty and the Great Libertarians* (1913; San
Francisco: Fox & Wilkes, 1995), 111.

101. One might argue that Stirner pushed a reductionist vision of what it meant to be a
strong individual ego. Surely feeling a strong commitment to moral values can be an individual ego's choice as much as rejecting them.

102. Wendy McElroy, "The Non-Economic Debates in *Liberty*," in Coughlin et al., eds.,
Benjamin R. Tucker, 133. As McElroy notes, Tucker later realized this problem with the
rights-created-only-by-contract argument.

103. As Tucker wrote, "Reform communities will either be recruited from the salt of
the earth, and then their success will not be taken as conclusive, because it will be said that
their principles are applicable only among men and women well-nigh perfect; or, with
these elect, will be a large admixture of semi-lunatics among whom, when separated from
the great mass of mankind and concentrated by themselves, society will be unendurable,
practical work impossible, and Anarchy as chaotic as it is generally supposed to be. But in
some large city fairly representative of the varied interests and characteristics of our heterogeneous civilization let a sufficiently large number of earnest and intelligent Anarchists,
engaged in nearly all the different trades and professions, combine to carry on their production and distribution on the cost principle and to start a bank through which they can
obtain a non-interest-bearing currency for the conduct of their commerce and dispose

their steadily accumulating capital in new enterprises, the advantages of this system of affairs being open to all who should choose to offer their patronage,—what would be the result? Why, soon the whole composite population, wise and unwise, good, bad, and indifferent, would become interested in what was going on under their very eyes, more and more of them would actually take part in it, and in a few years, each man reaping the fruit of his labor and no man able to live in idleness on an income from capital, the whole city would become a great hive of Anarchistic workers, prosperous and free individuals. It is such results as this that I look forward to, and it is for the accomplishment of such that I work. . . . I care nothing for any reform that cannot be affected right here in Boston among the every-day people whom I meet upon the streets." Quoted in Brooks, ed., *Individualist Anarchists*, 275–276.

Tucker's idea was to create shadow economic institutions within the modern industrialized world to achieve a working anarchy for those who wanted to live in it while avoiding the monopoly evils of currency and land, and it inspired the "agorist" movement in modern libertarianism, whose linchpin was Samuel E. Konkin III. The agorist movement condemns as a useless sellout of principle the political and policy machinations of the likes of the Libertarian Party and the Cato Institute. See Morgan Edwards, "Neither Bombs Nor Bullets: *Liberty* and the Strategy of Anarchism," in Coughlin et al., eds., *Benjamin R. Tucker*, 84.

104. Schuster, *Native American Anarchism*, 157.

105. Quoted in Watner in Coughlin et al., eds., *Benjamin R. Tucker*, 208.

106. See Schuster, *Native American Anarchism*, 173–177, for a brief discussion of the federal police war on anarchists in this period. See 180 for a list of suppressive public reactions against anarchists throughout American history.

107. Quoted in Hamilton in Coughlin et al., eds., *Benjamin R. Tucker*, 2. This sense of deep depression can be found in many libertarian agitators, looking back on a life that on some level can be seen as futile so long as the state continues to thrive.

108. Martin, *Men Against the State*, 167.

109. Martin, *Men Against the State*, 170.

110. Reichert, *Partisans*, 118–119.

111. Spooner also reportedly planned to kidnap the governor of Virginia and ransom him off for John Brown after Brown's attack on Harper's Ferry. See Reichert, *Partisans*, 122.

112. Lysander Spooner, *The Lysander Spooner Reader*, ed. George H. Smith (San Francisco: Fox & Wilkes, 1992), 51.

113. For a compact discussion of Garrison's life and career in a libertarian context, see Powell, *Triumph of Liberty*, 45–52. See also Schuster, *Native American Anarchism*, 61–65.

114. Spooner, *Lysander Spooner Reader*, 49. Disdain for Lincoln and a hint of sympathy on the right of secession (*only*; no support for slavery) has been a thread found in many libertarian writers ever since, though getting thinner as the years go by and the standard zeitgeist sees, any such sympathy as a sign of racism.

115. See Martin, *Men Against the State*, 175–180, for a discussion of Spooner's writings and agitation on finance matters.

116. This idea of jury power and responsibility has come on hard times in the modern American context, though it was widely accepted as true in early America. See Rakove, *Original Meanings*, 300. But the Supreme Court has seen it necessary, in *Sparf and Hanson v. United States* (1895), to insist the jury does *not* have that right. See Michael E. Coughlin, "The Jury: Defender or Oppressor," in Coughlin et al., eds., *Benjamin R. Tucker*, 49. In modern America jurors have been prosecuted for trying to exercise that power deliberately. A libertarian agitation group, the Fully Informed Jury Amendment, today proselytizes to inform jurors of their right to decide whatever they want, judging both the facts and the law as they please.

117. The secret ballot drew special derision from Spooner. "What is the motive of the secret ballot? This, and only this: Like other confederates in crime, those who use it are not friends, but enemies; and they are afraid to be known, and to have their individual doings known, even to each other. . . . This is avowedly the only reason for the ballot: for a secret government, a government by secret bands of robbers and murderers. And we are insane enough to call this liberty! To be a member of this secret band of robbers and murderers is esteemed a privilege and an honor! Without this privilege, a man is considered a slave; but with it a free man! With it he is considered a free man, because he has the same power to secretly (by secret ballot) procure the robbery, enslavement, and murder of another man, that that other man has to procure his robbery, enslavement, and murder. And this they call equal rights!" Spooner, *Spooner Reader,* 89–90.

118. Spooner, *Spooner Reader,* 78.

119. A thorough website dedicated to Spooner is run by libertarian anarchist legal philosopher Randy Barnett, and can be found at www.lysanderspooner.org.

120. For a reasonably thorough account of the small individualist anarchist periodicals that kept the faith after Tucker and until World War II, see Reichert, *Partisans,* pt. 3, chap. 4. Though Reichert wrote in the 1970s and continued his history of American anarchism past Tucker to communist anarchists such as Emma Goldman and Alexander Berkman, and postwar figures like Paul Goodman, he did not recognize or even mention Rothbard and modern libertarians as heirs of the Tuckerite individualist anarchist tradition. For insight on those connections, see DeLeon, *American as Anarchist,* chaps. 5–8. DeLeon recognizes and traces the connections between the Tucker tradition and the rising Rothbardian anarcho-capitalism of the 1960s and 1970s.

121. Rothbard called Spooner and Tucker "unsurpassed as political philosophers . . . nothing is more needed today than a revival and development of the largely forgotten legacy that they left to political philosophy." In Murray N. Rothbard, *Egalitarianism as a Revolt Against Nature and Other Essays* (Washington, DC: Libertarian Review Press, 1974), 125. However, he discovered them while looking for forefathers for what he had already come to believe; they were no conversion experience for him.

122. Rothbard discussed his differences with Tucker and Spooner on land and currency issues in Rothbard, *Egalitarianism,* 128–135.

123. Kline, *Individualist Anarchists,* 104. Kline's thesis is that the individualist anarchists were not radicals breaking with standard American liberalism, were not presenting a critique of the American tradition, but were merely an anomalously pure expression of it.

124. Quoted in Robert M. Crunden, *The Mind and Art of Albert Jay Nock* (Chicago: Henry Regnery, 1964), 18.

125. Nock was a friend of young Buckley's father and an occasional guest in the family home. Buckley biographer John Judis says that Nock's *Memoirs of a Superfluous Man* was Buckley's favorite book, and that "Nock's view of society and the state and of democracy and politics would run through Bill's politics over the next four decades." John Judis, *William F. Buckley, Jr.: Patron Saint of the Conservatives* (New York: Touchstone, 1990 [1988]), 46. Be that as it may, Buckley was never as anarchistic, as opposed to modernity, or as anti-war as Nock. Nock's elegant anti-authoritarianism was something Buckley may have aspired to; in reality, he went for the plums of influence and respectability that Nock always eschewed.

126. Michael Wreszin, *The Superfluous Anarchist: Albert Jay Nock* (Providence: Brown University Press, 1971), 150.

127. For more on Nock on this state/government distinction, see Albert Jay Nock, *Our Enemy, The State* (1935; New York: Free Life Editions, 1977), 19–22.

128. Wreszin, *Superfluous Anarchist,* 4.

129. Albert Jay Nock, *The Book of Journeyman: Essays from the New Freeman* (New York: Publishers of the New Freeman, 1930), 73–74.

130. For an overview of Nock's early life, education, and ministry, see Wreszin, *Superfluous Anarchist*, 8–17; and Crunden, *Mind and Art,* 4–11.

131. Frank Chodorov, *Out of Step: The Autobiography of an Individualist* (New York: Devin-Adair, 1962), 144.

132. Crunden, *Mind and Art,* 36. The editors of *The American* in their mission statement said they wanted the magazine to "reflect a happy, struggling, fighting world, in which, as we believe, good people are coming out on top." Quoted in Crunden, 45.

133. Crunden, *Mind and Art,* 40.

134. Michael Wreszin, *Oswald Garrison Villard: Pacifist at War* (Bloomington: Indiana University Press, 1965), 147.

135. Details on this in Wreszin, *Oswald Garrison Villard,* 97–98. Wreszin says that Villard "was secretly delighted at this public proof of his charge that freedom of the press was dead in America" (97).

136. Crunden, *Mind and Art,* 58.

137. Crunden, *Mind and Art,* 94.

138. Wreszin, *Superfluous Anarchist,* 54.

139. Susan Turner, who wrote a book about the Nock *Freeman,* stated: "That a magazine which is intrinsically so good and so representative of a turning point in American cultural history should have won such minor notice from literary and cultural historians is puzzling." Lewis Mumford once wrote to Van Wyck Brooks that a *Freeman* essay of Brooks's made him fall in love with America, and said Nock's *Freeman* was one of the four major American intellectual magazines of its time, along with the *Dial,* the *Nation,* and the *New Republic.* Quoted from a memo prepared for the Liberty Fund by Charles Hamilton on the history of the *Freeman,* whose purpose was to convince them to republish the magazine's entire run in book form. (It failed to do so.) Memo, Institute for Humane Studies Archives, Charles Hamilton folder.

140. Crunden, *Mind and Art,* 72.

141. Charles H. Hamilton, foreword in Albert Jay Nock, *The State of the Union: Essays in Social Criticism,* ed. Charles H. Hamilton (Indianapolis: LibertyPress, 1991), xix.

142. After his wife's death, Francis Neilson became quite bilious on the subject of Albert Jay Nock. Neilson wrote a long journal article on the history of the *Freeman* in which he obliquely accused Nock of stealing his writings wholesale and directly accused him of being a painfully ignorant, oversexed, scheming double-dealer who didn't know how to sit up properly at the dining table. Francis Neilson, "The Story of The Freeman," *American Journal of Sociology,* October 1946 (supplement).

143. See Wreszin, *Superfluous Anarchist,* 114–125, for an extended discussion of Cram and his influence on Nock.

144. "The idea that [literacy] is an absolute good is one of the oddest and most indefensible superstitions rampant in our superstition-ridden society. To prove this, one has but to look at what our literates mostly read, and what their reading habits are." In Nock, *Book of Journeyman,* 18. Nock repeated this notion frequently.

145. Nock, *State of the Union,* 133. This attitude so infected some early libertarian institutions that one of them, the Institute for Humane Studies, had employees who believed that they should not even have a listed phone number.

146. Henry George has sadly thin secondary literature explaining and contextualizing his work and the movement it inspired. One decent one, mostly dedicated to discussing how various other schools of thought dealt with George, is Steven B. Cord, *Henry George: Dreamer or Realist?* (Philadelphia: University of Pennsylvania Press, 1965).

147. This distinction has remained a favorite of libertarians ever since, and Oppen-heimer's *The State* was brought back into print in the 1970s by a specifically libertarian-anarchist publishing house, Free Life Editions.

148. Albert Jay Nock, *Journal of Forgotten Days, May 1934–October 1935* (Hinsdale, IL: Henry Regnery, 1948), 94.

149. See the unsigned preface to Nock, *Letters from Albert Jay Nock*, 7–9, for details on his relationship to the Evans family, major supporters of Nock's final decades.

150. Abraham Ellis, interview by author, October 12, 1998.

151. Nock, *Book of Journeyman*, 38.

152. Nock, *Letters from Albert Jay Nock*, 75

153. Albert Jay Nock, *Free Speech and Plain Language* (New York: William Morrow, 1937), 168–169.

154. Nock, *Free Speech,* 275.

155. Nock called FDR's death "the biggest public improvement that America has expe-rienced since the passage of the Bill of Rights." In Nock, *Letters from Albert Jay Nock*, 211.

156. Nock, *Journal of Forgotten Days*, 29–30.

157. Nock, *Book of Journeyman*, 139.

158. Nock, *Letters from Albert Jay Nock*, 171.

159. Nock, *Letters from Albert Jay Nock*, 95.

160. Nock, *Letters from Albert Jay Nock*, 105.

161. Nock, *Journal of Forgotten Days*, 33.

162. Nock, *Memoirs*, 25.

163. Crunden, *Mind and Art of Nock*, 39.

164. Walter E. Grinder, introduction to Nock, *Our Enemy, The State*, xxv.

165. Sheldon Richman, "New Deal Nemesis: The 'Old Right' Jeffersonians," *Indepen-dent Review*, Fall 1996, 202.

166. For a fair, though not ultimately sympathetic, look at the history, goals, and failures of the Liberty League, see George Wolfskill, *The Revolt of the Conservatives: A History of the American Liberty League, 1934–1940* (Boston: Houghton Mifflin, 1962). Also Frederick Rudolph, "The American Liberty League, 1934–1940," *American Historical Review*, Octo-ber 1950, featured a measured take, which summed it up this way: "The Liberty League was as indigenously American as the New Deal which it was determined to destroy. Its unsuccessful efforts to unseat Franklin Roosevelt, its philosophy and program, the tech-niques which it used in order to survive as long as it did—these are not the materials of an un-American movement. . . . The Liberty League represented a vigorous and well-stated defense of nineteenth century individualism and liberalism, a more explicit and deter-mined elaboration of that position than will be found elsewhere in American history. . . . there was too much of a thoroughly American character in the movement to permit the conclusion that it was an unimportant, flash-in-the-pan combination of undercover polit-ical party and overt pressure group" (20–21). For a modern libertarian writing on its his-tory and noting the lack of pure laissez-faire bona fides on the part of the businessmen who financed and ran the Liberty League, see Sheldon Richman, "A Matter of Degree, Not Principle: The Founding of the American Liberty League," *Journal of Libertarian Stud-ies*, Spring 1982.

167. While often lumped in with other anti–New Dealers and anti-interventionists as a proto–libertarian old righter, the Flynn portrayed in the most recent and most thorough book about him, John E. Moser, *Right Turn: John T. Flynn and the Transformation of American Liberalism* (New York: New York University Press, 2005), shows a powerful yen for state in-tervention in the economy to halt what he saw as the depredations of unrestricted capital-ism. By the end of his career, principled noninterventionism had morphed into an obsession with stopping communism in the Far East.

168. See his essay "The Revolution Was," in Garet Garrett, *The People's Pottage* (Caldwell, ID: Caxton, 1953).

169. See Justin Raimondo, *Reclaiming the American Right* (Burlingame, CA: Center for Libertarian Studies, 1993), 58, 66–67 for some of Garrett's heresies from a libertarian perspective regarding autarchy and immigration.

170. John Chamberlain, *The Turnabout Years: America's Cultural Life, 1900–1950* (Ottowa, IL: Jameson, 1991), 39.

171. Quoted in Murray Rothbard, "H. L. Mencken: The Joyous Libertarian," *New Individualist Review*, Summer 1962, 27. Rothbard was sure he detected Mencken's obvious sympathy with sometimes obscure anarchists from the nineteenth century in a book of quotations edited by Mencken, since he included entries from the likes of Tucker, Stirner, and Sumner.

172. Barnes had some well-known supporters; Papa Joe Kennedy once wrote him a congratulatory note: "Your summary of the rapid drift towards Socialism under the screen of war psychology is the best I have seen. . . . I admire your courage in continuing the fight." Joseph Kennedy to Harry Elmer Barnes, January 26, 1951. Institute for Humane Studies Archives, Barnes folder.

173. Martin, in his attempt to adjust standard historical understandings of war and war guilt, shifted into questioning the veracity of standard anti-German atrocity stories, including the standard details of the Holocaust. This unfortunate shading over into Hitler apologetics has stained the term "revisionism" with one particular offshoot of it, "Holocaust revisionism." They are not coterminous, though it is true that some World War II revisionists also shaded into Holocaust revisionism. Martin discussed his doubts about the standard Holocaust story in "Introducing Revisionism: An Interview with James J. Martin," *Reason,* January 1976, 16: "I don't believe that the evidence of a planned extermination of the entire Jewish population of Europe is holding up." A current Holocaust revisionist group had adopted Barnes's name for one of its magazines, *Barnes Review.*

174. Childe on the definitions of magic and religion quoted in Muller, *Freedom in the Ancient World,* 10. In pragmatic terms, ancient eastern theocracy of the Egyptian variety is the type of state that seemed to "work" best; it lasted for many thousands of years.

175. For a modern liberal's complaint about how Flynn's work was propagandistically spread in the early 1950s by right-wing pressure groups, see Karl Schriftgeisser, *The Lobbyists: The Art and Business of Influencing Lawmakers* (Boston: Little, Brown, 1951), 205–206.

176. Sheldon Richman pointed out that by the time Mencken's edited diaries were released in 1989, most standard American literary intellectuals reviewing it could not figure out where Mencken was coming from. The old right was so dead that even well-educated people had no idea that, as recently as forty years ago, people with such outrageous ideas as being opposed to FDR and World War II really walked the earth, much less that so revered, if dimly remembered, a name as Mencken could have been one of them. Richman, "New Deal Nemesis," 201–202.

CHAPTER 2

1. F. A. Hayek, introduction to Carl Menger, *Principles of Economics* (1871; Grove City, PA: Libertarian, 1994), 15.

2. Hayek, introduction, 16.

3. It is always difficult to be certain that any apparent innovator is a real first. It is settled intellectual history that the three "inventors" of marginalism were not directly influenced by (or, less charitably, did not steal from) each other; see Richard S. Howey, *The Rise of the Marginal Utility School* (1960; New York: Columbia University Press, 1989), 215–216. Scholars have traced back many of the subjectivist and marginalist innovations of Menger,

Jevons, and Walras to precursors both far and near. See Murray N. Rothbard, "New Light on the Prehistory of the Austrian School," in Edwin G. Dolan, ed., *The Foundations of Austrian Economics* (Kansas City: Sheed & Ward, 1976); Alexander H. Shand, *The Capitalist Alternative: An Introduction to Neo-Austrian Economics* (New York: New York University Press, 1984), 46; Erich W. Streissler, "The Influence of German Economics on the Work of Menger and Marshall," in Bruce J. Caldwell, ed., *Carl Menger and His Legacy in Economics* (Durham, NC: Duke University Press, 1990); Erich W. Streissler, "German Predecessors of the Austrian School," in Peter J. Boettke, ed., *The Elgar Companion to Austrian Economics* (Brookfield, VT: Edward Elgar, 1994); Ludwig von Mises, *Human Action: A Treatise on Economics,* 3rd rev. ed. (1949; San Francisco: Laissez-Faire, 1990), 219.

4. See Erich W. Steissler, "To What Extent Was the Austrian School Marginalist?" *History of Political Economy,* Fall 1972; and Karen Vaughn, *Austrian Economics in America: The Migration of a Tradition* (Cambridge: Cambridge University Press, 1994), chap. 2, for an analysis of the unique aspects of Menger that led to the distinctive Austrian style of economics.

5. The connections between the Austrian school of economics and classical liberalism are explored in Ralph Raico, "The Austrian School and Classical Liberalism," *Advances in Austrian Economics,* vol. 2A, 1995.

6. Erich W. Streissler, "Carl Menger on Economic Policy: The Lectures to Crown Prince Rudolf," in Caldwell, ed., *Carl Menger and His Legacy.*

7. Menger's own book-length contribution to the debate was Carl Menger, *Investigations into the Method of the Social Sciences* (1883; Grove City, PA: Libertarian Press, 1990). For a modern interpretation of the *Methodenstreit* cognizant of post-Mengerian developments in Austrian economics, see Bruce Caldwell, *Hayek's Challenge: An Intellectual Biography of F.A. Hayek* (Chicago: University of Chicago Press, 2004), chap. 3.

8. Ludwig von Mises, *Ludwig von Mises, Notes and Recollections* (Spring Mills, PA: Libertarian Press, 1978), 35.

9. Wieser's credit for the term comes, appropriately enough for an Austrian economist, through a roundabout method of production: Wieser used the German term *Grenznutzen,* which was his German translation of Jevons's term for the concept of terminal utility. When Wicksteed translated Wieser into English, he translated it as "marginal utility." Howey, *Rise of the Marginal Utility School,* 145–146.

10. Details on Wieser's life and thought from F. A. Hayek, *The Fortunes of Liberalism: Essays on Austrian Economics and the Ideal of Freedom,* ed. Peter G. Klein (Chicago: University of Chicago Press, 1992), chap. 3; also Jacob Oser and William C. Blanchfield, *The Evolution of Economic Thought,* 3rd ed. (New York: Harcourt Brace Jovanovich, 1975), 241–246.

11. Hayek, *Fortunes of Liberalism,* 29. Mises thought Wieser "never really understood the gist of the idea of Subjectivism in the Austrian School of thought" (Mises, *Notes and Recollections,* 36). Mises also objected to Wieser's calculation of the total value of an object as a multiple of marginal value times the number of available units. To Mises, value represents nothing more than a rank ordering of possibilities made by an individual at a given point in time. It is necessarily ephemeral and represents nothing more than a position in a list of options—an ordinal number, not a cardinal one (cardinal being the kind that can be added, subtracted, multiplied, or divided—the difference between "being fifth" and the number five. You can add five and five; you cannot add "being fifth" to anything else meaningfully.).

12. As one history of economic thought text summed up the Böhm-Bawerkian message, "In brief, interest *can* be paid by the entrepreneur, because the more roundabout the process of production, the more productive and efficient it becomes. Interest *must* be paid because people prefer present to future consumption." Oser and Blanchfield, *Evolution of Economic Thought,* 247.

13. See Leland B. Yeager, "An Interview," *Austrian Economics Newsletter*, 9: "The interest rate is determined by interaction between time preference and productivity of roundaboutness. I don't know why this view should be considered anti-Austrian. Böhm-Bawerk and Hayek explicitly recognized both time-preference and productivity. I don't quite understand how the pure subjectivist or pure time-preference theory came to be regarded as a key part of Austrian doctrine. . . . Maybe people thought that since subjectivism is good, the more subjectivism the better."

14. An understandable explanation of the Misesian pure time preference theory is in Israel Kirzner, "The Pure Time Preference Theory of Interest: An Attempt at Clarification," in Jeffrey M. Herbener, ed., *The Meaning of Ludwig von Mises: Contributions in Economics, Sociology, Epistemology, and Political Philosophy* (Norwell, MA: Kluwer, 1993). American economist Frank Fetter independently developed the same idea, evolving from a similar Böhm-Bawerkian background; see Gerald P. O'Driscoll, "Frank A. Fetter and 'Austrian' Business Cycle Theory," *History of Political Economy*, Winter 1980; and Murray N. Rothbard, introduction to Frank A. Fetter, *Capital, Interest, and Rent: Essays in the Theory of Distribution* (Kansas City: Sheed Andrews & McMeel, 1977).

15. Quoted in Ludwig M. Lachmann, *The Market as an Economic Process* (New York: Basil Blackwell, 1986), 23. A good example of how Mises critiqued his masters, Menger and Böhm-Bawerk, for certain failures to be sufficiently subjectivist in their analysis is in Ludwig von Mises, *Epistemological Problems of Economics* (1960; New York: New York University Press, 1981), chap. 5.

16. Details on Böhm-Bawerk's attack on Marxian value theory from Caldwell, *Hayek's Challenge*, 102–106. Böhm-Bawerk quote from 103.

17. Quoted in Peter J. Boettke, "Why Are There No Austrian Socialists? Ideology, Science, and the Austrian School," *Journal of the History of Economic Thought*, Spring 1995, 37.

18. Mises, *Notes and Recollections*, 37. Mises biographer Jorg Guido Hulsmann says the same is true of Mises himself. "Mises made no efforts to stimulate discipleship, and in fact had no disciples during his Vienna years. . . . Steeped in the idealism of Schiller, Herder, and other classical German authors, Mises considered the free development of the individual to be the supreme goal of human achievement. . . . After 1926, when he succeeded Wieser as the main contact of the Rockefeller Foundation in Vienna. . . . he did not use this power to raise epigones. Noble as this attitude was, it gave a competitive edge to some of his rivals who didn't have the same scruples." Jorg Guido Hulsmann, "The Last Knight of Liberalism: An Intellectual Biography of Ludwig von Mises" (unpublished manuscript in author's possession), 384.

19. Mises was actually the first member of his family to be born with the "von" attached, a family honorific that began when Ludwig's great-grandfather was ennobled just before Ludwig was born and thus was automatically attached to his descendants. Noble titles were abolished in Austria in 1918, and consequently he was legally merely "Ludwig Mises." However, he continued to use the "von" in his professional writings. Hulsmann, *Last Knight*, 6, 22.

20. Hulsmann, *Last Knight*, 11.

21. This first book of Mises's has not been translated into English, though its English title would be *The Development of the Relationship Between Peasant and Lord of the Manor in Galicia, 1772–1848* (1902).

22. Details on Mises's early life from Margit von Mises, *My Years with Ludwig von Mises*, 2nd enl. ed. (1976; Cedar Falls, IA: Center for Futures Education, 1984), 199–201; Eamonn Butler, *Ludwig von Mises: Fountainhead of the Modern Microeconomics Revolution* (Brookfield, VT: Gower, 1988), 7–8; Murray N. Rothbard, *Ludwig von Mises: Scholar, Creator, Hero* (Auburn, AL: Ludwig von Mises Institute, 1988), 7–11; details on chamber of

commerce in Mises, *Notes and Recollections*, 6, 71–72. Mises's relentless liberalism wasn't so much heeded at the chamber; "Mises would always stress that all of his influence was through literary work and public lectures. The monetary stabilization of 1922 was the only time official policy met with his approval." Hulsmann, *Last Knight,* 379.

23. Mises, *Notes and Recollections*, 30–31.

24. Mises, *Notes and Recollections*, 66.

25. Hayek, *Fortunes of Liberalism*, 132.

26. Hayek, *Fortunes of Liberalism*, 133.

27. It is commonly thought that Mises's social rationalism, his tracing of all human action to conscious individual choice, leaves no room for Hayek's evolutionary sociology based on human action having results that man could not have intended. For an exposition on this viewpoint, see Joseph T. Salerno, "Mises as Social Rationalist," in Herbener, ed., *Meaning of Mises.*

At times Mises sounds more Hayekian. He seems to appeal to Hayek's notion (before Hayek) of societies as surviving through evolutionary struggle: "More highly developed societies attain greater material wealth than the less highly developed; therefore they have more prospect of preserving their members from misery." Ludwig von Mises, *Socialism* (1922; Indianapolis: LibertyClassics, 1981), 272. He also presages the Hayekian notion of reason as being coterminous with civilization: "The development of human reason and the development of human society are one and the same process" (Mises, *Socialism*, 258). He seems to embrace the Hayekian notion that overarching social structures arise unbidden from individual purposes: "Men who create peace and standards of conduct are only concerned to provide for the needs of the coming hours, days, years; that they are, at the same time, working to build a great structure like human society, escapes their notice. Therefore the individual institutions, which collectively support the social organism, are created with no other view in mind than the utility of the moment" (Mises, *Socialism*, 467). Also: "The market economy was not designed by a master mind; it was not first planned as a utopian scheme and then put to work. Spontaneous actions of individuals, aiming at nothing else than at the improvement of their own state of satisfaction, undermined the prestige of the coercive status system step by step," in Ludwig von Mises, *The Ultimate Foundations of Economic Science: An Essay on Method* (1962; Kansas City: Sheed Andrews & McMeel, 1978), 109. Also: "The individual does not plan and execute actions intended to construct society. His conduct and the corresponding conduct of others generate social bodies" (Mises, *Human Action*, 188). The distinction between Mises the rationalist and Hayek the irrationalist evolutionist is not as clear-cut as some make it.

28. A reasonably thorough look at the many precursors to Mises's role in the socialist calculation debate and their specific contributions can be found in Richard Ebeling, "Economic Calculation Under Socialism: Ludwig von Mises and His Predecessors," in Herbener, ed., *Meaning of Mises.*

29. Quoted in Alan Ebenstein, *Friedrich Hayek: A Biography* (New York: Palgrave, 2001), 90.

30. The chandelier detail from Alec Nove, *The Soviet Economy: An Introduction* (New York: Praeger, 1961), 157.

31. This is one of the most discussed and most hotly debated elements of Mises's thought, with two books written on the subject alone. See Don Lavoie, *Rivalry and Central Planning: The Socialist Calculation Debate Reconsidered* (Cambridge: Cambridge University Press, 1985); and David Ramsey Steele, *From Marx to Mises: Post-Capitalist Society and the Challenge of Economic Calculation* (LaSalle, IL: Open Court, 1992).

32. Peter Boettke, interview by author, February 10, 1997.

33. Steele, *Marx to Mises*, 107.

34. Steele, *Marx to Mises*, 2.

35. Hayek's classic essay on the role of local knowledge and the price system is "The Use of Knowledge in Society," which can be found in Chiaki Nishiyama and Kurt R. Leube, eds., *The Essence of Hayek* (Stanford: Hoover Institution Press, 1984), 211–224.

36. "Thus Professor Hayek and Professor Robbins have given up the essential point of Professor Mises' position and retreated to a second line of defense. On principle, they admit, the problem is soluble, but it is to be doubted whether in a socialist community it can be solved by a simple method of *trial and error*, as it is solved in the capitalist economy." Oskar Lange, "On the Economic Theory of Socialism," *Review of Economic Studies*, October 1936, 56. For Rothbard's view, see Rothbard, *Mises: Scholar, Creator*, 38. For commentary on Salerno's arguments, see Steele, *Marx to Mises*, 121–122.

37. Lavoie, *Rivalry and Central Planning*, 180–181.

38. Robert Heilbroner, "After Communism," *New Yorker*, September 10, 1990, 92. Despite this, Heilbroner just can't abide Mises altogether. He called him "impossible" (like socialism) and said, "I just don't buy the practicality of his theory of praxeology. I can't take his book *Human Action* seriously. He said socialism is impossible, and he turned out to be right. But he was not terribly convincing to me. He was so dogmatic." *Forbes*, "Just Because Socialism Has Lost Does not Mean That Capitalism Has Won," May 27, 1991, 134.

39. For a discussion of this controversial point, see David L. Prychitko, "Comparative Economic Systems," in Boettke, ed., *Elgar Companion*.

40. Mises, *Notes and Recollections*, 77.

41. A thorough account of Mises's role at the chamber through the crisis-ridden postwar years in Austria can be found in Richard M. Ebeling, "The Economist as the Historian of Decline: Ludwig von Mises and Austria Between the Two World Wars," in Richard M. Ebeling, ed., *Globalization: Will Freedom or World Government Dominate the International Marketplace?* Champions of Freedom Series, vol. 29 (Hillsdale, IL: Hillsdale College Press, 2002).

42. John Maynard Keynes gave the book a decent review in the *Economic Journal* but found nothing new in it. He later admitted this was because of his meager grasp of German. See Mises, *Notes and Recollections*, 61–62.

43. Mises, *Notes and Recollections*, 79–83, 91–92.

44. Ludwig von Mises, *Liberalism in the Classical Tradition,* 3rd ed. (1962; Irvington-on-Hudson, NY: Foundation for Economic Education, 1985), 88–89.

45. Mises, *Liberalism*, 4.

46. During World War II, Mises wrote *Omnipotent Government,* a history of the rise of German warmongering during the twentieth century, which set forth this argument in a more detailed and specific way.

47. Mises, *Liberalism*, 55–56.

48. Mises, *Liberalism*, 19.

49. Mises, *Epistemological Problems*, 24.

50. Mises, *Epistemological Problems*, 29.

51. David L. Prychitko, "Praxeology," in Boettke, ed., *Elgar Companion*, 81–82. For an example of the attitude Prychitko is referring to here, see this comment by Rothbard disciple Hans-Hermann Hoppe: "It is manifestly impossible to ever dispute or falsify the validity of Mises's insights." In Hans-Hermann Hoppe, "On Praxeology and the Praxeological Foundations of Epistemology and Ethics" in Herbener, ed., *Meaning of Mises*, 146. Milton Friedman has also floated this critique of Misesian praxeology, anytime he brought up the topic.

52. Mises, *Epistemological Problems*, xxv.

53. Mises, *Epistemological Problems*, 3.

54. Mises, *Epistemological Problems*, 200.

55. Margit von Mises, *My Years*, 203.

56. Hayek, *Fortunes of Liberalism*, 26.

57. Despite Mises's later reputation for intolerance and arrogance—a reputation spread by his fellow economics and libertarian luminary Milton Friedman—no reminiscence of these days has Mises as anything more than a helpful "first among equals." "We formed neither school, congregation, nor sect," Mises recalled. "We helped each other more through contradiction than agreement. But we agreed and were united on one endeavor: to further the sciences of human action. Each one went his own way, guided by his own law. . . . There was greatness in this unpretentious exchange of ideas; in it we all found happiness and satisfaction." Mises, *Notes and Recollections*, 98.

For more details on Mises's Vienna seminar, see Gottfried Haberler, "Mises' Private Seminar," in Ludwig von Mises, *Planning for Freedom and 16 Other Essays and Addresses* (South Holland, IL: Libertarian Press, 1980), 276–278; Margit von Mises, *My Years*, appendix 1, 202–211; Hayek, *Fortunes of Liberalism*, 25–34; and Mises, *Notes and Recollections*, 97–100. The Ludwig von Mises Institute in Auburn, Alabama, occasionally stages performances of some of Kaufmann's songs about and for the *Miseskreis* (Mises circle).

58. Quoted in Bettina Bien Greaves, ed., *Austrian Economics: An Anthology* (Irvington-on-Hudson, NY: Foundation for Economic Education, 1996), 77.

59. Quoted in Margit von Mises, *My Years*, 41.

60. Mises, *Notes and Recollections*, 95.

61. Mises, *Notes and Recollections*, 95. Mises was kept out of an official job systematically, Earlene Craver concluded in her study of the Viennese economists of the 1920s and 1930s, because of his intransigent liberalism and his Jewishness, and because "he was difficult to the point that many people thought him 'personally obnoxious.'" Earlene Craver, "The Emigration of the Austrian Economists," *History of Political Economy*, 1986, 5.

62. Details on their courtship from Margit von Mises, *My Years*, 13–20, 35–36.

63. Details on the Miseses' escape from Europe in Margit von Mises, *My Years*, 51–56. Mises left all his papers in his Viennese apartment when he took the job in Geneva; he assumed the Nazis had destroyed them. In fact, they preserved them in a document depot that was captured by the Soviets at the end of the war. The Soviets catalogued and preserved them in KGB archives, unknown to any Western Mises scholar until 1996. Then they were discovered and microfilmed and the films brought back to the United States by Austrian economist, and current president of the Foundation for Economic Education, Richard Ebeling. For details, see Brian Doherty, "Mises Papers Recovered," *Reason*, May 1997, 19–20.

64. Mises, *Liberalism*, 180.

65. Mises, *Notes and Recollections*, 115.

66. See, for example, "Politics and Ideas," in Ludwig von Mises, *Economic Policy: Thoughts for Today and Tomorrow* (Irvington-on-Hudson, NY: Free Market, 1995); and von Mises, "Trends Can Change," in *Planning for Freedom*.

67. Ludwig von Mises to F. A. Hayek, June 18, 1941, Hoover Institution, F. A. Hayek Collection, Box 38.

68. Quoted in Margit von Mises, *My Years*, 58.

69. Ronald Reagan to Henry Hazlitt, November 16, 1984. Henry Hazlitt Archives, FEE.

70. Quoted in Margit von Mises, *My Years*, 205. For details on Mises's early years in New York, see Margit von Mises, *My Years*, 58–63.

71. Rothbard, *Mises: Scholar, Creator*, 58–60.

72. Bettina Bien Greaves and Robert W. McGee, *Mises: An Annotated Bibliography* (Irvington-on-Hudson, NY: Foundation for Economic Education, 1993), 45–47.

73. "In a letter to Hayek of December 22, 1940, Mises blames his age for some of the difficulties he experienced trying to integrate himself into a new academic culture."

Vaughn, *Austrian Economics in America*, 65 n. 7. This idea was also expressed by Boettke, interview by author.

74. Rothbard, *Mises: Scholar, Creator*, 81 n. 51.

75. Vaughn, *Austrian Economics in America*, 66 and 66 n. 9.

76. Rose Wilder Lane, *Economic Council Review of Books*, October 1949, 3.

77. Henry Hazlitt, "The Case for Capitalism," *Newsweek*, September 19, 1949, 70.

78. Alfred Sherrard, "The Free Man's Straightjacket," *New Republic,* January 9, 1950, 18–19.

79. "Fabulous Survival," *Economist,* December 31, 1949, 1464.

80. J.E., "Das dummste Buch des Jahres," *Aufbau,* October 14, 1949. This translation from Greaves and McGee, *Mises*, 112.

81. Mises, *Human Action*, 67.

82. Mises, *Human Action,* 255.

83. Later Austrian economist Dominick Armentano, who did most of his work in monopoly theory, points out the libertarian implication of Mises's definition of monopoly price: if it only arises as a side effect of people's demand curves, which are a result of their voluntary demand, you can't say that even a monopoly price is actually harming consumers. See D. T. Armentano, "A Critique of Neoclassical and Austrian Monopoly Theory," in Louis Spadaro, ed., *New Directions in Austrian Economics* (Kansas City: Sheed Andrews & McMeel, 1978).

84. Margit von Mises, *My Years*, 109. For the full saga of Mises's relationship with Yale University Press, see 99–111.

85. Margit von Mises, *My Years*, 110.

86. For details on *Human Action*'s publishing history, see Greaves and McGee, *Mises,* 20–22.

87. The libertarian scholarly support organization, the Institute for Humane Studies, used Hayek's image on their postcards. The libertarian policy think tank the Cato Institute named its auditorium after him. It is most likely a combination of his complicated, scholarly, respectable defense of liberty, his Nobel Prize, and his relative freedom from association with conservatism or the Republican Party as compared to his greatest living "competitor" in this sense—Milton Friedman—that elevates him thusly.

88. F. A. Hayek, *Hayek on Hayek: An Autobiographical Dialogue,* ed. Stephen Kresge and Leif Wenar (Chicago: University of Chicago Press, 1994), 114.

89. Nick Gillespie, "Liberating Liberal," *Reason,* June 1995, 48.

90. The limits of Hayek's reason and knowledge apparently limited the extent to which he felt confident in condemning state action. Pierre Goodrich, later founder of the Liberty Fund and then already a big donor to libertarian causes, complained to Hayek about how much room he allowed for the state in early drafts of *Constitution of Liberty*. Hayek responded, "I don't think it is considerations of political expediency or possibility or any temporizing which make me draw the line at a point which admittedly still leaves much that I dislike inside the range of the permissible [state action]. The fact is that in my present state of thinking I cannot yet state with any clarity a general criterion which would exclude all that I dislike. I believe much would be gained and further drift prevented if agreement among sensible people could be achieved on criteria which I suggest, even if in the long run they should not be proven altogether sufficient. It may be that by much further thought I shall succeed in developing a more satisfactory criterion; but that is a matter of years." F. A. Hayek to Pierre Goodrich, April 4, 1959, Institute for Human Studies Archive, Liberty Fund folder.

91. F. A. Hayek, *Individualism and Economic Order* (Chicago: University of Chicago Press, 1948), 180.

92. Quoted in Bruce Caldwell, introduction to *Contra Keynes and Cambridge: Essays, Correspondence* (Chicago: University of Chicago Press, 1995), 31.

93. Hayek, *Hayek on Hayek*, 48. When asked how he got interested in the social sciences, Hayek replied, "I think the decisive influence was really World War I, particularly the experience of serving in a multinational army, the Austro-Hungarian army. That's when I saw . . . the great empire collapse over the nationalist problem. I served in a battle in which eleven different languages were spoken. It's bound to draw your attention to the problems of political organization."

94. Hayek, *Hayek on Hayek*, 7. From the introduction by Stephen Kresge: "The American newspaper stories of the war were accurate and revealing in a way that the Austrian accounts had not been. The truth about the course of the war had been largely kept from the Austrian people. We can date Hayek's skepticism toward the actions and motives of government from this point."

95. Hayek, *Hayek on Hayek*, 1. From the introduction by Stephen Kresge: "It has largely been the intellectual and cultural eruptions from Vienna and Central Europe to which the rest of the world has been forced to respond."

96. Details on Hayek's genealogy can be found in Hayek, *Hayek on Hayek*, 37–40; and Kurt R. Leube, "Friedrich August von Hayek: A Biographical Introduction" in Nishiyama and Leube, eds., *Essence of Hayek*, xvii.

97. Amusing details of Hayek's relationship with his famous cousin Wittgenstein can be found in Hayek, *Fortunes of Liberalism*, 176–181.

98. Hayek, *Hayek on Hayek*, 42–43.

99. Hayek, *Hayek on Hayek*, 45–46.

100. Hayek, *Hayek on Hayek*, 47.

101. Hayek's doctoral thesis in political science was on a topic that would now only be appropriate in an economics program: the problem of imputation of value from finished consumer products back to the producers' goods that go into making them. Hayek "rather hope[s] that no copies of the thesis have survived." Hayek, *Hayek on Hayek*, 65.

102. Hayek, *Hayek on Hayek*, 67.

103. Hayek, *Hayek on Hayek*, 66.

104. G. R. Steele, *The Economics of Friedrich Hayek* (New York: St. Martin's Press, 1993), 4.

105. Norman Barry, *Hayek's Social and Economic Philosophy* (London: Macmillan, 1979), vii.

106. Hayek, *Hayek on Hayek*, 77. Hayek's move to London, followed by the rise of Hitler, meant the book was never completed. The four chapters Hayek did finish were eventually published as chapters 9–12 in F. A. Hayek, *The Trend of Economic Thinking: Essays on Political Economists and Economic History,* ed. W. W. Bartley III and Stephen Kresge (Chicago: University of Chicago Press, 1991).

107. F. A. Hayek, "The Keynes Centenary: The Austrian Critique," in Caldwell, ed., *Contra Keynes*, 248.

108. Caldwell, introduction to *Contra Keynes*, 38.

109. Keynes's ideas fell within an old tradition in economics known as "underconsumption" theory. Hayek had made a sustained attack on a then-current wave of underconsumptionist theory sweeping America from a pair named William Foster and Waddill Catchings, which first drew Lionel Robbins's attention to Hayek. All the details of the Hayek/Keynes underconsumptionist debate are explained and reprinted in Caldwell, ed., *Contra Keynes*, introduction and Parts I–II. See also B. J. McCormick, *Hayek and the Keynesian Avalanche* (New York: St. Martin's, 1992), especially chaps. 3 and 8.

110. F. A. Hayek, *Money, Capital, and Fluctuations*, ed. Roy McClaughry (Chicago: University of Chicago Press, 1984), 110.

111. "The assumption that all goods and factors are available in excess makes the whole price system redundant, undetermined, and unintelligible . . . some of the most orthodox disciples of Keynes appear consistently to have thrown overboard all the traditional theory of price determination and of distribution . . . and in consequence . . . have ceased to understand any economics." F. A. Hayek, "Personal Recollections of Keynes and the 'Keynesian Revolution,'" in Caldwell, ed., *Contra Keynes*, 243.

112. "Indeed the ultimate motive of Keynes efforts was to find a roundabout method of reducing wages too high to allow employment of all seeking jobs." F. A. Hayek, "Symposium on Keynes: Why?" in Caldwell, ed., *Contra Keynes*, 238.

113. F. A. Hayek, "The Keynes Centenary: The Austrian Critique," in Caldwell, ed., *Contra Keynes*, 254–255.

114. Steele, *Economics of Hayek*, xi. "I graduated in economics in 1967, but another twenty years were to pass before I first read Hayek. I am not untypical of my generation. Even now, when I turn to the index of any recent textbook produced for the current crop of undergraduates, a citation for Hayek is a rare exception."

115. John Hicks, *Critical Essays in Monetary Theory* (Oxford: Oxford University Press, 1967), 203.

117. See Caldwell, ed., *Contra Keynes*, chaps. 12–13, for varying versions of why Hayek didn't criticize Keynes's *General Theory* thoroughly upon its release.

116. Quoted in Caldwell, introduction to *Contra Keynes*, 36.

118. Hayek's gradual departure from equilibrium analysis is discussed at greater length in Bruce J. Caldwell, "Hayek's Transformation," *History of Political Economy* 20, no. 4 (1988).

119. F. A. Hayek, "Use of Knowledge in Society," in Nishiyama and Leube, eds., *Essence of Hayek*, 223.

120. For Hayek's shift away from Misesian praxeology, see Caldwell, *Hayek's Challenge*, 220–223; for Hayek and Popper's delicate dance on method, as well as the context in Hayek's later thought that occasionally brought him in opposition to Popper, see 309–312.

121. Hayek, *Hayek on Hayek*, 116. Speaking in 1945, "that the monetary system must be under central control has never, to my mind, been denied by any sensible person." F. A. Hayek, *Denationalisation of Money* (London: Institute for Economic Affairs, 1976), is devoted to denying that contention. Both Friedman and Hayek became more skeptical about government involvement in the money supply the more they studied it.

122. Milton Friedman, introduction to F. A. Hayek, *The Road to Serfdom*, 50th anniversary ed. (1944; Chicago: University of Chicago Press, 1994), ix.

123. Hannes H. Gissurarson, "'The Only Truly Progressive Policy . . .'" in Norman Barry et al., *Hayek's Serfdom Revisited: Essays by Economists, Philosophers, and Political Scientists on 'The Road to Serfdom' after 40 Years* (London: Institute of Economic Affairs, 1984), 4.

124. Hayek, *Fortunes of Liberalism*, 190. See also Friedman, introduction, in Hayek, *Serfdom*.

125. Hayek, *Serfdom*, xxiii.

126. Hayek, *Serfdom*, xxiv.

127. Hayek, *Serfdom*, 253–257. Mises made a similar statement from a pure liberal perspective: "Liberalism, with its fundamental antagonism to warfare, wants to give the whole world some state form of organization." In Mises, *Socialism*, 140–141. Hayek later reversed his opinion on the positive value of a world government. See Hayek, *Hayek on Hayek*, 152.

128. The most vivid example was Herman Finer's *Road to Reaction*, a book even longer than Hayek's, dedicated entirely to shredding it, quite uncharitably. It's the most thorough exposition of what mainstream European and American political thinking could find objectionable about Hayek in his first bloom of fame (though not all of Hayek's opponents would have agreed with all of it, or with its tone). Finer's initial bill of particulars: that "Hayek's apparatus

of learning is deficient, his reading incomplete; that his understanding of the economic process is bigoted, his account of history false; that his political science is almost nonexistent, his terminology misleading, his comprehension of British and American political procedure and mentality gravely defective; and that his attitude to average men and women is truculently authoritarian." Herman Finer, *Road to Reaction* (Boston: Little, Brown, 1945), xii.

With that in the introduction, it's not surprising that the book concludes more or less advocating the murder of Hayek and all who think like him: "The system of competition is by its very nature a system of insecurity for all; and if unqualified in practice, it could stand for not more than a few days, after which there would be insufficient lampposts for its pedantic and trifling apologists" (222).

129. Quoted in Caldwell, introduction to *Contra Keynes*, 45–46.

CHAPTER 3

1. John Chamberlain, *A Life with the Printed Word* (Chicago: Regnery Gateway, 1982), 136.

2. David Boaz, ed., *The Libertarian Reader: Classic and Contemporary Readings from Lao-tzu to Milton Friedman* (New York: Free Press, 1997), 31.

3. As quoted in Stephen Cox, "Introduction to the Transaction Edition," in Isabel Paterson, *The God of the Machine* (1943; New Brunswick, NJ: Transaction), 1993, il.

4. Stephen Cox, *The Woman and the Dynamo: Isabel Paterson and the Idea of America* (New Brunswick, NJ: Transaction), 2004, 14.

5. Cox, *Woman and the Dynamo*, 15.

6. Cox, *Woman and the Dynamo*, 16.

7. Quoted in Cox, *Woman and the Dynamo*, 55.

8. Biographical details on Paterson from Cox, "Introduction," in Paterson, *God of the Machine*, x–xv.

9. Cox, *Woman and the Dynamo*, 77.

10. Cox, *Woman and the Dynamo*, 77.

11. Quoted in Cox, *Woman and the Dynamo*, 81.

12. Quoted in Cox, "Introduction," in Paterson, *The God of the Machine*, xviii.

13. Quoted in Cox, "Introduction," in Paterson, *The God of the Machine*, xxiii.

14. Cox, *Woman and the Dynamo*, 113.

15. Cox, *Woman and the Dynamo*, 112.

16. Cox, *Woman and the Dynamo*, 176.

17. Cox, *Woman and the Dynamo*, 195.

18. Cox, *Woman and the Dynamo*, 243.

19. Cox, *Woman and the Dynamo*, 244.

20. Information on *God's* publishing history from Stephen Cox, interview by author, March 6, 2002.

21. Cox, *Woman and the Dynamo*, 263.

22. Paterson, *The God of the Machine*, 140.

23. Paterson, *The God of the Machine*, 62.

24. Paterson, *The God of the Machine*, 12–13.

25. Paterson, *The God of the Machine*, 134.

26. Paterson, *The God of the Machine*, 196.

27. Ayn Rand grew to think that her former friend Isabel Paterson took from her "why the morality of altruism and sacrifice is evil and improper to man. Until I explained my theory to you, you believed—as you told me—that the morality of altruism was proper, but men were not good enough for it." Berliner, ed., *Letters of Ayn Rand*, 211. Paterson denied this, responding to Rand (in a rejoinder included in Rand's letters collection, which as a matter of course printed only Rand's side of the correspondence, at the firm insis-

tence of Paterson's estate) that "I always thought that proposition was a manifest absurdity—it would be an absurdity for *any* kind of morality, a contradiction in terms—and how could it be a morality, a rule of conduct *for* human beings, if human beings were *incapable* of practicing it. As well say sawdust is a proper diet for human beings only they can't digest it." Berliner, ed., *Letters of Ayn Rand*, 214–15. Paterson's biographer Stephen Cox says that "Rand looking back after the fact tried to represent herself as teacher instead of student, which is what she was." Cox, interview by author.

28. Paterson, *The God of the Machine*, 206.

29. Paterson, *The God of the Machine*, 218.

30. The chapter was excerpted in Boaz, ed., *Libertarian Reader*, 31–35.

31. Paterson, *The God of the Machine*, 241.

32. Paterson, *The God of the Machine*, 242.

33. Paterson, *The God of the Machine*, 66.

34. Paterson, *The God of the Machine*, 250.

35. Paterson, *The God of the Machine*, 45.

36. Paterson, *The God of the Machine*, 255, 258.

37. Paterson, *The God of the Machine*, 275.

38. Paterson, *The God of the Machine*, 291–292.

39. Quoted in Cox, *Woman and the Dynamo*, 282.

40. Quoted in Cox, *Woman and the Dynamo*, 287.

41. Rose Wilder Lane, *National Economic Council Review of Books*, February 1946, 2.

42. Quoted in Cox, *Woman and the Dynamo*, 289.

43. Quoted in Cox, *Woman and the Dynamo*, 294

44. Berliner, ed., *Letters of Ayn Rand*, 215.

45. Cox, "Introduction" in Paterson, *The God of the Machine*, xx.

46. See note 27 for Rand's attitude toward what she saw as Paterson's intellectual borrowings.

47. Berliner, ed., *Letters of Ayn Rand*, 211.

48. For details on the final break between Rand and Paterson, see Barbara Branden, *The Passion of Ayn Rand* (Garden City, NY: Doubleday, 1986), 203–205.

49. Cox, *Woman and the Dynamo*, 313.

50. Paterson, *The God of the Machine*, 55.

51. Cox, interview by author.

52. Berliner, ed., *Letters of Ayn Rand*, 184

53. Cox, "Introduction" in Paterson, *God of the Machine*, xxviii.

54. The *Freeman* earned a wonderful Paterson mal mot, quoted by William F. Buckley in the obituary he wrote for her in *National Review*, January 28, 1961: "That sort of handout reminds me of nothing so much as a lot of Tierra del Fuegans gnawing at the carcass of a stranded whale, the carcass of capitalism."

55. Isabel Paterson to Henry Hazlitt, undated. Henry Hazlitt Archives, FEE.

56. Isabel Paterson to Leonard Read, February 6, 1945. FEE Archives.

57. Letter from William F. Buckley to Isabel Paterson, April 16, 1956. In William F. Buckley Papers (Part III), Group 576, Series 111, Box 148, Yale University. Shown to author by Sam Tanenhaus.

58. Note from January 2, 1958. In William F. Buckley Papers (Part III), Group 576, Series 111, Box 148, Yale University. Shown to author by Sam Tanenhaus.

59. Letter from William F. Buckley to Isabel Paterson, September 16, 1959. In William F. Buckley Papers (Part III), Group 576, Series 111, Box 148, Yale University. Shown to author by Sam Tanenhaus.

60. Quoted in Stephen Cox, "Representing Isabel Paterson," *American Literary History* 17, no. 2 (2005): 237.

61. Cox, "Introduction" in Paterson, *The God of the Machine*, xxix.

62. Details of Rose's early years can be found in William Holtz, *The Ghost in the Little House: A Life of Rose Wilder Lane* (Columbia: University of Missouri Press, 1993), chap. 1.

63. For Rose's adolescence in Mansfield, see Holtz, *Ghost,* chap. 2.

64. For Rose's marriage, see Holtz, *Ghost,* chap. 3.

65. Lane's correspondence with Thompson is collected in William Holtz, ed., *Dorothy Thompson and Rose Wilder Lane: Forty Years of Friendship, Letters 1921–60* (Columbia: University of Missouri Press, 1991). Some of her European adventures are described in greater detail in Rose Wilder Lane, *Travels with Zenobia: Paris to Albania by Model T Ford* (Columbia: University of Missouri Press, 1983). For Lane's European travels, also see Holtz, *Ghost,* chaps. 6, 7, and 9.

66. In its original serialized magazine version, the novel has a conventionally happy ending with the heroine remarried to a childhood sweetheart. Holtz, *Ghost,* 77. The book version is more like Lane's own life, with the heroine finding happiness as an independent journalist. Strangely, Rose's heir, Roger MacBride, republished *Diverging Roads* with the characters' names changed and presented it as an actual autobiography of Rose. See R. W. Bradford, "Freedom's Rose," *Liberty,* March 1994, 54.

67. William Holtz, Lane's only substantial biographer, launched a big literary controversy when he gathered what he considered incontrovertible evidence that Rose substantially rewrote her mother's artless reminiscences and gave them their gemlike literary sparkle. Many who adored the myth of the strangely articulate sixty-year-old uneducated frontier lady Laura Ingalls Wilder were angered, apparently garnering Holtz a stray death threat or two.

Lane's heir, Roger MacBride, did his best to keep the Holtz book from being sold at an official Laura Ingalls Wilder Museum. Lane herself publicly denied any role in her mother's success. For details on the evidence and the controversy, see Holtz, *Ghost in Little House*, chap. 11 and appendix. See also William Holtz, "The Ghost in the Little House Books," *Liberty,* March 1992; and Bradford, "Freedom's Rose." Chilton Williamson Jr., "Lizzie Borden's Mama Was No Writer," *Chronicles,* September 1993, defends Laura against what he sees as Holtz's attacks on her integrity and reputation. Williamson argues that what Holtz found evidence for is more properly known as editing than ghostwriting.

68. See Holtz, "Ghost in the Little House Books," *Liberty,* 54.

69. Quoted in Holtz, *Ghost,* 260.

70. Roger Lea MacBride, ed., *The Lady and the Tycoon: The Best of Letters Between Rose Wilder Lane and Jasper Crane* (Caldwell, ID: Caxton, 1973), 169.

71. Holtz, *Ghost,* 271.

72. Holtz, *Ghost,* 268.

73. She referred to the needlework articles, perhaps jokingly, as "a really Right Wing Extremist series of articles on needlework in *Woman's Day.*" MacBride, ed., *Lady and Tycoon,* 285.

74. Rose Wilder Lane, *The Discovery of Freedom: Man's Struggle Against Authority* (1943; New York: Laissez-Faire, 1984), xi–xii.

75. Cox, *Woman and the Dynamo,* 285–287, for Cox's opinion of Lane as compared to Paterson.

76. Lane also thought Mises was soft on democracy in her review of his *Omnipotent Government* in the *National Economic Council Review of Books,* November 1945.

77. Lane, *The Discovery of Freedom,* 38–39.

78. Lane, *The Discovery of Freedom,* 109.

79. Lane, *The Discovery of Freedom,* 250.

80. Lane, *The Discovery of Freedom,* 208, 211.

81. Roger MacBride, "What They Are Teaching Us," *Educational Review,* April 15, 1950, 1.

82. For details on MacBride as legislator, see MacBride, ed., *Lady and Tycoon*, 313–314.

83. The account of her encounter with the Social Security thought police from William Holtz, "The Woman vs. the State," *Liberty*, March 1991, 46–7.

84. "I am FOR any and every way of diminishing the size, the activity, the extent of Government per se, and all respect for Government, to the eventual end of eliminating Government totally. Anarchy is absence of Earthly authority over human beings, by definition and etymology; so I am an anarchist." MacBride, ed., *Lady and Tycoon*, 268.

85. Holtz, *Ghost*, 377.

86. Holtz, *Ghost*, 328. Though the tone of such references seems unmistakably hostile, Holtz unaccountably claimed in a letter to the libertarian movement magazine *Liberty* to have "admiration" for the later Lane's politics. See William Holtz, "The Quirky Libertarian," Letters, *Liberty*, May 1994, 4.

87. MacBride, ed., *Lady and Tycoon*, 12.

88. Holtz, ed. *Dorothy Thompson and Rose Wilder Lane*, 195.

89. MacBride, ed., *Lady and Tycoon*, 216–217.

90. Richard Cornuelle, "The First Libertarian Revival and the Next: Where We Were and Where We Are," *Critical Review Update*, April 1993, 2.

91. MacBride, ed., *Lady and Tycoon*, 88.

92. MacBride, ed., *Lady and Tycoon*, 192.

93. MacBride, ed., *Lady and Tycoon*, 227–228, 333 for Lane's thoughts on the Soviet "threat."

94. Lane modestly insists that LeFevre gave her too much credit. See MacBride, ed., *Lady and Tycoon*, 294: "Bob LeFevre has a fantastically mistaken feeling about me because *he* changed all his ideas and the rest of his life while reading *The Discovery of Freedom*. I am not responsible for what he thought and did; and this isn't an opinion, it is demonstrable fact. He is not the only reader of that book, and all the others haven't made Freedom Schools. It isn't even a good book." Lane was always unhappy with *Discovery* and planned to rework it later, but never finished the project. The book did not sell well, and was not well reviewed. Lane even returned her advance, embarrassed at its poor sales.

95. MacBride, ed., *Lady and Tycoon*, 205–209 for Lane's early experiences with and support of LeFevre.

96. See Holtz, *Ghost*, chapter 20 for details on Rose's Vietnam trip.

97. MacBride, ed., *Lady and Tycoon*, 210.

98. Holtz, ed., *Dorothy Thompson and Rose Wilder Lane*, 190.

99. MacBride, ed., *Lady and Tycoon*, 15.

100. Rand's early life is detailed in B. Branden, *Passion of Ayn Rand*, chaps. 1–3.

101. Rand's college years are discussed in B. Branden, *Passion of Ayn Rand*, chap. 4.

102. B. Branden, *Passion of Ayn Rand*, 61–62.

103. B. Branden, *Passion of Ayn Rand*, 60.

104. B. Branden, *Passion of Ayn Rand*, chapter 6, for Rand's Chicago experience.

105. Berliner, ed., *Letters of Ayn Rand*, 31–33. Rand, grateful for the help at this early stage of her career, later donated money to and wrote a fund-raising letter for the continuation of the club.

106. Details of some of Rand's earliest film scenario attempts can be found in David Harriman, ed., *Journals of Ayn Rand* (New York: Dutton, 1997), 4–20.

107. Harriman, ed., *Journals*, 20–48. Rand wanted this book to show "all the filth, stupidity, and horror of the world. . . . Show how insignificant, petty, and miserable the 'good' in the world is, compared to the real horror it masks. . . . Show that *humanity is petty*. That it's small. That it's dumb. . . . Show *that humanity is utterly illogical*, like an animal that cannot connect the things it observes. . . . Show that humanity has and wants to have: existence instead of life, satisfaction instead of joy, contentment instead of happiness,

security instead of power, vanity instead of pride, attachment instead of love" (Harriman, ed., *Journals*, 23–25). Rand's sense of life was more bitter than admitted in her later novels.

108. Details on DeMille and early courtship with Frank O'Connor in B. Branden, *Passion of Ayn Rand*, chap. 8.

109. Berliner, ed., *Letters of Ayn Rand*, 13.

110. *Red Pawn* is printed in Leonard Peikoff, ed., *The Early Ayn Rand* (New York: New American Library, 1984).

111. Rand made some unacknowledged changes in the original 1936 text of *We the Living* when it was republished in 1959 by Random House (and the next year in paperback by New American Library). For example, in the original Kira says, "If one believes one's right, one shouldn't wait to convince millions of fools, one might just as well force them." And "I loathe your ideals [to a communist official] because I know no worse injustice than justice for all." For discussion of the meaning of these changes, see Sciabarra, *Russian Radical*, 100–106. Her *Journals* also contain a somewhat Nietzschean statement about replacing liberal democracy with a "democracy of superiors only." Harriman, ed., *Journals*, 74.

112. Ayn Rand, *The Night of January 16th,* paperback ed. (New York: Signet, 1971). This version is a restored text, Rand approved. The introduction explains the tortured, to Rand, history of the play's production.

113. Rand, *Night of January 16th*, 98.

114. B. Branden, *Passion of Ayn Rand*, 143–144. Rand also studied railroads and steel mills extensively for her later novel *Atlas Shrugged*, spending time in examples of each.

115. B. Branden, *Passion of Ayn Rand*, 187–188.

116. Rand undoubtedly changed lives. Barbara Branden reports that to this day that is the statement she hears more than any other from people who know of her connection with Rand. However, that change is not always in the direction of making libertarian activists. Nathaniel Branden wryly reports about appearing on a TV show with a former Berkeley student activist leader from the free speech days, who told him excitedly how much she and her compatriots on the barricades adored Rand. Branden was nonplused. "Sure!" she exclaimed. "*Atlas Shrugged!* Fight the system! Do your own thing!" (Creators cannot control how their message will be received.) Nathaniel Branden, interview by author, April 22, 1998.

117. Both plays are reprinted in Peikoff, ed., *Early Ayn Rand*.

118. Berliner, ed., *Letters of Ayn Rand*, 308.

119. Berliner, ed., *Letters of Ayn Rand*, 56–57.

120. Barbara Branden describes their relationship as one in which Rand was largely the student, almost the acolyte, on matters of American history. Paterson thought of Rand as a "genius," though she disliked her as a novelist. See B. Branden, *Passion of Ayn Rand*, 164–166, 204.

121. A discussion of Rand's relations with fellow individualists in this context can be found in B. Branden, *Passion of Ayn Rand*, 162–164.

122. Berliner, ed., *Letters of Ayn Rand*, 54.

123. Details on the difficulties of selling *The Fountainhead* can be found in B. Branden, *Passion of Ayn Rand*, 155–157; 168–171.

124. B. Branden, *Passion of Ayn Rand,* 173–174 n.

125. Cox, *Woman and the Dynamo*, 304.

126. B. Branden, *Passion of Ayn Rand*, 132.

127. B. Branden, *Passion of Ayn Rand*, 134.

128. Toohey was modeled, in appearance and manner, on British Labor Party panjandrum Harold Laski, and in ideology and style on popular columnist Heywood Broun and architectural critic Lewis Mumford. See B. Branden, *Passion of Ayn Rand*, 139–140. See also Harriman, ed., *Journals*, 102–115, 122–129.

129. Ayn Rand, *The Fountainhead* (New York: Bobbs-Merrill, 1943), 390–391.

130. Rand, *The Fountainhead,* 685–686.

131. Harriman, ed., *Journals,* 86.

132. Berliner, ed., *Letters of Ayn Rand,* 73.

CHAPTER 4

1. Rand contacted Wright while writing *The Fountainhead* and received a brief (and uncomprehendingly negative) response to the first three chapters, objecting to Roark's name and hair color. See Berliner, ed., *Letters,* 108–111. After actually reading the finished product, Wright was very impressed, writing, "Your thesis is *the* great one." For details on the unbuilt home he designed for her, see *Letters of Ayn Rand,* 117–119. For Rand's later personal view on Wright, see Harriman, ed., *Journals,* 412–415.

2. Only two of the scripts Rand wrote for Wallis were filmed—*Love Letters* and *You Came Along,* both Paramount Pictures from 1945. *You Came Along* was scripted by Rand from an original story by another writer, concerning a dying World War II pilot who falls in love and marries a female Treasury agent traveling around the country with him selling war bonds. *Love Letters* is more Randian, concerning a Keating/Roarkesque (and Cyranoesque, of course) situation where a woman falls in love with and marries a soldier because of love letters written by one of his buddies. She becomes disgusted with the reality of the man, so much less than his wonderful letters, and gets embroiled in melodrama when her husband is murdered and she, now amnesiac on top of it all, is accused of the crime. Things work out in the end, including her eventual marriage to the real letter writer. For more details on Rand's film script work and career, see Stephen Cox, "The Films of Ayn Rand," *Liberty,* August 1987.

3. Leonard Read to Marge Lindley, July 19, 1949, FEE Archives.

4. For Read's reminiscences on the *Tuscania* sinking, see Mary Sennholz, *Leonard E. Read: Philosopher of Freedom* (Irvington-on-Hudson, NY: Foundation for Economic Education, 1993), 18–20.

5. Sennholz, *Leonard E. Read,* 41–42.

6. Quoted in Andrew A. Workman, "Manufacturing Power: The Organizational Revival of the National Association of Manufacturers, 1941–1945," *Business History Review,* Summer 1998, 294.

7. Sennholz, *Leonard E. Read,* 57–59.

8. Details on Mullendore's background and character are from Leonard E. Read, "The Independent Mr. Mullendore," *Freeman,* September 1955.

9. By the end of his career, Taft supported federal subsidies (though not federal control) to the states for education, housing, and health. See Russell Kirk and James McClellan, *The Political Principles of Robert A. Taft* (New York: Fleet, 1967), 135–153. Despite his isolationist reputation, he supported the United Nations, "a more energetic prosecution of the war in Korea," and a "diversionary attack on the Chinese mainland" by Taiwan with U.S. backing, as well as the Marshall Plan and aid to Greece and Turkey, and even a peacetime draft. See Ronald Radosh, *Prophets on the Right* (New York: Free Life Editions, 1975), 166–167.

10. W. C. Mullendore to Grover Collinson, July 14, 1952, University of Oregon Special Collections, W. C. Mullendore Collection, Box 1, Grover Collinson folder.

11. W. C. Mullendore to Kenton Collinson, June 20, 1951, University of Oregon Special Collections, W. C. Mullendore Collection, Box 1, Correspondence C folder.

12. W. C. Mullendore to Henry Ford II, January 18, 1951, University of Oregon Special Collections, W.C. Mullendore Collection, Box 1, Correspondence F folder.

13. Other Pamphleteers publications included Rose Wilder Lane's *Give Me Liberty.* Read's partners in the venture were, besides Mullendore, L.A. chamber of commerce

economist V. Orval Watts, downtown L.A. attorney James Ingebretsen of Musick, Burrell, and Ingebretsen, William H. Courtney, and George F. Rogers.

14. For Perlstein's apt description of these types of men, which this paraphrases, see Rick Perlstein, *Before the Storm: Barry Goldwater and the Unmaking of the American Consensus* (New York: Hill & Wang, 2001), 3–6.

15. Leonard Read, address to National Coal Association Convention, October 7, 1949, FEE Archives.

16. Sennholz, *Leonard E. Read,* 69.

17. Leonard Read to James Fifield, August 9, 1945, FEE Archives.

18. NAM executive director Walter Weisenburger "believed NAM should abandon the hope . . . of obliterating the New Deal." Workman, "Manufacturing Power," 290. Leonard Read would not abandon that hope, then or ever. Mises, who had been on NAM's economic advisory board, resigned over their heresies on inflation in 1948. Hulsmann, *Last Knight,* 641.

19. For Sloan's influence on FEE founding, see Alfred P. Sloan to Henry Hazlitt, September 11, 1946; and Henry Hazlitt to Hamilton Owens, September 18, 1946, both in Henry Hazlitt Archives at FEE. Sloan had been running a service in NAM that was trying to do roughly what FEE did, the National Industrial Information Committee.

20. Sennholz, *Leonard E. Read,* 70.

21. Leonard Read to W. C. Mullendore, March 1, 1946, University of Oregon Special Collections, W. C. Mullendore Collection, Box 2, Leonard Read 1946 folder.

22. The list of unlibertarian events of March 7 gleaned from the *New York Times*, March 7 and March 8, 1946.

23. Leonard Read to W. C. Mullendore, June 7, 1955, FEE Archives.

24. Read quotes from his typical form response to financial cutoffs in his Journal, May 22, 1958, FEE Archives.

25. Leonard Read to J. W. Clise, June 12, 1958, FEE Archives.

26. "Discussion of Statement in Re: Possibility of Writing a Book, Dinner Meeting, The Conference Board, February 8, 1946," typescript, FEE Archives.

27. There were indeed some randomly scattered ears. A little personal newsletter (a zine, in modern terms) dedicated to a decidedly modern libertarianism was already coming out in late 1946, under the title *Individualist*, edited and written by C. O. Steele of Forest Hills, New York. He was a fan of Spencer, Nock, and Garrett, had a delightfully light touch and cheerful, optimistic, open, unfearful demeanor, not obsessed with communists or war, was sound on all libertarian issues—pro-immigrant, antibureaucrat and antiprice control, pro–Betty Grable getting all she earns in a free market, anti-Republicans who sell out free enterprise, with a sensibility not the slightest bit cramped, hateful, or frightened. He signed his subscription solicitation as "Formerly Editor The Freeman," the Henry George Society *Freeman* that Frank Chodorov edited earlier. Steele shows some signs of Georgism in his discussion of land rent in one of the issues I've seen in the FEE archives.

28. Leonard Read, FEE memo to board, undated (but context clues indicate it must be from 1953 to 1954), FEE Archives.

29. Leonard Read to A. Cyril Daldy, March 21, 1960, University of Oregon Special Collections, W. C. Mullendore Collection, Box 1, FEE 1960–1961 folder.

30. Benjamin Rogge, "The Foundation for Economic Education: Success or Failure?" *Freeman*, May 1996, 384.

31. This tale of the redeemed labor organizer from Leonard Read, *How to Advance Liberty: A Learning, Not a Selling, Problem,* FEE pamphlet, undated; and from Bettina Bien Greaves, "FEE and the Climate of Opinion," *Freeman*, May 1996, 342.

32. Robert Hessen, interview by author, November 8, 1998.

33. Williamson Evers, interview by author, November 9, 1998.

34. Harper joined the same fraternity as his brother, a full-haired young man ironically dubbed "Baldy" by his fraternity brothers. When young Floyd Arthur joined the same fraternity, he was of course "Baldy Jr." and later just Baldy. He too retained a full head of hair throughout life.

35. See Tom Reiss, "The First Conservative," *New Yorker*, October 24, 2005, for an overview on Viereck and his influence (or lack of it) on contemporary conservatism.

36. Felix Morley, *For the Record* (South Bend, Ind.: Regnery/Gateway, 1979), 417.

37. For details on *Human Events* founding, see Morley, *For the Record,* 396–397.

38. Morley, *For the Record*, 428.

39. Felix Morley, *The Power in the People* (1949; Los Angeles: Nash, 1972), 255.

40. Morley, *For the Record,* 428.

41. Morley, *For the Record,* 437.

42. Details of Hoiles's beginnings from Jordana Milbauer, "A Libertarian Dynasty: Publishers of *The Orange County Register,* 1935–1987," master's thesis, California State University, August 1988. Copy in *Orange County Register* archives.

43. For Orange County's radical role in late-twentieth-century American political history, with some focus on Hoiles and on its ironic, inescapable ties with the modern megastate, see Lisa McGirr, *Suburban Warriors: The Origins of the New American Right* (Princeton: Princeton University Press), 2001. For specific discussion of Hoiles's influence and the tension between his libertarianism and the standard conservatism or anticommunism of his Orange County audience, see 152–155 and 163–167. See also Brian Doherty, "The Orange Revolution," *Reason*, October 2001.

44. Arnold Forster and Benjamin R. Epstein, *Danger on the Right* (New York: Random House, 1964), 170.

45. R. C. Hoiles to Leonard Read, September 6, 1946, FEE Archives. When challenged by a college student about why he paid taxes if he considered them illegitimate, he snapped back, "I can't help further free enterprise if I'm in jail." Quoted in Milbauer, "Libertarian Dynasty," 157.

46. R. C. Hoiles, *Santa Ana Register,* October 14, 1942.

47. Quoted in Milbauer, "Libertarian Dynasty," 125.

48. For Ashby's brief stint living with Rand and Frank O'Connor, see Branden, *Passion of Ayn Rand*, 197–198.

49. Quoted in Carl Watner, "To Thine Own Self Be True: The Story of Raymond Cyrus Hoiles and His Freedom Newspaper," *Voluntaryist,* May 1986, 4.

50. "Hoiles, A Conservative Publisher, Tells Views," *New York Times*, October 6, 1964.

51. Quoted in Watner, "To Thine Own Self Be True," 1.

52. R. C. Hoiles to Leonard Read, August 17, 1946, FEE Archives.

53. Murray Rothbard to F. A. Harper, May 22, 1955, Murray Rothbard Archives, Ludwig von Mises Institute.

54. Leonard Read to Pierre Goodrich, January 23, 1956, FEE Archives.

55. For a fellow anticommunist's flaying of Hart's anti-Semitism, see Isaac Don Levine, "The Strange Case of Merwin Hart," *Plain Talk,* February 1950.

56. The iconoclastic and super-Austrian Bettina Bien Greaves was a decades-long FEE employee and one of Mises's closest acolytes. After his wife Margit died, she became his heir. Greaves asserts that as far as she's concerned, the John Birch Society was better on libertarian economics than, say, Milton Friedman. (She's slightly defensive on the matter, as her husband, Percy Greaves, wrote for the Birch magazine *American Opinion*.)

57. Leonard Read to Harvey Campbell, October 29, 1959, FEE Archives. Robert Welch wrote to one of his field coordinators who overheard Read complaining about the JBS to tell him that "Leonard has been a good friend of mine for many years" and that no JBS member should ever, "by any stretch of the imagination or to any slightest extent, harbor

any resentment against Leonard Read, or ever make the least remark anywhere about his own work . . . that is not entirely and unreservedly favorable. For I am sure that Leonard Read was stating what he actually believed about the Society and . . . no man should be condemned for that. Also, the Foundation for Economic Education has been doing too good a job, at its own level and in its own way, for too many years, for any of us on the same side to want to detract one iota from its acceptance or support." Robert Welch to Thomas N. Hill, May 3, 1960, FEE Archives.

58. Harper privately confessed to Hoiles his realization that any sort of taxation violated liberalism in 1949, though he said he was not yet willing to discuss the matter publicly. F. A. Harper to R. C. Hoiles, July 18, 1949, FEE Archives.

59. Leonard Read, *Government: An Ideal Concept* (1954; Irvington-on-Hudson, NY: Foundation for Economic Education), 1997.

60. "First, imagine 160,000,000 dead persons arranged in a huge circle, their hands clasped to a conduit capable of transmitting every conceivable type of physical and human energy. No energy would be put into the conduit by the dead persons. None could, therefore, be withdrawn." Read, *Government*, 27.

61. Read, *Government*, 46.

62. Read, *Government,* 59. In a footnote on the same page, he claims weakly that a *progressive* tax "is, in fact, a form of aggressive confiscation." He later tries to explain that this same thinking does *not* mean conscription is okay because we all have a right to choose *not* to live: "the obligation to pay for an agency of common defense is imposed on those who choose to take advantage of their right to life. There is no such obligation, obviously, on those who choose not to live" (63 n.). This seems to imply that anyone who chooses not to be drafted has only one legitimate way out: suicide. This is *not* what Read means to suggest. As he admits in the footnote, "This is an extremely difficult point for me to 'think through.'" Harper and others recognized that the way Read chose to argue his point about why forced taxation is justified gives away the libertarian game on almost every level. If "society" has the right to force you to pay for anything you "need" that it chooses to provide, there is not much left of the limited-government argument.

63. F. A. Harper to Murray Rothbard, February 25, 1955, MRA, LVMI.

64. R. C. Hoiles to Leonard Read, August 13, 1954, FEE Archives.

65. Herbert Cornuelle, *Mr. Anonymous: The Story of William Volker* (Caldwell, ID: Caxton, 1951), 180–182.

66. Apparently William Volker was proximately responsible for creating the first municipal Department of Public Welfare in the United States, according to Cornuelle, *Mr. Anonymous,* 93. Though, as Cornuelle reports, seeing how politicians associated with the Pendergast machine used it for their own gain helped sour him on this sort of government do-goodism (96–97).

67. Loren B. Miller to Leonard Read, January 28, 1947, FEE Archives. Miller also worried that Earhart lacked enough solid, unshakable beliefs in what is to be done about America's political quandary to be an effective donor. See memo, Loren B. Miller to H. B. Earhart, January 28, 1947, FEE Archives.

68. F. A. Hayek, *Socialism and War: Essays, Documents, Reviews,* ed. Bruce Caldwell (Chicago: University of Chicago Press, 1997), 225, 227.

69. Hayek, *Socialism and War,* 235.

70. Richard Cornuelle, interview by author, September 15, 1996.

71. Volker ran a program called the National Book Foundation which gave away free copies of selected books to libraries. The fund prompted requests by sending reviews summing up the book's virtues; libraries often throw away books sent to them unsolicited. Among the dozens of books Volker thus sponsored were collections of John Calhoun's papers, books by Isaiah Berlin, Leo Strauss, Arthur Ekirch, Roscoe Pound, Peter Bauer, Felix

Morley, Mises, Hayek, Böhm-Bawerk, Wilhelm Röpke, Forrest McDonald, Henry Hazlitt, and Murray Rothbard.

72. Cornuelle, interview by author.

73. Richard Cornuelle to Murray Rothbard, June 17, 1952, MRA, LVMI. Leonard Read once advised James Ingebretsen of *Faith and Freedom* to run a review of a FEE antitariff book, to similarly mark libertarianism's independence from mere business cheerleading.

74. Harry Elmer Barnes to William Neumann, September 14, 1956, Institute for Humane Studies Archives.

75. See Harriman, ed., *Journals*, chap. 9, for Rand's notes on the atomic bomb movie.

76. Harriman, ed., *Journals*, 355–367.

77. Harriman, ed., *Journals*, 381.

78. Branden, *Passion of Ayn Rand,* 202.

79. Harriman, ed., *Journals*, 381–386.

80. For some of Rand's notes on *The Moral Basis of Individualism*, see Harriman, ed., *Journals*, chap. 8.

81. Leonard Read, memo to FEE staff, September 4, 1946, University of Oregon Special Collections, W. C. Mullendore Collection, Box 1, Foundation for Economic Education 1946 folder.

82. Berliner, ed., *Letters*, 121. Rand sent an early draft of Francisco D'Anconia's famous money speech from *Atlas Shrugged* to Mullendore for vetting and comments.

83. Berliner, ed., *Letters*, 308.

84. Berliner, ed., *Letters of Ayn Rand*, 299. Rand's marginal comments in certain of her books were published as Robert Mayhew, ed., *Ayn Rand's Marginalia: Her Critical Comments on the Writings of Over 20 Authors* (New Milford, CT: Second Renaissance, 1995). She thinks Hayek's definition of a person's "own sphere" in which his views are supreme could be narrowed down to "mere breathing" (146); Hayek's rejection of "dogmatic laissez-faire attitude" gets him called "The God Damned abysmal fool" (149). When Hayek accepts that certain goods, like roads and pollution abatement, need to be supplied by government, he is "so saturated with all the bromides of collectivism that it is terrifying" (149). When Hayek talks of the "very defined limits" in which individualism "allows" people to follow their "own values and preferences rather than somebody else's," Rand thunders, "Oh God damn the total, complete, vicious bastard! This means that man does exist for others, but since he doesn't know how to do it, the masters will give him some 'defined limits' for himself" (151).

85. Mayhew, ed., *Rand's Marginalia* contains Rand's unhappy thoughts on Mises's *Human Action* and *Bureaucracy*, and Hazlitt's didactic free market novel, *Time Will Run Back.*

86. Rand's discussion of social morality is in Harriman, ed., *Journals*, 610–612. Ronald E. Merrill, *The Ideas of Ayn Rand* (La Salle, IL: Open Court, 1991), 106–109, includes a brief argument: If Objectivist ethics state that morality is a matter of choosing goals and that the goals chosen ought to be those that sustain life, then there is no cleavage at all between "ought" in a technological sense ("you ought to format a new disk before attempting to write a file to it") and "ought" in a moral sense. Every fact of the universe imposes a moral necessity in Objectivist ethics.

87. Berliner, ed., *Letters of Ayn Rand*, 187.

88. Berliner, ed., *Letters of Ayn Rand*, 100.

89. Ayn Rand, *The Voice of Reason: Essays in Objectivist Thought*, ed. Leonard Peikoff (New York: New American Library, 1988), 162.

90. Branden, *Passion of Ayn Rand*, 35.

91. Rand speculated once in her journals that "man may be the highest form, the crown and final goal of the universe, the form of spirit and matter in which the spirit predominates

and triumphs. (If there's any value in 'feelings' and 'hunches'—God! How I feel that *this* is true!)" Harriman, ed., *Journals*, 466.

92. Berliner, ed., *Letters of Ayn Rand*, 237.

93. Berliner, ed., *Letters of Ayn Rand*, 257.

94. Berliner, ed., *Letters of Ayn Rand*, 300.

95. Berliner, ed., *Letters of Ayn Rand*, 319.

96. Berliner, ed., *Letters of Ayn Rand*, 327.

97. Berliner, ed., *Letters of Ayn Rand*, 332.

98. See Berliner, ed., *Letters of Ayn Rand*, 320–327, for the details of Rand's complaint against the booklet. Strangely, the editor of the Rand letters volume never identified the famous authors of the booklet that raised her ire. David Friedman, Milton's son, says that they probably didn't know who wrote it.

99. What Friedman and Stigler wrote was: "The fact that, under free market conditions, better quarters go to those who have larger incomes or more wealth is, if anything, simply a reason for taking long-term measures to reduce the inequality of income and wealth. For those, like us, who would like even more equality than there is at present, not alone for housing but for all products, it is surely better to attack directly existing inequalities in income and wealth at their source." Quoted in Leonard Read to Herbert Nelson, August 28, 1946, FEE Archives.

100. More than a decade later, the pamphlet was still annoying FEE donors. Pierre Goodrich expressed hope in a letter he wrote to Leonard Read in 1958 that Friedman realized that "society by government is not a free society" and complained about *another* bit of the pamphlet, where Friedman and Stigler list "heavy taxation, governmental economies, and control of the stock of money" as "fundamental weapons to fight inflation." Goodrich, from a more anarcho-Austrian perspective than Friedman and Stigler's Chicago one, notes that inflation *only* occurs as a result of government money supply mismanagement, and thus that "in a truly free society you could not . . . normally have monetary inflation." Men as bright as these two young economists should realize that there's a tension, not to say a contradiction, between those first two weapons. Pierre Goodrich to Leonard Read, January 9, 1958, FEE Archives. Years later Stigler floated the interestingly unlibertarian theory that any long-lasting government institution or intervention was efficient toward achieving the (morally and politically untroublesome, to Stigler) "goals adopted by society through its government." For a libertarian critique of this later Stigler position, see Donald J. Boudreaux, "Was Your High-School Teacher Right After All? Donald Whitman's *The Myth of Democratic Failure*," *Independent Review*, Spring 1996. Friedman denies the seemingly obvious implication of his and Stigler's statement that we "attack directly existing inequalities in income and wealth at their source" in his and his wife Rose's autobiography. He said that they regarded Read's footnote "which in effect accused us of putting equality above justice and liberty, as inexcusable." Subsequently he became estranged from Read and FEE. Milton and Rose Friedman, *Two Lucky People: Memoirs* (Chicago: University of Chicago Press, 1998), 151.

101. Leonard Read to Herbert Nelson (executive vice president of the National Association of Real Estate Boards), August 28, 1946, FEE Archives.

102. Representative Schwab of Oklahoma did this with Hazlitt's *Will Dollars Save The World?* about the bad thinking behind the Marshall Plan.

103. Leonard Read to Rep. Ralph Gwinn, March 23, 1948, FEE Archives.

104. See Henry Hazlitt, *Will Dollars Save the World?* (Irvington-on-Hudson, NY: Foundation for Economic Education, 1947).

105. Leonard Read to Rep. Ralph Gwinn, March 5, 1948, FEE Archives.

106. Privately held electric utilities were supplying 2 percent of FEE's income at certain times, for example, 1966.

107. W. C. Mullendore to Rep. Frank Buchanan, telegram, June 5, 1950. Copy of text in FEE Archives.

108. To further complicate the history of the *Freeman* title, Chodorov had during his George School days run a journal for them under that title (until he was fired for being too anti-war), and Read and his cohorts had used it as a umbrella title for their Pamphleteers series, which included Bastiat, Rand, and Lane.

109. Bonner Fellers, "The Lessons of Korea," *Freeman,* November 2, 1950, 7.

110. *World War III? Correspondence Between a Congressman and Constituent Excerpts from a Speech by Ralph W. Gwinn* (United States Government Printing Office, 1948, 783593–24851, 3).

111. Arlington House released an anthology from *Plain Talk* in 1976, after Solzhenitsyn's revelations made it seem particularly prescient. Isaac Don Levine, ed., *Plain Talk: An Anthology from the Leading Anti-Communist Magazine of the 40s* (New Rochelle, NY: Arlington House, 1976). During FEE's first year, Read wanted to take over *Plain Talk.* See Leonard Read to James W. Fifield, November 27, 1946, FEE Archives.

112. For details on *Freeman* finances, see Leonard Read to Gardner Miller, February 2, 1959, FEE Archives.

113. Frank Chodorov, *Fugitive Essays: Selected Writings of Frank Chodorov,* ed. Charles Hamilton (Indianapolis: LibertyPress, 1980), 63. The article reprinted originally appeared in the February 1947 *analysis.*

114. Chodorov, *Fugitive Essays,* 172–178. The article reprinted originally appeared in the December 1946 *analysis.*

115. From Charles Hamilton, introduction to Chodorov, *Fugitive Essays,* 12.

116. Frank Chodorov, "Things Are Looking Up," *Freeman,* October 1954, 117.

117. Frank Chodorov, *Out of Step: The Autobiography of an Individualist* (New York: Devin-Adair, 1962), 75–77.

118. Chodorov, *Out of Step,* 79. Will Lissner, one of his supervisors at the Henry George School, says it was Chodorov's truculent inability to work well with nonindividualist fellow Georgists that got him canned. See Will Lissner, "Frank Chodorov: Director," *Fragments,* January–March 1967. Hamilton, introduction to *Fugitive Essays,* also discusses Chodorov's firing from the Henry George School.

119. Chodorov, *Fugitive Essays,* 337–349. The article reprinted originally appeared in the April 1947 issue of *analysis.* Representative Howard Buffett entered it, titled "A Byzantine Empire of the West," into the *Congressional Record* on April 29, 1947.

120. Chodorov, *Out of Step,* 80.

121. Abraham Ellis, interview by author, October 12, 1998.

122. Chodorov, *Out of Step,* 260–261.

123. For details on Chodorov's intentions with ISI, see Chodorov, *Out of Step,* 251–261.

124. Lee Edwards, *Educating for Liberty: The First Half-Century of the Intercollegiate Studies Institute* (Washington, DC: Regnery, 2003), 4.

125. Edwards, *Educating for Liberty,* 17.

126. For details on the ISI/FEE relationship, see Edwards, *Educating for Liberty,* 24–27.

127. Edwards, *Educating for Liberty,* 310.

128. Frank Chodorov, "An Editorial Problem," *Freeman,* September 1955, 630.

129. Frank Chodorov, "Reds Are Natives," *Freeman,* August 1954, 45–46.

130. William F. Buckley, "A Dilemma of Conservatives," *Freeman,* August 1954, 52.

131. Quoted in Hamilton, introduction to *Fugitive Essays,* 29.

132. James Ingebretsen of Spiritual Mobilization and R. C. Hoiles both also wanted to nab the *Freeman* before FEE took it on.

133. Details on donor base and *Freeman* circulation from Leonard Read to Richard Ware, February 12, 1958, FEE Archives.

134. Between 1948 and 1969, the seminar met every Thursday of the school year, from 7:25 to 9:25 P.M. Mises never missed one. He arranged any other speaking or lecturing responsibility around it. See Margit von Mises, *My Years,* 140. Over the years, the seminar met in three different NYU buildings. Each year, Mises would pick a general topic. Bettina Bien Greaves, who attended the seminar religiously for eighteen years, remembers topics such as "capitalism, epistemology, praxeology, bureaucracy, interventionism, socialism, Marxism, capital theory, monetary theory, interest theory, prices and competition, monopoly and monopoly prices, institutional economics, the profit and loss system, as well as various theories of the trade cycle." Regardless of the general theme, to Mises all economics was a unified edifice. It was impossible to stick strictly to one narrow topic, as everything was related. See Bettina Bien Greaves, "Mises's New York University Seminar," *Libertarian Review,* September 1981, 24.

135. Cornuelle, interview by author.

136. Israel Kirzner, interview by author, February 9, 1997.

137. Robert J. Smith, interview by author, March 17, 1999.

138. Quoted in Dyanne M. Peterson, "The Mises Centennial Celebration," *In Pursuit of Liberty*, February 1982, 3.

139. Bettina Bien Greaves, interview by author, September 6, 1996.

140. Cornuelle, interview by author. Something Mises wrote regarding the Böhm-Bawerk seminars he attended in Austria is telling on his attitude toward how to run a student seminar: "Unfortunately, the extraordinary freedom to speak which [Böhm-Bawerk] granted to every member was occasionally abused by thoughtless talkers. . . . Stronger use of the responsibilities inherent in a chairmanship would often have improved the situation, but Böhm-Bawerk wanted no part of it. In science he believed, as did Menger, that everyone should be permitted to speak." Mises, *Notes and Recollections*, 40–41.

141. Greaves, "Mises's New York Seminar," 23–24.

142. Greaves, interview by author.

143. Cornuelle, interview by author.

144. Milton Friedman, interview by author, January 21, 1995. Similar accusations are thrown at other libertarian luminaries, such as Ayn Rand. Bettina Bien Greaves, who watched them all come and go from her berth at FEE, admits that for better or worse the libertarian movement has been led by a series of prima donnas. Greaves, interview by author.

145. Hans Sennholz, interview by author, February 10, 1997.

146. Sennholz, interview by author.

147. Greaves, interview by author.

148. Margit von Mises, *My Years*, 143. Margit's memoir of her life with Mises paints a human—perhaps all too human—portrait of the great scholar. He's shown as hopelessly incompetent in many day-to-day details of life, from driving to preparing food for himself to remembering to not flood the bathroom when shaving—the stereotypical absent-minded professor.

149. Kirzner, interview by author.

150. Margit von Mises, *My Years*, 93.

151. Rothbard, *Mises*, 63.

152. Kirzner, interview by author.

153. Margit von Mises, *My Years*, 222.

154. Hayek, *Fortunes of Liberalism*, 233. Hayek was remembering fondly an attempt at a similar organization launched before the war, which had only two meetings before World War II made it impossible to continue. That group was the brainchild of French philosopher Louis Rougier and was called Colloque Walter Lippman, after the American writer whose book *The Good Society* excited Rougier. Hayek and Mises were among the twenty-

six founding members from eight countries. Twelve of those twenty-six were early Peler-ines as well. See R. W. Hartwell, *A History of the Mont Pelerin Society* (Indianapolis: Liberty Fund, 1995), 20–21.

155. On the Pelerin founding, see Hartwell, *History of Mont Pelerin*, 27–33.

156. Hartwell, *History of Mont Pelerin*, 44.

157. Hartwell, *History of Mont Pelerin*, 41.

158. Hartwell, *History of Mont Pelerin*, 42.

159. Leonard Read to Fred R. Fairchild, May 27, 1948. Fairchild was a Yale economist of mostly FEE and libertarian bona fides. Read was discussing Fairchild's invitation to join MPS. Finally Read said that he loved the idea of Fairchild being part of a group he, Read, is in, but he himself would not now join Pelerin if he weren't already a member, given his judgment of the first meeting. He adds, "I hope none of the others who are invited to membership write me, because I don't like the role of being such a wet blanket."

160. Leonard Read's Journal, July 1949, FEE Archives.

161. Hartwell, *History of Mont Pelerin*, 214–215. For the reaction of standard economic wisdom of the mid-1940s to Erhard's bold and ultimately successful, act, see Hayek, *Fortunes of Liberalism*, 13–14.

162. Leonard Read to Pierre Goodrich, January 14, 1958, FEE Archives.

163. Leonard Read to J. Howard Pew, September 23, 1954, FEE Archives.

164. J. Howard Pew to Leonard Read, August 15, 1955, FEE Archives.

165. Leonard Read to Jasper Crane, November 24, 1954, FEE Archives. For a thorough attack from an Austrian-libertarian perspective on Henry Simons's free enterprise bona fides, see Walter Block, "Henry Simons Is Not a Supporter of Free Enterprise," *Journal of Libertarian Studies,* Fall 2002. Simons thought Mises was "the greatest living teacher of economics" and "the toughest old liberal or Manchesterite of his time," but because of his radicalism and intransigence, also "perhaps the worst enemy of his own libertarian cause." Quoted in Hulsmann, *Last Knight*, 662.

166. For Mises on Pelerin, see Hulsmann, *Last Knight*, 668.

167. Hayek, *Fortunes of Liberalism*, 192.

168. For details on the personality wars, fights over expense accounts, and general over-wrought absurdity whose cause is difficult for outsiders to accurately identify or sum up at all, see Hartwell, *History of Mont Pelerin*, chap. 5. If your appetite is whetted, the R. W. Hartwell collection at the Hoover Institution has even more details about actions by Al-bert Hunold that almost split the Society in the early 1960s. For the lesser, but equally childish, Jewkes–Leoni wars of the mid-1960s, see Hartwell, *History of Mont Pelerin*, 138–142. For debate about whether to shut down MPS, see Hartwell, *History of Mont Pelerin*, 200–203.

169. Mach was a pure phenomenalist, trying to reduce all human psychology to "simple and pure sensations." "A revelation came to me similar to one that Mach describes from his own experience," Hayek wrote, "when he suddenly recognized that the concept of 'things in themselves' in Kant's philosophy served no purpose. . . . I had the revelation that Mach's concept of 'simple and pure sensations' in his sensory psychology was equally meaningless. Since Mach had qualified so many of the connexions between sensations as 'relations,' I was finally forced to conclude that the whole structure of the sensory world was derived from 'relations' and that one might therefore throw out altogether the concept of pure and simple sensations, which plays such a large role in Mach." Hayek, *Fortunes of Liberalism,* 174. For larger context about Hayek and Mach, see 172–175.

170. Quoted in F. A. Hayek, "Philosophical Consequences," in Nishiyama and Leube, eds., *Essence of Hayek*, 228. Hayek biographer Alan Ebenstein identifies its importance to Hayek's work like this: "In both Hayek's economic and psychological thought, the limits of knowledge are key. The sensory, as societal, world is complex. In both the sensory and

societal worlds, the idea of complexity is, in Hayek's thought, paramount. Complexity prevents detailed prediction and control." Ebenstein also links Hayek's later interest in evolution and biology to his psychological thoughts in *Sensory Order*. He believed that consciousness also arises through an evolutionary process in which our perceptual apparatus arises and is shaped by experience. Ebenstein, *Friedrich Hayek*, 163. Caldwell, on the other hand, thinks the *Sensory Order* is in many ways antievolutionary because it implies ultimately that our entire body of knowledge becomes tautological, with everything we know "defined in terms of each other" and thus that no further growth in knowledge would be possible through experience. Caldwell, *Hayek's Challenge*, 275. Of arguing over what Hayek meant there is no end.

171. F. A. Hayek, *The Counter-Revolution of Science: Studies on the Abuse of Reason* (1952; Indianapolis: LibertyPress, 1979), 277. See chapters 13–14 for full exposition on why Hayek sees Saint-Simon as the father of modern socialism. Hayek traces direct connections of influence from Saint-Simon, Comte, and their followers to the young Hegelians in Germany, Thomas Carlyle and John Stuart Mill in England, and of course Karl Marx, in chapters 15–16.

172. Leube, "Biographical Introduction," in Nishiyama and Leube, eds., *Essence of Hayek*, xxiv.

173. John Nef, chairman of the University of Chicago's Committee on Social Thought, mentioned in his autobiography that it was the polemical stain of *Serfdom* that made Hayek uncongenial. In his recent Hayek biography, Alan Ebenstein insists that was not true, that his interviews with Friedman and others from Chicago indicate it was merely a lack of appreciation of Hayek's economic method, as well as a desire for departmental independence from outside sources, that led to Hayek's failure to get an economics post. See Ebenstein, *Hayek*, 185–188.

174. Hayek, *Hayek on Hayek*, 126.

175. Ralph Raico, interview by author, August 26, 1996. For more details on Hayek's Chicago seminars, see Shirley Robin Letwin, "The Achievement of Friedrich A. Hayek," in Fritz Machlup, ed., *Essays on Hayek* (New York: New York University Press, 1976), 147–149.

176. F. A. Hayek, *The Constitution of Liberty* (Chicago: University of Chicago Press, 1960), 6.

177. Hayek, *Constitution*, 20–21.

178. F. A. Hayek, *Law, Legislation, and Liberty: A New Statement of the Liberal Principles of Justice and Political Economy*, vol. 1, *Rules and Order* (Chicago: University of Chicago Press, 1973), 75.

179. Hayek, *Law, Legislation*, 1: 98–101.

180. Hayek, *Law, Legislation*, 1: 17.

181. This essay is necessary reading for anyone trying to understand Hayek. See F. A. Hayek, "The Use of Knowledge in Society," in Nishiyama and Leube, eds., *Essence of Hayek*, 211–224.

182. Not all scholars are able to make perfect sense of this Hayekian distinction. See Detmar Doering, "Hayek on Constructivism: Is the English Tradition a Sufficient Guide to Liberalism?" in Frei and Nef, eds., *Contending With Hayek*. Former Hayek student and historian of liberalism Ralph Raico admitted during an interview by the author, "I don't know what Hayek means by that distinction."

183. See Hayek, *Law, Legislation, and Liberty*, 1: 20–22. Also see Hayek, *Trend of Economic Thinking*, chaps. 6–8. Also see Hayek, *Individualism and Economic Order*, chap. 1.

184. Quoted in Hayek, *Trend of Economic Thinking*, 92.

185. Quoted in Hayek, *Trend of Economic Thinking*, 113.

186. The anarcho-capitalist Murray Rothbard, whose views are discussed more fully in Chapter 5, was vetting manuscripts for Volker, including the yet unpublished *Constitution of Liberty*. Rothbard hated the book and thought that its concessions to the state combined with Hayek's reputation as a great libertarian made it "surprisingly and distressingly, an extremely bad, and I would even say evil, book." Rothbard found Hayek's obeisance to the rule of law overwhelming support for liberty per se, as in Hayek's belief that any state intervention applied equally and with announced rules was thus noncoercive. He also thinks Hayek's disdain for the natural law/natural rights tradition in favor of the rule of law misses what is most important in libertarianism. As a Misesian, Rothbard found Hayek's mistrust of the use of reason in forming social and political philosophies leading Hayek to a combination of errors: Kirkian tradition worship combined with a Millian fascination with the meaning of our inherent ignorance. But Rothbard argues that Hayek's very knowledge of markets leads him astray here: "To Hayek, the market is an example of a social institution which works better than any individual knows, and . . . it is needed because of each person's ignorance. But while a subtle, this too is a fallacious, argument. For there is nothing really mysterious about the market: the fact that Hayek can explain its workings shows that reason can comprehend it; and since every single transaction benefits both parties and reward rationality, it is not surprising that the *sum* of all market transactions is a beautiful and rational instrument." Rothbard concludes that "if I were a young man first getting interested in political questions, and I should read *this* as the best product of the 'extreme right', I would become a roaring leftist in no time, and so I believe would almost anyone." Murray N. Rothbard, "Memorandum to the Volker Fund: Re: F. A. Hayek's *Constitution of Liberty*," January 21, 1958, MRA, LVMI. There is some rhetorical truth to this. Hayek is often used as a club to beat back more radical libertarianism, to the point where the anarchistic libertarian, weary of hearing his name, might think that ol' F. A.'s first name was actually "Even," as in, "Even Hayek admits that" such and such a state action is legitimate or necessary.

CHAPTER 5

1. Rand's break with Paterson is discussed in B. Branden, *Passion of Ayn Rand*, 203–206.
2. B. Branden, *Passion of Ayn Rand*, 218.
3. Merrill, *Ideas of Ayn Rand*, 2–3.
4. See a particularly rough-and-tumble attack from Rand's then-leading disciple Nathaniel Branden: "There is only one class of men who receive moral condemnation [in Rand's fiction]: the men who demand any form of the unearned, in matter or in spirit; who propose to treat other men as sacrificial animals; who claim the right to rule others by physical force. . . . If those who charge Ayn Rand with 'hatred,' feeling themselves to be its object, choose to identify and classify themselves with the men she condemns—doubtless they know best. But then it is not Ayn Rand—or humanity—whom they have damned." Nathaniel Branden, *Who Is Ayn Rand?* (New York: Paperback Library, 1962), 116. The most notorious of these is Whittaker Chambers in the pages of the conservative magazine *National Review*. Chambers wrote that "From almost any page of *Atlas Shrugged*, a voice can be heard, from painful necessity, commanding: 'To a gas chamber—go!'" Whittaker Chambers, "Big Sister Is Watching You," *National Review*, December 28, 1957, 596. From then on she and the magazine had a continuing mutual enmity.

But Chambers's reaction at least took the book somewhat seriously; many other gatekeepers of the popular intelligentsia couldn't even muster that. The *New Yorker* mocked it broadly, referring to a couple of Rand's fictional flourishes as reminiscent of Swift, then revealing he meant, of course, Tom Swift; refers to the gang of heroes as "the Utopia branch of the N.A.M." and writes of the climax that "apparently [the heroes] are now satisfied that the bulk of the globe's two billion or so incompetents, having starved to death, will at last know better than to fool around with businessmen." Donald Malcolm, "The New Rand Atlas," *New Yorker,* October 26, 1957, 194–198.

Still, some intelligentsia couldn't just write Rand off with an ironic chuckle; they knew better and were *scared.* In *Esquire,* Gore Vidal, alarmed that in his recent run for the House of Representatives, Rand was "the one writer people knew and talked about," complained that Rand's "'philosophy' is nearly perfect in its immorality, which makes the size of her audience all the more ominous." Gore Vidal, comment, *Esquire,* July 1961, 26–27. *Time* grumbled that Rand's "philosophy must be read to be disbelieved . . . Nietzsche's inversion of all Christian values, with an admixture of Adam Smith economics and David Hume ethics, both carried to absurd extremes . . . [a] weird performance . . . not so much capitalism as its hideous caricature." "The Solid Gold Dollar," *Time,* October 14, 1957, 128–130.

5. One can see how Rand evoked this sort of reaction. For some examples, of which there are plenty, Hank Rearden thinks of a man who buys out his mines when a government edict forbids certain vertical business integrations, that he ought to "step on the obscene thing which was Larkin and grind every wet bit of it out of existence." Ayn Rand, *Atlas Shrugged* (New York: Signet, 1957), 213–214; Dagny says of people who would dare complain about billboards blocking views of unmarred nature: "They're the people I hate" (267). A striker tells Hank that he's "abandoned at the bottom of a pit of subhuman creatures who are all that's left of mankind" (544).

6. B. Branden, *Passion,* 230–231.

7. Rand constantly hammered the notion that thinking must be rooted in the rational processing of sensory data. Since Rand believed in the primacy of existence, not consciousness, everything a man thought or knew must be reducible to sense perceptions. Men think and reason using concepts, and that is what defines man's identity—the proper definition of *man* being *rational animal.* Thus Rand thought hard about how to link concepts to sensory data. Rand took it as an axiom that our senses give us purely true and valid data. Arguing this point is an easy way to strike at the structure of Objectivism because everything else Rand had to say about concept formation falls without the base of unfailingly accurate sensory data to support it. Rand's theory on concept formation, the only part of her philosophy she wrote a whole book about, deserves more attention, even if only in a footnote. We must define, she said, by *fundamental* characteristics.

Thus for *man,* the idea that man is rational explains more about what makes him distinctive than the notion that he has two legs, has opposable thumbs, or laughs. While Rand's system is Aristotelian in many ways, she differs from him on the concept of *essence.* To Aristotle, *essence* is metaphysical; to Rand, it is epistemological—the essence of something is that which condenses and sums up what we know about it. Certain concepts come to us naturally and automatically. You can tell a concept is axiomatic "by observing the fact that an axiomatic concept has to be accepted and used even in the process of any attempt to deny it." Ayn Rand, *Introduction to Objectivist Epistemology,* 2nd ed. (New York: Meridian, 1990), 86. Mises used a similar strategy in praxeology. It is hard to argue against the idea of consciousness and existence as an existing, conscious being. Humans need concepts, because our minds can only grasp a certain number of units before becoming a jumble. Conceptual thinking allows us to reduce the innumerable concrete facts of reality into a manageable number of chewable nuggets, recombine them, and apply our knowledge of concepts back to the existents that make them up, extending our knowledge infinitely. Without concepts, humans couldn't grasp distances larger than they see; by conceptualizing "length" and particular terms of it, they can deal with distances spanning light-years.

David Gordon has pointed out, though, that it's hard to see how a child can abstract out the conceptual common denominator of various objects as being "length" without *already* having some idea, somehow, of what length is. How can one abstract a quality that one has not yet conceptualized? See David Gordon, review of *Objectivism: The Philosophy of Ayn Rand* by Leonard Peikoff, *Journal of Libertarian Studies,* Spring 1995, 138.

8. Ayn Rand, *The Voice of Reason: Essays in Objectivist Thought* (New York: New American Library, 1988), 3.

9. The novel was to be titled *To Lorne Dieterling*, and was supposed to be set in the world of dance, expressing the philosophic principles of "Atlas who did not go on strike," the problem of keeping up a heroic sense of life in a rotten culture. It was also a story of unrequited love. The notes are in Harriman, ed., *Journals,* 706–715.

10. B. Branden, interview by author, April 20, 1998.

11. Nathaniel Branden, *Judgment Day: My Years with Ayn Rand* (Boston: Houghton Mifflin, 1989), 17.

12. N. Branden, *Judgment Day*, 39.

13. N. Branden, *Judgment Day,* 40.

14. N. Branden, *Judgment Day*, 40.

15. B. Branden, *Passion of Ayn Rand*, 238.

16. Peikoff, who became a philosopher, would end up the last of Rand's circle, and her financial, literary, and intellectual heir. Later when he told the story, Peikoff merely says he was introduced by an unnamed "mutual friend." See *Intellectual Activist*, "TIA's Interview with Leonard Peikoff," June 30, 1982, 2.

17. For details on the early years of the Rand/Brandens relationship, see B. Branden, *Passion of Ayn Rand*, chaps. 20–21; N. Branden, *Judgment Day*, chaps. 3–6.

18. Social metaphysics is explained further in N. Branden, *Judgment Day*, 129–31; also in Nathaniel Branden, *The Psychology of Self-Esteem* (New York: Bantam, 1969), chap. 10.

19. N. Branden, *Judgment Day*, 131. Branden's first published work, in the June 1955 issue of the Chodorov *Freeman,* was "The Age of Un-Reason," a Randian discussion of how contemporary academia is out to destroy the mind and rationality that never mentions Rand. Since she surely knew of the article, it casts an interesting light on Rand, clearly not as controlling or obsessed with strict property rights and credit for her ideas as she was later perceived to be.

20. N. Branden, *Judgment Day*, 137. In some letters written by old associates after her death—bitter letters that aired a lifetime of closeted resentment—Rand is portrayed as never referring to Mises as anything other than "that old fool." Henry Hazlitt allegedly told a story (which he denied while the principles were alive but then said was mostly true) of Mises and Rand getting so angry at each other during an argument at the Hazlitts' home that an exasperated Mises called her "just an ignorant Jewish girl."

21. For details on the beginnings of the Rand/Branden affair, see B. Branden, *Passion of Ayn Rand*, 256–264; N. Branden, *Judgment Day*, 142–166.

22. Greenspan was "outed" as a Randian by *Time* when he was appointed chair of President Ford's Council of Economic Advisers. *Time*, "The Chairman's Favorite Author," September 30, 1974, 87–88. For a good overview of Rand's influence on Greenspan's career in public service, see R. W. Bradford, "Greenspan: Deep-Cover Radical for Capitalism?" *Liberty*, November 1997.

23. For details on the initial coalescing of the Collective, see B. Branden, *Passion of Ayn Rand*, 254–255; N. Branden, *Judgment Day*, 128–134.

24. B. Branden, *Passion of Ayn Rand,* 291–292.

25. Ayn Rand, *The Romantic Manifesto: A Philosophy of Literature* (New York: World, 1970), 177.

26. See note 4.

27. N. Branden, *Judgment Day*, 224.

28. For details on the beginnings of NBI, see N. Branden, *Judgment Day*, 235–238; also B. Branden, *Passion of Ayn Rand*, 306–308.

29. Nathaniel Branden, interview by author, April 22, 1998.

30. R. W. Bradford, editor of *Liberty* magazine, suggests that this approach encouraged NBI's cultish aspect, since people could not go back and reread or relisten to the tapes to consider their cogency, and had no one to ask challenging questions to upon hearing them. See R. W. Bradford, "Who Is Nathaniel Branden?" *Liberty*, July 1989, 62.

31. Nathaniel Branden, "A Report to Our Readers—1964," *Objectivist Newsletter*, December 1964, 51.

32. Nathaniel Branden, "A Report to Our Readers—1965," *Objectivist Newsletter*, December 1965, 57.

33. B. Branden, *Passion of Ayn Rand*, 324.

34. Murray Rothbard wrote an essay, "The Sociology of the Ayn Rand Cult," full of such observations—the joyless obsession with making sure all pleasures served "rational values," a woman booted from the Randian circle for marrying someone the leaders disapproved of, the constant reporting back to Branden and Rand about what everyone else was saying and thinking, and the belief that not showing eager support for these excommunications was an excommunicable offense itself. Libertarian movement magazine *Liberty* gave that essay away as a subscription premium in the late 1980s and early 1990s. To this day, Rand's critics get a lot of mileage from mocking the notion of a devotee of absolute reason giving birth to another nutty cult. While it doesn't use the word "cult," an early *Newsweek* article about NBI is an ancestor of all following Rand-mocking journalism. It quotes one young communicant as saying "her books are so good that most people should not be allowed to read them" and refers to Rand as a "she-messiah" in the style of Aimee McPherson. *Newsweek*, "Born Eccentric," March 27, 1961, 104–105.

For an extended rant analogizing Objectivism and a religious cult, see Albert Ellis, *Is Objectivism a Religion?* (New York: Lyle Stuart, 1968). For a survey of articles on Rand and the Rand cult, see Mimi Reisel Gladstein, *The Ayn Rand Companion* (Westport, CT: Greenwood, 1984), 93–95. More recent extended takes on this theme appear in Jeff Walker, *The Cult of Ayn Rand* (La Salle, IL: Open Court, 1998); and in Michael Schermer, *Why People Believe Weird Things* (New York: W. H. Freeman, 1997), chap. 8, "The Unlikeliest Cult."

35. Merrill, *Ideas of Ayn Rand*, 3–4. "Never did I encounter a single one of the cape-wearing, cigarette-holder-wielding cultists who were allegedly so omnipresent in the movement. Certainly I did meet a number of self-appointed guardians of ideological purity. But I, and the vast majority of my friends in the movement, regarded these characters with amused tolerance rather than quaking fear. . . . The smokers I knew within the movement would certainly have been surprised and pleased if they'd only known that [according to Rothbard] 'smoking, according to the cult, was a moral obligation'; they were used to being criticized by the rest of us for irrational and self-destructive behavior."

36. Robert Hessen, interview by author, November 8, 1998.

37. Jerome Tuccille, *It Usually Begins with Ayn Rand* (New York: Stein & Day, 1971), 33.

38. Joan Kennedy Taylor, interview by author, September 7, 1996.

39. N. Branden, *Judgment Day*, 172.

40. N. Branden, *Judgment Day*, 255–256.

41. Taylor, interview by author.

42. Hessen, interview by author.

43. N. Branden, *Judgment Day*, 315–316.

44. Hessen, interview by author.

45. N. Branden, *Judgment Day*, 244.

46. These collected pieces comprise most of her remaining books: *The Virtue of Selfishness* (1964); *Capitalism: The Unknown Ideal* (1966); *The Romantic Manifesto* (1970); *The New Left: The Anti-Industrial Revolution* (1971); *Philosophy: Who Needs It?* (1982); and the posthu-

mous *The Voice of Reason* (1988). Many of the books were fleshed out with approved essays by her acolytes that had also appeared in official Rand-edited Objectivist publications. Branden, Peikoff, Greenspan, and Hessen all contributed.

47. Ayn Rand, *For the New Intellectual* (New York: Signet, 1961), 53.

48. Rand, *New Intellectual*, 57.

49. This principle defined *Atlas*: each of the novel's three sections, in a repetition of the ultimate unity of its theme, is named after a restatement of this Aristotelian truth: "Non-contradiction," "Either-or," "A is A."

50. Ayn Rand, *The Virtue of Selfishness* (New York: Signet, 1964), 17.

51. An entertainingly scabrous argument against Rand and other libertarian natural rights theorists can be found in L. A. Rollins, *The Myth of Natural Rights* (Port Townsend, WA: Loompanics, 1983).

52. Once Leonard Peikoff, in a Rand fiction writing workshop, guessed that a character must be essentially evil because he was a priest. "But Leonard," Rand admonished, "you are forgetting Thomas Aquinas!" Ralph Raico, interview by author, October 10, 1998.

53. Harriman, ed., *Journals*, 254, 276.

54. Reporting on specific current events sometimes gave flesh to Rand's philosophical principles, as in her obituary for Marilyn Monroe, written for Rand's short-lived attempt at a newspaper opinion column for the *Los Angeles Times* in 1962. (For details on this short-lived column, see B. Branden, *Passion of Ayn Rand*, 318.) Her elegy to the innocent greatness Monroe represented is powerful and affecting. (See Rand, *Voice of Reason*, chap. 16.) Her essay on the wonders of the Apollo 11 launch (Rand, *Voice of Reason*, chap. 17), while evocative, lovely, and passionate reporting, cannot help but smell funny coming from a woman who is supposed to defend the right of the individual to what is his. The woman who earlier wrote of the "monstrous absurdity" of the "'conquest of space' by some men, when and if it is accomplished by expropriating the labor of other men who are left without means to acquire a pair of shoes," (Rand, *Virtue of Selfishness*, 84) and who insists on absolute consistency and integrity, ought not later scornfully mock anti-Apollo protesters who complain that it was done at their expense. She missed her own mark in some other notorious essays, including her masculinist attempt to explain why no woman, even one as brilliant and capable as Rand herself, would or could ever want to be president. That piece is not so much reasoned as cried—a feminine cry for a man she could and must look up to, from a woman trapped in a marriage with a kind man who had never done much of anything on his own, certainly not something the likes of Rand could look up to (Rand, *Voice of Reason*, chap. 26).

On art, Rand fiercely defended her own romanticism. "Romantic art is the fuel and the spark plug of a man's soul; its task is to set a soul on fire and never let it go out. The task of providing that fire with a motor and a direction belongs to philosophy" (Rand, *Romantic Manifesto*, 150). Only romantic art presents man as he should be and ought to be: a purposeful, competent being who faces challenges and conquers them. The modern thriller, Rand thought, is the only living survivor of that tradition in the 1960s context, though it is flawed by its lack of serious intellectual content to accompany its heroes moving purposefully through exciting and unusual plots. Rand's favorite author was Victor Hugo, but in the modern world, largely bereft of her preferred type of writing, a simple but precise thriller writer like Mickey Spillane was to her the literary superior of obscurantists like Thomas Wolfe or grim sewer dwellers such as Joyce and Kafka or pretentious, absurd nonentities such as Gertrude Stein. In fact, Rand's very favorite piece of fiction was from a French children's adventure magazine she read as a child, called "The Mysterious Valley." "No work of literature has ever impressed me quite that much," Rand told *Mademoiselle*. *Mademoiselle*, "Disturber of the Peace: Ayn Rand," August 1962, 194.

55. Ayn Rand, *Capitalism: The Unknown Ideal* (New York: Signet, 1966), chap. 22.

56. Ayn Rand, *Voice of Reason*, chap. 12. This piece, called "Global Balkanization," was originally given as a lecture at Boston's Ford Hall Forum, Rand's favorite place to speak, where she gave yearly lectures for many years. In it, among very prescient quotes about how the welfare state manufactures ethnic grievances and ethnic pressure groups that tend to help only their own elites and not the rank-and-file minority members, is an amusing quote against native culture, which Rand found "excruciatingly boring . . . [you see] one set of people clapping their hands while jumping up and down, you've seen them all"(120). That sort of biting assault is the only kind of humor Rand indulged in in her later writings, though portions of *The Fountainhead* are very funny, particularly involving Toohey, a far more witty villain than the pathetic slugs in *Atlas Shrugged*. "Humor is not an unconditional virtue," Rand wrote. "Its moral character depends on its object. To laugh at the contemptible, is a virtue; to laugh at the good, is a hideous vice." Rand, *Romantic Manifesto*, 126. In her personal life, says Barbara Branden, Rand didn't seem to get the logical reversal that so much humor depends on. But her portrayals of Toohey and Dominique in *Fountainhead* show that Rand, at least once, had a masterly command of irony. For more of Rand on multiculturalism, see Ayn Rand, *Philosophy: Who Needs It?* (Indianapolis: Bobbs-Merrill, 1982), 51.

57. Rand, *Voice of Reason*, 343.

58. Rand, *Philosophy: Who Needs It*, chap. 13.

59. Rand, *Capitalism*, chap. 24.

60. Murray N. Rothbard, "Life in the Old Right," *Chronicles*, August 1994, 15.

61. Rothbard, "Life in the Old Right," *Chronicles*, 15.

62. Quoted in Justin Raimondo, *An Enemy of the State: The Life of Murray N. Rothbard* (Amherst, NY: Prometheus, 2000), 59–60.

63. Quoted in Raimondo, *Enemy of the State*, 60–61. Not necessarily opposition to labor unions in principle, but certainly a strong emphasis on their misbehaviors and dark side, is a thread running through most of the major libertarian intellectual leaders, and their supporters—many of them industrialists with personal experience in resenting unions.

64. Rothbard, "Life in the Old Right," *Chronicles*, 16.

65. Quoted in Raimondo, *Enemy of the State*, 41.

66. Murray N. Rothbard, "Recommended Reading," *Libertarian Forum*, June 1971, 5.

67. Quoted in Raimondo, *Enemy of the State*, 47.

68. Murray N. Rothbard, "What's Wrong with the Liberty Poll; or, How I Became a Libertarian," *Liberty*, July 1988, 55.

69. Richard Cornuelle to Henry Hazlitt, December 19, 1955, Henry Hazlitt Archives, FEE.

70. Murray Rothbard to Richard Cornuelle, January 6, 1954, MRA, LVMI.

71. Murray Rothbard to Frank Meyer, May 15, 1967, MRA, LVMI.

72. Although Rothbard was happily calling himself an anarchist privately by the mid-1950s, he was still cagey and wary about it publicly, since few understood his unique anarcho-capitalist synthesis. In a 1955 letter to R. C. Hoiles, he congratulated the radical newspaper magnate for an article Rothbard saw in the May 8 *Colorado Springs Gazette Telegraph*, which used the term proudly: "This is the first time one of us 'right-wing anarchists' has had the courage to come right out and call our philosophy by its proper name. . . . The name 'anarchist' has been stolen from us by leftists in a similar way as the term 'liberal.' Those who call themselves anarchists now are not really anarchists at all, but a wild type of communist" (Murray Rothbard to R. C. Hoiles, September 11, 1955, MRA, LVMI). In a 1958 letter to Bill Buckley, he'd say to those who accused him (and in this case Frank Meyer, to whom it did not apply) of philosophical anarchy: "What is it supposed to be, and who are the 'philosophers' sponsoring it? Is it Prince Kropotkin, who wanted to abolish private property and organize all production in workers' collectives and peasants' com-

munes? . . . Are we and Mr. Meyer similar to the Spanish Anarchists who, during the Civil War, imposed the death penalty on anyone caught using money, as contrasted to barter? In what way, then, are we to be called Anarchists? But what *is* it then, that libertarianism resembles? Who are *its* founding philosophers?" Rothbard pointedly leaves the question unanswered. Murray Rothbard to William F. Buckley, September 18, 1958, MRA, LVMI.

73. Raico, interview by author.

74. George Reisman, *Capitalism: A Treatise on Economics* (Ottawa, IL: Jameson, 1996), xliii.

75. Llewellyn H. Rockwell Jr., ed., *Murray N. Rothbard: In Memoriam* (Auburn, AL: Ludwig von Mises Institute, 1995), 3. In contemporaneous correspondence, strangely, Rothbard credits *Raico* with the bon mot.

76. Murray N. Rothbard, "My Break with Branden and the Rand Cult," *Liberty*, September 1989, 27.

77. Cornuelle, interview by author.

78. Quoted in Raimondo, *Enemy of the State*, 82–83.

79. Raico wrote mostly on historical figures of the European classical liberal tradition and wrote and lectured for libertarian institutes such as Cato (where he was books editor and briefly publisher for its magazine *Inquiry* in the late 1970s and early 1980s), the Institute for Humane Studies, and the Ludwig von Mises Institute.

80. Hessen wrote a book on a free market defense of the corporation, *In Defense of the Corporation* (Stanford: Hoover Institution Press, 1979).

81. Hamowy taught history for most of his career at the University of Alberta, after a stint in the late 1960s lecturing at Stanford.

82. In the 1980s, Liggio served as president at the Institute for Humane Studies, and in the early 1990s joined the Atlas Foundation, the think tank created by Britain's Antony Fisher to help guide and support free market think tanks across the globe. He also served as president of the Mont Pelerin Society in the early twenty-first century. It strikes some as unusual that such a radical Rothbardian managed to achieve positions of respect in the institutional small-government libertarian movement that never did, and never would, come Rothbard's way. Liggio was even more far-out, in conventional movement terms, on issues of war and land reform than was Rothbard. Old friends credit it with his mild, lovable manner as compared to Rothbard's deliberate, outrageous scabrousness.

83. Mrs. Rothbard, known as Joey, apparently extracted from the night owl Rothbard a New Year's resolution in 1954 to be asleep every night before 5:00 A.M., and to arise by 1:30 P.M. See Powell, *Triumph of Liberty*, 276. The Volker Fund's Kenneth Templeton delighted in showing up at the Rothbards' apartment unannounced from a West Coast flight. Thanks to the time change, he'd have three more hours of vitality than Rothbard and could talk him under the table until the morning light. Kenneth Templeton, interview by author, September 18, 2005.

84. Ronald Hamowy, interview by author, October 7, 1998.

85. Rockwell, ed., *Rothbard: In Memoriam*, 97. Hamowy added that Rothbard was "*always* and unwaveringly on [a victim of injustice's] side, demanding that justice be done."

86. Hessen, interview by author.

87. Liggio, interview by author.

88. Raico, interview by author.

89. Liggio, interview by author.

90. Liggio, interview by author.

91. Murray Rothbard to Frank Meyer, May 15, 1967, MRA, LVMI.

92. Murray Rothbard to William Johnson, August 19, 1954, MRA, LVMI.

93. Details on the Cohn memorial event speech from Murray Rothbard to Thaddeus Ashby, August 19, 1954, MRA, LVMI.

94. The patrician Buckley, for a while at least, took Rothbard's upbraidings in stride and good humor. In rejecting one article of Rothbard's making an isolationist case, Buckley wrote, "not that I love you any the less, you perverse old anarchist. But don't worry, when the Communists come, I'll run interference." William F. Buckley to Murray Rothbard, May 13, 1959, MRA, LVMI.

95. E. W. Dykes to William Buckley, December 19, 1955, FEE Archives.

96. Murray Rothbard to Kenneth Templeton, December 30, 1956, MRA, LVMI.

97. Murray Rothbard to Richard Cornuelle, February 2, 1955, MRA, LVMI.

98. Dennis L. Lythgoe, *Let 'Em Holler: A Political Biography of J. Bracken Lee* (Salt Lake City: Utah State Historical Society, 1982), 6.

99. Lythgoe, *Let 'Em Holler,* 179.

100. Lythgoe, *Let 'Em Holler,* 182.

101. Rothbard, "Life in the Old Right," *Chronicles,* 17. Third parties were a fascination of Rothbard's; he kept up with every random twitch of possibly libertarian-leaning action in the obscure political scene in long memos written for the Volker Fund in the 1950s.

102. Liggio, interview by author.

103. Murray Rothbard to Thaddeus Ashby, May 8, 1955, MRA, LVMI.

104. Murray Rothbard to Herbert Cornuelle, November 12, 1952. The right's awfulness on these issues, as well as the standard conflation of libertarian individualism as a movement of the right, made critics mistake the very libertarian Mencken for a progressive leftist, Rothbard complained.

105. Murray Rothbard to Thaddeus Ashby, May 8, 1955, MRA, LVMI.

106. Howard Buffett to Murray Rothbard, February 9, 1956, MRA, LVMI.

107. Murray Rothbard to Richard Cornuelle, February 10, 1954, MRA, LVMI.

108. Rothbard wrote to a friend regarding these antinuke activities: "I realize that this is heresy for a professional economist to say, but I think the issue of peace vs. nuclear annihilation of the world is considerably more important than whether we have a 2% or 4% per annum rise in prices, or whether taxes on the upper income brackets are raised or lowered by 2%." Murray Rothbard to William Allen, [late 1950s], MRA, LVMI.

109. William F. Buckley, in an ill-tempered attack obituary on his old friend, said that Rothbard stood in the street and physically cheered Khrushchev as he drove by. There is no documentary evidence for this allegation, which is denied by Rothbard's friends from the time. See William F. Buckley Jr., "Murray N. Rothbard R.I.P.," *National Review,* February 6, 1995, 19–20. A more nuanced explanation of why Rothbard metaphorically "cheered" a Khrushchev visit went like this: "Yes, yes, Nikita Sergeyevitch Khrushchev is a Bloody Butcher. On the Day of Judgment he will answer for his crimes, and roast a thousand years in hellfire. But there are a lot of bloody butchers around; the world reeks with them, is universally run by them, has been run by them, more or less, for many centuries. Lord Acton, the great British libertarian historian, once said that the Muse of the historian is not Clio, but Rhadamanthus, the avenger of innocent blood. I agree. . . . Khrushchev *is* a Bloody Butcher, but so is Churchill, and DeGaulle, and Franco . . . and countless other 'bastions of the Free World.'. . . Certainly, Winston Churchill slaughtered far more men in his lifetime than had Nikita. So did F.D.R. Harry S. Truman, Butcher of Hiroshima and Nagasaki, is not far behind. Out task should be: to reduce the annual quantity of butchery as much as possible. How do we do this, we anti-Butchers? By reviling Khrushchev or Kosygin as much as possible, and thereby making a peaceful *détente* impossible, and nuclear extermination ever closer? Or by seeing to it that peace prevails, and that therefore there is no mass international butchery to worry about? The chief instrument of butchery by state rulers over innocent civilians is *war;* refrain from war, work for peace, and we shall have done our part in reducing butchery in the world." Murray N. Rothbard, "Myths of the Cold War," *Rampart Journal of Individualist Thought,* Summer 1966, 70–71.

110. Murray Rothbard to Kenneth Templeton, May 19, 1959, MRA, LVMI.

111. E. W. Dykes to Leonard Read, September 16, 1963. Memo sent to the FEE board of trustees on September 20, 1963, FEE Archives.

112. See Raimondo, *Enemy of the State,* 109–114 for Rothbard's initial reactions to Rand.

113. Murray Rothbard to Richard Cornuelle, August 11, 1954, MRA, LVMI.

114. Raimondo, *Enemy of the State,* 117–118.

115. Murray Rothbard, "My Break with Branden and the Rand Cult," *Liberty*, September 1989, 28.

116. Bruce Goldberg got his revenge with his review "Ayn Rand's 'For the New Intellectual,'" *New Individualist Review*, November 1961. He criticized it for "the paucity of rational arguments, the frequency with which nonsense is offered as self-evident truth, the hysterical ranting against opponents who have had their views distorted beyond recognition." (17) Nathaniel Branden, appalled by this hooliganish attack, wrote Hayek, a faculty adviser to the magazine at the University of Chicago, to get him to denounce the magazine; Hayek declined to do so.

117. Tuccille, *It Usually Begins with Ayn Rand,* 21.

118. Rothbard, "Rand Cult," 29.

119. Murray Rothbard to Bruce Goldberg, June 23, 1958, MRA, LVMI.

120. The essay originally appeared in Helmut Schoeck and James W. Wiggins, eds., *Scientism and Values* (Princeton, NJ: Van Nostrand, 1960). It was reprinted in Murray N. Rothbard, *The Logic of Action One: Money, Method, and the Austrian School* (Cheltenham, UK: Edward Elgar, 1997).

121. Rothbard, "Rand Cult," *Liberty*, 31.

122. Rothbard, "Rand Cult," *Liberty*, 31.

123. Rothbard, "Rand Cult," *Liberty*, 32.

124. Hessen, interview by author.

125. Murray Rothbard to Kerry Thornley, May 18, 1965, MRA, LVMI.

126. The play concerns Keith Hackley, a young fan of Carson Sand's masterpiece *The Brow of Zeus,* visiting her home and being flummoxed with, among other things, talk of a "particularly rational brand" of cigarettes, and being told how wrong it is that he admires "Beethoven, Mozart, who reek of naturalism, whose whole work tramples on values, whose every note displays the malevolent universe premise."

127. His later sparring partner Milton Friedman expressed his regret: "I am sorry that you decided not to apply for a Post Doctoral Fellowship. I am sure we would have benefited at least as much as you to have an opportunity to have you around." Milton Friedman to Murray Rothbard, April 17, 1956, MRA, LVMI.

128. Rothbard also received a one-year grant from the Earhart Foundation for this project.

129. Murray N. Rothbard, *Man, Economy, and State: A Treatise on Economic Principles* (1962; Los Angeles: Nash, 1970), 585–586.

130. Mises, *Human Action,* 359.

131. Rothbard, *Man, Economy, and State,* 604–615, for the illusion of monopoly price.

132. Rothbard, *Man, Economy, and State,* 701–703, for Rothbard against fractional-reserve banking.

133. Rothbard, *Man, Economy, and State,* 765–766.

134. In the acknowledgments Rothbard thanks nineteenth-century French liberal economist Gustave de Molinari and nineteenth-century American individualist anarchist Benjamin Tucker for being part of "that small fraction of . . . men who began to demonstrate how a totally free, Stateless market might operate successfully." Murray Rothbard, *Power and Market: Government and the Economy,* 2nd ed. (Kansas City: Sheed, Andrews & McMeel, 1977), unnumbered acknowledgments page.

135. Rothbard, *Power and Market*, 1.

136. Rothbard breaks down state intervention into three categories: autistic, where an individual is coerced, attacked, or ordered to do or not to do something; binary, when someone is forced into an exchange with the intervener (e.g., taxation); and triangular, where two or more parties are forced to engage or not engage in an exchange (e.g., minimum wage laws).

137. Rothbard's discussion of libertarian class analysis in Rothbard, *Power and Market*, 14–16.

138. Rothbard, *Power and Market*, 16.

139. Rothbard, *Logic of Action One*, 89.

140. For a critique of Rothbard's ideas about social utility, see Bryan Caplan, "The Austrian Search for Realistic Foundations," *Southern Economic Journal*, April 1999, 832–836. Caplan argues that it is absurd to say that all preferences must and can only be expressed through action. "At every moment, by introspection we are aware of unrevealed preferences" (834). Caplan used one of the Austrians' own tropes—introspection as a way to useful knowledge—against Rothbard.

141. Rothbard's most direct attack on the free rider problem can be found in Rothbard, *Logic of Action One*, 251: "A and B decide to pay for the building of a dam for their uses; C benefits though he did not pay. A and B educate themselves at their expense and C benefits by being able to deal with educated people, and so on. This is the problem of the Free Rider. Yet it is difficult to understand what the hullabaloo is all about. Am I to be specially taxed because I enjoy the sight of my neighbor's garden without paying for it? A's and B's purchase of a good reveals that *they* are willing to pay for it; if it indirectly benefits C as well, no one is the loser. If C feels that he would be deprived of the benefit if only A and B paid, then he is free to contribute too. In any case, all the individuals consult their own preferences in the matter. In fact, we are *all* free riders on the investment, and the technological development, of our ancestors. Must we wear sackcloth and ashes, or submit ourselves to State dictation, because of this happy fact?"

142. Quoted in James Dale Davidson, "A Libertarian Rebuttal: Conservatism Examined," *Libertarian Forum*, April 1971, 7.

143. For Rothbard on Hoover's actual policies and attitudes toward laissez-faire, see Murray N. Rothbard, *America's Great Depression,* 3rd ed. (Kansas City: Sheed & Ward, 1975), chaps. 7–8. Rothbard's version of the Great Depression's cause is not widely accepted in the economics profession, but popular historian Paul Johnson, in his huge history of the twentieth century, *Modern Times,* credits Rothbard with the most believable theory of its causes. It stands as one of the few attempts to show the Austrian business cycle theory in action during an actual historical incident.

144. A somewhat hostile but reasonably informative history of Spiritual Mobilization can be found in Eckard V. Toy Jr., "Spiritual Mobilization: The Failure of an Ultraconservative Ideal in the 1950s," *Pacific Northwest Quarterly,* April 1970.

145. *The Christian's Political Responsibility,* pamphlet in Hoover Institution, George Koether Collection, Box 2, Spiritual Mobilization folder.

146. For the saga of Pew's and the National Lay Committee's failures to stem the social gospel, see E. V. Toy Jr., "The National Lay Committee and the National Council of Churches: A Case Study of Protestants in Conflict," *American Quarterly*, Summer 1969.

147. James Fifield to Norman Vincent Peale, May 10, 1944, FEE Archives.

148. A list of authors and themes in *Faith and Freedom* can be found in John Cody, "Some Spiritual Dimensions in Modern Libertarianism: The *Faith and Freedom* Circle" (paper delivered at a 1984 Libertarian Scholars Conference). Hoover Institution, Center for Libertarian Studies Collection, Box 1.

149. Leonard Read, "A Thought on War," *Faith and Freedom,* April 1951, 6.

150. In the mid-1950s, editor William Johnson briefly handed over control of *Faith and Freedom*'s book review section to the Circle Bastiat.

151. Ralph Lord Roy, *Apostles of Discord: A Study of Organized Bigotry and Disruption on the Fringes of Protestantism* (Boston: Beacon, 1953), 285.

152. Roy, *Apostles of Discord*, 285.

153. Roy, *Apostles of Discord*, 289.

154. Armstrong County was absorbed into neighboring Dewey County in 1951 by South Dakota's state legislature because it was being used as a tax haven for cattle barons in neighboring counties, who would drive their herds into Armstrong to avoid levies. Peter Steele, "Armstrong County R.I.P.," *Faith and Freedom*, April 1953.

155. The case was appealed to the Supreme Court, but cert was denied. Ingebretsen leaned on Rothbard and Rose Wilder Lane for research into the topic of compulsory education for the case.

156. James C. Ingebretsen, *Apprentice to the Dawn* (Los Angeles: Philosophical Research Society, 2003), 27.

157. Ingebretsen, *Apprentice*, 28.

158. See Ingebretsen, *Apprentice,* 28–40, for the curious narrative of his spiritual awakening.

159. Jay Stevens, *Storming Heaven: LSD and the American Dream* (New York: Harper & Row, 1987), 37.

160. Leonard Read to W. C. Mullendore, May 25, 1956, FEE Archives.

161. Leonard Read to R. C. Hoiles, July 8, 1948, FEE Archives.

162. Leonard Read to W. C. Mullendore, March 14, 1955, FEE Archives.

163. W. C. Mullendore to Leonard Read, August 18, 1956, FEE Archives.

164. Regarding Read and acid, the context of the journals shows that he expected, even intended, that his children should read it, so some level of self-censorship may have been at work. See his March 29, 1962, journal entry: "WCM [Mullendore] seems to be greatly impressed with LSD experiments, something that has no attraction for me. During his recent experience in which a greater consciousness is apparent, the message is, 'You are invited to partake.'"

165. Leonard Read Journal, November 5, 1962, FEE Archives.

166. W. C. Mullendore to Louis Dehmlow, July 11, 1962, University of Oregon Special Collections, W. C. Mullendore Collection, Box 1, Correspondence D folder.

167. W. C. Mullendore to Louis Dehmlow, April 22, 1964, University of Oregon Special Collections, W. C. Mullendore Collection, Box 1, Correspondence D folder.

168. Murray Rothbard to Kenneth Templeton, August 8, 1956, MRA, LVMI.

169. Murray Rothbard to Kenneth Templeton, December 7, 1956, MRA, LVMI.

170. Robert LeFevre to Murray Rothbard, February 2, 1959, MRA, LVMI.

171. After the 1961 collapse of Spiritual Mobilization, Greenfield ended up personal minister to Walter Knott, one of Orange County's famously antigovernment businessmen, on Knott's Berry Farm.

172. "Sometimes, through distortion, misunderstanding, or jealous rivalry, my liberalism is called 'radical,' my conservatism, 'reactionary.' But the labels do not matter, for I am a spirit rather than dogma. Wherever chains are being broken, whether ancient or new, and whether political, material, or moral, the Liberating Spirit is there. I was there when the Greeks lifted their singing temples to the sky. I was on the lips of the Nazarene as he flung his winged words to the world. . . . I was the wind that blew the ships to Jamestown and Plymouth . . . I was in the dauntless, hardy, sometimes ruthless and fool-hardy, avalanche of energy that won the West and built such industry, abundance, and freedom as never before had been known on earth." This definition of the new spirit of Spiritual Mobilization from *The Liberating Spirit of Spiritual Mobilization* pamphlet, no author or date listed, probably Ingebretsen in 1958. Copy in FEE Archives.

173. Some libertarians think that Rothbard's view of the extension of libertarianism is too limited, even given his intellectual frame of reference. John Cody delivered a paper at a Center for Libertarian Studies conference in 1984 entitled "Some Spiritual Dimensions in Modern Libertarianism: The *Faith and Freedom* Circle," in which he argues that Rothbard and those who try to keep libertarianism focused on the world, not the individual mind and spirit, are missing the point. Did not Etienne de la Boetie talk of "'voluntary servitude,' our own self-enslavement by succumbing to fear and the hypnotic propaganda that legitimizes statist ideology? The individual may prove inadequate theoretically to explain the genesis of how the state was able to usurp an individual's personal freedom. Nor does it seem likely that such an exclusively 'outer liberty' focus can offer any practical or effective techniques to empower individuals to bring about social change and move us from state domination. . . . My own researches time and again impressed on me that what the *'outer liberty'* paradigm tended to programmatically filter out as of secondary significance or irrelevant to 'libertarian' concerns were, in fact, the vital, motivating dimensions in the rise and evolution of human freedom: namely, the *'inner freedom'* dimensions of psychological autonomy, spiritual and religious insights and commitments . . . the predominantly political economy paradigm of libertarian scholarship tended to silently neglect or quickly pass over without analysis the deeply spiritual or psychological forces which historically nutured individual liberty."

Cody says this overpoliticization of libertarian thinking and scholarship reads out of the movement such important figures as William Blake, Emerson, Thoreau, Allen Ginsberg, and others who fought to extend freedom in mostly non–explictly political directions. The very fact that this discussion is in a footnote lends some credence to Cody's complaint—such figures have not been embraced by most movement libertarians as part of their team. Cody's essay goes on to give a gnostic interpretation of *Faith and Freedom's* Heardian turn. The typescript of this unpublished paper is in the Hoover Institution, Center for Libertarian Studies Collection, Box 1.

174. Leonard E. Read, *Elements of Libertarian Leadership* (Irvington-on-Hudson, NY: Foundation for Economic Education, 1962), 156–157.

175. Read, *Libertarian Leadership*, 157.

176. Read, *Libertarian Leadership*, 158.

177. Read, *Libertarian Leadership*, 158–159.

178. Read, *Libertarian Leadership*, 159.

179. "I, Pencil" first appeared in the December 1958 issue of *Freeman*. It was later distributed as a pamphlet.

180. Although they knew they were ideological outliers, Liggio didn't feel libertarians had been reduced to the Nockian "remnant" holding the truths of liberty and individualism alive in a completely hostile world in the mid-1950s. FEE then, as Liggio notes, had a mailing list of over 50,000 people. "If it was to be seen as a remnant, our remnant was not 10 people, it was tens of thousands of people in touch and interested in these ideas, and a good chunk of business leaders and intellectuals and even some political people. It did seem to me that subsequently those numbers became smaller, and the early '60s really did see a retrenchment." Liggio, interview by author.

181. Murray Rothbard to William Johnson, March 19, 1956, MRA, LVMI.

182. Some deeper analysis of Harper's poll results helps show where the libertarian movement stood on the cusp of the 1960s. Harper's twenty-five respondents listed 184 libertarian thinkers. Harper had asked for the names of "outstanding persons of our time in the United States in accomplishing education for the cause of human liberty" in "any form and process of education the person may have used." Only one-quarter of those picked were Ph.D. holders functioning in academic settings. Half of them had been helped in a major way by the Volker Fund directly or through an organization that Volker helped,

and one-quarter of them had been helped with lesser grants, amounting to three-quarters with some Volker connection. Institutions strongly represented on the list of names Harper received in response include FEE, the University of Chicago, NYU, the *Wall Street Journal*, LeFevre's Freedom School, and Spiritual Mobilization. Of those who received votes, 105 had written books, 83 taught academically, and 13 were in politics. The responses to Harper's poll are in Hoover Institution, F. A. Harper Collection, Box 12.

183. Murray Rothbard to F. A. Harper, January 3, 1961, MRA, LVMI.

184. Virgil Jordan to F. A. Harper, October 15, 1961, Hoover Institution, F. A. Harper Collection, Box 12. Four years later, Jordan killed his wife and himself.

CHAPTER 6

1. The first board of the Institute for Humane Studies consisted of Luhnow, James Doenges (an Indiana physician, one of the founders of the Association of American Physicians and Surgeons, a professional group that fought socialized medicine), Pierre Goodrich (an Indianapolis business man with interests in banking and other areas, who started his own Liberty Fund with a similar mission, though different tactics, than the institute), and Morris Cox, an old Volker board member.

2. Leoni, who was murdered in 1967 by one of his tenants, would be pleased to know that at the end of the twentieth century his book *Freedom and the Law* was still bought in bulk and given away by the Institute for Humane Studies. It is ideal, especially in dealing with students and thinkers from formerly communist countries, in explaining the meaning of law and legal institutions in a free society. (I received my own copy at an institute seminar in 1988.)

3. Information and quotes regarding the February 1–3, 1962, meeting, known as the Villa meeting, about the Institute for Humane Studies all from "Institute for Humane Studies: History and Progress," Memorandum 7 in a typescript bound in a folder called "Defensive Memorandums 1–11, April 20–21–22, 1962," in the author's possession. The document is unsigned, but context clues indicate Baldy Harper or George Resch, or the two in collaboration, authored it.

4. H. W. Luhnow, untitled and undirected memo, William Volker Fund stationery, March 15, 1962. Copy in author's possession. This was not, however, the end. Some of the Volker funds went into a failed Center for American Studies, run briefly by Ivan Bierly and dedicated to exploring the spiritual roots of American liberty, which Luhnow was now saying was always his primary concern. That operation never achieved much, and within a couple of years Bierly was selling real estate in the Burlingame/Menlo Park area, garnering this Rothbardian jibe: "The great negative burden of having Ivan in the field will be lifted from the libertarian movement. From now on, Ivan will no longer be a burden to us; the people with problems will be the customers, who will have to ponder the question: 'Do I want to buy a house from this man?'" Murray Rothbard to F. A. Harper, November 26, 1964, MRA, LVMI. As late as 1973, Luhnow's successor as chairman of the fund board, Morris A. Cox, was still writing letters on Volker Fund stationery to the likes of Henry Hazlitt regarding possible support of projects, but its active programs along libertarian lines died in March 1962 (except for a continuation of its commitment to Mises at NYU for two more years). Most of the fund's money was transferred to the Hoover Institution in the late 1960s.

5. For a brief summation of reconstructionist thinking and internal controversies, see Anson Shupe, "Prophets of a Biblical America," *Wall Street Journal*, April 12, 1989. For a longer one from a libertarian perspective, see Jeffrey A. Tucker, "Puritanism Comes Full Circle," *Liberty*, July 1989.

Reconstructionism had not been fully formulated by the early 1960s, but Bierly was sending copies of Rushdoony's early books to libertarian colleagues. George Resch recalls

Bierly making sly references to what a shame it was that certain of his Volker colleagues weren't going to church, and that Rothbard was attempting to craft a libertarian natural rights theory that wasn't explicitly theological.

6. Murray Rothbard, "Toward a Strategy for Libertarian Social Change" (undated, unpublished ms. in author's possession), 141.

7. Kenneth Templeton, interview by author, September 18, 2005.

8. George Resch, interview by author, December 19, 2005.

9. Murray Rothbard to F. A. Harper, March 22, 1962, MRA, LVMI.

10. For the story of United Student Aid Funds losing out to federal efforts, see Richard Cornuelle, *Reclaiming the American Dream* (1965; New Brunswick, NJ: Transaction, 1993), 186–189.

11. T. George Harris, "A New Conservative Manifesto," *Look*, December 29, 1964.

Cornuelle, in the afterword to a 1993 reprint of *Reclaiming the American Dream*, apologized for calling himself a conservative rather than a libertarian. He regrets framing the book in a way that fit "into the context of the then current debate in a way it did not entirely deserve, and also to give the book a false confessional air, as if a dangerous reactionary had suddenly seen the error of his ways and tearfully accepted the then fashionable agenda of what we were just then beginning to call the Liberal Establishment. I admitted I had been a right-wing extremist who had swallowed the conservative doctrine whole. I hadn't been and didn't, but because the public had not even begun to distinguish between the gathering conservative movement and the then practically invisible libertarian movement of which I was a proud and industrious functionary, it seemed reasonable to borrow the conservative designation. This was a mistake, but it was not as reprehensible as it sounds now: the vague and mistaken public image of a libertarian, if one existed at all, was of a cloaked and bearded figure with a bomb behind his back and a dirty book in his pocket." Cornuelle, *Reclaiming the American Dream*, 171.

12. Nixon's HUD secretary George Romney took the helm on the program. Its unveiling is reported in Don Oberdorfer, "Voluntary Attack Mapped on Social Ills," *Washington Post,* January 26, 1969. Cornuelle wrote a book on the topic in collaboration with Nixon's HEW Secretary Robert Finch: Richard Cornuelle and Robert H. Finch, *The New Conservative/Liberal Manifesto* (San Diego: Viewpoint, 1968).

13. "In addition to being safe and non-controversial, it is also a highly self-righteous revolution, as are all ideologies of charity of the 'let's you help him' variety. With all the vast proliferation of private charity in recent years, oddly coinciding with a great increase in living standards, it is also a clearly superfluous revolution on any count; surely what America does *not* need most is one more charity and one more set of charity-mongers." Murray Rothbard to the editor of *Look* magazine, December 20, 1964, MRA, LVMI. In an even harsher judgment on Cornuelle's new turn, Rothbard complained, "How many noses of Kentucky hillbillies would you suppose that RCC [Cornuelle] has wiped personally?" Murray Rothbard to George Resch, December 20, 1964, MRA, LVMI.

14. Meant to be a one-volume text covering all of American history, it ballooned into a five-volume work only on colonial history, ending with the Constitution. Mostly written in the mid-1960s, it was not published until the mid-1970s by right-wing publisher Arlington House, under the omnibus title *Conceived in Liberty*. The fifth volume has not yet been published; it was apparently dictated onto a now obsolete playback system for which parts cannot be found.

15. A letter from Kenneth Templeton in response to a request for the Lilly Endowment to pick up Mises's tab at NYU indicated the depth of the anger the Volker breakup caused. "I don't know if you have any real idea of the enormity of the way in which 'the marbles were scattered around' in the demise of the Volker Fund. I for one am not about to suggest that Lilly Endowment or other foundations pull all the chestnuts out of the

fire resulting from that action, and I hope I never again have to see such a flagrant demonstration of irresponsibility, duplicity, and hypocrisy on 'our side of the fence.' Considering all the sweet talk that has been going on about the necessity of revitalizing 'values and principles' and about the evils of relativism and materialism, I think a lot of us had better look to our own side first before we start preaching the virtuous life to college students and the heathens of collectivism." Kenneth Templeton to Leonard Read, June 14, 1963, FEE Archives.

16. See "Letters," *Policy Review*, Fall 1994, 90, where Friedman has a letter exchange with editor Adam Meyerson. *Policy Review* was then published by the flagship conservative think tank, the Heritage Foundation. (It is now run by the Hoover Institution, coincidentally Friedman's current institutional home.) Meyerson tells Friedman, "You are a conservative too. Sorry." Friedman, as always, and like his former Chicago colleague Hayek, begged to differ.

17. Details on Friedman's early life and education from Milton Friedman, "Milton Friedman," in William Breit and Roger W. Spencer, eds., *Lives of the Laureates: Ten Nobel Economists*, 2nd ed. (Cambridge: MIT Press, 1990), 79–83. For a more leisurely and detailed discussion of the same period, see Milton and Rose Friedman, *Two Lucky People: Memoirs* (Chicago: University of Chicago Press, 1998), 19–35.

18. M. Friedman, interview by author, January 28, 1995.

19. Friedman in Breit and Spencer, eds., *Lives of the Laureates*, 85.

20. M. Friedman, interview by author, January 28, 1995. He discusses this period in more detail in Friedman and Friedman, *Two Lucky People*, 59–62. The techniques he learned there he credits as the base of his favorite bit of technical economics, his work on the consumption function (66).

21. George Stigler, *Memoirs of an Unregulated Economist* (New York: Basic, 1988), 68.

22. Stigler, *Memoirs*, 70. For Friedman on this, see Friedman and Friedman, *Two Lucky People*, 71–72.

23. M. Friedman, interview by author, January 28, 1995.

24. M. Friedman, interview by author, January 28, 1995.

25. Alan Walters, "Friedman, Milton," in John Eatwell et al., eds., *The New Palgrave: A Dictionary of Economics* (New York: Stockton, 1987), 2:422. For more on sequential sampling, see Friedman and Friedman, *Two Lucky People*, 140–142.

26. Ronald Coase, "George Stigler," in Edward Shils, ed., *Remembering the University of Chicago: Teachers, Scientists, and Scholars* (Chicago: University of Chicago Press, 1991), 470.

27. Friedman served as a visiting professor at Cambridge (1953–1954), Columbia (1964–1965), UCLA (1967), and the University of Hawaii (1972). Friedman in Breit and Spencer, eds., *Lives of the Laureates*, 92.

28. See Friedman and Friedman, *Two Lucky People*, 182.

29. For Friedman in defense of floating exchange rates, see Milton Friedman, *Capitalism and Freedom* (Chicago: University of Chicago Press, 1962), 67–69.

30. Details on the inspiration and genesis of *Capitalism and Freedom* and his ideology from M. Friedman, interview by author, January 28, 1995; also Friedman, *Capitalism and Freedom*, preface.

31. Ronald Hamowy, interview by author, May 11, 1995; R. W. Bradford, interview by author, January 11, 1995.

32. Milton Friedman, interview by author, January 29, 1995.

33. *Reason*, "An Interview with Milton Friedman," December 1974, 5.

34. Milton Friedman, "Value Judgments in Economics," in Leube, ed., *Essence of Friedman*, 4–5. Also Milton Friedman, "Inflation and Unemployment," in Leube, ed., *Essence of Friedman*, 347–350. His wife Rose disagrees, finding that she can predict people's positions on a wide variety of seemingly non–value related positions by their value judgments.

35. M. Friedman, *Capitalism and Freedom*, 2.

36. M. Friedman, interview by author, January 29, 1995. See also Chuck Freadhoff, "Economist Milton Friedman: Gaining New Respect, Followers for Free-Market Ideas," *Investor's Business Daily*, January 14, 1994, 1; Jonathan Peterson, "The Captain of Capitalism," *Los Angeles Times Magazine*, December 14, 1986, 18.

37. For Friedman's debunking of the Keynesian multiplier effect, see M. Friedman, *Capitalism and Freedom*, 79–83.

38. Friedman has gotten more libertarian on the issue of compulsory schooling between this book and his similar 1980 tome *Free to Choose*, no longer believing it necessary; characteristically, he insists it was new evidence, not just a more hard-core ideology, that made him change his mind. M. Friedman, interview by author, January 28, 1995.

39. Michael Barone, *Our Country: The Shaping of America from Roosevelt to Reagan* (New York: Free Press, 1990), 418, 473–474.

40. ISI soon tired of the magazine's libertarianism; later support came from Ingersoll, the Lilly Endowment, and Pierre Goodrich.

41. Ralph Raico, "Benjamin Constant," *New Individualist Review* 3, no. 2 (n.d.).

42. Ralph Raico, "Wilhelm von Humboldt," *New Individualist Review*, April 1961.

43. Ronald Hamowy and William F. Buckley Jr., "'National Review': Criticism and Reply," *New Individualist Review*, November 1961, 7.

44. Hamowy and Buckley, "'National Review,'" 7, 9.

45. F. A. Hayek to senior tutor, Balliol College, March 5, 1963. (A letter of recommendation for Hamowy.) Hoover Institution, Hayek Collection, Box 23, Folder 23–16. Despite their more-libertarian-than-thou attitude toward their teacher, Hayek seemed to enjoy these radical kids. Upon hearing that Hayek had called Raico one of his two best students ever, Rothbard in his best S. J. Perelman mode joked, "So there you are! Congratulations! I guess it's a good thing that you didn't tell Hayek he was a 'dirty Commie' after all." Murray Rothbard to Ralph Raico, November 25, 1959, MRA, LVMI.

46. Edward C. Facey, "Conservatives or Individualists: Which Are We?" *New Individualist Review*, Summer 1961.

47. Harry Elmer Barnes, "A. J. P. Taylor and the Causes of World War II," *New Individualist Review*, Spring 1962.

48. James M. O'Connell, "The New Conservatism," *New Individualist Review*, Spring 1962.

49. Robert M. Hurt, "Sin and the Criminal Law," *New Individualist Review*, Spring 1962.

50. Howard Buffett, "An Opportunity for the Republican Party," *New Individualist Review*, Summer 1962, 13.

51. Joe Michael Cobb, "Emigration as an Alternative to the Draft," *New Individualist Review*, Spring 1967.

52. Robert M. Hurt, "Antitrust and Competition," *New Individualist Review*, Winter 1962.

53. The spring 1963 issues featured takedowns of the Interstate Commerce Commission, the Civil Aeronautics Board, and the Federal Communications Commission on grounds of economic inefficiency.

54. Yale Brozen, "Wage Rates, Minimum Wage Laws, and Unemployment," *New Individualist Review*, Spring 1966.

55. Perlstein, *Before the Storm*, xiii.

56. Ayn Rand, "A Suggestion," *Objectivist Newsletter*, October 1963; and Rand, "Check Your Premises: How to Judge a Political Candidate," *Objectivist Newsletter*, March 1964.

57. J. William Middendorf to Leonard Read, August 5, 1964, FEE Archives.

58. Butler Shaffer, interview by author, March 28, 2002.

59. See, for example, these lines from Barry Goldwater, *The Conscience of a Conservative* (1960; New York: McFadden Capitol Hill Books, 1963): "A tolerable peace . . . must *follow*

victory over Communism" (92); "We must . . . make it the cornerstone of our foreign policy: that we would rather die than lose our freedom" (93); "No nation at war, employing an exclusively defensive strategy, can hope to survive for long. Like the boxer who refuses to throw a punch, the defense-bound nation will be cut down sooner or later" (96–97); "In addition to parrying [the Soviets'] blows, we must strike our own. In addition to guarding our frontiers, we must try to puncture his. In addition to keeping the free world free, we must try to make the Communist world free. To these ends, we must always try to engage the enemy at times and places, and with weapons, of our own choosing" (122); "We should make every effort to achieve decisive superiority in small, clean nuclear weapons" (122); "We would invite the Communist leaders to choose between total destruction of the Soviet Union, and accepting a local defeat" (125).

60. Benjamin Rogge, "Note on the Election," *New Individualist Review,* Spring 1965, 28. What those conservatives could justly point out is that the failure in 1964 set off events and energies that resulted in the election of a very Goldwaterish candidate in 1980, Ronald Reagan. The truly confused premise in this libertarian/conservative argument over presidential politics is the one that these conservative/Republican politicians would succeed in implementing true libertarian goals; they wouldn't and didn't.

61. Garry Wills, *Nixon Agonistes: The Crisis of the Self-Made Man* (Boston: Houghton Mifflin, 1970), 553.

62. Wills, *Nixon Agonistes,* 555–556.

63. See Raimondo, *Enemy of the State,* 104–105, for details on Rothbard's efforts on Adlai Stevenson's behalf.

64. Murray N. Rothbard, "Repartee," *Innovator,* August 1964, 1–27.

65. A couple of those scams are detailed in Robert LeFevre, *A Way to Be Free: The Autobiography of Robert LeFevre,* vol. 1, *The Making of a Modern American Revolutionary* (Culver City, CA: Pulpless, 1999), 116–118, 187–191.

66. For details on the ritual and beliefs of the Mighty "I AM," see William J. Whalen, *Minority Religions in America* (Staten Island, NY: Alba, 1972), 77–93; and Gerald B. Bryan, *Psychic Dictatorship in America* (Los Angeles: Truth Research Publications, 1940). LeFevre's account of his involvement with "I AM" in LeFevre, *Way to Be Free,* vol. 1, chaps. 23–40.

67. For details on that Supreme Court case, see Leo Pfeffer, "The Legitimation of Marginal Religions in the United States," in Irving I. Zaretsky and Mark P. Leone, eds., *Religious Movements in Contemporary America* (Princeton: Princeton University Press, 1974), 20–21.

68. For LeFevre's discovery of Rose Wilder Lane's *Discovery of Freedom,* see Robert LeFevre, *A Way to Be Free: The Autobiography of Robert LeFevre,* vol. 2, *The Making of a Modern American Revolutionary* (Culver City, CA: Pulpless, 1999), 168–169.

69. Marion Murphy, "And the Right Shall Triumph," *Freeman,* October 1954. The height of his notoriety—a true American distinction—was LeFevre being caricatured in a Herblock cartoon as threatening and frightening a bunch of little girls. See LeFevre, *A Way to Be Free,* 2:214.

70. For LeFevre's time (and disillusionment) with Merwin Hart, see LeFevre, *A Way to Be Free,* 2:217–223.

71. Thaddeus Ashby, "Is Anybody Listening?" *Faith and Freedom,* June 1955, 10.

72. The filthy-minded could also have fun with one of LeFevre's later books, *Lift Her Up, Tenderly,* a strange account of how he tutored an alluring nymphet who fell into his care in free market economics—at least partially based on real experiences, as per LeFevre, *A Way to Be Free,* 2:461–463. The Lolita angle is never explicit but is hard to miss, to those who like looking for such things.

73. For Baldy Harper's reluctance to work with LeFevre, see LeFevre, *A Way to Be Free,* 2:387. Colorado locals had their own rumors about the Freedom School. LeFevre's wife Loy remembers drunken college-age youth skidding in their old jalopies onto the

grounds, shouting for the nudist colony they heard was nestled somewhere hereabouts. Lois LeFevre, interview by author, March 2, 2002. The Freedom School celebrated the eccentricities of its devotees. Its newsletter once reported straightfacedly on a Rampart graduate who had spent 1,500 hours of spare time (and what a rich abundance of spare time he must have had) building a miniature but precise model of Stonehenge. "Grad Creates Exact Replica of Stonehenge," *Rampart College Newsletter,* October 15, 1966, 2.

74. For LeFevre on the evil of retaliation, see Robert LeFevre, *The Fundamentals of Liberty* (Santa Ana, CA: Rampart Institute, 1988), 355.

75. LeFevre, *A Way to Be Free,* 2: 411.

76. LeFevre, *A Way to Be Free,* 2: 334–336.

77. LeFevre once thanked his trustees for letting him "espouse a completely moral position and to hold to it without compromise even when my views were unpopular and even detrimental to the well-being of the institution." Robert LeFevre, "President Expresses Thanks," *Rampart College Newsletter,* August 15, 1968, 4.

78. The acerbic Ronald Hamowy, recalls Loy LeFevre, would mutter while this nut went on and on, "It's getting cold in here, let's throw another Jew on the fire." Lois LeFevre, interview by author.

79. Robert LeFevre, "Rampart Profile," *Rampart College Newsletter,* August 15, 1968, 2.

80. Sterling L. Smith to Leonard Read, December 9, 1964, FEE Archives.

81. Vern Hansen, "The Radical Inactivist," *Libertarian Review,* April 1981, 12.

82. Robert J. Smith, interview by author.

83. LeFevre, *A Way to Be Free,* 2: 422. The most extreme reaction of this sort to LeFevre—initial attraction followed by a realization that it doesn't hold up—came from his former Rampart lecturer, the wunderkind Roy Childs. Childs was later advising his partners in the Society for Individual Liberty to *not* sell LeFevre lecture tapes. LeFevre's home study course, Childs asserted, was "evil in essence . . . a group of doctrines so evil as to be capable of destroying libertarianism as an ideology, not to mention the pushing upward of a man who surely deserves to bite the dust as far as influence goes." Further, LeFevre's ideas were the "intellectual equivalent of rat poison . . . nobody has been stupid enough to ever propose, in any semi-serious vein, such a bunch of inane garbage as this— not in the entire history of the world." Roy Childs to Jarret Wollstein and Don Ernsberger, January 1, 1970, Hoover Institution, Roy Childs Collection, Box 42, LeFevre folder. Childs was a vibrant rhetorician who turned similar invective of a more personal nature on mentor and guru Murray Rothbard in the early 1980s.

84. Dean Russell did grant in his letter to Jasper Crane that if LeFevre can convince him that "he positively does believe in limited government in some traditional and understandable sense, and that he is actively working for it, I will apologize to him and ask you to destroy this letter." Dean Russell to Jasper Crane, January 6, 1964, MRA, LVMI.

85. Read had earlier told J. Howard Pew that, while he had been a booster of LeFevre, he had come to realize that there were two reasons he could no longer in good conscience recommend people support his operation: anarchism and atheism. Leonard Read's Journals, August 1962, FEE Archives.

86. Rothbard felt sandbagged by Russell during one student session in 1962, when FEE's kids were brought down to his apartment in New York for a lecture on economics. Russell accompanied the students, and when questions arose about competitive courts and defense, he heckled. Rothbard found this revealing and appalling, since surely Russell knew this would come up, and he could only assume his whole purpose in bringing the kids to Rothbard was to give Russell a chance to attack Rothbard's anarchism as they heard it. Rothbard thought this meant that "it is *not* simply that we favor privately competitive courts and that *they* favor taxation for monopoly courts. If they were really heart-and-soul libertarians, for example (e.g., Russell, Read) then they would be anxious to get

the state out of the protection field, and would be at least interested in our ideas, even if they think them impractical. . . . They are people . . . who do not, in any sense, hate the State. In a profound sense, they are just as bemused with State-worship, and 'democracy' worship, and Supreme Court worship, as any average American. . . . I am beginning to come to the conclusion that, in basic socio-political outlook, there is far more difference between us and the Read-Russell people, than there is between *them* and say, the average member of the Republican Party." Murray Rothbard to F. A. Harper, August 13, 1962, MRA, LVMI.

87. Rose Wilder Lane to Jasper Crane, January 18, 1964, MRA, LVMI.

88. Irene G. Phillips, William Aleks et al. to Rockford, Illinois, Chamber of Commerce, September 1, 1959, Hoover Institution, F. A. Harper Collection, Box 30, 2263—Freedom School folder.

89. F. A. Harper to Murray Rothbard, April 21, 1964, MRA, LVMI.

90. LeFevre, *A Way to Be Free*, 2:473.

91. Roy Childs, "The Contradictions in Objectivism," *Rampart Journal of Individualist Thought,* Spring 1968.

92. Maurice C. Bryson and William R. McDill, "The Political Spectrum: A Bi-Dimensional Approach," *Rampart Journal of Individualist Thought,* Summer 1968.

93. Aslam Effendi, "Pakhtun Tribesmen and Their Free Society," *Rampart Journal of Individualist Thought,* Spring 1968.

94. W. H. Hutt to Robert LeFevre, July 16, 1967, Hoover Institution, F. A. Hayek Collection, Box 45, folder 43–43, Rampart College.

95. Libertarian Jeff Riggenbach wrote an affecting account of seeing the former Freedom School in 1981 as essentially a prison for juveniles. See Jeff Riggenbach, "LP/10 Considered As a Work of Art," *Libertarian Review,* November–December 1981, 40–41.

96. Tuccille, *Usually Begins with Ayn Rand*, 70–71.

97. Harry Browne, "Freedom's Unknown Guru," *Liberty,* November 1997, 57.

98. You could consult (though it would not help explain why so many skilled professionals loved him so much) the posthumously printed collection of some of Galambos's course notes. Andrew J. Galambos, *Sic Itur Ad Astra: This Is the Way to the Stars,* ed. Peter N. Sisco (San Diego: Universal Scientific Publications, 1998).

99. Harry Browne, "Freedom's Unknown Guru," 58.

100. Ric Villanueva, "A Positive Program for Responsible Extremists," *Liberal Innovator,* July 1964, 1–21.

101. *Liberal Innovator,* February 1964, 1–1.

102. Editor Tom Marshall, writing under his El Ray pseudonym, noted that the libertarian's mission is to "define operationally as well as conceptually the objectives toward which we are striving, predict the consequences of the societal structure we envision, and test out our theories, when possible, in small-scale developments. If libertarians proceed with care and deliberation, the millennium will be ours." El Ray, "The Time to Design a Free Society," *Liberal Innovator,* April 1964, 1–11.

103. For more on Thornley, see Adam Gorightly, *The Prankster and the Conspiracy: The Story of Kerry Thornley and How He Met Oswald and Inspired the Counterculture* (New York: Paraview, 2003); Brian Doherty, "Historia Discordia," *Reason,* August–September 2004.

104. Thornley's correspondent Robert Anton Wilson, later of *Playboy* and the *Illuminatus!* trilogy, profiled the cult in Ralph Ginzburg's notorious *Fact* magazine. Robert Anton Wilson, "The Religion of Kerista and Its 69 Positions," *Fact,* July–August 1965.

105. Kerry Thornley, "How Our Movement Began: Extremism in the Defense of Liberty Part II," *New Libertarian,* April 1985, 13.

106. The account of Vonu training and the last (known) days of Tom Marshall by Benjamin Best is available at www.benbest.com/travel/vonuweek.html.

107. Thornley, "How our Movement Began, Part II," 13.

108. Rand, *Virtue of Selfishness*, 13.

109. Leonard Peikoff, *Objectivism: The Philosophy of Ayn Rand* (New York: Meridian, 1993), 219–220.

110. Allan Blumenthal, who practiced Objectivist psychotherapy for years, finally concluded that Objectivists tended to become "afraid of the judgments that they and other Objectivists would have to pass. They experienced, to an unwarranted degree, feelings of inadequacy and guilt and consequently, they repressed massively. This led to a tragic loss of personal values. Instead of living for their own happiness—one of the ideas that attracted them to Objectivism in the first place—they sought safety by living to be 'moral,' to be what they were 'supposed' to be and, worse, to feel 'appropriate' emotions. Because they had learned the philosophy predominantly from fiction, the students of Objectivism thought they had to be like Ayn Rand heroes: they were not to be confused, not to be unhappy, and not to lack confidence. And because they could not meet these self-expectations, they bore the added burden of moral failure. . . . In that atmosphere it was difficult to deal with the real problems." B. Branden, *Passion of Ayn Rand*, 388.

The Objectivist tendency toward psychologically damaging moralism is explored from a perspective hostile to Objectivism in Albert Ellis, *Is Objectivism a Religion?* (New York: Lyle Stuart, 1968); and from a perspective friendly to Objectivism in George H. Smith, *Atheism, Ayn Rand, and Other Heresies* (Buffalo: Prometheus, 1991), 216–229.

111. This is the standard version of the psychological dynamic leading to the Rand/Branden break adhered to by both Brandens in their biographies and memoirs regarding Rand. Late in the writing of this book, some new revelations arose from a revisionist account based on Rand's unpublished journal entries in James S. Valliant, *The Passion of Ayn Rand's Critics* (Dallas: Durban, 2005).

Valliant was granted access by Rand's heir Leonard Peikoff to her unedited, unpublished journals. Valliant's book presents a lawyerly brief that reverses the apparent virtues of the Brandens' biographical writings on Rand. The fact that they had over a decade of almost exclusive firsthand contact with her means most of what they say is unverifiable, and the fact that those loyal to Rand or Peikoff refuse to speak to them means that any further reporting or research in the form of interviewing others was bound to come up with only corroboration for their self-serving vision of Rand as an irrational terror, controlling her associates' lives and then tossing them into outer darkness with inexplicable rage.

He denies the Brandens' vision of a Rand ruthlessly controlling her friends or demanding irrational obedience (53–59), even on their own evidence, where he points out that Branden himself describes the demands of unquestioning obedience to all of Rand's whims and preferences among her circle as "implicit." (Valliant is being naive in assuming that a strong-willed person can't make such a demand very clear even without saying so explicitly.) Valliant's interpretation of Branden's affair with Patrecia Wynand and the break with Rand, backed up interestingly with Rand's contemporaneous diaries, is that Rand was perfectly willing to accept that their sexual relationship might have to be put aside permanently, and even that Branden might want a sexual relationship with a younger woman; it was his continued lying and hiding it for years that drove her to turn on him with such rage. Branden's keeping the secret, in Valliant's reading, was not to protect Rand's feelings, so delicate that she could not handle the truth; it was to protect his own position as her right-hand man and the commercial life of NBI. (See Part II, "Documenting the Rape of Innocence.") Valliant uses journal excerpts to show that Rand was aware that their romantic relationship was over before the angry break (194); that she did not believe that not being sexually attracted to her would be a moral failing on Branden's part (196); and that she even suggested he have an affair with someone else to help solve his emotional and sexual problems (199). Valliant's interpretation of the situation is of a man deceiving and playing with an older woman's heart for years for his own gain. (It is unfortunate that so far Peikoff's policy is not to allow free and open scholarly access to all of Rand's papers to help others explore these matters independently.)

112. Quote from B. Branden, *Passion of Ayn Rand,* 347. For the larger context of the end of the affair, see B. Branden, *Passion of Ayn Rand,* 332–347; also N. Branden, *Judgment Day,* 375–388.

113. Rand's heir Leonard Peikoff finally wrote that book himself, which was published as Peikoff, *Objectivism: The Philosophy of Ayn Rand.*

114. A summation of the damage caused by the Rand/Branden split from an Objectivist movement follower who knew neither personally is found in Merrill, *Ideas of Ayn Rand,* 160–161. "The NBI lectures, and the clubs and discussion groups which grew out of them, brought isolated Objectivists together. The movement began to become not just an arena for learning and debate, but a social meeting ground. We started to learn how to interact with other people in a new way; we took the first steps toward building a rational society. Then it was all destroyed. . . . If Objectivism is to begin moving again, we must reestablish an Objectivist subculture. The influence of Objectivists as isolated individuals is too limited. More important, to maintain Objectivist ideals as a lone and lonely individual is too stressful . . . we do need social institutions which allow us to meet with one another."

115. Ayn Rand, "To Whom It May Concern," *Objectivist,* May 1968, 3.

116. "For the Record," *Objectivist,* May 1968, 9.

117. Nathaniel Branden, *In Answer to Ayn Rand,* October 16, 1968, 6. Pamphlet issued by the Nathaniel Branden Institute.

118. B. Branden, *Passion of Ayn Rand,* 351.

119. B. Branden, *Passion of Ayn Rand,* 352.

120. Taylor, interview by author.

121. At the beginning of his career Branden dubbed his psychiatric approach "biocentric" since, like Objectivism, it began with what was best for the living being. Branden, following Rand, thought that what was best for a living human was productivity and through it, self-esteem. Objectivism still permeated Branden's popular psychology; he retained its notions about sexual attraction, the need for a reasoned moral code, and the constant need for unconditional reality-bound cognitive functioning.

The pragmatically eclectic Branden later abandoned labels for his technique. Some of his earlier books, like *The Disowned Self,* are about the youthful causes of adult neuroses and read as direct ancestors of the current pop-therapeutic concern with the "inner child."

122. Branden considers his ultimate statement on issues of psychology and self-esteem to be in Nathaniel Branden, *The Six Pillars of Self-Esteem* (New York: Bantam, 1994). The more popular version of the importance of self-esteem has evolved (or devolved, as Objectivists might have it) from Branden's vision, which was roughly that, since humans need self-esteem, they must do what is necessary to earn it. The more modern liberal, welfare state version of self-esteem states more or less that since people need it, it is everyone else's obligation to make sure they get it, by any means necessary.

123. B. Branden, *Passion of Ayn Rand,* 350.

124. Rothbard wrote to revisionist historian Harry Elmer Barnes in 1964 that "the political differences between myself and the other Misesians are so enormous that relations are getting pretty strained all around." He was especially annoyed that a speech in favor of Western imperialism had gotten good reactions from the Mises crowd. Quoted in Raimondo, *Enemy of the State,* 141–142.

125. Rothbard's cadre obsession failed him here. Hayek, merely through the force of his scholarly work and not through any deliberate attempt to form a gang, team, or movement,

created many important Hayekians in the decades to come—Margaret Thatcher most prominent among them.

126. R. W. Bradford, later editor of the movement magazine *Liberty,* tells me that in his Michigan student libertarian group in the mid-1960s, no one really considered the war the main issue. "We were just as upset at having an 80 percent marginal tax rate on the books, or drug laws, or a million other degradations that libertarians can and do get pissed off about." R. W. Bradford, interview by author, April 2, 1999.

127. Murray N. Rothbard, *Left and Right: The Prospects for Liberty* (San Francisco: Cato Institute, 1979), 7.

128. Murray N. Rothbard, "Liberty and the New Left," *Left and Right,* Autumn 1965, 43–44.

129. "Ernesto Che Guevara, R.I.P," *Left and Right,* Spring–Autumn 1967, 3.

130. Liggio, interview by author.

131. Ronald Hamowy, "Left and Right Meet," *New Republic,* March 12, 1966, 15. He also singled out *Left and Right* and his own *New Individualist Review* as "the only elements resisting" the right's shift from classical liberalism to statist militarism (14) and upbraided the new leftists clinging to their naive belief that the public sector really was necessarily on the side of the poor or disadvantaged or the "public" at all. All the "public sector" ultimately means, Hamowy argued, are bureaucrats and police, far more likely to be the tools of the powers-that-already-be. Decentralization, as per Paul Goodman, was the real answer.

132. "The noble task of Revisionism is to de-bamboozle," Rothbard explained, "to penetrate the fog of lies and deception of the State and its Court Intellectuals, and to present to the public the true history of the motivation, the nature, and the consequences of State activity. By working past the fog of State deception to penetrate to the truth, to the reality behind the false appearances, the Revisionist works to delegitimate, to desanctify, the State in the eyes of the previously deceived public. By doing so, the Revisionist, even if he is not a libertarian personally, performs a vitally important libertarian service. . . . since the State cannot function, cannot command majority support vital to its existence without imposing a network of deception. Revisionist history becomes a crucial part of the tasks of the libertarian movement. Crucial especially because Revisionism goes beyond pure theory to expose and reveal the specific lies and crimes of the State as it exists in concrete reality." Murray N. Rothbard, "Revisionism and Libertarianism," *Libertarian Forum,* February 1976, 3.

133. Rothbard's interest in pinning the blame, so to speak, seemed to grow as his career progressed. See the differences, for example, between his 1963 book about central banking and government manipulation of money, *What Has Government Done to Our Money?* (originally written for FEE in the mid-1950s, but Leonard Read chose not to publish it) and a 1994 return to the same theme, *The Case Against the Fed.* The latter not only discusses the workings of central banks and how they inflate the currency and generate business cycles, but tells in detail the story of the founding and growth of the Federal Reserve in terms of the specific banking families and politicians who benefited from it.

"From the 1890s until World War II," Rothbard wrote regarding the history of the Federal Reserve, "much of American political history, of programs and conflicts, can be interpreted not so much as 'Democrat' versus 'Republican,' but as the interaction or conflict between the Morgans and their allies on the one hand, and the Rockefeller-Harriman-Kuhn, Loeb alliance on the other." See Murray N. Rothbard, *The Case Against the Fed* (Auburn, AL: Ludwig von Mises Institute, 1994), 92. He traces the public and intellectual agitation for a central bank back before the Panic of 1907, which standard histories say taught America of the need for a Federal Reserve. Rubbish, Rothbard says. "The Panic of 1907 provided a convenient handle to stir up the public and spread pro-Central Bank propaganda. In actuality, the banker agitation for a Central Bank began as soon as the 1896 McKinley victory over Bryan was secure. . . . The banks desperately desired a Central Bank, not to place fetters on their own natural tendency to inflate, but, on the contrary, to enable them to inflate and expand together without incurring the penalties of market competition" (83).

134. Murray Rothbard to Ronald Hamowy, February 2, 1966, MRA, LVMI.

135. Rothbard to Hamowy, February 2, 1966.

136. Walter Block, interview by author, January 27, 1999.

137. Carl Oglesby to Murray Rothbard, October 14, 1966, MRA, LVMI.

138. Certain new leftists were attracted, like Oglesby, but not many. In the *Innovator,* one young libertarian sold by Rothbard's praise for SDS and the new left attended an SDS conference and ran up hard against one very dominant type that was never going to be turned to anarcho-capitalism—the "social worker" element, whose whole goal was organizing mass public campaigns to help those they thought needed helping in the way they thought they needed to be helped. (This was the idea behind a famous chapter of Isabel Paterson's *God of the Machine,* titled "The Humanitarian with the Guillotine.") To them, nothing but the Great Society and the welfare state would do. Marick Payton, "Searching the Soul of SDS," *Innovator,* November 1966.

139. Quoted in Murray Rothbard to Louise Lacey, September 24, 1966, MRA, LVMI.

140. Murray N. Rothbard, "Confessions of a Right-Wing Liberal," *Ramparts,* June 15, 1968, 48.

141. Rothbard, "Confessions," 50. By the 1990s, Rothbard would be sounding a tune similar to the one he here condemned the new conservatives for singing.

142. Rothbard, "Confession," 52. *National Review* jabbed back at Rothbard in a response to a letter from him upbraiding James Burnham for being a flag waver for the Party of Order versus Rothbard's Party of Liberty. They claimed to no longer run Rothbard's articles because "however shrewd or useful his occasional apercus in economics" they "declined to inhabit, along with Mr. Rothbard, the overcrowded quarters of Freak House." Letters, *National Review,* August 13, 1968, 778–779.

143. Murray Rothbard to Kenneth Templeton, September 21, 1959, MRA, LVMI.

144. Kolko's most thorough work on the topic is Gabriel Kolko, *The Triumph of Conservatism: A Reinterpretation of American History, 1900–1916* (1963; Chicago: Quadrangle Paperback, 1967).

145. Murray Rothbard to W. D. Pringle, September 13, 1966, MRA, LVMI.

146. Block, interview by author.

147. Quoted in Raimondo, *Enemy of the State,* 172.

148. Murray N. Rothbard, "The Student Revolution," *Libertarian,* May 1, 1969, 2.

149. In the age of blogs, the amateur press association (APA) had gone from certainly obscure to almost certainly unknown. Arising from science fiction fandom (the early editors of *Libertarian Connection,* going under the noms de revolution of Skye D'Aureous and Natalee Hall, were SF fans as well), this was a publication consisting of mimeo pages submitted by a handful to dozens of contributors, all compiled into one zine by the editors and mailed to all APA contributors and members.

150. Murray N. Rothbard, "Toward a Strategy for Libertarianism," *Libertarian Connection,* February 10, 1969, 5–7.

151. Murray Rothbard to "Alex and Sara," August 15, 1969, MRA, LVMI. Rothbard also noted his crankily traditionalist objection to almost any drug whatsoever, not just illegal drugs, and opined that in an increasingly sensate and decidedly unpuritanical culture, in which the wonders of science and medicine were pushed every which way you looked, he was actually inclined to *believe* dire establishment warnings about the dangers of psychedelics.

152. For a representatively vitriolic take on Hess, see Justin Raimondo, "The Legacy of Karl Hess," *Rothbard/Rockwell Report,* August 1994. Raimondo saw a sinister conspiracy on the part of the media who eulogized Hess to elevate his variety of left-leaning, "cultural" libertarianism above the real hard-core Rothbardian stuff—which by the time of Hess's death in 1994 meant a strict cultural conservatism combined with anarcho-capitalism.

153. For more insight on the libertarian decentralist tradition in which Hess was enmeshed, see Mildred J. Loomis, *Alternative Americas* (New York: Free Life Editions/Universe Books, 1982). See also Staughton Lynd, *Intellectual Origins of American Radicalism* (New York: Pantheon, 1968), 162–169.

154. See Karl Hess, *Mostly on the Edge: An Autobiography* (Amherst, NY: Prometheus, 1999), 245–247, for Hess's exposition on why toolmakers are more important than social thinkers.

155. Hess, *Edge,* 45.

156. Hess, *Edge,* 58–59.

157. For details on Hess's early print journalism jobs, quite amusingly told, see Hess, *Edge,* 83–107. Hess tells of a managing editor whose "career high came on a Christmas Eve. He fired one of the staff. When someone asked him why, of all times, he'd chosen this day to fire the guy, [the editor] replied, 'Well, look, it was Christmas Eve, it was snowing, the guy had a sick kid at home, his wife was about to leave him. Christ, I just couldn't resist it'" (90).

158. For Hess's *Newsweek* days, see Hess, *Edge,* 109–118.

159. Hess, *Edge,* 128–130.

160. Hess, *Edge,* 145.

161. Hess, *Edge,* 117–118. For Ralph de Toledano's account of this, see Toledano, ed., *Notes from the Underground: Chambers-de Toledano Letters,* 136–139, 145.

162. Hess, *Edge,* 133–148, for his anticommunist activism and writing.

163. Raico, interview by author. Raico says Hess used to tell this story during his days hanging around with Rothbard.

164. For the leftist Hess's jaundiced look at corporate life at Champion, see Karl Hess, *Dear America* (New York: William Morrow, 1975), 47–51.

165. Hess, *Edge,* 170.

166. For Hess's account of the beginnings of his attraction to both the new left and anarcho-capitalism, see Hess, *Edge,* 183–197.

167. Ralph Raico recalls him pandering to lefty student anger, saying that the South's problems would be solved when the blacks and whites got together to string up the capitalists.

168. Hess, *Edge,* 194. Hess wrote: "I wore [the ring] for several months as a symbol of opposition to the Vietnam War, until it dawned on me that I was celebrating the death of a warrior. I was ashamed. The war was bad, but never could it have been so bad as to deserve the boasting of a countryman's death—the death of a neighbor, a friend, a loved one."

169. Donald Meinshausen, interview by author, May 15, 2004.

170. Meinshausen, interview by author.

171. Donald Meinshausen, statement submitted to House Internal Security Committee, August 6, 1969. In author's possession.

172. "Informer on S.D.S. Vexes House Unit," *New York Times,* August 17, 1969, 52. Meinshausen wrote of his experiences working for HISC in Don Meinshausen, "Confessions of a Spy: SDS Experience Converts HUAC Spy to New Left," *Los Angeles Free Press,* October 10, 1969, 3. He wrote of turning in loads of publicly available information to a committee obsessed with the notion of external communist subversion. "The names they could have gotten just by asking on a campus who the SDS people were," he wrote.

173. Meinshausen, interview by author.

174. Karl Hess, "Letter from Washington: My Taxes," *Libertarian*, May 1, 1969, 3.

175. Hess, *Edge*, 39.

176. Karl Hess, "The Death of Politics," *Playboy*, March 1969.

177. Rothbard and Hess appeared together in 1987, in ads for the movement magazine *Liberty*. The ads riffed humorously off the notion that the two grand old men of the movement had nothing in common, save their love for *Liberty*.

178. James Boyd, "From Far Right to Far Left—and Farther—with Karl Hess," *New York Times Magazine*, December 6, 1970.

179. Tony Lang, "Karl Hess Is Aflame with the Idea That a Man Can Run his Own Life," *Washington Post Potomac*, December 6, 1970, 20. Goldwater's reaction to this praise is unrecorded. He was probably not flattered.

180. The story of Hess and Goldwater's encounter during the protest is told in Lee Edwards, *Goldwater: The Man Who Made a Revolution* (Washington, DC: Regnery Gateway, 1995), 359.

181. Lang, "Karl Hess Is Aflame," 14.

182. *Liberty* magazine editor R. W. Bradford controversially denies that Rothbard was considered an important figure by any young libertarians outside New York City until the 1970s. Bradford, interview by author.

183. Gary Greenberg, interview by author, September 7, 1996.

184. One of them, Gus DiZerega, was given Mises books at a Wichita American Opinion bookstore by later libertarian financier, the billionaire Charles Koch. Gus DiZerega, interview by author, November 3, 2005.

185. Tuccille, *Usually Begins with Ayn Rand,* 59.

186. Murray Rothbard, "Listen, YAF," *Libertarian Forum*, August 15, 1969, 2.

187. Durk Pearson and Sandy Shaw, interview by author, November 29, 2005.

188. Karl Hess Jr., interview by author, November 11, 2005.

189. Meinshausen, interview by author.

190. Hess Jr., interview by author.

191. Rebecca E. Klatch, *A Generation Divided: The New Left, the New Right, and the 1960s* (Berkeley: University of California Press, 1999), 232.

192. Tuccille's reporting on St. Louis—attacked in later accounts by people also present as overestimating the role of the anarchist caucus and underestimating the libertarian caucus—is in Jerome Tuccille, *Radical Libertarianism* (1970; San Francisco: Cobden, 1985), 97–109.

193. Roy A. Childs Jr., "Objectivism and the State: An Open Letter to Ayn Rand," in Joan Kennedy Taylor, ed., *Liberty Against Power: Essays by Roy A. Childs, Jr.* (San Francisco: Fox & Wilkes, 1994). Bill Bradford, later editor of *Liberty* magazine and then a student libertarian in Michigan, claims that this was no revelation to anyone. He and his friends already knew that Objectivism implies anarchism. R. W. Bradford, "It Really Didn't Begin with Roy Childs," *Liberty*, June 1999. Nonetheless, it has gone down in movement lore as a bombshell revelation.

194. Block, interview by author.

195. Block, interview by author. While Block knows many people think Rothbard was habitually vicious toward anyone who disagreed with him, he recalls that for the first five or six years of their comradeship, he poo-poohed most of the methodology and tenets of Rothbard's beloved Austrian economics (though he later became a hard-core Rothbardian Austrian himself), and suffered no abuse or excommunication for it.

196. Tuccille, *Usually Begins with Ayn Rand,* 110.

197. Tuccille, *Usually Begins with Ayn Rand,* 110.

198. Tuccille, *Usually Begins with Ayn Rand,* 114.

199. Tuccille, *Usually Begins with Ayn Rand,* 118–119.

200. Murray Rothbard to Gerald O'Driscoll, October 18, 1969, MRA, LVMI.

201. All quotes and details regarding the end of the Columbus conference from Rothbard to O'Driscoll, October 18, 1969.

202. Cobb's thoughts on anarcho-property in Joe Cobb, "Individualism, After the Revolution," typescript, n.p., n.d., MRA, LVMI. Context and placement in archive indicate a 1969 or 1970 date of composition.

203. Tuccille, *Usually Begins with Ayn Rand*, 108.

204. Jonathan Schoenwald, "No War, No Welfare, and No Damn Taxation: The Student Libertarian Movement, 1968–1972," in Marc Jason Gilbert, ed., *The Vietnam War on Campus: Other Voices, More Distant Drums* (Westport, CT: Praeger, 2001), 33.

205. Rothbard, "Toward a Strategy for Libertarian Social Change," 160. Conversation with one of the young libertarians who did this, Gus DiZerega, clarified its humorous, though still respectful, intent. DiZerega, interview by author.

206. Rothbard, "Toward a Strategy for Libertarian Social Change," 160–161.

207. Liggio, interview by author.

208. Alice Widener, "For a Radical America: The Sixth Annual Conference of Socialist Scholars," *Barron's*, July 13, 1970, 12.

209. See Murray N. Rothbard, "Ultra-Leftism," *Libertarian Forum*, November 15, 1969, for Rothbard's critique of libertarians subsuming themselves in leftist lifestyle or organizations.

210. Murray N. Rothbard, "The Task Ahead," *Libertarian Forum*, February 15, 1970, 1.

211. Klatch, *A Generation Divided*, 234.

212. Stan Lehr and Louis Rossetto Jr., "The New Right Credo—Libertarianism," *New York Times Magazine*, January 10, 1971. They drag Spinoza into the libertarian pantheon because of something he said against victimless crime laws.

213. William F. Buckley, "The Right-Radicals," *National Review*, February 9, 1971, 162.

214. Jerome Tuccille, interview by author, October 7, 1998.

215. The series included reprints of Rose Wilder Lane's *Discovery of Freedom,* Isabel Paterson's *God of the Machine,* John Flynn's *As We Go Marching,* Franz Oppenheimer's *The State,* and William Graham Sumner's *What Social Classes Owe to Each Other*; biographies of Josiah Warren; of a late-nineteenth-century hard money–free trade New York congressman, Bourke Cockran; of George Logan, an anti-war Quaker at the turn of the nineteenth century against whom the Logan Act, banning private diplomatic negotiations with foreign powers, was aimed; and of Edward Atkinson, leader of the Anti-Imperialist League at the turn of the century; as well as works by Benjamin Tucker, Harry Elmer Barnes, and H. L. Mencken.

216. Tuccille, interview by author.

217. J. Neil Schulman, interview by author, March 9, 2002.

218. For discussion and defense of the idea that libertarian ideas and ideological activists were key in ending the draft, see Gary North, "The Libertarian Roots of the All-Volunteer Military," LewRockwell.com, www.lewwrockwell.com/north/north235.html. For the account of Friedman's direct role, see Friedman and Friedman, *Two Lucky People,* 377–381. Karl Hess, in collaboration with Thomas Reeves, also came out with a book of arguments against the draft in 1970. Thomas Reeves and Karl Hess, *The End of the Draft* (New York: Random House, 1970).

For the idea that an all-volunteer fix was already in on the Gates Commission, see Robert K. Griffiths Jr., *The U.S. Army's Transition to the All-Volunteer Force, 1968–1974* (Washington, DC: Center of Military History, United States Army), 29–30. The official name of the commission was President's Commission on an All-Volunteer Force.

219. Quoted in Griffiths, *U.S. Army's Transition*, 43.

220. Klatch, *A Generation Divided*, 235.

221. Quoted in Schoenwald, "No War, No Welfare," 38.

222. Quoted in Schoenwald, "No War, No Welfare," 39.

223. In the late 1980s, SIL folded into Libertarian International, a group with an international focus on conferences and activism that takes it beyond the strictly American focus of this book, and formed the International Society for Individual Liberty.

224. Gary North's horrific experience at the libertarian conference is related in "Anarchism: Left and Right," Institute for Humane Studies Archives, Gary North file. Context clues indicate the essay may have appeared in a newsletter, *Chalcedon Report No. 46,* but I have been unable to find that periodical to confirm.

225. Tom Palmer, interview by author, July 8, 1998.

226. *Reason* used to publish annual financial issues dedicated to these matters, but stopped in the 1980s as its audience and the hard money audience diverged.

227. A sample of Congressman Rohrabacher's song lyrics: "Lots of people in this town/Trying to help us sinful folks/By outlawing everything from magazines/To telling dirty jokes/Oh, they think that they're helping people/By regulating what they do/But they're just putting people in jail/Folks like me and you." Reprinted in *New Libertarian Notes,* 36, 23.

228. Murray N. Rothbard, *For a New Liberty: The Libertarian Manifesto,* rev. ed. (New York: Collier, 1978), 10.

229. Rothbard, *For a New Liberty,* 23

230. Rothbard, *For a New Liberty,* 39.

231. Rothbard, *For a New Liberty,* 68.

232. When I first read the book, as a nineteen-year-old who had long harbored antistatist sympathies but was relatively fresh to the libertarian movement synthesis, I found it both bracing and frightening—with a hint of the thrill of the forbidden—when I realized what Rothbard was up to here.

233. For Peden's most thorough work on Ireland's "stateless" law, see Joseph R. Peden, "Property Rights in Celtic Irish Law," *Journal of Libertarian Studies* 1, no. 2 (1977).

234. See Rothbard, *Logic of Action One,* 144–153, where he attacks Hayek's reliance on spontaneous order as an explanatory device. Rothbard even questions, based on work by Mises Institute fellow David Gordon, the favorite "spontaneous order" trope—the idea that language was not rationally created but just developed (151).

235. Rothbard, *For a New Liberty,* 234.

236. Rothbard, *For a New Liberty,* 237–241.

237. Rothbard, *For a New Liberty,* 259.

238. Rothbard, *For a New Liberty,* 259.

239. Reisman, *Capitalism,* 1 n. 15.

240. Rather than seeking communist victories, Rothbard argues that "In order to preserve peaceful relations between Russia and the West, Stalin consistently tried to hold back the success of various Communist movements. He was successful in France and Italy, where Communist partisan groups might easily have seized power in the wake of the German military retreat; but Stalin ordered them not to do so, and instead persuaded them to join coalition regimes headed by anti-Communist parties. . . . Russia . . . governed Eastern Europe as military occupier after winning a war launched against her. Russia's initial goal was not to communize Eastern Europe on the backs of the Soviet army. Her goal was to gain assurances that Eastern Europe would not be the broad highway for an assault on Russia, as it had been three times in half a century. . . . Even in the other Eastern European countries, Russia clung to coalition governments for several years after the war and only fully communized them in 1948—after three years of unrelenting American Cold War pressure to try to oust Russia from these countries." Rothbard, *For a New Liberty,* 286–287. Elsewhere he wrote, "Given the black record of American aggression in the

Cold War and elsewhere, I must say that [communists] have a point: not in the inevitability of capitalism begetting imperialism, but in a wariness over the possibly aggressive intentions of American imperialism. In short, there is infinitely more evidence of an American military threat to Russia than vice versa: and the 'announced intentions' of Marxism-Leninism confirm rather than rebut this conclusion." Murray N. Rothbard, "The Editor Rebuts," *Libertarian Forum*, February 1973, 5.

241. Rothbard, *For a New Liberty*, 294.

242. Rothbard, *For a New Liberty*, 304.

243. Baldy Harper had his quirks, but they were more charming than alarming. He invented a new cataloguing system for libraries. In order to save the trouble of shifting the books on hundreds of shelves every time new ones got stuck in the middle of the collection, he suggested simply whole numbering every acquisition based on when it entered the collection. That way you only needed to add books at the end. He admitted there would be some loss in search serendipity with no guarantee that the books on the same shelf as the one you were looking for would have anything to do with the same or similar topics. But it could also open up wider, wilder, random serendipity.

Not the type to impose on others experiments he wouldn't try himself, Harper's own papers at the Hoover Institution are filed this way. One has no idea what the topic of the next clip or letter might be as one works through the files. I was slightly disappointed to discover that the excellent libertarian library at the Institute for Humane Studies today does *not* follow the Harper filing system.

244. In his celebration of proprietary communities and the value added by the property manager, MacCallum's book shows surprising (for a libertarian) lack of faith in the coordinating properties of spontaneous orders in free markets for land. For example, he writes that "it should be apparent that the decision how and by whom the land can be used to best advantage is an on-going process and involves no less than planning the whole economic structure of the community." Spencer Heath MacCallum, *The Art of Community* (Menlo Park, CA: Institute for Humane Studies, 1970), 65.

See also his discussion on page 57 about how, with land ownership spread among different people, effective land use planning that maximizes everyone's land values is impossible. He seems to believe that singular ownership of all land in a community is a positive good, not merely an interesting way to approximate "government" in a private property market. Some libertarians thought the MacCallum idea smacked of company-townism, and despite Harper's enthusiasm, the Heath and MacCallum ideas are not much discussed in the movement today.

245. David Friedman is not, however, a utilitarian himself. He merely wished, as per Hayek and Mises, to show that ethical arguments need not come into arguments over free markets (though his market is much freer than that of either of those old Austrians). In assuming that most people want a world of plenty, opportunities, and relative peace, he thinks his efficiency arguments show that anarchy is the best way to reach that world. As he says, "I have never met a socialist who wanted the kind of society that I think socialism will produce." David Friedman, *The Machinery of Freedom: Guide to a Radical Capitalism* (New York: Harper Colophon, 1973), 223.

246. David Friedman was in a poetry course at Harvard when Goldwater lost, and he wrote a lament about it, which his parents kindly reprinted in their memoirs; see Friedman and Friedman, *Two Lucky People*, 371–372. As a sign of how acceptable Goldwaterism was at Harvard, his teacher responded to the poem—with lines such as, "The night will fall; all must from free decline/Cannot the sun forever shine?/Or if in time the sun must fall/Why must my time be that, of all/The times I might have chanced in? . . . I know that all of this is empty wind./As empty as the wind that sweeps the sky/Of Arizona, where our dreams will die"—with: "How can anyone feel this way?"

Friedman also remembers a friend quipping to an economics professor from whom he'd taken a course at Harvard that he came into the university a Rockefeller Republican, and of *course* Harvard changed his mind on all that; he was leaving Harvard a *Goldwater* Republican. The professor insisted he must be joking; after all, he had done well in his class. David Friedman, interview by author, December 2, 2005.

247. See D. Friedman, *Machinery of Freedom*, chap. 6.

248. D. Friedman, *Machinery of Freedom*, 207–210.

249. "People who want to control other people's lives are rarely eager to pay for the privilege; they usually expect to *be* paid for the 'services' they provide for their victims. And those on the receiving end—whether of laws against drugs, laws against pornography, or laws against sex—get a lot more pain out of the oppression than their oppressors get pleasure. They are willing to pay a much higher price to be left alone than anyone is willing to pay to push them around. For that reason the laws of an anarcho-capitalist society should be heavily biased toward freedom." D. Friedman, *Machinery of Freedom*, 174.

250. D. Friedman, *Machinery of Freedom*, 195.

251. D. Friedman, *Machinery of Freedom*, xii.

CHAPTER 7

1. The earliest mention I've found of the concept of a third party using the name "Libertarian Party," strangely enough came from the publicly apolitical Leonard Read. He wrote in his journal about wanting "to get some friend of mine to send out a letter" that would propose this: "'I am suggesting the organization of a Libertarian Party, getting it officially recognized in the several states, and preparing for a convention in the summer of 1956. The convention would adopt a libertarian platform and would nominate its candidates." Leonard Read Journal, 1952, 89, FEE Archives.

2. David Nolan, interview by author, December 11, 2005. Nolan also was keeper of what he thinks was an even more important list to the libertarian youth movement in the late 1960s: a six-hundred-name Liberty Amendment Committee student list, which he supplied to Jarret Wollstein to help build the Society for Rational Individualists, which then merged with YAF's libertarian caucus to form the Society for Individual Liberty.

3. For a libertarian movement take on Vivien Kellems's career and significance, see Joan Kennedy Taylor, "Preaching at the Juggernaut: The Constitution and the IRS," *Libertarian Review*, April 1981.

4. After David Nolan announced the LP's formation, Rothbard wrote, "It should be clear that . . . any talk of a libertarian party is grossly premature, and will be for many years to come." Murray N. Rothbard, "The Party," *Libertarian Forum*, March 1972, 1. Some former friends of Rothbard suspect a bit of "not invented here" syndrome in this opposition. Rothbard had a sense of hard-earned ownership of the movement that made him tend to be unsupportive of efforts not arising from him or his immediate circle. Nolan doesn't agree with this interpretation; he believes Rothbard genuinely thought it was a premature idea and might embarrass the movement by revealing how small its mass constituency really was. He also thinks Rothbard might have been kicking himself when eventual candidate John Hospers actually received an electoral vote.

Only after attending out of curiosity and being impressed by a convention of the New York State LP in 1973 did Rothbard become actively involved with the party. He quickly threw himself into party action and became a fixture on the national LP platform committee and a major party gadfly until 1989, when he left in a huff.

5. Anthony Ripley, "New Party Makes a Debut in Denver," *New York Times*, February 6, 1972.

6. See John Hospers, "Conversations with Ayn Rand," *Liberty*, July–September 1990, for his account of his relationship with Rand, and its end.

7. Printed at website of the Ayn Rand Institute, "Ayn Rand's Q & A on Libertarians," www.aynrand.org/site/PageServer?pagename=education_campus_libertarians.

8. On MacBride and the Electoral College, see Bill Kauffman, "The Elector Defector," *American Enterprise,* March 2001.

9. Tonie Nathan, interview by author, December 16, 2005.

10. MacBride's account of the experience of voting for Hospers/Nathan in Roger L. MacBride, "One Small Step," *Reason,* December 1975.

11. Edward Crane III, interview by author, July 7, 1998. For an overview of Crane's career, see Richard Morin, "Free Radical," *Washington Post,* May 9, 2002.

12. Crane, interview by author.

13. Manuel Klausner, interview by author, January 11, 1999.

14. David Bergland, interview by author, February 15, 1998.

15. Crane, interview by author.

16. George Smith, interview by author, November 7, 1998.

17. Konkin was an inveterate phrasemaker, having given the movement that term as well as "minarchist" and "Kochtopus."

18. Konkin was so sure that my vision of the libertarian movement, in which such organizations as the LP, Cato, and Reason were central, was completely off base that he refused my entreaties for an interview for this book. We sparred lightheartedly when we ran into each other at events or parties at mutual friends' homes, and I held out hope that he'd eventually give in. Alas, Sam Konkin died in February 2004, uninterviewed by me.

19. "The New Gypsies," *Esquire,* September 1970, 110.

20. For a mostly firsthand account of life as a would-be Atlantean, see Roy Halliday, "Operation Atlantis and the Radical Libertarian Alliance: Observations of a Fly on the Wall," *Formulations,* Summer 2001. For more details on some of the pre-Oliver attempts at creating libernations, see John L. Snare, "The Nation Builders' Struggle," *Reason,* December 1972.

21. Details on Oliver's thought and background from "Designing a Free Country: An Interview with Mike Oliver," *Reason,* December 1972.

22. For the story of Minerva, see "Designing a Free Country," *Reason;* and Erwin S. Strauss, *How to Start Your Own Country* (Port Townsend, WA: Breakout, 1999), 114–117.

23. For details on libertarian hopes for Abaco, see Lynn Kinsky and Robert Poole Jr., "Abaco: Birth of a New Country?" *Reason,* October 1974.

24. Erwin Strauss estimates Oliver and the foundation spent as much as $130,000 in aiding Stevens's rebels. Strauss, *How to Start Your Own Country,* 121.

25. For a detailed history of Stevens's rebel movement as it intersected the libertarian world, see Patrick Cox, "Wun Niu Fela Kuntri," *Reason,* September 1980. Erwin Strauss thinks that American libertarian media overemphasized Oliver and the Phoenix Foundation's influence on Stevens's movement; he notes that American libertarians' lack of detailed knowledge of the local situation meant that "there was no significant role to be played by any libertarian new-country promoters with no more than one or two hundred thousand dollars to play with." Strauss, *How to Start Your Own Country,* 123.

26. Despite past failures in the artificial ocean city field, some bright folk are still counting on the fact that many will want to live in one, and be willing to pay dear first-adapter prices to do so. Patri Friedman, grandson of Milton and son of anarcho-theorist David, is even today actively planning to launch artificial sea platform communities, which he's calling seasteads, currently hoping to start small with one in San Francisco Bay. That's the spirit of America, as John Adams never quite said: may I advocate classical-liberal limited government, so that my son may advocate anarcho-capitalism, and that my grandson may plan to build new artificial countries in the ocean.

27. Even now, some people in both the Limon province of Costa Rica and in Somalia are raising funds and raising consciousness about creating free market enclaves in a statist world.

28. Strauss, *How to Start Your Own Country*, 111.

29. Bergland, interview by author.

30. Roy A. Childs Jr., "Victory in California," *Libertarian Review*, July 1978, 18.

31. Some details on the Koch family's background from David Koch, interview by author, December 17, 2005. The Kochs are press shy and have not been written about commensurate with their wealth; but see Elliot Blair Smith, "The Billionaires' Brawl," *USA Today*, April 8, 1998; and Leslie Wayne, "Pulling the Wraps off Koch Industries," *New York Times*, November 20, 1994, for accounts of the family's personal and business history.

32. D. Koch, interview by author.

33. Koch's earliest institution building came with the Center for Independent Education, pursuing research in the failure of state-run schools, run in collaboration with a longtime Koch friend and fellow supporter of libertarian causes, Bob Love, a fellow Bircher who ran his own independent private prep school in Wichita. It ended up being folded into first the Institute for Humane Studies, then Cato, then faded away.

34. The Koch family became notorious for a bitter and expensive series of lawsuits over two of the brothers, William and Fred, deciding they'd been cheated when Charles bought them out of the company in 1981. Details can be found in Wayne, "Pulling the Wraps," *New York Times*.

35. Charles Koch, interview by author, January 12, 2006.

36. *Libertarian Review* evolved from Robert Kephart's *Books for Libertarians* book review and sales catalog from the early to mid-1970s, which Childs also worked on. Kephart was a former publisher of *Human Events* and publisher of many hard money newsletters who had been converted to anarcho-capitalism by Rothbard and Karl Hess. Kephart sold *Libertarian Review* to Koch in 1976.

37. Charles Hamilton, interview by author, January 28, 1999.

38. D. Koch, interview by author.

39. C. Koch, interview by author.

40. More recently, in what could be seen as a more pragmatic taking care of the Koch family's business, they have become big donors to Republican candidates such as Dole and George W. Bush while continuing more radical libertarian funding.

41. Williamson Evers, interview by author, November 9, 1998.

42. Evers, interview by author.

43. "Reminiscences and Prognostications," *Reason*, May 1978, 45.

44. Crane, interview by author.

45. Ernest van den Haag, "Libertarians and Conservatives," *National Review*, June 8, 1979.

46. Crane, interview by author.

47. When Rothbard was drawn into Lew Rockwell's Ludwig von Mises Institute, founded in 1982, he gleefully declared that Rockwell was who Crane was *supposed* to be, a dedicated professional adult with institution-building skills and an impregnable libertarianism. Both Crane and Rockwell have been extraordinarily successful in their respective ways, though they have aimed their institutions in different directions and toward different audiences.

48. Crane made an impassioned case in a January 22, 1979, letter to the LP's National Committee against a science fiction emphasis at the convention, which he thought would give the party's its biggest chance yet to explain itself to the American people: "Why *can't* a convention devoted to the 'real world' of politics be exciting? What does it take to charge people's batteries—spaceships or freedom? Were the American revolutionaries driven by a vision of horseless carriages in their future or by a passion for liberty? Was Thomas Paine fighting for the chance to see television one day or for the dignity of free men and women?"

49. Quoted in David Nolan, "Clark for President: A Campaign Critique," *Libertarian Forum*, September–December 1980, 14.

50. Murray N. Rothbard, "Nuclear Power Crisis," *Libertarian Forum*, July–August 1979, 1.

51. Murray N. Rothbard to Jule Herbert, May 29, 1979, MRA, LVMI.

52. Murray N. Rothbard, "The Menace of Opportunism," *Libertarian Forum*, November–December 1979, 2.

53. Murray N. Rothbard, "The Presidential Campaign: The Need for Radicalism," *Libertarian Forum*, March–April 1980, 2.

54. Murray N. Rothbard, "The Clark Campaign: Never Again," *Libertarian Forum*, September–December 1980, 1.

55. See Murray N. Rothbard, "It Usually Ends with Ed Crane," *Libertarian Forum*, January–April 1981, for Rothbard's account of his departure from the Cato Institute. From Crane's point of view, it was impossible working with a man who was traducing him in every forum public and private that he could access; that Rothbard had failed to deliver a book on the Progressive Era that Cato had paid him for, and that the taking back of a founder's shares was indeed allowed for in Cato's bylaws. Rothbard's counter to that point was that the taking of the shares had to occur at a duly constituted board meeting, and that didn't happen in his case. Complaining that he didn't have the funds to go toe to toe with a billionaire in a legal dispute, Rothbard had only complaining about it as an option.

56. Justin Raimondo, interview by author, September 25, 1999. Students for a Libertarian Society was, for a few years in the late 1970s and early 1980s, a genuine revival of student libertarian activism, with dozens of active chapters, and played a major role in the (ultimately failed) campus-based campaign against reinstituting draft registration.

57. Raimondo, interview by author.

58. Crane machiner Chris Hocker in a 1982 memo to party activists, state chairs, and NatCom members, tried to remind them that "Crane . . . was the LP National Chair from 1974 to 1977. He was elected twice to this position by delegates to national conventions (as opposed to, say, having arisen from Hell in a cloud of sulphur smoke, as some have been led to believe)." Chris Hocker, "Response to David Bergland Memo of August 11," August 17, 1982. Memo in the author's possession.

59. Earl Ravenal quoted in Robert K. Landers, "The Party's Over," *Washington Weekly*, September 17, 1984.

60. Eric O'Keefe, interview by author, August 4, 1998.

61. In the presidential race, Crane was not technically campaign manager, but everyone knew he was in charge.

62. According to Roger MacBride, Gene Burns ensured his own lack of support by not seeking it intelligently. He claims that Burns had gathered around $10,000 to $20,000 prior to dropping out but never bothered to approach MacBride, Crane, or the Kochs, who had up until then been the party's main power brokers and financiers. Quoted in Richard Murray Borchers, "The Libertarian Party: Headed Where?" master's thesis, University of Colorado, 1986, 28.

63. Details on the negative reactions to Bergland's nomination from Bergland, interview by author.

64. Crane, interview by author.

65. Sennholz, interview by author.

66. Boettke, interview by author.

67. Kirzner, interview by author.

68. A brief exposition on the Austrian "middle ground" perspective on equilibrium (and other things) is in Roger W. Garrison, "Austrian Economics as the Middle Ground: Comment on Loasby," in Israel Kirzner, ed., *Method, Process, and Austrian Economics: Essays in Honor of Ludwig von Mises* (Lexington, MA: Lexington Books, 1982).

69. Ludwig M. Lachmann, *Capital, Expectations, and the Market Process* (Kansas City: Sheed Andrews & McMeel, 1977), 323–336.

70. A good discussion of how the kaleidic version of Austrianism must lead to agnosticism about the benefits of free markets can be found in Brian J. Loasby, *The Mind and Method of the Economist: A Critical Appraisal of Major Economists in the 20th Century* (Brookfield, VT: Edward Elgar, 1990), chap. 10.

71. Lachmann, *Capital, Expectations*, 284.

72. Good expositions from Kirzner on the connection between free markets and his entrepreneurial vision are in Israel M. Kirzner, *Perception, Opportunity, and Profit* (Chicago: University of Chicago Press, 1979), chaps. 9, 13; and Kirzner, *The Meaning of Market Process: Essays in the Development of Modern Austrian Economics* (London: Routledge, 1992), chap. 2. This divergence between Kirzner and Lachmann's views—are we tending always toward equilibrium or floating through a kaleidic haze?—is made the linchpin of Karen Vaughn's history of the Austrian tradition in America. To her, the future of Austrian economics will involve some attempt to resolve or decide this conflict between the Kirznerian and Lachmannian visions. See Vaughn, *Austrian Economics in America*, chaps. 7–8.

While Kirzner acknowledges the disagreement with his dear friend Lachmann, he doesn't give it the same significance as Vaughn does. "Vaughn and some others have seen this issue as being one that has riven Austrian economics down the middle and that everything revolves around this issue. I'm not convinced that that's the case, though it makes a neat dramatic development in a story."

73. Kirzner, interview by author. A collection of talks given at the Royalton conference was later published in a volume edited by Edward Dolan and called *The Foundations of Austrian Economics*, which is a good place to look for a sense of the Austrian landscape immediately after Mises. Edwin G. Dolan, ed., *The Foundations of Modern Austrian Economics* (Kansas City: Sheed & Ward, 1976).

74. Vaughn, *Austrian Economics in America*, 108.

75. Dolan, ed., *Foundations of Modern Austrian Economics*, 4.

76. Details on South Royalton conference from Richard Ebeling, interview by author, June 25, 2005.

77. Israel Kirzner to Leonard Liggio, January 27, 1983, Institute for Humane Studies Archives, Israel Kirzner file.

78. Louis M. Spadaro, "Toward a Program of Research and Development for Austrian Economics," in Louis M. Spadaro, ed., *New Directions in Austrian Economics* (Kansas City: Sheed Andrews and McMeel, 1978).

79. Later on, more conservative foundations such as Scaife and Bradley also helped fund Austrian programs at NYU. While Kirzner doesn't like to link Austrianism with politics of any sort, he could note to potential funders that "if you are interested in a free society, you'll be interested in a body of thought that we believe can demonstrate the advantages of a free market, and it makes a lot of sense for those interested in classical liberal values to make sure this way of thinking, this tradition, is not lost."

80. Mario Rizzo, interview by author, September 1, 1996. Despite Rizzo's lament, NYU is still an academic center of Austrianism in the United States, featuring a weekly colloquium of Austrians where papers are presented and discussed. Even so, Austrian economics is not its own degree track; any student seeking a graduate degree at NYU must take all the required courses anyone else must take.

81. Sennholz was not known for providing the best preparation for high-level grad programs. Walter Grinder studied under him on Leonard Read's recommendation and regretted it. He claims Sennholz didn't encourage you to learn much more than he was prepared to tell you. "If you read anything besides Mises and Böhm-Bawerk, you were

suspect. Even Hayek was a problem." Walter Grinder, interview by author, October 6, 1998.

82. Boettke, interview by author.

83. Boettke, interview by author.

84. Boettke, interview by author.

85. Mises, *Epistemological Problems*, 214.

86. Israel M. Kirzner, "The 'Austrian' Perspective on the Crisis," in Bell and Kristol, eds., *Crisis in Economic Theory*, 115.

87. For a thorough Austrian critique of this, see Roger W. Garrison, "Mises and His Method," in Herbener, ed., *Meaning of Mises*.

88. See Lawrence H. White, "Mises, Hayek, Hahn, and the Market Process: Comment on Littlechild," in Kirzner, ed., *Method, Process*, 108.

89. Lachmann, *Capital, Expectations*, 114.

90. For a thorough modern Austrian exposition, including a summation of where older Austrians stood on this issue, see Roy Cordato, *Welfare Economics and Externalities in an Open Ended Universe: A Modern Austrian Perspective* (Boston: Kluwer Academic, 1992).

91. Gerald P. O'Driscoll, "Spontaneous Order and the Coordination of Economic Activities," in Spadaro, ed., *New Directions*.

92. Kirzner, interview by author.

93. "The New Generation: Part 1, Interview with Edward Stringham," *Austrian Economics Newsletter*, Summer 2002, 4–5.

94. Stavros Ioannides, *The Market, Competition, and Democracy: A Critique of Neo-Austrian Economics* (Brookfield, VT: Edward Elgar, 1992), 141.

95. Robert Nozick, "On Austrian Methodology," *Synthese*, 1977, 376.

96. Boettke, interview by author.

97. Boettke, interview by author. Arguments between Boettke and other Austrians as to whether Austrians' relative lack of success in academia is attributable to methodological and political prejudice or simply the Austrian academics' lack of sensible professional entrepreneurship (or world-class talent) continue to this day on listservs where Austrians gather.

98. Boettke, interview by author.

99. Boettke, interview by author. Rothbard and the economists and philosophers surrounding him at the Ludwig von Mises Institute at Auburn and their journal, the *Quarterly Journal of Austrian Economics* (originally *Review of Austrian Economics*), stayed mostly entrenched in the Misesian tradition until Rothbard's death and later. Most of the other big Austrian revival figures have followed some variation of Boettke's call for "pollution" of the Austrian tradition with other ideas, even if they might not put it that way. Vaughn maintains in her history that Rothbard's attempt to hold firm to pure Misesianism trapped him in his own side pool from the flowing stream of the modern Austrian revival, making him largely irrelevant (Vaughn, *Austrian Economics in America*, 139 n. 1).

Kirzner has attempted to explain in more modern terms the Misesian concept of the entrepreneur, and how the entrepreneur's constant alertness to profit possibilities others have missed keeps the economy moving toward, but never reaching, equilibrium. Lachmann brought in Shackle and even a Keynesian influence in his focus on the subjectivity of expectations, and the damage this does to any assumption of even a path toward equilibrium. Rizzo and O'Driscoll explain the basics of the entire Austrian paradigm in new and more contemporary terms in their 1985 book *The Economics of Time and Ignorance*. The book defines the Austrian approach as *radically* subjectivist, compared to the standard neoclassical static subjectivism. As Vaughn puts it, "Dynamic subjectivism . . . recognizes the creativity and nondeterminate nature of human choice. . . . It was dynamic subjectivism that could account for the open-endedness of economic processes" (Vaughn, *Austrian Economics in America*, 134–135).

That open-endedness is inherent in the real changes that occur as real time passes, and the inevitable changes in knowledge and expectations that come with the passing of time.

100. Rand, *Philosophy: Who Needs It?*, 15.

101. Berliner, ed., *Letters of Ayn Rand*, 664.

102. Rand acolyte Peter Schwartz's total condemnation of libertarians as amoral, nihilistic whim worshipers was canonized in the pages of a mostly Rand-authored posthumous essay collection, *The Voice of Reason*. It originally appeared as Peter Schwartz, "Libertarianism: The Perversion of Liberty," *Intellectual Activist*, May 10, 1985, 2–15; June 25, 1985, 2–7; December 4, 1985, 4–11. The version that appeared in *Voice of Reason* was edited and condensed.

103. Ayn Rand, "Check Your Premises: How to Judge a Political Candidate," *Objectivist Newsletter*, March 1964, 9.

104. Schwartz, "Libertarianism: The Perversion of Liberty," *Intellectual Activist*, May 10, 1985, 9.

105. Schwartz, "Libertarianism: The Perversion of Liberty," *Intellectual Activist*, May 10, 1985, 12.

106. Schwartz, "Libertarianism: The Perversion of Liberty," *Intellectual Activist*, June 25, 1985, 7.

107. Schwartz, "Libertarianism: The Perversion of Liberty," *Intellectual Activist*, December 4, 1985, 9–10.

108. N. Branden, interview by author. Barbara Branden speculates that in the 1970s Rand was connected to the real world almost solely through the *New York Times* and through Peikoff, and was ignorant of the extent to which libertarians respected her and made valuable contributions toward turning the world, at least the political world, in the direction she preferred. B. Branden, interview by author.

109. Schulman, interview by author.

110. Klausner, interview by author.

111. Within five years, that would no longer be true of most of them. As the years have gone by, it is less and less likely that a random gathering of ten important libertarian activists would care much about the LP at all.

112. "Reminiscences and Prognostications," *Reason*, May 1978, 47.

113. "Inside Ronald Reagan: A Reason Interview," July 1975, 6.

Chapter 8

1. See, for example, Karen Lehrman, "The Dope on Dana: From Anarchism to Neoauthoritarianism," *New Republic*, November 5, 1990.

2. Dana Rohrabacher, "The Goals and Ideals of the Reagan Revolution," in B. B. Kymlicka and Jean V. Matthews, eds., *The Reagan Revolution?* (Chicago: Dorsey, 1988), 27.

3. Nathaniel Branden, interview by author.

4. Ed Crane, "Reagan Never Meant What He Said," *Washington Post*, August 19, 1982, A19. Robert Poole at *Reason*, in the meantime, said in 1983 that the magazine was studiedly easy on Reagan in the beginning. Noting his friendship with many free marketers Reagan recruited at the start, Poole got the idea that "it might be wiser, at least in the first two years, to give more of the benefit of the doubt and to encourage the positive tendencies when they were so much under attack from people who fundamentally disagreed with even the best parts of Reagan's agenda. In other words, maybe we could help get more accomplished by trying to counteract that climate of hysteria whipped up by the liberals." "Reason Interview: Robert W. Poole, Jr.," *Reason*, May 1983, 60.

5. Sheldon Richman, "Bonzo's Bedtime Reading," *Inquiry*, February 15, 1982, 11.

6. Murray Rothbard, "Ronald Reagan: A Political Obituary," *Liberty*, August 2004, 20. For the most heated libertarian denunciations of Reagan's legacy, see that whole article and Jeff Riggenbach, "Ronald Reagan, R.I.H.," *Liberty*, August 2004.

7. Anderson's book about the Reagan years presents the most optimistic, best-case assessment of Reagan from a roughly libertarian perspective. See Martin Anderson, *Revolution* (San Diego: Harcourt Brace Jovanovich, 1988).

8. Doug Bandow, interview by author, October 6, 1998.

9. Jeff Riggenbach, interview by author, September 26, 1998.

10. A more specifically movement-oriented magazine, *Liberty,* launched in 1987, still lives as the second most popular and long-lived libertarian magazine; its circulation maxed out at around 14,000, but has since shrunk to 5,000.

11. Sidney Blumenthal, "Jack Wheeler's Adventures with the 'Freedom Fighters,'" *Washington Post,* April 16, 1986, D1. The strangest article *Reason* ran in what might be called its military era was a cover story in the mid-1980s proposing seriously that the key to Middle East peace was building a wall around Israel filled with pipes of radioactive waters and gases, so that if anyone ruptured it they'd be zapped with deadly radiation.

12. Ed Crane, interview by author.

13. Robert Poole, interview by author, July 5, 1998.

14. The idea of *Byline*, Riggenbach explained to me, "was to have people identified as liberals like Nat Hentoff and Nicholas von Hoffman, and people identified as conservatives, like Tom Bethell and Howard Jarvis, we'd pick people from either side who weren't apt to emphasize things libertarians would find offensive, then slip in libertarians among them as if they were of equal stature with the others, and pull the wool over the public's eye and win the revolution. So far as I've been able to ascertain, it didn't work."

15. John L. Kelley, *Bringing the Market Back In: The Political Revitalization of Market Liberalism* (New York: New York University Press, 1997), 194, 225 n. 43.

16. Friedman has referred to Hayek as the most influential modern libertarian. Milton Friedman, interview by author, January 29, 1995.

17. "The Evolution of the Chicago School of Economics," *Chicago Maroon,* April 3, 1992.

18. Bernard D. Nossiter, "The Prize," *Washington Post,* November 6, 1976, B1–2.

19. "Friedman's Laurel Wreath," *Nation,* November 20, 1976, 516.

20. Melville J. Ulmer, "Friedman's Currency," *New Republic,* November 6, 1976, 8–9.

21. Robert H. Nelson, *Economics as Religion: From Samuelson to Chicago and Beyond* (University Park: Pennsylvania State University Press, 2001), 114.

22. A concise explanation in movement libertarian terms on the importance of Yale Brozen in particular and by implication the Chicago School in general on antitrust and regulatory issues can be found in David R. Henderson, "In Memoriam: Yale Brozen," *Freeman,* June 1998.

23. An eclectic libertarian economist who both admires and criticizes aspects of both schools has written an entire book on the similarities and divergences of the Austrian and Chicago schools of free market economics. See Mark Skousen, *Vienna and Chicago: Friends or Foes? A Tale of Two Schools of Free-Market Economics* (Washington, DC: Capital, 2005).

24. Central to Keynes's theory was the idea that money velocity was far more variable than Friedman found it to be; debate about the stability of velocity continues apace, however, though leaning more toward Friedman's side.

25. In other contexts Friedman has granted that any amount of money can be optimal; money's "usefulness to the community as a whole does not depend on how much money there is." Milton Friedman, *Money Mischief: Episodes in Monetary History* (New York: Harcourt Brace Jovanovich, 1992), 28.

26. There is more to Friedman's monetarism than this short sketch presents. For good nontechnical summations of Friedman's thought on this topic, see Milton Friedman, "The Quantity Theory of Money: A Restatement," "The Supply of Money and Changes in Prices and Output," "A Monetary History of the United States: A Summing Up," "Inflation and Unemployment," "Notes on the Quantity Theory of Money," all in Leube, ed.,

Essence of Friedman, 285–384. See also Milton Friedman, *Money Mischief*, chap. 2. A good collection of his writings on money is Milton Friedman, *Monetarist Economics* (London: Basil Blackwell, 1992).

For good commentary on and summation of Friedman's monetary thought, see Eamonn Butler, *Milton Friedman: A Guide to His Economic Thought* (New York: Universe, 1985), chaps. 2–10; also, Henri Lepage, *Tomorrow Capitalism* (La Salle, IL: Open Court, 1982), chap. 9.

27. M. Friedman, interview by author, January 29, 1995.

28. A good but brief nontechnical discussion of the consumption function appears in Thomas J. Sargent, "Rational Expectations," in Henderson, ed., *Fortune Encyclopedia of Economics*, 156–157.

Friedman has rarely tackled the topic nontechnically, but the brave who don't want to tackle his entire original book on the topic can see Milton Friedman, "Consumption and Permanent Income," in Leube, ed., *Essence of Friedman*, chap. 12.

29. Leonard Silk, "Milton Friedman: Nobel Laureate," *New York Times,* October 17, 1976, sec. 3, p. 16.

30. M. Friedman, interview by author, January 29, 1995.

31. Alexander Rosenberg, *Economics: Mathematical Politics or Science of Diminishing Returns?* (Chicago: University of Chicago Press, 1992), 57–60.

32. Milton Friedman, "The Methodology of Positive Economics," in Leube, ed., *Essence of Friedman*, 163. Friedman's position on economic methodology has been much commented on and attacked, and others have attempted to refine it for him, which he has chosen not to do. Mario Rizzo, from an Austrian perspective, says that attempting to apply testability criteria to economic theories is impossible because the ceteris paribus assumptions (about what other things can be assumed to stay the same as we try to test the one theoretical proposition we are trying to test) themselves need to be tested, leading to a potential infinite regress and a thorny problem of trying to figure out whether the theory being tested has failed or whether ceteris paribus conditions didn't apply. Mario J. Rizzo, "Praxeology and Econometrics: A Critique of Positivist Economics," in Spadaro, ed., *New Directions in Austrian Economics*, 42–49. Alexander Rosenberg says Friedman was missing the point by defending unrealistic assumptions; "no economist has ever questioned the assumptions of neoclassical theory just because they are unrealistic, and the real reason many have done so is because of dissatisfaction with what Friedman assumes to be beyond question, the predictive success of neoclassical economic theory." Rosenberg, *Economics: Mathematical Politics*, 60. Hayek scholar Bruce Caldwell criticizes Friedman for seeming to fall back on realism as a deciding factor in theories in his later career in Bruce Caldwell, *Beyond Positivism: Economic Methodology in the Twentieth Century* (London: George Allen & Unwin, 1982), 182–183. Friedman, meanwhile, just kept doing his work.

33. "Monetarists Succeed in Pushing Basic Ideas but Not Their Policies," *Wall Street Journal,* December 10, 1984, 1. See also Murray Rothbard, "Is There Life After Reaganomics?" in Llewellyn H. Rockwell, ed., *The Free Market Reader* (Burlingame, CA: Ludwig Von Mises Institute, 1988), 378.

34. Friedman thinks that these sort of intellectual battles are never really won; some people will hold on to certain errors forever. M. Friedman, interview by author, January 29, 1995.

35. For a discussion of Friedman's policy successes as a reaction to crisis, see Allan H. Meltzer, "Choosing Freely: The Friedmans' Influence on Economic and Social Policy," in Mark A. Wynne, Harvey Rosenbaum, and Robert L. Formaini, eds., *The Legacy of Milton and Rose Friedman's Free to Choose: Economic Liberalism at the Turn of the 21st Century* (Dallas: Federal Reserve Bank of Dallas, 2004), 195–198.

36. Friedman collected these *Newsweek* columns into three more books of popular political science and economics: *An Economist's Protest: Columns on Political Economy* (1972), revised and republished as *There's No Such Thing as a Free Lunch* (1975), and *Bright Promises, Dismal Performance: An Economist's Protest* (1983).

37. The *Free to Choose* documentary was made by Video-Arts of London, a video production firm run by a man who was familiar with Friedman through an interview with *Playboy* in 1973. It is always hard to predict exactly how ideas will incubate and spread.

38. Information on background of *Free to Choose* TV series from Milton and Rose Friedman, *Free to Choose* (New York: Harcourt Brace Jovanovich, 1980), ix–xii; also M. Friedman, interview by author, January 29, 1995.

39. Friedman and Friedman, *Free to Choose*, ix.

40. Kenneth J. Arrow, *New Republic*, March 22, 1980, 26.

41. Elton Rayack, *Not So Free to Choose* (New York: Praeger, 1987), 9–13.

42. Anderson, *Revolution*, 172.

43. For an anti-Friedman perspective on his relations with Chile from the vantage point of the mid-1980s, see Rayack, *Not So Free*, chap. 5. For a more evenhanded discussion of the actual nature of Friedman's involvement in Chile and the controversy it caused, see William Frazer, *Power and Ideas: Milton Friedman and the Big U-Turn*, 2 vols. (Gainesville, FL: Gulf/Atlantic, 1988), chap. 10. For a discussion of the un-Friedmanite nature of the 1970s Pinochet regime, see Jonathan Marshall, "Did Milton Friedman Really Ruin Chile?" *Inquiry*, August 1983, 18–21.

Friedman's own explanation and defense of his role in Chile is in Friedman and Friedman, *Two Lucky People*, 591–602.

44. Murray Rothbard, "Milton Friedman Unraveled," *Individualist*, February 1971, 3–7. Being called a statist by Rothbard is better than being called a fascist, as Lyndon LaRouche and David Goldman did in their amusingly bizarre book of conspiracy mongering linking Friedman to a centuries-old conspiracy run by the British to push the economics of stagnation and drugs, *The Ugly Truth About Milton Friedman*, which eerily mimics, in its economics, many supply-sider arguments against Friedman.

45. William J. Baumol and Alan S. Blinder, *Economics: Principles and Policy* (San Diego: Harcourt Brace Jovanovich, 1985), 861.

46. Rothbard, *For a New Liberty*, 27.

47. Sheldon Richman, "Commentator on Our Times: A Quest for the Historic Rothbard," in Walter Block and Llewellyn H. Rockwell, eds., *Man, Economy, and Liberty: Essays in Honor of Murray N. Rothbard* (Auburn, AL: Ludwig von Mises Institute, 1988), 357.

48. M. Friedman, interview by author, January 28, 1995. It was not only the anarchist wing of the movement that took Friedman to task for some of his gradualist policy prescriptions. Henry Hazlitt dedicated a chapter in one of his books to poking holes in Friedman's negative income tax, arguing that it is politically and historically naive, that the tax would be bound to grow, and could not realistically be held back to Friedman's plan that someone with zero income receive from the government only half of what's calculated as a bare minimum survival income. Henry Hazlitt, *Man vs. the Welfare State* (New Rochelle, NY: Arlington House, 1969), chap. 12.

49. For Friedman's more radical later thoughts about money, see Milton Friedman, "Has Government Any Role in Money?" in Leube, ed., *Essence of Friedman*, chap. 26.

50. Bettina Bien Greaves, interview by author, May 15, 1995. F. A. Hayek, whom Friedman has never publicly attacked for intolerance, shared Mises's strong antipathy toward parts of Friedman's thought. Hayek considers Friedman's great contribution to economic methodology, *Essays in Positive Economics*, to be as dangerous a book as Keynes's *General Theory*. See Hayek, *Hayek on Hayek*, 145.

51. Butler, *Friedman: Guide to Thought*, 232, 242–245.

52. Ralph Raico, interview by author; see also Ralph Raico, "The Austrian School and Classical Liberalism," in Peter J. Boettke and Mario J. Rizzo, eds., *Advances in Austrian Economics* (Greenwich, CT: JAI Press, 1995), 2: 9–11.

53. Milton Friedman, "Say 'No' to Intolerance," *Liberty,* July 1991, 17–20.

54. Milton Friedman, *Dollars and Deficits: Living with America's Economic Problems* (Englewood Cliffs, NJ: Prentice-Hall, 1968), 3.

55. David Friedman, interview by author, May 22, 1995.

56. M. Friedman, interview by author, January 28, 1995.

57. D. Friedman, interview by author, May 22, 1995.

58. Quoted in Skousen, *Vienna and Chicago,* 225.

59. For an interesting example of average libertarians attacking Friedman, see "Letters," *Reason,* March 1975, 37–39.

60. David Reisman, *The Political Economy of James Buchanan* (London: Macmillan, 1990), 167.

61. Gordon Tullock et al., *Government Failure: A Primer in Public Choice* (Washington, DC: Cato Institute, 2002), 11.

62. For a concise and nontechnical discussion of this rent-seeking idea, pioneered though not named by Gordon Tullock, see Tullock et al., *Government Failure,* chap. 4, "The Cost of Rent Seeking."

63. James M. Buchanan, *Better Than Plowing and Other Personal Essays* (Chicago: University of Chicago Press, 1992), 97.

64. Buchanan, *Better Than Plowing,* 107.

65. Thomas Sowell, *A Personal Odyssey* (New York: Free Press, 2000), 282, 296.

66. Thomas Sowell, *Knowledge and Decisions* (New York: Basic, 1980), 331–368.

67. Soma Golden, "Greenspan, Economist, Is Believer in Laissez-Faire Capitalism," *New York Times,* July 24, 1974, 57.

68. For details and analysis of how true Greenspan was to his Objectivist-libertarian roots in his professional career, see R. W. Bradford, "Alan Greenspan and Ayn Rand," *American Enterprise,* September–October 1997.

69. Doug Casey, interview by author, August 9, 2005.

70. "Interview with Harry Browne," *IRI Insight,* March–April 1981.

71. Details on Blanchard background and career from "Reason Interview: James U. Blanchard III," *Reason,* June 1983.

72. Casey, interview by author.

73. Antony Fisher to Leonard Read, April 30, 1949, FEE Archives.

74. Frost, *Antony Fisher,* 118–133.

75. Joseph Bast, interview by author, August 5, 1998.

76. Charles Murray, interview by author, July 3, 1998.

77. Charles Murray, *In Pursuit of Happiness and Good Government* (New York: Touchstone, 1988), 303.

78. Murray, interview by author.

79. Tom G. Palmer, "The Literature of Liberty," in David Boaz, ed., *The Libertarian Reader: Classic and Contemporary Writings from Lao-Tzu to Milton Friedman* (New York: Free Press, 1997), 417.

80. Robert Nozick, *Anarchy, State, and Utopia* (New York: Basic Books, 1974), xv.

81. Ralph Raico, "Robert Nozick: A Historical Note," *Lew Rockwell.com,* available at www.lewrockwell.com/raico/raico15.html.

82. "How Is Business Different from Sex? A Talk with Philosopher Robert Nozick," *Forbes,* March 15, 1975, 23.

83. Julian Sanchez, "Interview with Robert Nozick, Pt. 2," available at www.laissezfaire-books.com/index.cfm?eid=359.

84. Nozick, *Anarchy*, x.

85. Sanchez, "Interview with Nozick, Pt. 2."

86. For Nozick at the LP convention in 1975, see Kelley, *Bringing the Market Back In*, 123.

87. Jan Narveson, *The Libertarian Idea* (Philadelphia: Temple University Press, 1988), 5.

88. Loren Lomasky, *Persons, Rights, and the Moral Community* (New York: Oxford University Press, 1987), 106.

89. See Nozick, *Anarchy*, 12–17, for Nozick's account of protection agencies and how and why a dominant one would arise.

90. See Nozick, *Anarchy*, 57–84, for Nozick's long explanation and defense of his principles dictating when you can prohibit risky activity on the part of others, and what compensation is due under what circumstances.

91. On procedural rights, see Nozick, *Anarchy*, 96–101.

92. The state enters via these arguments in Nozick, *Anarchy*, 110–115.

93. Taylor, ed., *Liberty Against Power: Essays by Roy A. Childs, Jr.*, 166.

94. John Rawls, *A Theory of Justice* (Cambridge: Belknap/Harvard University Press, 1971), 62.

95. Nozick, *Anarchy*, 177.

96. See Nozick, *Anarchy*, 160–165, for the Chamberlain example.

97. Nozick, *Anarchy*, 226.

98. Nozick, *Anarchy*, 231.

99. Nozick, *Anarchy*, 312.

100. Some critics have noted that to truly function, this utopian framework might require a specific kind of moral education in liberal, tolerant values to ensure that people would honor its libertarian aspects, thus making it not quite as wide-open and all-embracing of different ways of life as Nozick suggests. See Mark Fowler, "Stability and Utopia: A Critique of Nozick's Framework Argument," in J. Angelo Corlett, ed., *Equality and Liberty: Analyzing Rawls and Nozick* (New York: St. Martin's, 1991), for a good example of this argument.

101. Murray Rothbard, "Robert Nozick and the Immaculate Conception of the State," *Journal of Libertarian Studies* 1, no. 1 (1977): 56–57.

102. The essay whose argument I summarize here is Roy Childs, "The Invisible Hand Strikes Back," *Journal of Libertarian Studies* 1, no. 1 (1977). Reprinted in Taylor, ed., *Liberty Against Power.*

103. The argument summarized here and below is in Rothbard, "Robert Nozick and the Immaculate Conception of the State."

104. Rothbard, "Robert Nozick," 49.

105. Rothbard, "Robert Nozick," 51. Rothbard is undoubtedly thinking of himself here.

106. Some examples: Andrew Valls, "The Libertarian Case for Affirmative Action," *Social Theory and Practice*, Summer 1999, tries to prove that Nozick's theory of rectification of past injustices in property rights transfers provides a grounding for affirmative action; Brian Lund, "Robert Nozick and the Politics of Social Welfare," *Political Studies* 44 (1996), posits that Nozick's principle of boundary violations with compensation being morally permissible should leave room for state-provided medical care and other elements of the welfare state; Aletheia Jackson, "For the Love of Whizdom," *Critical Review*, Summer 1990, agrees that "the arguments of *Anarchy, State, and Utopia* are not sufficient to establish libertarian conclusions because their basic premises better support the welfare state" (355). A similar argument that Nozick is, unknown to himself, providing a defense of the welfare state is in Michael Davis, "Nozick's Argument for the Legitimacy of the Welfare State" in Corlett, ed. *Equality and Liberty;* Justin Schwartz, "From Libertarianism to Egalitarianism," *Social Theory and Practice*, Fall 1992, argues that "a labor theory of property entitlements of the sort advocated by Locke and Nozick" in fact "supports not liber-

tarianism but a strong form of egalitarianism" (259). Gregory S. Kavka, "An Internal Critique of Nozick's Entitlement Theory" in Corlett, ed., *Equality and Liberty*, also argues that Nozick's entitlement theory of property cannot defend private property against redistribution by the state as long as he accepts the principle that full compensation can justify rights violations.

The specific arguments behind most of these assertions are as complicated and nuanced as Nozick's original, and fairly explaining them goes beyond the capacity of this note. The interested reader is referred to the articles in their entirety.

107. Brian Barry, Review of *Anarchy, State, and Utopia, Political Theory,* August 1975, 331.

108. Sanchez, "Interview with Robert Nozick, Pt. 2." Rothbard, one of Nozick's greatest critics on this matter and others, lived in a rent-controlled apartment in New York City, though he never filed suit to defend this unlibertarian privilege.

109. See Robert Nozick, "On the Randian Argument," *Personalist,* Spring 1971; and Nozick, "On Austrian Methodology," *Synthese* 36 (1977). Both essays are reprinted in Robert Nozick, *Socratic Puzzles* (Cambridge: Harvard University Press, 1997). For a countercritique from the Austrian perspective, see Walter Block, "On Robert Nozick's 'On Austrian Methodology,'" *Inquiry* 23.

110. *The Examined Life* received the most across-the-board critical drubbings of any of Nozick's books, and, unlike *Anarchy,* not for verboten political ideas. Nozick's drippingly and unctuously earnest attempts to "speak to [the readers] whole being, and to write from mine," drew some very sharply worded criticisms.

For example: Aletheia Jackson referred to the book's "constant oscillation—in ever-widening swings—between solemnly pronounced tautologies and dizzying emotional outbursts, between extravagant metaphysical absurdities and embarrassing personal confessions, between gassing—and gushing," in Jackson, "For the Love of Whizdom." Kenneth Minogue wrote that Nozick here "seems to be operating on the formula: quantification + mysticism = profundity," in Kenneth Minogue, "Pisher's Progress," *National Review,* December 31, 1989, 38. Jim Holt writes that "the greater part of Nozick's musings, however, issues in solemnly reported platitudes and sheer blather. Nothing, said Descartes, is so absurd that it was not said by one of the philosophers; to this I would add that nothing is so banal that Nozick does not bother to say it," in Jim Holt, "Is *The Examined Life* Worth Reading?" *American Scholar,* Summer 1990, 461.

On the whole, Nozick's attempt to, for example, schematicize the "matrix of reality" as a polyhedron featuring such categories as "thereness," "infinitude," "peace that passeth understanding," and the amazing "[unnamed]" row, seems less intellectual bravery than foolhardy hubris.

111. Robert Nozick, *The Examined Life* (New York: Simon & Schuster, 1989), 286.

112. Nozick, *Examined Life,* 290.

113. Nozick, *Examined Life,* 292.

114. Sanchez, "Interview with Robert Nozick, Pt. 2."

115. From "Anarchy at Harvard: Robert Nozick," an interview with Nozick in Giovanna Borradori, *The American Philosophers* (Chicago: University of Chicago Press, 1994), 75.

116. Jonathan Wolff, *Robert Nozick: Property, Justice, and the Minimal State* (Stanford: Stanford University Press, 1991), vii. Jeffrey Friedman, former movement libertarian and editor of *Critical Review,* an academic journal dedicated to some degree to critiques of libertarianism, has a more cynical view of the significance of Nozick in academic political philosophy. "Nobody agrees with him, but he's widely taught as someone to beat up on. There's a tendency for liberals and people on the left to exaggerate the importance of libertarianism. Ideologues seem to attribute more coherence and rationality to politics than there really is, so intellectuals conclude that if people voted for Reagan they must have understood what he stood for. The intellectuals don't understand him and they find him indistinguishable

from Nozick, therefore they think the majority of America agrees with Nozick." Friedman gave Nozick credit for swaying the direction of contemporary political philosophy in one respect; he credits the popularity of communitarian arguments in liberal political philosophy in the past couple of decades to Nozick's influence. "The point [the communitarians] are making is that liberalism in the Rawlsian sense is vulnerable to the Nozickian critique, so they must abandon the individualist basis of liberalism that Rawls uses and adopt a communitarian basis, based on an exaggerated fear about how Nozick undermined the welfare state." Jeffrey Friedman, interview by author, July 13, 1999.

117. Narveson, *Libertarian Idea*, 175. Narveson's sense of these "more extravagant implications" is uniquely peculiar; in this book (though he recanted this notion in conversation with this author) he judges Canadian-style national health care as acceptable (255) and also posits that using force to stop a parent from killing its born child is unjustified (274). He accepts zoning laws if reasonably applied (306–307), but also advocates privatized streets (309–313). Narveson is doing his own thinking here. Narveson also agrees with Nozick critics who say Nozick's argument for the minimal state justified far more than a minimal state (220–221).

118. Narveson, *Libertarian Idea*, 183–184.

119. Jan Narveson, interview by author, September 19, 2002.

120. Randy Barnett notes regarding his own major work of libertarian political philosophy, the anarchistic *The Structure of Liberty*, that he hoped it would become "the next big footnote" when it came to libertarian philosophy. He regrets that he hasn't noticed it happening yet.

121. Barnett presents the very complicated case for his anarchism, rooted in a long discussion of the nature of rights, in Randy Barnett, *The Structure of Liberty: Justice and the Rule of Law* (Oxford: Clarenden, 1998), showing how a regime of liberty is best equipped to cope with the three main dilemmas of human social life: knowledge, interest, and power.

122. Randy Barnett, *Restoring the Lost Constitution: The Presumption of Liberty* (Princeton: Princeton University Press, 2004), 45. The book as a whole is the most thorough discussion, including many specific case citations and reasoning through such cases, of a libertarian approach to real constitutional law in America.

123. Anthony de Jasay, *Against Politics: On Government, Anarchy, and Order* (London: Routledge, 1997), 11–36.

124. De Jasay, *Against Politics*, 196–198.

125. Rothbard addressed the question of whether his tort approach to pollution could mean the end of industrial civilization in his essay "Law, Property Rights, and Air Pollution," which appears in Murray Rothbard, *The Logic of Action II: Applications and Criticisms from the Austrian School* (Cheltenham: Edward Elgar, 1997), 148–153. Roughly, he says that invasions have to cause "*damage* beyond the mere fact of invasion itself" (150).

126. Thomas Szasz, *Insanity: The Idea and Its Consequences* (New York: John Wiley, 1987), 359.

127. Thomas Szasz, "An Autobiographical Sketch," in Jeffrey A Schaler, ed., *Szasz Under Fire: A Psychiatric Abolitionist Faces His Critics* (Chicago: Open Court, 2004), 1–3.

128. Szasz, "Autobiographical Sketch," 4.

129. Thomas Szasz, *The Myth of Psychotherapy: Mental Healing as Religion, Rhetoric, and Repression* (Garden City, NY: Anchor, 1978), 97.

130. Details on Szasz's troubles getting into medical school in Szasz, "Autobiographical Sketch," 14–15.

131. Thomas Szasz, interview by author, May 10, 2002.

132. Szasz, "Autobiographical Sketch," 32.

133. Thomas Szasz, *The Manufacture of Madness: A Comparative Study of the Inquisition and the Mental Health Movement* (New York: Harper & Row, 1970), 41.

134. Szasz, interview by author.

135. Szasz, interview by author.

136. Szasz, interview by author.

137. Szasz, interview by author.

138. Thomas Szasz, *The Myth of Mental Illness: Foundations of a Theory of Personal Conduct,* rev. ed. (1961; New York: Harper & Row, 1974), 262.

139. Maggie Scarf, "Normality Is a Square Circle or a Four-Sided Triangle," *New York Times Magazine,* October 3, 1971, 43.

140. Szasz, *Insanity,* ix.

141. Szasz, *Insanity,* 23.

142. Details on influential and admired authors from Szasz, interview by author.

143. In his major work from this period of cultural prominence, *The Manufacture of Madness* (1970), Szasz used one of his favorite techniques—the extended metaphor (he saw most mental illnesses as in fact metaphorical)—to compare the current treatment of the mentally ill with the treatment of witches in premodern times. He debunks the popular notion among the liberal-minded that the witches of old were "really" mentally ill. In this book Szasz can often be read, as some of his counterculture fans preferred to read him, as if he thinks of the mentally ill as oppressed for their deviance. In other contexts, Szasz would be less kind in his own moral judgments on the "mentally ill."

144. Thomas Szasz, *The Therapeutic State: Psychiatry in the Mirror of Current Events* (Buffalo: Prometheus, 1984), 26. For an extended discussion of Szasz's differences with Laing and the antipsychiatrists, see Thomas Szasz, *Schizophrenia: The Sacred Symbol of Psychiatry* (New York: Basic, 1976), chap. 2. "Anti-Psychiatry: The Model of the Plundered Mind."

145. Szasz, *Insanity,* 126.

146. See Thomas Szasz, *Law, Liberty, and Psychiatry* (1963; Syracuse: Syracuse University Press, 1989), xi, on this point.

147. Szasz, *Insanity,* 355.

148. Thomas Szasz, *The Second Sin* (Garden City, NY: Anchor, 1974), 35.

149. Maggie Scarf, "Normality Is a Square Circle or a Four-Sided Triangle," *New York Times Magazine,* October 3, 1971.

150. A collection of such journalism, including many pieces Szasz wrote for the Cato Institute's late 1970s and early 1980s libertarian journal *Inquiry,* and for Roy Childs's *Libertarian Review,* can be found in Szasz, *Therapeutic State.*

151. Leary quote regarding *Myth of Mental Illness* in a July 17, 1961, letter from Leary to Szasz, available at www.enabling.org/ia/szasz/leary.html. The dying Leary once asked me if I could tell Szasz to call him. Dawdling and aware (as Leary seemed not to be) that the admiration was not mutual, I failed to get around to relaying the message before Leary's prostate cancer killed him in May 1996. This has remained one of my deepest regrets. Of all the things not to procrastinate on, fulfilling a dying man's wishes should top the list. Szasz, informed of Leary's wish after it was too late, seemed glad to hear of it and sorry I had not told him before it was too late.

152. Szasz, interview by author.

153. The standard popular history of deinstitutionalization's dire effects credits Szasz as the primary direct influence on Bruce Ennis, who did pioneering work with the New York Civil Liberties Union on fighting for the rights of the mentally ill. It also refers to the fact that "Szasz is quoted constantly and at length" in "precedent-setting briefs and judicial decisions that effected this transfer of power" over mental patients from psychiatrists to lawyers. See Rael Jean Isaac and Virginia C. Armat, *Madness in the Streets: How Psychiatry and the Law Abandon the Mentally Ill* (New York: The Free Press, 1990), 109–111, 34.

154. See Thomas Szasz, *Cruel Compassion: Psychiatric Control of Society's Unwanted* (New York: John Wiley, 1994), chaps. 9–10 for an extended discussion of what Szasz sees as the causes of, realities of, and problems with deinstitutionalization. For his defense of himself from critics who blame him for the current state of deinstitutionalization, see 190–92.

155. Szasz, *Cruel Compassion*, 184.

156. Szasz, interview by author.

157. In other contexts—for example, in a critique of R. D. Laing in his essay "Models of Madness," reprinted in Szasz, *Therapeutic State*, 22–27, Szasz seems to take the more standard libertarian view that one is wronging society at large by supporting the so-called insane in public institutions. "Economically, Laing has . . . replaced the coercion of the mental patient by psychiatry on behalf of the citizen with the coercion of the taxpayer by the government on behalf of the mental patient" (26).

158. Letter from Lynn Kinsky, November 14, 1973, in the author's possession.

159. Szasz wrote a book about what he sees as the failures of libertarian thinkers to grapple effectively with the psychiatric issues that have been his bread and butter. Thomas Szasz, *Faith in Freedom: Libertarian Principles and Psychiatric Practices* (New Brunswick, NJ: Transaction, 2004).

160. For a comprehensive yet respectful summation of psychiatric critiques of Szasz, with a thorough bibliography, see Eric J. Damann, "'The Myth of Mental Illness': Continuing Controversies and their Implications for Mental Health Professionals," *Clinical Psychology Review* 17, no. 7 (1997).

161. Robert M. Leibert and Michael D. Spiegler, *Personality: Strategies and Issues,* 6th ed. (Pacific Grove, CA: Brooks/Cole, 1990), 12.

162. See Meg Jay, *The Princeton Review: Cracking the GRE Psychology Test,* 5th ed. (New York: Random House, 1999), 106: "Thomas Szasz viewed the schizophrenic world as simply misunderstood or artistic. He felt that they should not be treated."

163. Szasz, *Cruel Compassion*, 201–202, for Menninger letter to Szasz.

164. Szasz, interview by author. For an interesting example of this, Horacio Fabrega wrote that he does not accept the "wholesale rejection and condemnation on Dr. Szasz's part of such ideas as psychiatric illness, psychiatric disease, the biomedical theory of psychiatry" yet still somehow manages to say that "my thinking was very much influenced by his early work, and I continue to be admiring and respectful of the fertility of his mind, the breadth of his scholarship, and the high level of productivity he has shown." Horacio Fabrega, "Lack of Reference to the Work of Thomas Szasz, Dr. Fabrega Replies," *American Journal of Psychiatry*, December 1989, 1648.

165. See, for example, M. L. Zupan, "Is Mental Illness a Myth?" *Reason*, August 1973; and Ralph Slovenko, "The Trouble with Szasz," *Liberty*, August 2002.

166. Quote and explication of the statue metaphor in Szasz, *Schizophrenia*, 82–83.

167. Paul Jacob, interview by author, July 8, 1998.

168. In some states, some years, the LP candidate is technically on the ballot as an independent rather than a Libertarian, since in many cases that makes getting on the ballot easier. Any generalization about the fifty states' ballot access laws would be misleading, which is part of what makes coping with them so onerous.

169. In the mid-1970s, a Nevada LP candidate who could only get on the ballot as a Republican legally changed his name to James Libertarian Burns. See Eric Garris, "Frontlines," *Reason,* January 1975. For similar reasons of its being easier to get on the ballot under a different party name, in California in 1974 many LPers made a concerted invasion of the Peace and Freedom Party's ballot line.

170. By 1994, running a full national slate of congressional and presidential candidates for the LP would have required gathering 3.5 million signatures. Because of constant

changes in state requirements—often prompted by lawsuits or lobbying by third party activists—this figure is always shifting.

171. "Means and Paul Launch Campaigns," *American Libertarian*, March 1987, 2.

172. Details on Marrou's peccadilloes from Michael Emerling, "Why the Libertarian National Committee Must Remove Andre Marrou from the Libertarian Presidential Ticket," memo in the author's possession.

173. Todd Seavey, "Stern und Drang," *National Review*, June 13, 1994, 28.

174. Kevin Sack, "With Eyes Wide Open, Libertarians Choose Stern," *New York Times*, April 24, 1994, 40.

175. Harry Browne's time in the party was mired in mild scandal when Jacob Hornberger began publicizing the many interlocking payments and supposed conflicts of interest between Browne's campaign and various party officials, and Browne's brief decision, quickly rescinded, to openly refuse to file FEC-required information on donors and expenses.

176. Ronald Bailey, *Liberation Biology: The Scientific and Moral Case for the Biotech Revolution* (Amherst, NY: Prometheus, 2005).

177. Not that Wilson considered himself an enemy of the libertarian Austrians. In an interview with Sam Konkin's *New Libertarian Notes*, he was challenged on his various differences with orthodox libertarian economists. He explained those differences but concluded that "this is turning into a diatribe against the group I find least obnoxious in the whole politico-economic spectrum. . . . The orthodox conservatives and liberals, not to mention Nazis and Marxists, are really pernicious, and the Austrian libertarians are basically okay." Jane Talisman and Eric Geislinger, "Illuminating Discord: An Interview with Robert Anton Wilson," *New Libertarian Notes/Weekly*, September 5, 1976, 6.

178. Robert Shea and Robert Anton Wilson, *Illuminatus! Part II: The Golden Apple* (New York: Dell, 1975), 248–251.

179. Shea and Wilson, *Illuminatus! Part II*, 121.

180. Paulina Borsook, *Cyberselfish: A Critical Romp Through the Terribly Libertarian Culture of High-Tech* (New York: Public Affairs, 2000). See also my review and critique of her theory, Brian Doherty, "Cybersilly," *Reason*, August–September 2000.

181. Michael L. Rothschild, *Bionomics: The Inevitability of Capitalism* (New York: Henry Holt, 1990).

182. For a recent example from a libertarian scholar of this sort of historical analysis of how the state has helped hold down blacks in some generally obscure economic regulation areas, see David E. Bernstein, *Only One Place of Redress: African Americans, Labor Regulations, and the Courts from Reconstruction to the New Deal* (Durham, NC: Duke University Press, 2001).

183. For a sampling of such libertarian feminist theory, history, and criticism, see Wendy L. McElroy, ed., *Freedom, Feminism, and the State*, 2nd ed. (Oakland, CA: Independent Institute, 1991); Joan Kennedy Taylor, *Reclaiming the Mainstream: Individualist Feminism Reconsidered* (Amherst, NY: Prometheus, 1992); and Sharon Presley and Crispin Sartwell, eds., *Exquisite Rebel: The Essays of Voltairine de Cleyre: Anarchist, Feminist, Genius* (Albany, NY: SUNY Press, 2005).

184. John Baden, "The Nature Market: Why Listen to the New Resource Economics?" *Northern Lights*, Fall 1992.

185. A general survey of free market environmentalist thinking can be found in Terry L. Anderson and Donald R. Leal, *Free Market Environmentalism*, rev. ed. (New York: Palgrave, 2001).

186. Brian Doherty, "Selling Air Pollution," *Reason*, May 1996.

187. Lynn Scarlett, interview by author, October 25, 2005.

188. C. Koch, interview by author.

189. Fred Smith, interview by author, July 10, 1998.

190. Fred Smith, interview by author.

191. Ed Regis, "The Doomslayer," *Wired*, February 1997.

192. The most thorough summation of Simon's thinking and research is Julian Simon, *The Ultimate Resource 2* (Princeton: Princeton University Press, 1998).

193. Deirdre R. Schwiesow, "The GenX Philosophy," *USA Today*, July 26, 1995, A1.

194. Quoted in David Boaz, ed., *The Libertarian Reader* (New York: Free Press, 1997), xi.

195. Quoted in Boaz, ed., *Libertarian Reader*, xi.

196. Knowing I was skeptical of the idea that term limits would necessarily lead to a more libertarian legislature (that belief requires the secondary assumption that a citizens legislature would be more libertarian, which seems to imply that the citizenry is more libertarian than I suspect it is), Crane dryly informed me, "It's a silver bullet. It will make us all live longer, have better health. . . . They hate it *so much* here inside the beltway, the lobbyists hate it, the bureaucrats hate it, the core of the political class are so passionate in their hatred of term limits. I could make all the theoretical arguments to you, but that's all you need to know."

197. Quoted in Nina Easton, *Gang of Five: Leaders at the Center of the Conservative Crusade* (New York: Simon & Schuster, 2000), 147. Easton was unaware of the song's provenance with the Circle Bastiat.

198. Grover Norquist, interview by author, June 21, 2006.

199. Ron Paul, interview by author, September 28, 2005.

200. Dana Rohrabacher, interview by author, September 28, 2005.

CHAPTER 9

1. B. Branden, *Passion of Ayn Rand*, 386–388.

2. Hessen, interview by author.

3. B. Branden, *Passion of Ayn Rand*, 372–377.

4. B. Branden, interview by author.

5. For overarching details on Rand's last years, see B. Branden, *Passion of Ayn Rand*, chaps. 30–32.

6. Hessen, interview by author.

7. These have included *The Early Ayn Rand* (1984) (a collection of unshot screenplays, early short stories, and excised portions from the novels), *Journals of Ayn Rand* (1997) (incomplete portions of her notes on philosophy and her novels), and *The Letters of Ayn Rand* (1995) (only Rand's side of the correspondence, and similarly edited by unrevealed methods). Independent Rand scholar Chris Sciabarra has complained publicly about the unacknowledged editing on Rand's published journals. See Chris Sciabarra, "Bowdlerizing Ayn Rand," *Liberty*, September 1998.

Peikoff controls all access to Rand's papers and materials. A Peikoff-approved documentary, *Ayn Rand: A Sense of Life*, actually copped an Oscar nomination in 1998, though its authorized nature made it a one-sided and in many ways colorless assessment of Rand's life. An attractive picture book was produced to accompany the film. Michael Paxton, *Ayn Rand: A Sense of Life* (Layton, UT: Gibbs-Smith, 1998).

8. Mimi Reisel Gladstein, *The Ayn Rand Companion* (Westport, CT: Greenwood, 1984), 4.

9. Harriman, ed., *Journals*, 298.

10. James Baker, *Ayn Rand* (Boston: Twayne, 1987). Roy Childs's inexplicable praise for this book in the Laissez-Faire Books catalog earned him sheaves of angry letters, dutifully preserved in his papers at the Hoover Institution.

11. Robert Hessen remembers Rand as "a painfully slow reader. She read everything like a contract. It took her five minutes to write a check for $10 dollars." Thus it was al-

ways Nathaniel Branden, not Rand, who vetted books for sale by NBI Book Service. Hessen, interview by author.

12. B. Branden, interview by author.

13. J. Charles King, "Life and the Theory of Value: The Randian Argument Reconsidered," in Douglas J. Den Uyl and Douglas B. Rasmussen, eds., *The Philosophic Thought of Ayn Rand* (Urbana: University of Illinois Press, 1984). David Gordon offers an interesting twist on the notion that the indestructible can have no values, pointing out the implication that there's no reason to prefer heaven to hell, since in each one will be indestructible. If you believe, as per Rand, that the chance of death is necessary to pursue values, Gordon writes, "'Depart from me, ye cursed, into everlasting fire' portends nothing better or worse than 'This day shalt thou be with me in Paradise.'" See David Gordon, review of Peikoff's *Objectivism, Journal of Libertarian Studies,* Spring 1995, 141.

14. Eric Mack, "The Fundamental Moral Element of Rand's Theory of Rights," in Den Uyl and Rasmussen, eds., *Philosophic Thought of Rand.*

15. Sciabarra, *Russian Radical,* 129. Sciabarra's is the first sympathetic, serious attempt to bring Rand into the philosophical tradition—and in a way, as Rasmussen said in his blurb for the book, that shows her as a "postmodern thinker" who "overcame the dichotomies of modernity: empiricism/rationalism; facts/values; body/mind; and prudence/morality." For those interested in understanding Rand in the context of contemporary philosophy, Sciabarra's book is important, though the specifics of his insights go beyond the scope of this book.

16. Ellis, *Is Objectivism a Religion?,* 103.

17. Ellis, *Is Objectivism a Religion?,* 274.

18. N. Branden, *Who Is Ayn Rand?,* 51.

19. Harriman, ed., *Journals,* 25.

20. Harriman, ed., *Journals,* 437.

21. Ayn Rand, *The New Left: The Anti-Industrial Revolution* (New York: Signet, 1971), chap. 9.

22. B. Branden, *Passion of Ayn Rand,* 244.

23. Berliner, ed., *Letters of Ayn Rand,* 584.

24. Rand, *Voice of Reason,* chap. 6.

25. Rand, *Voice of Reason,* ix.

26. B. Branden, interview by author.

27. Harriman, ed., *Journals,* 694.

28. In unpublished private correspondence after Rand's death, at least two longtime members of her inner circle expressed heatedly negative assessments of her. One called her "the cruelest and most destructive (person) I have ever known." Another wrote that the notion Rand had a benevolent sense of life to be "the greatest fiction surrounding Ayn Rand," and that "life with Ayn was so abnormal that it left us all affected in many and strange ways" and that Rand was "very harmful to all aspects of my personal life."

29. Hayek, *Law, Legislation, and Liberty,* 1:55.

30. F. A. Hayek, *Law, Legislation, and Liberty: A New Statement of the Liberal Principles of Justice and Political Economy,* vol. 2, *The Mirage of Social Justice* (Chicago: University of Chicago Press, 1976), 97.

31. The further restrictions and specifications Hayek lays down for those dual legislative houses are curious. The lower house could be run by the current methods of party politics, since it deals with the specifics of government that involve conflicting interests. The upper house should be free of the passions and push-pull of partisan politics and frequent elections. Hayek recommends that its legislators be selected for fifteen-year terms from a single age cohort; he recommends forty-five-year-olds. They should be granted honorable sinecures for life after turning sixty and retiring. Every year new members would come in as others were rotated out.

In Hayek's preferred version, only forty-five-year-old candidates are eligible for election, and only forty-five-year-olds are eligible to vote. His coevals are in the best position to judge the probity and ability of any candidate for office, Hayek argues. Uncharacteristically for a writer who tends so strongly to the abstract as Hayek, he painstakingly presents every practical and specific detail for this curious scheme. See F. A. Hayek, *Law, Legislation, and Liberty: A New Statement of the Liberal Principles of Justice and Political Economy*, vol. 3, *The Political Order of a Free People* (Chicago: University of Chicago Press, 1979), chap. 17.

Regarding his usual abstractness of thought, which this constructivist scheme goes against, Hayek has criticized that tendency in himself. See Hayek, *Hayek on Hayek*, 75: "That in fact I was led into the life almost of a pure scholar was not entirely a matter of inclination and would certainly not have happened if I had stayed in Austria. But transferred into an entirely different environment, my factual knowledge was inevitably so much inferior to that of my colleagues that I got pushed rather farther than was entirely to my liking into an entirely theoretical and bookish field." And: "It has been to a large extent the external circumstances of living in foreign countries . . . which . . . as a scholar drove me from the more concrete and empirical to the more abstract aspects of scientific work" (137).

32. Hayek suffered from intermittent bouts of depression during the 1960s and early 1970s. See Hayek, *Hayek on Hayek*, 130. In a 1983 speech printed as F. A. Hayek, "The Origins and Effects of Our Morals: A Problem for Science," in Nishiyama and Leube, eds., *Essence of Hayek*, 330, Hayek said: "The present trend of opinion makes it seem quite possible that men, because they do not like it, will destroy the moral order that keeps them alive." This is the essay in which Hayek explains how both instinct and reason work against private property most thoroughly.

33. F. A. Hayek, "Origins and Effects of Our Morals," 329–330.

34. Thomas W. Hazlett, "The Road from Serfdom: An Interview with F. A. Hayek," *Reason*, July 1992, 31.

35. James L. Rowe Jr., "Myrdal, Austrian Hayek Get Economics Nobel," *Washington Post*, October 10, 1974, A27.

36. F. A. Hayek, *New Studies in Philosophy, Politics, Economics, and the History of Ideas* (Chicago: University of Chicago Press, 1978), 23.

37. Hayek, *New Studies*, 34.

38. F. A. Hayek, "Socialism and Science," in Nishiyama and Leube, eds., *Essence of Hayek*, 124. "I have to admit that, after vainly waiting for upwards of 40 years to find a respectable intellectual defence against objections raised to socialist proposals, I am becoming a little impatient. Since I have always acknowledged that the socialist camp included many people of good will, I have tried to deal with their doctrines gently. But the time is overdue to proclaim loudly that intellectually the foundations of socialism are as hollow as can be, and that opposition to socialism is based, not on different values or on prejudice, but on unrefuted logical arguments. . . . Instead of reasoning logically to meet the substantial objections they have to answer, socialists impugn the motives and throw suspicion on the good faith of defenders of what they choose to call 'capitalism'. . . . the socialist counter-critique seems often to be more concerned to discredit the author than to refute his arguments."

Also, in "Two Pages of Fiction," in Nishiyama and Leube, eds., *Essence of Hayek*, 56, Hayek writes in discussing the assertion that a socialist government could have at its disposal all the same information as an entrepreneur in a market society: "I am afraid this is a blatant untruth, an assertion so absurd that it is difficult to understand how an intelligent person could ever honestly make it."

39. F. A. Hayek, *A Conversation with Friedrich A. Von Hayek: Science and Socialism* (Washington, DC: American Enterprise Institute, 1979), 5.

40. For a discussion on the controversy over how much of *Fatal Conceit* is Hayek's work and how much may be Bartley's, see Caldwell, *Hayek's Challenge*, 316–319. See also Alan Ebenstein, "The Final Deceit," *Liberty*, March 2005. Ebenstein says that the papers deposited by Hayek's longtime secretary at the Hoover Institution prove that the final work should at least be marked as coauthored by Hayek and Bartley. At one point Hayek, who slipped in and out of lucidity in the final seven years of his life, demanded that it be so identified but later backed down (31).

41. Ronald Hamowy, "Hayek's Concept of Freedom: A Critique," *New Individualist Review*, April 1961, 28–31.

42. See "Economics, Politics, and Freedom: An Interview with F. A. Hayek," *Reason*, February 1975, 9: "I think Hamowy was right to the extent that my definition of the rule of law which would secure freedom was too wide. It's not sufficient that government coercion is limited to the enforcement of general rules because that might well include such things as control of religious beliefs and the like, but now I think the definition has to be extended. Government coercion is to be confined to the rules with a regard to conduct towards other people."

43. Hayek, *Constitution of Liberty*, 258.

44. For more on the problems that Hayek's allowance of a welfare state creates for his policies, see Raymond Plant, "Hayek on Social Justice: A Critique," in Jack Birner and Rudy van Zijp, eds., *Hayek, Co-Ordination, and Evolution: His Legacy in Philosophy, Politics, Economics, and the History of Ideas* (London: Routledge, 1994), 176. "Once Hayek has conceded the case for a minimal welfare state . . . he fails to explain how this welfare state and the conception of needs implicit within it will be immune to precisely the same interest group pressures which in his view pose a fatal political objection to social-democratic ideas of distributive justice . . . he has given us no clue as to how to define the class of acceptable satiable basic needs and those that are not so satiable. Until this is done it is not clear that Hayek has at all a consistent position."

45. Hayek, *Law, Legislation, and Liberty*, 3:156.

46. Karen I. Vaughn, "The Constitution of Liberty from an Evolutionary Perspective," in Norman Barry et al., *Serfdom Revisited*, 127–128.

47. For a thorough exposition of the change in Hayek's thinking from pure a priorism to Popperianism, see T. W. Hutchinson, *The Politics and Philosophy of Economics* (Oxford: Basil Blackwell, 1981), 210–224.

48. For Hoppe's complaints about Hayek's irrationalism, see Hans-Hermann Hoppe, "F. A. Hayek on Government and Social Evolution: A Critique," *Review of Austrian Economics* 7, no. 1 (1994).

49. F. A. Hayek, *The Fatal Conceit*, ed. W. W. Bartley III (Chicago: University of Chicago Press, 1988), 63. This turn to tradition peeved some young libertarian scholars. David Hart, then a historian supported by the Institute for Humane Studies, thought Hayek was going off the reactionary deep end in his emphasis on tradition in his later work. Hart wrote that "libertarianism is rationalist, iconoclastic towards authority and tradition, individualistic, and personally liberating. If we want to appeal to people who share these views then we will surely offend them by talking about gerontocracies and slavish adherence to traditions which have given us a privileged and corporatised society and a population which is all too willing to march off to war and kill at the state's behest. So you can see, I am suspicious of Hayek." David Hart to Walter Grinder, November 16, 1984, Institute for Human Studies Archives, David Hart folder.

50. Hayek, *Individualism and Economic Order*, 26. "It must remain an open question whether a free or individualistic society can be worked successfully if people are too 'individualistic' in the false sense, if they are too unwilling voluntarily to conform to traditions and conventions."

51. Hayek, *Constitution of Liberty*, 61.

52. Hayek, *Constitution of Liberty,* 145.

53. Spontaneous orders can lead to results that need positive legislation to change, Hayek writes, when "the development of the law has lain in the hands of members of a particular class whose traditional views made them regard as just what could not meet the more general requirements of justice. There can be no doubt that in such fields as the law on the relations between master and servant, landlord and tenant, creditor and debtor, and in modern times between modern business and its customers, the rules have been shaped largely by the views of one of the parties . . . when it is recognized that some hereto accepted rules are unjust in light of more general principles of justice it may well require the revision not only of single rules but of whole sections of the established system of case law. This is more than can be accomplished by decisions of particular cases in the light of existing precedent." Hayek, *Law, Legislation, and Liberty*, 1:89.

54. Hoppe, a Rothbard disciple, says this quality in Hayek, which he dismisses as incoherence, accounts for Hayek's reputational advantage over Mises and Rothbard, whose social theories are clearer and more definitive. Hoppe suspects that "Hayek's fame has little to do with his importance as a social theorist, but rather with the fact that his theory poses no threat whatsoever to the currently dominating statist ideology of social democracy, and that a theory which is marked by contradiction, confusion and vagueness provides an unlimited reservoir for hermeneutical endeavors." Hoppe, "Hayek on Government," *Review of Austrian Economics*, 93.

55. Hayek, *Counter-Revolution of Science*, 399–400.

56. Hess proselytized for what became known as "appropriate technology," even serving on a West Virginia state advisory committee to the governor on the topic. His curious status as rural small-tech anarchist earned him the attention of documentary filmmakers Peter Ladue and Roland Halle, whose short film about Hess, *Toward Liberty*, won an Academy Award for Best Short Documentary in 1981.

57. Hess, *Edge*, 242–243.

58. Hess, *Dear America*, 112.

59. Hess, *Dear America*, 271–272.

60. Hess, *Dear America*, 42–43.

61. Hess, *Dear America*, 68.

62. Charles Murray conducted long interviews with Hess to gather materials that became part of his posthumous autobiography. That book, more autobiographical than the earlier *Dear America*, was published in 1999 as *Mostly on the Edge*. Murray lamented that Hess didn't have an accurate memory for chronology in recalling his life. Murray was disappointed that he wasn't able to get much fresh material that wasn't already in *Dear America*. But he had no regrets; "I was so immediately taken with Karl that I was happy to do whatever Karl wanted." Murray, interview by author.

63. While Hess's days as a minor celebrity were long over, his death was noted even outside the libertarian movement. In the *New Republic* he was praised as the kind of libertarian who "believed in the visible hand of the craftsman, not in the invisible hand of the market." John Judis, "After You've Gone: Three Wise Men," *New Republic*, May 30, 1994, 21.

64. Hess, *Edge*, 247.

65. The libertarian supper club in Los Angeles, for example, is named in Hess's honor.

66. Roche's tenure at Hillsdale came to a hideous end when his daughter-in-law killed herself after publicly stating she'd been having a long-term affair with Roche. See Sam Tanenhaus, "Deadly Devotion," *Vanity Fair,* March 2000, for a detailed account of the suicide and its aftermath.

67. Rothbard contributed dozens of articles to *Free Market* from 1984 until his death, many of them collected in his 1995 volume, *Making Economic Sense*.

68. Walter Block, interview by author.

69. Rothbard, *Ethics*, xlv. Rothbard received support through the decades for the project from the Institute for Humane Studies and from Charles Koch, who financed a year off from teaching for Rothbard in 1974–1975 to work on it.

70. Murray N. Rothbard, "Land Reform: Portugal and Mexico," *Libertarian Forum*, January 1977, 6.

71. Rothbard, *Ethics*, 85–86.

72. Rothbard, *Ethics*, 86. The willingness of libertarian thinkers to toy with the notion of "just slavery," whether as punishment or even as the farthest extension of the rights of people to contract out their efforts freely has led at least one libertarian-leaning academic to walk away from the movement in disgust.

73. Rothbard, *Ethics*, 98.

74. For a detailed exposition on Benjamin Tucker's child-as-property argument and the controversy it caused among other individualist anarchists, see Brooks, ed., *Individualist Anarchists*, chap. 9, "Children as Property." Frequent contributor to Tucker's *Liberty*, J. William Lloyd, was so exasperated by what he saw as Tucker's inhuman insistence on this theoretical principle that he wrote, "[Tucker's] position on this issue, if adhered to, will strike the death-blow to philosophical anarchism. It is suicidal. Modern civilization will never accept it." (Quoted in Brooks, ed., *Individualist Anarchists*, 219.) He further adds that if belief in children as property is necessary to be an individualist anarchist—and he grants that Tucker is "the accredited head of that philosophy" and thus has the right to dictate its tenets—then "Henceforth I am no Anarchist, but a Free Socialist!" (Quoted in Brooks, ed., *Individualist Anarchists*, 221.)

75. Rothbard, *Ethics*, 262.

76. *Reason* did publish, to some controversy, a Rothbard column in July 1975, "Death of a State," in which he cheered the collapse of South Vietnam, on the grounds that the death of *any* state is worth celebrating from a libertarian perspective. This was an example of what many libertarians have condemned as moral blindness on Rothbard's part, not to mention strategic foolhardiness.

77. Murray N. Rothbard, *Economic Thought Before Adam Smith: An Austrian Perspective on the History of Economic Thought* (Brookfield, VT: Edward Elgar, 1995), 1:117–122, for Rothbard on Mariana.

78. Llewellyn H. Rockwell Jr., "The Case for Paleo-Libertarianism," *Liberty*, January 1990, 34.

79. Rockwell, "Case for Paleo-Libertarianism," 34–35.

80. Rockwell, "Case for Paleo-Libertarianism," 35.

81. Rothbard wrote on such topics frequently in the pages of *Libertarian Forum*. He judged Woody Allen's *Manhattan* the best movie of the 1970s because it wittily skewed the sewer of modern cultural and ethical values. Murray N. Rothbard [Mr. First Nighter], "'S Wonderful, 'S Marvelous," *Libertarian Forum*, May–June 1979.

82. Murray N. Rothbard, Comment, *Libertarian Forum*, August 1971, 5. In a posthumous new edition of *Ethics of Liberty*, the Mises Institute attempts to reconstitute Rothbard's older work within this new paleolibertarian dispensation. In his new introduction to the 1998 New York University republication of *Ethics*, Hans-Hermann Hoppe, a protégé of Rothbard's in the Economics Department at UNLV, wrote that the book "revealed libertarianism as a fundamentally conservative doctrine" for such details as its advocacy of proportional punishment for property rights violations, and such "old-fashioned institutions as compulsory labor and indentured servitude for convicted criminals, and for debtor's prisons; and his analysis of causation and liability, burden of proof, and proper assumption of risk invariably displayed a basic and staunch moral conservatism of strict individual responsibility and accountability." See Hans-Hermann Hoppe, introduction to Rothbard, *Ethics*, xxxviii–xxxix.

Hoppe also notes, presumptively as per Rothbard, that "libertarianism could and should be combined exclusively with traditional Western bourgeois culture; that is, the old-fashioned idea of a family-based and hierarchically structured society of voluntarily acknowledged rank orders of social authority" (xxxix). *Ethics* is about strictly political liberty and says little or nothing about moral issues beyond that. But there is little in its tone and examples to suggest admiration for "acknowledged rank orders of social authority." It recommended revolutionary changes in too many elements of traditional Western civilization for that to be true.

Still, this recognition of a cultural dimension to libertarianism beyond politics is part of what libertarian scholar Chris Matthew Sciabarra characterizes and praises as "dialectical" in Rothbard's thinking. Earlier in his career, Rothbard kept libertarianism culturally isolated, insisting that it was a purely intellectual ideology, a mere acceptance of principles and logic that could work universally in any human context. Chris Matthew Sciabarra, *Total Freedom: Toward a Dialectical Libertarianism* (University Park: Pennsylvania State University Press, 2000), 348–349, for a discussion of Rothbard's earlier acultural libertarianism.

But political philosophy oughtn't be merely an ahistorical, acontextual embrace of a philosophical vision of Lockean rights, Sciabarra argues. Rothbard's corpus shows a greater grappling with specific historical circumstances and shifting political realities than most other major libertarian thinkers. Still, Sciabarra thinks that "Rothbard's substantive commitment to cultural conservatism was problematic. Why? Quite simply because an intransigent cultural conservatism cannot be a viable foundation for a free society. While the market may depend on various cultural and legal precedents for its functioning, it is also a spontaneous ordering that challenges, and may topple, traditions. The innovative adaptability of the market to changing circumstances is matched only by the staggering changes it can bring about to those societies it touches" (361).

83. As early as 1972, Rothbard wrote that "the libertarian movement, in its program for getting the government off the backs of the individual, aims to be the fulfillment of the aspirations of . . . Middle America." Murray N. Rothbard, "No, No McGovern," *Libertarian Forum*, October 1972, 2.

84. Tuccille, interview by author.

85. William F. Buckley Jr., "Murray N. Rothbard R.I.P.," *National Review*, February 6, 1995, 19–20.

86. Regarding libertarian movement unity, Rothbard once wrote that "keeping the faith on vital issues can only be sustained by polemicizing against error and deviation wherever it rears its head." Murray N. Rothbard, "Unity or Cadre?" *Libertarian Forum*, October 1972, 8.

87. Gary Greenberg, interview by author, September 7, 1996.

88. Hamowy, interview by author. Jeff Tucker of the Mises Institute once told me wistfully that when Rothbard was around, every cause seemed vital and exhilarating, every event a charged celebration, everything going on exciting, worth noting, worth cheering, or worth booing. After Rothbard was gone, the world was merely what the world was. That sense of constant thrills and excitement was not inherent in it but was Rothbard's unique contribution to it.

89. Quoted in Raimondo, *Enemy of the State,* 294–295.

90. Robert Poole Jr., interview by author, June 5, 1998.

91. R. W. Bradford, "The Rise of the New Libertarianism," *Liberty*, March 1999, 44.

92. Chris Sciabarra, interview by author, October 4, 1998.

93. Crane, interview by author.

94. Nozick, *Anarchy, State, and Utopia*, xv. "It was a long conversation about six years ago with Murray Rothbard that stimulated my interest in individualist anarchist theory."

95. Randy Barnett, interview by author, May 15, 2005.

96. Norman Barry, *On Classical Liberalism and Libertarianism* (New York: St. Martin's, 1987), 173.

97. Ronald Reagan to FEE, Western Union mailgram, May 16, 1983. FEE Archives.

98. FEE's financial loss figure from a memo that Hans Sennholz gave to FEE Board of Trustees, December 14, 1992, FEE Archives. John Sparks, Read's first successor, who left amid acrimony and lawsuit threats, later wrote and staged a romantic musical, *Along Came a Frenchman,* about life in a celibate intentional community of Zoarites in Tuscarawas, Ohio. The musical had a brief run at Malone College Performing Arts Center in Canton, Ohio.

99. Gary North to Hans Sennholz, January 27, 1993, FEE Archives.

Epilogue

1. Kozinski's article is available online at www.cato-unbound.org/2005/12/09/alex-kozinski/reply-to-buchanan–2.

2. N. Branden, interview by author.

3. Nick Gillespie, "Jayhawk Down: Economic Freedom May Be Just Another Word for Nothing Else to Do," *Reason Online,* November 18, 2004, www.reason.com/links/links111804.shtml.

4. A couple of books by libertarian or libertarian-friendly writers that are popular with libertarian audiences make the case for a continually richer world in detail: W. Michael Cox and Richard Alm, *Myths of Rich and Poor: Why We Are Richer than We Think* (New York: Basic, 2000); and Julian L. Simon and Stephen Moore, *It's Getting Better All the Time: 100 Greatest Trends of the Last 100 Years* (Washington, DC: Cato Institute, 2000).

5. For more on the Free State Project, see Brian Doherty, "Revolt of the Porcupines," *Reason,* December 2004.

6. Andrew Rich, *Think Tanks, Public Policy, and the Politics of Expertise* (Cambridge: Cambridge University Press, 2004), 82.

7. John Stossel, interview by author, June 22, 2006.

8. Neal Boortz, interview by author, June 28, 2006.

9. Boortz has lately been at odds with many in the LP and the larger libertarian movement over his steadfast support of the war in Iraq, which has become a serious fault line in the movement. While a supporter of drug legalization, he thinks the LP overemphasizes it to its detriment, and recommends the fight against eminent domain as the politically winning issue the LP ought to embrace.

10. See on these topics Robert C. Ellickson, *Order Without Law: How Neighbors Settle Disputes* (Cambridge: Harvard University Press, 1991); Bruce Benson, *The Enterprise of Law: Justice Without the State* (San Francisco: Pacific Research Institute, 1990); and Robert Axelrod, *The Evolution of Cooperation* (New York: Basic, 1984).

11. For Coase and Smith contextualized in a libertarian context, see interviews with them in *Reason*: Thomas W. Hazlett, "Looking for Results: Nobel Laureate Ronald Coase on Rights, Resources, and Regulation," *Reason,* January 1997; and Mike Lynch and Nick Gillespie, "The Experimental Economist: Nobel Laureate Vernon Smith Takes Markets Places They've Never Been Before," *Reason,* December 2002.

12. See Brian Doherty, "'It's So Simple, It's Ridiculous': Taxing Times for 16th Amendment Rebels," *Reason,* May 2004, on this "tax honesty" movement.

13. For details and documentation on these cases, see these on the Institute for Justice website: www.ij.org/schoolchoice/ohio_ussc/index.html; www.ij.org/economic_liberty/ny_wine/index.html; and www.ij.org/private_property/connecticut/index.html.

14. For de Soto's most recent take on the topic, see Hernando de Soto, *The Mystery of Capital* (New York: Basic, 2000). De Soto won the second Milton Friedman Prize, a $500,000 cash prize given by the Cato Institute to reward those who have done the most for freedom around the world.

15. See George Ayittey, *Africa Unchained: The Blueprint for Africa's Future* (New York: Palgrave Macmillan, 2005).

16. R. J. Smith, interview by author.

17. James Miller, *The Passion of Michel Foucault* (New York: Simon & Schuster, 1993), 310.

18. Tyler Cowen, "Why Does Freedom Wax and Wane? Some Research Questions in Social Change and Big Government," Mercatus Center, 11.

19. See Thomas Frank, *One Market Under God: Extreme Capitalism, Market Populism, and the End of Economic Democracy* (New York: Doubleday, 2000); and David Harvey, *A Brief History of Neoliberalism* (Oxford: Oxford University Press, 2005). For attacks on this progressive myth of the victory of laissez-faire, see Brian Doherty, review of *One Market Under God, Freeman,* December 2001; and Brian Doherty, "Laissez-Faire Fiction," *Reason,* June 2001.

20. Bandow, interview by author.

21. Quoted in Jasper Crane to William Mullendore, December 30, 1960, University of Oregon Special Collection, William Mullendore Collection, Box 1, Jasper Crane folder.

22. Bandow, interview by author.

23. Cornuelle, interview by author.

24. Ebeling, interview by author.

25. Steve Chapman, interview by author, November 9, 2005.

26. Bergland, interview by author.

27. LP vote totals from Micah L. Sifry, *Spoiling for a Fight: Third Party Politics in America* (London: Routledge, 2003), 298.

28. Greenberg, interview by author.

29. See Randy Langhenry, "Billions Saved: LP in LA Leads Bond Measure Defeat," *LP News,* July 1994. Purist libertarians could complain—and rightly, in purist libertarian terms—about the fact that the pamphlet was printed and distributed at taxpayer expense.

30. Once the LP "spoiled" things for Democrat senatorial candidate Wyche Fowler, who got more votes than his GOP opponent Paul Coverdell in the 1992 Georgia Senate race, but not the legally required 50 percent for victory because the Libertarian candidate, Jim Hudson, pulled 3.1 percent. In the runoff, Coverdell won, with Libertarian Hudson's endorsement. The Democrats running the state legislature promptly changed the percentage required for victory in a U.S. Senate race to just 45 percent. For an account of the LP's potent role as spoiler in Georgia, see Tim Bentley, "Spoilers," *South,* February 1998. Why Georgia? Many credit the effect of local favorite radio talk show host, and outspoken LP supporter, Neal Boortz.

31. Riggenbach, interview by author.

32. For a summation of Mackey's approach, see his speech at FreedomFest in 2004, John Mackey, "Winning the Battle for Freedom and Prosperity," *Liberty,* June 2006.

33. For a discussion that situates these critics of public schools in a libertarian context, see Sheldon Richman, *Separating School and State* (Fairfax, VA: Future of Freedom Foundation, 1994), 70–77, 90–95.

34. Joel Spring, *A Primer on Libertarian Education* (New York: Free Life Editions, 1975), 9.

35. "Reason Interview: Robert W. Poole, Jr.," *Reason,* May 1983, 61.

36. David Padden, interview by author, August 5, 1998.

37. George Pearson, interview by author, April 1, 1999.

38. Crane, interview by author.

39. C. Koch, interview by author.

40. Richard Fink, interview by author, September 29, 2005.

41. Cornuelle, interview by author.

42. For a discussion of doubts about the Hayekian pyramid in the libertarian context, see R. W. Bradford and Murray Rothbard, "Eyeing the Top of the Pyramid," *Liberty,* May 1989.

43. C. Koch, interview by author.

44. George Smith, a learned natural rights historian and libertarian philosopher, very deliberately pursued a career as an unaffiliated "market intellectual." In the 1970s, he'd lecture on philosophy to people in their homes for a fee. Rothbard used to advise him to bite the bullet and get the intellectual union card of a university degree, but Smith held fast to the market intellectual experiment. With no small humor, he tells me that "I felt an obligation as a social experiment to carry it out to the end, even if I'd end up like Poe, dead in a gutter."

45. Memo, Ed Crane to Roy Childs and Don Lavoie, December 29, 1983, Hoover Institution, Roy Childs Collection, Box 23, Cato Institute folder.

46. Ted Galen Carpenter, interview by author, September 30, 2005.

47. For a recent book summing up Bauer's foreign aid views, see Peter Bauer, *From Subsistence to Exchange and Other Essays* (Princeton: Princeton University Press, 2000).

48. Carpenter, interview by author.

49. Milton Mueller, "The Movement," *Libertarian Review,* April 1979, 18.

50. Raimondo, interview by author.

51. Crane, interview by author.

52. For Riggenbach on these ideas, see Jeff Riggenbach, "The Politics of Aquarius," *Libertarian Review,* March 1981; and Jeff Riggenbach, *In Praise of Decadence* (Amherst, NY: Prometheus, 1998).

53. John Perry Barlow, "Declaration of the Independence of Cyberspace," http://homes.eff.org/~barlow/Declaration-Final.html.

54. Cowen, "Why Does Freedom Wax and Wane?" 26.

55. Libertarian economist Don Lavoie argued that the twentieth century left had been fooled by the dominant powers-that-be into accepting government planning as liberatory for the masses when in fact it was a tool for plutocrats: "It is not correct to say that planning was modified from its Marxist origins to take on its modern, noncomprehensive form. It would be more accurate to say that comprehensive planning and the radical movement it inspired were utterly defeated and replaced root and branch by an entirely different idea with an entirely different heritage, by a movement driven not by popular resistance to oppression but by ruling groups themselves. . . . The real fathers of planning, *as it has actually been practiced in this century,* are neither Marx and Engels nor Lange and Lerner, but Bernard Baruch, David Lloyd George, and General Erich Ludendorff . . . for the purpose of fighting World War I." Don Lavoie, *National Economic Planning: What Is Left?* (Cambridge: Ballinger, 1985), 220.

56. Louis Rossetto, interview by author, December 7, 2005.

57. Murray N. Rothbard, "Social Darwinism Reconsidered," *Libertarian Forum,* January 1971, 3.

SELECTED BIBLIOGRAPHY

Since much of the libertarian movement's history has not yet been dealt with in book form, archives and periodicals supplied my richest historical sources. The archives I used are listed in full in the acknowledgments. I was particularly educated by the Foundation for Economics Education and Henry Hazlitt archives at FEE's Irvington-on-Hudson, New York, headquarters; the Murray Rothbard archives at the Ludwig von Mises Institute in Auburn, Alabama; and various collections at the Hoover Institution archives at Stanford University, especially the Roy Childs, Williamson Evers, Milton Friedman, F. A. Harper, and F. A. Hayek collections.

Libertarian periodicals are where many important aspects of the movement's history and ideology have unfolded. This is a selected list of the ones I found most useful. The ideas and stories told in these periodicals offer a rich libertarian education indeed.

- *Faith and Freedom*
- *The Freeman*
- *New Individualist Review*
- *The Innovator*
- *Reason*
- *Libertarian Forum*
- *SIL News/Individual Liberty*
- *New Libertarian Weekly*
- *Libertarian Review*
- *LP News*
- *Update*
- *Frontlines*
- *American Libertarian*
- *Liberty*

The endnotes should be examined for the full range of sources relied on. What follows is a *very* selected bibliography meant to guide the reader to books that cover the most important aspects of the life and thought of the major libertarian thinkers and institutions as discussed in this book. These volumes cover just the basics, focusing on the book's five central intellectual influences: Ludwig von Mises, F. A. Hayek, Ayn Rand, Murray Rothbard, and Milton Friedman, and also trying to touch on the major lines of thought and important figures in the movement's ideological and institutional history. In many cases, multiple editions of these books exist; I list the editions I personally relied on.

Barnett, Randy. *The Structure of Liberty: Justice and the Rule of Law.* Oxford: Clarenden, 1998.

Berliner, Michael S., ed. *Letters of Ayn Rand.* New York: Dutton, 1995.

Boaz, David, ed. *The Libertarian Reader: Classic and Contemporary Readings from Lao-tzu to Milton Friedman.* New York: Free Press, 1997.

_____. *Toward Liberty: The Idea That Is Changing the World.* Washington, DC: Cato Institute, 2002.

Branden, Barbara. *The Passion of Ayn Rand.* Garden City, NY: Doubleday, 1986.

Branden, Nathaniel. *Judgment Day: My Years with Ayn Rand.* Boston: Houghton Mifflin, 1989.

Brooks, Frank H., ed. *The Individualist Anarchists: An Anthology of Liberty (1881–1908).* New Brunswick, NJ: Transaction, 1994.

Caldwell, Bruce. *Hayek's Challenge: An Intellectual Biography of F. A. Hayek.* Chicago: University of Chicago Press, 2004.

Casey, Douglas R. *Crisis Investing: Opportunities and Profits in the Coming Great Depression.* New York: Stratford Press, 1980.

Childs, Roy. *Liberty Against Power: Essays by Roy A. Childs, Jr.* Edited by Joan Kennedy Taylor. San Francisco: Fox & Wilkes, 1994.

Chodorov, Frank. *Fugitive Essays: Selected Writings of Frank Chodorov.* Edited by Charles Hamilton. Indianapolis: LibertyPress, 1980.

Cox, Stephen. *The Woman and the Dynamo: Isabel Paterson and the Idea of America.* New Brunswick, NJ: Transaction, 2004.

Ebenstein, Alan. *Friedrich Hayek: A Biography.* New York: Palgrave, 2001.

Foundation for Economic Education. *Cliches of Socialism.* Irvington-on-Hudson, NY: Foundation for Economic Education, 1970.

Friedman, David. *The Machinery of Freedom: Guide to a Radical Capitalism.* New York: Harper Colophon, 1973.

Friedman, Milton. *Capitalism and Freedom.* Chicago: University of Chicago Press, 1962.

Friedman, Milton, and Rose Friedman. *Free to Choose: A Personal Statement.* New York: Harcourt Brace Jovanovich, 1980.

_____. *Two Lucky People: Memoirs.* Chicago: University of Chicago Press, 1998.

Gillespie, Nick, ed. *Choice: The Best of Reason.* Dallas: BenBella, 2004.

Hartwell, R. W. *A History of the Mont Pelerin Society.* Indianapolis: Liberty Fund, 1995.

Hayek, F. A. *The Constitution of Liberty.* Chicago: University of Chicago Press, 1960.

_____. *The Counter-Revolution of Science: Studies on the Abuse of Reason.* 1952. Indianapolis: LibertyPress, 1979.

_____. *The Fatal Conceit.* Edited by W. W. Bartley III. Chicago: University of Chicago Press, 1988.

_____. *The Fortunes of Liberalism: Essays on Austrian Economics and the Ideal of Freedom.* Edited by Peter G. Klein. Chicago: University of Chicago Press, 1992.

_____. *Hayek on Hayek: An Autobiographical Dialogue.* Edited by Stephen Kresge and Leif Wenar. Chicago: University of Chicago Press, 1994.

_____. *The Road to Serfdom.* 50th anniversary ed. Chicago: University of Chicago Press, 1994.

Hazlitt, Henry. *Economics in One Lesson.* New York: Harper, 1946.

Hess, Karl. *Mostly on the Edge: An Autobiography.* Amherst, NY: Prometheus, 1999.

Holtz, William. *The Ghost in the Little House: A Life of Rose Wilder Lane.* Columbia: University of Missouri Press, 1993.

Kelley, John L. *Bringing the Market Back In: The Political Revitalization of Market Liberalism.* New York: New York University Press, 1997.

Lane, Rose Wilder. *The Discovery of Freedom: Man's Struggle Against Authority.* 1943. New York: Laissez-Faire Books, 1984.

LeFevre, Robert. *A Way to Be Free: The Autobiography of Robert LeFevre, The Making of a Modern American Revolutionary.* 2 vols. Culver City, CA: Pulpless, 1999.

Leube, Kurt R., ed. *The Essence of Friedman.* Stanford, CA: Hoover Institution Press, 1987.

MacBride, Roger Lea, ed. *The Lady and the Tycoon: The Best of Letters Between Rose Wilder Lane and Jasper Crane.* Caldwell, ID: Caxton, 1973.

Martin, James J. *Men Against the State: The Expositors of Individualist Anarchism in America, 1827–1908.* 1953. Colorado Springs, CO: Ralph Myles, 1970.

Mises, Ludwig von. *Epistemological Problems of Economics.* 1960. New York: New York University Press, 1981.

_____. *Human Action: A Treatise on Economics.* 1948. 3rd rev. ed. San Francisco: Laissez-Faire Books, 1990.

_____. *Liberalism in the Classical Tradition.* 1927. 3rd ed. Irvington-on-Hudson, NY: Foundation for Economic Education, 1962.

_____. *Ludwig von Mises, Notes and Recollections.* Spring Mills, PA: Libertarian Press, 1978.

_____. *Socialism.* 1922. Indianapolis: LibertyClassics, 1981.

Mises, Margit von. *My Years with Ludwig von Mises.* 2nd enl. ed. Cedar Falls, IA: Center for Futures Education, 1984.

Morley, Felix. *For the Record.* South Bend, IN: Regnery/Gateway, 1979.

Murray, Charles. *In Pursuit: Of Happiness and Good Government.* New York: Simon and Schuster, 1988.

Nishiyama, Chiaki, and Kurt R. Leube, eds. *The Essence of Hayek.* Stanford: Hoover Institution Press, 1984.

Nock, Albert Jay. *Our Enemy the State.* 1935. New York: Free Life Editions, 1973.

Nozick, Robert. *Anarchy, State, and Utopia.* New York: Basic, 1974.

Paterson, Isabel. *The God of the Machine.* 1943. New Brunswick, NJ: Transaction, 1993.

Powell, James. *The Triumph of Liberty.* New York: Free Press, 2000.

Radosh, Ronald. *Prophets on the Right.* New York: Free Life Editions, 1975.

Raimondo, Justin. *An Enemy of the State: The Life of Murray N. Rothbard.* Amherst, NY: Prometheus, 2000.

Rand, Ayn. *Atlas Shrugged.* New York: Random House, 1957.

_____. *The Fountainhead.* Indianapolis: Bobbs-Merrill, 1943.

_____. *The Romantic Manifesto: A Philosophy of Literature.* New York: World, 1970.

_____. *The Virtue of Selfishness: A New Concept of Egoism.* New York: New American Library, 1964.

Read, Leonard E. *Elements of Libertarian Leadership.* Irvington-on-Hudson, NY: Foundation for Economic Education, 1962.

_____. *Government—An Ideal Concept.* 1954. Irvington-on-Hudson, NY: Foundation for Economic Education, 1997.

Rockwell, Llewellyn H., Jr., ed. *Murray N. Rothbard: In Memoriam.* Auburn, AL: Ludwig von Mises Institute, 1995.

Rothbard, Murray N. *For a New Liberty: The Libertarian Manifesto.* Rev. ed. New York: Collier, 1978.

_____. *Man, Economy, and State: A Treatise on Economic Principles.* 1962. Los Angeles: Nash, 1970.

_____. *Power and Market: Government and the Economy.* 2nd ed. Kansas City: Sheed Andrews and McMeel, 1977.

Sennholz, Mary. *Leonard E. Read: Philosopher of Freedom.* Irvington-on-Hudson, NY: Foundation for Economic Education, 1993.

Shea, Robert, and Robert Anton Wilson. *Illluminatus! Trilogy: The Eye in the Pyramid, The Golden Apple, and Leviathan.* New York: Dell, 1988.

Sowell, Thomas. *Knowledge and Decisions.* New York: Basic, 1980.

Spooner, Lysander. *The Lysander Spooner Reader.* Edited by George H. Smith. San Francisco: Fox & Wilkes, 1992.

Sprading, Charles T., ed. *Liberty and the Great Libertarians.* 1913. San Francisco: Fox and Wilkes, 1995.

Szasz, Thomas. *Insanity: The Idea and Its Consequences.* New York: John Wiley, 1987.

Tannehill, Morris and Linda. *The Market for Liberty.* 1970. San Francisco: Fox and Wilkes, 1993.

Tuccille, Jerome. *It Usually Begins with Ayn Rand.* New York: Stein and Day, 1971.

Vaughn, Karen. *Austrian Economics in America: The Migration of a Tradition.* Cambridge: Cambridge University Press, 1994.

ACKNOWLEDGMENTS

The first and most vital thanks are due to all who allowed me to interview them about libertarianism and the libertarian movement in the course of researching this book. They provided the bulk of the understanding, anecdotes, and observations that informed it, even if they are not all quoted by name in the text. They all gave generously of their time, memories, and insights, and in some cases their papers and documents. They are listed in alphabetical order: John Baden, Doug Bandow, John Perry Barlow, Randy Barnett, Joseph Bast, David Bergland, Walter Block, Burt Blumert, John Blundell, David Boaz, Alan Bock, Peter Boettke, Neal Boortz, Don Boudreaux, Mark Brady, R. W. Bradford, Barbara Branden, Nathaniel Branden, Harry Browne, Scott Bullock, Gene Callahan, Ted Galen Carpenter, Doug Casey, Susan Chamberlain, Steve Chapman, Edward Clark, Joe Cobb, Richard Cornuelle, Tyler Cowen, Stephen Cox, Edward Crane III, Douglas Den Uyl, Gus DiZerega, Richard Ebeling, Abraham Ellis, Don Ernsberger, Williamson Evers, Paul Feine, Richard Fink, David Friedman, Jeffrey Friedman, Milton Friedman, Mary Frohman, David Gordon, Bettina Bien Greaves, Gary Greenberg, Kenneth Gregg, Walter Grinder, Charles Hamilton, Ronald Hamowy, Karl Hess Jr., Robert Hessen, Michael Holmes, Jacob Hornberger, Jeffrey Rogers Hummel, Sam Husbands, Paul Jacob, David Kelley, Israel Kirzner, Manuel Klausner, Charles Koch, David Koch, George Koether, Timothy Leary, Lois LeFevre, Leonard Liggio, Spencer Heath MacCallum, Tibor Machan, Randall McElroy, Wendy McElroy, Donald Meinshausen, Charles Murray, Jan Narveson, Tonie Nathan, David Nolan, Grover Norquist, Eric O'Keefe, Emilio Pacheco, David Padden, Tom Palmer, Ron Paul, Durk Pearson, George Pearson, Robert Poole Jr., Virginia Postrel, Sharon Presley, Ralph Raico, Justin Raimondo, George Resch, Andrea Rich, Howard Rich, Sheldon Richman, Jeff Riggenbach, Mario Rizzo, Llewellyn H. Rockwell Jr., Dana Rohrabacher, Louis Rossetto, James Sadowsky, Ryan Sager, Lynn Scarlett, J. Neil Schulman, Dave Schumacher, Chris Sciabarra, Hans Sennholz, Butler Shaffer, Jane Shaw, Sandy Shaw, Mark Skousen, Fred Smith, George H. Smith, L. Neil Smith, Robert J. Smith, John Stossel, Thomas Szasz, Chris Talley, Jason Talley, Joan Kennedy

Taylor, Kenneth Templeton, David Theroux, Jerome Tuccille, Jesse Walker, Chris Whitten, Walter Williams, Robert Anton Wilson, Richard Winger, Anne Wortham, and Marty Zupan.

While it may usually begin with Ayn Rand, in this book's case it began with Chris Whitten. In a longish bull session on matters libertarian back at the Cato Institute in the early 1990s, he decided that a book like this needed to be written and that I was competent to do it. He brought the idea, and me, to the attention of Andrea Rich, one of the administrators of the Roy Childs Memorial Scholars Fund. The Childs Fund graciously (and patiently) provided me with financial assistance to cover some of the costs of travel, books, and other expenses of researching and writing this book. I would like to thank the fund and all its administrators and contributors, particularly Andrea Rich, the late Robert Kephart, Anita Anderson, and David Boaz.

That support paid off because of the belief, support, and encouragement of Peter Osnos, one of the last of the great independent publishers, and Lisa Kaufman, my brilliant editor, both of PublicAffairs, who took a chance on a curious and sometimes disreputable topic. Kaufman was a skilled and skeptical set of intelligent and observant eyes that helped make this book much better than it otherwise might have been; any errors and infelicities of course remain my responsibility. Thanks also to my agent William Clark for his usual cheerful and encouraging efficiency in making it all happen.

Many friends, colleagues, and interview subjects supplied much needed hospitality during research trips to visit archives and interview subjects that spanned a decade. The travel would have become prohibitively expensive, and soul deadening, without the kindness of (in alphabetical order): Jon Asfour, Bob Bannister, Jude Blanchette, Philip Bonham, Barbara Branden, Krista Avril Bray, Greg Ceton, Ana Marie Cox, Celia Farber, Nick Gillespie, Kip Haugen, Jeffrey Rogers Hummel, Shari Linnick, Joe Martin, Candace Nelson, Ivan Osorio, Kevin Regan, John Rinaldi, Joyce Slaton, Karen Solomon, Tertia Speiser, Jessica Spicer, Matthew Schaefer, Kenneth and Lois Templeton, Silke Tudor, Karrin Vanderwal, Danni Watt, and Chris Whitten. The Ludwig von Mises Institute kindly provided lodging during my stay at the institute examining the Murray Rothbard Archives in its possession.

Thanks also to those who gamely volunteered to read portions of earlier drafts of the book and gave valuable advice and some correction along the way: Jude Blanchette, David Boaz, Bryan Caplan, Angela Keaton, the late Robert Kephart, Tom Palmer, and Andrea Rich. For any errors that might remain, I am of course entirely and solely to blame.

My research relied heavily on the resources of the Hoover Institution's archives at Stanford University; the Labadie Collection at the University of Michigan; the Special Collections at the University of Oregon; and the Libertarian Party Archives at the University of Virginia. Jeffrey Rogers Hummel graciously allowed me full access to his ambitious and thorough private collection of libertarian periodicals. Louis Carabini lent me his very rare volume of Andrew Galambos's writings. The Reason Foundation in Los Angeles, the Foundation for Economic Education in Irvington-on-Hudson, New York (special thanks to the organizing efforts and guidance of Jude Blanchette, and to Richard and Anna Ebeling), the Ludwig von Mises Institute in Auburn, Alabama (special thanks to Pat Barnett, Lew Rockwell, and Jeff Tucker), the Institute for Humane Studies in Arlington, Virginia (special thanks to Elaine Hawley, Gary Leff, and Marty Zupan), and the *Orange County Register* (special thanks to Sharon Claremont and Dick Wallace of Freedom Communications) were generous in allowing me access to their archives, files, and libraries.

The reader should be aware that I write this book on the institutional and intellectual history of American libertarianism as an insider. I have been employed by, or written for, or received fellowships at, or spoken at conferences under the sponsorship of, or been sent to seminars by, many libertarian institutions, including the Reason Foundation (my current employer; I am senior editor at *Reason* magazine, which they publish), the Cato Institute (where I worked from 1991 to 1994), the Competitive Enterprise Institute (I was their 1999 Warren Brookes Fellow in Environmental Journalism), the Foundation for Economic Education, the Institute for Humane Studies, Liberty Fund, and the Ludwig von Mises Institute. This experience and access has deepened and strengthened my understanding of the facts and circumstances of libertarian intellectual and institutional history. But all opinions or interpretations expressed here are, unless otherwise specifically attributed, my own. They are neither the responsibility of, nor dictated by, any of those organizations.

Reason magazine's 2004 Burton C. Gray Memorial intern Hanah Metchis helped with interview transcriptions and digging up needed sources and information; *Reason*'s 2006 Burton C. Gray Memorial intern Taylor Buley was also wonderful in digging up citations and information under severe deadline pressure. All my colleagues at *Reason*, past and present, have been marvelously supportive of the project and patient with the long absences from daily work responsibilities that it required, for which I'd like to thank Nick Gillespie, David Nott, Jesse Walker, Kerry Howley, Julian Sanchez, Jacob Sullum, Charles Paul Freund, Matt Welch, Sara Rimensnyder, Barbara Burch, Murielle Schultz, and Mary Toledo.

Thanks to the owners and staff of Abbot's Habit (day shift), and Roman's (evening shift), both on fabulous Sunset Boulevard, Hollywood, California, where much of this book was written, for their patient hospitality and great drinks and food. Thanks also to fellow Hollywood writer Ben Schwartz for keeping me company in various coffee shops in and around Hollywood and Silver Lake, where much of the reading related to this book was done.

Libertarians like to talk about libertarianism and other libertarians. I have been fortunate over the years, for more years than I was consciously working on this book, to have various friends guide and influence my thinking and education on matters libertarian, outside the context of a formal taped interview. With the sad thought that I am undoubtedly neglecting some imparter of important insight, wisdom, or comedy, I'd like to thank the following for their (often unwitting) guidance through the thickets of libertarian ideas and history: Phil Blumel, Thomas D. Walls III, Sean Landon, J. Mark Hardy, Ivan Osorio, Allan Sawyer, Nick Gillespie, Bryan Caplan, Timothy Virkkala, Adam Chacksfield, Andrew Farrant, Margaret Griffis, Jude Blanchette, Brink Lindsey, Timothy Lynch, Jerry Taylor, and my wife, Angela Keaton.

All of my professional work has depended in some way on the support and encouragement of my family: parents Frank and Helene Doherty, brother Jim, sister-in-law Beth, and nephew Gram.

INDEX

BRIAN DOHERTY is a senior editor at *Reason* magazine. His work has appeared in the *Washington Post*, the *Wall Street Journal*, the *Los Angeles Times, Mother Jones, Spin, National Review, The Weekly Standard*, the *San Francisco Chronicle*, and dozens of other publications. In addition to *Radicals for Capitalism*, he is the author of *This Is Burning Man* (Little, Brown, 2004). Doherty received a bachelor's degree in journalism from the University of Florida. He also played bass in several punk rock bands in the early 1990s, including The Jeffersons and Turbo Satan. He founded Cherry Smash Records in 1993. He lives in Los Angeles.

a publishing house founded in 1997. It is a tribute
rds, values, and flair of three persons who have
ntors to countless reporters, writers, editors, and
of all kinds, including me.

ɴᴇ, proprietor of *I. F. Stone's Weekly*, combined a com-
to the First Amendment with entrepreneurial zeal and
ng skill and became one of the great independent journal-
American history. At the age of eighty, Izzy published *The
of Socrates*, which was a national bestseller. He wrote the
k after he taught himself ancient Greek.

ᴇɴᴊᴀᴍɪɴ C. Bʀᴀᴅʟᴇᴇ was for nearly thirty years the charis-
natic editorial leader of *The Washington Post*. It was Ben who
gave the *Post* the range and courage to pursue such historic
issues as Watergate. He supported his reporters with a tenacity
that made them fearless and it is no accident that so many
became authors of influential, best-selling books.

Rᴏʙᴇʀᴛ L. Bᴇʀɴsᴛᴇɪɴ, the chief executive of Random House
for more than a quarter century, guided one of the nation's premier publishing houses. Bob was personally responsible for
many books of political dissent and argument that challenged
tyranny around the globe. He is also the founder and longtime
chair of Human Rights Watch, one of the most respected human
rights organizations in the world.

·   ·   ·

For fifty years, the banner of Public Affairs Press was carried by its
owner Morris B. Schnapper, who published Gandhi, Nasser, Toyn-
bee, Truman, and about 1,500 other authors. In 1983, Schnapper
was described by *The Washington Post* as "a redoubtable gadfly."
His legacy will endure in the books to come.

Peter Osnos, *Founder and Editor-at-Large*